Sans-Culottes

Sans-Culottes

AN EIGHTEENTH-CENTURY EMBLEM

IN THE FRENCH REVOLUTION

Michael Sonenscher

PRINCETON UNIVERSITY PRESS

PRINCETON AND OXFORD

PUBLISHED BY PRINCETON UNIVERSITY PRESS, 41 WILLIAM STREET,
PRINCETON, NEW JERSEY 08540

IN THE UNITED KINGDOM: PRINCETON UNIVERSITY PRESS, 6 OXFORD STREET,
WOODSTOCK, OXFORDSHIRE OX20 1TW

LIBRARY OF CONGRESS CATALOGING-IN-PUBLICATION DATA

SONENSCHER, MICHAEL.
SANS-CULOTTES : AN EIGHTEENTH-CENTURY EMBLEM IN THE FRENCH
REVOLUTION / MICHAEL SONENSCHER.
P.   CM.
INCLUDES BIBLIOGRAPHICAL REFERENCES AND INDEX.
ISBN 978-0-691-12498-8 (HARDCOVER : ALK. PAPER)   1. SANSCULOTTES.
2. FRANCE—INTELLECTUAL LIFE—18TH CENTURY.   3. SYMBOLISM IN
POLITICS—FRANCE—HISTORY—18TH CENTURY.   4. POLITICS AND
CULTURE—FRANCE—HISTORY—18TH CENTURY.   5. FRANCE—HISTORY—
REVOLUTION, 1789–1799.   I. TITLE.
DC158.8.S64   2008
944.04—DC22   2007051699

BRITISH LIBRARY CATALOGING-IN-PUBLICATION DATA IS AVAILABLE

THIS BOOK HAS BEEN COMPOSED IN JANSON TYPEFACE

PRINTED ON ACID-FREE PAPER. ∞

PRESS.PRINCETON.EDU

PRINTED IN THE UNITED STATES OF AMERICA

1 3 5 7 9 10 8 6 4 2

CONTENTS

LIST OF ILLUSTRATIONS   vii

ACKNOWLEDGEMENTS   ix

ABBREVIATIONS AND A NOTE ON TRANSLATIONS   xi

1. Introduction: "One of the Most Interesting Pairs of Breeches
Recorded in Modern History"   1

2. An Ingenious Emblem   57

New Year's Gifts and an Eighteenth-Century French Joke   57
Fashion's Empire: The Moral Foundations of Salon Society   77
*A "Poor Devil": The Short, Unhappy Life of
    Nicolas-Joseph-Laurent Gilbert*   101
*Mercier and Rousseau: Vitalist and Contractual Conceptions
    of Political Society*   110

3. Diogenes and Rousseau: Music, Morality, and Society   134

Diogenes and the Ambiguities of Cynic Philosophy   134
Jean-Jacques Rousseau and the Politics of Public Opinion   147
Rousseau and His Cynic Critics   164
John Brown and the Progress of Civilisation   178
*"That Subtle Diogenes": Immanuel Kant and
    Rousseau's Dilemmas*   195

4. Property, Equality, and the Passions in Eighteenth-Century
French Thought   202

Reform, Revolution, and the Problem of State Power   202
Property and the Limits of State Power   221
Physiocracy, Reform, and the Fruits of the Tree of Life   248
John Law's Legacy and the Aftermath of Physiocracy   260
*Dominique-Joseph Garat, the Modern Idea of Happiness,
    and the Dilemmas of Reform*   273

5. The Entitlements of Merit   283

Visions of Patriotism   283
The Army and Its Problems in the Eighteenth Century   288
Constitutional Government, Taxation, and Equality   296
Political Liberty, Public Finance, and Public Worship   305
Etienne Clavière, Law's System, and French Liberty   315
Feuillants and Brissotins   324
Antoine-Joseph Gorsas and the Politics of Revolutionary Satire   338

6. Conclusion: Democracy and Terror   362

   Politics and History in Jacobin Thought   362
   Rousseau and Revolution   367
   Mably, Rousseau, and Robespierre   372
   Epilogue   407

BIBLIOGRAPHY   425

INDEX   475

ILLUSTRATIONS

FIGURE 1. Sans-Culottes, as Remembered by Posterity   2

FIGURE 2. François-Jacques-Barthélemy Dequevauviller,
L'assemblée au salon   6

FIGURE 3. Jacques Réattu, *The Triumph of Civilisation*   27

FIGURE 4. Jacques Réattu, *The Triumph of Liberty*   56

FIGURE 5. Charles Bonnet, Palengenesis, and the Great
Chain of Being   122

FIGURE 6. Antoine-Joseph Gorsas, *Mais . . . qu'est-ce qu'un
sans-culotte?*   360

ACKNOWLEDGEMENTS

I AM grateful to the Provost and Fellows of King's College, Cambridge for the many different resources that they have made available to me and, more particularly, to John Dunn, Istvan Hont, and Gareth Stedman Jones for their help and advice over the years. I have an additional debt to Istvan Hont both for many illuminating conversations about Rousseau's moral and political thought (although he certainly bears no responsibility for any of the descriptions that follow), and, more generally, for a style of intellectual gregariousness that can truly be said to be *sans pareil*. I am glad, too, to record my thanks to the British Arts and Humanities Research Council, and, in its former incarnation, the British Academy, for the financial support that allowed me to collect much of the material that I have used in this book. In one sense, the impetus to write it came from a chance discovery of an eighteenth-century joke, a discovery I made while looking for something entirely different in what was then the North Library of the British Museum. In another sense, however, that sort of chance discovery, as well as the subsequent investigation of its surprisingly extensive implications, would not have been possible without the wealth of information housed not only by the British Library, but also by the Cambridge University Library and the Bibliothèque nationale de France. I am most grateful to the many people working there for their professional kindness and help.

Rafe Blaufarb kindly sent me comprehensive answers to my questions about French army reform in the eighteenth century; David Garrioch did the same to my questions about Parisian finance and politics after 1789; Edward Castleton gave me helpful guidance to modern scholarship on Charles-François Dupuis; while Katie Scott directed me to a recent edition of some of Antoine-Joseph Gorsas's salon criticism. Thanks, too, to Béla Kapossy, Isaac Nakhimovsky, and Richard Whatmore for a great deal of helpful advice and information over the years. Ed Hundert and Colin Jones read earlier versions of the whole text, and I owe a great deal to them, not only for their helpfully critical comments, but also for the time and care that this involved. I have tried, too, to respond as fully as possible to the equally helpful comments supplied by Princeton's other, still anonymous, reader, and owe her a particular debt for the constructive spirit in which her advice was offered. I am especially grateful to Raymond Geuss, not only for reading the whole text, and for correcting some of the more egregious blunders in my treatment of aspects of ancient Greek and Roman thought, as well as a further array of equally horrible mistakes in German names and titles, but also, from his own work, for giving me some idea of what, historiographically, to aim for.

No one has given me more encouragement to write this book than Elizabeth Allen, and I hope that the outcome does not fall too far short of her own idea of what it should have been. I also owe a great deal to Mark Goldie and the late Robert Wokler for inviting me to write what (after rather a long time) became chapter 16 of *The Cambridge History of Eighteenth-Century Political Thought*. Although that chapter had nothing to say about the *sans-culottes* as such, much of the argument of this book is a modified and more comprehensive version of the argument outlined there, with, as will be shown in chapter 4, a much sharper focus on a widely recognised, theologically inspired antithesis between Gothic government and absolute government as the initial framework in which a surprisingly large number of eighteenth-century justifications of an egalitarian property regime arose. One, very short, version of this book would be to say that the *sans-culottes* emerged when, for specifiable historical reasons, this long-standing antithesis between Gothic government and absolute government no longer made sense, and when, as a result, an old, rather austere way of thinking about moral integrity and royal reform—one sometimes associated with the ancient philosophical sect called the Cynics—became a vision of a more republican, and ultimately democratic, set of social and institutional arrangements. This book is a story about how and why these things happened, and, by extension, a description of what the French Revolution begins to look like in the light of the full version of the story.

Ian Malcolm at Princeton has been a patient and encouraging editor in helping me to get to its point, and I am most grateful to him, particularly for his willingness to tolerate my propensity to abuse the resources of modern electronic communication. Lauren Lepow has been extraordinarily meticulous in turning the typescript into a publishable book, and I am, again, extremely grateful to her for the time and trouble that this has involved. To some extent, this is a book about lost possibilities and disappointed hopes, even if, as is suggested in its final chapter, this may not be entirely a matter for regret. Although my own background may have given me something of a disposition to this way of approaching the past, I owe my initial awareness of its historiographical possibilities to the time when, nearly forty years ago, I was given the opportunity to study in Venice, where I was able to read *Il Doge Nicolò Contarini*, Gaetano Cozzi's marvellous book about, among other things, the Venetian Reformation that never was. I am still grateful to the late John Hale, Warwick University's first professor of history, and to Michael Mallett, for making that opportunity available, as well as to Robin Clifton for the advice that, on the eve of a particularly alarming examination, helped me to take advantage of it. As these acknowledgements are also intended to indicate, whatever merits this book might have are certainly the work of others, while its faults are still, emphatically, my own.

ABBREVIATIONS
AND A NOTE ON TRANSLATIONS

ABBREVIATIONS USED IN FOOTNOTES

A. N. Archives nationales, Paris
B. L. British Library, London
B. N. Bibliothèque nationale de France, Paris
CUP Cambridge University Press
OUP Oxford University Press
PMLA *Publications of the Modern Language Association*
SVEC *Studies on Voltaire and the Eighteenth Century* (in 2000 the abbreviation became the title of an annual series, published by the Voltaire Foundation, Oxford, with each issue numbered according to the year to which it belongs, as in, e.g., *SVEC* 2004: 04, meaning the fourth issue of SVEC published in 2004, and, where no subsequent pagination is indicated, this means that the issue in question consists of a single monograph).
UP University Press

A NOTE ON TRANSLATIONS

I have used a wide variety of editions of the works of individuals like Fénelon, Fleury, Mably, Mercier, Pluche, Poiret, or Rousseau, and have frequently made use of eighteenth-century English translations when citing passages from them, partly because these are sometimes more precise, or vivid (or both) than more recent translations, but mainly because they often give more consistently determinate renditions of words like *âme*, *esprit*, *lumières*, *sentiment*, *moeurs*, *état*, *amour-de-soi*, or *amour-propre* than are available in modern translations, and, by doing so, help to clarify the concepts that words like these were intended to indicate. References to modern translations are also supplied where these exist, and minor modifications to their wording in the light of eighteenth-century translations have, if they occur, been indicated. Translations from works not given either recent or eighteenth-century translations are my own, and, when I have been aware that my rendition of a French word may be tendentious, I have supplemented it with the French original in brackets. Full details of the editions used are available in the bibliography.

Sans-Culottes

∞ 1 ∞

INTRODUCTION: "ONE OF THE MOST INTERESTING PAIRS OF BREECHES RECORDED IN MODERN HISTORY"

THIS is a book about the *sans-culottes* and the part that they played in the French Revolution.[1] It is also a book about Rousseau, and, no less centrally, a book about salons. Its aim is to try to show how the three subjects were connected, and by doing so, to begin to piece together the historical and intellectual setting in which the republican politics of the French Revolution first acquired their content and shape. This, in the first instance, entails going back quite a long way into the eighteenth century. It also involves trying to get behind many of the events and images now associated with what the *sans-culottes* became. These centre mainly on the crowds who stormed the Bastille in Paris in July 1789 and, more specifically, on the mixture of direct democracy and physical force that, according to an established range of historical interpretations, either was orchestrated deliberately or erupted spontaneously among the artisans and small shop-keepers of urban France during the violent period of political conflict that occurred after the Parisian insurrection of 10 August 1792, and the trial and execution of Louis XVI in January 1793. By then, France had become a republic and, again according to the same range of established historical interpretations, the *sans-culottes* are usually described either as its social and political vanguard, or as the largely unwitting instruments of its Jacobin-dominated politics.[2] In one guise or another, however, the *sans-culottes*

---

[1] It is also an attempt to correct some of the gaps or mistakes in Michael Sonenscher, "The *Sans-Culottes* of the Year II: Rethinking the Language of Labour in Revolutionary France," *Social History* 9 (1984): 301–28; *Work and Wages: Politics, Natural Law and the Eighteenth-Century French Trades* (Cambridge, CUP, 1989), ch. 10; and "Artisans, Sans-Culottes and the French Revolution," in Alan Forrest and Peter Jones, eds., *Reshaping France: Town, Country and Region during the French Revolution* (Manchester, Manchester UP, 1991), pp. 105–21.

[2] For these characterisations of the *sans-culottes*, see, for more emphasis on spontaneity, Albert Soboul, *Les sans-culottes parisiens en l'an II* (Paris, Clavreuil, 1958); George Rudé, *The Crowd in the French Revolution* (Oxford, OUP, 1959); Richard Cobb, *Les armées révolution-naires: instrument de la terreur dans les départements*, 2 vols. (The Hague, Mouton, 1961–3); and, for more emphasis on orchestration, François Furet, *Interpreting the French Revolu-tion* [1978] (Cambridge, CUP, 1981); Patrice Gueniffey, *La politique de la terreur. Essai sur la violence révolutionnaire 1789–1794* (Paris, Fayard, 2000); and (with more emphasis on

FIGURE 1. Sans-Culottes, as Remembered by Posterity. (*Left*) French School, *The Sans-Culotte*, nineteenth century, © Bibliothèque des Arts Décoratifs, Paris, France / Archives Charmet / The Bridgeman Art Library; (*Right*) James Gillray, *A Paris Beau*, published by Hannah Humphrey in 1794, © Courtesy of the Warden and Scholars of New College, Oxford / The Bridgeman Art Library.

continue to be remembered (figure 1) as the hardworking, plain-speaking, moustache-wearing members of the popular societies, local militias, and revolutionary committees that proliferated in France between the spring and autumn of 1793, when the republic lurched from war into civil war, and as the institutions responsible for the Terror of 1793–4—from the French Convention's two great committees of public safety and general security, to the revolutionary tribunal, the maximum on prices, and the law of suspects—were put cumulatively into place. Evaluations may differ, but the *sans-culottes* are still normally identified with the Jacobin phase of the French Revolution.

This book tells a different story, both about the *sans-culottes* and about the French Revolution. It is a story about how to make property generally

orchestration by local elites), Richard M. Andrews, "Social Structures, Political Elites, and Ideology in Revolutionary Paris, 1792–1794: A Critical Evaluation of Albert Soboul's *Les sans-culottes parisiens en l'an II*," *Journal of Social History* 19 (1985): 71–112.

available, and what can happen if things go wrong. It starts with the sub-ject of culture, or what, beyond property, may be required for people to have better lives. It ends with the subject of necessity, or what, also beyond property, may be required politically just for people to survive. By de-scribing the original, eighteenth-century setting to which the phrase *sans culottes* first belonged, and by piecing together the steps involved in giving the phrase its more familiar connotations, the aim of this book is to open up a way towards the real political history of the French Revolution itself. It is still, of course, a history with the same protagonists and the same sequence of events. But, in the one set out here, both the goals and values of the protagonists, and the historical significance of the events themselves will all look rather different. So, too, will the weight given both to economic and social, and to political and ideological explanations of their content and course. Part of the point of this book is, therefore, to start a long overdue process of historiographical realignment by integrating both the politics and the economics of the French Revolution into a single, but still causally differentiated, historical narrative. Its focus is on a mixture of modern debt-based economics and ancient republican politics and, more specifically, on how the first came to be seen in the eighteenth century as the means to revive the second. In this vision of the future, public credit appeared to supply a way to reinstate merit, talent, and individual ability as the only legitimate criteria of social distinction, relegating property, privilege, and inherited advantage to positions commensurate with their status as what, in eighteenth-century language, were usually called goods of fortune. Using the modern funding system in this way appeared to offer the prospect of re-viving the ancient virtues, but without the violence of ancient politics, and, at least to some, to hold out the further prospect of a post-Machiavellian world, based firmly on purely natural, pre-Machiavellian, moral and politi-cal principles. From this perspective, modern public finance could look like the key to establishing a world made up of nations, not states, where the old phrase "the law of nature and nations" had been stripped, both theoretically and practically, of the state-centred set of connotations and arrangements that it had been given in the modern natural jurisprudence of the Dutch humanist Hugo Grotius and his seventeenth- and eighteenth-century fol-lowers ("sorry comforters," as the German philosopher Immanuel Kant called them in 1795).[3]

---

[3] For Kant's phrase, see Immanuel Kant, *Toward Perpetual Peace* [1795], in Immanuel Kant, *Practical Philosophy*, trans. and ed. Mary J. Gregor (Cambridge, CUP, 1996), p. 326. The phrase, it should be noted, was the original title of the Carlyle Lectures given by Richard Tuck at Oxford University that were published subsequently as *The Rights of War and Peace: Political Thought and International Order from Grotius to Kant* (Oxford, OUP, 1999). In this sense, what follows amounts to part of the other side of the relationship between Machiavelli, Machia-vellianism, and modern natural jurisprudence described by Tuck both in that book and in

In this sense, the narrative that follows is a story about a number of different eighteenth-century assessments of public debt, and about the way they
came to be connected to an older and broader array of eighteenth-century
evaluations of human nature, human history, and the part played by human
feelings, or the passions, in both. Explaining how and why these connections
occurred entails describing a number of subjects that now look quite specialised, but which were, in fact, considerably more central to eighteenth-
century thought than they may now seem. Some have to do with early
modern assessments of Ciceronian and Cynic moral philosophy, and, more
generally, with the part played by ancient thought in eighteenth-century
intellectual life. Some deal with what, in the eighteenth century, was usually
called enthusiasm, and, more specifically, with the idea that music, dance,
and poetry, rather than scarcity, need, and utility, were once the original
bonds of human association. Some are concerned with eighteenth-century
investigations of the very first forms of government, long before Rome set
its seal on Europe's history, and with the possibility that the Scythians, Germans, Celts, or Saxons were once subject to forms of rule unknown in either
republican or imperial Rome. Some involve heterodox early eighteenth-
century Protestant and Catholic discussions of the origins and nature of
property, and their bearing on the subject of love. Some centre on late
eighteenth-century scientific speculations about the nature of life, and the
part played by the soul in giving the body its complex internal organisation.
Some, finally, involve the eighteenth-century afterlife of the ideas of the
early eighteenth-century Scots financier John Law. Together, they add up
to a story about the origins and nature of late eighteenth-century French
republicanism and, more broadly, about how and why eighteenth-century
evaluations of the ancient Greek idea of democracy turned from negative
to positive, to become part of the political vocabulary and, more elusively,
the political practice of modernity.[4] Quite a large number of the features

---

his earlier *Philosophy and Government, 1572–1651* (Cambridge, CUP, 1993), as well as by
Istvan Hont, in his *Jealousy of Trade: International Competition and the Nation-State in Historical
Perspective* (Cambridge, Mass., Belknap Press, 2005), especially pp. 1–156, 447–528. For a
recent examination of eighteenth-century discussions of natural law, see André Charrak, "La
question du fondement des lois de la nature au dix-huitième siècle," *SVEC* 2006: 12, pp. 87–
99. For stronger emphasis on the differences between rights-based and virtue-based political
theories, see, classically, J.G.A. Pocock, *The Machiavellian Moment: Florentine Political Thought
and the Atlantic Republican Tradition* [1975], 2nd ed. (Princeton, Princeton UP, 2003).

[4] The argument of this book is, therefore, intended to complement that in Michael Sonenscher, *Before the Deluge: Public Debt, Inequality, and the Intellectual Origins of the French Revolution* (Princeton, Princeton UP, 2007). There, as indicated in the subtitle, the focus fell on the
subject of inequality; here, the focus falls on the subject of equality; but both had a bearing
on the broader subject of the nature and future of a world made up of states, wars, and public
debts. For the most sustained interest in democracy as a historical problem (irrespective of
the other types of problem it might present), see John Dunn, *Setting the People Free: The Story*

of this story about democracy's second life have disappeared from modern historiography, perhaps because they do not seem to have had much to do with the Enlightenment, or with the history of political thought, or with the emergence of political economy, or even with the history of the French Revolution itself. Much of the content of this book is designed to show that they did. Rousseau's part in the whole story is, however, quite complicated, because, as will be shown, many of its components came from Rousseau's critics, and not from Rousseau himself. But, without Rousseau, it is not clear that there would have been anything like this story at all.

The key initial ingredient in the story is, however, the original meaning of the phrase *sans culottes* and, with this in place, its bearing on the sequence of events that led from the fall of the Bastille to the beginning of the Terror. This is because the name *sans-culottes* was actually a neologism with a rather curious history. Although it can be taken initially to refer to someone simply wearing ordinary trousers, rather than the breeches usually worn in eighteenth-century public or professional life (since this, literally, is all that the French words mean), the words themselves also had a more figurative sense. In this latter usage, the condition of not having breeches, or being *sans culottes*, had very little to do with either everyday clothing or ordinary artisans, because it had, instead, much more to do with the arrangements and values of eighteenth-century French salons. In this setting, the condition of not having breeches, or being *sans culottes*, was associated with a late seventeenth- or early eighteenth-century salon society joke. As with all jokes, the context matters. But, stripped of the details that, for a surprisingly long period of time, made the joke worth repeating, and of the initial story that made it amusing, as well as the now rather inaccessible moral point that both the story and the details were intended to make (these can all come later), the joke relied on the fact that in the eighteenth century a writer who had a patron—in this case a woman who kept a salon—might be given a pair of breeches, while one who did not, would not, and would, therefore, be *sans culottes*.

The word *salon* is also a neologism. Before the nineteenth century, salons were usually called *sociétés*, *sociétés particulières*, *académies bourgeoises*, or *assemblées*, with no metaphorical significance attached to the name of the room in which they often met, as can be seen in the engraving (figure 2) entitled *L'assemblée au salon* published in 1783 by a Parisian engraver named François-Jacques-Barthélemy Dequevauviller, and based on an earlier gouache by a Swedish, but also Parisian, court painter

of Democracy (London, Atlantic Books, 2005). For a recent overview of "social" and "political" interpretations of the French Revolution, see Peter Davies, *The Debate on the French Revolution* (Manchester, Manchester UP, 2006), and, for a further round of the debate, see Henry Heller, *The Bourgeois Revolution in France 1789–1815* (New York, Berghahn Books, 2006).

FIGURE 2. François-Jacques-Barthélemy Dequevauviller, *L'assemblée au salon*, 1783. Bibliothèque nationale de France, Paris.

named Niclas Lafrensen.[5] But whatever they were called, salons are now mainly remembered as one of the more distinctive informal institutions of eighteenth-century France, and the often rather ornate setting in which women played a major part in establishing and maintaining the mixture of culture, civility, intrigue, and patronage that made up much of the unofficial life of the old French monarchy. It is not usual to think that there was much of a connection between eighteenth-century salons and the *sans-culottes* of the period of the French Revolution (beyond, perhaps, mutual disdain). This is why the first objective of this book is to try to show that

---

[5] Discussion of the furnishings depicted in the engraving can be found in Mimi Hellman, "Furniture, Sociability, and the Work of Leisure in Eighteenth-Century France," *Eighteenth-Century Studies* 32 (1999): 415–45. An early nineteenth-century account—Sophie Gay, *Salons célèbres* (Brussels, 1837)—began with a chapter on the salon of Mme de Staël but could still report that in the eighteenth century both Mme du Deffand and Mme Geoffrin had "un salon où l'on faisait des édits et des académiciens" (p. 8). On the large literature on salons, see below, p. 62n12.

there really was, and that it was historically significant, and, in the light of
this, that it is worth trying to explain how and why it occurred. The details
of how, when, and by whom the connection came to be made are set out,
first in chapter 2, and then in chapter 5. A large number of further details
are involved both in trying to explain why the connection was made and,
more importantly, in trying to describe what the point of making it might
have been. These form the subject matter of chapters 3 and 4.

These details are, however, parts of a broader argument, whose first step
is partly chronological and partly prosopographical. It is still usual to associate the *sans-culottes* with the year 1793 and the period of the French
Revolution that began with the final phase of the conflict between the former lawyer and republican political journalist Jacques-Pierre Brissot, and
his political allies on the one side (a loose alliance still sometimes called the
Girondins), and the better-known figure of Maximilien Robespierre, and
his Jacobin political allies on the other (a conflict that Robespierre and his
allies won). But it is not difficult to find quite a large amount of historical
evidence to show that the term *sans-culottes* was one of a number of now
less well-known figures of speech that were used somewhat earlier in the
French Revolution, specifically during the autumn and winter of 1791–2, to
try to attract the kind of popular support that, by 1793, came to be associated more or less exclusively with the name *sans-culottes* (*hommes à piques*, or
pikemen, was one, while *bonnets de laine*, or what, in English, might be called
flat-cap wearers, was another). Further historical evidence also indicates that
one reason why the words *sans-culottes* caught on, to become the name of a
political force, while the other names fell gradually out of use, was because
the words themselves had a resonance that was readily available to anyone
who knew anything about eighteenth-century French salons (the evidence is
set out in chapters 2 and 5). It may not be possible to count up the number
of people who actually did know much about eighteenth-century French
salons, but it is still possible to show that some of those who did were the
political actors who were largely responsible for turning the words *sans culottes* into the name of a political force (with a hyphen to connect the two
parts of the name). They were, in fact, Jacques-Pierre Brissot and his political allies, and they did so during the winter of 1791–2. A now forgotten
early nineteenth-century tradition once had it that the ministry made up of
Brissot's political allies that Louis XVI appointed in March 1792 was known
as the *sans-culotte* ministry.[6]

This chronological and prosopographical point has two implications.
First, it pushes back the starting point of any historical explanation of

[6] See, for example, François-Auguste-Marie-Alexis Mignet, *History of the French Revolution
from 1789 to 1814* [1824] (London, 1846), p. 128; and M. Touchard-Lafosse, *Souvenirs d'un
demi-siècle*, 6 vols. (Brussels, 1836), 2:262.

the part played by the *sans-culottes* during the French Revolution to the period that preceded the fall of the French monarchy and the beginning of the Terror. Second, it shifts the initial focus of attention away from Robespierre and his political allies towards Brissot and *his* political allies.[7] Together, they raise an obvious question about the type of connection that could have existed between Brissot, his political allies, and whatever the *sans-culottes* were supposed to be and do. The initial incongruity of the name itself makes the question more intriguing. Before 1789, Phrygian bonnets, pikes, or liberty trees all had a recognisable republican pedigree. They could be associated either with the ancient Roman republic and the liberty cap, or *pileus*, that was used to mark the emancipation of a slave, or with the popular militias, patriotic spirit, and egalitarian political arrangements commemorated in histories of the sixteenth-century Dutch and Swiss republics and the seventeenth-century English commonwealth. In this guise, they could all, for example, be found in the elaborate array of engraved emblems carefully chosen by the "strenuous Whig" Thomas Hollis to decorate the bindings of the many books that he sent all over Britain, Europe, and the United States in the middle of the eighteenth century to promote the republican moral and political values that he himself admired.[8] The phrase *sans culottes*, however, had no such past political resonance. It belonged fully and firmly to the world of the salon, where, well before the French Revolution, it was simply part of a joke.

Explaining how and why a joke about breeches could have become a republican emblem calls, initially, for piecing together a number of early eighteenth-century arguments about culture, civility, fashion, and trade, because these were the arguments that first supplied a connection between the various purposes that salons were taken to serve, and someone who was said to be not wearing breeches and was therefore *sans culottes*. The arguments in question (described in detail in chapter 2) amounted to a strong endorsement of the part played by the arts, in the broad eighteenth-century sense of the term, not only in making commerce, not conquest, one of the keys to the difference between the ancients and the moderns, but also in supplying reasons for thinking that the continuous traffic in goods and services that

---

[7] For a recent study of Brissot, see Leonore Loft, *Passion, Politics, and* Philosophie*: Rediscovering Jacques-Pierre Brissot* (Westport, Conn., Greenwood Press, 2002). On Brissot and his political allies, see Gary Kates, *The Cercle Social, The Girondins, and the French Revolution* (Princeton, Princeton UP, 1985); and François Furet and Mona Ozouf (eds.), *La Gironde et les Girondins* (Paris, Payot, 1991).

[8] See Caroline Robbins, "The Strenuous Whig, Thomas Hollis of Lincoln's Inn" [1950], in her *Absolute Liberty*, ed. Barbara Taft (Hamden, Conn., Archon Books, 1982), pp. 168–205 (especially pp. 180–2). According to a notice on Hollis published in the *Chronique de Paris*, no. 21 (13 September 1789), he commissioned the "famous Italian antiquarian" the abbé Venuti to write a dissertation entitled *de Pileo libertatis* (On the Liberty Cap) that was to be dedicated to the English nation.

was one of the more conspicuous features of the modern world could still be compatible with political or even moral virtue. In this context, it was not so much the interests that served to neutralise the passions, as the arts.[9] Here, the analytical focus fell less immediately on property and the productive uses to which it might be put, than on the way that fashion, and the mixture of public display and social conformism that it served to promote, worked to offset many of the more potentially pernicious effects of private property. From this point of view, what, in the early eighteenth century, came to be called "fashion's empire" could be said to have produced a rather benign form of subjection, where slavery to fashion (or being a fashion slave, as the modern phrase goes) was more metaphorical than real.

Property itself was divisive. "Mankind may live in peace," wrote Charles-Irénée Castel, abbé de Saint-Pierre, at the beginning of his *Project for Settling an Everlasting Peace in Europe* in 1713, "so long as they have nothing of any sort to be disputed or divided between them."

> They mutually obtain and procure to each other several conveniences, several considerable advantages, by means of the commerce they have with one another, and this unites them. But when they have anything to be disputed or divided between them, each of them, about the possession of the whole, or the greater or lesser share in the division, generally deserts from equity, which alone is able to serve them for a rule in the decision and for a preservative against general disunion.

"Thus mankind," Saint-Pierre concluded, "who seem to be created only to enjoy the blessings which society procures, are often obliged, for the possession of these same blessings, to re-enter into a state of division."[10] But, as both he and his friend, a Jesuit named Louis-Bertrand Castel, argued in a public discussion in 1725, the arts and sciences, and the technically innovative, fashion-based system of industry and trade that they had brought in their wake, housed a capacity to neutralise property's more divisive effects.[11] They did so, as several other early eighteenth-century

---

[9] On this theme in eighteenth-century thought, see Albert Hirschman, *The Passions and the Interests: Political Arguments for Capitalism before Its Triumph* (Princeton, Princeton UP, 1977).

[10] Charles-Irénée Castel, abbé de Saint-Pierre, *A Project for Settling an Everlasting Peace in Europe. First Proposed by Henry IV of France, and Approved of by Queen Elizabeth ... and now Discussed at Large and Made Practical by the Abbot St. Pierre* [sic] [1713] (London, 1714), pp. 2–3. For the original, see Charles-Irénée Castel, abbé de Saint-Pierre, *Projet pour rendre la paix perpetuelle en Europe* [1713], ed. Simone Goyard-Fabre (Paris, Garnier, 1981), pp. 2–5. For a helpful recent examination of theories of property, see Peter Garnsey, *Thinking about Property: From Antiquity to the Age of Revolution* (Cambridge, CUP, 2007).

[11] See, by way of introduction, the "Lettre sur la politique adressée à Monsieur l'abbé de Saint-Pierre, par le P. Castel Jésuite," *Journal de Trévoux*, April 1725, pp. 698–729, as well as Saint-Pierre's various essays on trade, beginning with his "Sur le commerce par rapport à l'état," reprinted in Charles-Irénée Castel de Saint-Pierre, *Les rêves d'un homme de bien, qui*

writers also argued, not only because of the price-making power that fashion supplied, or even simply because of the prosperity that fashion could produce (since prosperity could be redescribed less positively as luxury), but because of the way that it tapped those parts of human nature, like the feelings of surprise, wonder, or curiosity, that had little to do with immediate utility or purely physical pleasure. Here, as will be shown in more detail in chapter 2, it ·was usually the seventeenth-century philosopher René Descartes's analysis of the passions of the human soul that supplied a foil to the dark picture of human nature that was so prominent a feature of the strand of seventeenth-century Catholic theology that came to be called Jansenism. Cartesian moral theory helped to make it easier to claim that the arts and sciences, along with fashion, industry, and trade, fell on the right (honourable) side of the long-established distinction, usually associated with Cicero, between the honourable (*honestum*) and the useful (*utile*). Fuller explanations of these technicalities will be supplied in chapter 2. What matters here is simply the positive evaluation of fashion that they entailed. As was registered by another early eighteenth-century writer, Jean-Baptiste Dubos, in an influential book on poetry, painting, and music published in 1719, this type of evaluation cut across the old division between the liberal and mechanical arts (Dubos himself seems to have made a deliberate point of ignoring that older division).[12] Both, in certain respects, could be associated readily with the Ciceronian notion of decorum, just as, in a related gesture towards ancient philosophy's modern relevance, eighteenth-century salons could sometimes be identified with Plato's eponymous *Symposium*. The same conceit could also turn a *salonnière* into a modern version of a Greek courtesan, or *hetaira*. "Even the least celebrated of authors," as one, not entirely sympathetic, eighteenth-century commentator put it, "will still have his Aspasia."[13]

---

peuvent être réalisés (Paris, 1775), pp. 195–254. On Saint-Pierre's milieu, and its intellectual concerns, see Istvan Hont, "The Early Enlightenment Debate on Commerce and Luxury," in Mark Goldie and Robert Wokler, eds., *The Cambridge History of Eighteenth-Century Political Thought* (Cambridge, CUP, 2006), pp. 379–418, and, recently, Henry C. Clark, *Compass of Society: Commerce and Absolutism in Old-Regime France* (New York, Lexington Books, 2007), pp. 96–9. On Castel, see Catherine M. Northeast, "The Parisian Jesuits and the Enlightenment 1700–1762," *Studies on Voltaire and the Eighteenth Century* 288 (1991), and below, chapter 3.

[12] On the broad background to this vast subject (including a discussion of Dubos), see the classic article by Paul Oskar Kristeller, "The Modern System of the Arts: A Study in the History of Aesthetics," *Journal of the History of Ideas* 12 (1951): 496–527; 13 (1952): 17–46. For its eighteenth-century bearing, see, equally classically, Friedrich Meinecke, *Historism: The Rise of A New Historical Outlook* [1936] (New York, 1972), and, for a discussion, Allan Megill, "Aesthetic Theory and Historical Consciousness in the Eighteenth Century," *History and Theory* 17 (1978): 29–62. For further details, see below, chapter 2.

[13] Charles Palissot de Montenoy, *Les Courtisanes*, reprinted in his *Oeuvres complètes*, 6 vols. (Paris, 1809), 2:178. For further examples, see chapter 2.

Quite a large number of moves were required to turn evaluations like these into anything to do with republicanism. An initial indication of how they occurred can be found in a pamphlet that was published much later in the eighteenth century, because it touched on both the joke about breeches, and on what the joke became during the period of the French Revolution, in a rather oblique way. Since it supplies a substantial amount of information about some of the real historical figures with whom the joke was initially associated, and about those involved in its subsequent transformation, it is a helpful introduction both to some of the individuals described in this book, and to the mixture of political purpose, moral theory, and cultural criticism that they used to turn the joke about breeches into the now more recognisable figure of a *sans-culotte*. The pamphlet in question was actually a history of the Bastille or, as was indicated by its title (*Mémoires de la Bastille, sous les règnes de Louis XIV, Louis XV et Louis XVI*), a collection of accounts written by a number of individuals during the reigns of Louis XIV, Louis XV, and Louis XVI describing their periods of incarceration in the famous French fortress.[14] It was published in 1784 and was clearly designed to capitalise on the success of a pamphlet with a very similar title that had been published a year earlier, in 1783. This earlier pamphlet, entitled *Mémoires sur la Bastille* (or *Memoirs of the Bastille*, as the English translation, published in the same year, put it) was also an account of a period of incarceration in the royal prison, this time by a single individual, a lawyer named Simon-Nicolas-Henri Linguet. The largely satirical use to which the *Mémoires de la Bastille* put Linguet's own *Mémoires sur la Bastille* not only makes it a helpful initial guide to the related subjects of salons, breeches, and *sans-culottes*, but also supplies an introduction to the various types of satire that could be applied to these subjects in eighteenth-century France. Some aimed to emulate the works of the Roman satirist Horace, who wrote at the time when the Roman republic's last stormy years had given way to Augustus Caesar's empire, while others could be modelled in tone and content on the works of the later satirist of imperial Rome Juvenal. Both types of satire, however, took their cue from the ancient Roman conflation of the Greek and Latin pronunciations of the name (the Greek word indicated someone lewd, or a satyr, while the Latin word *satura* indicated a mixture or melange), to

---

[14] For a recent study of the Bastille, see Hans-Jürgen Lüsebrink and Rolf Reichardt, *The Bastille: A History of a Symbol of Despotism and Freedom* [1990], trans. Norbert Schürer (Durham, N.C., Duke UP, 1997). The pamphlet has sometimes been conflated with an earlier, much shorter pamphlet published (with no place of publication) in 1774 under the title of *Remarques historiques et anecdotiques sur le château de la Bastille*, and attributed in some library catalogues to an individual named Joseph-Marie Brossais du Perray. It was translated into English in 1780 and 1784 under the auspices of the prison reformer John Howard, and was then reissued in both French and English in 1789.

refer to a collection of miscellaneous, sometimes scatological, subjects that were treated with wit, style, and linguistic dexterity, either to highlight the distinction between rustic vulgarity and urbane decorum or, more fiercely, to underline the real moral difference between virtue and vice. In different ways, both types of satire had a bearing on the subjects of salons and breeches.

Linguet is quite well known to specialists of eighteenth-century French history, and of the history of eighteenth-century political thought.[15] He made his name as a lawyer by using the techniques of the theatre to turn legal proceedings into the dramatic rhetorical and emotional public spectacles that, in many parts of the world, they still are. He also made his name as a political writer by turning Jean-Jacques Rousseau's attack on the poisonous effects of private property into a justification of a centrally managed system of common ownership that, he argued provocatively, would be controlled by an absolute royal government similar in structure to the actually existing system of government of the Ottoman Empire. Both types of notoriety played a part in his imprisonment in the Bastille on 27 September 1780. Linguet's courtroom theatrics led him to be struck off the register of the Parisian order of advocates, while the literary and political journal, the *Annales politiques, civiles et littéraires*, that he had begun to publish in 1777 rapidly brought him to the attention of the French police authorities. The journal attained notoriety both for its violent attacks on certain named royal ministers and for its ferocious denunciations of the highest appeal courts in the kingdom, the thirteen royal parlements, as corrupt bastions of the financial and personal privilege that, he argued, ruled out justice from almost all legislative and political decisions made in the king's name. Linguet made great play of the sinister activities of his ministerial and his magisterial enemies in the account of his twenty-month incarceration in the Bastille that he published in 1783. In doing so, however, he rather overplayed his hand. On his account, not only had he been imprisoned in "a lion's den," where many of his earlier counterparts had been tortured or poisoned, but he had also suffered the indignity of being confined for two whole months without breeches (*sans culottes*).

Here, as Linguet emphasised, the date of his incarceration was what mattered. He had been arrested in late September, when it was still warm,

---

[15] For recent studies, see Darlene Gay Levy, *The Ideas and Careers of Simon-Nicolas Henri Linguet: A Study in Eighteenth-Century French Politics* (Urbana, University of Illinois Press, 1980); Sarah Maza, *Private Lives and Public Affairs: The* Causes Célèbres *of Prerevolutionary France* (Berkeley and Los Angeles, University of California Press, 1993), pp. 23–4, 45–50, 57, 279–80; David A. Bell, *Lawyers and Citizens: The Making of a Political Elite in Old Regime France* (Oxford, OUP, 1994), pp. 134–6, 146–7, 151–5, 159–62; and Miriam Yardeni, "Linguet contre Montesquieu," in Louis Desgraves, ed., *La fortune de Montesquieu* (Bordeaux, Bibliothèque municipale, 1995), pp. 93–105.

and, since he was about to go to the country to dine, all that he had at his disposal was his summer wardrobe. By November, however, it was getting much colder. "During that month, which in 1780 was extremely rigorous," as the English translator of his pamphlet put it, "I was reduced to the necessity of either condemning myself to close confinement in my cell, or of going naked, literally naked, to brave in my walk the violence of the cold." Although he offered "to *buy* the breeches which, I was informed, they *gave* to others," nothing happened until the end of November, when a Parisian silk merchant named Lequesne (a further object of Linguet's ire, but also, as will be shown, a name of some significance) sent over a winter collection (or *convoi d'hiver*) consisting of stockings "which a child of six years could scarcely have got on, with the rest of the habiliments in the same proportion." "Doubtless," Linguet commented, "they concluded I must have fallen away prodigiously," meaning, in more modern language, that he must have become exceedingly small and thin. The arrival of this unwelcome attire led Linguet to complain bitterly to the governor of the Bastille about "being derided in this manner." The result, he reported, was an explosion. The governor said "sharply" that "*je pouvais m'aller faire f**, qu'il se f** bien de mes culottes*" (or, as Linguet's translator put it more decorously, "that I might go to the *** and that he did not care a *** about my breeches"), adding as an afterthought that Linguet either ought to have taken more care to avoid being thrown into the Bastille or, once there, should have known how to put up with it.[16]

The story resurfaced in several satirical or more serious publications produced in response to Linguet's description of his ordeal at the hands of what he was only too willing to call ministerial despotism. The content of the more serious reaction can be left to chapter 6, because it has a bearing on understanding the political thought of the abbé Gabriel Bonnot de Mably. The satirical reaction, however, supplies an initial clue as to what a Parisian silk merchant might have been doing by sending Linguet a set of tiny stockings and breeches. It appeared in the *Mémoires de la Bastille*, the pamphlet published in 1784 to capitalise on Linguet's best-selling account of his victimisation. Its anonymous author made a point of highlighting the story about Linguet's run-in with the governor of the Bastille by setting it alongside a number of other famous stories about breeches. The first could be found in an episode in Voltaire's mock-heroic poem about Gothic barbarism and religious superstition, *La pucelle d'Orléans* (The Maid of Orléans) of 1756. In this episode, Joan of Arc had crept into the tent in which John Chandos was lying asleep in a drunken stupor and had

---

[16] Simon-Nicolas-Henri Linguet, *Mémoires sur la Bastille, et sur la détention de M. Linguet, écrits par lui-même* (London, 1783), pp. 155–6, and, in English translation, *Memoirs of the Bastille* (London, 1783), p. 156.

stolen his breeches, adding insult to injury as she left by drawing a *fleur de lys* on the English knight's equally somnolent servant's naked bottom. The breeches were then stolen again, this time by the volatile Agnès Sorel so that she could disguise herself as a man and, in this guise, resume her tryst with her heart's desire, Charles VII, king of France, by gaining entry to his armed camp. Before she could do so, however, she was captured by the English and brought face-to-face with the owner of the breeches, John Chandos, just as he was waking from his drunken stupor. How, Voltaire wrote, would you feel if you were to awake to see "so beautiful a nymph" at your side, wearing your *grègues*, just as sleep gives way to wakefulness, and as the senses begin to stir desire into voluptuousness? Before answering this entirely self-evident question, Voltaire inserted a pseudoerudite note to explain that the word *grègues* was an old Celt word for breeches. These, he wrote, were quite unlike modern breeches in appearance, since they were, in fact, long. The word itself, Voltaire explained, was a corruption of the old Celt word *brag*, and had then become the Latin word *bracca*, as in *Gallia braccata*, or *Gaule enculotté* (Gaul in breeches), the term once used to refer to the part of Gaul that was not ruled directly by the Romans, in contradistinction to *Gallia togata*, or the part of Roman Gaul that was subject to the authority associated with the togas worn by Gaul's imperial rulers. The word *brag*, Voltaire noted, actually referred to the upper part of the breeches, or to what was once called the codpiece, and is now usually associated with the fly-buttons (or *braguettes* in French). This part of the breeches, he explained, was usually of immense size, possibly out of necessity, but equally possibly because of vanity. Our ancestors, he continued, "kept oranges, sugared almonds and sweetmeats in them to give the ladies pleasure" (the author of *Memoirs on the Bastille* here, helpfully, referred readers to a picture published in the January 1783 entry of the *Almanac de Gotha*). This line of thought clearly fitted John Chandos's behaviour. The result, as Voltaire put it, was that Agnès Sorel's "modesty suffered greatly," and a good deal more happened too.[17]

John Chandos's breeches, the satirist noted, were "undoubtedly one of the most interesting pairs recorded in modern history."[18] There were,

---

[17] [Anon.], *Mémoires de la Bastille, sous les règnes de Louis XIV, Louis XV et Louis XVI* (London, 1784), pp. 68–71. See also François-Marie Arouet de Voltaire, *La pucelle d'Orléans* [1756] (Paris, 1766), cantos 2 and 3, pp. 40–2, 60–72. On the distinction between *Gallia braccata* and *Gallia togata*, see, for example, Thomas Carte, *A General History of England*, 4 vols. (London, 1747–55), 1:19–20: "The name of *Gallia Braccata*, by which the Narbonensis was called, being given to distinguish it from other parts of Gaul, was taken from the peculiar dress of the inhabitants of those provinces, who wore Braccae, trousers striped, and of various colours, serving for both hose and breeches, as the ancient Britons did of old, and the Irish, as well as the highlanders of Scotland continued to do till within living memory."

[18] [Anon.], *Mémoires de la Bastille*, p. 72.

however, several others. At the battle of Parma in 1734, the satirist observed, French forces had been surprised by those of the Holy Roman Empire, but their commander, Marshal Broglie, had earned himself lasting fame by appearing in the field without his breeches (*sans culottes*) to issue the orders that won the day. Nor was this the last story to be listed, because, the satirist continued, "Mme de Tencin's breeches are no less famous." These had nothing to do with the celebrated early eighteenth-century salonnière's own attire but consisted, instead, "of a pair of velvet breeches that the lady gave as a New Year's Day present to each of the wits (*beaux esprits*) who frequented her house, beginning with M. de Fontenelle. She was the most amiable woman of her age, and the breeches that she distributed have become proverbial." Alongside this "illustrious frippery," there were also "the old, henceforth famous, breeches" that had once been consigned to the *Annals* of the eighteenth century but were now destined "not to occupy the lowest of ranks among memorable breeches" (this, too, as will be shown shortly, was an allusion to Linguet). Finally, and "if the subject were not so serious (*grave*)," room on the list might also be found for the once-celebrated pair of breeches described in the old comic opera *Arlequin, roi de Sérendib* (Harlequin, King of Serendipity), where Harlequin's identity was revealed not only by his tears but, even more obviously, by the cut of his breeches.[19]

Not all these stories about breeches have a bearing on the connection between Simon Linguet's encounter with the governor of the Bastille in 1780 and whatever the *sans-culottes* were supposed to be or do during the period of the French Revolution. Marshal Broglie's breeches did have a short afterlife in Franco-British war propaganda at the time of the War of the Austrian Succession (from one point of view, they served to symbolise the French flair for nonchalant courage, while, from another, they helped to highlight French proneness to abject cowardice, since, in this version of the story, Marshal Broglie had simply deserted the battlefield, *sans culottes*).[20] The breeches' association with the family name may also have had some bearing on the younger Marshal Broglie's aversion to Prussian-style

[19] [Anon.], *Mémoires de la Bastille*, pp. 72–4. On Marshal Broglie's breeches, see also Barthélémy-François-Joseph Mouffle d'Angerville, *Vie privée de Louis XV*, 4 vols. (London, 1781), 2:13–4.

[20] Modern technology allows Broglie's breeches to be found in a widely reprinted poem entitled "Marshal Broglie's Breeches," in, for example, *The Englishman's Miscellany* (London, 1742), pp. 29–30; *The New Ministry* (London, 1742), p. 30; *The Summer Miscellany* (London, 1742); and Samuel Silence, *The Foundling Hospital for Wit* (London, 1743), pp. 46–7. The story was also rehearsed in John Winstanley, *Poems* (Dublin, 1742), p. 259; [Anon.], *An account of the birth, life and negotiations of the Marechal Bellisle* (London, 1745), p. 13; [Anon.], *Flanders Delineated* (London, 1745), p. 266; [Anon.], *Beauty's Triumph, or The Authority of the Fair Sex Invincibly Proved* (London, 1751), p. 247. It could still be found in Frederick II, King of Prussia, *Letters between Frederick II and M. de Voltaire*, 3 vols. (London, 1789), 2:322.

military discipline, as against French-style military flair, during the long argument over French army reform that punctuated much of the reigns of Louis XV and Louis XVI, as well as on the same younger Broglie's doubts about the merits of turning the guns of the French army on the population of Paris, just before the Bastille fell.[21] But, as will be shown in chapter 5, other reasons mattered more. A more recognisable set of evaluations occurred in the autumn of 1793, when the etymological distinctions involved in Voltaire's pseudoerudite footnote on *bracca* and *Gallia braccata* resurfaced as an entirely unsatirical evocation of the moral principles of the indigenous Gallic society that had once existed beyond the confines of *Gallia togata*. In this guise, the ordinary attire once worn by the Gauls (without any reference to the size of their *braguettes*) came to stand for the difference between an old, but now new, republican morality and its corrupt modern counterpart, as symbolised by Versailles. It also meant, in the light of a related, more or less scholarly tradition, that Hercules had originally been a Gaul. These, accordingly, became the reasons why the last five days of the new era's calendar came to be named *sans-culottides*, with each day celebrating a special feature of the French republic's moral qualities, beginning (on Robespierre's insistence) with virtue, followed by intelligence, work, repute, and memorable actions.[22] But, by the autumn of 1793, it was already quite clear what a *sans-culotte* was.

[21] On the younger Broglie's views on the French army, see his "Mémoire sur l'état de l'armée" of 1769, printed in Albert Latreille, *L'armée et la nation à la fin de l'ancien régime* (Paris, 1914), pp. 343–93, and, on his views in 1789, see L. Hartmann, *Les officiers de l'armée royale et la révolution* (Paris, 1910), pp. 37, 46, 53; and, in more detail, Munro Price, *The Fall of the French Monarchy* (London, Macmillan, 2002). On the subject of army reform, see below, chapter 5.

[22] The initial proposal had "genius" as the first subject to be celebrated in the five holidays, but Robespierre insisted on "virtue" (perhaps because Fabre d'Eglantine's first suggestion was too redolent of the thought of Helvétius). On the discussion, see Jacques Guillaume, ed., *Procès-verbaux du comité d'instruction publique de la Convention Nationale*, 6 vols. (Paris, 1891–1907), 2:704–5. On the idea of a Gallic Hercules, see, for example, Pierre de Longchamps, *Tableau historique des gens de lettres*, 6 vols. (Paris, 1767–70), and the review of it in the *Journal des beaux arts et des sciences* 1 (1768): 126–42, as well as Louis Poinsinet de Sivry, *Origine des premières sociétés, des peuples, des sciences, des arts et des idiomes anciens et modernes* (Amsterdam and Paris, 1769). Two further associations are worth noting. According to a satirical pamphlet entitled *Le parchemin en culotte* (Amsterdam, 1789), "forty years ago, workers in towns and villages wore sheepskin breeches." These then cost three livres but now cost three times as much, because of the large amounts of sheepskin required to make the parchment used in legal and fiscal documents. Less litigation, and fewer fiscal disputes, the pamphlet suggested, would make sheepskin less dear, "et les ouvriers auront des gants, des tabliers et des culottes" (p. 61). According to another pamphlet, also published in 1789, generals who were soldiers of fortune were called "leather breeches" (*culottes de peau*) by courtiers who relied on intrigue and patronage for promotion to high military office, which was why Chevert, "*une culotte de peau*," never became a marshal of France: see *Le premier aux grands, ou suite du Fanal* (n.p., 1789), 14, note.

Although, with hindsight, John Chandos might seem to have been the very first *sans-culotte*, the story that actually had the most considerable initial bearing on what the *sans-culottes* became was the one about Mme de Tencin and her "proverbial" practice of giving "the wits who frequented her house" a pair of velvet breeches on New Year's Day. To see why it did, two further pieces of information are required. Both concern the *sans-culottes* in their more familiar guise and can be found in two accounts of the origin of the name that were published in 1799 by a playwright, essayist, novelist, and moralist named Louis-Sébastien Mercier in a collection of short essays to which, echoing the earlier success of his *Tableau de Paris* (a multivolume description of Paris and its assorted inhabitants that began to appear in 1781), he gave the name *Le Nouveau Paris*, or a *New Picture of Paris*, as the English translation of 1800 was entitled. The first account of the term's source is quite well known and appeared in a chapter headed *Sans Culottes*.[23] "We are in general ignorant of the origin of this name," Mercier wrote.

> It is this. The poet Gilbert, perhaps the most excellent versifier after Boileau, was very poor. He had trimmed [mocked] some philosophers in one of his satires. An author who was desirous of paying his court in order to be of the Academy wrote a little satirical piece, which he called the *Sans Culotte*. Gilbert was rallied [ridiculed] on it, and the rich readily adopted this denomination against all authors who were not elegantly dressed.
>
> At the time of the Revolution, they remembered the term, adopted it, and employed it as an invincible spear against all those whose writings or discourses tended to a great or speedy reform.
>
> They thought it an excellent joke, and that they might laugh at it as they did twenty years ago. But politicians are more invulnerable than poets, and they took with a good grace the title which was given them. I was inscribed on the first list of sans-culottes, at which I only laughed.[24]

A great deal more can be said about the satirical poet Nicolas-Joseph-Laurent Gilbert and the bearing that his life and unhappy career may have

[23] The passage is reproduced in Annie Geffroy, "Sans-culotte(s)," in Annie Geffroy, Jacques Guilhaumou, and Sylvia Moreno, eds., *Dictionnaire des usages socio-politiques* (Paris, Klinck-sieck, 1985), pp. 159–86.

[24] Louis-Sébastien Mercier, *Le Nouveau Paris* [2 vols., 1799] (reprinted, Paris, 1862), 1:425–9, and, in the contemporary English translation, Louis-Sébastien Mercier, *New Picture of Paris*, 2 vols. (London, 1800), 1:420. Mercier's statement that his name appeared on a "list of *sans-culottes*" can be corroborated from the anonymously published *Liste des Sans-Culotte* [sic] (Paris, 1791), where it appears on p. 4 (along with eighty others, including Georges Danton, Antoine-Joseph Gorsas, Jean-Jacques Rutledge, Camille Desmoulins, François-Xavier Lanthénas, Fréron, Tallien, Jean-Paul Marat, Louis Carra, Joseph-Marie Prudhomme, Fabre d'Eglantine, Nicolas Bonneville, Anacharsis Cloots, François Robert, and François Momoro, to list those names that will be familiar to specialists of the French Revolution).

had on what the *sans-culottes* became (some is available in chapter 2). So far, however, no trace has been found of "the little satirical piece" called the *Sans Culotte* to which Mercier referred.

One possible reason may be that the piece in question was never actually published because it did not refer to Gilbert at all, but to Simon Linguet, and may, in fact, have been the cause of the episode that took place in the Bastille in 1780. Somewhat earlier in his *New Picture of Paris*, Mercier presented a rather different account of the origin of the name. This one appeared in a description of the background to or, as Mercier put it, the "first symptoms" of the Parisian insurrection of 10 August 1792, the day that marked the overthrow of the French monarchy and the beginning of the first French republic. To describe them, he gave them a specific geographical, and social, location. "The tempest rolled at a distance in hollow murmurs," Mercier wrote. "The inhabitants of the fauxbourgs [the suburbs mainly on the eastern side of Paris] made up a formidable corporation under the name of *sans-culottes*, which had been given them as a mark of derision by Laceuil, and which they afterwards preserved as a title of glory."[25] Again, no trace of any Laceuil has ever been found, although there was a marquis de Laqueuille, whose name is similar enough to the name Lequesne—the silk merchant responsible for sending Simon Linguet the set of tiny stockings and breeches during his incarceration in the Bastille—to suggest a possible confusion.[26] Linguet's outburst about "being derided in this manner" is also similar enough to Mercier's description of the name's being used as "a mark of derision" to suggest, too, that Linguet's story about his breeches may have been the source of this version of the origin of the term.

Whether or not, and also with hindsight, Gilbert or Linguet could lay claim to the title of being the first *sans-culotte*, both stories indicate that someone without breeches, or *sans culottes*, could become an object of derision. As will be shown in more detail in chapter 2, the derision applied particularly to a certain type of man of letters. It was an outcome of Mme de Tencin's widely publicised practice of giving a pair of velvet breeches on New Year's Day to the men of letters who frequented her salon. Linguet himself certainly knew of the custom, since he published an article in the December 1777 issue of his *Annales politiques* to correct a mock obituary notice that had appeared in the London *Morning Post*. According to that notice, the recent death of another *salonnière*, Mme Geoffrin, meant, as the English newspaper put it, that "about two hundred poetasters" would, "in all probability, never wear velvet again" ("no less than four thousand

---

[25] Mercier, *New Picture of Paris*, 1:126.

[26] On the marquis de Laqueuille, see Edna Hindie Lemay, *Dictionnaire des constituants*, 2 vols. (Oxford, Voltaire Foundation, 1991), 2:525–6.

pair of velvet breeches," it explained, "have been worn out in the poetical service of that lady"). As Linguet pointed out in reply, "the glory of the academic breeches" belonged first to Mme de Tencin, not Mme Geoffrin, even though, he wrote, the latter might have continued "so wise an institution." Perhaps, he continued, the name of the *order of the breeches* (*ordre de la culotte*), emblematised by a miniature pair of breeches garlanded with pink or puce ribbons suspended from the buttonhole, might one day replace the name of the French Academy, which was already looking rather worn out and had lost much of its lustre.[27] But whomever they were associated with (and they were, in fact, associated with both), the gift meant that someone who enjoyed either Mme de Tencin's or Mme Geoffrin's friendship and patronage had a pair of breeches, while those who did not were *sans culottes*.

Both Gilbert and Linguet could be associated with this latter category, which, as will also be shown in chapter 2, had come to have a broadly generic sense in the second half of the eighteenth century (although Mme de Tencin died in 1749, Linguet was not the only individual to indicate that the memory of her breeches lived on). Sending a set of miniature breeches and stockings to Linguet was, from this point of view, rather similar to writing "a little satirical piece called *The Sans Culotte*" about Gilbert, or even, perhaps, a satirical gesture towards Linguet's own joke about establishing an order of the breeches to replace the Académie française (this, presumably, was the point of the allusion to the "annals of the eighteenth century" made by the author of the *Mémoires de la Bastille*). In this sense, both of Mercier's two accounts of the origin of the name *sans-culotte* can be connected to this now largely forgotten story, and, since both referred to events that had occurred well before the French Revolution, it is entirely possible that, by 1799, Mercier's memory was no longer very accurate. He might, quite simply, have conflated the stories about Gilbert and Linguet by turning the name of the silk merchant Lequesne into Laceuil as a misremembered version of the name Laqueuille, a real individual whose hostility to the events of the revolution was of more recent memory. He might, equally plausibly, have conflated the name of the fortress in which Linguet had been imprisoned with the mysterious Laceuil's putative remark about the inhabitants of the suburb known as the *faubourg* Saint-Antoine, because the *faubourg* Saint-Antoine adjoined Linguet's prison in the Bastille.[28] It also happened to be the case that Gilbert, too, had been

---

[27] Simon-Nicolas-Henri Linguet, *Annales politiques, civiles et littéraires du dix-huitième siècle* (London, 1783), December 1777, pp. 405–8, commenting on the notice published in the *Morning Post* of 3 November 1777, from which the statement about "two hundred poetasters" and "four thousand pair of velvet breeches" is cited.

[28] On the silk merchant Pierre Lequesne (or Le Quesne, as the name was spelt in contemporary publications), who was the French distributor of Linguet's *Annales Politiques* at the time of Linguet's arrest in 1780, but then, like many others, became embroiled in a lawsuit

incarcerated in 1780, but in the Parisian Hôtel-Dieu, not the Bastille, and for his own protection rather than as punishment, because while Linguet was imprisoned for libel, Gilbert had gone mad.

There may, however, have been other reasons for the two versions of the origin of the term. Connecting the origin of the name to Gilbert, rather than Linguet, may have had the merit of eliminating any allusion to Linguet's despotic political propensities (highlighted, so his opponents claimed, by his call for a royal debt default in the August 1788 issue of his *Annales politiques* as a first step towards putting private property under state control).[29] But the possibility that Mercier's memory was more than simply garbled is still not the whole story. A little later in the chapter on *sans-culottes* in his *New Picture of Paris*, he went on to offer an explanation of why the term had become part of the political currency of the French Revolution. "All this," he began, referring to the story about the poet Gilbert, "took place before the Revolution. Who would have thought that republicans would have adopted this term, and made it a point of rallying?"

> It was certainly in order to annex contempt, hatred, and execration to the word, to the idea of republic, to the quality of republican, to the only government which can be avowed by reason, justice, and social reason. It was to render the natural rights of liberty and equality detestable that the Jacobins imagined and put in vogue the ignoble *sans-culottisme* and the *sans-culottide fêtes*.[30]

Here, what was at issue was certainly more than memory loss because it was, in fact, Mercier himself who had played a prominent part in encouraging "republicans" to adopt the term and "made it a point of rallying." The details of how he went about achieving this goal are set out in chapter 2. As Mercier also did not say, even though this memory was of equally recent vintage, his own efforts to identify the word *sans-culotte* with "the quality of republican" had been matched by an equally vigorous campaign (described in chapter 5) by another man of letters, an art critic and political journalist named Antoine-Joseph Gorsas, to do the same thing. These

---

with him, see Levy, *Linguet*, pp. 1, 190–206, 236. On the marquis de Laqueuille's hostility to the new regime, see B. L. F33 (13), a satirical pamphlet entitled *Décret important de l'assemblée nationale* (n.p., n.d. but 1790 from the contents), p. 13. It may also be worth noting that the story about Linguet and his breeches was repeated in the *Journal des Révolutions de l'Europe en 1789 et 1790*, 14 vols. (Strasbourg, 1789), 2:32–34. "A la vérité," the journal noted (p. 32), "les culottes de M. Linguet vont devenir fameuses, et ce ne sera pas un petit aliment pour ceux qui lui reprochent avec fondement un égoïsme dont le fiel orgueilleux perce à travers toutes les beautés dont fourmillent ses ouvrages."

[29] On this aspect of Linguet's career, see Michael Sonenscher, "The Nation's Debt and the Birth of the Modern Republic: The French Fiscal Deficit and the Politics of the Revolution of 1789," *History of Political Thought* 18 (1997): 64–103, 267–325.

[30] Mercier, *New Picture of Paris*, 1:421.

further details suggest that Mercier's story about Gilbert was rather more than the outcome of a hazy recollection of distant events, but was instead an effect of a more deliberate interest in highlighting one aspect of a more complicated set of memories. Gorsas's campaign, which took place during the winter of 1791–2, also had its starting point in the story about Mme de Tencin, her salon, and her breeches (although one of Gorsas's political opponents pushed the story back even earlier, to the seventeenth-century fable writer Jean de Lafontaine and his patron, Mme de la Sablière).[31] For both Gorsas and Mercier, far from its being the case that their aim in recycling the story had been "to annex contempt, hatred, and execration to the word, to the idea of republic," their initial purpose had been the exact opposite. Mercier himself made this particularly clear in the context of a full-blown endorsement of civil war that he published in July 1792, but which he had, in fact, first made public many years before the French Revolution in a satirical novel entitled *L'an 2440, rêve s'il en fut jamais* (The Year 2440, a Dream If Ever There Was One), published during the last, decaying, years of the reign of Louis XV (who died in 1774). If, as Mercier claimed in 1799, the word *sans-culotte* had nothing to do with "the quality of republican," this had certainly not been the case in 1792.

Although he did not quite put it like this, the most charitable interpretation of Mercier's various memory lapses is that republicanism in its Jacobin guise, or the republicanism of Robespierre, Saint-Just, and the revolutionary government of 1793–4, had entirely discredited whatever the term *sans culottes* once stood for. The substantive aim of this book is, accordingly, to describe what the term really did once stand for, before the image of the *sans-culottes* came to be set in its more familiar historical guise. In this sense, finding out about someone who was *sans culottes* before the *sans-culottes* became a political force (here, the hyphen is important) may help to open up a way to find out more about what republicanism in late eighteenth-century France once looked like, before it was given a real existence by the first French republic itself.[32] Doing so, however, first requires a further story. This one is about Plato and the ancient Cynic philosopher Diogenes of Synope. By the eighteenth century, however, it had also become a story about salons and men of letters, since, as the

---

[31] See below, p. 358.

[32] For two recent ways in to the large subject of republicanism, and a helpful reminder of the subject's historicity, see David Wootton, "The True Origins of Republicanism, or *de vera respublica*," in Manuela Albertone, ed., *Il repubblicanismo moderno. L'idea di republicca nella riflessione storica di Franco Venturi* (Naples, Bibliopolis, 2007), and his earlier review of Quentin Skinner and Martin Van Gelderen, eds., *Republicanism: A Shared European Heritage*, 2 vols. (Cambridge, CUP, 2002), in *English Historical Review* 120 (2005): 135–9. See, too, Paschalis M. Kitromilides, ed., *From Republican Polity to National Community: Reconsiderations of Enlightenment Political Thought*, SVEC 2003: 09.

early eighteenth-century French philosopher André-François Boureau Deslandes observed, the latter could be associated quite readily with both the poverty and satire of the Cynic way of life. "As for men of letters," Deslandes wrote, "it is well known that it is generally their lot to be at odds with fortune. Diogenes is of all ages, and his empty tub is but too often the patrimony of wit, which is, however, a kind of fatality hardly to be lamented, since penury and distress give one an air of vivacity which is wanting in a flowing felicity." The wit sometimes went along with moral criticism. "Every age, and especially our own," wrote the better-known philosopher Jean Le Rond d'Alembert in the context of a discussion of the relationship between men of letters and the great, "stands in need of a Diogenes, but the difficulty is in finding men who have the courage to be one, and men who have the patience to endure one."[33] In this particular story about Diogenes, Cynic wit was applied to Plato's taste for high living and his willingness to consort with unjust rulers, notoriously with the ruler of Sicily, Dionysius the Tyrant. Diogenes, whose own views on tyrants are best known from his curt request to Alexander the Great to get out of his sunlight, was said to have made a point of showing his disdain for Plato by trampling on his purple carpets, or, in other versions, his purple cloak, with his bare, filthy, feet. The choice of object could be taken to indicate either that Diogenes was rejecting the power associated with the imperial office, or that he was spurning the luxury associated with the imperial court. Both, more unequivocally, meant that he took Plato to be up to no good. By the eighteenth century, however, the story had acquired a more metaphorical significance. Just as a salon could be described as a reincarnation of an ancient Greek symposium, so a moral critic of salon society could be described as a reincarnation of a Cynic. If, according to the story about Mme de Tencin and her breeches, salon society supplied men of letters with a pair of *culottes*, then someone who made it a point of honour to avoid this type of patronage not only had no breeches in a literal sense but also was *sans culottes* in a Cynic sense.

From one point of view, not having breeches in this latter sense could amount to an ostentatious display of Cynic pride. But from another, it could also imply a strong endorsement of Cynic moral and political independence. It is not difficult to see how either characterisation could have been applied to the thought of Jean-Jacques Rousseau, as well as to Rousseau's

[33] [André-François Boureau Deslandes], *Réflexions sur les grands hommes qui sont morts en plaisantant* [1714] (Rochefort, 1755), p. 12. I have used what seems to be an original English version, published as *A Philological Essay, or Reflections on the Death of Free-Thinkers, with the Characters of the Most Eminent Persons of Both Sexes, Ancient and Modern, that Died Pleasantly and Unconcern'd* (London, 1713), p. 8. D'Alembert's statement can be found in his *Essai sur la société des gens de lettres et des grands* [1754], translated in Jean Le Rond d'Alembert, *Miscellaneous Pieces in Literature, History and Philosophy* (London, 1764), pp. 153–4.

own descriptions of himself (many of his critics did exactly that).[34] The remorseless eloquence of Rousseau's *Discourse on the Origin of Inequality* can make it easy to forget the ferocity of his wit (the most famous story of all about the French Revolution actually began as an episode in his *Confessions*, where, long before the remark came to be associated with Marie Antoinette, Rousseau described "a great princess" reacting to the news that "the peasants had no bread" by saying "let them eat cake," or, in the original, *qu'ils mangent de la brioche*).[35] But, as will be shown in chapter 3, the Cynic label that was often applied to Rousseau was also applied to a number of other, now much less well-known, writers, including Louis-Sébastien Mercier himself. One of them was one of Rousseau's earliest and most savage critics, the Jesuit Louis-Bertrand Castel, now perhaps known less for his friendship with the abbé de Saint-Pierre than for his lifelong efforts to find a way to invent a clavichord, or piano, that would play colours, not sounds. Another was also one of Rousseau's critics, this time a high Anglican English political moralist named John Brown, whose *Estimate of the Manners and Principles of the Times*, first published in 1757, was translated into almost every major European language during the following decade. A third, the abbé Gabriel Bonnot de Mably, was also one of Rousseau's critics, and a strong admirer of Brown. The title of his best-known work, *Phocion's Conversations*, was also a gesture towards Cynic philosophy, since Phocion, according to the *Encyclopédie* entry on the sect, was one of the later Cynics. They were, the entry concluded, "enthusiasts of virtue."[36] So, too, according to Robespierre a generation or so later, was Rousseau. But the generic term "virtue" could encompass a wide variety of different evaluations of human behaviour, and an equally wide range of assessments of their causes and effects. As will be shown from chapter 3 onwards, quite a large number of historically contingent moves were required to bring them into moral and political alignment.

From a distance Rousseau, Mably, and Brown may all have looked quite similar. All three subscribed to a three-stage model of the development of human association, even if their respective descriptions of the social arrangements corresponding to each stage were still significantly different. All three were invited in 1762 by the Swiss Patriotic Society to contribute entries to one of its prize competitions on the subject of moral and political reform, while the argument of Brown's *Thoughts on Civil Liberty, on Licence*

---

[34] "By a morality, apparently of a severe kind, by leading the life of a cynic, and by writings replete with fire, eloquence, and genius, he has influenced some minds of more sensibility than strength": Louis Dutens, *The Tocsin, or an appeal to good sense* [1769] (London, 1800), p. 19. For other examples, see below, chapter 3.

[35] Jean-Jacques Rousseau, *Les Confessions* [1783], 3 vols. (London, 1786), vol. 2, bk. 6, p. 296.

[36] Denis Diderot and Jean Le Rond d'Alembert, eds., *Encyclopédie*, vol. 4 (Paris, 1755), pp. 598–9.

and Faction of 1765 was used, when it was published in French translation in 1789, to endorse what its translator emphasised was the idea of moral improvement supplied by Rousseau's more slippery concept of *perfectibilité*.[37] But on closer inspection, their moral and political theories were actually very different. For Mably, Rousseau's imaginative reach far exceeded his analytical grasp, resulting too often in "shocking disparities" and "those paradoxes that are so displeasing to sound minds." "We are born," he wrote, "for honest sufficiency (*médiocrité*). A virtue carried too far becomes a vice, just as all the qualities that form genius degrade it, if, through an unbalanced mixture, one of them has too much of an empire over the others."[38] This was Rousseau's failing, and, as will be shown in chapter 6, the basis of Mably's sustained criticism of his moral and political thought. Reconstructing both the similarities and the differences between Rousseau and his critics is a way not only to identify what Cynic moral philosophy may have stood for in the eighteenth century, but also, and in contradistinction to Rousseau, to begin to describe what, in the eighteenth century, a noncontractual theory of a republican polity might once have looked like.

Here, too, the various types of moral evaluation involved in having or not having breeches form a helpful starting point, because they make it easier to highlight two contrasting conceptions of human decency. Just as, from a Ciceronian point of view, the first condition could be associated with the cultivation of the arts and sciences, and the civility and decorum that they brought in their wake, so, from a Cynic point of view, could the second condition be associated with a more natural set of human qualities and, more particularly, with the idea that the peculiarly human capacity for music, dance, and poetry was once the primary bond of society. To its critics, as will also be shown in chapter 3, this way of thinking about the very first forms of human association fully deserved the Cynic label. But

[37] [John Brown], *De la liberté civile et des factions* (n.p., 1789), p. 11. The content of Brown's 1765 pamphlet was made available earlier in a translation of the attack on it by Joseph Priestley in his *Essay on a Course of Liberal Education for Civil and Active Life* (London, 1765) that was published by the former Jesuit Jean-Baptiste-René Robinet in his *Dictionnaire universel des sciences morale, économique, politique et diplomatique, ou Bibliothèque de l'homme d'état et du citoyen*, 30 vols. (London, 1772–83) under the rubric "éducation libérale." On Brown, Rousseau, Mably, and the Swiss patriotic society, see below, chapter 4.

[38] Gabriel Bonnot de Mably, "Des talents," in Gabriel Bonnot de Mably, *Collection complète des oeuvres*, 15 vols. [1794–5], ed. Peter Friedemann (Aalen, Scientia Verlag, 1977), 14:178–81. For an overview of the relationship, see Giuseppe A. Roggerone, "Rousseau-Mably: Un rapporto umano e culturale difficile," *Il Pensiero Politico* 23 (1990): 219–39. According to one (eccentric) defender of absolute government, Mably was the source of "l'économie des systèmes de vos nouveaux disciples, car vous êtes leur oracle et le créateur de la jurisprudence politique que nos auteurs nouveaux ont embrassé et voudraient nous faire adopter": [Augustin-Jean-François Chaillon de Jonville], *Apologie de la constitution française, ou états républicains et monarchies comparés dans les histoires de Rome et de France*, 2 vols. (n.p., 1789), 2:29.

Rousseau's Jesuit opponent Louis-Bertrand Castel called it "naturalism" (he also blamed Montesquieu for having led Rousseau astray), while John Brown wrote two versions of the same book (soon translated into French) to show that the original union between music, dance, and poetry that, he argued, was still visible in French Jesuit missionaries' descriptions of the North American Hurons, as well as in the recently discovered poems of the Celtic bard "Ossian," indicated that the very first manifestation of human culture had to be the hymn.[39] One of Voltaire's admirers wrote a large satirical novel, entitled *Le Diogène moderne* (The Modern Diogenes), to suggest that Rousseau's thought was simply Brown, minus Brown's religious dogma. Brown's own suicide, the novel suggested, merely underlined the untenable quality of both types of moral philosophy.

But whether Cynic moral theory was taken to be sceptical, as with Rousseau, or dogmatic, as with Brown, it still relied heavily, at least according to this characterisation, on the claim that the arts in their original form had nothing at all to do with fashion and display, but derived instead from the various types of intense emotion involved in "enthusiasm," as, for example, these were described by another widely read English (and also Anglican) moralist, Edward Young, in his *Conjectures on Original Composition* of 1759.[40] In this context, the arts were not the offspring of necessity, but the outcome of the feelings of wonder, awe, or reverence produced by the human capacity to respond emotionally to what was sacred or sublime. From this more spiritually charged point of view, as Young wrote in 1742 in his equally celebrated *Night Thoughts*, "passion is reason; transport temper *here*."[41] Seen like this, the arts, and the emotions from which they

[39] On Brown, and the broader subject of Ossian, see below, chapter 3, and Paul Van Tieghem, *Ossian en France*, 2 vols. (Paris, 1917), 1:241–2. For a recent overview, but with more emphasis on the origins of later musical categories, see Matthew Gelbart, *The Invention of "Folk Music" and "Art Music": Emerging Categories from Ossian to Wagner* (Cambridge, CUP, 2007).

[40] On Young, see the best edition of his *Night Thoughts* [1742], ed. Stephen Cornford (Cambridge, CUP, 1989), and, on Young's French reception, see, for the best study, Fernand Baldensperger, "Young et ses *Nuits* en France," in his *Etudes d'histoire littéraire*, 4 vols. (Paris, 1907–39), 1:55–109. See, too, Walter Thomas, *Le poète Edward Young 1683–1765. Etude sur sa vie et ses oeuvres* (Paris, 1901); Paul Van Tieghem, *Le Préromantisme*, 3 vols. (Paris, 1948), 2:3–203; John McManners, *Death and the Enlightenment* (Oxford, OUP, 1981), pp. 335–8. For a starting point on Young's ideas and readership, see H. B. Nisbet and Claude Rawson, eds., *The Cambridge History of Literary Criticism* (Cambridge, CUP, 1997), pp. 141–9, 165–6, 629–32.

[41] Young, *Night Thoughts*, ed. Cornford, p. 107, night 4, line 640 (the italics are in the original). On this aspect of Young's thought, see Shaun Irlam, *Elations: The Poetics of Enthusiasm in Eighteenth-Century Britain* (Stanford, Stanford UP, 1999), and, for its reverberations in German Pietist circles, including Young's friend, the poet Friedrich Klopstock, see Jonathan Sheehan, *The Enlightenment Bible: Translation, Scholarship, Culture* (Princeton, Princeton UP, 2005), pp. 152–81 (especially pp. 156–8). "Je veux du mal au sublime Young d'avoir infecté le monde du poison de son imagination transcendante et noire," wrote the Swiss political essayist Georg Ludwig Schmid d'Auenstein to his friend Johann Georg Zimmermann in

derived, could be associated with an entirely different moral universe from the one described, for example, in Voltaire's poem *Le Mondain* (The Man of the World), or even, as Young noted in his early (1728) *Vindication of Providence*, from "the wrong bias" given to the treatment of the emotions by Descartes in his study of the passions of the human soul.[42] Here, culture was less a matter of acquired civility than the authentic voice of human dignity. Brown was the first writer in the English-speaking world to pick up the recently coined French word *civilisation* to describe this type of moral universe, and when, towards the end of the eighteenth century, the painter Jacques Réattu began the painting that he was to call *The Triumph of Civilisation* (see figure 3), the moral values that it was intended to endorse were substantially nearer to Brown than they were to Voltaire.[43] The two points of view did share a measure of common ground, since both dealt with the related subjects of human association and morality, or what in the eighteenth century was usually called sociability, in terms of something other than indigence, need, and utility. But, despite this initial similarity, the differences were more pronounced. For the first, the arts polished and embellished primitive human nature, while for the second, they were real evidence of humanity's original natural dignity. One, put very crudely, pointed to the value of culture. The other, put equally crudely, pointed to the value of nature. Both terms require much fuller explication (also supplied in chapter 3). But in a remote yet still real sense, the *sans-culottes* could be described as the product of Cynic criticism of Ciceronian moral philosophy, as both were construed in the eighteenth century.

Setting Rousseau's moral and political thought against this large and now rather neglected strand of eighteenth-century thought (which Castel, in the eighteenth century, called "naturalism," but which, in the first half of the twentieth century, came to be called "primitivism") helps to highlight Rousseau's subtleties and ambiguities. Both were captured memorably by the German philosopher Immanuel Kant in his description of Rousseau as

---

1756 (Nieder-Sachsische Staastarchiv, Zimmermann papers, MS XLII, 1933, AII, 83, fol. 115, Schmid to Zimmermann, 1 December 1756). Young's "genius," wrote Anna Laetitia Barbauld in 1794, "was clouded over with the deepest glooms of Calvinism, to which system however he owed some of his most striking beauties." See her "Essay on Akenside's Poem," in Mark Akenside, *The Pleasures of Imagination* (London, 1796), p. 15.

[42] Edward Young, *A Vindication of Providence, or a True Estimate of Human Life. In Which the Passions are Considered in a New Light* [1728], in Young, *Works*, 6 vols. (Edinburgh, 1774), 6:preface (unnumbered pages). For an interesting suggestion that this type of "enthusiasm" had a bearing on Tom Paine's thought, see Joe Lee Davis, "Mystical versus Enthusiastic Sensibility," *Journal of the History of Ideas* 4 (1943): 301–19 (318).

[43] On the eighteenth-century concept of "civilisation," see, most recently, Bertrand Binoche, ed., *Les équivoques de la civilisation* (Seyssel, Champ Vallon, 2005). On Brown's use of the term, see below, pp. 180, 191. On Jacques Réattu, see Katrin Simons, *Jacques Réattu (1760–1833), peintre de la révolution française* (Paris, Arthéna, 1985).

FIGURE 3. Jacques Réattu, *The Triumph of Civilisation*, ca. 1794–98, © Hamburger Kunsthalle, Hamburg, Germany / The Bridgeman Art Library.

"that subtle Diogenes."[44] Both, too, were visible in Rousseau's historically conjectural treatment of human nature and property. To many of his early readers, Rousseau's morally attenuated treatment of the first appeared to align his moral theory with that of the seventeenth-century English political philosopher Thomas Hobbes, while his morally charged treatment of the

[44] For Kant's description, see Immanuel Kant, *Lectures on Ethics*, ed. Peter Heath and J. B. Schneewind (Cambridge, CUP, 1997), p. 45. The ambiguities in Rousseau's stance were captured in a different way in an entry on "civilisation," aimed at Rousseau, that was published by an obscure teacher named Alexandre Bacher in the aftermath of the coup d'état that brought Napoleon to power. Both "the titled factions" and "the intrusive factions" responsible for the revolution's violent course had, he wrote, "appealed to your paradoxes": Alexandre Bacher, *Cours de droit public*, 4 vols. (Paris, 1801), 1:394. The idea of "civilisation," he went on to claim, nullified the argument of Rousseau's second *Discourse*. On "primitivism," see Arthur O. Lovejoy and George Boas, *Primitivism and Related Ideas in Antiquity* [1935] (Baltimore, Johns Hopkins UP, 1997); George Boas, *Primitivism and Related Ideas in the Middle Ages* [1948] (Baltimore, Johns Hopkins UP, 1997); Lois Whitney, *Primitivism and the Idea of Progress in English Popular Literature of the Eighteenth Century* (Baltimore, Johns Hopkins UP,

second appeared to rule out any possibility of moral and political reform, at least as far as an absolute monarchy like France was concerned. As Rousseau reiterated repeatedly, all that the great states of modern Europe could look forward to was an age of crisis and revolution, from which there might be no way back.[45] The underlying reason followed the historical logic that he set out in his anti-Montesquieuian *Discourse on the Origin of Inequality*, with its step-by-step account of the emergence of the distinctions between the strong and the weak, the rich and the poor, and the powerful and the powerless. "The general spirit of laws in every country," he wrote in a note to his *Emile*, "is to favour the strong against the weak, and the rich against the poor; this inconveniency is inevitable and admits of no exception."[46] The diagnosis was easily applicable, particularly in France. "If the system remains, and foodstuffs (*les vivres*) stay as dear as rent, and the people continues to suffer, either there will be a violent crisis that will overturn the throne, and give us another form of government, or there will be a kind of lethargy, just like death," wrote one of Rousseau's admirers, the future Manon Roland, in response to the first apparent corroboration of his predictions, in 1776.[47] Chapter 4 is an examination of how Rousseau's critics and admirers (the line dividing the one from the other was often fairly hazy) tried to come to terms with this prospect, as well as the broader set of claims about human nature and history on which it was based. If, as one of Rousseau's readers put it, "nature gave men feelings (*sentiments*) that made them sociable," but those same feelings could be "corrupted and destroyed by society itself," then the prospects for the future were unusually bleak.[48] One way out pointed towards the political thought of Emmanuel-Joseph Sieyès during the period of the French Revolution.[49] Others, however, pointed towards the kind of republicanism that Louis-Sébastien Mercier came to espouse.

1934); Gilbert Chinard, *L'Amérique et le rêve exotique dans la littérature française du xviie et xviiie siècles* (Geneva, Droz, 1934); and Arthur O. Lovejoy, *Reflections on Human Nature* (Baltimore, Johns Hopkins UP, 1961). On Kant's assessment of Rousseau, see below, chapter 3.

[45] On this way of thinking about revolution, see Sonenscher, *Before the Deluge*, pp. 1–9, 23–32, 41–52, 192, 254, 317, 354, and below, chapters 4 and 6. More broadly, see Reinhart Koselleck, *The Practice of Conceptual History* (Stanford, Stanford UP, 2002), chs. 5–10, 12–14; J.G.A. Pocock, *Barbarism and Religion: The First Decline and Fall* (Cambridge, CUP, 2003), chs. 14–16; Malcolm Jack, *Corruption and Progress: The Eighteenth-Century Debate* (New York, AMS Press, 1989), pp. 63–112.

[46] Jean-Jacques Rousseau, *Emilius, or An Essay on Education*, trans. Thomas Nugent, 2 vols. (London, 1763), 1:360.

[47] Gita May, *De Jean-Jacques Rousseau à Madame Roland* (Geneva, Droz, 1964), p. 63. The comment was prompted by the so-called flour war of that year.

[48] Dominique-Joseph Garat, *Éloge de Michel de l'Hôpital, chancelier de France* (Paris, 1778), p. 4.

[49] On Sieyès's political thought, see Sonenscher, *Before the Deluge*, pp. 10–21, 67–94, 349–71, and Christine Fauré, ed., *Des manuscrits de Sieyès*, 2 vols. (Paris, Champion, 1999–2007), as well as the further bibliographical guides to secondary literature set out there.

Two subjects loomed large in this vision of a republic. The first was morality, while the second was the modern funding system, or the growing eighteenth-century practice of using public debt to fund the costs of war. Rousseau showed no interest at all in thinking in any positive way about how the two could be combined, but many of his critics or admirers did. Detailed descriptions of the claims about human nature, private property, and emotional peace of mind involved in this mixture of morality and debt finance—as well as of the largely theological context in which these claims first arose—are contained in chapters 3 and 4. But an initial indication of what this mixture entailed is best set out by dealing, in the rest of this introduction, with the two subjects in turn. The first involved finding a number of different, but complementary, ways to put more morality into Rousseau's highly attenuated characterisation of human nature, and the abstentive moral theory that it implied. As several of his critics pointed out, Rousseau's attempt, in his *Discourse on the Origin of Inequality*, to use the Anglo-Dutch freethinker Bernard Mandeville's description of the prereflective emotion of pity as the basis of a purely negative morality (involving doing one's own good, with the least harm, rather than the most good, to others) begged too many questions about natural human capabilities and motivation to be plausible. It seemed either to rule out anything recognisable as altruism, or to require a very highly developed imaginative ability to be able to work. The only "true model" of human happiness that Rousseau appeared to offer, noted his Genevan acquaintance Jean-André Deluc, was "the absence of any positive bond within the human race." Rousseau's moral maxim of doing the least possible harm to others was undoubtedly a "natural rule" because it had its basis in pity, but, Deluc complained, it made "the human disposition to beneficence quite useless."[50] The same type of objection came from the other side. As another of Rousseau's critics commented, getting pity to work in the way that Rousseau claimed that it did presupposed a level of imaginative agility that was incompatible with his other claims about the rudimentary qualities of the original features of human nature. Far from being natural, Rousseau's idea of pity was simply "the pure eloquence of a soul embellished (*orné*) by an acquired enlightenment."[51] It relied on far too many

---

[50] Jean-André Deluc, *Lettres sur l'histoire physique de la terre adressées à M. le professeur Blumenbach* (Paris, 1798), pp. cii–ciii.

[51] [Claude-François-Xavier Millot], *Histoire philosophique de l'homme* (London, 1766), p. 250. See, too, pp. 40, 256–7: "Si M. Rousseau eût pris son modèle dans l'enfant à la mamelle, il aurait vu que son homme naturel pouvait être environné des cadavres ensanglantés de son père, de sa mère, de tous ceux avec qui il avait coutume de vivre, se trouver inondé de leur sang, et ne sentir cependant que cet étonnement irraisonné, cette frayeur machinale qui arrachent des cris aux enfants à la vue d'hommes armés, menaçants, bruyants, vêtus extraordinairement pour eux, et se conduisant d'une manière toute opposée à celle des hommes avec qui ils sont

unacknowledged primary human feelings and ideas to be credible. Getting behind the acquired features of human nature called, it could be claimed, for an even more determined effort than Rousseau had been either willing or able to make.

The difficulties involved in identifying what was innate or acquired in Rousseau's characterisation of human nature were compounded by the fact that two of the key parts of what he described repeatedly as his system were published only posthumously. These were the *Essay on the Origin of Languages*, which, it is now clear, Rousseau began to draft in 1754, initially as a part of the *Discourse on the Origin of Inequality*, and the *Considerations on the Government of Poland*, which Rousseau wrote some fifteen years later, during the winter of 1770–1, but which also entered the public domain only with the posthumous publication of the Geneva edition of his collected works in 1781.[52] In one sense, the appearance of the two works added to the ambiguity. In part this was because of the striking difference between Rousseau's description of the feeling of pity in the *Discourse on the Origin of Inequality* and his examination of the same emotion in the *Essay on the Origin of Languages*. In part, too, it was because of the quite emphatic endorsement of monarchy that could be found in the *Considerations on the Government of Poland*. The first of these apparent discrepancies in Rousseau's thought has attracted the most attention, but, once clarified, it helps to make sense of the second. Where, as many of Rousseau's early critics noted, pity in the second *Discourse* worked in purely negative terms, as an aversion to the sight or sound of others' pain, Rousseau gave it a more positively sympathetic, or compassionate, content in the *Essay*. The discrepancy puzzled Rousseau's later readers and has continued to do so

---

accoutumés, et dont ils n'ont éprouvé que les caresses." For a helpful examination of another contemporary reaction to Rousseau's pity-based moral theory (by the Basel magistrate Isaak Iselin), see Béla Kapossy, *Iselin contra Rousseau: Sociable Patriotism and the History of Mankind* (Basel, Schwabe, 2006), pp. 218–45.

[52] On the chronology, see Robert Wokler, "Rameau, Rousseau, and the *Essai sur l'origine des langues*," *Studies on Voltaire and the Eighteenth Century* 117 (1974): 179–238; Elizabeth Duchez, "*Principe de mélodie* et *Origine des langues*: Un brouillon inédit de Jean-Jacques Rousseau sur l'origine de la mélodie," *Revue de musicologie* 60 (1974): 33–86; and, for Wokler's revised view, Robert Wokler, *Rousseau on Society, Politics, Music and Language: An Historical Interpretation of His Early Writings* (New York, Garland Press, 1987), pp. 306–7. For bibliographical details of the large literature on Rousseau's *Essay*, see John T. Scott, introduction to Jean-Jacques Rousseau, *The Collected Writings*, vol. 7. *Essay on the Origin of Languages and Writings Related to Music* (Hanover and London, University Press of New England, 1998), pp. xxvii–xxxvi, 560–1, 566. Scott's own examination of pity tends to conflate Rousseau's distinctions between its abstentive and compassionate qualities with its innate and acquired properties: see John T. Scott, "Rousseau and the Melodious Language of Freedom," *Journal of Politics* 59 (1997): 803–29, and his "The Harmony between Rousseau's Musical Theory and His Philosophy," *Journal of the History of Ideas* 59 (1998): 287–308.

ever since.[53] It can, however, be reconciled if both characterisations of pity are positioned within the broader framework of Rousseau's historical treatment of property on the one hand, and of music, language, and morality on the other. Setting the two alongside each other makes it easier to see the two different conjectural histories of humanity that lay at the heart of Rousseau's moral and political thought. One had property at its centre, but the other did not. The details of these two histories will be developed in the next two chapters, but, put summarily, one pointed towards the despotic outcome of the *Discourse on the Origin of Inequality*, while the other pointed towards the set of economic and political arrangements outlined in the *Considerations on the Government of Poland* and, less generalisably, in the *Social Contract*. Analytically, the switch from largely self-sufficient to interdependent households occurred when one household owned enough to feed two, and when a property-based social contract served to magnify the resulting spiral of dependence. Historically, however, Rousseau also implied that the switch would happen in real time and involve a step back to a less socially interdependent political order. In this vision of the future, the self-sufficient arrangements and inward-looking emotions that he described in his books about Poland and Corsica would form the surviving pockets of what had once been Europe in the wake of the revolution that he first predicted at the end of the *Discourse on the Origin of Inequality* and amplified upon in many of his later publications.

There would still be property, but its legal character would be defined by the general will as what belonged to others, not to oneself. As an individual possession, property would be limited by need and utility (plus, as will be shown in chapter 3, good taste) because acquisitive emotions and behaviour would be cancelled out by conscience, or the developed form of pity that Rousseau began to discuss in the second *Discourse* but explained more fully in the *Essay on the Origin of Languages*. The difference between the two was connected to his historical and political vision. Pity in its first, abstentive, guise was a presocial emotion, common to animals as much as to humans. It was present among the very first humanoids, who, Rousseau emphasised in the *Essay*, originated in the hot climate of the South (roughly speaking, Egypt). The mechanism responsible for giving pity its fuller, more actively sympathetic, content was, initially, love. Love, Rousseau argued,

<hr/>

[53] For an example of the continuing hostility towards Rousseau's self-centred treatment of pity, one that set his moral theory against that of his self-proclaimed disciple Jacques-Henri Bernardin de Saint-Pierre, see George-Marie Raymond, *Essai sur l'émulation dans l'ordre social, et sur son application à l'éducation* (Geneva, 1802), pp. 56–65. For a particularly fascinating discussion of Rousseau's treatment of the related subjects of pity, music, and language, see Jacques Derrida, *Of Grammatology* [1967] (Baltimore, Johns Hopkins UP, 1974). See, too, Charles Porset, "L'inquiétante étrangeté de l'*Essai sur l'origine des langues*: Rousseau et ses exégètes," *Studies on Voltaire and the Eighteenth Century* 154 (1976): 1715–54.

was a passion, not a need (unlike the need for sex itself). As such, it was not an original feature of human nature. It, too, began in the hot climate of the South, where, at streams or oases, it was given its initial expression in the first, musical, language, or, as Rousseau put it more floridly, "from the pure crystal of fountains came the first fires of love."[54] This passion-generated language, he claimed, was the first social bond.

The reason why it was had a great deal to do with the properties of music. Music, Rousseau explained, consists of sounds, but sounds alone cannot be music, just as, he added, colours alone cannot be paintings. Colours require design to be paintings, while sounds require melody to be music. Both, in other words, were composite entities. But there was also a significant difference between painting and music, because paintings exist in space, while music exists in time (which, he explained, was why harmony was a late, Gothic, musical aberration). If, as Rousseau claimed, love first found expression in musical form, then melody was the primary source of the self, because it added the dimensions of time and continuity to the eternal present of humanity's natural state (as he emphasised, it was possible to envisage a more or less entirely silent human aggregation, with no passions, and with natural gestures, and, at most, natural cries allowing individuals to communicate their intermittent needs or short-term alarms). The resulting melodiously generated awareness of the continuous character of human life served to bring memory and the imagination into play, and, with working memories and imaginations, humans could think of others, as well as themselves.

With these acquisitions in place, the first durable form of human interaction, with its initial motivation in the desire for love (or *aimez moi* as Rousseau put it), could then be transposed, by way of population growth and migration, to the harsher physical environment of the North, where the desire for love took second place to the need for help (or *aidez moi* in Rousseau's phrase).[55] Here, pity could work in more positive ways, because, with their newly acquired memories and imaginative capacities, humans could identify with others' needs, since these would now be expressed in emotionally meaningful ways. Further migration, this time from the North to the South, served to bring this array of acquired capacities back to humanity's original starting point, while, at the same time, limiting their motivational power to the inner life of the many different linguistic communities that now made up the human race. In this sense, the *Essay on the Origin of Languages* formed a real bridge between Rousseau's

[54] Jean-Jacques Rousseau, *Essay on the Origin of Languages. In Which Melody and Musical Imitation are Treated*, in Jean-Jacques Rousseau, *Collected Writings*, vol. 7, ed. John T. Scott, ch. 9, p. 314.
[55] Rousseau, *Essay on the Origin of Languages*, ch. 10, p. 316.

two early *Discourses* and both the *Social Contract* and the *Considerations on the Government of Poland*. Its historical treatment of the character of most human emotions, and their basis in memory and the imagination, was broader in scope than the one contained in the *Discourse on the Origin of Inequality*, because it was not tied to the subject of property. Viewed alongside one another, the two works set out two differently sequenced histories of humanity, with property and the division of labour forming the basis of the historical bifurcation (the significance of Rousseau's treatment of the division of labour is described in detail in chapter 2). Sieyès was the first to call the perspective that they appeared to open up *science sociale*, or social science.[56]

Hindsight makes it easy to overlook the generation-long period separating the appearance of the *Discourse on the Origin of Inequality* from the publication of both the *Essay on the Origin of Languages* and the *Considerations on the Government of Poland*. Irrespective of the difficulties and uncertainties involved in putting their respective arguments together (Rousseau himself never really did), the long delay meant that his earlier treatment of human history and its potentially catastrophic outcome was by far the more obvious. The result (described in outline in chapter 2, and then in further detail in chapters 3 and 4) was a small explosion of conjectural investigation into the putatively original attributes of human nature, and their bearing on the question of whether, as Rousseau himself put it in his *Discourse on the Origin of Inequality*, the advantages and disadvantages of every type of government outweighed the rights of the natural state (his first English translator wrote "the rights of man in a state of nature").[57] As

---

[56] Emmanuel-Joseph Sieyès, *Political Writings*, ed. Michael Sonenscher (Indianapolis, Hackett, 2003), pp. ix–x. On the term, see Brian W. Head, "The Origins of 'la science sociale' in France," *Australian Journal of French Studies* 19 (1982): 115–32, and, for recent work on this aspect of Rousseau's thought, see Awen A. M. Coley, "The Science of Man: Experimental Routes to Happiness in Duclos and Rousseau," *SVEC* 2000:08, pp. 235–327, and Michael O'Dea, "Philosophie, histoire et imagination dans le *Discours sur l'origine de l'inégalité* de Jean-Jacques Rousseau," *SVEC* 2001: 04, pp. 340–60.

[57] Jean-Jacques Rousseau, *A Discourse upon the Origin and Foundation of the Inequality among Mankind* (London, 1761), p. 171. For the French version, see Jean-Jacques Rousseau, *Discours sur les sciences et les arts. Discours sur l'origine et les fondements de l'inégalité parmi les hommes*, ed. Jacques Roger (Paris, Garnier Flammarion, 1971), p. 231. Rousseau's question supplied much of the initial intellectual setting for the subjects discussed by Pierre Vidal-Naquet in his *Politics Ancient and Modern* (Cambridge, Polity Press, 1995), and by Lynn Hunt in her *Inventing Human Rights: A History* (New York, Norton, 2007). For recent indications of the range of publications that it entailed, see, in addition to Kapossy, *Iselin contra Rousseau*, Bertrand Binoche, *Les trois sources des philosophies de l'histoire (1764–1798)* (Paris, Presses universitaires de France, 1994); and Annette Meyer, "The Experience of Human Diversity and the Search for Unity: Concepts of Mankind in the late Enlightenment," *Studi Settecenteschi* 21 (2001): 244–64. For an indication of the research agenda, see Benjamin Carrard, *Essai qui a remporté le prix de la société hollandaise des sciences de Haarlem en 1770 sur cette question: 'Qu'est-ce qui est requis dans l'art*

should now be apparent, much of the content of this book is an examination of how and why the arguments generated by this type of investigation could look quite similar to Rousseau's own, but, on closer inspection, were actually rather different. Carrying out this examination requires a double process of clarification, first of Rousseau's thought, and then of the thought of a host of now less well-known eighteenth-century authors, in order to show how a line of thought that really did derive from Rousseau was then turned into a rather different type of argument. This is the procedure that has been followed throughout this book in describing the ideas of some less familiar figures in the intellectual life of the eighteenth century.

A number of initial examples may help to introduce both some of the arguments involved in this double process of clarification and some of the individuals who made them. Some, like Mercier himself, turned to the findings of the strand of modern natural philosophy that has come to be called vitalism, and which in the last third of the eighteenth century was sometimes identified with the thought of the seventeenth-century German philosopher Gottfried Wilhelm Leibniz. As will be shown in the next chapter, this strand of natural philosophy came to highlight a mixture of physiology and spirituality that, its supporters argued, made it appropriate to describe human beings as "ensouled bodies" rather than, as in more orthodox theology, "embodied souls," and, by extension, made it possible to envisage human culture as part of a progressively developing, and ever more spiritually oriented, great chain of being. This new perspective made it easier to suggest that many of Rousseau's claims about the original properties of human nature could be revised and corrected to produce a different, noncontractual explanation of social cohesion. But it is important to see, too, that the perspective in question remained one that was still compatible with the broader argument of Rousseau's *Discourse on the Origin of Inequality*. A different starting point and a different set of causal mechanisms could still give rise to an outcome that could look quite similar to Rousseau's own indictment of modernity but, because of the initial differences, could then also entail a rather different set of remedies.

Another initial example of the same mixture of similarity and difference can be found in the late eighteenth-century vogue for mesmerism. Here, too, vitalist natural philosophy supplied a different starting point from Rousseau's treatment of human nature, but could still be compatible with his own style of social and cultural criticism even if the moral and political

---

d'observer, et jusqu'où cet art contribue-t-il à perfectionner l'entendement?' (Amsterdam, 1777), and, for an interesting example of the results, informed by a late eighteenth-century education at the universities of Glasgow and Oxford, see Charles-Athanase Walckenaer, *Essai sur l'histoire de l'espèce humain* (Paris, 1798).

conclusions remained rather different. "You were saying," wrote one of Mesmer's supporters, a man named Charles de Villers who was later to become one of the early French admirers of Kant (as, too, was Mercier), "that the soul gives life to matter to form man." "Yes," the conversation continued, "the soul unites itself to matter, and this union gives birth to the combination of matter called organisation. The greater the proportion of the soul in it, the more perfect the organisation will be."[58] As Villers emphasised, this reversal of the usual approach to the mind-body problem made Mesmer's own speculations about a mysterious magnetic fluid largely redundant. Mesmer's claims about the healing powers of animal magnetism were certainly wrong, wrote Jean-Louis Carra (one of Mercier's friends and, later, one of his political allies), but they still pointed towards "correct and consequential applications of the relationship of this fluid to the organisation and vital principle of living beings," not for spurious medical purposes, but for more modest scientific explanations of the workings of the whole animal economy.[59] Animal magnetism may, or may not, have existed, but the important thing, as even mesmerism's opponents recognised, was its initial perspective on the mind-body problem, and the way that it seemed to open up to explain the observable power that mind sometimes seemed to have over matter. Here, as will be shown in chapters 3 and 6, Rousseau's interest in music, dance, and public festivities could be given a rather different inflection. From this perspective, Emmanuel-Joseph Sieyès may have had something quite precise in mind when, in 1788, he warned that it was a mistake to apply the methods of the natural sciences to the subjects of morality and politics.[60]

Whether or not this was the point of Sieyès's remark, many of his contemporaries were quite willing to claim that this type of vitalist natural philosophy really did seem to have established a genuine foundation for morality. As another supporter of Mesmer, this time a man named Jean-Baptiste Salaville, wrote in 1784, "the celebrated author of the discovery of animal magnetism has done to love what Newton did to the system of the world; his doctrine explains all its phenomena; one can study its filiations,

[58] Charles de Villers, *Le Magnétiseur amoureux* [1787], ed. François Azouvi [1978], 2nd ed. (Paris, Vrin, 2006), p. 109.

[59] Jean-Louis Carra, *Examen physique du magnétisme animal* (London, 1785), pp. 10–1. On mesmerism, see, classically, Robert Darnton, *Mesmerism and the End of the Enlightenment in France* (Cambridge, Mass., Harvard UP, 1968), with, pp. 98–100, 107–11, 163–7, further details on Carra's own ideas. Darnton's book is unsurpassed, but both he and Azouvi, in his introduction to Villers's book, do not bring this aspect of the mind-body problem as clearly into focus as does the contemporary literature itself. For further discussion of its implications, see pp. 119–26 below.

[60] Emmanuel-Joseph Sieyès, *Views of the Executive Means available to the Representatives of France in 1789*, in Emmanuel-Joseph Sieyès, *Political Writings*, ed. Michael Sonenscher (Indianapolis, Hackett, 2003), p. 16.

travel along its chain, and go back to its primary cause."[61] Here, the antithesis was between love as a brute physical passion, and love in its more spiritual and altruistic guise, with Mesmer's new science supplying an explanation of the switch between the two. For a time, Salaville was part of the carefully selected circle of writers and thinkers gathered together by Honoré-Gabriel Riqueti, comte de Mirabeau, the dominant figure in the French National Assembly during the first year of the French Revolution, in what seems to have been a deliberately eclectic way (alongside Salaville were the Genevans Etienne Dumont and Etienne Clavière, as well as the priest Adrien-Antoine Lamourette, the journalist Camille Desmoulins, the political economist the marquis de Casaux, and, more remotely, Emmanuel-Joseph Sieyès himself). Later, he was one of several possible French translators of William Godwin's *Inquiry concerning Political Justice* and, later still, the author of a highly charged endorsement of the spiritually ennobling effects of war. As he went on to argue in his *De la perfectibilité* (On Perfectibility) of 1801, knowledge of the sensible world never seemed to exhaust human curiosity, indicating that knowledge of the suprasensible was the real goal of humanity's restless striving. The fact that familiarity really did breed contempt meant, Salaville wrote, that the more intellectual riches increased, the more physical riches would start to lose their value, and, as they did, the status and distinctions attached to them would also begin to lose their hold on people's lives. One day, he suggested, cupidity and social envy would no longer drive human behaviour.[62] It was a rather more morally straightforward version of whatever Rousseau may have meant in coining the neologism "perfectibility" (as will be shown in chapter 3, Rousseau's own idea involved a postrevolutionary reversion to a less spiritually charged set of social arrangements).

[61] Jean-Baptiste Salaville, *Le moraliste mesmérien, ou Lettres philosophiques sur l'influence du magnétisme* (London, 1784), p. 8.

[62] Jean-Baptiste Salaville, *L'homme et la société, ou nouvelle théorie de la nature humaine et de l'état social* (Paris, an VII/1799), pp. 339–54 (on war), and (on the gradual subordination of the sensible to the spiritual), see his *De la perfectibilité* (Paris, 1801), pp. 28–39. On Salaville's involvement with Mirabeau, see Tony Davis, "Borrowed Language: Milton, Jefferson, Mirabeau," in David Armitage, Armand Himy, and Quentin Skinner, eds., *Milton and Republicanism* (Cambridge, CUP, 1995), pp. 254–71 (268), and, on his interest in Rousseau, see his *De l'organisation d'un état monarchique, ou considérations sur les vices de la monarchie française et nécessité de lui donner une constitution* (Paris, 1789). Godwin's other failed translators were Benjamin Constant and a man named François-Xavier Lanthénas, the author of a curious description, to be found in chapter 3, of what on Cynic premises a *sans-culotte* might be, and why, on the same premises, the ancient republican principle of selection by lot, rather than by vote, should be the principle underlying elections to office in the first French republic. See also his mesmerist-inspired *Motifs de faire du 10 août un jubilé fraternel* (Paris, 1793). For an earlier argument about the ennobling effects of war (produced during the War of American Independence), see [Auffray], "Réflexions sur la guerre," *Courier de l'Europe*, 8, no. 30 (13 October 1780).

Speculations like these were not confined to France. As will be indicated in chapter 2, Kant's critic Johann Gottfried Herder was a strong supporter of this spiritualised version of natural philosophy. Nor were they limited to examination of the intricacies of human character formation, as this was developed by one of the sources of Salaville's highly spiritual version of perfectibility, the Swiss physiognomist Johann Caspar Lavater (whose ideas, as will also be shown in chapter 2, Mercier greatly admired). Jean-Paul Marat, for example, a native of Switzerland and a practising doctor, subscribed strongly to the new type of dualism—putting the soul ahead of the body—as a way of criticising both Claude-Adrien Helvétius, "for reducing everything in man to moral causes," and Rousseau, for his un-warranted claims about the purely natural, presocial, character of pity. So, too, did the circle of late eighteenth-century British moral and political re-formers associated with Erasmus Darwin and the Birmingham Lunar So-ciety. Jacques-Pierre Brissot also made use of natural philosophy (derived, in this case, from the French natural historian Georges Leclerc, comte de Buffon, and from Rousseau's interpreter Jacques-Henri Bernardin de Saint-Pierre) to argue, against Linguet, that Rousseau's attack on inequal-ity did not rule out possession and use as the basis of an attenuated, but still naturally individuated, property system.[63] Yet others, like the Protestant pastor and future Girondin leader Jean-Paul Rabaut Saint-Etienne, relied on the findings of modern science to argue that early astronomy supplied a set of clues to the prepolitical and agricultural origins of morality, first

[63] On Erasmus Darwin, see Maureen McNeil, *Under the Banner of Science: Erasmus Darwin and His Age* (Manchester, Manchester UP, 1987), pp. 153–67. On Marat, see [Jean-Paul Marat], *A Philosophical Essay on Man. Being an Attempt to investigate the Principles and Laws of the Reciprocal Influence of the Soul on the Body*, 2nd ed., 2 vols. (London, 1775), 1:xiv–xv, 33–57, 95–6, 128–9, 141–5. It may be worth noting that Marat's criticisms of Rousseau found favour with the Jesuit Nicolas-Silvestre Bergier, *Traité historique et dogmatique de la vraie religion*, 12 vols. (Paris, 1780), 4:149. Jacques-Pierre Brissot, *Recherches philosophiques sur le droit de la propriété considéré dans la nature, pour servir de premier chapitre à la "Théorie des loix" de M. Linguet* (n.p., 1780), pp. 46, 49–52 (for Buffon), 62–3 (for Bernardin de Saint-Pierre). Brissot, it is worth noting, was also familiar with the ideas of Antoine Court de Gebelin (on whom see below, chapter 4): see Jacques-Pierre Brissot, *Mémoires de Brissot*, ed. Adolphe Mathurin de Lescure (Paris, 1877), pp. 13, 32–3. Buffon's theory of generation, it is worth noting too, was sometimes taken to be a more empirically based synthesis of Leibniz and Epicurus and, in this light, seen as dangerously similar to Rousseau's own putative Epicureanism: see, for example, the self-explanatory title of the book by the German philosopher Hermann Samuel Reimarus, *The Principal Truths of Natural Religion Defended and Illustrated in Nine Disserta-tions, wherein the Objections of Lucretius, Buffon, Maupertuis, Rousseau, La Mettrie and Other Ancient and Modern Followers of Epicurus are Considered and their Doctrines Refuted* (London, 1766), with, pp. 316–25, specific discussion of Rousseau. For a similar claim about Buffon, see, too, the introduction (by the Physiocrat Paul Abeille) to Chrétien-Guillaume de Lamoi-gnon de Malesherbes, *Observations sur l'histoire naturelle et générale et particulière de Buffon et Daubenton*, 2 vols. (Paris, an VI/1798), 1:xix–xx.

by indicating the way that agriculture had supplied humans with an incentive to acquire a knowledge of the seasons from the movements of the heavens, and second by showing how the need to preserve and transmit this knowledge had turned on the language instinct that allowed humans living in settled communities to become quite different from animals.[64] Still others, like the future minister of justice of the first French republic, Dominique-Joseph Garat, preferred to highlight the difference between the primary moral values of the ancient and modern worlds to make the claim now usually associated with Louis-Antoine Saint-Just's famous assertion in 1794 that "happiness is a new idea in Europe."[65] It was new, not really because it was recent, but mainly because it was natural, and because the slavery and brutality of the feudal age had given it a value that had been redundant in the ancient republics of Europe's more remote past. In free states, happiness could be taken for granted, which was why its new value began only with Europe's postrepublican, and postfeudal, history. Here, too, Rousseau supplied the starting point for a broader range of arguments about the difference between common glory or collective security as the core values of the slave-based republics of the ancient world, or the serf-based military despotisms of the feudal world (Roman legions and medieval fortresses symbolised the difference), and modernity's compatibility with the more naturally individuated value of happiness. In this setting, happiness, with its basis in a natural balance among needs, abilities, and the feeling of self-liking, or *amour de soi-même*, was not only what, in the first instance, was all that was required to make life worth living, but, in the second instance, was also the real, though hidden, underlying moral value of the great, postfeudal states.

Revising and correcting Rousseau in these parallel ways made it easier to accept his indictment of property and inequality without also having to endorse his bleak assessment of the prospects facing the modern world. This, in turn, made it easier to inject a stronger moral content into the idea of revolution. Instead of the catastrophic breakdown of human society that Rousseau predicted so frequently, revolution could be taken to be the prelude to reform. From this perspective, Rousseau's political thought could be detached almost entirely from its early association with Hobbes, and brought into closer alignment with the eighteenth century's great blueprint of moral and political reform, François de Salignac de la Mothe Fénelon's

---

[64] For an examination of the broader concerns of this type of investigation, see Albert J. Kuhn, "English Deism and the Development of Romantic Mythological Syncretism," *PMLA* 71 (1956): 1094–116.

[65] On this phrase, see, helpfully, Raymond Geuss, *Outside Ethics* (Princeton, Princeton UP, 2005), pp. 97–110. On the substance of these arguments, see below, chapter 4. On the large subject of Rousseau's reception, see, most recently, Raymond Trousson, *Jean-Jacques Rousseau jugé par ses contemporains* (Paris, Champion, 2000).

Adventures of Telemachus, Son of Ulysses. The steps involved in this shift away from the Hobbes-Rousseau pairing towards the Rousseau-Fénelon pairing are described in detail in chapter 4. But two aspects of the process are worth highlighting here. The first was a revival of the emphasis on the comprehensive programme of royal reform that was a prominent feature of *Telemachus*, but which was largely foreign to Rousseau's own political thought. Before 1789, almost all the more sanguine predictions of revolution to appear in print, including those published by Mercier, Garat, and Rabaut Saint-Etienne, took this form. So, too, as will be shown in chapter 4, was that published by Robespierre in the early spring of 1789, possibly as a reply to the royal government's own upbeat poetic propaganda.

But the second aspect of the Rousseau-Fénelon pairing actually had little to do with the moral or political thought of either Rousseau or Fénelon. This was a revival of interest in the monetary and financial theories of the early eighteenth-century Scottish financier John Law.[66] Some three generations after the failure of his system, Law's ideas about the ability of public credit to promote prosperity, but reduce inequality, came back comprehensively as the basis of a new set of claims about the modern world's capacity to turn need, possession, and occupation into the sole criteria governing the legitimate ownership of property, leaving virtue, not the goods of fortune, as the basis of moral authority, and merit, not inheritance, as the real criterion of the right to rule.[67]

The details of Law's original system, with its Mississippi Company and its French Royal Bank, are set out towards the end of chapter 4, while

---

[66] This aspect of late eighteenth-century thought, and its bearing on the origins of Jacobin republicanism, is not discussed in recent, more or less charitably minded, studies of Jacobinism. For less charitable approaches, see Lucien Jaume, *Le discours jacobin et la démocratie* (Paris, Fayard, 1989), and Gueniffey, *La politique de la terreur*; for more charitable approaches, see Jean-Pierre Gross, *Fair Shares for All: Jacobin Egalitarianism in Practice* (Cambridge, CUP, 1997); Patrice Higonnet, *Goodness beyond Virtue: Jacobins during the French Revolution* (Cambridge, Mass., Harvard UP, 1998); James Livesey, *Making Democracy in the French Revolution* (Cambridge, Mass., Harvard UP, 2001). For a recent examination of Law's legacy during the French Revolution, see Rebecca L. Spang, "The Ghost of Law: Speculating on Money, Memory and Mississippi in the French Constituent Asssembly," *Historical Reflections* 31 (2005): 3–35.

[67] For some examination of these themes in eighteenth-century thought, see Jay M. Smith, *The Culture of Merit: Nobility, Royal Service, and the Making of Absolute Monarchy in France, 1600–1789* (Ann Arbor, University of Michigan Press, 1996); Ken Alder, "French Engineers Become Professionals: or, How Meritocracy Made Knowledge Objective," in William Clark, Jan Golinksi, and Simon Schaffer, eds., *The Sciences in Enlightened Europe* (Chicago, University of Chicago Press, 1999), pp. 94–125; Rafe Blaufarb, "The Social Contours of Meritocracy in the Napoleonic Officer Corps," in Howard G. Brown and Judith A. Miller, eds., *Taking Liberties: Problems of a New Order from the French Revolution to Napoleon* (Manchester, Manchester UP, 2002), pp. 126–46; John Carson, *The Measure of Merit: Talents, Intelligence, and Inequality in the French and American Republics, 1750–1940* (Princeton, Princeton UP, 2007).

an account of its French Revolutionary afterlife forms part of the subject matter of chapter 5. But it is important, at the outset, to give an initial indication of how the subject of public debt became the second of the two subjects that, as has been said, loomed large in the type of republican vision to which many of Rousseau's critical admirers subscribed. It is also important to emphasise how broadly based these claims about Law and public credit actually were, and how significant a feature of thinking about politics and political economy they became in the decade or so that preceded the French Revolution. They could draw some sustenance from Adam Smith's treatment of Law's ideas in his *Inquiry into the Nature and Causes of the Wealth of Nations* of 1776, and, more comprehensively, from the earlier speculations about the properties of public debt set out in 1767 in the *Inquiry into the Principles of Political Economy* by the Jacobite exile Sir James Steuart. In France, they were carried through particularly strongly into the period of the French Revolution by one of Jacques-Pierre Brissot's allies, the Genevan political exile and financial expert Etienne Clavière, who became the most influential advocate of the creation of a paper currency modelled on Law's system, but based on the bonds (or *assignats*) that the French government decided to issue in December 1789, after the National Assembly's decision to nationalise the property of the French church on 2 November 1789. Here, too, however, it is important to emphasise both the broad initial approval of Clavière's ideas and the equally widely shared recognition of Law as their source. Saint-Just, for example, publicly endorsed Clavière's "wise views" on the uses to which the *assignat* could be put, before going on to make his own assessment of Law in his *Esprit de la revolution et de la constitution de la France* (The Spirit of the Revolution and the Constitution of France) written in 1790, but published in 1791. "One could say in Law's justification," Saint-Just wrote, "that he was simply imprudent." His one mistake had been to assume that a people of swindlers (*fripons*), with no real laws, was capable of morality. "If," he concluded, "the depravity of the government had not undermined Law's system, it would have led to liberty."[68] Saint-Just's verdict was by no means unusual. Mercier was also a strong admirer of Law, as, too, well before 1789, was the future "Gracchus" Babeuf.[69] But so, it also needs to be emphasised, was Adrien Duport, one of the leading figures of the group of French politicians who, after their secession from the Parisian Jacobin club in July 1791, came to be known as the Feuillants.

[68] Louis-Antoine Saint-Just, *Esprit de la revolution et de la constitution de la France* [1791], ed. Michel Vovelle (Paris, Editions 10/18, 2003), p. 122.

[69] On Mercier and Law, see below, chapter 2; and, on Babeuf, see Michael Sonenscher, "Property, Community and Citizenship," in Mark Goldie and Robert Wokler, eds., *The Cambridge History of Eighteenth-Century Political Thought* (Cambridge, CUP, 2006), pp. 465–94 (489).

"Some," Duport told the French National Assembly a little under a year earlier, in a speech on the *assignat* on 29 September 1790, "have tried to frighten you by reminding you of Law's system, and by reviving that hereditary terror that he succeeded in transmitting down to us." But, he continued, the "imaginary Mississippi" on which Law's system had been based had now been replaced by one that was real, since it consisted of the recently nationalised property of the French church. With land, not foreign trade, as the basis of this variation on Law's system, Duport argued, economic prosperity and political stability would go hand in hand. The comparison between the two sources of financial stability allowed Duport to end his speech with a further comparison, this time between Britain and France, that was much to the advantage of the latter. "You have been told," he said, "that it is necessary to bind every individual interest to the constitution and one example may serve to persuade you of the strength of this argument."

> England does not dare to try to make any change to a constitution whose vices are recognised by all. The well-known primary cause of this is that almost every individual is directly or indirectly interested in the public establishment (*la chose publique*), and that even the smallest of shocks to the public fortune might destroy private fortunes. This is the cement that holds together all the parts of the English political edifice. Think, Gentlemen, about the power of such a bond once it has come to hold together a free constitution, one that already favours reason and justice, as well as every interest. *Walpole* made the English contract debts to bind them to the House of Brunswick, while we pay ours to bind the French to the work of their representatives, thus uniting justice to politics in an indissoluble manner.[70]

The immediate source of the claim, at least in this context, was a pamphlet entitled *An Essay on the Constitution of England* that was published in London in 1765. The details of its origins (in some sense in David Hume's *History of England*), and its later French reception, are described in chapter 5, but its salience here lies in the broad principle underlying its whole argument, namely, as the anonymous author of the pamphlet put it, that "*the constitution of every country constantly changes with its constituent powers*."[71] Once, what the pamphlet called "the constituent power" in

---

[70] Adrien Duport, *Des assignats* (Paris, 1790), pp. 14, 26. On the speech, see Georges Michon, *Essai sur l'histoire du parti feuillant. Adrien Duport* (Paris, 1924), p. 129, even if, despite the similarities described in chapter 4 below, it imputes a more strongly Physiocratic point of view to Duport than the evidence warrants. On the earlier decision, in April 1790, to add to the initial issue of 400 million livres by issuing a further 1,200 million livres, see Timothy Tackett, *Becoming a Revolutionary: The Deputies of the French National Assembly and the Emergence of a Revolutionary Culture (1789–1790)* (Princeton, Princeton UP, 1996), pp. 265–9.

[71] [Anon.], *An Essay on the Constitution of England* (London, 1765), p. 23 (the passage is italicised in the original). Reference to the pamphlet is made in David Williams, "French

England had been in the hands of the landowners, but with the growth
of Britain's public debt an entirely new constituent power had emerged.
"With the debt of the nation," the pamphlet stated, "so grew, in proportion to its credit, and by degrees produced a new set of constituents who,
without being necessarily connected with the land, with the trade, with either of the Houses of Parliament, or with any corporation or regular body
of men in the kingdom, became no less formidable than they were useful
to the government."[72] The language, which was carried through into two
French versions of the pamphlet published in 1789 by a man named Jean
Chas, who was to become a prominent pro-Feuillant political journalist
in 1791–2, chimed readily with the more familiar distinction between the
constituting and constituted powers of a nation made at the same time
by the abbé Emmanuel-Joseph Sieyès both in his *Views on the Executive
Means Available to the Representatives of France in 1789*, and in his more famous *What Is the Third Estate?*[73] It also, however, gave what Sieyès's critics
called the "metaphysical" character of his terminology a more substantive
economic and social content by linking it to the claim, made famous by
the seventeenth-century English Commonwealthman James Harrington,
that the balance of political power followed the balance of property. Put
summarily, public debt was the new cement of society.

One example of the sort of institutional and financial arrangements that
this type of claim could entail can be found in the political thought of
Jacques-Pierre Brissot's friend, an Anglo-Welsh political reformer named

---

Opinion concerning the English Constitution in the Eighteenth Century," *Economica* 30 (1930):
295–308 (307–8), but I have not been able to find any others in the large literature dealing with
discussions of the so-called English constitution in the eighteenth century, either in Britain or
in France. On this, see, classically, Elie Carcassonne, *Montesquieu et le problème de la constitution française au xviiie siècle* (Paris, 1927); and Laurence L. Bongie, *David Hume: Prophet of
the Counter-Revolution* [1965] (Indianapolis, Liberty Fund, 2000); Charles E. McClelland,
The German Historians and England: A Study in Nineteenth-Century Views (Cambridge, CUP,
1971), pp. 12–23; J. R. Jones, ed., *Liberty Secured? Britain before and after 1688* (Stanford, Stanford UP, 1992); Ellis Sandoz, ed., *The Roots of Liberty: Magna Carta, Ancient Constitution, and
the Anglo-American Tradition of Rule of Law* (Columbia, University of Missouri Press, 1993);
J.C.D. Clark, *The Language of Liberty 1660–1832: Political Discourse and Social Dynamics in the
Anglo-American World* (Cambridge, CUP, 1994); Edouard Tillet, *La constitution anglaise, un
modèle politique et institutionnel dans la France des lumières* (Aix-en-Provence, Presses univer-
sitaires d'Aix-Marseille, 2001). The best guide to the similarities and differences between
Hume's own thought and the more Harringtonian inflection it was given in the *Essay on the
Constitution of England* (although it does not discuss that pamphlet) is Duncan Forbes, *Hume's
Philosophical Politics* (Cambridge, CUP, 1975), pp. 194–223, 229–30, 260–307, 311–23.

[72] [Anon.], *Essay*, pp. 10 (for the phrase "the constituent power"), 70–1.

[73] The translation was published anonymously, first under the title of *Réflexions sur la constitution de l'Angleterre* (London, 1789), and then under the more explicitly didactic title of *A
l'assemblée des états-généraux, ou coup d'oeil sur la constitution, sur le prêt et l'emprunt* (London,
1789).

David Williams, who, in 1793, was invited to submit his views on the nature of the future French republican constitution to its founding Convention.[74] By then, Williams's ideas were well established. As the title of a pamphlet that he published in 1790 indicates (*Lessons to a Young Prince on the Present Disposition in Europe to a General Revolution*), their prime concern was to promote reform in order to avert the potentially catastrophic effects of the type of revolution that Rousseau was by no means the only individual to have predicted. "That the great body of the people; on whose labour, industry and talents, the whole state depends," Williams wrote in his *Letters on Political Liberty* of 1782 (later incorporated extensively into a work by Brissot's other friend, Jerome Pétion, *Avis aux François*, or *Advice to the French*, in 1789), "that the PEOPLE properly arranged; organized into sensibility or judgment; having the strongest and best principles of self-preservation,—should be incapable of acting on them—is an impossible supposition."[75] To realise this vitalist conception of the body politic, where the whole political system could, in a not entirely metaphorical sense, feel the condition of its constituent parts and, as a result, take the appropriate corrective action, Williams advocated the creation of a republican system of government based on the old Saxon divisions of tithings, hundreds, and thousands. "Political bodies, to have one soul, one spirit, one interest," he wrote in 1789, "should have their members and parts united vitally, and not by such feeble bandages as contracts and treaties."[76] This was the aim of establishing the cone-shaped set of interlocking political units modelled on the ancient Saxon system of government that Williams recommended for both Britain and France. It was designed not only to create a better system of political representation, but to prevent the government, or any other partial association, from usurping political sovereignty. As Williams's hostility towards social contract theory indicated, the type of vital unity involved in this political system would answer the unsolved problems in the political thought of the man who, elsewhere, he called "that wise, enchanting, whimsical guide, Mr Rousseau."[77]

[74] On Williams, see James Dybikowski, "On Burning Ground: An Examination of the Ideas, Projects and Life of David Williams," *Studies on Voltaire and the Eighteenth Century* 307 (1993), and, on his relations with Brissot, the same author's "David Williams (1738–1816) and Jacques-Pierre Brissot: Their Correspondence," *National Library of Wales Journal* 25 (1987–8): 71–97, 167–90. Further information on these circles can be found in A. N., F⁷ 4774⁷⁰, dossier Pétion.

[75] David Williams, *Letters on Political Liberty and the principles of the English and Irish Projects of Reform*, 3rd ed. (London, 1789), p. 54.

[76] David Williams, *Lectures on Political Principles; The Subjects of Eighteen Books in Montesquieu's "Spirit of Laws"* (London, 1789), p. 114.

[77] David Williams, *Lectures on the Universal Principles and Duties of Religion and Morality* (London, 1779), p. 134. Rousseau's heart, he wrote elsewhere, "atoned for the caprices of his head": Williams, *Lessons to a Young Prince on the Present Disposition in Europe to a General Revolution* (London, 1790), pp. 56–7.

The reformed government would still have a king (as Alfred the Great had been), but sovereignty would belong to the whole body politic. The "immediate object" of the entire system, Williams wrote, was not only to establish "representation for the purpose of a legislature," but also "to form political powers in the body of the people, to control, balance, or give stability to the legislature and crown; and to effect the purposes of defensive and internal police." It was, he explained, the "want of this political power" that had been felt in the ancient republics of Greece and Rome, because it was something that the checking power of popular magistracies like Sparta's ephors or Rome's tribunes of the people had not been able to supply.[78]

Williams gave Harrington a higher intellectual rating than Montesquieu (the "plan of the Oceana," he wrote, "is, perhaps, the best imaginable to improve the institutions of mankind").[79] He was also a strong admirer of the works of Sir James Steuart (describing him as "the most profound and original of all writers on political subjects," even if, as he wrote elsewhere, Steuart's *Inquiry into the Principles of Political Economy* was "clogged with prejudices, and obscured by a stile uncouth and almost unintelligible").[80] He singled out Steuart's remarks on public credit for particular attention, highlighting the way that they showed how public debts made taxation a permanent necessity, and how taxation, in turn, served to prevent "profits from being consolidated with price," so that "the fruits of industry might be brought to market on proper terms," leaving "the artisan . . . easy or happy" and "the state with funds."[81] The Swiss banker and French finance minister Jacques Necker, Williams noted, had understood this aspect of the relationship between public debt, fiscal policy, and manufacturing industry very well. Debt entailed taxation, which forced manufacturers to innovate, which led to new products, which led to expenditure by the owners of fixed property, which allowed the producers of manufactured goods to raise prices, which were, in turn, restrained by taxes, resulting in a virtuous circle that would offset the divisive effects of private property. Williams also endorsed Steuart's projection of a continually increasing, but domestically funded, public debt, arguing that the perpetual rotation of assets that would arise once the annuitants replaced the landed proprietors as the ultimate owners of the national income could become the basis of a genuinely integrated state.[82] Provided that borrowing was purely domestic, a state could become prosperous, but entirely self-sufficient. Since the annuitants would have to spend in order to live, the tax revenue raised from every other class, and paid out to them as interest payments,

[78] Williams, *Letters*, p. 61.
[79] Williams, *Lectures on Political Principles*, p. 203.
[80] Williams, *Lectures on Political Principles*, pp. 247–8.
[81] Williams, *Lectures on Political Principles*, pp. 251–2.
[82] Williams, *Lectures on Political Principles*, pp. 253 (on Necker), 256–61.

would circulate back through the whole economy, while the tax burden itself would be equitably managed by the reformed political system. The combination of Williams's interpretation of the Saxon system of government with Steuart's analysis of the properties of public credit led, in this way, to a peculiarly debt-based version of the idea of the body politic as a kind of organism. According to one of his French admirers, his idea of the body politic corresponded "perfectly" to "the admirable, multiple, and symmetrical" divisions and subdivisions of the physical body's nervous system, and could be taken as an illustration of how politics might aspire to the same type of image of ideal beauty, or *beau idéal*, motivating the achievements of painters and sculptors. As Williams's late didactic poem, *Egeria*, served to show, it was a position that he maintained to the end of his life.[83] It amounted to adding modern finance to ancient politics to produce a self-sufficient state, with a unitary debt, and a unitary set of underlying fundamental interests.

The idea is now often associated with the German idealist philosopher Johann Gottlieb Fichte's *Closed Commercial State* of 1800.[84] But Fichte's version of the idea was, in fact, a more intellectually sophisticated revival of a style of speculation about the properties of modern public finance that predated the French Revolution by several decades, and which was to remain the key component of one vision of national independence and republican self-government up to the revolutions of 1848, and beyond. One aspect of this style of political speculation was a claim that, for all his apparent hostility towards the vision of an ideal republic set out in Harrington's *Oceana*, Montesquieu was actually a covert, neo-Machiavellian, republican. A careful (proto-Straussian) reading of his *The Spirit of Laws* would, from this point of view, reveal that Law was a victim of absolute government (and not, as Montesquieu actually wrote, its accomplice), and that, under a different political regime, modern public finance really could bring about the type of agrarian law that Harrington had commended.[85] Once in place,

---

[83] François-Xavier Lanthénas, *Bases fondamentales de l'instruction publique et de toute constitution libre, ou moyens de lier l'opinion publique, la morale, l'éducation, l'enseignement, l'instruction, les fêtes, la propagation des lumières, et le progrès de toutes les connaissances, au Gouvernement national républicain* (Paris, 1793; 2nd ed. Paris, Vendémiaire an III), pp. 57, 70–4. The book was a compilation of earlier publications, including, as Lanthénas emphasised here, his *Inconvénients du droit d'ainesse* of August 1789. On Williams's view of public debt, and its basis in Steuart's projections, see Sonenscher, *Before the Deluge*, pp. 58–64, 256.

[84] Johann Gottlieb Fichte, *Der Geschlossene Handelsstaat* [1800]; translated as *L'état commercial fermé*, ed. Daniel Schulthess (Lausanne, L'âge d'homme, 1980).

[85] For examples of this type of claim, see Jean-Jacques Rutledge, *Eloge de Montesquieu* (London, 1786); *Journal encyclopédique* (September 1785): 330–1, reviewing a translation of an English-language parallel between Montesquieu and Machiavelli, and concluding that both were "true friends of liberty and human kind"; and Philippe-Antoine Grouvelle, *De l'autorité de Montesquieu dans la révolution présente*, reprinted in the *Bibliothèque de*

it would open up a way to self-sufficiency at home, and cooperation abroad. In this earlier incarnation (as well as in Fichte's more Rousseau-inspired version), the idea of self-sufficiency had nothing to do with the type of Napoleonic concern with *Machtpolitik* with which it came to be associated later in the nineteenth century, and a good deal more to do with its opposite. Here, the emphasis fell not on trade as an instrument of power politics, but on bringing power politics to an end, with public credit forming the means to make foreign trade voluntary and reciprocal, rather than necessary and competitive. Fair trade would then complement free trade. From this perspective, the monetary and fiscal policies that public credit entailed (expressed most simply by the eighteenth-century French political economist Jean-François Melon's metaphor of the left hand lending to the right) appeared to indicate that states could use the modern funding system to promote prosperity at home, and export their surpluses abroad without, at the outset, having to rely on price competitiveness or productivity gains to establish and maintain a presence in world markets. Prosperity at home would simply allow domestic surpluses to be traded for surpluses abroad. Although, as Sieyès noted somewhat viciously in 1795, Duport had been a strong supporter of Mesmer before 1789, there is no real evidence that either he or Barnave was ever as fascinated as were Brissot, Pétion, Clavière, and Mercier by this type of political vision.[86] But, as will be shown in

---

l'homme public, 12 vols. (Paris, 1790), 7:22. A variation on the theme can be found in the French republican Bertrand Barère's argument about Montesquieu's intellectual debt to the seventeenth-century English Commonwealthman Walter Moyle. On this, see Eric Nelson, *The Greek Tradition in Republican Thought* (Cambridge, CUP, 2004), pp. 136, 138, 159, 193. According to Barère, in his *Montesquieu peint d'après ses ouvrages* (Paris, an V/1797), pp. 67, note 2, 70, the hidden message of Montesquieu's book was brought out into the light of day by Claude-Adrien Helvétius, in his *De l'esprit*. Helvétius, also according to Barère, knew that Montesquieu's critics had spotted the truth, since, Barère wrote, one of them told Helvétius that if he were a king, he would have had Montesquieu drowned in his own blood (p. 129, note 2). For a more cautious version, see Pierre-Claude-François Daunou, *Le contrat social des français* (Paris, 1789), p. 15. According to the English former supporter of the French Revolution Henry Redhead Yorke, this was never Robespierre's view: "'The *Spirit of Laws*', said he, is the production of a fanatic and a weak mind, replete with dogmas and ignorance. If Montesquieu were now alive, he would have been either an emigrant, or very soon *less by a head*, for he was *un parlementaire, non pas un bon républicain*." Similarly, according to Robespierre, "the doctrines of Machiavel established tyranny over the whole of Europe": Henry Redhead Yorke, *Letters from France in 1802*, 2 vols. (London, 1804), 1:273–6.

[86] For Sieyès's comments on Duport, see [Conrad Engelbert Oelsner], *Notice sur la vie de Sieyès* (n.p., 1795), pp. 15–6 (it is worth noting that Sieyès corresponded with Duport on the subject of mesmerism before 1789 and, on Duport's advice, undertook an unsuccessful, and disillusioning, mesmerist cure for his backache). Saint-Just, it is also worth noting, referred to Williams approvingly in his famous speech advocating the confiscation of the property of "enemies of the revolution" in Ventôse of the Year II: see Saint-Just, *Oeuvres complètes*, ed. Michèle Duval (Paris, Editions Gérard Lebovici, 1984), p. 706.

chapter 5, there is still enough evidence to indicate that they were, none-theless, part of what began as a broad early consensus in favour of a set of views about public credit that could be associated loosely with Law's system. It amounted to what became the mainstream of patriot political thinking in France in the immediate aftermath of the fall of the Bastille.[87]

Usually, the historical focus has tended to fall on two other ways of thinking about France and its political future in the immediate aftermath of the events of the summer of 1789. The first, advocated by a lawyer from Grenoble named Jean-Joseph Mounier and the group of individuals who came to be known as the Monarchiens, involved trying to establish a British-style system of mixed, or balanced, government in France. The second, advocated by Emmanuel-Joseph Sieyès and, more erratically, by Mirabeau, involved trying to establish an entirely new system of representative government and, in tandem, an entirely new social elite. Neither Mounier nor Sieyès showed any interest at all in Law's system. In Mounier's case, this was because the actually existing system of British government (as described by the Genevan political exile Jean-Louis Delolme) made Law's ideas irrelevant. In Sieyès's case, it was because the unavoidable nature of modern, debt-based, war finance made public credit a necessary evil, rather than either a social cancer or, still less, a positive good, and this in turn required the creation of a system of government that would be less exposed to the risks of public debt than, it was widely claimed, the British system might be.[88] Although they differed very radically in their assessments of the political risks associated with adding a debt to a state, both points of view focused on the constitutional arrangements that, it could be claimed, were compatible with the real world fact of public debt.

As will be shown in chapter 5, by the early winter of 1789, it was clear that there was no real support for either of these constitutional alternatives. To its critics, Mounier's system appeared to rely too heavily on patriotic self-sacrifice by the powerful and privileged to be able to prevent inequality from becoming embedded in the British-style political system that he advocated. His own argument, that France after 1789 could do in a matter of years what it had taken the British several hundred years to do, could be turned all too easily against itself, particularly in the light of the glaring differences between the tiny British peerage and the huge French nobility. To *its* critics, Sieyès's more politically subtle attempt to bypass these problems looked like Mounier's system at one remove. The strategy that he envisaged consisted of two related steps. The first relied

---

[87] On the idea of an early consensus, and its gradual breakdown between the autumn of 1789 and the spring of 1791, see William Doyle, *The Oxford History of the French Revolution* [1990], 2nd ed. (Oxford, OUP, 2002), pp. 136–58.

[88] On these views of Britain's future, see Sonenscher, *Before the Deluge*, pp. 41–52, 174, 357.

on arguing that the idea of representation meant that the constituting
power of the nation could be represented entirely by its self-proclaimed
national and constituent assembly, without having to refer back, at least
in any binding sense, to the nation itself. The second involved using this
constituting power to create an entirely new hierarchy of representative
institutions, but to do so from the bottom upwards, starting with a new
set of municipal institutions, before proceeding step by step towards the
creation of a new national legislature, using a system of election that came
to be called "graduated promotion." The newly constituted legislature
would, as it came into being out of the hierarchy of municipal, district,
and departmental levels of representation, sidestep existing economic and
social divisions, allowing the political structure of the new regime to rise
up gradually alongside the old, while the staggered sequence of elections
that it required would entrench the legitimacy of the new social and political elite that Sieyès envisaged as the outcome of this non-British-style
system of representative government.

This strategy soon, however, came to look too much like a long-term
political gamble to be worth taking. In a mirror image of the objections
to Mounier, Sieyès's argument in favour of using the mechanisms of representation to circumvent the political problems that existing inequalities
might cause could be redescribed all too easily either as political miscalcu-
lation in the face of impending social collapse, or as blind indifference to
real merit. Sieyès's constitutional proposals, wrote the Monarchien Stanislas de Clermont-Tonnerre, amounted to changing the monarchy into "a
multitude of separate little portions, each with their own interests, partiali-
ties, and internal regime, obeying no one, and looking at what remains of
the executive power as a common enemy, instead of a centre of reunion."[89]
Inversely, however, it also appeared to offer too little of an immediate basis
for grounding public life on genuinely well-deserved individual distinction. "Some excellent writers," wrote the abbé Claude Fauchet, later one
of the leading figures in the loose Parisian moral and political association
named the Cercle social (Social Circle), in his *De la religion nationale* (On
National Religion) published early in 1789, "among others the author of
What Is the Third Estate?, conclude from the principles of national unity,
that there should be no different orders of citizens in the kingdom's representation." This, Fauchet wrote, was "outrageous." Once, he argued,
the existing nobility had been stripped of its hereditary privileges, and an
agrarian law had been applied to the excessive amounts of property that
it owned, the way would be open to establish a true nobility based upon

---

[89] Stanislas-Marie-Adelaide de Clermont-Tonnerre, *Réflexions sur l'opinion de M. l'abbé Sieyès, concernant les municipalités et le veto* (Paris, 1789), cited in Charles Du Bus, *Stanislas de
Clermont-Tonnerre et l'échec de la révolution monarchique* (Paris, 1931), p. 159.

real merit and genuine public service. Here, Fauchet suggested, a combination of popular nomination and royal selection could be used to elect what in modern British terms would be called a life peerage, to form the moral core of a reformed system of royal government.[90] Set against this type of vision of the future, Mounier's constitutional proposals appeared to entrench inequality, while Sieyès's constitutional proposals appeared to rule out moral distinction. In this sense, the two sets of proposals cancelled each other out.

This double failure supplies the initial context for the sequence of conflicts that led, in 1791–2, to the transformation of the salon society joke into a republican emblem. The details of how the transformation occurred are set out in chapter 5. Here, for the last time (at least in this introduction), the story about breeches can be used as a helpful entry point. If having a pair of breeches could be associated with Ciceronian decorum, and not having breeches could be associated with whatever Cynic morality was taken to be, the same antithesis could also be associated with two different types of satire. From one point of view, worldly sophistication could mock unworldly naivety (this, in fact, was the real point of the joke about breeches). But from the opposite point of view, moral integrity could mock self-serving hypocrisy (which was the point of the story about Diogenes and Plato's purple carpets). In these different senses, satire, in eighteenth-century language, could be either urbane or sublime. The difference was sometimes registered in terms of the opposition between a satirist like Horace and one like Juvenal, who, in the eighteenth century, was sometimes described as a kind of Cynic. "Juvenal," in the words of a late eighteenth-century expert on satire named Jean Dusaulx (who was also an admirer of Mably and a critic of Voltaire), "began his satiric career where the other finished, that is to say he did for morals and for liberty, what Horace had done for decorum and taste."[91] True satire aimed not "to raise a laugh at vice" but "to hold up the vicious as objects of reprobation and scorn for the example of others who may be deterred by their sufferings."[92] In this sense, the rhetorical techniques involved in both Cynic morality

[90] Claude Fauchet, *De la religion nationale* (Paris, 1789), pp. 160, 161–5.

[91] Jean Dusaulx, *Satires de Juvénal* [1770], 2 vols. (Paris, 1803), 1:clxvii. I have used a translated version of this passage, as cited in William Gifford, "An Essay on the Roman Satirists," which introduces his translation of *The Satires of Decimus Junius Juvenalis* (London, 1802), p. liii. On Juvenal's Cynic sympathies, as noted approvingly by Fénelon, see below, p. 240.

[92] Gifford, "Essay," p. xlviii. For discussion of the standing of Horace and Juvenal in the eighteenth century, see W. B. Carnochan, "Satire, Sublimity and Sentiment: Theory and Practice in Post-Augustan Satire," *PMLA* 85 (1970): 260–70; Thomas B. Gilmore and W. B. Carnochan, "The Politics of Eighteenth-Century Satire," *PMLA* 86 (1971): 277–80; William Kupersmith, "Juvenal as Sublime Satirist," *PMLA* 87 (1972): 508–11; W. B. Carnochan, "Juvenal as Sublime Satirist," *PMLA* 87 (1972): 1125–6; William Kupersmith, "Juvenal as Sublime Satirist," *PMLA* 88 (1973): 144; Thomas Lockwood, "On the Relationship of Satire

and Cynic satire were two sides of the same coin (both, as Diogenes himself was supposed to have said, were designed to "deface the currency").

This was the type of rhetoric that was brought into play in the winter of 1791–2 by Louis-Sébastien Mercier and, particularly, by Antoine-Joseph Gorsas. Gorsas was an unusually gifted exponent of Cynic satire, as can be seen from some of his prerevolutionary publications, which included a curious parody of *Telemachus*, with an art critic as its eponymous hero, and a donkey as his Mentor (described in the final part of chapter 5). It is worth remembering, however, that the young Saint-Just also tried his hand at the same genre, both in his enormous satirical (and pornographic) poem, *Organt*, and in a comedy called *Arlequin Diogène* (Harlequin as Diogenes).[93] By the late summer of 1791, however, Cynic satire had become more directly political. One reason for this transformation was that, by then, it had become clear that the vague word "republican," which, in 1790, was used quite often to refer to the policies espoused by Barnave as much as Robespierre, could refer to a very broad range of social and political arrangements that were not, in fact, mutually compatible. Here, the main source of division was the subject of trade, and the extent to which a debt-based system of public finance required a continuous supply of tax revenue. From one point of view, it did, which was why the Feuillants began to argue with growing urgency that France still had to rely on the tax revenue generated by trade, even if this meant accepting the continued existence of a slave-based colonial empire. It also meant, as the trickle of emigration from France began to grow, that inducements or threats were required to bring back the *émigrés*, and to prevent a potentially disastrous erosion of the kingdom's tax base. The alternatives, they argued, involved either higher taxation of income from the land, with the risk that this would simply be passed on in the form of higher prices, leaving more economic and political power in the hands of the landowners, or borrowing even more, with the risk that the resulting inflationary spiral would destroy the tax base completely. The problem was complicated further by the electoral system established by the French National Assembly in 1790. This made both the right to vote and eligibility for election subject to the payment of specified levels of taxes. Although the initial threshold, consisting of the payment of taxes equivalent to the local level of three days' wages, was not high, rising prices caused by a depreciating currency threatened not only to eat into popular purchasing power but also,

---

and Poetry after Pope," *Studies in English Literature, 1500–1900* 14 (1974): 387–402; and, with less emphasis on morality, Dror Wahrman, "Gender in Translation: How the English Wrote Their Juvenal, 1644–1815," *Representations* 65 (1999): 1–41.

[93] These are available in Louis-Antoine Saint-Just, *Oeuvres complètes*, ed. Anne Kupiec and Miguel Abensour (Paris, Gallimard, 2004).

perversely, to reduce the size of the electorate. From this point of view, currency stability was required not only to prevent the already large gap between the rich and the poor from growing wider, but also to maintain the political viability of the new regime. The result (described in detail in chapter 5) was an increasingly bitter clash between different assessments of the underlying sources of political stability of the new regime, and of the extent to which its survival was bound up either with the survival of the empire, and concessions to the *émigrés*, or with maintaining popular purchasing power to prevent the gradual erosion of its electoral base.

The king's flight in June 1791 set the seal on these increasingly intense arguments over the related subjects of empire and emigration, and precipitated the final collapse of the initial patriot consensus. By early 1792, after the first wave of insurrection in the French colonies in the Caribbean, Clavière was calling openly for a partial debt default, to keep the *émigrés* out, and, with Brissot, for a preemptive war to eliminate the threat to domestic political stability. Without an empire, or the *émigrés*, this left the people as the only available pillar of the new regime. The broad aim of chapter 5 is to describe how Brissot and his political allies set about trying to build up a popular following to ensure that it was. In this sense, the emergence of the *sans-culottes* as both a name and a political force was a product of the gradual disintegration of what, in 1789, had begun as a broad consensus in favour of using the power of modern public finance to promote more equality in France, against the inegalitarianism that could be imputed both to Mounier and the Monarchiens on the one side, and to Sieyès and the dwindling number of his political allies on the other. As that consensus collapsed, Cynic satire became the first weapon to be used by one type of republican against another, because, to the one, the other had revealed its apostasy. By 1792, as the political trajectories of Adrien Duport and his Feuillant political allies could be said to have shown, this type of republican had thrown in its lot with the French monarchy and signed up to a political alliance with France's queen. This, finally, was why what, in the early eighteenth century, started out as a salon society joke ended up as Cynic satire on the new political clients of the old French monarchy.

In broad terms, the rest of the story is quite familiar and is described at greater length in chapter 6. The so-called *sans-culotte* ministry came to power in March 1792 with a commitment to maintain financial stability at home by embarking on what, it assumed, would be a short, preemptive war. Events, however, proved otherwise, and, as the costs of war began to be added to the ordinary costs of government, what was left of the broad early consensus in favour of the compatibility between public debt and political unity collapsed completely. As it did, much of the somewhat illusory timelessness of the idea of a republic (one that could accommodate the idea of a royal executive, or a balanced government, or even a patriot king) collapsed too. France became a real republic, but then had to face many of the problems of political survival and public safety usually assigned, even by republicans, to a powerful reforming monarchy. Here, the parallels between the ancients and the moderns of the early eighteenth century acquired a different type of political salience, as, too, did both Rousseau's grim predictions of modernity's future and Mably's more explicit politics of crisis management (the combination is described more fully in chapter 6). As the command structure of what Robespierre and his allies called the system of revolutionary government acquired more of the features of an absolute monarchy, it was not difficult for Robespierre's enemies to claim that this, indeed, might be its final goal (it served to justify the coup against him in late July 1794).

One aspect of the story is, however, less familiar. When, in June 1794, Robespierre organised his famous Festival of the Supreme Being, Johann Arnold Ebert, the German translator of Edward Young's *Night Thoughts*, was surprised to discover that the hymn sung on the occasion by the whole assembled crowd was strikingly similar to the thirty-eighth verse of the first of Young's *Nights*. Since, Ebert observed, the hymn's appeal to the deity to strike wisdom and love in every heart involved a rather unusual combination of metaphorical images—notably one comparing God to a spark that had turned dark nothingness into dazzling sunlight—it was hard not to think that it owed more than a little to Young, while, Ebert also noted, its beginning and end were rather like Alexander Pope's *Universal Prayer*.[94] It is well known that the festival itself was organised in something of a rush, and that the author of the hymn, a man named Théodore Desorgues, was chosen almost at the last minute by Robespierre himself, to replace the man he sacked, the better-known republican playwright Joseph-Marie Chénier.[95] In this sense, desperation, not intellectual homage, may have been the real reason for the rather surprising afterlife of Young's poem. But whatever the reason may have been, its appearance in this setting was not entirely incongruous. As Robespierre emphasised in his speech on the same occasion, religion was the real

[94] Edward Young, *Klagen, oder Nachtgedanken*, trans. Johann Arnold Ebert (Leipzig, 1794), p. xxii, referring to what is now in Young, *Night Thoughts*, ed. Cornford, p. 38, lines 38–41. The similarity applies to the sixth verse of the *Hymn*: "O toi, qui du néant, ainsi qu'une étincelle, / Fis jaillir dans les airs l'astre éclatant du jour, / Fais plus . . . verse en nos coeurs ta sagesse immortelle, / Embrase nous de ton amour!"; this can be compared to Young's "O thou! whose word from solid darkness struck / That spark, the sun; strike wisdom from my soul." For the text of the hymn, see Michel Vovelle, *Théodore Desorgues, ou la désorganisation. Aix-Paris, 1763–1809* (Paris, Seuil, 1985), p. 225, although Vovelle appears to have been unaware of Ebert's comments on Desorgues's hymn. Ebert's remarks were noticed by Young's only intellectual biographer, Thomas, *Le poète Edward Young 1683–1765*, p. 539, note 3. I am grateful to Isaac Nakhimovsky of Harvard University for finding a copy of this edition of Ebert's translation in Harvard University Library and for translating the relevant pages.

[95] On Desorgues and the background to the Festival of the Supreme Being, see Vovelle, *Théodore Desorgues*.

cement of society, because, stripped of its more parochial superstitions, it alone gave humans a genuine motivation for altruism. It was not quite Brown's argument, because, as Robespierre said on 16 June 1790 during the National Assembly's debate on the civil constitution of the French clergy, it was "inexact" that "the clergy performs the most important function in society; the most important function in society is that of the legislator."[96] This was rather more like Rousseau. Unlike Rousseau, however, Robespierre's idea of a legislator was inside, rather than outside, the society in question.

Nor was this the only way in which Robespierre went further than Rousseau. He also argued consistently from 1789 onwards in favour of using public finance to enable every citizen to play an active part in public life. From one point of view, the argument was simply a rehearsal of other, more widely voiced calls to provide travel and attendance allowances for the many, often long-drawn-out, electoral meetings that were a feature of public life after 1789.[97] But from Robespierre's point of view, using public funds in this way had a more ambitious moral and political objective. It was, he argued, the real alternative to Sieyès's idea of representative government, and the only way to secure full political accountability. Coupled with the principles underlying the attenuated right to private property that he set out in his draft Declaration of the Rights of Man of 10 May 1793, and with the programme of redistributive taxation that, he envisaged, would be tied to the new, republican system of public education, it would give formal equality a real content.[98] "Despotism," Robespierre was reported to have said in August 1791, was preferable to what he called "absolute representative government," where, he continued, the nation was no longer free nor, in any real sense, even extant.[99] The "bizarre system of absolute representative government," he repeated in October 1792, was "the most unbearable of all despotisms" because it had "no counterweight in the sovereignty of the people."[100] For Robespierre, securing the sovereignty of the people meant, above all, removing the many obstacles that inequality had placed in their way, in order to enable them to play a real

[96] *Archives parlementaires*, ed. M. J. Mavidal, M. E. Laurent, and M. E. Clavel, 82 vols. (Paris, 1878–1913), 16 (16 June 1790): 235.

[97] For an example, see Malcolm Crook, "Citizen Bishops: Episcopal Elections in the French Revolution," *Historical Journal* 43 (2000): 955–76 (958).

[98] On these, see Sonenscher, "Property, Community and Citizenship," pp. 489–91.

[99] Maximilien Robespierre, speech to the National Assembly, 10 August 1791, reprinted in his *Oeuvres*, ed. Victor Barbier, Marc Bouloiseau, Jean Dautry, Gustave Laurent, Georges Lefebvre, Georges Michon, Albert Soboul, and Charles Vellay, 10 vols. (Paris, 1910–69), 7:615. For a recent, but largely ahistorical, contribution to the ongoing argument over Robespierre's significance, see the selection from his published works made by Jean Ducange, ed., *Robespierre: Virtue and Terror*, introduced by Slavoj Žižek (London, Verso, 2007).

[100] Maximilien Robespierre, *Lettres de Maximilien Robespierre à ses commettants* (19 October 1792), in Robespierre, *Oeuvres*, 5:19.

part in the nation's affairs. He first made the argument in favour of financial allowances in March 1789 at the meeting of the electoral assembly of the town of Arras that elected him to represent the Third Estate at the forthcoming Estates-General, saying that "humanity and justice" called for compensating "artisans" for the four days "necessary to their subsistence" that they had lost attending the assembly.[101] It was an argument that he went on to make consistently. "When salaries are paid to representatives of the people, to judges or financial officials," he said at a charged meeting of the Jacobin club in June 1791, and "when the head of the executive (Louis XVI) is given twenty-five millions, why should a salary not also be given to that interesting part of the citizenry that sacrifices its time and its labour?"[102] Here, however, the point was more than purely financial. It was made soon after Louis XVI's flight from Paris, and in opposition to Sieyès's alternative proposal to circulate a voluntary declaration of allegiance to the new French constitution as a guide for voters in the forthcoming elections to the new legislature. From Robespierre's point of view, real people, not vacuous declarations, were what counted at elections.

He repeated the point on the eve of the elections to the Legislative Assembly in August 1791 and developed it fully and forcefully two years later in his great speech on the new French republic's constitution on 10 May 1793. What weight, he told the Convention then, could be attached to the idea of equality of rights "if the most imperious of all laws, necessity, forces the major (*la plus saine*) and most numerous part of the people to renounce public affairs." It followed, he argued, that everyone who lived from their work should, like all public officials, be indemnified for attending public meetings. These, too, should be genuinely public. "A splendid and majestic building, open to twelve thousand spectators," Robespierre said, "should be the site of sessions of the legislative body." Ensuring that all public debates and decisions were underpinned both by a real popular presence and by an institutionalised popular tribunal, he emphasised, was the only way to turn "the virtue of the people and the authority of the sovereign into the necessary counterweight to the passions of the magistrate, and government's tendency towards tyranny." "In this way," he concluded, "you will have solved the still unresolved problem of popular economy (*l'économie populaire*)."[103] Two days later, on 12 May, he repeated the call, this time in the context of a speech advocating the establishment of a popular republican militia, or

[101] Robespierre, *Oeuvres*, 6:15–6.

[102] Maximilien Robespierre, *Adresse de la Société des Amis de la Constitution aux Sociétés qui lui sont affiliées* (Paris, 1791), printed in F. A. Aulard, *La Société des Jacobins. Recueil de documents pour l'histoire du club des Jacobins de Paris*, 6 vols. (Paris, 1889–97), 2:519–20.

[103] Maximilien Robespierre, speech to the Convention, 10 May 1793, reprinted in his *Oeuvres*, 9:503 (on the size and appearance of a legislative building), 506–7 (on indemnifying the people). On his earlier call for an indemnity, on 30 August 1791, see Robespierre, *Oeuvres*, 7:689.

armée révolutionnaire, made up of *sans-culottes*. As he had already emphasised in an earlier speech, its members would not wear braid breeches. "He who has braid breeches (*culottes dorées*) is the born enemy of all *sans-culottes*." Nor, he now said, could genuine *sans-culottes* be expected to handle "trowels and arms" simultaneously. They would form "a reserve army" that would remain in Paris and would, therefore, have to be paid by the public treasury.[104] Both proposals, for a fully paid Parisian *sans-culotte* militia, and for a forty-sous-a-day indemnity for participation in public life, were put into effect six months later, in September 1793. From Robespierre's perspective, with these in place, religion could then be relied upon to supply the altruistic motivation required for full participation in civic life.

This switch from political satire to moral politics is one indication of how it might be possible to begin to position Jacobin ideology in a setting made up of a range of now largely forgotten ways of addressing some of the better-known themes in eighteenth-century thought. Some were concerned with property, markets, and prices; others focused on states, laws, and governments; while yet others concentrated on morality, equality, and justice. All these themes were captured in the titles of the two paintings that the late eighteenth-century French artist Jacques Réattu called *The Triumph of Liberty* and *The Triumph of Civilisation* (figures 3 and 4). The difficulty, on Rousseau's premises, was to see how to have both, and in more than a figurative sense. Much of the content of this book is an examination of how, after Rousseau, this question was discussed. Since both liberty and civilisation were not self-explanatory concepts, the ways in which the question *was* discussed fell comprehensively beyond the binary terms of enlightenment versus counterenlightenment, or class versus sovereignty, or the public sphere versus the private sphere, that still hang quite heavily both over the historiography of the French Revolution and, in related ways, over Rousseau's moral and political thought.[105] From the point of view of the great philosophies of history of the nineteenth century, those terms may matter. But in the eighteenth century, the subjects to which they came to be applied were often discussed in less strongly polarised terms, involving arguments with more than just two sides. One reason why they did was that the ways of thinking about history were themselves rather different. As will be shown in more detail in chapter 6, some of them had a bearing not only on the politics of the Terror, but also on the later, early nineteenth-century, history of the type of republicanism that, as indicated by Louis-Sébastien Mercier's struggles with his own memory, the events of the Terror helped to efface. But the events of the Terror also effaced rather more. In doing so, they

---

[104] Robespierre, *Oeuvres*, 9:490, 514–5.

[105] For an earlier attempt to avoid these types of antithesis, this time in the context of the eighteenth-century French trades, see Sonenscher, *Work and Wages*, p. 2.

FIGURE 4. Jacques Réattu, *The Triumph of Liberty*, ca. 1798, © Musée Réattu, Arles, France / Archives Charmet / The Bridgeman Art Library.

became the starting point of what still remains one of the most widely assumed sets of received ideas about the French Revolution. This is that its content and course are best described in terms of growing political radicalism, either liked or misliked, with the Feuillants taken to be more radical than the Monarchiens, the Girondins more radical than the Feuillants, and the Jacobins the most radical of all. This type of characterisation of the French Revolution may fit the philosophies of history of the nineteenth century, since this (in much more sophisticated form) is where it comes from. It is less clear, however, that it fits the different types of historical assessment of the eighteenth century, and the more varied range of outcomes envisaged in its now more unfamiliar historical evaluations of political possibilities and constraints. It may be somewhat disconcerting to think that a salon society joke was once part of this multifaceted set of arguments, and that the joke in question also had something to do with the content and course of the French Revolution, but it may still be true. Even more, however, than the concepts of enlightenment, class, or sovereignty, jokes make sense only in some sort of context. This, to begin with, is what this book is intended to supply.

❦ 2 ❧

AN INGENIOUS EMBLEM

NEW YEAR'S GIFTS AND AN EIGHTEENTH-CENTURY FRENCH JOKE

THE NAME *sans-culottes*, and the emblem with which it was associated, first came to public prominence on 20 June 1792, the day that a Parisian crowd invaded the Tuileries Palace and forced Louis XVI to don a red, Phrygian liberty cap. Eyewitness accounts of the events of the day are not particularly easy to find, but one of the most detailed descriptions of what happened was compiled some weeks later by an English physician and prolific travel writer named John Moore, who went to Paris in early August, mainly to find out more about the looming catastrophe that the French Revolution looked likely to become. According to Moore, the day began with a procession that formed at 9 a.m. on the site of the Bastille, the once-imposing royal fortress that had been demolished after the most famous of all French insurrections, on 14 July 1789. The procession was headed by members of the National Guard of the *faubourg* Saint-Antoine, the suburb that lay immediately to the east of the ruined fortress. They were followed by their counterparts from the adjoining *faubourg* Saint-Marcel. Between them was a cortege made up of people carrying banners. One stated, *Tremblez tyrans, ou soyez justes et respectez la liberté du peuple* (Tremble tyrants, or be just and respect the liberty of the people); a second contained the words *Louis, le peuple est las de souffrir* (Louis, the people is tired of suffering); a third warned, *Tremblez tyran, ta dernière heure est venue* (Tremble tyrant, your last hour has come); a fourth, connected more obviously to the crisis caused by the king's dismissal of several of his still nominally royal ministers that had precipitated the events of 20 June, demanded, *Le rappel des ministres, la sanction ou la mort* (Recall the ministers, the sanction, or death). "Other banners were carried," Moore reported, "ornamented with vile allegorical figures and suitable inscriptions. Among other ingenious emblems, a pair of old black breeches were carried on a pole, with this comfortable inscription, *Libres—et sans-culottes* (Free—and without breeches)."[1]

---

[1] John Moore, *A Journal during a Residence in France from the Beginning of August to the Middle of December 1792*, 2 vols. (London, 1793), 2:204–6. See also François-Emmanuel Toulangeon, *Histoire de France depuis la révolution de 1789*, 7 vols. (Paris, 1801), 2:166: "Un homme, couvert d'habits déchirés, tenait élevés au haut d'une pique des lambeaux d'une

Used as a noun, the hyphenated word *sans-culottes* has a straightforward literal meaning. It means, as Moore wrote, someone not wearing breeches, and who was, therefore, *sans culottes*. In this sense, anyone not wearing the breeches and stockings worn by men in public or professional life in eighteenth-century France could be described as *sans culottes*. Oddly, however, the words were never joined together by a hyphen to form a simple substantive noun (as, for example, was done with the words *gagne-deniers*, meaning a casual worker). Although most men in rural France, and many of the ordinary male inhabitants of towns and cities, usually wore trousers for going about their daily lives, and wore breeches and stockings only on more formal or festive public occasions, it was never the case that they were described as *sans-culottes*. The noun cannot be found in any seventeenth- or eighteenth-century French dictionary. But this does not mean that the term *sans-culottes* was purely a product of the French Revolution and, in particular, of the part played by artisans and shopkeepers in the sequence of Parisian insurrections that led, first, to the fall of the French monarchy on 10 August 1792 and then to the period of intense political conflict that culminated in the Terror in 1793 and 1794—although this, of course, is the meaning that the noun now has.[2] The term did exist before the French Revolution, but it did not have a hyphen, and it meant something else. Before the French Revolution someone who was *sans culottes* was a writer without a patron. The writer was usually male; the patron was usually female. In seventeenth- and eighteenth-century France, and Paris in particular, there was said to be a New Year's Day custom among some of the ladies who presided over salons to give the men of letters whom they protected a piece of silk or velvet cloth to be made into a pair of breeches. A man of letters who did not frequent a salon and who had, instead, to rely on his wit, talent, and industry to earn his keep was, therefore, *sans culottes*.

There is a particular French word (*étrennes*) for a New Year's gift. But the only type of New Year's gift in which breeches were involved centred upon the distinctively French institution that, in the seventeenth and eighteenth centuries, turned the name of a room into the name of a cultivated

---

culotte noire. On lisait écrit: Tremblez tyrans! Voici les sans-culottes." The description is reproduced verbatim in the abbé Jean-Gabriel-Maurice Rocques de Montgaillard, *Histoire de France*, 9 vols. (Paris, 1827), 3:92.

[2] See, most famously, Albert Soboul, *Les sans-culottes parisiens en l'an II* (Paris, Clavreuil, 1958), part of which was translated by Gwynne Lewis as *The Parisian Sans-Culottes and the French Revolution* (Oxford, OUP, 1964). For a readable English-language summary, see Gwyn A. Williams, *Artisans and Sans-Culottes* [1968], 2nd ed. (London, Libris, 1989), and, for a more recent examination of both the term and what a *sans-culotte* might have looked like, see Richard Wrigley, *The Politics of Appearances: Representation of Dress in Revolutionary France* (Oxford, Berg, 2002), especially pp. 186–227.

literary gathering, the salon. Although the word itself acquired its generic sense only in the nineteenth century, the arrangements and activities to which it referred were all in existence by the eighteenth century.[3] Most salons were presided over by women. Most of those present were men. One example of the custom to which this relationship gave rise can be found in a comedy entitled *Le Bureau d'esprit* (The Office of Wit) written by a man named Jean-Jacques (or John James) Rutledge, a member of an Irish Jacobite family that had settled in France, and who was later to become quite an influential member of the Parisian Cordeliers club in 1789 and 1790. The play was published in 1776 and was reprinted twice in slightly modified form in 1777 (it is not clear whether it was ever actually performed).[4] It was immediately identified by contemporaries as a rather vicious satire on one of the most prestigious Parisian salons of the third quarter of the eighteenth century and its presiding figure, Mme Geoffrin. It also acquired a reputation for very bad taste, mainly because it appeared (entirely inadvertently) just a few weeks after Mme Geoffrin had suffered a stroke. "I do not know what kind of scum has just printed a comedy entitled *Le Bureau d'esprit* where that poor dying woman has been blackened so strongly, but in truth so poorly, that the whole thing is unreadable," the mathematician and *philosophe* Jean Le Rond d'Alembert informed Voltaire in November 1776.[5] The comedy was the kind of moral drama about mistaken judgement, falsehood unmasked, and love triumphant that Molière had made famous in *Les Femmes savantes*. The Geoffrin figure in Rutledge's comedy is a character named Mme de Folincourt. She, mistakenly, has become an

---

[3] On the use of the term, see Steven Kale, *French Salons: High Society and Political Sociability from the Old Regime to the Revolution of 1848* (Baltimore, Johns Hopkins UP, 2004), pp. 218, 237, note 4.

[4] It has been republished quite recently (without any commentary on the episode described here). See Jean-Jacques Rutledge, *Le Bureau d'esprit* [1776], ed. Pierre Peyronnet (Paris, Champion, 1999). On Rutledge, see most recently, Rachel Hammersley, *French Revolutionaries and English Republicans: The Cordeliers Club, 1790–1794* (Woodbridge, Suffolk, The Royal Historical Society and The Boydell Press, 2005), pp. 83–115, and her earlier publications cited there. More generally, see Ira O. Wade, *The "Philosophe" in the French Drama of the Eighteenth Century* (Princeton, Princeton UP, 1926), including pp. 46–9 on Rutledge.

[5] Cited in Rutledge, *Le Bureau d'esprit*, ed. Peyronnet, p. 12, note 9. On Mme Geoffrin, see, for sympathetic treatment, André Morellet, ed., *Eloges de Mme Geoffrin, par MM Morellet, Thomas et d'Alembert* (Paris, 1812), and A. Tornezy, *Un bureau d'esprit au xviiie siècle. Le salon de Madame Geoffrin* (Paris, 1895) (see pp. 262–4 for the episode described here). Simon Linguet, however, described Mme Geoffrin as "a sophist in skirts" and wrote a vicious fable, entitled "Le convoi de la pie," describing her funeral convoy accompanied by the braying of an ass: "Oraisons funèbres de Mme Geoffrin," *Annales politiques, civiles et littéraires du xviiie siècle* 3 (London, 1777): 122–35. For an illuminating initial examination of the values that Mme Geoffrin herself may have admired, see Emma Barker, "Mme Geoffrin, Painting and *Galanterie*: Carl Van Loo's *Conversation Espagnole* and *Lecture Espagnole*," *Eighteenth-Century Studies* 40 (2007): 587–614.

admirer of the antiquarian researches presented to her salon by a particularly scheming man of letters named M. Cocus (modelled, according to some, on Denis Diderot) and, foolishly, has decided to marry Henriette, one of her two daughters, to him, despite the fact that Henriette is in love with someone else. Midway through the drama, Mme de Folincourt interrupts proceedings to ask Henriette to read out an invoice from a tailor who is expecting payment for a bill. As Henriette begins to read it out, spluttering with laughter as she speaks, it becomes clear that the bill is for the supply of fifty pairs of velvet breeches to be given, so the invoice reads, as a New Year's gift (*étrennes*) to all the "gentlemen" (*messieurs*) who attend Mme de Folincourt's salon. Henriette collapses with laughter and is ordered to spend the day in her room for making so "frightful a display" of her convent-girl manners, with the added threat of a return to the convent if her behaviour does not improve. Just as she is leaving, however, M. Cocus arrives, wearing a pair of black velvet breeches. Henriette curtsies to him deeply, laughing wildly as she leaves.[6]

The opposite of this state of affairs can be found in an article about the English periodical press written and published by the future French republican leader Jacques-Pierre Brissot in the first issue of his *Journal du lycée de Londres* (Journal of the London Lyceum) in 1784. According to Brissot, periodical publications in England followed exactly the same principles as those that obtained on the European mainland, where the proprietor owned the work of his hired pens and exploited them as much as he could. "It would seem," Brissot wrote, "that they are all imbued with the spirit of that bookseller of the rue Saint-Jacques who said so nicely, 'Would that I could keep Voltaire, Rousseau, and Diderot in my loft *sans culottes*. How I would make them work! And how I would be able to earn!'"[7] Brissot probably took the story from Louis-Sébastien Mercier's

---

[6] Rutledge, *Le Bureau d'esprit*, ed. Peyronnet, pp. 134–5 (pp. 47–51 in the Liège, 1776, edition). On the claim that Cocus was meant to be Diderot (presumably because of his role as an art critic), see Friedrich-Melchior Grimm and Jacques-Henri Meister, *Correspondance secrète, politique et littéraire*, 18 vols. (London, 1787–90), 4:22.

[7] Jacques-Pierre Brissot, *Journal du lycée de Londres* 1 (1784): 11–2. The passage in question reads: "Il semble que tous soient imprégnés de l'esprit de ce libraire de la rue Saint-Jacques qui disait si plaisamment: que puis-je tenir dans mon grenier Voltaire, Rousseau, Diderot, sans culottes. Comme je les ferais travailler! Comme je gagnerais!" (I have modernised the spelling and punctuation in this and subsequent citations from eighteenth-century French.) The passage reappears in the compilation published posthumously by Brissot's descendants under the title of *Mémoires de Brissot*, ed. Adolphe Mathurin de Lescure (Paris, 1877). These were given a critical edition by Claude Perroud in 1911 (see Jacques-Pierre Brissot, *Mémoires de Brissot*, ed. Claude Perroud, 2 vols. [Paris, 1911], 1:317, for the passage in question). As Perroud recognised, a substantial part of the memoirs were pieced together by Brissot's widow and son, both from Brissot's surviving papers and from extracts from his daily newspaper, the *Patriote français*. Perroud did not, however, notice that others, as this passage indicates,

Tableau de Paris (Picture of Paris) where, in a slightly different form, it had been published in 1781 in a chapter dealing with booksellers.[8] The same story was also used to illustrate the definition of an "egoist" in a collection of essays published in 1783 by the future Parisian revolutionary prosecutor Pierre-Louis Manuel.[9] The words attributed to the bookseller were not used as a noun, but the meaning was still the same. Writers who were said to be without *culottes* lived in garrets and wrote for what they could get. Writers said to be with *culottes* had an altogether more comfortable time. As one pamphlet put it in 1771, "Parisian society now has a man who has won his breeches (*un homme qui a gagné ses culottes*), a furnished house, a carriage, a *name*, and 10,000 louis in an evening."[10] The breeches that individuals like these might perhaps be given on New Year's Day were marks of the mixture of financial security, social arrival, and literary status that the patronage of those with great wealth was able to supply. But whether the breeches were a sign of success or a subject of scorn, the noun that the words *sans culottes* became had its origins in an eighteenth-century salon society joke. As indicated, much of what follows is designed to try to explain how and why the joke turned into an emblem of republican politics during the period of the French Revolution, and to show how the cluster of values and social arrangements that the emblem came to signify was connected to a way of thinking about morality and politics that has largely disappeared from historical view.

One way of approaching the subject was set out by Robert Darnton in an immensely influential article published in the historical journal *Past & Present* in 1971. In it, Darnton highlighted the salience of the distinction articulated in the article's title—"The High Enlightenment and the Low-Life of Literature in Pre-Revolutionary France"—to the subsequent dynamics of revolutionary politics. Some writers, like Jean-Baptiste-Antoine Suard, were very successful. Others, like Jacques-Pierre Brissot, were not. This difference, coupled with a claim about the divergences in values and beliefs that it helped to cause, became the basis of an argument about political conflict during the French Revolution. "Once the revolution came," Darnton wrote, "the opposition between the high- and low-life of literature had to be resolved. Grub Street rose, overthrew *le monde*, and requisitioned the positions of power and prestige. It was a cultural revolution, which

---

seem to have been taken from some of Brissot's prerevolutionary publications, including the *Journal du lycée de Londres*.

[8] Louis-Sébastien Mercier, *Tableau de Paris* [1781], 12 vols. (Amsterdam, 1782–8), 2:126–7.

[9] [Pierre-Louis Manuel], *Essais historiques, critiques, littéraires et philosophiques* (Geneva, 1783), p. 155. For the passage, see [François Métra], *Correspondance secrète, politique et littéraire*, 18 vols. (London, 1787–90), 15:70.

[10] [Charles Théveneau de Morande], *Le philosophe cynique, pour servir de suite aux anecdotes scandaleuses de la cour de France* (London, 1771), p. 36.

created a new elite and gave them new jobs."[11] In that argument, the emphasis fell upon the circumstances and motivations of writers themselves. Here, the emphasis is upon a joke. Although there is a substantial overlap between the subjects of being a hack writer or not, and of having *culottes* or not, the joke about breeches was not just a joke about writers. It was also a joke about a particular type of cultivated woman and about a way of thinking about civility, politeness, and morality that resonated both to ancient distinctions between the *honestum* and the *utile*, and to early-modern conceptions of honour, honesty, and *honnêteté*. The joke about writers and *culottes* was connected to this large family of related concepts because these, in turn, were connected to the emergence of French salon society in the seventeenth century.[12] In the account of the *sans-culottes*, and the part that they played in the French Revolution set out here, the joke, not the writers, is the significant part of the story. Getting the point of the joke about breeches throws a different light on the point of being *sans culottes*, and this, in turn, opens up a way to recover a range of connections between seventeenth- and eighteenth-century moral theory and the republican politics of the French Revolution. When, in August 1793, the republican bishop of Blois, Henri Grégoire, told the French Convention that "true genius is almost always *sans-culotte*," he was making more than a point about writers, just as when, a little earlier in the same speech, he said that "we must seek out indigent merit in its basement or its sixth floor abode," he was making more than a point about their circumstances.[13] Once the point becomes

[11] The article was originally published in *Past & Present* 51 (1971): 81–115. I have quoted from the reprinted version in Robert Darnton, *The Literary Underground of the Old Regime* (Cambridge, Mass., Harvard UP, 1982), pp. 1–40 (see pp. 37–8 for the passage cited). For a full recent assessment, see Simon Burrows, *Blackmail, Scandal, and Revolution: London's French libellistes 1758–92* (Manchester, Manchester UP, 2006).

[12] For recent studies of salons, and further bibliographical information, see Dena Goodman, *The Republic of Letters: A Cultural History of the French Enlightenment* (Ithaca, Cornell UP, 1994); Daniel Gordon, *Citizens without Sovereignty: Equality and Sociability in French Thought, 1670–1789* (Princeton, Princeton UP, 1994); Miriam Maître, *Les Précieuses. Naissance des femmes de lettres en France au xviie siècle* (Paris, Champion, 1999); Jacqueline Hellegouarc'h, *L'Esprit de société. Cercles et 'salons' parisiens au xviiie siècle* (Paris, Garnier, 2000); Siep Stuurman, *François Poulain de la Barre and the Invention of Modern Equality* (Cambridge, Mass., Harvard UP, 2004); Wendy Ayres-Bennett, *Sociolinguistic Variation in Seventeenth-Century France* (Cambridge, CUP, 2004); Kale, *French Salons*; Benedetta Craveri, *The Art of Conversation* (New York, New York Review, 2005), and the review of it by David A. Bell, *London Review of Books* 28, no. 9 (2006): 17–9; Antoine Lilti, "Sociabilité et mondanité: Les hommes de lettres dans les salons parisiens du xviiie siècle," *French Historical Studies* 28 (2005): 415–45, and his *Le monde des salons. Sociabilité et mondanité à Paris au xviiie siècle* (Paris, Fayard, 2005). This last work is the fullest study of the subject and the only one that (p. 35) mentions the joke about breeches.

[13] Henri Grégoire, *Rapport et projet de décret présenté par le comité d'instruction publique à la séance du 8 août* (Paris, 1793), pp. 8, 10.

clear, it also becomes clear that the archetype of a *sans-culotte* was not a vengeful literary hack but the ancient Greek Cynic philosopher Diogenes of Sinope; while the archetype's significance was its connection to the very ambivalent attitude towards the compatibility between culture and morality on the one hand, and wealth and justice on the other, that, in the eighteenth century, Cynic philosophy was taken to have.

Many historians have pointed out the widespread presence of ancient philosophy in eighteenth-century thought, even though it is not particularly clear why it was so ubiquitous, or why so much of the political rhetoric of the period of the French Revolution took its cue so readily from ancient Greece or Rome (the fact that an eighteenth-century education was a classical education begs as many questions as it answers). One theme running throughout this book is an unavoidably crude attempt at an explanation. Put schematically, ancient philosophy was the only available alternative to Christianity for thinking about the relationship between morality and politics. According to one influential school of political philosophy, one usually associated with the name of Leo Strauss, it may still be.[14] Christianity, it has often been said, captured much of the bleakness and contingency of human life and, in conjunction with its argument about the soul's immortality, gave politics its justification. But without the story of the Fall, and its complicated point about human depravity and divine redemption, it was not clear what the foundations of politics might be, or how power and morality could be reconciled.[15] From the vantage

[14] For commentary, counterposing Strauss's "political philosophy" to Carl Schmitt's "political theology," see Heinrich Meier, *Carl Schmitt and Leo Strauss: The Hidden Dialogue* (Chicago, University of Chicago Press, 1995), and his *Leo Strauss and the Theologico-Political Problem* (Cambridge, CUP, 2006), ch. 1, and, on Strauss's early interest in Christianity and its predicaments, see Samuel Moyn, "From Experience to Law: Leo Strauss and the Weimar Crisis of the Philosophy of Religion," *History of European Ideas* 33 (2007): 174–94. For a recent, balanced, guide, see Steven B. Smith, *Reading Leo Strauss: Politics, Philosophy, Judaism* (Chicago, University of Chicago Press, 2006). In a weaker sense, the claim could be extended to include the legacy of Hannah Arendt. For the two sets of claims, compare, for example, J.G.A. Pocock, *The Machiavellian Moment: Florentine Political Thought and the Atlantic Republican Tradition* [1975], 2nd ed. (Princeton, Princeton UP, 2003), to Eric Nelson, *The Greek Tradition in Republican Thought* (Cambridge, CUP, 2004). For a neo-Roman variation on the theme, see Quentin Skinner, *Liberty before Liberalism* (Cambridge, CUP, 2000). For a helpful recent overview of ancient and Christian themes in early modern moral philosophy, see Susan James, "The Passions and the Good Life," in Donald Rutherford, ed., *The Cambridge Companion to Early Modern Philosophy* (Cambridge, CUP, 2006), pp. 198–220.

[15] Here, the moral and political thought of John Locke has often been taken to be a particularly rich guide to the broader set of problems: see John Dunn, "From Applied Theology to Social Analysis: The Break between John Locke and the Scottish Enlightenment," in Istvan Hont and Michael Ignatieff, eds., *Wealth and Virtue: The Shaping of Political Economy in the Scottish Enlightenment* (Cambridge, CUP, 1983), pp. 119–35, and, more recently, Jeremy Waldron, *God, Locke, and Equality: Christian Foundations of Locke's Political Thought* (Cambridge,

point of the eighteenth century, one way out was to go back to ancient philosophy—not, however, in pursuit of something that, in the nineteenth and twentieth centuries, came to be called "the Enlightenment," but, in a more open-ended and argumentative manner, to try to find ways to fit the many different, and often blatantly arbitrary, aspects of prevailing economic, social, and political arrangements into some broader normative (or "enlightened") framework.[16] Much of what is still interesting in eighteenth-century thought lies in the types of question that this sort of concern produced, if only because it is not entirely clear whether the twenty-first century has got much further in answering them. It may well be somewhat misguided to try to use a joke to discuss this kind of concern, but it may be equally misguided to try to deal with it head-on.

One way in can be supplied by another example of the joke. This time the joke was associated not with the salon kept by Mme Geoffrin but with the earlier, equally celebrated, salon held by Mme Claudine-Alexandrine Guérin de Tencin during the period of the Regency and the first half of the reign of Louis XV. The later salon was, in fact, a more or less direct successor of the earlier one. Mme de Tencin (whose illegitimate son was d'Alembert) died in 1749, but the memory of her annual New Year's Day practice of giving two ells of velvet to be made into breeches to the men of letters who frequented her salon was still alive more than fifty years later. Before the revolution, wrote the author of a life of the royalist man of letters Antoine de Rivarol, published in 1802, almost every neighbourhood in Paris housed two or three salons, or *bureaux de bel esprit*. There was one on the rue Saint-Honoré held by a dress designer (*artiste en robe*) named Mme Moreau, where plays were performed, as was also the case with one held by a shoemaker's wife named Mme Charpentier on the rue du-roi-de-Sicile. But, wrote Rivarol's biographer, none of the *habitués* of these gatherings could expect to receive a pair of velvet breeches of the kind that Mme de Tencin had been accustomed to bestow upon her acolytes.[17] Not only was Mme de Tencin said to give the men of letters who frequented her salon a pair of breeches on New Year's Day; she was also, as the editor

---

CUP, 2002). For an earlier, much less sophisticated, example of this type of concern, see Richard Winn Livingstone, *Greek Ideals and Modern Life* (Oxford, 1935).

[16] For these themes, see John Robertson, *The Case for the Enlightenment: Scotland and Naples 1680–1760* (Cambridge, CUP, 2005), and, for an older set of claims, see Peter Gay, *The Enlightenment, an Interpretation* [1966], 2 vols. (London, Wildwood House, 1970). For a recent overview, see Darrin M. McMahon, *The Pursuit of Happiness: A History from the Greeks to the Present* (London, Allen Lane, 2006).

[17] Sulpice Imbert de la Platière, *Vie Philosophique, politique et littéraire de Rivarol* (Paris, 1802), p. 121. For corroboration of Mme Moreau's "assemblies," see David Garrioch, *The Making of Revolutionary Paris* (Berkeley and Los Angeles, University of California Press, 2002), pp. 246–7.

of an edition of her collected works published in 1786 noted, said to refer to them occasionally as her *bêtes*.[18] As an earlier commentator noted, "the taste for this type of menagerie has not quite passed, and the *bêtes* who now compose them are even more submissive and tame than those of Mme de Tencin's time, although it must be said that their new superintendents are far from being as farsighted or agreeable."[19] The French word *bête* cannot be turned straightforwardly into the English word "beast" because, although both words do mean "animal," the French word also has connotations of clumsiness, stupidity, and unmanageability that are associated more readily with the related Anglicism, "menagerie" (you can talk about your menagerie in English in the same way as you might talk about your *bêtes* in French, but you would not be saying the same thing if you were to say *Je suis bête* in French and "I'm an animal" in English).

As was explained in a series of articles about Mme de Tencin and her unusual presents, published in the *Journal de Paris* in 1787 under the names of the "Recluse of the Pyrenees" and the "Recluse of Migneaux," the word *bête* was meant, in the first instance, to be a joke about wit and intelligence. Mme de Tencin's habit of calling Fontenelle or Montesquieu (the most distinguished members of her salon) her "beasts" was like calling the younger of the immensely rich Crozat brothers "Crozat the pauper" because he had a fortune worth no more than two million livres while his brother had one worth six million, or like calling the marquis d'Argenson "d'Argenson the blockhead" (*d'Argenson la bête*) to distinguish him from his equally able, but more socially sparkling brother, the comte d'Argenson. It was also a joke about worldliness. As the "Recluse of the Pyrenees" explained, Mme de Tencin, who was an accomplished intriguer, and who, he added, would never have written any novels if she had been in a position to write royal decrees, was very proud of her skill in a department in which men of letters were notoriously incompetent, or *bêtes*.[20] Her "sweet manner," another

[18] Antoine-François Delandine, "Observations sur les romans et en particulier sur ceux de Mme de Tencin," in Mme de Tencin, *Oeuvres*, 7 vols. (Paris, 1786), 1:xxxii–xxxiii.

[19] Antoine Sabatier de Castres, *Les trois siècles de notre littérature*, 3 vols. (Amsterdam, 1772), 3:320, as cited in "Vie privée de M. l'abbé de Mably," in Gabriel Bonnot de Mably, *Oeuvres complètes*, 13 vols. (London, 1789–90), 13:225–6.

[20] On the unworldliness of men of letters, see the compilation dealing with the question "pourquoi les gens de lettres sont communément dans l'indigence," in *L'abeille, ou recueil de philosophie, de littérature et d'histoire* (The Hague, 1755), pp. 7–25. The articles on Mme de Tencin were published as part of a series of letters to the *Journal de Paris* signed by "Le Solitaire des Pyrénées" starting on 25 June 1787 (issue 176) and continuing on 11 July 1787 (issue 192); 8 August 1787 (issue 220); 11 September 1787 (issue 254); 5 October 1787 (issue 278)—where the jokes about Crozat and d'Argenson can be found; and 15 October 1787 (issue 288). The issues of 3 and 16 November 1787 (307 and 320) contain two replies containing the pseudoerudite history of *étrennes* signed by "Le Solitaire de Migneaux." On Mme de Tencin, see particularly Jean Sareil, *Les Tencin* (Geneva, Droz, 1969), and the works mentioned in note 24 below.

commentator noted, simply meant that "if she had an interest in poisoning you, she would choose the sweetest poison."[21] As for the breeches, according to the "Recluse of Migneaux" (who may have been Jean-Baptiste-Antoine Suard, the man whose reputation now probably owes more to Professor Darnton than it does to himself), these were simply a variant of the widespread custom of giving presents on New Year's Day. The French word *étrennes*, the "Recluse" explained, adopting a tone of learning designed to match the subject at hand, came from the Latin word *strenna*, the branches cut from trees in a wood devoted to the goddess of strength, Strenna, which were given to Tatius, king of the Sabines, on the first day of the New Year. Examples of the custom, including the practice of giving items of clothing, could be found in many parts of the ancient and modern worlds. In Athens, the "Recluse" observed, Aristophanes referred to the practice of rewarding a poet by giving him a garment (*habit*) for his praise of the city. According to Martial, the Romans also rewarded their poets with a new garment, and, the erudite "Recluse" continued, the practice was also widespread in thirteenth- and fourteenth-century Italy when the country was divided among feudal lords like the Gonzaga of Mantua. The Arabs, he noted, still reward their poets in the same way.[22]

But this display of erudition did not tell the whole story. "It would be easy for me," the "Recluse of the Pyrenees" added as an aside, "to explain

---

[21] Sébastien-Roch-Nicolas Chamfort, *Maximes, pensées, caractères et anecdotes* (London, 1796), p. 143.

[22] *Journal de Paris*, 3 November 1787 (issue 307): 1322–3; 16 November 1787 (issue 320): 1373–5. The whole sequence of articles was reprinted in Jean-Baptiste-Antoine Suard, *Mélanges de littérature*, 2nd ed., 5 vols. (Paris, 1806), 1:346–50, 374–83, indicating that he was probably the "Recluse of Migneaux," and that Louis Ramond de Carbonnières was the "Recluse of the Pyrenees." For the source of many of these examples, see the research of the seventeenth-century antiquarian Jacob Spon, *De l'origine des étrennes* [1674] (Paris, 1781). For a similar, slightly earlier, further source, but not one mentioned in this exchange, see the fascinating essay by the seventeenth-century French bishop Pierre-Daniel Huet, "De l'origine des romans," that appeared as the preface (1:5–67) to *Zayde, histoire espagnole*, 2 vols. (Paris, 1671), a novel published under the name of Jean-Regnaud de Segrais but now attributed to Mme de Lafayette. As Huet wrote there (pp. 51–3), ancient Oriental kings gave their robes to the winners of the great poetry competitions held at the city of Fez, a custom also observed by later French lords in giving one of their garments to an admired troubadour. Huet's description throws more light on the association between salons and troubadours made by Mme de Tencin's admirer the comte de Tressan, as described below, p. 70. In doing so, it shows both how the conceit associating a *salonnière* with an ancient Greek courtesan could be extended to include the world of the troubadours, and how the gift of a pair of breeches could be associated, presumably more ironically than sincerely, with medieval chivalry (but with the further, less ironic, implication that someone who opted to be *sans culottes* might be truly chivalrous, as can be inferred from the satires published by Antoine-Joseph Gorsas described in chapter 5 below).

how velvet breeches became fashionable forty or fifty years ago, and why Mme de Tencin wanted to make reasonable men adopt so minor an elegance, an elegance that simplicity of manner, not thrift, might have led them to refuse. But these details would be too fastidious and would not seem *fitting* to readers who make a point of propriety."[23] The additional information is not hard to guess. The breeches were not just a New Year's gift. They also covered men's bottoms. This, too, was part of the joke. It was a deliberately vulgar way of highlighting the refinement of Mme de Tencin's salon, and the way that it could polish the rough, awkward, or clumsy manners of her *bêtes*. In this sense, the joke was an emblem of urbanity. The mixture of vulgarity and refinement that made it a joke was captured quite well in a poem about giving their hostess a straw hat written by one of the salon's *habitués*, the poet Alexis Piron.

Nous sentons, en faisant du mieux que nous pouvons,
Combien encore nous redevons.
Que vous donnons-nous? rien qui vaille.
Laissons-là tous ces beaux discours;
Nous emportons votre velours
Et vous présentons de la paille.
Du reste notre droit est clair
Et la représaille est honnête.
Vous nous couvrez le c . . . l'hiver;
L'été nous vous couvrons la tête.[24]

It was, as Piron put it, an "honourable reprisal." To summarise what he wrote in the poem, she gave them velvet; they gave her straw. She covered their bottoms in winter, and they covered her head in summer.

The sexual undertone was quite easy to spot (Mme de Tencin was famously promiscuous. "I was young; I was beautiful; what more should I

---

[23] "Il me serait aisé de vous expliquer comment les culottes de velours étaient devenues à la mode il y a quarante ou cinquante ans, et pourquoi Mme de Tencin avait voulu faire adopter cette petite élégance à des hommes raisonnables qui s'y refusaient par simplicité, non par économie; mais ces détails seraient trop fastidieux, et ne paraîtraient pas de *bon ton* aux lecteurs qui s'en piquent." *Journal de Paris*, 15 October 1787 (issue 288): 1244–5. See also Suard, *Mélanges*, 1:357.

[24] Alexis Piron, *Oeuvres complètes*, 7 vols. (Paris, 1776), 7:81–2. The poem is also printed in Charles de Coynart, *Les Guérin de Tencin (1520–1758)* (Paris, 1910), p. 303. See also Hellegouarc'h, *L'Esprit de société*, pp. 68, 467, note 5. A mock posthumous poem, entitled "Regrets de Madame de Tencin en mourant," that was published in *La Bigarrure, ou Meslance* [sic] *curieux, instructif et amusant* (The Hague, 1753), p. 103, struck a similar tone. In it, Mme de Tencin's breeches were given to all forty members of the Académie française, who, after her death, were now condemned to having to display their bare bottoms: "J'ai donné, tant que j'ai vécu, / Une culotte à chacun des Quarante. / Respectable Senat dont j'étais Présidente, / Vous allez donc montrer le C!"

confess?" she was said, late in life, to have asked her confessor). This allowed the custom to appear in a different light. "Such gifts," commented her biographer in 1786, "were as barely decent on the part of a woman as they were vile on the part of those who deigned to accept them."[25] "Every year on New Year's Day," a later compilation noted, the members of her salon received "two ells of velvet to be made into an article of clothing that an English lady would have been as careful not to point to as she would have been to name."[26] As the earlier comment implies, the gift could say something about the recipient as well as the giver. "Mme de Tencin had nine wits (*beaux esprits*) whom she called her Parnassus, to whom she gave each a pair of velvet breeches on the first day of each year," noted one later critic. "When the lackeys saw them coming, they would say derisively, 'Here's one of our pensioners, or even a man in knickers (*ou bien un homme à la culotte*).' "[27] This type of man could easily be described as someone "vile," someone who was rather like the hypocritical character of M. Cocus in Rutledge's comedy or, more memorably, like Trissotin in Molière's *Les femmes savantes*. This sort of evaluation sometimes went along with a more elaborate judgement. Here, disapproval of the gift was part of a broader condemnation of the whole panoply of conventions on which it was based.

The fullest description of this set of attitudes (at least as they pertained to Mme de Tencin and her salon) can be found in a short essay entitled "Summary Reflexions on Wit" ("Réflexions sommaires sur l'esprit") published in a posthumous edition of the miscellaneous works of an expert on chivalry and troubadour poetry named the comte de Tressan. By the time that he wrote them, Tressan (who was born in 1705 and died in 1783) was the last survivor of the two overlapping generations to have frequented the salon.[28] The elegiac tone of the essay was a deliberate and somewhat pointed evocation of an age that he knew had passed. There were, he wrote, any number of different ways of violating the rules of polite society. Some people were too calculating (*fin*), or too frivolous, or too obviously acting a part, while

[25] Delandine, "Observations," pp. xxxii–xxxiii.

[26] "Tous les ans, aux étrennes, ces derniers recevaient d'elle deux aunes de velours pour se faire le vêtement, qu' une Anglaise se serait aussi bien gardée d'indiquer que de nommer": [Guillaume-Edouard-Désiré Monnais, ed.], *Ephémérides universelles*, 13 vols. (Paris, 1828–33), 12:99.

[27] François-Antoine Chevrier, *Oeuvres*, 3 vols. (London, 1774), 2:221. As Chevrier commented earlier in the same text, the practice of engaging men of letters to deal with the diplomatic correspondence of foreign embassies meant that "ce petit commerce semi-politique leur vaut quelques culottes à la fin de l'année, et de là ils se croient autorisés à se qualifier *chargés d'affaires* et d'*agents* de tels ministres" (p. 53).

[28] A biography and list of Tressan's principal publications can be found in Jean-Benjamin Laborde, *Essai sur la musique ancienne et moderne*, 4 vols. (Paris, 1780), 4:413–25.

others were simply "*anglomanes*."[29] But the worst of all were "the kind of people who affect a stoic severity or the most crude cynicism."

> Diogenes, covered in rags, his legs bare, his feet covered in filthy mud, marches into Plato's abode and fouls his purple carpets. "I am here," he says, "to trample Plato's pride underfoot." "Bravely done, Diogenes," replies the Sage, "but bear in mind that you seem to be trampling them with more pride than, to me, these carpets may be worth."[30]

Cynicism, Tressan commented, was "the most vile mask behind which the man of pretensions, or someone superb, can hide."[31] A Stoic was no more than a pedant and a dull dispenser of dissertations who, for all these shortcomings, might still be someone whose character was true. But the character of a Cynic was always false. His harsh, crude tone and his abject and unusual appearance always hid a man of bad faith, someone whose aim was always to subjugate his interlocutor without any self-restraint or effort to please. "A shrewd, pretty, and amusing woman or a wealthy, liberal, and witty man can easily unmask these show philosophers" (*philosophes d'apparat*), Tressan wrote, dismissively.[32]

This, he continued, was what Mme de Tencin had invariably been able to do. She had a quite unusual talent for being able to see people for who they really were, and for talking to them in just the right way, no matter whether the person in question was Fontenelle or Réaumur, "her intimate friends," or "a young, beautiful woman preoccupied with her attire and her lover."[33] "No woman," Tressan wrote, "was ever better at joining the elevated gift of being able to please and enlighten at one and the same time. Never did a means of making herself useful to her friends elude her: she was always better at imagining how best to find a way to succeed than they were themselves."[34] It was in her society, he added immediately,

---

[29] Louis-Elizabeth de la Vergne, comte de Tressan, "Réflexions sommaires sur l'esprit" in his *Oeuvres choisis*, 12 vols. (Paris, 1787–91), 12:119.

[30] "Diogène couvert de haillons, les jambes nues, les pieds couverts d'une boue infect, entre chez Planton, et souille ses tapis de pourpre: Je viens, dit-il, fouler aux pieds l'orgueil de Platon.—Courage, Diogène, lui répondit le Sage; mais songe que tu les foules avec plus d'orgueil que je ne mets de prix à ces tapis": Tressan, "Réflexions," p. 122. For a pithier version of the story, see François de Salignac de la Mothe Fénelon, *The Lives and Most Remarkable Maxims of the Ancient Philosophers* [1726] (London, 1726), p. 199: "I tread, said he [Diogenes], on the vanity of Plato. True, Diogenes, cried Plato, but with a greater vanity." Another version of the story had Diogenes tearing off Plato's handsome cloak, or mantle, and trampling it underfoot: see Henry Grove, *A System of Moral Philosophy*, 2 vols. (London, 1749), 2:290.

[31] Tressan, "Réflexions," p. 122.

[32] Tressan, "Réflexions," p. 123.

[33] Tressan, "Réflexions," p. 123.

[34] Tressan, "Réflexions," p. 123.

that he had encountered the characters of both the Stoic and the Cynic. The first was Fontenelle's nephew, René-François Richer d'Aube, "one of the most knowledgeable men in Europe," who, to the hilarity of Mme Tencin's circle, was to earn himself some kind of fame for misplaced self-importance by accusing Montesquieu of plagiarising his *Essai sur les principes du droit et de la morale* (Essay on the Principles of Law and Morality) when the latter's *De l'esprit des lois* (The Spirit of Laws) was published late in 1748. The second was a "semi-Cynic," with "hair matted like a spaniel," "trampling on the skirts of women who displeased him," talking to them "like a libertine monk," whom Tressan identified as the poet and dramatist Joseph Saurin.[35]

In keeping with the association that he made between salon society and Plato's purple carpets, Tressan extended the parallel to encompass the salon itself. In a poem entitled "Various Proofs of Metempsychosis Addressed to the Late Mme de Tencin," he presented her salon as a reincarnation of an ancient Greek philosophical symposium, or banquet. A young man (Tressan himself) contemplating suicide after the death of a woman he loved is restrained by Pythagoras from taking his own life. There is, Pythagoras informs him, a "temple in Paris, worthy of the finest days of Greece, where reason joins with laughter under wisdom's breast." As the Greek philosopher went on to explain, the morality once associated with Periander's banquet—a morality, Tressan added, that monarchies and republics had once both accepted—had been reborn, first among the troubadours of Provence, and now in the gatherings presided over by Mme de Tencin. This, although Tressan did not say so, implied that Mme de Tencin was a reincarnation of a Greek *hetaira*, or the distinctively cultivated type of courtesan whose musical skills, spinning wheels, and geisha-like presence featured quite prominently in descriptions of the mixture of conversation, drinking, and flirtation involved in an ancient Greek symposium. It was not a particularly unusual association to make. As the Jansenist-educated Simon Linguet noted in a hostile comment on salons, and the women who kept them, "of all the roles that the exaltation of wit makes them play in centuries in which what is called enlightenment (*lumières*) proliferates, the most common, and the easiest, is that of Aspasia."[36] The parallel between a *hetaira* and a *salonnière* was well enough known for M. Cocus, in a misplaced display of erudition, to compare Mme de Folincourt's salon to Plato's "banquet" in Rutledge's *Le Bureau d'esprit*, even though, as Rutledge himself pointed out in a pseudoerudite footnote, Aspasia, the most famous of all Greek *hetaerae*, was never mentioned at all in Plato's own *Symposium*. Cocus's blunder, Rutledge observed, was a

[35] Tressan, "Réflexions," pp. 123–4.
[36] Linguet, *Annales*, p. 379.

mark of "pedantic and gallant *préciosité*."[37] As the exchange suggests, the parallel owed something to seventeenth-century salon society, and to the fashion for *préciosité* with which it was associated (it was a parallel sometimes applied to the seventeenth-century *salonnière* Ninon de l'Enclos, who was certainly more of a genuine courtesan than Mme Geoffrin). The vogue for miniature spinning wheels, one of the many *articles de Paris* produced by fashionable Parisian lacquerware manufacturers like the Martin brothers, as well as the memorable portrait by the English painter George Romney of Lord Nelson's mistress, the courtesan Emma Hamilton, as a spinner (a painting that was probably commissioned in 1784 when she was still Emma Hart, and the mistress of Charles Grenville), are both indications of its enduring eighteenth-century resonance.[38]

Tressan did not describe the concept of morality that he associated with Periander, or explain what he meant by presenting an eighteenth-century salon as a reincarnation of an ancient Greek symposium. A description of the banquet to which he alluded could be found in Plutarch's *Moralia*, but a more significant remark about Periander and morality can be found in Plato's *Republic*, where Periander was identified with a notion of justice that involved helping one's friends and harming one's enemies.[39] If this

[37] Rutledge, *Le Bureau d'esprit*, ed. Peyronnet, p. 125, and note 1. The question of the nature and status of a Greek courtesan's activities gave rise to some scholarly (but also moral and political) discussion in the last years of the first French republic: see Pierre-Jean-Baptiste (Publicola) Chaussard, *Fêtes et courtisanes de la Grèce*, 4 vols. (Paris, 1801), 1:18; 3:64–6; 4:29–30, 45 (who argued in favour of the high honour in which Greek courtesans were held, and the part that they played in promoting "national luxury"). Chaussard's assessment was a reply to M. Jacobs, "Essai sur l'histoire des femmes, principalement des hétaires à Athènes," *Magasin encyclopédique* 5, issue 2 (1 Thermidor an VII/1799): 49–73 (who argued in favour of their low status).

[38] On the Martin brothers, see Michael Sonenscher, *Work and Wages: Politics, Natural Law and the Eighteenth-Century French Trades* (Cambridge, CUP, 1989), ch. 4, and Anna Czarnocka, "Vernis Martin: The Lacquer Work of the Martin Family in the Eighteenth Century," *Studies in the Decorative Arts* 2 (1994): 56–74. I am grateful to Elizabeth Allen for the information about Romney's painting. On the wider subject of courtesans (but not in France), see Sarah B. Pomeroy, *Goddesses, Whores, Wives and Slaves: Women in Classical Greece* (New York, Schocken, 1975); Martin Postle, " 'Painted Women': Reynolds and the Cult of the Courtesan," in Robyn Asleson, ed., *Notorious Muse: The Actress in British Art and Culture, 1776–1812* (New Haven, Yale UP, 2003), pp. 22–56; Martha Feldman and Bonnie Gordon, eds., *The Courtesan's Arts: Cross Cultural Perspectives* (Oxford, OUP, 2006).

[39] On Periander's banquet, see Plutarch, *Morals*, translated by several hands, 4th ed., 5 vols. (London, 1704), 2:1–36, and Isaac de Larry, *Histoire des sept sages*, 2 vols. (Rotterdam, 1714). On Periander's morality, see Plato, *Republic*, 1.336a, in Plato, *The Collected Dialogues*, ed. Edith Hamilton and Huntingdon Cairns (Princeton, Princeton UP, 1963), p. 586. According to Fénelon, *Lives*, p. 58, there may have been two Perianders, with the views of one conflated with those of the other. On the broader subject of the notion of justice that Plato associated with Periander, see Mary Whitlock Blundell, *Helping Friends and Harming Enemies: A Study in Sophocles and Greek Ethics* (Cambridge, CUP, 1989), and Bernard Williams, "Pagan Justice

was a conception of morality that Plato rejected, it was, nonetheless, one that fitted Tressan's characterisation of Mme de Tencin quite well. As he emphasised in his *Summary Reflexions on Wit*, her great gift was her ability to serve her friends without, however, making them feel obliged to serve her in return. The same capacity for disinterested friendship had been highlighted very strikingly in another description of Mme de Tencin and her salon (one that Tressan himself probably knew) published by the novelist Marivaux in his *La vie de Marianne*, an eleven-part novel that appeared between 1731 and 1742. Marivaux was a very subtle analyst of human emotions, and his description of Mme de Tencin and her salon (through the character of Mme Dorsin in the novel) is a miniature version of the much broader view of the relationship between morality and the passions that, according to many of his eighteenth-century readers, including David Hume and Adam Smith, was what made his work so fascinating. For the Anglican divine William Warburton, writing in 1748, the English novelists Fielding and Richardson were building largely on the techniques pioneered by the French, and by Marivaux in particular, to supersede "the first barbarous romances" of earlier times. "At length," Warburton wrote, "this great people (to whom, it must be owned, all science has been infinitely indebted) hit upon the true secret by which alone a deviation from strict fact, in the commerce of man, could be really entertaining to an improved mind, or useful to promote that improvement. And this was by a faithful and chaste copy of real *Life and Manners*."[40]

As Marivaux observed, we all need one another from time to time. But the transactions to which need can give rise usually involve a cluster of quite complicated feelings. Asking for someone's help can be embarrassing, which is why people often ask for less than they might actually need. Receiving someone's help can also create an awkwardness about how best to reciprocate, which is why people often forget how much they really owe. This, Marivaux suggested, is why it is often easier to ask for help from someone who either does not know you particularly well, or may not see all the reasons for the request.

> Most people, when they are obliged, would prefer not to have to feel either the price of the service rendered or the extent of the obligation that they have acquired. They would prefer one to be good without being enlightened, since this best suits their ungrateful delicacy. But this is exactly what they do

and Christian Love" [1993], now reprinted in his *The Sense of the Past: Essays in the History of Philosophy*, ed. Miles Burnyeat (Princeton, Princeton UP, 2006), pp. 71–82.

[40] [William Warburton], *Preface* to vol. 4 of the first edition of Richardson's *Clarissa*, as cited by R. S. Crane, "Richardson, Warburton and French Fiction," *Modern Language Review* 17 (1922): 17–23 (17–8). For further discussion, see James S. Munro, "Richardson, Marivaux, and the French Romance Tradition," *Modern Language Review* 70 (1975): 752–9.

not find with someone who has a great deal of wit and intelligence (*esprit*). The more wit they have, the more humiliating it is for those whom they help, because someone with a great deal of wit can see the point of being helpful all too well. Their intelligence is too exact, and perhaps too proud a witness, making any failure of gratitude feel all the more shameful. This in turn irritates those whom they help so much that they forget to be grateful, precisely because too much is known about what they owe. If they had to do with someone who knew less, they would have more gratitude.[41]

This, Marivaux explained, was one reason why it was easy to ask for help from another famous *salonnière*, the marquise de Lambert (Mme de Miran in the novel). Since she had a good nature, but no great insight, it was easy to ask her for just what was needed, and to be sure that her help would not give rise to the sort of anxiety involved in relying on someone with more wit and intelligence (*esprit*). The source of this "unjust delicacy," Marivaux wrote, was probably to be found in "the real greatness of our souls" and the likelihood, "if it can be put like this," that "the soul is of too high a condition to owe something to another soul." In this sense, "the title of benefactor" was one that really befitted only God.[42]

The remarkable thing, according to Marivaux, about Mme de Tencin was that not only did she have a great deal of wit and intelligence; she was also able to use these qualities to get round the difficulties that they might have been expected to produce. This was because she used her intelligence to foresee the ways in which she could be of service to her friends. By taking the initiative, she was able to feel a mixture of gratitude for the trust that her friends placed in her, duty towards a confidence that she felt could not be betrayed, and commitment to a duty that she felt obliged to fulfil. Her "sublime self-love" (*son sublime amour-propre*), as Marivaux put it, had the effect of reversing the usual emotions involved in giving and receiving.

> Thus, in the way that she saw it, it was not she who deserved your gratitude, but you who deserved hers, because it was you who counted upon her to help you. From this, she concluded that it was her duty to serve you, and she reached this conclusion with a pleasure that was her reward for all that she had done for you.

Perhaps, Marivaux concluded, "the exalted quality of these sorts of feelings" (*l'élévation de pareils sentiments*) was "too delicious," and God might, perhaps, forbid one to collude with them, but "morally speaking" it was an elevation that was "very respectable in the eyes of men."[43]

---

[41] Pierre Carlet de Chamblain de Marivaux, *La vie de Marianne* [1741], ed. Frédéric Deloffre (Paris, Garnier, 1963), pt. 5, p. 220.

[42] Marivaux, *La vie de Marianne*, p. 221.

[43] Marivaux, *La vie de Marianne*, p. 224.

It is not difficult to see why this kind of "sublime self-love" might not have been acceptable to either a Stoic or a Cynic. However quick-witted Mme de Tencin might have been, the combination of imagination and calculation that she relied upon to help her friends was grounded upon an emotional foundation that, from either point of view, was unlikely to be compatible with real virtue. It is also fairly easy to see that the qualities that Marivaux admired in Mme de Tencin were connected to a kind of Epicureanism, although it was a kind of Epicureanism that matched the claim Marivaux made about the "real greatness" of the human soul. In this respect, it was a rather more authentic version of Epicureanism than that sometimes associated with the type of self-love to which Catholic and Protestant theologians referred in describing the behaviour of fallen mankind.[44] That sort of self-love was not at all compatible with the "real greatness" of the human soul because its focus fell largely on the purely physical side of human nature, and on the motivating power of what, in the seventeenth century, was usually called "concupiscence," a concept that loomed very large in the disabused descriptions of human society to be found in the works of the great Jansenist theologians of the age of Louis XIV. It also fitted the strong emphasis on self-interest to be found in the moral theories of seventeenth-century "libertines" like the duc de la Rochefoucauld. In the view of Mme de Sablé, the Jansenist-leaning author of a *Discourse* on La Rochefoucauld's *Reflections, Sentences, and Maxims*, the significance that La Rochefoucauld attached to false virtue in his moral theory was not to be taken as an incitement to licence. It could, instead, fit Jansenist accounts of human nature. Just as, wrote Mme de Sablé, copper coin or paper money could stand in for the real thing if "need and misery" made them necessary, so, too, in human life could false virtues take the place of the genuine article, since they were "not without their merits and are, in some sense, worthy of our esteem, it being very difficult for mankind to have any better."[45]

The kind of self-love that Marivaux seems to have had in mind was rather different. Described in detail, it reveals one of the core values of salon society. It had an aesthetic dimension that went beyond the sort of purely self-centred calculation involved in the gratification of concupiscence, and the complicated, but providentially governed, chains of unintended consequences that, particularly in Jansenist discussions of morality, selfishness

[44] Compare Dale Van Kley, "Pierre Nicole, Jansenism, and the Morality of Enlightened Self-Interest," in Alan Charles Kors and Paul J. Korshin, eds., *Anticipations of the Enlightenment in England, France, and Germany* (Philadelphia, University of Pennsylvania Press, 1987), pp. 69–85, to Robertson, *The Case for the Enlightenment*, pp. 128–9.

[45] [Mme***], "Discours sur les Réflexions, sentences et maximes morales," in François, duc de la Rochefoucauld, *Réflexions, sentences et maximes morales*, ed. Amelot de la Houssaye (Paris, 1714), pp. 8–9.

served to promote. This, more aesthetically driven, kind of Epicureanism was a prominent feature of the moral philosophy to be found in René Descartes's *The Passions of the Soul* of 1649. Its significance lay in its demonstration of how a particular aspect of self-esteem, one produced by the feeling of having a free will, could become the basis of a genuinely altruistic morality. And, since the feeling applied to the soul, it made no assumptions about any moral differences between the sexes. (It is worth noting that Descartes was often associated, as a late eighteenth-century comedy called *The Ladies Club* put it, with replacing scholastic misogyny with "the most pleasing system of gentleness, love, and union among mankind," which was why the ladies choose a reincarnation of Descartes for their president.)[46] "I see only one thing in us which could give us just cause to esteem ourselves," Descartes had written in *The Passions of the Soul*, "namely, the use of our free will and the dominion we have over our volitions."[47] The feeling of having a free will was connected to self-esteem because of the wonder that the discovery of its existence was likely to provoke (wonder, according to Descartes, was the first of the six primary passions of the human soul).[48] It was also something absolute or self-determining, the one thing that made a human like God. Since, Descartes went on to add, this quality of the will meant that the source of the feeling of wonder was entirely freestanding, "those who have this knowledge and this feeling about themselves can readily believe that every other person can have the same knowledge and feeling about themselves, because there is nothing in either the knowledge or the feeling which depends on someone else."[49] Knowing and feeling this property of human nature could, with several additional moves, explain how those with a proper self-esteem (the basis, Descartes wrote, of "true generosity") would be able "to esteem nothing more highly than doing good to others and to despise their own self-interest."[50]

---

[46] [Anon.], *Le Club des Dames, ou les deux partis* (Avignon, 1787), pp. 12, 14–6. The play has been attributed to Mme de Genlis.

[47] René Descartes, *Les passions de l'âme* [1649], translated as *The Passions of the Soul* by Stephen H. Voss (Indianapolis, Hackett, 1989), §152, p. 103 (I have used the French version of Descartes, *Traité des passions*, ed. François Mizrachi [Paris, 1965], to make minor modifications to this and subsequent translations of the text). The rest of this paragraph owes a great deal to Patrick R. Frierson, "Learning to Love: From Egoism to Generosity in Descartes," *Journal of the History of Philosophy* 40 (2002): 313–48 (especially pp. 323–4). More generally see John Marshall, *Descartes's Moral Theory* (Ithaca, Cornell UP, 1998); Anthony Levi, *French Moralists: The Theory of the Passions 1585 to 1649* (Oxford, OUP, 1964); and, recently, Deborah J. Brown, *Descartes and the Passionate Mind* (Cambridge, CUP, 2006).

[48] See, helpfully, Philip Fisher, *Wonder, the Rainbow, and the Aesthetics of Rare Experiences* (Cambridge, Mass., Harvard UP, 1998), pp. 41–50.

[49] Descartes, *Passions*, §154, trans. Voss, p. 104.

[50] Descartes, *Passions*, §§153 and 156, trans. Voss, pp. 104–5. For Mme de Tencin's version of something like the same idea, see the letter that she wrote either to Fontenelle or to

The aesthetic aspect of Descartes's moral philosophy, and the significance that he attached to the feeling of wonder in providing a starting
point for arriving at disinterested moral evaluations, could be carried over
into a broader assessment of the role of the arts and sciences in human
affairs, and the way that their development could be explained in terms
of something more than physical necessity on the one side, but less than
providential design on the other. If, like the nature of the soul itself, the
ultimate truths of the physical world lay beyond human understanding,
this did not make the emotions sometimes aroused by natural phenomena
pointless, or curiosity superfluous (which was one reason why Voltaire
entitled one of his essays *Of Natural Law, and Curiosity*, and why, according to the entry on "antediluvian" in the *Encyclopédie*, quoting Denis
Diderot's translation of Shaftesbury's *Essay on Merit and Virtue*, the first
humans would not have been philosophers, since their habituation to the
routines of survival meant that they would not have noticed anything to
awaken their curiosity).[51] Some of the assumptions underlying this view
of human culture, and its basis in human curiosity and ingenuity, were
also taken to be a feature of Mme de Tencin's salon and the qualities associated with its members. Thus, in the "Proofs of Metempsychosis" that
he addressed to her, Tressan ended the poem with a verse celebrating her
salon's most glittering intellectual ornament, the philosopher Fontenelle
and his best-known work, *A Conversation on the Plurality of Worlds*. He
was, Tressan wrote floridly, "the swan whose voice can be heard in the
heart's depths."[52] In another poem, entitled "A Letter to M. the Comte
de Caylus on the Uncertainty of the Higher Sciences and of Systems,"
Tressan elaborated upon the various qualities that he associated with the
type of cultivated reasoner that Fontenelle epitomised. He was, first and
foremost, a sceptic. But this did not mean that he adopted a posture of
pure lassitude, towards either nature or society. If the truths of the divine
and natural orders lay beyond human reason's powers, their benefits still
remained, to be identified, improved, and embellished. Here, the models
were Voltaire, as the author of both the Epicurean poem *Le Mondain*
(The Man of the World) of 1736, and, with his mistress Emilie du Châtelet, the *Eléments de la philosophie de Newton* (The Elements of Newton's

Maniquet on Descartes and the relationship between *amour-propre* and "greatness of soul,"
published in Coynart, *Les Guerin de Tencin*, pp. 116–7.
    [51] François Arouet de Voltaire, "De la loi naturelle, et de la curiosité" [1768] in his *Dia-
logues philosophiques*, ed. Raymond Naves (Paris, Garnier, 1966), pp. 280–4; Denis Diderot
and Jean Le Rond d'Alembert, eds., *Encyclopédie*, 17 vols. (Paris, 1751–68), vol. 1, under
"antédiluvienne," citing Diderot's *Essai sur le mérite et la vertu*, p. 92.
    [52] Louis-Elizabeth de la Vergne, comte de Tressan, "Différentes preuves de la métempsy-
cose, adressées à feu Mme de Tencin," in Tressan, *Oeuvres choisis*, 11:91–5.

Philosophy), as well as Voltaire's patron, the duc de Richelieu. "Look," the poem ended, with Richelieu clearly in mind, "see him, like Maecenas, leaving the court for the *guinguette*, Pufendorf for Eloisa, countless highnesses for a *grisette*, and Xenophon, for the Opera."[53] It was a confident endorsement of the world to which Voltaire, Richelieu, and Tressan himself belonged.

Fashion's Empire: The Moral Foundations of Salon Society

Despite the myriads of different forms of private property that it contained, it was not seen as a strongly property-based world. One reason for this was the part that fashion was taken to have come to play both in establishing and maintaining French commercial competitiveness abroad, and in neutralising some of the more divisive effects of economic inequality and social envy at home. It was a development that, particularly in the first half of the eighteenth century, was sometimes registered as both a cause and an effect of the behaviour and values associated with the salon. The causal chain may have been difficult, if not impossible, to disentangle, but three of its features were usually singled out. The first was the way that fashion had the effect of injecting a layer of complexity into judgements based on what might otherwise have been no more than brute passion. The second was the way that fashion also served to insulate traded goods from the just as potentially brutal effects of price competition in both domestic and foreign markets. The third was the way that fashion could be taken to be as compatible with the decentralised character of salon society as with a centralised royal court, with the potentially additional advantage that the kind of competitiveness associated with fashion might, as a result, have more to do with emulation, in both an economic and a social sense, than with the more brutal, zero-sum struggles for influence and power that were the hallmark of the court-based politics of absolute governments. What made the chain more complicated was the question of the extent to which each, or all, of these developments owed something in turn to women, either as such, or as consumers, or as the presiding spirits of salons, or, in a broader historical sense connecting all three, as the real beneficiaries of the sixteenth-century renaissance of learning and the end of Gothic gloom. Together, all these aspects of the causes and effects of fashion added up to what, in the first half of the eighteenth century, some

---

[53] Louis-Elizabeth de la Vergne, comte de Tressan, "Lettre écrite de *** à M. le comte de Caylus sur l'incertitude des sciences élevées et des systèmes," in Tressan, *Oeuvres choisis*, 11:131–5 (A *guinguette* is a suburban tavern or pleasure garden; and a *grisette* a shop assistant, named for the colour of her attire, and often said to be of easy virtue).

French writers called *l'empire de la mode*, or "fashion's empire." In 1754 the Académie française awarded a prize for a poem on the subject, by a spur-maker's son named Antoine-Marin Le Mierre.[54] Historians have usually studied one or other of these aspects of fashion in isolation. By putting them together one can see the outlines of a very comprehensive justification of, if not the actual, at least of the possible type of political society that eighteenth-century France had become. The best examples of what that kind of justification might have looked like could, in one guise, be pieced together from the very generic treatment of the relationship between the arts, luxury, and morality made by Voltaire in *Le Mondain*, and, in another, from the more historical treatment of the same subjects (forming what amounted to a reply to Voltaire) made by Montesquieu in *The Spirit of Laws*.[55]

The idea that fashion could have the effect of neutralising strong convictions and of disarming social envy made an early appearance in a didactic poem entitled *Dialogue de la mode et de la nature* (A Dialogue between Fashion and Nature), published in 1662.[56] The poem was explicitly associated with the world of the salons and the vogue for *préciosité* that was gathering momentum in that decade (unusually, it was not a satire but a very positive endorsement of the values ascribed to *préciosité*). It may, in fact, have been written by Marie-Catherine Desjardins who, as Mme de Villedieu, was one of the most successful of the many French female writers of the

[54] The subject of fashion in eighteenth-century thought, particularly French fashion and assessments of its significance, has not been studied very fully. See, for some ways in, Daniel Leonhard Purdy, *The Tyranny of Elegance: Consumer Cosmopolitanism in the Age of Goethe* (Baltimore, Johns Hopkins UP, 1998); Daniel Leonhard Purdy, ed., *The Rise of Fashion: A Reader* (Minneapolis, University of Minnesota Press, 2004); Cissie Fairchilds, "Fashion and Freedom in the French Revolution," *Continuity and Change* 15 (2000): 419–33; Jennifer M. Jones, *Sexing La Mode: Gender, Fashion and Commercial Culture in Old Regime France* (Oxford, Berg, 2004); Karin A. Wurst, *Fabricating Pleasure: Fashion, Entertainment and Cultural Consumption in Germany 1780–1820* (Detroit, Wayne State UP, 2005); Maxine Berg, *Luxury and Pleasure in Eighteenth-Century Britain* (Oxford, OUP, 2005); Linda Levy Peck, *Consuming Splendor* (Cambridge, CUP, 2005); Katie Scott and Deborah Cherry, eds., *Between Luxury and the Everyday: Decorative Arts in Eighteenth-Century France* (Oxford, Blackwell, 2005); Florian Schui, *Early Debates about Industry: Voltaire and His Contemporaries* (Basingstoke, Palgrave Macmillan, 2005), and the further works listed in chapter 3, note 8.

[55] On the subject of luxury, see, helpfully, Istvan Hont, "The Early Enlightenment Debate on Commerce and Luxury," in Mark Goldie and Robert Wokler, eds., *The Cambridge History of Eighteenth-Century Political Thought* (Cambridge, CUP, 2006), pp. 379–418; and Jeremy Jennings, "The Debate about Luxury in Eighteenth- and Nineteenth-Century French Political Thought," *Journal of the History of Ideas* 68 (2007): 79–105. On Voltaire and Montesquieu on monarchy, see Michael Sonenscher, *Before the Deluge: Public Debt, Inequality, and the Intellectual Origins of the French Revolution* (Princeton, Princeton UP, 2007), pp. 108–49.

[56] All the passages cited in the rest of this paragraph have been translated from lines of [Anon.], *Dialogue de la mode et de la nature*, 2nd ed. (n.p., 1662). (It does not seem that any major library has a copy of the first edition, if it exists.)

second half of the seventeenth century.[57] As its preface stated, the poem was intended to show that fashion and nature were not as incompatible as they might seem. It began, however, by setting out the usual reasons for thinking that they were. From nature's point of view, fashion seemed to make "all the great qualities" look "frivolous or ridiculous." Reason, after all, was "uniform and invariable" and had a seriousness that fashion seemed to lack. Fashions changed, but values should not, so that giving fashion precedence over nature would be likely to lead to "disorder and intrigue." But from fashion's point of view, the argument was overstated. The rigidity that nature commended was incompatible with "urbanity and charming tenderness," especially because the days when military valour was the only virtue had long gone. Nor, moreover, were "disorder and intrigue" unknown in the warlike age of ancient Gaul. Fashion set no value on rustic crudeness, but instead valued "a fine air, fine manners, fine gestures, and fine feelings, whether tender or strong, and all kinds of fine things." This was why fashion was most appealing to the great and power-ful, and why they, not the ordinary inhabitants of towns and villages, were most subject to fashion's sway. It was also, the argument continued, why the most virtuous nations were also "the most opulent." Nor was fashion incompatible with moral stability. Instead, it had the effect of reconciling "the immoderate man" with "the wise man" (*l'extravagant et le sage*), be-cause of the way that fashion's imitative power was likely to lead the man of extremes to believe that behaving well was simply a new and captivating fashion. The imitative mechanism would also work in the opposite sense, so that under fashion's aegis a man of rigid principle would come to stand out as a "capricious" eccentric. In either sense, these recurrent shifts of perspective meant that jealousy, "that insatiable monster that can turn even the finest angel into a devil," could be neutralised by the perpetually changing array of goods and values that fashion displayed.

The connection between fashion and conformism could look quite strange. "Of all the singularities of the French," wrote the Swiss moralist Béat-Louis de Muralt in a tone of mildly horrified perplexity in his fre-quently reprinted *Lettres sur les anglais et les français* (Letters on the English and French Nations), which first appeared in 1725, "the greatest, and the one that includes most of the others, is fashion." While every people might be subject to custom, he observed, this was because custom usually consists of something settled. In France, however,

nothing in custom is fixed; it is a torrent that changes its course every time it spills over and, whenever it does, it floods the whole country. A custom

[57] The attribution can be found (without an indication of its basis) in Maître, *Les Précieuses*, p. 46, note 30. On Marie Catherine Desjardins, see Micheline Cuénin, *Roman et société sous Louis XIV. Madame de Villedieu*, 2 vols. (Lille, Atelier de reproduction des thèses, 1979).

that has run its course gives way to a new one, so that one is always subject to a custom that is fresh and vigorous; and men, amidst all these changes, are ceaselessly exercised and breathless to keep up, simply to be subjected once again. This exercise, which gives them so much pleasure, seems to them like liberty, just as prisoners whose chains are changed every day may come to believe that they are free.[58]

From a more positive perspective, however, the conformism generated by fashion could be taken to be fundamentally harmless. As the anonymous author of a real fashion column that began to appear in the *Mercure de France* in 1726 put it, partly to disarm Béat-Louis de Muralt's highly charged observation that fashion seemed, at least in this respect, to have brought France nearer than anything else to universal monarchy, "nothing authorised by fashion is ridiculous, just as everything on which fashion has not set its mark (*son attache*) seems disgusting and bizarre." Wisdom, as another early eighteenth-century compilation put it, had to be known before it could be appreciated, but fashion supplied its own self-explanatory rules or labels (*étiquettes*), to which everyone could conform. This, it went on to argue, was why fashion applied not just to the notion that champagne might be the best wine, or to the use of perfume by men, but also to the status of orators, poets, actors, and doctors.[59]

The five propositions embedded in the earlier *Dialogue between Fashion and Nature* (that fashion neutralises conflicting moral values; assuages jealousy; subjects the powerful to its influence; gives value to fine things; and makes rigidity look ridiculous) could all be associated with a range of ancient philosophical positions. They could, with some considerable weakening of the kind of knowledge involved, be subsumed under the broader idea of the skill and discernment required for knowing when, where, and how to do the right thing that formed the subject matter of Aristotle's *Nichomachean*

[58] Béat-Louis de Muralt, *Lettres sur les anglais et les français* [1725] (Lausanne, Bibliothèque romande, 1972), pp. 132–3, and, at greater length, see the reproduction of the 1728 edition, ed. Charles Gould (Paris, 1933), pp. 205–13, 345–7. On Muralt in this context, see Arthur Ferrazzini, *Béat de Muralt et Jean-Jacques Rousseau. Etude sur l'histoire des idées au xviiie siècle* (La Neuveville, Switzerland, 1951).

[59] The fashion column, with illustrations, appeared in the *Mercure de France*, February 1726, pp. 399–409; May 1726, pp. 946–59 (containing the passage cited here); January 1728, pp. 179–83; March 1729, pp. 611–20; October 1730, pp. 2311–21. On fashion's *étiquettes*, and the conformism that it entailed, see the comments on fashion in the review of a new edition of Montesquieu's *Persian Letters*, in [Antoine de La Barre de Beaumarchais], *Lettres sérieuses et badines sur les ouvrages des savants et sur d'autres matières*, 8 vols. (The Hague, 1729–33), 3:96–109. "Plus d'un auteur économique," as a later writer put it, in what amounted to a reply to Muralt, "a calculé les avantages réels des modes. Cette politique, qui n'a point changé en France, est la dernière preuve de la solidité du caractère de ses habitants": Thomas-Jean Pichon, *Le physique de l'histoire, ou considérations générales sur les principes élémentaires du tempérament et du caractère naturel des peuples* (Amsterdam, 1765), p. 223.

Ethics. They lent themselves particularly well, however, to the more strongly differentiated typology of moral judgements and behaviour to be found in Cicero's *On Duties* (*De Officiis*). "It is right to know," Cicero wrote, "that nature has, as it were, clothed us with two characters (*personae*).

> One is general and is founded on reason. It is something in which we all share insofar as it is this that distinguishes us from all the other animals. Everything that is honourable and seemly has its origins in this, and it is from this that we begin to arrive at a knowledge of our duty. The other type of character is purely personal and is a result of individual qualities. For, just as there are enormous bodily differences . . . so there are still greater differences in men's minds.[60]

In addition to these two characters (*personae*), Cicero continued, there were also two more. The third was one that we are given by chance or circumstance, while the fourth was one that was added by our own choice. Thus "thrones, all kinds of principality, nobility, honours, riches, and their opposites, depend on circumstance and are subject to events. But it is our will that determines the type of profession that we adopt."[61] Some virtues might be appropriate to humans simply as humans. But others were related to the

---

[60] Cicero, *On Duties*, bk. 1, §107, ed. M. T. Griffin and E. M. Adkins (Cambridge, CUP, 1991), p. 42. I have modified the translation of the passage in the light of the way that it was translated into French in the seventeenth century: "Il faut considérer aussi que la nature nous a, pour ainsi dire, revêtus de deux personnages. L'un est commun à tous les hommes, en ce qu'ils ont tous l'usage de la raison qui les relève par dessus les bêtes, qui est l'origine de la vertu et de la bienséance, et par laquelle nous connaissons ce qui est de notre devoir. L'autre est propre à chaque homme, et lui est particulièrement attribué": Cicero, *Des offices*, in Cicero, *Oeuvres*, trans. Pierre Du Ryer, vol. 9 (Paris, 1670), p. 150. I have used this translation to modify the modern English translation in all subsequent citations. It is worth comparing the passage in question to a late eighteenth-century translation: "Il est à propos de savoir que la nature nous a pour ainsi dire revêtus de deux caractères, l'un général est établi sur la raison, que tous nous avons en partage, qui nous distingue du reste des animaux, de laquelle l'honnêteté et la bienséance tirent leur origine, et dont nous partons pour arriver à la connaissance du devoir; l'autre, particulier à l'individu, résulte de ses qualités personnelles": Cicero, *Des devoirs de l'homme*, trans. Emmanuel Brosselard (Paris, an IV/1796), §30, pp. 64–5. On Cicero in seventeenth-century France, see Maurice Magendie, *La politesse mondaine et les théories de l'honnêteté en France au xviie siècle, de 1600–1660*, 2 vols. (Paris, 1925), especially pp. 306–7.

[61] Cicero, *On Duties*, bk. 1, §115, p. 45. "Mais à ces deux personnages dont nous disions tantôt que l'homme était revêtu, nous en pouvons ajouter un troisième, qui lui est donné par la fortune ou par le temps, comme d'être riche et de commander aux autres; et un quatrième qui lui est donné par lui-même, comme quand il détermine par son jugement quelle condition il doit embrasser": Cicero, *Des Offices* (1670), pp. 157–8. Compare to the late eighteenth-century translation: "Aux deux caractères dont j'ai parle plus haut, il s'en joint un troisième que nous recevons du hasard ou des circonstances, et nous en ajoutons encore un quatrième de notre choix; ainsi les trônes, les principautés en tout genre, la noblesse, les honneurs, les richesses, et leurs contraires dépendent des circonstances, et sont subordonnés aux événements; mais notre volonté décide du genre de profession que nous embrassons": Cicero, *Des Devoirs*, §33, p. 70.

several different types of character (*personae*) to be found in every actual person and what, in the light of these, the right thing to do or say might be. The result was an emphasis upon seemliness and decorum that, in conjunction with the stress upon the values of legality and moderation in his more directly political theory, made Cicero an obvious foil to the darker picture of both human nature and politics to be found in the seventeenth century's other ancient intellectual icon, Tacitus. In France in particular (but in Britain, the Italian states, the Netherlands, and the German-speaking world too), the late seventeenth and early eighteenth centuries saw a small wave of books emphasising the value of what, in French, was called *convenance* or what was *convenable*, words that, since they were the French equivalents of the Latin *decorum*, mean something "seemly," "fitting," or "decorous," as well as just "suitable" or "convenient." For a time, the terms looked as if they might open up a way to a kind of moral code (based, according to Voltaire's friend the marquis d'Argenson, upon the *droit de convenance*, or law of decorum) that was unlikely to offer too many intellectual hostages to revealed religion on the one hand, but was sufficiently attentive to human culture and civility on the other to be able to avoid the strong emphasis upon sheer self-preservation associated with Spinoza and Hobbes.[62] Justice, wrote the young Montesquieu in the eighty-third of his *Persian Letters* (expressing a view that he was later to abandon), "is a relationship of fitness (*convenance*) that actually exists between two things."[63] From this perspective Cicero was to any number of late seventeenth- and early eighteenth-century thinkers— from Lambert van Velthusyen in the Netherlands, to Samuel Pufendorf and Christian Thomasius in Germany, to Joseph Addison in Britain, or the marquis d'Argenson in France—what Tacitus was to Hobbes.[64]

[62] René-Louis de Voyer de Paulmy, marquis d'Argenson, *Considérations sur le gouvernement ancien et présent de la France* (Amsterdam, 1764), p. 18.

[63] Charles-Louis de Secondat, baron de Montesquieu, *Lettres persanes* [1721], ed Paul Vernière (Paris, 1960), letter 83, p. 174. On Montesquieu's early admiration for Cicero, particularly as a foil to Hobbes, see Paul Dimoff, "Cicéron, Hobbes et Montesquieu," *Annales Universitatis Saraviensis (Philosophie-Lettres)* 1 (1952): 19–47; David Fott, " 'Preface' to Translation of Montesquieu's 'Discourse on Cicero,' " *Political Theory* 30 (2002): 728–32 (as well as the translation of Montesquieu's "Discourse on Cicero" that follows).

[64] Lambert van Velthusyen, *Epistolica Dissertatio de Principiis Justi, et, Decori* [1651]; translated as *Des principes du juste et du convenable*, ed. Catherine Secrétan (Caen, Presses Universitaires de Caen, 1995). The emphasis on decorum was particularly strong in the revised (1680) version of the text. The idea of justice as *convenance* can also be found in Gottfried Wilhelm Leibniz, *Essais de Théodicée* [1709], ed. Paul Janet, 2 vols. (Paris, 1866), 2:147–58. On Cicero in eighteenth-century thought, see M. A. Stewart, "The Stoic Legacy in the Early Scottish Enlightenment," in Margaret J. Osler, ed., *Atoms, Pneuma, and Tranquillity: Epicurean and Stoic Themes in European Thought* (Cambridge, CUP, 1991), pp. 273–96 (288–89); Gunter Gawlick, "Cicero and the Enlightenment," *Studies on Voltaire and the Eighteenth Century* 25 (1963): 657–82, and, on the aspect of Cicero's moral theory described here, see Christopher Gill, "Personhood and Personality: The Four *Personae* Theory in Cicero, *De Officis* I," *Oxford*

If the idea of *convenance* as a real principle soon ran into the sands (applied to international relations it lent itself far too readily to justifications of all kinds of boundary changes for reasons of convenience or suitability), the metaphor of clothing as character still had substantial early eighteenth-century resonances.[65] Its availability allowed the third earl of Shaftesbury to use dress as a metaphor for institutional specialisation, John Gay to compare the rules of clothing to the rules of writing, and Jonathan Swift to use clothes as symbols of the different kinds of religious allegiance that he satirised in his *Tale of a Tub*, a choice reinforced by the ease with which, as Swift showed, it could be illustrated by "French fashion."[66] It also, more substantively, supplied a way to show how one might connect the emotions involved in honour and shame to the subject of morality without having to rely on any particularly strong claims about the dignity of human reason, or to risk exposing this kind of claim about human reason to sceptical doubt. This, too, was available in Cicero. A comprehensive understanding of duty, he wrote, after describing the four types of *persona* to be found in any actual person, would supply answers to the questions "What is seemly?" and "What suits different characters, circumstances or ages?" This differentiated understanding of duty would impart a "seemliness," or decorum, that could be seen "in every deed and word, and indeed in every bodily movement or state." This seemliness, Cicero went on immediately to explain, "is based on three things: on beauty, order and on a certain kind of good grace suited to the action in question." Such things, he continued, "are quite difficult to express but are not too difficult to understand." If one considered them attentively, he added, "one would come to see that they contain the means to win men's esteem and to make us loved by those with whom and among whom we live."[67]

Studies in Ancient Philosophy 6 (1988): 168–99. For a recent discussion of these subjects in an eighteenth-century British context, see Stephen J. McKenna, *Adam Smith: The Rhetoric of Propriety* (Albany, State University of New York Press, 2006), pp. 53–72. On Pufendorf and Cicero, see Peter Garnsey, *Thinking about Property: From Antiquity to the Age of Revolution* (Cambridge, CUP, 2007), p. 214, note 27.

[65] For an example of the more expedient uses to which the idea could be put (in the context of the imminent War of the Austrian Succession), see Fréderic-Henri Strube de Piermont, *Recherche nouvelle de l'origine et des fondements du droit de la nature* (St. Petersburg, 1740).

[66] Anthony Ashley Cooper, Third Earl of Shaftesbury, *Characteristics of Men, Manners, Opinions, Times* [2nd ed., 1714], ed. Lawrence E. Klein (Cambridge, CUP, 1999), pp. 39–40; [John Gay], *The Guardian* [1714–5], no. 149, 3rd ed. 2 vols. (London, 1723), 2:240–6. For an overview of the uses to which clothing metaphors could be put (including some remarks on the *sans-culottes*), see Claude Rawson, "Revolution in the Moral Wardrobe: Mutations of an Image from Dryden to Burke," in his *Satire and Sentiment 1660–1830* (New Haven, Yale UP, 2000), pp. 133–98.

[67] Cicero, *On Duties*, bk. 1, §125, pp. 48–9. The 1670 French translation is rather clearer than the modern English version: "Mais comme cette bienséance se remarque en nos paroles,

To explain the point, Cicero turned to the human body. "From the beginning," he wrote, "nature itself seems to have been thoroughly rational
concerning our bodies: she has placed in sight those parts of our form and
features that have an honourable appearance, but has covered and hidden
the parts of the body that are devoted to the necessities of nature and
would have an ugly or dishonourable aspect." This "careful craftsman-
ship" was "mirrored in men's sense of shame." Usually, anyone "of sound
mind" was careful to keep out of sight the parts that "nature has hidden"
and to obey nature's necessities "as secretly as possible." This, Cicero
continued, was why it was wrong "to listen to the Cynics or to those Stoics who were almost Cynics, who criticise and mock us because we think
that, though some things are not themselves dishonourable, the words for
them are shameful, while we call by their own names those things that are
dishonourable. It is actually dishonourable to rob, to deceive, or to commit adultery, but to speak of them is not indecent." For the Cynic, however, since procreation was laudable, it made no sense not to speak of the
parts and acts involved in human sexuality. "They have many arguments
of the same sort, leading towards the total ruin of decency (*pudeur*) and
modesty." In these matters, Cicero concluded, it was important to avoid
doing anything either "effeminate or soft" on the one hand or "harsh and
uncouth" on the other. Even "actors," he pointed out, never "step on to
the stage without a breech-cloth" for fear that "if an accident occurred,
parts of the body might be revealed that it is not seemly to see." In the
complex dynamics of honour and shame that gave seemliness and deco-
rousness their value, Cicero emphasised, "nature herself is our mistress
and guide."[68]

This kind of concern with honour and shame could be assimilated quite
readily by the strongly Augustinian moral theories of seventeenth-century
Catholic theology. As a note attached to one late seventeenth-century
French translation of Cicero pointed out, the Cynics he attacked

> paid no attention to the way that the violence of the upward movement
> (*soulèvement*) of the inferior parts in these kinds of actions offends the dig-
> nity of reason, which then finds itself in the position of a queen trampled
> underfoot by her slave. It is this that gives rise to a feeling of shame that is

---

en nos actions, & même en notre contenance & au mouvement de notre corps. Comme en
l'établit sur trois choses, en la beauté, en l'ordre, & en une certaine bonne grâce, convenable
à l'action que l'on fait, il est bien difficile de l'exprimer & il n'est pas malaisé de la compren-
dre. Si même on considère attentivement ces trois choses, on connaîtra qu'elles contiennent
les moyens de gagner l'estime des hommes, et de nous faire aimer de ceux avec lesquels et
parmi lesquels nous vivons." Cicero, *Des Offices* (1670), pp. 167–8.

[68] Cicero, *On Duties*, bk. 1, §§126–9, pp. 49–50.

all the more well founded in that nothing is more damaging to a man than something that compels him despite his reason.[69]

But, with less emphasis upon reason's dignity, and more emphasis on Cicero's own evaluation of decorum, the same concern with honour and shame could also be compatible with a quite positive endorsement of fashion. As Cicero wrote, the human interest in searching for truth was matched by a capacity "that this one animal alone" has, namely, an ability to "perceive what order there is, what seemliness, what limit to words and deeds." No "other animal," he stated, was able to perceive "the beauty, the loveliness, the congruence of the parts of the things that sight perceives. Nature and reason transfer this by analogy from the eyes to the mind, thinking that beauty, constancy and order should be preserved, and much more so, in one's decisions and in one's deeds."[70] From this perspective, reason was not the only resource to be relied upon to distinguish the honourable from the merely useful, or to establish a scale of priorities in cases where different kinds of honour clashed. The human responsiveness to what was decorous supplied additional grounds for discrimination.

This emphasis on what was seemly or decorous could be fitted quite easily into a wider range of arguments about the relationship between the arts, morality, and civility. The key concept in this type of argument was often denoted by the word "sociability." Here, sociability referred to something more than mere conviviality, gregariousness, or politeness because it meant something more like an antonym of the word "state." To claim that humans were sociable was to deny that the primary form of human association was political. To claim that the primary form of human association was political was to deny that humans were sociable.[71] In the eighteenth century, this view was usually associated with the political thought of Thomas Hobbes and the argument that he made at the beginning of his *De Cive* that, since the two initial motivations for human association—utility and pride (or "vainglory")—were self-defeating, it was

---

[69] Cicero, *Des Offices* (The Hague, 1692), ch. 35, p. 141, notes 1 and 2: "ils ne prenaient pas garde que la violence du soulèvement de la partie inférieure, dans ces sortes d'actions, blesse la dignité de la raison, qui se trouve alors comme une reine sous les pieds de son esclave. C'est ce qui produit un sentiment de honte qui n'est que trop bien fondé, puisque rien n'en doit tant faire à l'homme, que ce qui l'entraîne malgré sa raison." The note referred to St. Augustine's *City of God*, bk. 14, chs. 17, 23, and 29, along with his *On Marriage and Concupiscence* and his *Contra Julien* for support.

[70] Cicero, *On Duties*, §14, p. 7.

[71] On sociability, see Istvan Hont, *Jealousy of Trade: International Competition and the Nation-State in Historical Perspective* (Cambridge, Mass., Belknap Press, 2005), pp. 39–45, 159–84, and Gordon, *Citizens without Sovereignty*, although it is sometimes not clear here whether the various authors whose work Gordon examines took sociability to be primary or to be derivative.

the fear associated with the overwhelming power of a sovereign state that
was the real cement of society. But it was a view that Jansenists could also
associate with Aristotle and his assertion, in his *Ethics*, that "man is by nature made for marriage, even more than he is a political creature."[72] This,
by extension, meant that properly political societies were the outcome of
a more protracted historical sequence of agreements and arrangements, a
view that could be associated with the political theories of Samuel Pufendorf and John Locke. From the anti-Aristotelian perspective underlying
much Jansenist thought, true sociability theory was to be found in a mixture of Plato, with his identification of justice with a fully formed array
of interlocking occupations and activities, and the providential message of
scripture. "This universal passion for society in man is as much a gift of
the Creator as are his very arms," thundered one early eighteenth-century
French Jansenist. This, he continued, was why it was quite false to attribute
"the origin of society to our reciprocal wants," and why it was also "quite
needless to derive the first duties and the true science of society from reasonings and a kind of philosophy always staggering and uncertain." "I will
never," he concluded, "take Aristotle or Pufendorf for my masters."[73]

Much of the early eighteenth-century interest in Ciceronian decorum
grew out of a concern to find a position somewhere between these stark
alternatives, by showing how the arts, and the emotions that could be
associated with them, made it easier to reinstate the historical gradual-
ism that could be associated with either Aristotle or Locke, against both
Hobbes and Plato. One of the clearest and most accessible versions of the
type of argument that this involved can be found at the beginning of the
abbé Jean-Baptiste Dubos's *Réflexions critiques sur la poésie et la peinture*, a
work that was first published in 1719 and appeared under the broader title
of *Critical Reflections on Poetry, Painting and Music* in English translation
in 1748. The work was mainly didactic in aim, setting out to describe the
most technically adroit ways of making poetry and painting (and music)
achieve the very broad range of effects (moral and political, as well as what
we might call aesthetic) that they were capable of having. To do so, Dubos
began by explaining why the arts could address subjects that would usually
be unbearable if they really were present. One example that he used to
illustrate the point was the painting by Poussin entitled *Et in arcadia ego*,
a title that Dubos translated as "And yet I was living in Arcadia." Even in
Arcadia, he explained, the image showed that humans could not escape

---

[72] Aristotle, *Ethics*, 1162a16 ff.

[73] Noël-Antoine Pluche, *Le spectacle de la nature, ou entretiens sur les particularités de l'histoire
naturelle*, 8 vols. (Paris, 1732–50). The citations are from the English translation published
as Noël-Antoine Pluche, *Spectacle de la nature: or Nature Displayed. Being Discourses on such
Particulars of Natural History as were thought most proper to excite the curiosity and form the minds
of youth. Containing what belongs to man considered in society*, 7 vols. (London, 1748), 6:8–12.

their knowledge of death.[74] The peculiar property of a painting like this (but one that applied to poetry, painting, and music in general) was its ability to turn something like the fact of death, and the knowledge that it really would occur (even in Arcadia), into something pleasurable.

Dubos's explanation of the phenomenon was based on a synthesis of ancient and modern moral philosophy, particularly the part of ancient philosophy that dealt with rhetoric, and the part of modern philosophy that, following Descartes, dealt with the passions of the human soul. The pleasure that painful subjects could produce when they were treated by a skilful artisan (Dubos made an explicit point of avoiding a distinction between artists and artisans) was, he argued, an effect of the artificial character of the paintings or poetry in question, and of how the knowledge that these really were artefacts would enable spectators or listeners to control passions that, were they to occur naturally, would simply be what their name meant, namely, the opposite of actions. The arts, in other words, made something like the old Stoic idea of self-command humanly feasible and gave a real content to the apparently incoherent idea of being able to manage the passions. They did so, Dubos argued, because they turned what was already available in nature into "beings of a new nature" or "objects which excite artificial passions in us that are able to occupy us at the moment that we feel them, but are unable to cause us real pain or true afflictions in their wake."[75] The first poems or pictures, he wrote, might have been produced simply to flatter our senses or our imagination, but the "phantoms of the passions" that they also produced subsequently gave them a different kind of effect.[76] Since they presented a copy of an object that could produce real passions, and since the copy of the object produced a copy of the passions, the passions in question were correspondingly less powerful. The result was a "pure pleasure" that could be distinguished from the emotions involved in real life.[77] Unlike the importunate quality of the latter, the emotions involved in artefacts could be turned on or switched off at will. As Dubos put it, "[t]he painter and the poet afflict

[74] Jean-Baptiste Dubos, *Réflexions critiques sur la poésie et la peinture* [1719]. I have used a Utrecht (1732) edition, sec. 6, p. 30. For some indications of the wider intellectual context to which Dubos's book belonged, see Annie Becq, *Genèse de l'esthétique française moderne 1680–1814* [1984] (Paris, Albin Michel, 1994); Jeffrey Barnouw, "Feeling in Enlightenment Aesthetics," *Studies in Eighteenth-Century Culture* 18 (1988): 323–42, and his "The Beginnings of 'Aesthetics' and the Leibnizian Conception of Sensation," in Paul Mattick Jr., ed., *Eighteenth-Century Aesthetics and the Reconstructions of Art* (Cambridge, CUP, 1993), pp. 52–95; Vernon Hyde Major, *The Death of the Baroque and the Rhetoric of Good Taste* (Cambridge, CUP, 2006); Ann Delehanty, "Mapping the Aesthetic Mind: John Dennis and Nicolas Boileau," *Journal of the History of Ideas* 68 (2007): 233–53.

[75] Dubos, *Réflexions*, sec. 3, p. 14.

[76] Dubos, *Réflexions*, sec. 3, p. 15.

[77] Dubos, *Réflexions*, sec. 3, pp. 16–7.

us only as much as we want, and make us love their heroes and heroines only as much as it pleases us."[78] While real objects meant that "we are not masters of the measure of our sentiments" or "of their vivacity or duration," it was generally the case that "our soul always remains master of those superficial emotions that verse and paintings excite in us."[79] This, in itself, was a cause of pleasure. As Descartes had suggested, pleasure began with the mind's awareness of its own reflective capacities.[80]

The arts might have had Epicurean origins, but their existence produced something like a Stoic outcome. Dubos supplied a concise, but clear, connection between the arts, the oddly voluntary character of the emotions that they produced, and the broader eighteenth-century idea of sociability. The point of the argument was to emphasise the way that the arts served to stabilise the potentially self-defeating character of several of the other obvious human motivations for society. The first of these was boredom. As Dubos put it, citing the Roman poet Horace, few people had the ability to learn that art that enabled them "to live in friendship with themselves," or had the strength of mind to concentrate so powerfully on something in particular that, "by dint of exercising their imagination, they could tame it so that, once made docile, it would do what it was asked."[81] The pain involved in this kind of effort was usually too hard to bear, which was why most people preferred either to busy themselves in an ultimately futile round of "frivolous occupations and useless affairs," or to look for satisfaction in "passions whose harmful effects they know."[82] The resultant erratic social behaviour had the further effect of making society look like an association made up of individuals who were deceitful or designing even if, in reality, they were actually no more than wilful or inconstant. The other obvious motivation for society—namely, the human ability to recognise and respond to others' emotions—was, Dubos argued, equally self-defeating. The "natural sensibility of the human heart" was certainly "the first foundation of society." But the way that self-liking (*amour de soi-même*) changed into "an immoderate fondness of oneself" (*amour-propre*) "as men advance in years," making them "too strongly attached to their present and future interests and too inflexible towards one another when

[78] Dubos, *Réflexions*, sec. 3, p. 17.

[79] Dubos, *Réflexions*, sec. 3, pp. 17–8.

[80] For later discussion of this Cartesian approach to the origins of pleasure, see Johann Georg Sulzer, *Nouvelle théorie des plaisirs, avec des réflexions sur les origines du plaisir par Mr Kaestner* (n.p., 1767), and Abraham Gotthelf Kaestner, "Réflexions sur l'origine du plaisir, où l'on tache de prouver l'idée de Descartes qu'il naît toujours du sentiment de la perfection de nous-mêmes," in *Le temple du bonheur, ou recueil des plus excellents traités sur le bonheur, extraits des meilleurs auteurs anciens et modernes*, 3 vols. (Bouillon, 1769), 3:191–204.

[81] Dubos, *Réflexions*, sec. 1, p. 5.

[82] Dubos, *Réflexions*, sec. 1, p. 6.

they enter deliberately upon any resolution," meant that something more was needed "that man should be easily drawn out of this situation."[83] The first motivations for society might be natural, but a stable society was not. This was why the arts mattered. They were, in a sense, a painless alternative to boredom, and a pleasurable surrogate for love. The "phantoms of the passions" that they produced could keep a society together without, at least in the first instance, giving rise to the need to bring in states and governments and laws.

Dubos's argument followed Descartes's emphasis upon the uniquely human ability to produce ideas and artefacts independently of the stimuli supplied by the passions or external events. The most compelling example of this ability was the way that human language amounted to a system of signs that did not need to have any connection at all to an individual's present state or survival needs.[84] Since the signs involved in language had no necessary connection to a human's present state, while those made by animals were a direct indication of their actual feelings or needs, language was a clue to the existence of other minds as well as other bodies, and an indication of the social capacities available to humans despite the fact that they were not equipped with the kinds of apparently automatic social instinct observable in animals. The freestanding character of language set human communication apart from animal communication and the purely physical or mechanical arrangements underlying the cries, calls, or gestures involved in animal life. Where animals were guided by instincts, humans were able to produce their own sources of guidance. In this sense, it was not so much the interests that served to neutralise the passions, as the arts, and the knowledge (*scientia*) from which the arts derived.[85] Natural objects produced natural passions that were both involuntary and difficult to control. Artificial objects, however, produced artificial passions that were more manageable because they were more voluntary. As with Descartes's moral philosophy, Dubos's treatment of the passions made no particularly strong claims about natural human benevolence or selflessness, but it still made it possible to see how the artificial passions produced by poetry, painting,

---

[83] Dubos, *Réflexions*, sec. 4, p. 21.

[84] For the broader arguments, see Noam Chomsky, *Cartesian Linguistics* (New York, Harper & Row, 1966), pp. 3–11, and, more recently, Fred Ablondi, *Gerauld de Cordemoy: Atomist, Occasionalist, Cartesian* (Milwaukee, Marquette UP, 2005), pp. 106–12.

[85] This dimension of the subject is absent from the classic study by Albert Hirschman, *The Passions and the Interests: Political Arguments for Capitalism before Its Triumph* (Princeton, Princeton UP, 1977). It is also likely to have formed much of the real intellectual setting for the much studied subject of politeness and Whiggism in early eighteenth-century Britain. On this, see Lawrence E. Klein, "Politeness and the Interpretation of the British Eighteenth Century," *Historical Journal* 45 (2002): 869–98, and, for a judicious reassessment, Markku Peltonen, "Politeness and Whiggism, 1688–1732," *Historical Journal* 48 (2005): 391–414.

or music could reduce the part played by real objects and real passions in human life. The arts added an extra, more malleable layer of concerns to the more strongly self-centred descriptions of human nature to be found both in Jansenist theology and in the political thought of Thomas Hobbes. Moreover, since the artificial passions associated with the arts did not have the same kind of intensity or necessity as those produced by natural objects, they took much of the drama out of the ordinary choices and preferences involved in daily life. They had the effect of producing a quite literal version of enlightened self-love, because the pleasure that even pain could produce was enlightened by a knowledge of its causes.

The obvious appeal of this additional dimension of discrimination was the way that it could be used to counter the strong emphasis upon human selfishness that modern historiography now usually associates with the political thought of Thomas Hobbes, but which, in reality, was far easier to find in some of the more dogmatic versions of Catholic or Protestant theology. From the perspective that Dubos presented, the arts kept both religion and politics at one remove from everyday life. They also supplied a way to bridge the gap between knowing and feeling as reasons for action and, by doing so, made it easier to bring the principles underlying Stoic and Epicurean moral theory into closer alignment. This was largely the point of Antoine-Marin Le Mierre's poem about fashion's empire. Fashion, he wrote, was born of the human disdain for nature's fecundity and an ungrateful propensity to see nature's variety as mere uniformity. But when fashion appeared, "everything sprang to life," and ardour, caprice, prejudice, vanity, and ridicule all found their place in life's affairs. Fashion ruled by example and imitation, bringing together the disparate admirers of a new taste like so many neatly arranged, freshly harvested sheaves of corn. Yet the price of conformity could be high. Fashion's "despotic spirit" could, when coupled with pride, lead to the "public misery" that had once ruined Rome. But fashion's very changeableness contained a self-correcting mechanism. One "absurd" taste would soon give way to another, making fashion itself fundamentally harmless. From this perspective, Cynic moralism was redundant. "The wise man," Le Mierre concluded, "will not be willing to applaud fashion's decrees, but he will also not need to be rigidly hostile towards them. He will put up with a yoke that the Cynic would spurn, never being her enemy, but never, too, her slave."[86] From this perspective, Epicurean enjoyment could be combined with Stoic serenity, leaving the Stoic side of Cicero's moral theory relatively

---

[86] Antoine-Marin Le Mierre, "L'empire de la mode" [1754] reprinted in his *Oeuvres*, 3 vols. (Paris, 1810), 3:271–4. The lines translated (from p. 274) run: "Le sage à tes décrets est bien loin d'applaudir, Et cependant contre eux il doit peu se roidir; Il supporte ton joug que le cynique brave, Jamais ton ennemi, mais jamais ton esclave."

undisturbed while, at the same time, disarming moral criticism of a society based so strongly on display. Fontenelle, in much the same vein, was sometimes described as the Seneca of the age of Louis XIV.[87]

The connection between beauty and morality in both Ciceronian and Cartesian moral theory, and the possibility that both might be compatible with fashion, was reinforced very strongly by a number of claims about the way that fashion offset the divisiveness of private property, as well as about the part it played in promoting opulence and prosperity without, however, having to rely solely on price competitiveness and the market-based imperatives of necessity. These, in turn, helped to distance trade from its more pejorative association with traffic, and the more sordid aspects of market transactions that it could still have in more orthodox moral theory, particularly the austere Augustinianism underpinning seventeenth-century French Jansenism. That God intended to "subject men to a hard condition" was evident from the distribution of nature's goods, wrote the Jansenist Noël-Antoine Pluche in his very successful *Spectacle de la nature* (or *Nature Displayed*, as the contemporary English translation was entitled), a multivolume work that began to appear in 1732.

> The actual disposition of nature visibly obliges men to work, to stir about and to have a mutual regard for each other. God is not the author of the malice of men, but he is the author of this disposition that keeps it within bounds. He is then likewise the author of that inequality of conditions which is the first result of the good and bad qualities of the different countries and of the necessity men are under to supply their own wants, by taking upon them to supply what is wanting to others. God is then willing that men should submit to an oeconomy on which their preservation depends and that they should vary the works which make them subsist. It is by an artifice of his providence, that these men, who love not one another, and who, from their hatred, are always ready, mutually, to destroy each other, yet meet together, and conspire to afford reciprocal helps one to another.[88]

The principle applied to "all the men who cover the earth," just as it could be seen among "the inhabitants of a populous town."[89] "Doubtless they

[87] See, for example, [André-Pierre Le Guay de Prémontval], *L'esprit de Fontenelle ou recueil de pensées tirés de ses ouvrages* (The Hague, 1753), p. iii. Diderot made a more positive evaluation of the parallel between Fontenelle and Seneca in his late *Essai sur les règnes de Claude et de Néron* [1780], in Denis Diderot, *Oeuvres*, 5 vols. (Brussels, Robert Laffont, 1994–7), vol. 1, *Philosophie*, ed. Laurent Versini, p. 1123.

[88] Pluche, *Le spectacle de la nature* (Paris, 1732–50), 6:116–7. On Pluche, see Benoit de Baere, *Trois introductions à l'abbé Pluche: sa vie, son monde, ses livres* (Geneva, Droz, 2002); and Françoise Gevrey, Julie Boch, and Jean-Louis Haquette, eds., *Ecrire la nature au xviiie siècle* (Paris, Presses de l'Université Paris-Sorbonne, 2006).

[89] Pluche, *Spectacle* (English translation), 6:117.

all work for themselves," Pluche continued, echoing an idea that had been
set out particularly memorably by Pierre Nicole and Jean Domat in the
second half the seventeenth century,

> and yet they are all of service to the whole body of society. One offers you a
> pair of shoes: another makes you a hat. This man will sell you some fish, or a
> piece of cloth, and another will bring some suits [trays] of drinks of all kinds
> to you. All the sign posts of London and Paris are so many offers of service.
> In these cities as well as elsewhere, every one thinks he works for himself: nor
> is he in that at all mistaken. But things happen to be so ordered and disposed
> from one end of the earth to the other, as if every inhabitant had no other
> view but the service of society.[90]

Fashion introduced a different perspective into this rather bleak picture.
It did so not only because of the mixture of novelty, technical ingenuity,
and social display on which it was based, but also because of the unusual
pricing policy that it allowed traders to adopt.

"France alone," wrote a German named Ernst Ludwig Carl who spent
some time in France during the period of the Regency and who published
the results of his inquiries in a three-volume *Traité de la richesse des princes
et de leurs états: et des moyens simples et naturels pour y parvenir* (A Treatise
on the Wealth of Princes and Their States) in 1722,

> has discovered a fine secret in changes of fashion. As merchandises fall out
> of use in the kingdom, neighbouring nations take them up with rapidity.
> Peru and Mexico also absorb a great quantity, while a further quantity of the
> clothes and trinkets discarded by the rich end up in the hands of the poor
> for a modest price. Without all this, frequent changes of fashion would have
> often been prejudicial to the kingdom, but, instead, such changes have been
> an opportunity to perfect the arts and enrich the state.[91]

The "secret" in question was the way that it was possible to charge very
high prices for fashionable goods at the beginning of the product cycle,
and then slash them drastically when the cycle was coming to an end and
a new set of products was about to appear. It was a secret that had been
mastered very adeptly by the silk industry of Lyon, with its four, seasonal,
cycles of products every year, but it was one that could be applied to a
very wide range of goods, from champagne to cognac, as well as Parisian
wares (*articles de Paris*) and other products of the urban trades (as the
Parisian mercers' guild pointed out much later in the eighteenth century,
goods manufactured all over France were often exported as *marchandises*

---

[90] Pluche, *Spectacle* (English translation), 6:117.

[91] [Ernst Ludwig Carl], *Traité de la richesse des princes et de leurs états: et des moyens simples et
naturels pour y parvenir*, 3 pts. (Paris, 1722–3), pt. 2, pp. 493–4.

de Paris).[92] As Carl recognised, international competitiveness could take two forms. Goods could compete on price, or compete on quality. But the two were not mutually exclusive, because fashion formed a bridge between them. Anyone who was first able to develop a new product would be able to take advantage of its initial positional rent by charging a high price when it first appeared and, having made a profit, would then be able to slash the price savagely to keep competitors out of the market, thus establishing the conditions for further cycles of innovation and improvement by broadening and deepening the market for traded goods beyond the initial circle of wealthy consumers. The two streams of income, one at the beginning and the other at the end of the product cycle, also made it easier to manage the erratic schedules of credit built into the elaborate networks of supply and sale formed by the many interdependent small businesses (or artisans) involved in the production of manufactured goods.[93] The repeatedly reiterated cycles of product or process innovation and substitution also helped to reduce the differences between goods that were necessary and those that were convenient, or luxurious. Over time, goods that might initially appear to be luxuries would become conveniences and then turn into necessities.

Fashion was thus a vital defence for a state that entrusted its fate to the market for internationally traded goods, both because of the competitive advantage that it supplied at the beginning of the product cycle, and because of the deeper and broader domestic and foreign markets for low-priced goods that it was able to tap as one product cycle gave way to the next. It acted as a kind of buffer, giving traders a pricing power that they might not otherwise have, while insulating them from some of the impact of price fluctuations that lay beyond their control. As a later, more hostile, commentator noted, the lapse of time built into the spreading ripples of geographical and social distribution made the cycles quite long lasting. A fashion might start at the court and then spread to Paris. Fully outfitted fashion dolls would then make it known in the provinces and abroad, so that "the fashion arriving in Amsterdam in 1768 had been born and died in Paris in 1766." The rush to send goods abroad began only when a fashion had fallen into discredit at home. "Until then, fashion merchants (*marchandes de modes*) do not reduce the stocks of the baubles and trinkets (*colifichets*) that they can sell in their own shops. But once the mode

---

[92] B. N. Collection Joly de Fleury, Mss. 1426, fol. 168, *Mémoire pour les marchands merciers, et les fabricants d'étoffes de soie, d'or, et d'argent de la ville de Paris* (Paris, 1772).

[93] On these, see Sonenscher, *Work and Wages*, especially ch. 4. For a parallel description of the fashion-driven arrangements of the Lyon silk trade, see Carlo Poni, "Fashion as Flexible Production: The Strategies of the Lyons Silk Merchants in the Eighteenth Century," in Charles F. Sabel and Jonathan Zeitlin, eds., *World of Possibilities: Flexibility and Mass Production in Western Industrialization* (Cambridge, CUP, 1997), pp. 37–74.

has passed, they are overstocked with a clutter that they then proceed to get rid of by sending it to countries where Paris's leftovers are still avidly received."[94] This capacity to generate regular cycles of new products, continually shifting the boundaries demarcating necessities, conveniences, and luxuries, was also predicated upon a high degree of occupational specialisation and a range of assorted and specialised skills whose productivity and interdependence served to create the combination of high living standards and shared values that Carl associated particularly with Holland and England. This, he explained, was why

> the more the prince separates the professions and the less he allows anyone to exercise two, the more he will place everyone under the necessity of being unable to do without one another, and the more life's commerce will become great and flourishing.[95]

It was astonishing, he noted, that the products of artisans in big cities like Paris were half as dear as those of artisans in small towns, even though the cost of food, rent, and other necessities and conveniences was twice as great.

> Despite this, the artisans of great cities are ordinarily much richer than those of little towns. I attribute this partly to the greater facility and speed with which work is done in big cities, given the separation of each trade into several branches, which means that each individual is more skilled (*habile*) and is able to make a larger number of products by being concerned with no more than a single, small object.[96]

To illustrate the point, Carl described the Parisian tailoring trade which, he said, was divided into several different branches. There were merchant tailors who, by dint of their wealth and credit, supplied and maintained the smaller tailors. These, in turn, were divided into tailors for men and tailors

---

[94] Jean-Baptiste Robinet, "De la parure et de la mode," in Société typographique de Bouillon, *Recueils philosophiques et littéraires*, 5 vols. (Bouillon, 1769–70), 1:320–40 (331–2, for the passages cited). See also the anonymous *Lettres sur les préjugés du siècle* (The Hague, 1760), pp. 22–3, for a description of the German "mania" for outdated Parisian wall-panelling, furniture, and carriage decorations, and the stimulating effects of "German folly" on the "new inventions" of manufacturers and "faiseuses de mode."

[95] [Carl], *Traité*, pt. 1, p. 401.

[96] [Carl], *Traité*, pt. 2, p. 242. For a later version of the same interest in technical proficiency, see an essay entitled "Sur les avantages que l'étude de la physique procure à l'oeconomie," *La nouvelliste oeconomique et littéraire, ou choix de ce qui se trouve de plus curieux, et de plus intéressant dans les journaux, ouvrages périodiques, et autres livres qui paraissent en France et ailleurs*, vol. 1 (The Hague, 1754), 5–19, with its celebration of the achievements of the Martin brothers, for their lacquerware; Mme Maubois, for her gilded snuffboxes; the Van Robais and Paignon, for their fabrics; and, more generally "les artistes de Paris," for their knowledge of physics, rather than the speculative sciences, as the basis of their inventiveness.

for women, while others were concerned solely with making the frames for women's clothes. There was also a separate body of seamstresses, also exclusively involved in making women's clothes. "This separation of the tailoring trade into several branches," Carl concluded, "performs a great good, both to those in the trade and to the public."[97]

> The more men of the same town see and have something to do with one another, the more sociable and humane they become. The more relations and commerce they have, the more consideration they have for one another. But since they will not do so voluntarily, there has to be something that obliges them to do so. This is what the separation of trades and professions contributes marvellously towards.[98]

The civility of manners generated by the division of labour (a term that Carl himself did not use) and the competitive advantage given by fashion were also connected to a particular theory of property. As Carl described it, private property could not be justified solely in terms of possession. It also had to be used in ways that were compatible with general well-being and justice.[99]

The true hallmark of property, Carl argued, was the easy enjoyment of a good, not its mere possession (anyone can take or keep something, but taking or keeping things cannot secure their ease of use). Possession itself—as anyone living in a state of isolation would rapidly discover—was not a sufficient condition for enjoyment. The manifold character of human needs meant that those who tried to meet all their needs themselves would have very many fewer goods than those who sought the assistance of others. Exclusive possession had, therefore, to take second place to a general system of social reciprocity and its propensity to increase the production of necessities, conveniences, and luxuries in a cumulative way. Here, too, fashion had a more positive influence than appearances might suggest. Over time, Carl pointed out, the changing character of human needs would serve to modify the distinctions separating the necessary, the convenient, and and the luxurious, while the potentially infinite capacity of human ingenuity in devising new fashions would serve to reinforce and magnify the recurrent displacements among the three types of good. The process would generate a kind of built-in switchback, as the high prices paid for luxury goods at the top end of the market generated higher

---

[97] [Carl], *Traité*, pt. 2, p. 246. For an interesting corroboration of Carl's description, see the details of the division of labour between tailors and *fripiers* (usually translated as old-clothes dealers) in mid-eighteenth-century Paris, as described in a lawsuit over the different types of ready-to-wear men's clothing that the latter were entitled to make and sell: B. N. Collection Joly de Fleury, Mss. 1426, fols. 110, et seq.

[98] [Carl], *Traité*, pt. 2, p. 254.

[99] [Carl], *Traité*, pt. 2, p. 415.

levels of expenditure on necessities and conveniences further back along
the chain, resulting in higher agricultural prices and output, broader and
deeper markets for manufactured goods, and increasing opportunities to
substitute expenditure on one kind of good for expenditure on others, thus
promoting more prosperity and power for France as a whole.

As Carl acknowledged, most of the ideas in his book were ones that
he had picked up during his time in France. Among the works that he
mentioned were those by Pierre Le Pesant, sieur de Boisguilbert, and
Charles-Irénée Castel, abbé de Saint-Pierre, both protégés of Fontenelle
and, like Fontenelle, both rather different types of thinker from the Jansenist theologians with whom they have sometimes been identified.[100] As
the abbé de Saint-Pierre noted, even Pierre Nicole, towards the end of his
life, had abandoned some of his earlier Augustinianism, mainly because
he had begun to have doubts about whether the concept of "efficacious
grace" that loomed so large in Jansenist soteriology could be reconciled
with any idea of human choice and, by extension, with any coherent view
of divine justice unless it was matched by some explanation of the human
capacity to follow the laws of nature by finding something motivating in
what was right and good. Humans, Nicole pointed out, have the physical
power to cast out their own eyes or cut off their noses, but almost never
actually do so. Something, therefore, had to explain why they used their
physical powers in ways that they found attractive or pleasing.[101] Without an explanation of this more than straightforwardly physical ability, it
was difficult either to explain the justice of divine retribution for human
sinfulness or to avoid the conclusion that "efficacious grace" worked in
purely arbitrary ways. Nicole, accordingly, began to move nearer to the
kind of aesthetic motivation involved in both Ciceronian and Cartesian
moral theory, describing what he took to be the universal human capacity
to find something pleasing in what was right and good as a "universal"
or "general grace" made available by God to all humans. Its existence
(exemplified, Nicole argued, by the kind of imperceptible thoughts that
occur when one is reading a work of imaginative fiction) made it easier
to see why it was not always necessary to know, in any strong sense, in
order to love. This, in turn, made it possible to explain why humans were
able to observe natural laws without having any fully formed concepts of
what they might be, and why their failure to do so was all the more rightly
imputable (inversely, however, the idea of general grace seemed to imply
that humans were not, naturally, sociable, a view that, according to his

<hr/>

[100] On Boisguilbert as a Jansenist, see Gilbert Faccarello, *Aux origines de l'économie politique
libérale: Pierre de Boisguilbert* (Paris, Anthropos, 1986).

[101] Pierre Nicole, *Traité de la grâce générale*, 2 vols. (Paris, 1715), 6 (continuous pagination).
On Nicole's use of Cicero (citing his *Tusculan Questions*) to endorse the idea of general grace,
or natural law, see pp. 224–6.

horrified Jansenist critics, made Nicole's revised position look alarmingly like Hobbes, while the stronger emphasis upon human choice involved in the idea of general grace meant, according to the same opponents, that he had also, inadvertently, opened a door to the heresy of Pelagianism).[102] Carl shared this kind of concern with the relationship between decorum and morality, without, however, showing any interest in its theological implications. The general improvement in prosperity, he emphasised, would result in less inequality, and a general improvement in manners and civility. "Is it not shameful for a state," he wrote, "that some should be covered with gold and silver, while others have nothing to cover their nakedness? . . . Is it not a reproach to those who call themselves polished and polite that there are still a great number of people who resemble savages?" If every individual, he continued, "really did understand his true interests, he would also be contributing to the true delectation of his senses by preventing them from encountering objects offensive to them, which would perfect the second level of riches, namely, the convenient or the agreeable."[103]

Fashion, from this perspective, was the antidote to the conflation of wealth with power of an earlier, more barbarous, age. Without "French elegance," wrote one apologist, much later in the eighteenth century, "Europe would still be Gothic, still entombed beneath its gold plate."[104] By then, however, claims like this had begun in their turn to look dated. Fashion's empire, wrote the great French Revolutionary orator the comte de Mirabeau, in the multiauthored examination of the Prussian monarchy under Frederick the Great that appeared under his name in 1786, had nothing to do with "that national authority that France has lost since the Peace of Utrecht" (of 1715). It was, instead, no more than the product of "the perfection of French taste in clothing, above all among women." In a nation "in which the fair sex holds the sceptre governing every success, and where men, deprived by the system of government of all influence in public affairs (unless it occurs by way of opinion, which women also govern), are all devoted, if not enslaved, to those seductive creatures, and generally esteem themselves only in terms of their ability to please, women are required to use a great deal of skill in bringing together everything suitable for maintaining their power." Elegant attire had been the surest means. It appealed to women's talent, inventiveness, and perseverance, all qualities, Mirabeau wrote, that were more pronounced in a sex noted for its natural

---

[102] Nicole, *Traité*, pp. 93–103. Jacques-Joseph Duguet and Hilarion Monnier, *Réfutation du système de M. Nicole touchant la grâce universelle* (Paris, 1716).

[103] [Carl], *Traité*, pt. 2, pp. 484–5.

[104] Louis-Antoine de Caraccioli, *Paris, le modèle des nations étrangères, ou l'Europe française* (Paris, 1777), pp. 119–20.

discrimination and readiness to put up with hard work. It also appealed to
the natural intelligence of all those whose subsistence or fortunes depended
upon "the fantasies of the rich and the needs of luxury." Since men took
so much pleasure, whether physical or "as a matter of vanity," in pleasing the opposite sex, they were willing "to do their utmost to invent new
finery, new designs for attire and jewellery, or, in a word, new fashions."
This "universal tendency" had given rise to "an immense superiority,"
to which other nations rendered homage, but to which "free peoples" had
no need to aspire, since they had less need for "real or imaginary pleasures
(*plaisirs*)" to fill the gaps left by the absence of "natural enjoyments (*jouissances*)." In this respect, Mirabeau noted disparagingly, French men were
rather like English Catholics. A foreigner, looking at the latter, might
conclude that their gallantry did honour to their religion, but would have
forgotten that "not having any part in government, they are forced to find
entertainment for their idleness in the *ritual* of the cult of love."[105]

Mirabeau's Rousseau-inspired evaluation was the other side of the coin
of an earlier, more positive view. Early in the seventeenth century, the
connection between civility and the salon was given a neologism. In the
view of Catherine de Vivonne who, as the marquise de Rambouillet, established the first, most famous salon of all, cultivated assemblies like the
one that she had established would *debrutaliser*.[106] The neologism itself

---

[105] Honoré-Gabriel Riqueti, comte de Mirabeau, *De la monarchie prussienne sous Frédéric le
Grand*, 4 vols. (London, 1786), 1:34–5, and note 1. As Mirabeau indicated in the note, the
comparison between French men and English Catholics could be found in the *Principes de la
législation universelle*, 2 vols. (Amsterdam, 1776) by the Swiss writer Georg Ludwig Schmid
d'Auenstein.

[106] On the neologism, see Wendy Ayres-Bennett, "Women and Grammar in Seventeenth-
Century France," *Seventeenth-Century French Studies* 12 (1990): 5–25 (pp. 11–2). On the
wider claim about salons and civility, see Jolanta T. Pekacz, *Conservative Tradition in Pre-
Revolutionary France: Parisian Salon Women* (New York, Peter Lang, 1999), and the works
referred to in note 12 above. A full version of the whole story would have to include the
argument about the relationship between novels and the manners of French women, as this
was set out by the theologian Pierre-Daniel Huet in his "De l'origine des romans" of 1671
(referred to in note 22 above). According to Huet, the elevated status of postfeudal French
women, the freedom accorded them by noblemen, and the highly internalised level of trust
that came accordingly to be placed in their sexual fidelity meant that, in contradistinction
to the procedures followed by men in Italy and Spain, where women were required to lead
rigorously secluded lives, French men were obliged to use more subtle seductive strategies
than the force or deceit that were usually sufficient in Italy or Spain. In this explanation of
the rise of the novel, with its emphasis on the romances of the seventeenth century as more
sophisticated versions of "the gay science" of troubadour poetry (one that was obviously
indebted to debates in post-Tridentine Catholicism), fiction became the modern way to a
woman's heart (see Huet, "De l'origine des romans," pp. 62–7). For a discussion of Huet's
essay, but without his emphasis on the status of modern (seventeenth-century) women, see
Peggy Kanuf, "The Gift of Clothes: Of Mme de Lafayette and the Origin of Novels," *Novel:
A Forum on Fiction* 17 (1984): 233–45. For a crisp description of the continuity of values,

never really caught on, but the claim that something about the part played by women in presiding over an assorted, mainly male, literary gathering could indeed have a "debrutalising" effect soon became much more widely accepted. It was a claim that survived into the nineteenth century, where it was given an emphatic endorsement both by the French eclectic philosopher Victor Cousin and by the rather less well-known liberal politician Pierre-Louis Roederer (whose *Memoirs towards the History of Polite Society in France* in fact gave Cousin his starting point). "I consider," wrote Roederer in 1835, "the eight hundred *précieuses* or *alcovistes* whose names and addresses were listed by Somaise in 1661 to be eight hundred academicians divided into different mixed societies, bound by decent gallantry and refined language."

> Imagine the multiplicity of feats, images, and movements that must have been produced by these conversations, where the senses, the imagination, and the heart were all in play, where self-love was stimulated by a striving to please and astound, and where criticism was no less excited by rivalry than was the need to produce by the striving to please.[107]

Roederer's own concern was to show how, from the late seventeenth century, this decentralised system had been swallowed up by the French court, and the massive, and ultimately lethal, system of rewards and patronage that had grown up at Versailles. Like many of his generation, including his political ally the marquis de Condorcet, he was also quick to single out France's last foreign queen, Marie Antoinette, as having played a particularly dangerous, if unwitting, part in accelerating the process.[108]

Roederer's description of the decentralised polite society of the seventeenth century relied quite strongly on the idea of self-love as the basis of its dynamics, and its inbuilt "striving to please." It was, however, a very

particularly the value of urbanity, from Mme de Rambouillet's early seventeenth-century salon to those of the early eighteenth century, see Elena Russo, *Styles of Enlightenment: Taste, Politics, and Authorship in Eighteenth-Century France* (Baltimore, Johns Hopkins UP, 2007), pp. 18–20, 35–41.

[107] Pierre-Louis Roederer, *Mémoires pour servir à l'histoire de la société polie en France* (Paris, 1835), p. 176 (reprinted in his *Oeuvres*, 2:452). The reference to "Somaise" is to Antoine Baudeau, sieur de Saumaize, *Le grand dictionnaire des prétieuses, historique, poétique, géographique, cosmographique et armoirique* (Paris, 1661). On Roederer's earlier views on a republican alternative to what he, too, called "fashion's empire," see his *De l'usage à faire de l'autorité publique dans les circonstances présentes* (Paris, 1797), p. 59. On similar, early nineteenth-century evaluations of the salons, see Kale, *French Salons*, pp. 218–9.

[108] For Condorcet's account of how "fifty or sixty" small gatherings (*sociétés*) all came to be subsumed under "one single and numerous society" dominated by the queen, see the compilation (based on Condorcet's correspondence with Suard) by Gaëtan de la Rochefoucauld-Liancourt, *Mémoires de Condorcet sur la révolution française*, 2 vols. (Paris, 1824), pp. 179–210.

different conception of self-love from the loosely Cartesian concept that Marivaux had used three generations earlier. As Roederer indicated in some of his earlier works, his own explanation of the mechanisms involved was strongly physiological. The human body, and the face in particular, are, he wrote, unusually expressive of emotional states. People shrink and turn pale when they are frightened, and blush or sweat when they are embarrassed or ashamed. This physical transparency makes it easy for most people to find corroboration of others' states of mind, and this kind of corroboration can itself be pleasurable even if the feeling on display is not. The mirroring mechanism could, as Roederer also argued, be coupled with claims about real physiological differences (or even acquired gender differences), and could be used, as he also showed, to explain many of the ordinary assertions made about the effects of female beauty, intuitiveness, grace, modesty, or sensitivity. The "decent gallantry and refined language" that were the hallmark of the salon had their origin, ultimately, in the physical transparency of human emotions.

In certain respects, the seventeenth century was more subtle. It was also less egalitarian. One example of how the two fitted together can be found in an early eighteenth-century compilation of seventeenth-century moral theory entitled a *Traité du vrai mérite de l'homme* (A Treatise on the Real Merit of Man), first published in 1734 and reprinted nearly twenty times over the following three decades. As its author, Charles-François-Nicolas Le Maître de Claville (whose "hero," he wrote, was the seventeenth-century moralist La Bruyère), pointed out, "of all the passions to which man is subject, none is more universally the dominant passion than love."[109] But Cartesian dualism made love a complicated matter. As Le Maître de Claville emphasised, love was spiritual as well as physical, which was why making sense of its nature was so difficult, especially when neither the purely physical nor the purely spiritual was predominant. As (he noted) La Bruyère had said, "a lively and pure liaison between two people of opposite sexes is a sort of passion that is not exactly either love or friendship. It is less than the one, and more than the other, and forms a class apart."[110] Beauty, and all the other external qualities usually associated with women, were not the source of this unusual passion. Instead, its source was to be found in women's *amour-propre*, and the care that they took to preserve their physical qualities by dressing well, dyeing their hair, or covering their faces with rouge or other makeup. As, tactlessly, Le Maître de Claville also noted, even the most perfect woman would have some sort of caprice, and even the most stupid man some sort of reason, the two qualities could complement one another. The

---

[109] Charles-François-Nicolas Le Maître de Claville, *Traité du vrai mérite de l'homme* [1734] (Amsterdam, 1759), p. 257 (the remark about La Bruyère is on p. 265).
[110] Le Maître de Claville, *Traité du vrai mérite*, p. 261.

efforts that women made to defy old age and death, efforts that also gave the lie to beauty's permanence, would have the effect of allowing reason and capriciousness to complement one another, supplying a space for the passion that La Bruyère had described as not exactly full-blown love, nor just friendship.

> If ladies who wanted to please went about it fully, we would be lost. What kind of resistance can there be against an enchanting exterior and a happy naturalness, or against a great deal of wit, politeness, modesty, and gentleness? Happily, some women have imagined a secret for making themselves more ugly, in the hope of appearing more beautiful or of remaining so for longer. It is an involuntary remedy that self-love, wrongly understood, seems to have suggested to them to our advantage. Art serves to shelter us from nature's graces.[111]

This Christian emphasis upon *vanitas* (in both its senses) could, without much difficulty, go along with an admiration for ancient Greek symposiums and ancient Roman seemliness. As the comte de Tressan's various acts of poetic homage to Mme de Tencin indicate, ancient decorum and chivalrous honour were no more mutually exclusive than were Plato's purple carpets and troubadour ballads. However ill-assorted they may now seem and however ill-founded some of the moral theories on which they were based may now appear, the combination of the ancient concern with what was *honestum* and the Christian concern with *vanitas* amounted to quite a solid foundation for the mixture of status, emotion, and decorum on which salon society was based.

A "Poor Devil": The Short, Unhappy Life of Nicolas-Joseph-Laurent Gilbert

The point of the joke about breeches was that someone without *culottes* had the wrong kind of all three. He had no status, displayed the wrong sort of emotions, and showed no decorum. One further reason for the joke's late eighteenth-century resonance was that it fitted a real writer remarkably well. The writer in question was the satirical poet Nicolas-Joseph-Laurent Gilbert. Gilbert seems to have led a life that was something like a literal version of the tale of literary ambition, abject poverty, and unscrupulous exploitation told by Voltaire in his satirical poem *Le pauvre diable* (The Poor Devil).[112] Voltaire's poem was published in 1760, but it

---

[111] Le Maître de Claville, *Traité du vrai mérite*, pp. 264–5.

[112] The following account of Gilbert's life is based on Ernest Laffay, *Le poète Gilbert (Nicolas-Joseph-Florent [sic]), étude biographique et littéraire* (Paris, 1898), and the biography

could almost have been an account of Gilbert's life. He was born the son
of a corn merchant in a small town near Nancy in 1750, and from there
moved first to Dôle, then to Lyon, where he began to write poems. Local
success encouraged him to travel to Paris, where he fell in with the group
of journalists and writers associated with the *Année littéraire* (The Literary
Annual). This was the group that had been the prime target of Voltaire's
vengeful poem, a tale of how a garret-living writer had been taken on "to
lie for ten crowns a month" by the *Année littéraire*, and had then stumbled
from ignominy to ruin (all at the hands of a detailed list of Voltaire's enemies) before ending up as a doorman. Gilbert's fate was worse. He was
a gifted poet and soon made a name for himself by submitting his poems
to the annual prize competition put on by the French Academy in 1771,
1772, and 1773. The following year he published the poem that was to
earn him notoriety, a viciously satirical attack on the spirit of the age,
entitled *Le Dix-huitième siècle* (The Eighteenth Century).

Both the subject and Gilbert's own treatment of it were well chosen.
The last years of the reign of Louis XV were marked by a combination of
political brutality and moral decay that lent themselves particularly well to
the style of neo-Roman satirical poetry that Gilbert made his own. The
themes of political brutality and moral decay overlapped almost perfectly.
A series of lawsuits involving the parlements of both Brittany and Paris
on one side, and the military governor of the province of Brittany, the
duc d'Aiguillon, on the other, had led to a royal coup against the parlements in 1771. Aiguillon and his ally, the duc de Richelieu, had also been
instrumental in procuring the king the last of his mistresses, the memorably beautiful courtesan Mme du Barry, and in using her influence both
to bring about the fall of the king's most powerful minister, the duc de
Choiseul, and to launch the assault on the parlements that, among other
things, prevented Aiguillon from being brought to trial.[113] It was not very
difficult, when Gilbert wrote his poem, to think of the parallels between
modern France and imperial Rome, or to imagine what Juvenal, Lucian,
or Petronius might have written about a king still, in official propaganda,
called *Louis le bien aimé* (Louis the well-beloved). Gilbert did it well. But
his very success played a part in his undoing. In the shifting constellations

---

introducing Gilbert's *Oeuvres complètes* (Paris, 1823). See also the comparison between Gilbert and a later satirist named Despaze in an article in the *Journal de Paris*, issue 12 (12
Vendémiaire an IX), p. 70. Voltaire's poem *Le pauvre diable* was published in *Le joli recueil
ou l'histoire de la querelle littéraire, où les auteurs s'amusent en amusant le public* (Geneva, 1760),
pp. 49–72.

[113] For an authoritative account, see Julian Swann, *Politics and the Parlement of Paris under
Louis XV, 1754–1774* (Cambridge, CUP, 1995), and, for a contemporary description, see
Jeffrey Merrick, "Corruption versus *Honnêteté*: Morellet's Assessment of the French Political
Scene in May 1774," *SVEC* 2005: 12, pp. 155–75.

of faction and intrigue that accompanied both the royal coup of 1771 and the aftermath of Louis XV's own death three years later, his violent indictment of the age gradually lost its lustre, as first one, then another, set of patrons found other subjects to promote. The new reign presented different prospects; as time passed, the poem itself began to look like the work of a hired pen and a product of the devout circle associated with Louis XV's queen, Maria Leczinska, and, until his death in 1765, his eldest son, the dauphin of France. Gilbert's growing isolation and his increasingly frantic efforts to find a protector soon made him an easy target for jibes about the gap between the moralism of his poetry and the opportunism of his life. It is not clear whether this was the cause of the drinking and insanity to which he succumbed or whether the causation went the other way round, but, by the end of the decade, it was clear that he had gone mad. He had become convinced that there was a conspiracy to steal his poems and, in 1780, was encouraged to enter the Paris Hôtel Dieu for his own protection. There, in desperation, he locked his papers in a casket and swallowed the key, choking himself to death. He was just thirty years old.

Gilbert's unhappy life fascinated nineteenth-century romantics (one early nineteenth-century literary critic made a point of comparing his last poems, with their gloomy intimations of his own, obscure, death, to Edward Young's *Night Thoughts*, a comparison, he wrote, that was much to Gilbert's advantage).[114] Before then, however, he was identified as the prototype of what was to become the *sans-culotte*. This, as has been shown, was the guise in which he appeared in the 1799 *Nouveau Paris* (New Picture of Paris) by the novelist, playwright, and essayist Louis-Sébastien Mercier.[115] But, as has also been shown, Mercier's account was both rather vague and rather self-referential. Although he did associate the origins of the word *sans-culotte* with the status and appearance of men of letters, he made no reference at all to the joke about breeches, or to its connection to the world of eighteenth-century salons. For someone like Mercier, who was entirely at home in late eighteenth-century Parisian literary circles, it is unlikely that either the joke or its provenance could have been particularly obscure. He himself had told the story about the bookseller who would have liked to keep Voltaire, Rousseau, and Diderot in his loft *sans culottes* in one of his own most successful works, the *Tableau de Paris*. The story about Mme de Tencin and the breeches had first been made public

[114] Abel-François Villemain, *Cours de littérature française. Examen des ouvrages de Thompson, Young, Hume, Robertson, Gibbon, Ossian, Beccaria, Filangieri, Alfieri, etc.* (Paris, 1828), IIème leçon, p. 31.

[115] See above, p. 17. Mercier's account became the standard version of the term's origin in the nineteenth century: see M. Touchard-Lafosse, *Souvenirs d'un demi-siècle*, 6 vols. (Brussels, 1836), 1:19; and the various contributions on the subject in the *Intermédiaire des chercheurs et curieux* 5 (1867): 31, 217; 12 (1879): 194, 249; 13 (1880): 616.

in two articles published in the *Nouvelles littéraires* in 1749 and 1751 by a literary critic named the abbé Nicolas Trublet (whom Voltaire was to immortalise in *Le pauvre diable* as the man who "compiled and compiled and compiled").[116] It had then been given a more substantial and recent airing in the articles published by the "Recluse of the Pyrenees" and the "Recluse of Migneaux" in the *Journal de Paris* in summer of 1787. Mercier may or may not have known about these articles, but there is every reason to think that he did. He also seems to have known Rutledge quite well (well enough, at any rate, for Mercier to write approvingly about Rutledge's *Bureau d'esprit* in his own *Tableau de Paris* in 1781, but for Rutledge to accuse Mercier in 1784 of lifting a passage from his journal, *Calypso,* and of publishing it under his own name in the same *Tableau de Paris*). The two men were neighbours on the rue des Noyers in Paris at the time when Mercier was the editor of the *Journal des Dames* (The Ladies' Journal), a journal that, among other things, specialised in theatre reviews, and when Rutledge wrote his *Bureau d'esprit* (Mercier was also sometimes said, wrongly, to be its author). He also knew Gilbert (one later tradition had it that he had even been present at Gilbert's death).[117] He was, in addition, the dedicatee of a collection of literary essays published in 1787 containing a discussion of the origin of *étrennes* that was almost identical to the one published in the *Journal de Paris* in the same year. Its editor, another minor literary figure named Antoine-François Delandine, was also the editor of the 1786 edition of Mme de Tencin's collected works in which the story about the breeches had again been rehearsed.[118]

---

[116] [Jean-Marie-Bernard Clément, ed.], *Les cinq années littéraires, ou nouvelles littéraires des années 1748, 1749, 1750, 1751 & 1752,* 4 vols. (The Hague, 1754), vol. 2, letter 44, 5 November 1749, p. 19; vol. 3, letter 89, 1 December 1751, p. 89. On Trublet, see Jean Jacquart, *L'abbé Trublet, critique et moraliste 1697–1770* (Paris, Auguste Picard, 1926).

[117] For these details, see Raymonde Monnier, "Tableaux croisés chez Mercier et Rutlidge. Le *Peuple* de Paris et le *Plébéien* Anglais," *Annales historiques de la révolution française* 339 (2005): 1–16 (4–5). The question of the authorship of the *Bureau d'esprit* is discussed in Erma Wolf, *Rutledge's "Bureau d'Esprit",* Giessener Beitrage zur Romanischen Philologie, 16 (Giessen, 1925), p. 6, and by Pierre Peyronnet in his edition of the play (above, note 4), pp. 27–30, 33–5. On Mercier and Rutledge, see Nina Rattner Gelbart, *Feminine and Opposition Journalism in Old Regime France* (Berkeley and Los Angeles, University of California Press, 1987), pp. 115, note 51, 230, 284–5. On Mercier and Gilbert, see Charles Monselet, *Les oubliés et les dédaignés. Figures littéraires de la fin du xviiie siècle,* 2 vols. (Alençon, 1857), 1:61. On Mercier's friendship with Gilbert, see also *Almanach littéraire, ou étrennes d'Apollon* (Paris, 1782), pp. 73–4. See, too, Enrico Rufi, "Le rêve laïque de Louis-Sébastien Mercier entre littérature et politique," *Studies on Voltaire and the Eighteenth Century* 326 (1995): 146, where Mercier is reported to have written, "J'ai vu Gilbert mourir, sans pain."

[118] M. de Mayer, "Origine des étrennes," in [Antoine François Delandine, ed.], *Le conservateur, ou bibliothèque choisie de littérature, de morale et d'histoire* vol. 1 (Paris, 1787), p. 1 et seq. The text is slightly different from the one published by the "Recluse of Migneaux" in the *Journal de Paris* of 3 and 16 November 1787 (issues 307 and 320).

It resurfaced once more in 1790 in an edition of the collected works of the abbé Gabriel Bonnot de Mably, edited, among others, by another of Mercier's acquaintances, the abbé Gabriel Brizard, with whom he was collaborating on a concurrent edition of Rousseau's collected works.[119] Two years later, in March 1792, the story appeared again, now in the *Journal de Paris*, although this time the breeches were said to have been given by a seventeenth-century *salonnière* named Mme de la Sablière (famed in her age, just as Mme de Tencin was in hers, for her wit, beauty, and promiscuity) to the celebrated author of fables Jean de Lafontaine.[120] Mercier, however, did not refer to any of this.

As has been shown, one possible reason for this vagueness is that Mercier knew a great deal more about the term's history than, in 1799, it might have been prudent to acknowledge. He had in fact played a fairly prominent part in turning the joke into an emblem of something quite different, and, more specifically, in associating the neologism that the name *sans-culottes* became with a broader justification of civil war. Here, he amplified very considerably on what Jean-Jacques Rousseau, in his *Social Contract*, had written about "periods of violence in the lifetime of states, when revolutions do to peoples what certain crises do to individuals, when horror of the past takes the place of forgetting, and when the state aflame with civil wars is, so to speak, reborn from its ashes and recovers the vigour of youth as it escapes death's embrace."[121] Mercier did so in the July 1792 issue of the Parisian monthly journal, the *Chronique du mois* (or Monthly Chronicle), where he published an article on the sixteenth-century French Catholic League that picked up the theme of civil war, and its potential benefits, from several of his earlier, prerevolutionary publications. The article, he wrote, had been written originally in 1781 (presumably with the war between Britain and her American colonies in mind), but it had actually been foreshadowed by an even earlier endorsement of civil war

---

[119] Gabriel Bonnot de Mably, *Oeuvres*, 13 vols. (London, 1789–90), 13:225–6. For bibliographical guidance on the parallel edition of Rousseau's collected works, see Raymond Birn, "Les 'oeuvres complètes' de Rousseau sous l'ancien régime," *Annales de la Société Jean-Jacques Rousseau*, 41 (1997): 229–62, and his *Forging Rousseau: Print, Commerce and Cultural Manipulation in the Late Enlightenment*, SVEC 2001: 08, as well as Jean-Claude Bonnet, "Louis-Sébastien Mercier et les *Oeuvres complètes* de Jean-Jacques Rousseau," *Studies on Voltaire and the Eighteenth Century* 370 (1999): 111–24.

[120] *Journal de Paris* 61 (supplément), 1 March 1792. According to one eighteenth-century story, a magistrate who was one of Mme de la Sablière's relatives reproached her for her many lovers, pointing out that animals (*bêtes*) had only one season. Which, Mme de la Sablière replied, was why they were *bêtes* (stupid): see Poullain de Saint-Foix, *Essais historiques sur Paris*, 5th ed., 5 vols. (Paris, 1776), 5:186.

[121] Jean-Jacques Rousseau, *The Social Contract*, bk. 2, ch. 8, in Jean-Jacques Rousseau, *The Social Contract and Other Later Political Writings*, ed. Victor Gourevitch (Cambridge, CUP, 1997), p. 72.

that Mercier had published in 1770 in his satirical novel *L'an 2440, rêve s'il en fut jamais* (The Year 2440, a Dream If Ever There Was One). In the version published in 1792, Mercier made a point of highlighting the connection between the subject matter of his earlier publications and the events of the day, notably the very recent Parisian insurrection of 20 June. "Thus," he wrote in a footnote,

> the aristocracy has given patriots the name of *sans-culottes* and they in turn, identifying themselves with the *Greeks* and *Romans*, all peoples who wore no *breeches*, have put a pair of *breeches* on parade, as if to tell the beneficiaries of the civil list and the chief public official [Louis XVI] that without us, you wouldn't have any *breeches*. The weapons used by miserable aristocrats whose sole strength is a play on words ought to be used to combat them.[122]

In the text itself, Mercier went on to argue that a civil war was the only kind of war that could, perhaps, "be useful and sometimes necessary." The "true origin" of the sixteenth-century Catholic League, he argued, had been not "the defence of the Catholic religion" but "the extreme wretchedness of the people." The "most irrefragable proof" of this was the fact that "all of France, from one end of the kingdom to the other," had risen in arms. "Peasants, citizens, artists, all rushed with ardour into this civil war."[123] It was this near unanimity, Mercier wrote, that supplied its justification.

He had first made the claim in 1770, during the events of the last years of the reign of Louis XV that had also supplied Gilbert with the material for his satires. "In certain states," Mercier had written then, "there is a time that can become necessary, a terrible, bloody time, but one that signals liberty." Civil war, he added, "makes use of the most obscure talents," causing "the most extraordinary men" to emerge and to become worthy of taking command.[124] He repeated the claim in 1787 in his *Notions claires sur*

---

[122] Louis-Sébastien Mercier, "De la ligue," *Chronique du mois*, July 1792, 58–80: "Ainsi l'aristocratie a nommé *sans-culottes* les patriotes, et ceux-ci s'assimilant aux *Grecs* et aux *Romains*, tous gens sans *culottes*, ont promené des *culottes*, et ont semblé dire à la liste civile, et au premier fonctionnaire public: sans nous vous n'aurez pas des *culottes*. Il faut combattre avec les mêmes armes les misérables aristocrates forts en jeux de mots" (p. 64, note 1).

[123] Mercier, "De la ligue." The passage is also reproduced in Louis-Sébastien Mercier, *Fragments of Politics and History*, 2 vols. (London, 1795), 2:338–9.

[124] Louis-Sébastien Mercier, *L'An deux mille quatre cent quarante quatre, rêve s'il en fut jamais* [1770], ed. Raymond Trousson (Bordeaux, Editions Ducros, 1961), ch. 36, p. 330, note 3. The passage was republished (without any indication of its source) in the curious compilation produced by Joseph de Lanjuinais, *Le monarque accompli, ou prodiges de bonté, de savoir et de sagesse qui font l'éloge de sa majesté impériale Joseph II*, 3 vols. (Lausanne, 1774), 1:117–9. On Mercier's views on civil war (but without making a connection to the remark about *sans-culottes*), see Marcel Dorigny, "Du 'despotisme vertueux' à la république," in Jean-Claude Bonnet, ed., *Louis-Sébastien Mercier (1740–1814). Un hérétique en littérature* (Paris, Mercure de France, 1995), pp. 247–77.

les gouvernements (Clear Notions of Government), backing it up by invoking the authority of the seventeenth-century English republican Algernon Sidney, and did so again in a further, three-volume compilation, published in 1792 as *Fragments de politique et d'histoire*, which also included his article on the Catholic League (it appeared in English translation in 1795 as *Fragments of Politics and History*).[125] "During civil wars the destruction of the state is not to be dreaded," he wrote there. "Notwithstanding that the people may be divided into factions," he continued, "it is far from being annihilated. It has, on the other hand, a superabundance of vital action."[126] Given this underlying vitalism (an important aspect of Mercier's broader moral and political theory), civil war was a "kind of fever that can drive away a dangerous stupor and is often able to reinforce the principle of life." Its legitimacy could be derived "from necessity and strict justice" in cases where there were "no alternative means available to the injured party," making it a form of action that was "truly undertaken for the safety of the state." Its effects, he added, were rarely harmful. "Nations emerge from these internecine debates in a redoubtable condition. Political enlightenment is more widespread; armed valour grows stronger with exercise. The very fury and violence of this kind of war makes it of short duration."[127] By 1799, all this may well have looked like the wrong thing to have said.

It is less clear what, beyond the allusion to the Greeks and Romans, and the fact that "patriots" supplied the breeches worn by those presently holding political power, Mercier actually did intend to say. The note that he added to his article on the French Catholic League was simply an exhortation to turn the joke against its authors. In this sense, the point was simply to do what Rutledge had already done. The target was certainly different (it was no longer simply a matter of making a joke about salons), but the effect was not necessarily political, even if putting the note at the foot of an essay about civil war gave it a very powerful political charge indeed. Mercier was not a particularly sophisticated political thinker ("he is famous for his habit of not saying, writing, or doing anything other than the opposite of reason and his own conviction," wrote Pierre-Louis Roederer, dismissively, in 1801).[128] Nor, even more obviously, was Gilbert.

---

[125] Louis-Sébastien Mercier, *Notions claires sur les gouvernements*, 2 vols. (Amsterdam, 1787), 1:196.

[126] Mercier, *Fragments of Politics and History*, 2:11–2 (I have modernised the translation slightly).

[127] Mercier, "De la ligue," pp. 64–5. The same passage appears in Mercier, *Fragments of Politics and History*, 2:341: "Two armed nations do therefore irreparable mischief to each other, and blood is shed in useless battle. But civil war is a sort of fever which expels a dangerous stupor and often strengthens the principle of life. . . . This war, which I would call sacred, is therefore really undertaken for the salvation of the state."

[128] *Journal de Paris*, 4 June 1801, reprinted in Pierre-Louis Roederer, *Oeuvres*, ed. A.-M. Roederer, 7 vols. (Paris, 1853–9), 4:171.

Both were moralists, using ridicule and satire to expose what they took to be vice in all its forms. They could, quite easily, be placed in the category that the comte de Tressan associated with the figure of the Cynic, Diogenes. Some of Mercier's early biographers did exactly that, describing his *Nouveau Paris* as "a work of cynicism and *sans-culottisme*."[129] Although Mercier did write a great deal about politics, he did so in a way that now seems curiously simpleminded (although he himself was not at all simpleminded, as can be seen both from his theatre criticism and from the use to which the German dramatist and philosopher Friedrich Schiller put his drama theory, as well as some of the content of Mercier's *Portrait of Philip II, King of Spain*, in his masterpiece, *Don Carlos*).[130] Yet both the moral message and the "revolution" that he predicted in the dream that formed his novel *The Year 2440* clearly struck a chord. The German writer Christoph Martin Wieland (also the author of a sympathetic study of Diogenes the Cynic) incorporated large passages from it into the description of moral and political reform that he set out in his *Golden Mirror*. It was also reproduced in a compilation published in 1774, dedicated to Emperor Joseph II, and resurfaced, too, in several French works supporting the developing Dutch insurrection against the House of Orange after 1783.[131] For all its daring rhetoric, the prospect of the future that it presented was oddly attractive.

The revolution that Mercier envisaged would, he wrote, be the work of a "philosopher king." Its outcome would be the abolition of "absolute sovereignty" and the establishment of a republic. The republic in question would still have a king, but his power and responsibilities would be drastically curtailed. The "assembled estates of the kingdom" would have the sole right to legislate. The day-to-day business of government would be entrusted to a senate, while the king would be entrusted with "the power of the sword" to enforce the execution of the laws. The senate would be responsible to the king, and both would be responsible to the assembly

[129] Monselet, *Les oubliés et les dédaignés*, 1:77.

[130] On Mercier and Schiller, see Hermann Hofer, "Mercier admirateur de l'Allemagne et ses reflets dans le préclassicisme et le classicisme allemands," in Hermann Hofer, ed., *Louis-Sébastien Mercier précurseur et sa fortune* (Munich, Fink, 1977), pp. 73–116 (pp. 91–3); Edmond Eggli, *Schiller et le romantisme français*, 2 vols. (Paris, 1927), 1:27–8, 79–81; and Sylvain Fort, *Les lumières françaises en Allemagne: le cas Schiller* (Paris, Presses universitaires de France, 2002), pp. 55–61, 122–47, 173–4, 185–98. On Schiller's early interest in physiology and morality, see the texts translated in Friedrich Schiller, *Medicine, Psychology and Literature*, ed. Kenneth Dewhurst and Nigel Reeves (Oxford, Sandford Publications, 1978).

[131] See, most helpfully, W. W. Pusey, *Louis-Sébastien Mercier in Germany: His Vogue and Influence in the Eighteenth Century* (New York, Columbia UP, 1939), and Raymond Trousson, introduction to Mercier, *L'An deux mille quatre cent quarante quatre*, ed. Trousson, pp. 65–6. [Joseph Mandrillon], *Révolutions des provinces unies sous l'étendard des divers stadhouders*, 3 vols. (Nijmegen, 1788), 1:257; Lanjuinais, *Le monarque accompli*, 1:117–20.

of estates, which would meet every two years. Citizens would have equal status and form "one body" with the body of the state. The new regime, as Mercier wrote later, fitted the idea of a "democratic monarchy" that had been outlined by Voltaire's friend the marquis d'Argenson, in his posthumously published *Considerations on the Present and Former Government of France*, but with the key difference that it would be the democracy, not the monarch, that would be sovereign.[132] The new regime would also be one where need, possession, and occupation would be the sole criteria governing the legitimate ownership of property, where virtue, not the goods of fortune, would be the basis of moral authority, and where merit, not inheritance, would be the ultimate principle of the right to rule. As Mercier put it in a long note attached to an essay on literature that he published in 1778—a note that he said he had intended to put into his futuristic novel—the "Roman law that prohibited any Roman from possessing more than five hundred acres (*arpents*) was a very wise one."[133] He repeated the recommendation in his *Tableau de Paris* in 1782. The upper limit, it should be emphasised, was quite considerable, but was still intended to be consonant with general equality. In the future, Mercier emphasised in the novel itself, the "only distinction" would be "the one that virtue, genius, and industry make naturally."[134]

The emblem of this new order was to be found in a simple village that Mercier dreamt he had visited on his way to inspect the ruins of Versailles ("Would that I had known," he found Louis XIV lamenting). There, he came upon a group of peasants about to bury one of their own. His funeral oration, given by the village pastor, set out what Mercier intended to show was a wholly admirable life. He had died at the age of ninety after many years of toil and industry. He had cleared more than two thousand acres (*arpents*) of land, planting some with vines and others with fruit trees, driven "not by avarice" but by the love of hard work and the "great and holy idea" that God was watching over him as he worked the land to feed his children. He had had twenty-five of them, and had raised them all with a respect for hard work and virtue, so that they had all become "honourable people" (*honnêtes gens*). He had found each a spouse, and all his grandchildren had been raised in his own house. On holidays, he had been the first to promote the sound of rustic music, and his face and voice were the first to herald "universal cheerfulness." He had never refused a request for help or been unfeeling towards public or private misfortune. He had never

[132] Louis-Sébastien Mercier, *De Jean-Jacques Rousseau, considéré comme l'un des premiers auteurs de la révolution* (Paris, 1791), p. 168.

[133] Louis-Sébastien Mercier, *De la littérature et des littérateurs* (Lausanne, 1778), pp. 83–5, note 41.

[134] Mercier, *L'An deux mille quatre cent quarante quatre*, ed. Trousson, ch. 36, pp. 332–3, 338.

shown indifference to his country. His heart belonged to it, and the image that he carried of it was the "soul of his conversation." He never spoke of it but to wish for its prosperity. He cherished the order that it housed because of his own inner feeling for virtue. If, Mercier commented, "those celebrated by Bossuet, Fléchier, Mascaron, and Neuville in *their* funeral orations had had a hundredth part of the virtues of that cultivator, I might be able to forgive their futile, pompous eloquence."[135]

MERCIER AND ROUSSEAU: VITALIST AND CONTRACTUAL CONCEPTIONS OF POLITICAL SOCIETY

The sense of the phrase *honnêtes gens* that Mercier used in his description of rural simplicity was quite different from the one that, for example, Montesquieu, in his *The Spirit of Laws*, gave to the idea of honour as the principle underlying the hierarchical system of government that he called monarchy. It was, equally obviously, entirely different from anything that could be associated with salon society. But, however simplistic it may now seem, the intellectual origins of the picture of a good society that Mercier presented were actually quite complicated. The usual explanation is that these had a great deal to do with the moral and political thought of Jean-Jacques Rousseau.[136] In some sense they did. In different ways, both took morality to be the real cement of society. "It is useless to draw a distinction between a nation's morals and the objects of its esteem," Rousseau wrote in the fourth book of his *Social Contract*, "for they all follow from the same principle and necessarily converge." That principle, he continued, was opinion. Once there were societies, Rousseau argued, it was opinion that decided that some things were honourable, while others were shameful.

> Among all the peoples of the world, not nature but opinion determines the choice of their pleasures. Reform men's opinions and their morals will be purified by themselves. One always loves what is fine or what is taken to be so. But it is in this judgement that one can be mistaken, which is why it is this judgement that has to be regulated. Whoever judges morals judges honour, and whoever judges honour takes opinion as his law.[137]

In a superficial sense, the assertion was quite compatible with Mercier's vision of the future, even if, unlike the focus on the eighteenth-century

---

[135] Mercier, *L'An deux mille quatre cent quarante quatre*, ed. Trousson, ch. 43, pp. 416–9.

[136] See, for example, Norman Hampson, *Will and Circumstance* (London, Duckworth, 1983), and Rufi, "Le rêve laïque de Louis-Sébastien Mercier."

[137] Rousseau, *The Social Contract*, bk. 4, ch. 7, in Jean-Jacques Rousseau, *The Social Contract and Other Later Political Writings*, ed. Victor Gourevitch (Cambridge, CUP, 1997), p. 141.

emergence of the public sphere of recent historiography, Rousseau took the power of public opinion to be a feature of the ancient, not the modern, world.[138] In a simple rural society, there was no reason to think that hard work, family life, and shared pleasures would not be real objects of esteem. Rousseau himself was quite willing to endorse a picture of rural virtue that was very similar to the one that Mercier described when the Swiss physician Johann Caspar Hirzel sent him a copy of his *Socrate rustique* (The Rural Socrates), a very successful treatise in favour of decentralised agricultural improvement that had been published in 1761. Hirzel's "philosophical peasant," Kleinjogg (or Kliyogg), may well have served as Mercier's model, and Rousseau had no hesitation in expressing his approval. "However astonishing the hero of your book may be," he informed Hirzel in 1764, "to my eyes, its author is no less so. There are many more respectable peasants than scholars who respect them and dare to say so. Happy the country where there are Kliyoggs who cultivate the land and Hirzels who cultivate letters."[139]

In a less superficial sense, however, Rousseau's and Mercier's positions were quite different. Picking out these differences, both here and in the next two chapters, may help to distinguish Rousseau's moral and political thought from that of his many critics or admirers, since the two could look quite similar. Although both Mercier and Rousseau were sometimes described as Cynics, the shared label actually conceals more than it reveals. Where Rousseau stressed the fact that, once there were societies, it was opinion, not nature, that determined the objects of people's esteem, Mercier argued something like the opposite. Even when there were societies, he wrote repeatedly, it was nature, not opinion, that supplied the real objects of people's esteem and, by extension, gave morality its content. Rousseau summarised his own view clearly and concisely in the *Letter to Christophe de Beaumont, Archbishop of Paris* that he published in 1763, soon after his *Emile* had been condemned by the church and banned by the parlement of Paris. Its starting point, he wrote, and the "fundamental principle of all

---

[138] See below, p. 161.

[139] Rousseau to Hirzel, 12 September 1764, in Jean-Jacques Rousseau, *Correspondance complète*, ed. R. A. Leigh, 52 vols. (Oxford: Voltaire Foundation, 1967–98), 22:46. On Hirzel and "the rural Socrates," see Paul H. Johnstone, "The Rural Socrates," *Journal of the History of Ideas* 5 (1944): 151–75; and, for the parallel interest that Hirzel's book aroused among the French Physiocrats, see Johann Caspar Hirzel, *Le Socrate rustique, ou description de la conduite économique et morale d'un paysan philosophe*, 2nd ed. (Zurich, 1764), with the published correspondence between Hirzel and the marquis de Mirabeau that it contains, and the commentary on it in August Oncken, *Der ältere Mirabeau und die ökonomische Gesellschaft in Bern* (Berne, 1886). Hirzel's description, and the correspondence with Mirabeau, were published in translation by Arthur Young in his *Rural Oeconomy* (London, 1770). For an indication of the enduring appeal of the "rural Socrates," see [Thomas Christie], *Miscellanies: Literary, Philosophical and Moral* (London, 1788), pp. 207–8.

morality" was that "man is naturally good."[140] This natural goodness was
not moral goodness but simple self-love, or *amour-de-soi*. It was, Rousseau
wrote, "the only passion which is born with man" and was "in itself indifferent either to good or evil." This, he emphasised, meant that he had been
able to explain the origins of evil in a way that was more coherent than the
Christian story of the Fall (explaining how someone truly innocent, like
Adam, could sin, Rousseau argued, either would have to be incoherent, or
would end up by turning God into the author of evil).[141] Since "none of
the vices imputed to the human heart are natural to it," he had, he wrote,
"traced, as it were, their genealogy" to show how "mankind are become
what they are," despite their original natural goodness. This "genealogy"
involved three stages or "states of mankind."[142] The first was presocial and
revolved around *amour-de-soi*. This feeling, Rousseau emphasised, was a
compound passion, with "two principles," not one.[143] The first applied to
the body and the satisfaction of its physical needs. But the second applied
to the mind and entailed a different type of pleasure from simple physical
well-being. The kind of intellectual satisfaction that this involved was the
product of what Rousseau called "the love of order," which, he continued,
"expanded and become active, is denominated conscience."[144] The first
principle gave rise to the purely self-centred feeling of pity, but the second
led to a more moral awareness of others.

   To Rousseau's critics, the claim was as implausible as his parallel claim
about the purely natural character of pity. "His love of order," wrote one
of them, "or notions of equity, acquired from social commerce, that the
injustices he has experienced, or seen committed, helped to engrave so
powerfully on his imagination made him believe that he, like every other
man, was born with a sentiment of justice. He is so predisposed towards
this opinion that, in his *Emile*, he attributes the anger and uncontrolled
bawling of an infant struck by its wet-nurse to this sentiment."[145] Rousseau himself was certainly prepared to keep an open mind about its apparently instinctive quality. As he wrote elsewhere in *Emile*, Condillac's claim
that instinct was a habit devoid of reflection, but acquired by reflecting,

[140] Jean-Jacques Rousseau, *An Expostulatory Letter from J. J. Rousseau, Citizen of Geneva, to Christopher de Beaumont, Archbishop of Paris* (London, 1763), p. 51.
[141] Rousseau, *Letter*, pp. 53–9.
[142] Rousseau, *Letter*, pp. 51, 52.
[143] Rousseau, *Letter*, p. 51.
[144] Rousseau, *Letter*, p. 51. For helpful insights into this aspect of Rousseau's thought, see Dieter Henrich, *Aesthetic Judgement and the Moral Image of the World* (Stanford, Stanford UP, 1992), pp. 12–6.
[145] [Claude-François-Xavier Millot], *Histoire philosophique de l'homme* (London, 1766), pp. 40–1. It is worth emphasising the fact, noted below, p. 126, that the word "sentiment," in both French and English eighteenth-century usage, could mean an opinion as much as a feeling.

seemed to imply that children reflected more than adults, a suggestion that looked less plausible than the more economical, if still mysterious, notion of instinct.[146] But Rousseau also made a connection between the initial feeling and a more developed taste for aesthetic order and symmetry. The character of Wolmar in his *Julie* was, accordingly, equipped with only one "active principle," namely, "a natural love of order," which, he said, "pleases me exactly like beautiful symmetry in a picture or like a piece well represented on the stage."[147] For Rousseau, the pleasure associated with regularity and proportion was the basis of the artificial passion of love (here to be distinguished from both *amour-de-soi* and *amour-propre*). But, as he also emphasised, love of order in the fullest sense of the term was a divine, not a human, capability, since it was "on such order that the connection and preservation of all things depend."[148] In human terms, the nearest approximation to God's love of order was an effect of true, rather than fashion-based, taste. "To consult only our most natural impressions," Rousseau wrote at the beginning of his famous description of the well-governed household established by Wolmar and Julie, "it seems that to despise luxury and parade, we need less of moderation than of taste." "Symmetry and regularity," he added, "are pleasing to everyone," but "vain pomp" could give "little pleasure to the spectator."[149] "A regularity in the disposal of things, every one of which is of real use, and all confined to the necessaries of life," he concluded in the same, rather Epicurean vein, "not only presents an agreeable prospect, but as it pleases the eye it at the same time gives content to the heart. For a man views them always in a pleasing light, as relating to, and sufficient for himself."[150]

The difficulty was to find a way to keep *amour-de-soi* and *amour de l'ordre* in balance. The human condition, as Rousseau described it, was the outcome of the double bind built into these two aspects of love. To get conscience going, there had to be some sort of knowledge of order. But to get knowledge

---

[146] Jean-Jacques Rousseau, *Emilius and Sophia*, 4 vols. (London, 1763), 3:76–7.

[147] Jean-Jacques Rousseau, *Eloisa, or a series of original letters collected and published by J. J. Rousseau*, 4 vols. (London, 1769), 3:148–9.

[148] Rousseau, *Emilius and Sophia*, 3:73. For Rousseau's analysis of the origins of love (meaning a love of preference, rather than either simple *amour-de-soi* or *amour-propre*), and why it was an artificial passion, see the passage from Pierre-Antoine Antonelle cited below, chapter 3, note 56.

[149] Rousseau, *Eloisa*, vol. 3, letter 136, p. 236, and, on the difference between "true taste" and fashion, p. 242.

[150] Rousseau, *Eloisa*, 3:237–8. The passage continues: "A small number of good-natured people, united by their mutual wants and reciprocal benevolence, concur by their different employments in promoting the same end; every one finding in his situation all that is requisite to contentment, and not desiring to change it, applies himself as if he thought to stay here all his life; the only ambition among them being that of properly discharging their respective duties."

going, there had to be relations and comparisons. Relations and comparisons, however, gave rise to *amour-propre*, which set the self and its interests alongside conscience and *amour-de-soi*. The two could coexist in a kind of precarious equilibrium for as long as common knowledge could override the individual self. So long, Rousseau wrote, "as the opposition of their interests is less than the concurrence of their knowledge, men are essentially good." This, he added, "is the second state of mankind" (and, it could be added, one that could accommodate either a rural Socrates or the arrangements established by Julie and Wolmar).[151] But, he continued, "when all the particular interests of individuals interfere and clash against each other, when self-love (*amour-de-soi*) is converted by its fermentation into self-interest (*amour-propre*), and opinion, by rendering the whole universe necessary to each individual, makes them all enemies from their birth and causes the happiness of one to depend on the misery of another," then conscience turned into "a mere empty word which mankind reciprocally make use of to deceive each other." This, Rousseau wrote, was humanity's "third and last state."[152] Dealing with it involved accepting what was now in place. Once there were selves and self-interests, the only available way out was a form of association that could make the public interest coincide with self-interest. As Rousseau put it,

> Then everyone pretends to sacrifice his own interest to that of his country, and all are liars. Not one is desirous of the public good, unless it coincides with his own; and hence this coincidence between the public and private good becomes the object of that true policy which alone is calculated to make men virtuous and happy.[153]

This was the idea underlying the *Social Contract*. What Rousseau called "true policy" in humanity's "third and last state" involved making the politics of public opinion the real foundation of political stability. Instead of setting the common good above the individual good, it made each individual's assessment of his own good the basis of the common good (and it really was his, not her, good, because, as Rousseau went on to explain, it was a contract among male household heads, underpinned by the nonpolitical, purely moral relationship between men and women, and the mixture of natural and artificial passions on which that relationship was based). Since individual preferences clashed, it made the multiple differences between these individual assessments the basis of the one good that was common to the whole, because it was the one that applied equally to all.

"In this inquiry," Rousseau wrote at the very beginning of the *Social Contract*, "I shall always try to unite what right permits with what interest

---

[151] Rousseau, *Letter*, p. 52.
[152] Rousseau, *Letter*, pp. 52–3.
[153] Rousseau, *Letter*, p. 53.

prescribes, so that justice and utility may not be disjoined."[154] The real possibility of this disjuncture was the reason why Rousseau rejected both Hobbes's and Montesquieu's ideas of representative sovereignty. On his terms, no externally supplied idea of the common good could take precedence over individuals' evaluations of their own good once individual survival needs had come to be locked into a social division of labour. As he pointed out at the beginning of his *Encyclopaedia* article on *Political Economy*, there was an essential difference between the government of a household and the government of a state. For the latter to be like the former, he wrote, "the father's talents, force, and all of his faculties would have to increase in proportion to the size of the family, and the soul of a powerful monarch would have to be in proportion to an ordinary man's soul as the extent of his empire is to a private person's inheritance."[155] Humans come in natural sizes. States, however, do not, but the resources at their disposal magnify human power enormously. The problem was less acute in what Rousseau called "the second state of mankind." Self-sufficient households could make resources available to rulers to settle disputes, or to deal with external security problems, and still meet their own needs, particularly if the resources in question were made up largely of time rather than money. But if households were interdependent, not independent, and if money, not time, was the prime social resource, then decisions affecting the availability of common resources might soon become a zero-sum game. The heads of independent households might be able to meet together, as Rousseau imagined, and make collective decisions without bringing their own interests into the picture, either openly or covertly. In this setting, each household head really could see and feel the needs of all its members, and, if individual survival needs were catered for solely by all the members of each household, the idea could be scaled up to fit societies based on independent households, like those headed by

[154] Rousseau, *The Social Contract*, ed. Gourevitch, bk. 1, p. 41. One of the clearest descriptions of Rousseau's examination of the relationship between individual survival needs and the general will remains Leo Strauss, "On the Interpretation of Rousseau," *Social Research* 14 (1947): 455–87 (especially 480–1). See, too, his "What Is Political Philosophy?" in Leo Strauss, *What Is Political Philosophy? and Other Studies* [1959] (Chicago, University of Chicago Press, 1988), pp. 9–56 (50–3), and, less clearly, *Natural Right and History* [1953] (Chicago, University of Chicago Press, 1965), pp. 252–94. The broader distinction between useful and speculative knowledge made by Strauss in the first of these publications can be compared to Henry Fuseli, *Remarks on the Writings and Conduct of J. J. Rousseau* (London, 1767), pp. 2–19. On how Rousseau thought that government, public opinion, and the feelings of honour and shame would work to keep the general will intact, see below, chapter 3.

[155] Jean-Jacques Rousseau, *Discours sur l'économie politique* [1755], in Jean-Jacques Rousseau, *Sur l'économie politique, Considérations sur le gouvernement de Pologne, Projet pour la Corse*, ed. Barbara de Negroni (Paris, Garnier Flammarion, 1990), pp. 57–8. For the translation, see Rousseau, *Social Contract*, ed. Gourevitch, p. 3.

Johann Caspar Hirzel's rural Socrates, or by Julie and Wolmar in the *Nouvelle Héloïse*.[156] These conditions still existed (in Corsica or the Swiss Valais, for example) but were not to be found in Rousseau's Geneva. Nor was Geneva like any of the ancient republics, because the existence of slavery among the ancients eliminated the tension between individual survival needs and the common good that, in the modern Swiss republic, was inescapable. "Among the Greeks," Rousseau wrote in the *Social Contract*, "all the people had to do, it did by itself; it was constantly assembled in the public square. It lived in a mild climate, it was not greedy, slaves did its work, its chief business was its freedom." But modern societies, like the republic of Geneva, no longer had "the same advantages." "Your harsher climates," Rousseau pointed out, "make for more needs, six months of the year you cannot stay out on the public square, your muted languages cannot make themselves heard in the open, you care more for your gain than your freedom, and you fear slavery less than you fear poverty."[157] In circumstances of social interdependence, either collective decision making or representative sovereignty would be self-defeating.

These circumstances amounted to what Rousseau called "humanity's third and last state." The absence of slavery, and a division of labour that encompassed the supply of basic necessities, meant that the survival needs of each household were now locked into all the rest. Under conditions of real social interdependence, old-style republican political decision making would simply entrench the interests of the rich and their dependents, while political representation in Hobbes's or Montesquieu's more modern sense (and it was Montesquieu's concept of representation that Rousseau singled out, by indicating that "the idea of representatives is modern: it comes to us from feudal government") would generate a potentially unmanageable tension between real individual needs and nominally shared common concerns.[158] This ruled out a representative sovereign, in either Hobbes's or Montesquieu's sense. But, like Hobbes, and, less forcefully, Montesquieu, Rousseau also rejected the idea of a purely natural, prepolitical, society.

[156] For a discussion, see Claire Pignol, "Rousseau et l'argent: autarcie et division du travail dans *La Nouvelle Héloïse*," *SVEC* 2004: 10, pp. 262–74.

[157] Rousseau, *Social Contract*, ed. Gourevitch, bk. 3, ch. 15, p. 115. On the Valais as an example of a household-based political community with a remote royal sovereign, see below, chapter 3.

[158] Rousseau, *Social Contract*, ed. Gourevitch, bk. 3, ch. 15, p. 114. On Montesquieu and the idea of representative succession, see Sonenscher, *Before the Deluge*, pp. 121–49. For an interesting discussion of the difficulties arising from Rousseau's criticism of the idea of representation, both for finding something that could give an independent definition of citizenship—once, as Rousseau recognised, the distinction between slaves and free men no longer applied—and for avoiding the potentially infinite regress involved in explaining how citizens could become citizens, see Germain Garnier, *De la propriété dans ses rapports avec le droit politique* (Paris, 1792), pp. 5–6.

This ruled out reverting to communal government. Sovereignty would have to remain, but, as Rousseau indicated, it would have to be represented solely by itself, and never by a real person or group of people. In this sense, Rousseau took the modern idea of sovereignty a step further, by making it more, not less, abstract, with the further implication that, to avoid the potential conflict between individual and collective claims upon social resources, political sovereignty would have to be democratic and republican by nature (government, it should be remembered, was another matter) to retain its legitimacy.

On Rousseau's terms, a free state was the only viable solution to social interdependence. Even then, however, social interdependence had to be roughly the same for all, which was why Rousseau began chapter 8 of book 3 of the *Social Contract* by endorsing what he called the "principle established by Montesquieu," that "freedom, not being the fruit of every clime, is not within the reach of every people." Only where each household produced enough of a surplus to make a positive contribution to the general surplus would it be possible to reconcile the rival claims on time, effort, or money required by being both a citizen and a subject. Time, Rousseau argued consistently, in the form of freely given or state-specified public service, was always preferable to paying taxes in money. And, to maintain the conditions underlying this socially differentiated collective effort, no household could exempt itself from decisions made by the sovereign. As, notoriously, Rousseau put it in chapter 8 of book 1 of the *Social Contract*, "whoever refuses to obey the general will shall be constrained to do so by the entire body: which means nothing other than that he shall be forced to be free."[159] With Rousseau, the idea of a republic became the real content of the generic term *res publica*, and, as Sieyès was to put it, every other correlate of the concept of sovereignty became a *ré-privé*, or the opposite of a *ré-publique*. The idea of the general will—the term that Rousseau took over both from earlier theological writing and, more immediately, either from Jean Barbeyrac's French translation of Samuel Pufendorf's *Law of Nature and Nations*, or from Montesquieu's *The Spirit of Laws*—helped to fill this practical and normative gap.[160] Since its authors were individuals,

[159] Rousseau, *Social Contract*, ed. Gourevitch, bk. 3, ch. 8, p. 100; bk. 1, ch. 8, p. 53.

[160] See Patrick Riley, *The General Will before Rousseau* (Princeton, Princeton UP, 1986), and, in more detail, Frederick Neuhouser, "Freedom, Dependence and the General Will," *Philosophical Review* 102 (1993): 363–95, and his "Rousseau on the Relation between Reason and Self-Love," *International Yearbook of German Idealism* 1 (2003): 221–39. For a helpful reassessment of the origins of the idea of the general will (which brings the phrase in Barbeyrac's translation of Pufendorf more fully into the picture), see Bruno Bernardi, *La fabrique des concepts. Recherches sur l'invention conceptuelle chez Rousseau* (Paris, Champion, 2006), pp. 393–434. The subject could be broadened in the light of Pufendorf's more directly theological use of the concept of the general will in his *The Divine Feudal Law: or Covenants*

its content had to come from each but had to apply to all, leaving no one better or worse off than he would have been before. Initially, Rousseau toyed with a chemical metaphor both to express the idea of a collective person, or *moi commun*, that this type of political association would entail and to capture the idea of a general will. Just as a chemical compound can be said to have properties that do not exist in any of its constituent parts, so, too, could the general will be described as something qualitatively different from the will of all, and more, therefore, than a simple aggregate. But the chemical metaphor was easier to use negatively, as a way of criticising the idea of a general society of mankind, than to use positively, because it remained vulnerable to the type of objection that Rousseau made privately towards Diderot's use of the idea of the general will in the latter's *Encyclopaedia* entry on Hobbes. Whatever it was, Rousseau argued against Diderot, a general will did not really have the properties of an organism, because an organism had a common set of sensory faculties that, at best, had no more than a metaphorical existence among real people.[161]

It was still, however, a kind of compound because, although it originated in each household head's assessment of his own interests, its content was based on comparison with the interests of all the rest, to see whether they still looked the same. Since, as Rousseau pointed out, each individual, under modern conditions, had more to fear from poverty than from slavery, the content of the general will would, minimally, have to fit that initial specification, and since assessments of relative wealth and poverty were not difficult to make, each household head could, accordingly, arrive independently at his own assessment of the general will, and decide how much better or worse-off its content was likely to leave him. Initially, the assessment would apply to the formation of political society itself, which was why the very first political decision would have to be unanimous, and why its outcome was the single, but collective, state person that Rousseau called the *moi commun*. Subsequently, however, individual assessments

---

with Mankind, Represented [1695], ed. Simone Zurbuchen (Indianapolis, Liberty Fund, 2002). On Sieyès's terminology, see Emmanuel-Joseph Sieyès, *Political Writings*, ed. Michael Sonenscher (Indianapolis, Hackett, 2003), p. xxi.

[161] On the chemical aspects of Rousseau's political thought, see particularly Bernardi, *La fabrique des concepts*, although it is not entirely clear whether Bernardi takes the chemical metaphor to be a foundational, or a transitional, aspect of Rousseau's political thought and, possibly, one of the reasons behind Rousseau's decision to abandon his *Institutions politiques*. On this aspect of the relationship between Rousseau and Diderot, see Alberto Postigliola, "De Malebranche à Rousseau: les apories de la volonté générale et la revanche du 'raisonneur violent,'" *Annales de la société Jean-Jacques Rousseau* 39 (1972–7): 123–38; and Robert Wokler, "The Influence of Diderot on the Political Theory of Rousseau," *Studies on Voltaire and the Eighteenth Century* 132 (1975): 55–111, and his *Rousseau on Society, Politics, Music and Language: An Historical Interpretation of His Early Writings* (New York, Garland Press, 1987).

could simply be aggregated, provided that they were not subject to any external influence. The numerical outcome could then be taken to indicate the one position at which every interest looked the same, because it would be the one point at which the same conditions applied equally to all. In these circumstances, majorities of different sizes, depending on the matter at hand, could be taken to be proxies for the general will. Government, public opinion, and the emotions of honour and shame would then have to keep its binding presence intact. But the idea of a *moi commun* was as difficult to understand then as it remains now. Intuitively, it appears to apply to the common identity assumed by the members of a choir, or a team, or, perhaps, a church. But it was harder, both in the light of Rousseau's own account of the sparse array of social capacities with which humans were naturally equipped, and of his rejection of representative sovereignty, to understand how it could be applied to the membership of a large territorial state unless the state in question also had a very complex federal structure, as he himself hinted, but never really showed, until the posthumous publication of his *Considerations on the Government of Poland*. The possibility that Rousseau was actually a "federalist" added to the ambiguities of his legacy, particularly in the embattled condition of the first French republic in 1793. As Rousseau himself acknowledged in his letter to Christophe de Beaumont, "I am now beginning to talk a strange language, as little understood by the majority of readers as by your Lordship."[162]

Mercier's language was rather less strange. But, despite its apparent simplicity, it relied on a range of quite complicated claims about the properties of human nature. These, in turn, made it easier to think of political society as a kind of organism. One indication of their provenance is the epigraph from Leibniz—"*le temps présent est gros de l'avenir*" (the present age is big with the future)—that Mercier chose to place at the beginning of his future-oriented satire, *L'an 2440*. If, in one sense, the epigraph may have been no more than a chance discovery of a particularly apt quotation from the posthumously published (1765) French edition of Leibniz's *New Essays on Human Understanding*, it is more likely to have been a real gesture towards a version of post-Leibnitzian natural and moral philosophy that Mercier seems to have found especially appealing. In a narrow sense, it was proper natural philosophy, or the mixture of biology, chemistry, and physics that could be found in the works of the Bernese natural philosopher

---

[162] Rousseau, *Letter*, p. 53. On the realisation that Rousseau might have been a "federalist," see the description of "ce système épouvantable de Rousseau concernant les difficultés de faire exercer la volonté générale sans l'esclavage, les confédérations, et la destruction des villes" that Mme Roland's lover, the Girondin deputy François-Nicolas-Léonard Buzot, was reported to have made during a conversation in the spring of 1793 (at least according to a pamphlet citing Mme Roland's own *Appel à l'impartiale postérité*). For this, see *De l'équilibre des trois pouvoirs, ou lettres au représentant du peuple Lanjuinais* (Paris, an III/1795), pp. 96–9.

Albrecht von Haller, his Genevan counterpart, Charles Bonnet, and Bonnet's Italian emulator, Lazzaro Spallanzani (Mercier, it is worth noting, was a significant cultural broker not only in French, Swiss, and German theatre criticism, but in natural and moral philosophy as well).[163] In a broader sense, however, it was also a mixture of psychology, moral theory, and theology that could be used to counter the more sceptical aspects of the moral and political thought of Voltaire, Montesquieu, and Rousseau, without, however, having to rely particularly closely on orthodox Christian dogma (Bonnet, it is worth remembering, was one of the many critics of Rousseau's second *Discourse*, writing, under the pseudonym of "Philopolis," to the *Mercure de France* in 1755 to argue that the historically contingent connotations of Rousseau's neologism "perfectibility" did not fit the providentially devised capacity for human improvement that, he argued, was built into natural society).[164] Just as the original Leibniz supplied a real alternative to the sceptical natural jurisprudence of Hobbes, Pufendorf, and Locke, so the posthumous Leibniz of the *New Essays on Human Understanding* offered something similar to nondogmatic critics of more recent French or British philosophy.[165]

---

[163] On Mercier's interest in Bonnet, Haller, and Spallanzani, see Louis-Sébastien Mercier, *Mon Bonnet de Nuit* [1784], trans. as *The Nightcap*, 2 vols. (London, 1785), 2:15–7, and the additions that he inserted into later editions of *L'an 2440*: see, for example, Louis-Sébastien Mercier, *Astraea's Return, or the Halcyon Days of France in the Year 2440* (London, 1797), ch. 47, pp. 274–9. More generally, see Hofer, "Mercier admirateur de l'Allemagne.", pp. 73–116, and Andreas Pfersmann, "Une 'gloire tudesque,'" in Jean-Claude Bonnet, ed., *Louis-Sébastien Mercier (1740–1814). Un hérétique en littérature* (Paris, Mercure de France, 1995), pp. 417–36. For a helpful examination of how Haller's physiology could be given a more vitalist inflection, see James L. Larson, "Vital Forces: Regulative Principles or Constitutive Agents? A Strategy in German Physiology, 1786–1801," *Isis* 70 (1979): 235–49. On Bonnet and Spallanzani, see, initially, John Bostock, *An Elementary System of Physiology* [1824], 3rd ed. (London, 1836), pp. 668–773; Bentley Glass, Owsei Temkin, and William L. Straus, eds., *Forerunners of Darwin 1745–1859* [1959] new ed. (Baltimore, Johns Hopkins UP, 1968), pp. 164–72; Jacques Roger, *Les sciences de la vie dans la pensée française du xviiie siècle* (Paris, Armand Colin, 1963), pp. 651–3, 712–31; Henry Harris, *The Birth of the Cell* (New Haven, Yale UP, 1999), pp. 56–9; and the works cited in note 171 below. It is worth noting, too, that in a number of essays on Leibniz, subsequently reprinted in Charles Bonnet, *Oeuvres d'histoire naturelle et de philosophie*, 18 vols. (Neuchâtel, 1779–83), 8:3–107, Bonnet made a point of highlighting the superiority of his own, spiritually and physically integrated system of natural philosophy over what he took to be Leibniz's earlier, parallel, system.

[164] See Florence Lotterie, *Progrès et perfectibilité: un dilemme des lumières françaises (1755–1814)*, SVEC 2006: 04, pp. 31–4.

[165] On Leibniz in his first incarnation, see Patrick Riley, *Leibniz' Universal Jurisprudence: Justice as the Charity of the Wise* (Cambridge, Mass., Harvard UP, 1996), and, on the rather underresearched subject of the posthumous Leibniz, W. H. Barber, *Leibniz in France from Arnauld to Voltaire: A Study in French Reactions to Leibnitzianism, 1670–1760* (Oxford, Clarendon Press, 1955); Catherine Wilson, "The Reception of Leibniz in the Eighteenth Century," in Nicholas Jolley, ed., *The Cambridge Companion to Leibniz* (Cambridge, CUP, 1995), pp. 442–74.

This aspect of the type of natural philosophy that Haller, Bonnet, and Spallanzani practised grew out of their investigations into the properties of matter, and living matter in particular. Careful examination of the mechanisms of transpiration in leaves, bone formation in animals, reflex action in muscles, or, more broadly, of the mysterious processes of generation itself, all pointed towards a way to connect the two types of simple, but internally complex and irreducibly distinct physical and spiritual entities that Leibniz had called monads. For Leibniz, the two types of entity existed in parallel. The correspondence between their respective states was the effect of a divinely created preestablished harmony (like two clocks, one spiritual, the other physical, keeping the same time).[166] But the kind of natural philosophy produced by Haller, Bonnet, and Spallanzani made the distinction less sharp. Muscles (like the heart) had an internal capacity for action and reaction (Haller called it irritability) that could not be explained in terms of matter and motion. Nerves, too, had a capacity (Haller called it sensibility) to respond to some stimuli, but to ignore others (the things that the eye saw seemed, remarkably, to have nothing at all to do with the things that the ear heard). With this type of starting point, it was possible to move beyond Leibniz's parallel universe towards the idea of something more integrated, and to do this by giving the old idea of a great chain of being a much fuller, but more spiritually oriented, content.[167] In the old version of the idea, humans stood at the top of the chain because they were embodied souls. In the new version, they occupied the same position because they were, as the German philosopher Johann Gottfried Herder put it, "ensouled bodies."[168]

Reformulating the mind-body problem in this way made it easier to put the spiritual ahead of the physical. Instead of having to explain how the body could house the soul, science now seemed to suggest that the soul shaped the body, and, by extension, that the soul's striving towards perfection was the key to understanding the graduated scale of increasingly complex forms of life visible in the great chain of being. It seemed to indicate that Leibniz's emphasis on the power of self-realisation, or

[166] For helpful introductions, see Donald Rutherford, "Metaphysics, the Late Period," in Jolley, *The Cambridge Companion to Leibniz*, pp. 124–75; the editors' introduction to Leibniz, *New Essays on Human Understanding* (Cambridge, CUP, 1981); and R. S. Woolhouse and Richard Francks, eds., *Leibniz's New System and Associated Contemporary Texts* (Oxford, OUP, 1997).

[167] See, classically, Arthur O. Lovejoy, *The Great Chain of Being* (Cambridge, Mass., Harvard UP, 1936), and, helpfully, Francis C. Haber, *The Age of the World: Moses to Darwin* (Baltimore, Johns Hopkins UP, 1959), pp. 137–59.

[168] Johann Gottfried Herder, "On the cognition and sensation of the human soul" [1778], in Herder, *Philosophical Writings*, ed. Michael N. Forster (Cambridge, CUP, 2002), pp. 187–243 (see pp. 206–7 for the phrase itself); see, too, p. 197, note 11: "Physiology is the shrine of the soul."

Figure 5. Charles Bonnet, Palengenesis, and the Great Chain of Being. From Charles Bonnet, *Oeuvres d'histoire naturelle et de philosophie*, quarto ed., 8 vols. (Neuchatel, 1779–83), 4:1.

self-expression, built into monads could be understood in more comprehensively developmental terms. Expressed crudely, the idea came to form the basis of Julien Offray de La Mettrie's *L'homme machine*, or *Man, a Machine* (which, to his discomfort, La Mettrie dedicated to Albrecht von Haller).[169] In a more sophisticated form, it lay behind Charles Bonnet's idea of palengenesis and the detailed description of the soul's creation of a hierarchy of ever more elaborate physiological structures in its rise towards the spiritual realm that Bonnet presented in his *Philosophical Palengenesis* (see figure 5). Mercier subscribed very strongly to this sort of natural philosophy (usually called vitalism) and, by extension, to the idea of an orderly ascent from the physical to the spiritual that it implied. It also, he argued, favoured the kind of fragmented style and powerful metaphorical imagery that he often used, because, he claimed, a laconic style could imitate the rapidity of thought and strike the more spiritually attuned faculty of the imagination more effectively than orderly prose or rhymed verse could do. This was one reason for Mercier's strong admiration of the English Anglican poet Edward Young's *Night Thoughts* and, particularly, of the prose French translation published by his friend Louis Le Tourneur, which, Mercier argued, captured the metaphorical power of

[169] For a recent discussion of La Mettrie's anti-Cartesian monism, see Eleni Filippaki, "La Mettrie on Descartes, Seneca, and the Happy Life," *SVEC* 2004: 10, pp. 249–72.

Young's description of a divinely ordered universe even more effectively than did Young's own blank verse.[170] At its most ambitious, this type of natural philosophy supplied the framework for the new, spiritualised version of physiognomy developed by the Swiss theologian Johann Caspar Lavater. Mercier's moral theory was similar ("your metaphysics are mine, just as your moral theory is mine," he informed Lavater in 1785).[171] Their joint insights, he wrote, were the reason why it was advisable to study the physiognomies of candidates for public office when they were asleep, rather than awake, and were thus unable to disguise their real moral characters. As with Lavater, human life was part of a vast, increasingly spiritual, hierarchy of beings, running from apparently inert matter to purely spiritual creatures, like angels. "You criticise, weak and audacious mortal, the plan of the universe," Mercier wrote, grandly. "Wait until thy being

[170] On Mercier, Le Tourneur, and Young, see Fernand Baldensperger, "Young et ses nuits en France," in his *Etudes d'histoire littéraire*, 4 vols. (Paris, 1907–39), 1:55–109 (74–7). For the best modern edition of Young's poem, see *Edward Young's "Night Thoughts"*, ed. Stephen Cornford (Cambridge, CUP, 1989).

[171] See the two letters from Mercier to Lavater of 27 April and 30 August 1785 published by Hofer, "Mercier admirateur de l'Allemagne," p. 81, and, more generally, Fernand Baldensperger, "Les théories de Lavater dans la littérature française," in his *Etudes d'histoire littéraire*, 2:51–91. On Lavater, see, helpfully, Robert E. Norton, *The Beautiful Soul: Aesthetic Morality in the Eighteenth Century* (Ithaca, Cornell UP, 1995), especially ch. 5; David Bindman, *Ape to Apollo: Aesthetics and the Idea of Race in the Eighteenth Century* (London, Reaktion Books, 2002), pp. 92–123; and, on some of the more tendentious features of his thought, Jeffrey Freedman, *A Poisoned Chalice* (Princeton, Princeton UP, 2002). On the broader subject of the relationship between eighteenth-century natural philosophy and moral theory, see, most notably, John P. Wright, "Metaphysics and Physiology: Mind, Body and the Animal Economy in Eighteenth-Century Scotland," in M. A. Stewart, ed., *Studies in the Philosophy of the Scottish Enlightenment* (Oxford, OUP, 1990), pp. 251–301; John P. Wright, "Locke, Willis and the Seventeenth-Century Epicurean Soul," in Margaret J. Osler, ed., *Atoms, Pneuma, and Tranquillity: Epicurean and Stoic Themes in European Thought* (Cambridge, CUP, 1991), pp. 239–58; John P. Wright, "Materialism and the Life Soul in Eighteenth-Century Scottish Physiology," in Paul Wood, ed., *The Scottish Enlightenment: Essays in Reinterpretation* (Rochester, N.Y., University of Rochester Press, 2000), pp. 177–97; John P. Wright and Paul Potter, eds., *Psyche and Soma: Physicians and Metaphysicians on the Mind-Body Problem from Antiquity to the Enlightenment* (Oxford, OUP, 2000). More generally, see Jacques Roger, "The Living World," in G. S. Rousseau and Roy Porter, eds., *The Ferment of Knowledge: Studies in the Historiography of Eighteenth-Century Science* (Cambridge, CUP, 1980), pp. 255–83; Elizabeth A. Williams, *The Physical and the Moral: Anthropology, Physiology and Philosophical Medicine in France, 1750–1850* (Cambridge, CUP, 1994); Alan Richardson, *British Romanticism and the Science of the Mind* (Cambridge, CUP, 2001); Thomas Ahnert, "The Soul, Natural Religion and Moral Philosophy in the Scottish Enlightenment," in James G. Buickerood, ed., *Eighteenth-Century Thought*, vol. 2 (New York, AMS Press, 2004), pp. 233–53; Peter Hans Reill, *Vitalizing Nature in the Enlightenment* (Berkeley and Los Angeles, University of California Press, 2005). On La Mettrie, and his medically inspired "materialism" (a word he publicly endorsed), see Ann Thomson, *Materialism and Society in the Mid-Eighteenth Century: La Mettrie's "Discours Préliminaire"* (Geneva, Droz, 1981), pp. 215, 217, 236.

CHAPTER TWO

is unfolded and that it passes all the necessary degrees to form it into the state to which it aspires."[172]

One reason for the very wide appeal of this kind of "sensuous idealism," as it has been called, was that it supplied a way to explain individual human personality (and its survival after death) without, on the one hand, having to endorse orthodox Christian dogma, but without, on the other, having to subscribe to Rousseau's highly historically contingent account of the sources of the self.[173] Instead of the "genealogy" that Rousseau began to set out in his *Discourse on the Origin of Inequality*, and went on to develop in several of his later works, human personality could simply be taken as a physiologically, but also spiritually, generated given. This, somewhat later in his career, seems to have been the main reason why Mercier responded to Kant's philosophy with such enthusiasm. Like many of Kant's less analytically proficient admirers, he dropped the critical part of Kant's critical philosophy and highlighted its focus on moral autonomy. "It is horrifying to see the repeated efforts that have been made to turn *conscience* and the *moral instinct* into accidents," Mercier wrote in an outline of Kant's philosophy that he presented to the French Institute in 1802 (here, his immediate target was *idéologie*, and the type of moral philosophy that he associated with Condillac and his followers). "Morality is the highest point of our nature, and its primordial sentiments, inherent in human nature, exist by virtue of the synthetic unity of the I (*Moi*)."[174] From this perspective, Kant

---

[172] Mercier, *The Nightcap*, 2:17. I owe the point about Mercier's advice to study the physiognomies of candidates for public office when they were asleep to Richard Wrigley, "Genre Painting with Italy in Mind," in Philip Conisbee, ed., *French Genre Painting in the Eighteenth Century* (Washington D.C., National Gallery of Art, 2007), pp. 245–55 (246).

[173] On the phrase, see Marion Heinz, *Sensualistischer Idealismus. Untersuchungen zur Erkenntnistheorie und Metaphysik des jungen Herder (1763–1778)* (Hamburg, Felix Meiner, 1994); Manfred Baum, "Herder's Essay on Being," in Kurt Mueller-Vollmer, ed., *Herder Today* (Berlin and New York, Walter de Gruyter, 1990), pp. 126–37. More generally, see Wulf Koepke, ed., *Johann Gottfried Herder: Academic Disciplines and the Pursuit of Knowledge* (Columbia, S.C., Camden House, 1996); John H. Zammito, *Kant, Herder and the Birth of Anthropology* (Chicago, University of Chicago Press, 2002), and, still interestingly, Alexander Gottfried Friedrich Gode von Aesch, *Natural Science in German Romanticism* (New York, Columbia UP, 1941). On some of the problems involved in thinking about the idea of resurrection, see Lucia Dacome, "Resurrecting by Numbers in Eighteenth-Century England," *Past & Present* 193 (2006): 73–110; and, for a bibliographically rich example of this type of Christian speculation on these subjects (where angels were a probable solution to Rousseau's conundrum about the origin of language), see the "Thoughts on the Origin of Human Knowledge, and on the Antiquity of the World," in [Christie], *Miscellanies*, pp. 233–326. Christie was a friend of Tom Paine and a correspondent of, among others, Pierre-Louis Roederer: see Ann Thomson, "Thomas Christie, Paine et la révolution française," in Bernard Vincent, ed., *Thomas Paine, ou la république sans frontières* (Nancy, Presses Universitaires de Nancy, 1993), pp. 17–32.

[174] *Magasin Encyclopédique*, issue 2 (1802):, 79–80, printed in Hofer, "Mercier admirateur de l'Allemagne," p. 105. On Mercier's membership of the institute, see S. A. Leterrier,

could be fitted quite easily into an already well-established framework. As the Genevan natural philosopher Charles Bonnet put it in his *Essai de psychologie* (An Essay on Psychology) of 1755, "the soul has several ideas so essentially present to it, that it is from the sentiment of the relationship between its present state and its antecedent states, that *personality* follows (*que découle la personnalité*)."[175] With this as a basis, it was easier to think about individual character and its manifold social settings without having to follow all the steps involved in their construction that Rousseau had laid out. The framework that it supplied lent itself readily to the kind of variegated picture of individuality, social diversity, and collective urban life that was the real accomplishment of Mercier's most enduringly successful work, the *Tableau de Paris* of 1781.

As has been indicated, this way of thinking about individual personality, and the power of mind over matter that it seemed to entail, played a major part in generating the late eighteenth-century interest in mesmerism. It also made it easier to shift the focus of attention in thinking about human nature from sociability to culture. One indication of this shift was the new meaning acquired by the word "anthropology." Instead of its original meaning as a mistaken (all-too-human) idea of God, it came, by the last quarter of the eighteenth century, to mean the study of mankind, as, with rather fewer spiritual connotations, it still does.[176] As another practitioner of the mixture of natural and moral philosophy that could be found in Bonnet or Spallanzani put it in 1778, anthropology was "that important branch of philosophical science" that "teaches us to know man's origins,

"Mercier à l'Institut," in Jean-Claude Bonnet, ed., *Louis-Sébastien Mercier (1740–1814). Un hérétique en littérature* (Paris, Mercure de France, 1995), pp. 295–326.

[175] Charles Bonnet, *Essai de psychologie* (London, 1755), p. 133. On this aspect of Bonnet's thought, see Alberto Postigliola, "Montesquieu e Bonnet: la controversia sul concetto di legge," in Paolo Casini, ed., *La Politica della Ragione* (Bologna, Il Mulino, 1978), pp. 43–69; John C. O'Neal, *The Authority of Experience: Sensationist Theory in the French Enlightenment* (University Park, Pennsylvania State UP, 1996), pp. 61–82; Roselyne Rey, "La partie, le tout et l'individu: science et philosophie dans l'oeuvre de Charles Bonnet," in Marino Buscaglia, René Sigrist, Jacques Trembley, and Jean Wüest. eds., *Charles Bonnet, savant et philosophe (1720–1793)*, *Mémoires de la société de physique et d'histoire naturelle de Genève* 47 (1994): 61–75; Raymond Savioz, *La Philosophie de Charles Bonnet de Genève* (Paris, Vrin, 1948); Serge Nicolas, " 'Sur la réminiscence': un manuscrit inédit de Charles Bonnet," *Corpus. Revue de philosophie* 29 (1995): 165–221, and his introduction to the recent edition of Bonnet's *Essai de psychologie*, ed. Serge Nicolas (Paris, L'Harmattan, 2006).

[176] On this shift in meaning, see Robert Wokler, "Anthropology and Conjectural History in the Enlightenment," in Christopher Fox, Roy Porter, and Robert Wokler, eds., *Inventing Human Science: Eighteenth-Century Domains* (Berkeley and Los Angeles, University of California Press, 1995), pp. 31–52. On the older sense, see Nicole, *Traité*, 1:240: "il suffit de dire que les anthropologies auxquelles se réduit Spanhemius pour défendre ses sentiments vont plus loin que celles du père Malebranche." (I have modernised the spelling).

the various states through which he passes, his qualities or affections, faculties or actions, in order to deduce from these a knowledge of his nature, his relationships, his destiny, and of the rules to which he should conform so that he can meet them in an appropriate way."[177] In a related sense, the word "sentiment" came to mean something more than an opinion or judgement, as it also still sometimes does. As the English periodical *The Looker-On* put it, sentiment had now become "a word of modern origin" that, as another writer put it, referred to "finer feelings" and "tenderer moral nerves."[178] But if physiology removed much of the need to explain how humans might have acquired these capacities, it also raised a new set of questions about the relationship between culture and politics on the one hand, and between culture and the arts on the other.

These, however, now looked more tractable. If humans were simply a more physiologically finely tuned, and therefore more highly spiritual, version of life, then many of the moral and political problems that Rousseau had raised about how individuals could be fully themselves in a common social setting seemed to be more easily surmountable. The way out did not have to look quite like the intensely self-contained political society that Rousseau continued to emphasise right up to his posthumously published *Considerations on the Government of Poland* ("At twenty," he wrote, "a Pole should not be just another man; he should be

[177] Jean-Baptiste-René Robinet, *Dictionnaire universel des sciences morale, économique, politique et diplomatique, ou Bibliothèque de l'homme d'état et du citoyen*, 30 vols. (London, 1772–83), 5 (1778): 333. The outlines of the new content of "anthropology," Robinet wrote, were to be found in Bonnet's *Essai de psychologie*, Buffon's *Traité de l'homme*, Condillac's *Traité des sensations*, Helvetius's *De l'homme*, and the marquis de Gorini Corio's *Anthropologie*. Robinet was also the author of the anonymously published *De la nature* (Amsterdam, 1757) that, interestingly, was taken by one of its German readers to have been written by Haller's follower the Lausanne physician Samuel Tissot. On this, see Samuel-Auguste-André-David Tissot and Johann Georg Zimmermann, *Correspondance 1754–1797*, ed. Antoinette Emch-Dériaz (Geneva, Slatkine, 2007), pp. 221, 839–40. On Robinet's own spiritualised version of the great chain of being, see his *Considérations philosophiques de la gradation naturelle des formes de l'être, ou les essais de la nature qui apprend à faire l'homme* (Paris, 1768), and his description of the progressive embodiment of a world of invisible forms into physical forces, and their gradual ascent towards the possibility of "pure intelligences" (p. 9), in much the same way, he wrote, as Winckelmann had shown how ancient art had evolved out of the construction of irregular blocks, columns, and rectangles to become the ability to make limbs and heads (pp. 12–3). Jean-André Naigeon, in his *Théologie portative, ou dictionnaire abrégé de la Religion chrétienne* (London, 1768), could still define anthropology (dismissively) as "a manner of expression used by sacred writers" that assumed that "the spirit governing the universe" had "eyes, hands, passions, wickedness, and malice" (p. 44).

[178] Susie I. Tucker, *Protean Shape: A Study in Eighteenth-Century Vocabulary and Usage* (London, Athlone Press, 1967), pp. 247–8. For a full description of this change, see Dugald Stewart, "Locke on the Sources of Human Knowledge," in Dugald Stewart, *Philosophical Essays*, ed. Sir William Hamilton, 4th ed. (Edinburgh, 1855), p. 84, note e to ch. 4 (I am grateful to Istvan Hont for this reference).

a Pole").[179] It could, instead, look rather more like the kind of harmonious concord between individuals and communities, town and country, rich and poor, men and women, and rulers and ruled that Mercier set out in his *L'an 2440* (unsurprisingly, Mercier was also a strong admirer of the moral theory of Anthony Ashley Cooper, third earl of Shaftesbury, with its emphasis upon finding a way to establish a balance between what Shaftesbury had called a "self-system" and a "social-system," a balance that vitalist natural philosophy now made easier to envisage). This lowering of the scale of the kind of political requirements needed to give morality and justice a real social presence went along with a striking transformation in Rousseau's own public image. Among Rousseau's own intellectual contemporaries, it was quite common to describe Rousseau as either as a Cynic or an extreme moral relativist, or to pair him with Thomas Hobbes. Thus, in his philosophical novel *Fabius and Cato* of 1774 (reissued in French translation in 1790 as "a complete refutation of the principles prevailing in the National Assembly"), the Swiss natural philosopher Albrecht von Haller turned Rousseau into a reincarnation of the Greek academic sceptic Carneades (the archetype, since the publication of Hugo Grotius's *Laws of War and Peace* in 1625, of the moral relativism that modern, Grotian, natural jurisprudence was designed to supersede).[180] "Hobbes's book, the *Leviathan*, provided him with part of his ideas," wrote Voltaire's friend the marquis de Saint Lambert, "and those are the most reasonable."[181] But, by the time the next generation came to intellectual maturity, the Rousseau-Hobbes pairing had been almost entirely forgotten; when it did resurface during the period of the French Revolution, it did so in ways that were often nearer to Mercier's idea of a moral community than to Rousseau's own, more morally disenchanted vision of politics.[182]

The differences and similarities were set out in Mercier's *De Jean-Jacques Rousseau, considéré comme l'un des premiers auteurs de la révolution* (On Jean-Jacques Rousseau Considered as One of the First Authors of the Revolution), which he published in June 1791. By then, events in France had reached the first of several major political turning points, so that Mercier's large pamphlet was written to influence the direction of future policy. Its

---

[179] Jean-Jacques Rousseau, *Considerations on the Government of Poland*, in Rousseau, *The Social Contract*, ed. Gourevitch, p. 189.

[180] B. L., R202 (23), *Fragment d'un roman philosophique du célèbre Haller sur les principes d'un bon gouvernement* (n.p., 1790), p. 1. Generally, see G. de Reynold, "J. J. Rousseau et la Suisse," *Annales de la société Jean-Jacques Rousseau* 8 (1912): 161–204.

[181] Jean-François, marquis de Saint Lambert, *Oeuvres philosophiques*, 5 vols. (Paris, an IX), vol. 1, "Discours préliminaire," pp. 38–9. More generally, see Mark Hulliung, *The Autocritique of Enlightenment: Rousseau and the Philosophes* (Cambridge, Mass., Harvard UP, 1994), and Raymond Trousson, *Jean-Jacques Rousseau jugé par ses contemporains* (Paris, Champion, 2000).

[182] See below, chapter 6.

starting point was the vitalist conception of society that separated his moral and political thought from Rousseau's. "The social contract," he wrote, "obscured by so many vague terms, renews itself naturally and materially every day; it binds the members of society because it exists independently of political laws."[183] As he put it elsewhere, "human societies are a species of *polyp* which live in all their parts."[184] This vitalist-based conception of society allowed him to avoid Rousseau's radical individualism and, at the same time, to make a far stronger endorsement of democracy than Rousseau himself had ever been willing to make. While Rousseau's *Discourse on the Origin of Inequality* was simply "a satire on polished society" (which, Mercier added, meant that society required more, not less, polish), the "only legitimate constitution" for a political society was the one "called a *democratic* state."[185] From Mercier's perspective, vitalist physiology allowed the two to go together seamlessly (and, as will be shown at the beginning of the next chapter, also allowed "industry" and "luxury" to complement one another). Since individual personality and social integration could be explained in largely nonpolitical terms, politics was mainly a matter of removing the obstacles to social harmony. These certainly included all the causes of inequality that Rousseau had singled out, but the way to remove them went far beyond anything that Rousseau suggested. Mercier highlighted three. The first, he wrote, was "the constituting power" (Mercier borrowed the term from the abbé Sieyès).[186] The second was right to insurrection, "that means" he wrote "recognised by the *Creator*, who gave man strength, just as he gave claws to animals to repel their enemies."[187] As Mercier went to some lengths to emphasise, this had been one of the major themes of all his publications ever since the appearance of *L'an 2440* in 1771. Together, the combination of democratic sovereignty and the

---

[183] Mercier, *De Jean-Jacques Rousseau*, pp. 72–3. The whole passage reads, "Le contrat social qu'on obscurcit sous tant de mots vagues, se renouvelle naturellement et matériellement chaque jour; elle lie les membres de la société, car elle existe indépendamment des loix politiques; elle réagit contre la force oppressive; le pouvoir législatif est visiblement infus dans tous les citoyens; et que la nation soit assemblée, qu'elle ne le soit pas, elle exerce toujours la souveraineté, parce que, comme la mer, elle rejette hors de son sein tout ce qui lui est étranger ou nuisible." For commentary on this work, see Roger Barny, *L'éclatement révolutionnaire du rousseauisme* (Paris, 1988), pp. 53–75; James Swenson, *On Jean-Jacques Rousseau Considered as One of the First Authors of the Revolution* (Stanford, Stanford UP, 2000), and the judicious review by Jean Starobinski, "Rousseau and Revolution," *New York Review of Books* 49, no. 7 (25 April 2002).

[184] Mercier, *Fragments of Politics and History*, 1:132.

[185] Mercier, *De Jean-Jacques Rousseau*, pp. 18, note 1, 55–6.

[186] Mercier, *De Jean-Jacques Rousseau*, p. 58. On Sieyès's concept of a "constituting power," see, in particular, his *Views of the Executive Means available to the Representatives of France in 1789*, trans. Michael Sonenscher, in Sieyès, *Political Writings*, ed. Sonenscher (Indianapolis, Hackett, 2003), p. 34, and his *What Is the Third Estate?* in the same volume, p. 136.

[187] Mercier, *De Jean-Jacques Rousseau*, pp. 60–1, and note 2; 127–8, and note.

ultimate threat of insurrection supplied a framework for a much simpler system of government than Rousseau had ever envisaged. In substance, it was not significantly different from the model that Mercier had outlined two decades earlier.

The third of the resources that Mercier singled out was a real novelty. This was the modern system of public credit. Rousseau, Mercier noted, "whose severe morality" made him the "enemy" of "*capitalists, financiers, and bankers*," did not have a monetary theory. He had, therefore, not been able to see how money, the naturally available means for "freeing land from its sterility, trade from its confines, and workers of every kind from their fatal idleness," could be supplemented by the additional monetary and financial resources generated by public credit. This "science, new in so many regards," Mercier now argued, was one of the keys to future prosperity and political stability.[188] Here, he had no hesitation in looking back favourably to the early eighteenth century and the system that had then been established by the Scottish financier John Law. Had Law been in the position of his more recent counterpart Jacques Necker (France's very recent director general of finance), Mercier wrote, "you would have seen the great man correct his plans, set himself all at once at the head of the revolution, and march majestically towards immortality."[189] The assertion followed on from a striking claim about public credit that Mercier had made in 1787. If, he wrote then, a state was able to maintain the credit of an artificial currency (*une monnaie factice*), "it would no longer have need for taxes or finance." But, he continued, for this to be possible, "the state would first have to be isolated." If this were the case, then the artificial currency could perform all the functions of metallic money more efficiently and, since the source of the money supply would now be entirely domestic, there would be no need to rely on exports, particularly the export of subsistence goods, to acquire metal currency. The result would be a virtuous circle, in which the artificial currency would "fertilise land that is susceptible to prodigious increase," and, "on this marvellous hypothesis," both the state and the individual would be winners. The "secret" was to find a way "to isolate a kingdom."[190] A dozen or so years later, the same idea emerged in Johann Gottlieb Fichte's *Der Geschlossene Handelsstaat* (The Closed Commercial State). For Mercier, as for many of his political allies in the summer of 1791, modern public finance looked like the way to make Rousseau's politics more readily applicable to the real world.

Another year was to pass before the combination came to be associated with the figure of the *sans-culotte*. Contrary to his later suggestion, Mercier

---

[188] Mercier, *De Jean-Jacques Rousseau*, pp. 79–81, note 1.
[189] Mercier, *De Jean-Jacques Rousseau*, p. 81, note 1.
[190] Mercier, *Notions claires*, 2:347–8.

was not, in fact, the first person to make the association. As will be shown later, the real author of the neologism was actually another satirist, Antoine-Joseph Gorsas. Unlike Mercier, Gorsas made no secret of his knowledge of the salon society joke about breeches and, in the winter of 1791–2, proceeded to use it to give the word *sans-culotte* the meaning it has now. In one sense, the question of authorship (if that is the right word) and its relationship to the original joke may not seem to matter. Like a popular song, the name *sans-culotte* simply caught on. But in another sense, knowing more about both the original joke and the authorship of the neologism may make it easier to explain not only why it caught on, but what it managed to catch. Here, the combination of the physical and the spiritual that was so marked a feature of Mercier's many works has a particular significance, not so much for what it might have implied about social division or civil war, but for what it assumed about social stability and political harmony. The kind of neo-Leibnitzian natural philosophy from which the vitalist combination of the physical and the spiritual derived made it easier to move away from some of the assumptions about social polarity that the comte de Tressan described, with Plato and his purple carpets standing for polish, civility, and salon society on the one hand, and the Cynic philosopher Diogenes of Sinope standing for filth, brutality, and gross indecency on the other. The joke made sense in that context. But the joke about the joke made sense in a different type of context. If, on the one hand, it did not have to rely for its point on the sorts of argument about human nature, the passions of the soul, the arts, and fashion with which Voltaire or Montesquieu could be identified (although Mercier, like James Rutledge and Antoine-Joseph Gorsas, argued that Montesquieu was actually a covert satirist of this type of claim about luxury and monarchy), it also did not have to rely on Rousseau's controversial claim that the state of society was a radically unnatural state for human beings. Nor did it have to involve endorsing all the details of the very specific set of political and institutional arrangements that Rousseau set out in his *Social Contract*.[191] It could, instead, be used to make a much more limited point about the real moral blemishes on what, in other respects, amounted to a healthy political society.

These were not difficult to identify. The real difficulty was to know how deep-seated they actually were. From one perspective, the perspective of the abbé Emmanuel-Joseph Sieyès and his followers, they were the price

---

[191] As Mercier put it, summing up his assessment of Montesquieu: "Il n'y a qu'une idée dominante, finement enveloppée, dans tout Montesquieu. Il démontre qu'il faut que la nation se gouverne elle-même, ou qu'elle soit gouvernée tyranniquement; mais il déguise toutes les conséquences de ce grand principe, en éludant à chaque page ce développement critique." Mercier, *Notions claires*, 1:81–2.

to be paid for a property-based world and the states, wars, and public debts that it housed. The way out, as a result, had to involve establishing a system of representative government that would be able to bypass property and all the many forms of inequality that it entailed.[192] But from another perspective, the moral blemishes in question were the more historically contingent products of recent French history, and of the labyrinthine structure of privilege that was its most glaringly obvious outcome. From this latter perspective, the problem was less deep-seated. Beneath the pathology of privilege, there was still a potentially robust society. The joke about the joke came out of this context. It caught on because it captured something obvious about the French monarchy, not only to those at the bottom of the social hierarchy, but to all those, however well-placed, who, for one reason or another, found themselves on the wrong side of the advantages that privilege could confer. "Almost everyone has had something to say about the causes of the Revolution," wrote one of the old regime's last insiders, the prince de Ligne, many years after it was all over.

> According to the devout, it happened because of reading the *Encyclopaedia*; to the knights of Saint-Louis, because M. de Saint-Germain maliciously disbanded the guards of the royal household; to the clergy, because the king did not have a distinguished confessor through whom he could govern; to the libertines, because he did not have a mistress; to the ministers, because he did not leave affairs entirely in their hands; to the young court nobles, because they were not given embassies; to devout noble ladies, because they were not able to intrigue as once they could; to less devout noble ladies, because the lovers they hoped to take had not been made marshals of France; to the parlements, because they had been told that they were not like the English parliament; to the lawyers, because, it was said, the constitution had often been changed; to the jewellers, because of the diamond necklace affair; to men of letters, because verse was not prized at court; to the traders, because there were not enough festivities and public holidays; to the peasants, because no one would get rid of the salt tax and labour service; to soldiers, because it was necessary to be a gentleman to be an army officer; and to the young pedants found in good society, because the queen did not like memoranda and projects and being bored.[193]

It may not have been the most sophisticated of analyses, but it does capture something of the context of the joke about the joke.

[192] See Sonenscher, *Before the Deluge*, pp. 67–94, 314–7.
[193] Charles-Joseph, prince de Ligne, *Mémoires et mélanges historiques et littéraires*, 5 vols. (Paris, 1827–9), 4:148–9. For a helpful recent overview of this type of approach to the origins of the French Revolution, see Munro Price, "The Court Nobility and the Origins of the French Revolution," in Hamish Scott and Brendan Simms, eds., *Cultures of Power in Europe during the Long Eighteenth Century* (Cambridge, CUP, 2007), pp. 269–88.

Here, the idea of helping one's friends and harming one's enemies that had once been associated with Mme de Tencin and her salon could begin to look less innocent. Interpreted less benignly, the same idea could be applied straightforwardly to court society, and to the way that, as Roederer and Condorcet were to describe it, the system of patronage centred on Versailles had engulfed the decentralised world of the salons (as well as, from a point of view that Mercier was not the only one to endorse, making an arsenal of favours available to an Austrian queen). Well before 1792, it was not particularly difficult to claim that it had. "In the past few years, the domination of certain societies" (here meaning salons), reported an anonymous pamphlet published in 1790, and entitled *Des principes et des causes de la révolution française* (On the Principles and Causes of the French Revolution), "turned Paris and, by ricochet effect, France, into an aristocratic state, governed by five or six women."[194] In this sense, the joke about the joke was also aimed at court society and the system of rewards and patronage that, it could be claimed, it had come to swallow up. It was a claim that could be applied to the legal and financial systems, to membership of one or other of the royal academies, or, particularly after the Ségur ordinance of 1781 and its controversial aftermath, to the army, and even to the royal ministry itself.[195] Sieyès's *Essay on Privileges*, written in the late autumn of 1788, was only one of hundreds of pamphlets published at that time to make the point, and, with his mastery of Rousseau's rhetorical skills, it was one that he made well. But where Sieyès's onslaught on privilege was intended to be the first step towards a more theoretically ambitious political transformation, it was also quite easy to attack privilege from a range of other, often quite different, points of view. By June 1792, it was one of these that came to be associated with the compound neologism *sans-culotte*. In the way that Mercier used it, the joke about the joke was a kind of satire on a satire, with a strong moral point. But beyond the position and character of France's queen, Marie Antoinette, and the questions about the uses and abuses of royal patronage with which she came to be associated—or even the vicious political conflict in which, by the autumn of 1791, she was now directly involved—lay a further range of questions that the joke could not really answer. The joke was a joke

---

[194] [Anon.], *Des principes et des causes de la révolution française* (London, 1790), p. 56.

[195] On this type of claim, heralding, according to its author, "the feudal dismemberment of the monarchy," see Philippe-Antoine Grouvelle, *De l'autorité de Montesquieu dans la révolution présente*, reprinted in the *Bibliothèque de l'homme public*, 12 vols. (Paris, 1790), 7:53–5. See also the complaint that "three hundred" noble families "hold all the places and all the dignities," while there were "over one hundred thousand noble families in France, all of whom, to varying degrees, have been merited by the fatherland": *Le disciple de Montesquieu à MM les députés aux états-généraux* (n.p., 1789), p. 33. On the Ségur ordinance and its aftermath, see below, chapter 5.

about distinction. In its first, salon-based, guise, it made fun of men of letters and their female patrons. In its second, more morally charged, guise, it made fun of patronage itself. In this guise, the clear alternative to patronage as a source of distinction was merit. But the questions that this left over were not only questions about how individual merit could coexist with economic and social inequality, but also about how, in the first place, and in the late eighteenth century, merit was best recognised and rewarded.

❦ 3 ❦

DIOGENES AND ROUSSEAU: MUSIC,
MORALITY, AND SOCIETY

DIOGENES AND THE AMBIGUITIES OF CYNIC PHILOSOPHY

T HE JOKE about breeches fitted into a way of thinking about human association that set decorum alongside justice, reciprocity alongside property, distinction alongside equality, fashion alongside price competition, equity alongside legality, *honnêteté* alongside charity, and "sublime" self-love alongside ordinary human selfishness. More fundamentally, it also fitted into the type of claim about the relationship between the passions and the arts that could be found in the works of Jean-Baptiste Dubos or Voltaire, and of how, in conjunction, they could keep morality alive. The story about the Cynic philosopher Diogenes of Sinope and Plato's purple carpets relied on a different set of evaluations of these subjects and, at the same time, formed a context for making a joke about the joke. It is not difficult to see where Rousseau would have been placed after the publication of his answer to the question posed by the Academy of Dijon in 1750 on "whether the restoration of the sciences and arts has contributed to the purification of morals." He reiterated his position in 1752 in the preface to his play *Narcissus*, his final reply to the storm of criticism that his first *Discourse* provoked. "All our writers," he wrote there, "regard the masterpiece of politics of our century to be the sciences, the arts, luxury, commerce, laws, and all the other ties, that, by tightening the bonds of society among men through self-interest, place them all in a position of mutual dependence, impose on them mutual needs and common interests, and oblige everyone to contribute to everyone's happiness in order to secure his own." These, he continued, were "fine ideas," but they were also "subject to a good many reservations." But the alternative that he began to indicate in the long note about the differences between "a savage" and "a European" that he inserted two paragraphs later in the same preface was not quite as straightforward as his indictment had been. "Among savages," he wrote, "self-interest speaks as insistently as it does among us, but it does not say the same things." The assertion fitted what, in his later *Letter to Christophe de Beaumont*, he called "the second state of mankind." Self-interest among savages gave rise to "love of society" and "care for their common defence," but did not entail "discussions about interests that divide them" or give rise to anything that "leads them to deceive one another," leaving "public esteem" as "the only good to which everyone aspires." In short, as Rousseau began to indicate, the alternative to "the masterpiece of politics of our century" involved a rather limited array of individual interests and relied heavily on the part played by public opinion in shaping social behaviour. With these in place, self-interest and the common interest would coincide, without requiring any further motivation to be supplied by benevolence or altruism. As Rousseau put it at the end of the note, "I say it reluctantly: the good man is he who has no need to deceive anyone, and the savage is that man."[1] On Rousseau's terms, he might have been good, but he had no need to be noble.

The ambiguity ran all the way through Rousseau's moral and political thought, and spilled over into the many responses to it. In one dimension, it raised a question about the human capacity for altruism and purely disinterested love. In another, it raised a question about the shape and direction of human history, and whether, as so many of Rousseau's critics claimed, his indictment of the sciences and the arts meant that social stability involved going backwards, not forwards. In a third, it raised a question about culture, and whether, beyond Rousseau's indictment of the way of life celebrated in Voltaire's *Man of the World*, there was still some kind of culture that was genuinely compatible with both individual and collective well-being. These, in turn, raised a further question about politics, and about the degree to which Rousseau's criticism of modernity's cultural hollowness could be extended to include the state-based systems of government that might, or might not, be its source. In one guise, states were vast political, military, and financial machines. In another, however, their ability to maintain the allegiance that gave them their power could make them look largely, or perhaps mainly, like ideas. One reason for the widespread interest in the type of natural philosophy that came to fascinate Louis-Sébastien Mercier was that it seemed to open up a different way of thinking about all these subjects, one in which Shaftesbury's terminology of self- and social-systems could be given a stronger, more immediately physiological, grounding. Here, since the idea of an "ensouled

---

[1] Jean-Jacques Rousseau, "Preface to *Narcissus*" [1752], in Jean-Jacques Rousseau, *The Discourses and Other Early Political Writings*, ed. Victor Gourevitch (Cambridge, CUP, 1997), pp. 100–1. I have modified the translation slightly in the light of the original text in Rousseau, *Oeuvres complètes*, ed. Bernard Gagnebin and Marcel Raymond, 5 vols. (Paris, Pléiade, 1959–95), 2:968–69. On this aspect of Rousseau's thought, see Nannerl O. Keohane, "'The Masterpiece of Policy in Our Century': Rousseau and the Morality of the Enlightenment," *Political Theory* 6 (1974): 457–84, and her *Philosophy and the State in France; From the Renaissance to the Enlightenment* (Princeton, Princeton UP, 1980). For Rousseau's later description of the compatibility between self-interest and the love of society as "the second state of mankind," see above, p. 114.

body" meant that the self was already in place, it was easier to emphasise the real convergence between what Shaftesbury had called the self- and social-systems, and, by doing so, to avoid the abyss at the end of the questions that Rousseau had raised. In another sense, however, it raised a further set of questions about the content of something other than what Rousseau had called "the masterpiece of politics of our century." However compelling his analytical demolition of "fashion's empire" might be, it still seemed to leave no more than self-interest as the cement of society. The difficulty was to identify some other source of human motivation in order to develop some other way of thinking about history, culture, and politics, to fill the gaps that Rousseau had prised open.

These difficulties and uncertainties were all visible in Mercier's view of the modern world. "Our age," he wrote,

> may be reproached for incredulity with regard to virtuous actions, and we are too much disposed to attribute the most splendid achievements to mean or interested motives. In France, especially, we are accustomed to consider all men as having the same pursuit and the same character. It is even alleged that there are only two classes in the world, the artful and the unfortunate.[2]

The remark could go along quite easily with the type of moralistic social commentary with which the figure of Diogenes was sometimes associated. Mercier was certainly familiar with the style. "The legislators of ancient republics," he wrote, "who, by way of distinction, particularly bestowed the title of virtues on a love of poverty and a contempt for riches would not be a little surprised, at this time, to see nations gaining an ascendancy by commerce alone." To the ancients, this "perfectly novel policy" would have looked like a formula for "certain destruction." "A book," he added, "such as that produced by M. Necker" (alluding to Jacques Necker's recently published *Of the Administration of Finances*) "would certainly have surprised Lycurgus," who "would certainly have been able to form no clear idea of an administration founded on more-or-less usurious calculation and whose whole stress was laid on money bags."[3]

But if Mercier was quite an adept exponent of the satirical rhetoric that was usually taken to be one of the hallmarks of a Cynic, he was never particularly impressed by Cynic claims about the value of extreme material simplicity. "Everyone," he wrote, "dreads abstinence, and Diogenes alone would fancy that, if well borne, it might equal abundance."[4] He made the remark in the context of a short essay on luxury, where he set out much of his ambivalence about the relationship between wealth and virtue. "Where

[2] Louis-Sébastien Mercier, *Fragments of Politics and History*, 2 vols. (London, 1795), 1:197–8.
[3] Mercier, *Fragments*, 1:106–7.
[4] Mercier, *Fragments*, 2:4.

is the boundary, the line of separation between laudable and pernicious luxury?" he began. "I am unable to mark it." While it was easy enough to disparage "frivolous pieces of furniture," "useless jewels," and "superfluous articles of decoration," it was not so easy to dismiss "wines" and "compound drinks" or "the fruits of the earth which, in the wild state, are poor and austere, but, by high cultivation, are brought to our tables independently of the seasons and acquire a plumpness and exquisite flavour." The indeterminacy of the word meant, Mercier wrote, that "I should at present be almost equally afraid either to abolish luxury or to give it a still greater extension." But, he continued, if "reproduction depends on luxury," if, "without this attraction, the hands of the cultivator would grow languid," and "if enchased watches be intimately connected with the procuring of food," then "let us tolerate trinkets that we may have cattle." The underlying causal mechanisms might be "incomprehensible," but it was still the case that "without luxury there would be no arts." "This reflection," Mercier commented, "reconciles us somewhat to the term. For music, poetry and dancing are delicious arts which touch the soul."[5]

Music, poetry, and dance threw a different light upon luxury. Under "another name," and "considered as a ferment of emulation diffused among men," what was now called luxury was better named "the spur of labour, the animator of empires and the comforter of the human race." In this new guise, it was to be found as much in republics as in monarchies. "London, Paris, Naples, Amsterdam, Vienna, Petersburg, Berne and Venice are," Mercier noted, "in this respect, nearly on a par." But there was still a loss as well as a gain. On the minus side, there was the loss of "the chivalric virtues." But on the plus side, there was "the knowledge proper to form a good legislation." Thus, Mercier concluded, "everything is compensated and a nation which no longer possesses the warlike virtues in the same vigour has at least for its support, maxims of policy which the administrators of nations will not dare to infringe."[6] There was little that was original in these observations, but this did not mean that the problems that Mercier highlighted really had been solved (or have yet).[7] The difficulty was to be sure that "everything" really had been compensated, and that "maxims of policy" really could make up for "chivalric virtues." More broadly, it

---

[5] Mercier, *Fragments*, 2:1–4.

[6] Mercier, *Fragments*, 2:5–10.

[7] See, for a wider view, Istvan Hont, "The Early Enlightenment Debate on Commerce and Luxury," in Mark Goldie and Robert Wokler, eds., *The Cambridge History of Eighteenth-Century Political Thought* (Cambridge, CUP, 2006), and his *Jealousy of Trade: International Competition and the Nation-State in Historical Perspective* (Cambridge, Mass., Belknap Press, 2005), pp. 115–9. On the context of Mercier's remarks, see Henry C. Clark, "Commerce, Sociability, and the Public Sphere: Morellet vs Pluquet on Luxury," *Eighteenth Century Life* 22 (1998): 83–103.

amounted to finding a way to make luxury less exclusive and more democratic, while still managing to avoid a more generalised version of the social conformism and moral shallowness that it seemed to bring in its wake.
From this perspective, there may well have been a consumer revolution in
the eighteenth century, but contemporary evaluations of its implications
were often less polarised between noble nostalgia for a bygone age and
retrospective bullishness about shopping's causal powers than the modern
historiographical phrase can sometimes suggest. Unsurprisingly, Mercier's
own views wavered, not only because of his suspicion of the professional
surrogate for "the warlike virtues" that standing armies had become, but
also because of his recognition that, even under another name, a more
socially inclusive version of luxury seemed to substitute the problem of
individual authenticity for the now apparently more tractable problem of
inequality.[8] The uncertainty lay at the heart of Mercier's long engagement
with Rousseau's moral and political thought. As has been said, both were
described at one time or another as Cynics, Rousseau for his *Discourse
on the Origin of Inequality*, and Mercier for his *Nouveau Paris*. The label
captured something of the tension between nature and culture that, in different ways, was a feature of the thought of both. It was one that applied
particularly strongly to the case of music, poetry, and dance because, as
Mercier acknowledged, the arts could all, in some sense, be said to be the
offspring of luxury. But they were also as much a part of his idea of a good
society as they were of the court at Versailles. The difficulty of deciding
how to disentangle the two, so that the culture produced by the arts could
be separated from the inequality and conformism associated with luxury,
raised a number of awkward questions not only about the line dividing
culture from nature, but, by extension, about whether the Cynic idea of
living in accordance with nature really did have a specifiable content.

A Cynic was someone who took the Socratic concern with self-knowledge
and self-sufficiency very literally (which was why, according to Plato,

---

[8] A "philosophical century," Mercier noted, would do well to eliminate the burgeoning
market for engravings and prints of original paintings or sculptures, and "the boring mo-
notony" they gave to houses, where "what is to be found in one has already been seen in the
other": Louis-Sébastien Mercier, *Tableau de Paris* [1781], ed. Jean-Claude Bonnet, Shelly
Charles, and Michel Schlupp, 2 vols. (Paris, Mercure de France, 1994), 2:841. I owe this to
Kristel Smentek, "Sex, Sentiment, and Speculation: The Market for Genre Prints on the Eve
of the French Revolution," in Philip Conisbee, ed., *French Genre Painting in the Eighteenth
Century* (Washington D.C., National Gallery of Art, 2007), pp. 221–43 (235–6). For strong
versions of the claim about the effects of the consumer revolution of the eighteenth century,
see, classically, Neil McKendrick, John Brewer, and J. H. Plumb, *The Birth of a Consumer
Society: The Commercialisation of Eighteenth-Century England* (London, Europa, 1982), and, in
this context, Colin Jones, "The Great Chain of Buying: Medical Advertisement, the Bourgeois Public Sphere, and the Origins of the French Revolution," *American Historical Review*
101 (1996): 13–40. For further literature, see the works listed in chapter 2, note 54, above.

Diogenes of Sinope was *Socrates out of his senses*, a phrase that the German writer Christoph Martin Wieland was to turn into the title of a philosophical tale, ostensibly about Diogenes, but also about Jean-Jacques Rousseau).[9] This, in the first instance, entailed an ostentatious disdain for material goods and comforts, and a determination to rely on as little as possible to meet the ordinary needs of everyday life (it is not clear whether Diogenes actually owned the famous tub, since his only relatively permanent possessions were usually said to be no more than a cloak, a staff, and a lamp).[10] There was, accordingly, no room in the Cynic way of life for the fine arts, or for the company of courtesans (which was why Diogenes was said to have defaced the statue of Phryne, the famous Greek courtesan used as a model for several statues of Venus, by engraving the words "this is the fruit of Greek corruption" at her feet). Living like a Cynic also implied an indifference to family ties, and local laws and customs. Just as, according to Diogenes, it was possible to learn any trade by repeated application, so it was also possible to learn the habits of virtue by repeated exposure to the physical hardship and psychological independence of the Cynic way of life. A Cynic could be at home anywhere because he (but also she) lived in accordance with nature (*physis*), rather than with law (*nomos*), and had no reason to feel any allegiance to the particular set of social arrangements and conventions that the law upheld. In this sense, the *cosmos*, not any particular polity, was a Cynic's natural home. Living in accordance with nature also meant, notoriously, that no shame could be

[9] This was the English title of the 1771 translation of Christoph Martin Wieland, *Sokrates mainomenos oder die Dialoge des Diogenes von Sinope* [1770]. The title of the French translation— *Socrate en délire, ou dialogues de Diogène de Synope* (Paris, 1772)—is the most graphic. On Cynicism, see Donald R. Dudley, *A History of Cynicism* [1937], 2nd ed. with a foreword and bibliography by Miriam Griffin (Bristol, Bristol Classical Press, 1998). A good recent guide to Cynic thought is R. Bracht Branham and Marie-Odile Goulet-Cazé, eds., *The Cynics: The Cynic Movement in Antiquity and Its Legacy* (Berkeley and Los Angeles, University of California Press, 1996) and, more specifically, the chapter in that collection (pp. 329–65) by Heinrich Niehues-Pröbsting entitled "Diogenes in the Enlightenment." On the uses to which the Diogenes figure was put in the period of the French Revolution, see Klaus Herding, "Diogenes als Bürgerheld," *Boreas* 5 (1982): 232–54, and his "Diogenes, Symbolic Hero of the French Revolution," in Michael Vovelle, ed., *L'image de la révolution française*, 5 vols. (Oxford, Pergamon Press, 1989), 3:2259–71. See, too, Antoine de Baecque, *The Body Politics: Corporeal Metaphor in Revolutionary France, 1770–1800* [1993] (Stanford, Stanford UP, 1997), pp. 238–9. On Wieland's tale, see W. Daniel Wilson, "Wieland's *Diogenes* and the Emancipation of the Critical Intellectual," in Hansjörg Schelle, ed., *Christoph Martin Wieland* (Tübingen, Max Niemeyer Verlag, 1984), pp. 149–79.

[10] The standard ancient sources on Diogenes of Sinope were (in the modern editions that I have used) Diogenes Laertius, *Les vies des plus illustres philosophes de l'antiquité*, 3 vols. (Amsterdam, 1758), 2:14–53; 3:251–2 (on Hipparchia), and Claudius Aelianus, *His Various Histories*, trans. Thomas Stanley (London, 1665), bk. 3, ch. 29 (on Diogenes and property); bk. 9, chs. 19, 34 (on Diogenes and wealth); bk. 14, ch. 33 (on Plato and Diogenes).

attached to any natural function (which was why Crates and Hipparchia could have sexual intercourse in public, just as Diogenes famously masturbated in the Athenian marketplace).[11] A Cynic life was, therefore, a dog's life (the same Greek word described them both) and involved living in much the same kind of way, with no property, family, or fixed abode, but with the important difference that a Cynic could never be owned (another of the charges that Diogenes levelled against Plato).[12] One question raised by this way of life was whether a Cynic was capable of love, and, if so, what kind of love this might be (this was the subject matter of Wieland's philosophical tale about Diogenes, and Rousseau).

Living like a Cynic also went along with using a particular rhetorical style. A Cynic was adept at satire, and the kind of satire that a Cynic practised was distinguished by its emphasis on parody. Cynic satire was intended to mock what was incoherent or taken for granted in prevailing norms and orthodox pieties by carrying them to grotesque or absurd extremes (like a dog, Cynic satire was intended to bite). This, rather dark, form of satire came, in the Renaissance, to be known as Menippean satire, a name derived from the Cynic Menippus (the ancient satirical poet Lucian was an admirer of Menippus, just as many of the poets or dramatists of the last, satire-suffused, years of the reign of Louis XV, including Nicolas-Joseph-Laurent Gilbert, were admirers or imitators of Lucian and Juvenal).[13] The multiple levels of parody and the jumble of different attitudes

[11] On these episodes, see François de Salignac de la Mothe Fénelon, *The Lives and Most Remarkable Maxims of the Ancient Philosophers* [1726] (London, 1726), pp. 197, 210, 226; Raymond Geuss, *Public Goods, Private Goods* (Princeton, Princeton UP, 2001), pp. 12–33. On cosmopolitanism, see John Moles, "Cynic Cosmopolitanism," in Bracht Branham and Goulet-Cazé, *The Cynics*, pp. 105–20, and, for an eighteenth-century characterisation of Diogenes as a "cosmopolitan," see the *Epitre à la Westphalie* by the comte de Bar, cited in the anonymous *Lettres sur les préjugés du siècle* (The Hague, 1760), p. 136.

[12] Claudius Aelianus, *Histories*, bk. 14, ch. 33. In seventeenth- and eighteenth-century engravings or paintings, Diogenes was often given a broad, full-toothed, smile, an appearance usually taken to denote brutishness. I owe this to Colin Jones and his research on teeth and smiles in eighteenth-century Paris, foreshadowed in his "The French Smile Revolution," *Cabinet* 17 (2005): 97–100.

[13] One of the most famous examples of the genre was the anonymously published *Satyre ménippée, de la vertu du Catholicon d'Espagne et de la tenue des Etats de Paris* (Tours, 1594), a satirical attack on the French Catholic League by the *politique* writers Nicolas Rapin, Jean Passerat, and Florent Chrestien, which continued to be reprinted until the second half of the eighteenth century. More generally, see Joel C. Relihan, "Menippus in Antiquity and the Renaissance," in Branham and Goulet-Cazé, *The Cynics*, pp. 265–93; Kirk Freudenberg, ed., *The Cambridge Companion to Roman Satire* (Cambridge, CUP, 2005); and Howard D. Weinbrot, *Menippean Satire Reconsidered: From Antiquity to the Eighteenth Century* (Baltimore, Johns Hopkins UP, 2006). For some initial approaches to satire in a French context, see Elisabeth Bourguinat, *Le siècle du persiflage 1734–1789* (Paris, Presses universitaires de France, 1998), and Antoine de Baecque, *Les éclats du rire. La culture des rieurs au xviiie siècle* (Paris, Calmann-Lévy, 2000).

that were features of Menippean satire relied on ignoring the usual uni-
ties of time, place, and action of conventional narrative, so that the same
subject could be presented from a number of different spatial, temporal,
or personal points of view (including some that were very remote, like
heaven, hell, or chaos, or simply nowhere, or *utopia*). Swift's *Tale of a Tub*,
Lawrence Sterne's *Tristram Shandy*, and Denis Diderot's *Jacques le fataliste
et son maître* all owed something to the resources of the genre. The mixture
of different narratives, arguments, and points of view produced by looking
at the inside from the outside in so many dissimilar ways (a dialogue of the
dead was another way of doing this) also lent itself to the kind of informal
and analytically loose type of philosophical discourse known more generally as the diatribe.[14] Cynic rhetoric relied on presenting orthodox social
conventions in surprising and unexpected ways and, by doing so, sought
to persuade its listeners (or, later, readers) to change their way of life very
radically by giving up most of the false, but largely unrecognised, beliefs
on which that way of life was based. "Only by making vice blush can one
force it to hide," wrote the author, or "Diogenes" as he styled himself, of
a pamphlet entitled *Le philosophe cynique* (The Cynic Philosopher) that was
published in 1771, and which was probably the source of the story about
Mme Geoffrin, the tailor's bill, and the supply of velvet breeches that
Jean-Jacques Routledge was to use five years later in his *Bureau d'esprit*.
(According to the pamphlet, the bill showed that in the space of two years
Mme Geoffrin had bought some four hundred pairs of breeches to give
to her protégés on New Year's Day, mainly, it suggested, because the
breeches were soon worn out as a result of their owners' having to sit
through the interminable sessions of her salon.)[15] Shaming vice, from this
point of view, would leave nature free of shame. The aim of this kind of
shock therapy was, as Diogenes was said to have put it, "to deface the currency" and break free from the common moral currency of the day.[16] In
this sense, the goal of Cynic philosophy was a kind of self-knowledge that
could be reached only by overturning all the details of the unquestioned
assumptions involved in everyday life.

   One example of the dilemmas to which this sort of self-knowledge
could lead can be found in Denis Diderot's *Rameau's Nephew*, the not entirely fictitious conversation that Diderot described as having taken place

---

[14] On the connection between dialogues of the dead and Menippean satire, see Frederick
M. Keener, *English Dialogues of the Dead: A Critical History, an Anthology, a Check List* (New
York, Columbia UP, 1973), pp. 9–12, 71, 92.

[15] [Charles Theveneau de Morande], *Le philosophe cynique, pour servir de suite aux anecdotes
scandaleuses de la cour de France* (London, 1771), pp. ix, 67, and note xv (on Mme Geoffrin and
her gifts). The story, as noted above, pp. 18–9, resurfaced in the 3 November 1777 issue of
the *Morning Post*, after Mme Geoffrin died.

[16] Diogenes Laertius, *Vies*, 2:49, and note 1.

between *lui* (Rameau's nephew) and *moi* (Diderot himself) in the gardens of the Palais Royal some time towards the end of the reign of Louis XV. It is important to remember, however, that Diderot's masterpiece first appeared in public in a German translation (by Goethe) only in 1805 and was not published in French until 1823 (the first manuscript-based edition appeared only in 1891). It was, however, an unusually vivid examination of the ambiguities of Cynic philosophy when it was applied to the moral and political concerns of the eighteenth century. It has also sometimes been taken to be Diderot's final verdict on Jean-Jacques Rousseau.[17] For the German philosopher Georg Friedrich Wilhelm Hegel, Diderot's dialogue epitomised *"pure culture,"* or the condition that arises when individuals come to see themselves as persons who can be distinguished both from their naturally individuated physical attributes and from the status given to them by an estate- or court-based social hierarchy (as in those in the tiny worlds of the German princely states), but who still cannot find a way to get round the general character of the norms associated with the occupational labels used to describe their putatively distinct individual attributes.[18] Calling someone a doctor, teacher, philosopher, or musician, for example, still fails to capture the personality of the individual in question. The nephew's breathtakingly shameless lucidity grew out of his insight into this condition. Since all the labels used to describe individuals who did similar sorts of things could refer indiscriminately to one person as much as another, individual survival was best achieved by serial simulation. This was not only a matter of playing a part, but also of playing the kind of part that made an individual look like a particularly authentic example of the activity or occupation in question. Since individual distinction was never simply a matter of an occupation and its norms, but of the occupational idiosyncrasies (or *idiotismes*) that its exponent displayed, so the accomplished life artist had to be a virtuoso performer of this sort of occupational idiosyncrasy in order to create the illusion of familiarity with its underlying norms. Simulating individuality meant using his (or her) skills of observation and imitation to create as many personifications of proficiency as successful survival

[17] On the Cynic dimension of the satire, see the helpful editorial introduction to Denis Diderot, *Le Neveu de Rameau*, ed. Jean Fabre (Geneva, Droz, 1950), and Jacques D'Hondt, "Le cynisme de Rameau," *Recherches sur Diderot et sur l'Encyclopédie* 36 (2004): 125–37. On Rousseau as its target, see, for example, Donal O'Gorman, *Diderot the Satirist* (Toronto, University of Toronto Press, 1971), especially pp. 136–84. For an interesting small example of how Diderot incorporated real individuals into his fictions, and his more abstract works, see R. L. Ritchie, "Le 'père Hoop' de Diderot: Essai d'identification," in Mary Williams and James A. Rothschild, eds., *A Miscellany of Studies in Romance Languages and Literatures* (Cambridge, Heffer, 1932), pp. 409–26.

[18] Georg Friedrich Wilhelm Hegel, *Phenomenology of Spirit* [1807], trans. A. V. Miller (Oxford, OUP, 1977), p. 316. For a parallel reading, see Herbert Dieckmann, "The Relationship between Diderot's *Satire I* and *Satire II*," *Romanic Review* 43 (1952): 12–26.

required. This, until the fatal moment when he had spoken the truth, was the art that Rameau's nephew had mastered. It was an art that matched Rousseau's description of the pathology of modern society and his claim that, once humans had acquired an ability to evaluate each other in terms of property, rank, wit, beauty, strength, skill, merit, or talents, "to be and to appear to be (*être et paraître*) became two entirely different things."[19] Rameau's nephew used that insight to make a real life out of illusion.

As Diderot himself emphasised in the final part of his dialogue, the nephew's insight was a kind of Cynic insight, one that chimed both with the style of neo-Roman satire and cultural criticism that flourished in the last years of the reign of Louis XV, and with the broader way of life of the wealthy patrons and cultured mercenaries who formed the nephew's social world. But, as Diderot also emphasised, it was an insight that was finally self-defeating. Cultural criticism (even, perhaps, in the hands of a Rousseau) could not be separated from the culture that gave it its life, which was why the modern incarnation of Diogenes really was Rameau's worldly nephew, and not a man who could live in a tub.[20] The point at which Cynic satire shaded into cynical hypocrisy was extremely fine, and this, in turn, made it hard to be sure whether Cynic morality was anything more than Cynic pride. It was a charge that could be applied quite readily to Rousseau. "I finally believe," noted the Basel magistrate Isaak Iselin in 1752, adverting to the story about Plato and his purple carpets, "that the good Rousseau is like the honest Diogenes. He tramples Plato's pride underfoot, but does so with even greater pride. He reveals himself to be a real hater of mankind (*Menschenfeind*)."[21] Hegel's verdict was the same, if not on Rousseau, then certainly on Cynic cultural criticism. "Finally," he wrote, "should the plain mind demand the dissolution of this whole world of perversion, it cannot demand of the *individual* that he remove himself from it, for even Diogenes in his tub is conditioned by it, and to make this demand of the individual is just what is reckoned to be bad, viz. to care for *himself qua* individual."[22] The individual solution pointed all the way back to the state of nature. The way out had to come from the side of culture,

[19] Jean-Jacques Rousseau, *Discourse on the Origin and the Foundations of Inequality among Men* [1755], in Rousseau, *The Discourses*, ed. Gourevitch, p. 170. (I have modified the translation slightly.)

[20] Denis Diderot, *Le Neveu de Rameau*, ed. Henri Coulet, in Denis Diderot, *Oeuvres complètes*, vol. 12 [of 23 so far published] (Paris, Hermann, 1989), pp. 192–3. On the differences between Diderot's work and that of other contemporary satirists, see what remains the best edition of *Le Neveu de Rameau*, namely, the one edited by Fabre, p. lxi.

[21] Isaak Iselin, *Pariser Tagebuch 1752*, ed. Ferdinand Schwarz, *Basler Jahrbuch* (Basel, 1923), pp. 136–7. I have followed the translation given by Béla Kapossy, *Iselin contra Rousseau: Sociable Patriotism and the History of Mankind* (Basel, Schwabe, 2006), p. 82.

[22] Hegel, *Phenomenology*, p. 319.

and from a further step up in the mechanisms of human association that, in a real sense, would make the skills of the life artist redundant. The details of Hegel's solution were very complicated (and had a great to do with God, as well as with property, the law, and the state), but the simpler message was clear. Once there was society, there was culture, and once there was culture, even a Cynic could not live in accordance with nature.

There was nothing particularly political about Cynic philosophy. In most respects, it was ostentatiously antipolitical. But the figure of Diogenes could still sometimes be identified with something republican. Thus, in the June 1792 issue of the monthly republican journal the *Chronique du mois* (the journal in whose next issue Louis-Sébastien Mercier published his justification of civil war), and under the heading "Diogenes Lives!" one of the leading members of the loose Parisian moral and political association known as the Cercle social, a man of letters named François-Xavier Lanthénas, presented the archetype of virtue as a Parisian market porter named Quatorze-oignons, or Fourteen-Onions.[23] Quatorze-oignons had almost no property. He slept in his large, wicker basket and sheltered from the elements under the arches of the central market. He was, in short, free because he had no durable ties and lived entirely independently. He was also a model of virtuous self-denial, who was always willing to share his modest possessions or help anyone who had fallen into misfortune. Nine months later, in March 1793, Lanthénas revisited these concerns in a compilation of his publications entitled *Bases fondamentales de l'instruction publique* (The Fundamental Bases of Public Instruction). In this later version, the modern incarnation of Diogenes was identified explicitly as the archetype of a *sans-culotte* (as well as an example of Stoic rather than Cynic virtue), and the model of the type of republican that Lanthénas claimed he had presented to "all of France" at a time when the monarchical constitution of 1791 still dominated political views.[24] By then, the point of turning the virtuous market porter Quatorze-oignons into a personification of a *sans-culotte* was largely to rescue the idea of the type of republic that Lanthénas envisaged from the real threat of the type of republic that he now associated with

---

[23] François-Xavier Lanthénas, "De l'influence de la liberté sur la santé, la morale et le Bonheur," *Chronique du mois*, June 1792, p. 85. For further information on Lanthénas's egalitarian concerns, see Claude Perroud, ed., *Lettres de Madame Roland*, 2 vols. (Paris, 1900–2), 2:688–708.

[24] "Je t'adjure ici, vrai SANS-CULOTTE que j'ai montré pour modèle à toute la France, dans un temps où une constitution monarchique royalisait encore presque toutes les âmes; je t'adjure, toi dont je célébrais alors la vertu stoïque, la vertu vraiment républicaine; apparais et prononcez, avec l'indépendance de ta vie et celle du tombeau": François-Xavier Lanthénas, *Bases fondamentales de l'instruction publique et de toute constitution libre, ou moyens de lier l'opinion publique, la morale, l'éducation, l'enseignement, l'instruction, les fêtes, la propagation des lumières, et le progrès de toutes les connaissances, au Gouvernement national républicain* [Paris, 1793], 2nd ed. (Paris, Vendémiaire an III), p. 367.

Robespierre and his increasingly powerful political support. What, in June 1792, had begun as an "ingenious emblem" was, by March 1793, part of an intensifying political struggle, which, in the very short term, was one that Lanthénas, like his Girondin political allies Jacques-Pierre Brissot, Jean-Marie Roland, Jerome Pétion, and Etienne Clavière, was to lose.

Despite this identification of the figure of Diogenes with a *sans-culotte*, the personification could still have quite different connotations, even after the Jacobin phase of the French Revolution. Thus, in the very first issue of the journal *Le Catholique*, which began to appear in 1826, Diogenes resurfaced as a rather unusual kind of royalist. The issue began with a dialogue between a "liberal" and a "philosopher," and its very first word—*Capucinade!* ("Monkery!"), uttered by the liberal—served to highlight the journal's provocative title and the liberal hostility that it was intended to arouse. But, according to the philosopher, the point of the provocation was that the predictable reaction was in need of revision. Monks were not the only individuals to have beards and wear cloaks. So, too, had Diogenes, and he had paid even less attention than a monk might do to how he actually looked. Philosophy, the philosopher continued, did not need "to be clothed according to the latest taste or follow a fashion freshly released from the hands of one of the capital's famous tailors, or have a box at the opera, or converse with ease and grace with our fine beauties." Its currency was wisdom, not fashion. This, the philosopher added surprisingly, was why Diderot, the liberal idol, was a real philosopher. Some of his works displayed "Cynicism in the grand style," one that was even "more original than Diogenes." Diderot's crudeness might be unforgivable, but his creative abilities remained undeniable. Just as St. Jerome could admire Aristophanes, so his modern Catholic counterparts could also admire Diderot. As with the Cynicism of Aristophanes, Diderot's Cynicism lay in "the power of the conception of his ideas." It was this that was the opposite of "vulgar commonplaces" (*la pensée du vulgaire*).[25] From the point of view of *Le Catholique*, Cynic shock therapy also applied to liberals.

Le Catholique was not a conventional royalist journal. Its editor, the self-styled baron d'Eckstein, was a fluent German-speaker and may, therefore, have known of Goethe's translation of *Rameau's Nephew* and, more particularly, of the use to which it was put by Hegel in his *Phenomenology of Spirit*, independently of the recently published original version.[26] Although

---

[25] *Le Catholique* 1 (Paris, 1826), *Préface en trois dialogues*, pp. vi–viii, x.

[26] On Eckstein (or "Baron Buddha" as he was sometimes known), see Louis Le Guillou, *Le "baron" d'Eckstein et ses contemporains. Correspondances avec un choix de ses articles* (Paris, Champion, 2003), which, somewhat regrettably, does not reprint any of his contributions to *Le Catholique*. See, too, Kenneth R. Stunkel, "India and the Idea of a Primitive Revelation in French Neo-Catholic Thought," *Journal of Religious History* 8 (1974–5): 228–39, and Nicolas Burtin, *Un semeur d'idées au temps de la restauration: le baron d'Eckstein* (Paris, 1931).

Hegel's solution was quite different from Eckstein's more conventional royalism, the German philosopher's analysis of the moral and social problems of commercial society could be adapted to the broader onslaught on modernity and its "civilisation in miniature" that *Le Catholique* set out to undertake.[27] But if *Rameau's Nephew* may have been the reason for Eckstein's admiration of Diderot's "Cynicism in the grand style," one of Diderot's other works, the *Supplément au voyage de Bougainville* (A Supplement to Bougainville's Voyage), could still be described as "the true source of *sans-culotterie*," with a view of human nature that, it was claimed, was entirely consonant with the republican populism of two of the most notorious *sans-culotte* leaders of 1793–4, Anaxagoras Chaumette and Jacques-René Hébert, when it was first published posthumously in 1796 (one of the editors of the collection in which it appeared was the ubiquitous Jean-Baptiste-Antoine Suard).[28] The two works were, however, very similar. Both were parodies. The first was a parody of a Cynic. The second was a parody of the idea of living in accordance with nature. The problem with parody is that it can also be taken literally. It has been much easier to do this with the *Supplément au voyage de Bougainville* than with *Rameau's Nephew*, and it is still possible to find interpretations of the former work that, despite its dialogic structure, take it to be a more or less straightforward endorsement of the South Sea society that Diderot described.[29]

Closer inspection, as well as the dialogue's subtitle—"On the Inappropriateness of Attaching Moral Ideas to Certain Physical Acts That Do Not Admit of Them"—suggest something different. The people of Tahiti epitomised something like the opposite of the state of "pure culture" that Hegel was to associate with *Rameau's Nephew*. They lived in something more like a state of pure nature. In this version of the state of nature, however, they also lived in a society with a clear set of moral values, a visible social hierarchy, and a common system of rules of behaviour. But the peculiar property of this set of arrangements was that they were all physically determined.

[27] The phrase "civilisation in miniature" (also described as a "civilisation for egoists") can be found in [Anon.], "De l'influence des doctrines matérielles sur la civilisation moderne," *Le Catholique* 3 (Paris, 1826): 304. For a broad overview, see E. J. Hundert, "A Satire of Self-Disclosure: From Hegel through Rameau to the Augustans," *Journal of the History of Ideas* 47 (1986): 235–48.

[28] Jean-Baptiste-Antoine Suard and Simon-Jérôme Bourlet de Vauxcelles, eds., *Opuscules philosophiques et littéraires* (Paris, 1796), p. 271. See also the review of the collection in *Nouvelles politiques nationales et étrangères*, 2 Messidor an IV/16 July 1796, and the defence of Diderot in Jean-André Naigeon, *Mémoires historiques et philosophiques sur la vie et les ouvrages de D. Diderot* (Paris, 1821), p. 393.

[29] For an overview, see Peter Jimack, *Diderot. Supplément au Voyage de Bougainville* (London, Grant and Cutler, 1988). For an example of this type of naturalistic interpretation, see the introduction to Diderot, *Political Writings*, ed. Robert Wokler and John Hope Mason (Cambridge, CUP, 1992), p. xviii.

Instead, however, of being determined by age, strength, dexterity, agility, or some other form of physical prowess, they were determined solely by virility and fecundity (in an earlier work, the *Letters on the Blind* of 1749, Diderot had produced a similar sort of speculation about the relationship between the physical and the moral, writing that in a society of the blind, where primary judgements would depend upon touch, either men and women would live in common, or the most rigid rules of chastity would have to apply).[30] In Tahiti, respect and authority were given to the men who were the most virile lovers and the women who were the most fertile mothers. As Diderot went to some lengths to emphasise, it was this state of affairs that was most morally baffling to Bougainville and his companions, just as, in *Rameau's nephew*, *lui*'s insight into the nonindividuated nature of most apparently individual qualities baffled *moi*'s more conventional moral philosophy. It is not clear how far the two works were intended to form part of a larger collection of Cynic-style conversations on the related themes of culture and nature (and perhaps, by extension, on the dichotomous position that they occupied in Rousseau's thought).[31] But the satirical point of the latter work is not difficult to see. Living in accordance with nature could, quite easily, be described in purely physical terms, and could, equally easily, point to a purely physical version of morality. If this was the case, then, at least on Cynic premises, size may have mattered rather more than a Cynic might see.

JEAN-JACQUES ROUSSEAU AND THE POLITICS OF PUBLIC OPINION

Rousseau may or may not have been the target of Diderot's satirical speculations, but the unusually positive way in which he used the figure of Diogenes to symbolise the broader historical and moral transformation that he described in his *Discourse on the Origin of Inequality* of 1755 ("the reason why Diogenes could not find a man," he wrote, "was that he sought among his contemporaries a man of an earlier age") was something like an open invitation to an examination of the tension between nature and culture that so many of his critics went on to highlight (notoriously in

[30] For an overview of the questions that Diderot was addressing in that work, see Jessica Riskin, *Science in the Age of Sensibility* (Chicago, University of Chicago Press, 2002), pp. 23–62. For a parallel reading of this interpretation of the *Supplément*, see Katerina Deligiorgi, *Kant and the Culture of Enlightenment* (New York, State University of New York Press, 2005), pp. 26–8.

[31] It is usually accepted that the *Supplément* followed on from two other tales, *Ceci n'est pas un conte* and *Madame de la Carlière*. All three were circulated in Frederic Melchior Grimm's *Correspondance littéraire* in 1773 (see Jimack, *Diderot. Supplément*, pp. 11–2), one of the several dates suggested as the date of the composition of *Rameau's Nephew*.

the scene in which he appeared on all fours in Charles Palissot's satire, *Les philosophes*).[32] It was an invitation that was reiterated three years later with the publication in 1758 of the text that signalled Rousseau's public break with both Diderot and Parisian philosophical society, the *Lettre à M. d'Alembert sur les spectacles* (or *A Letter from M. Rousseau of Geneva to M. d'Alembert of Paris, Concerning the Effects of Theatrical Entertainments on the Manners of Mankind*, as the contemporary English translation was entitled). The range of subjects that Rousseau dealt with in the *Letter* make it something like a proxy for a great deal of his moral and political theory. Its best-known feature is its detailed description of what Rousseau took to be a good society and, by extension, of what something that might be called a natural culture would look like. "I remember in my younger days," he wrote, "to have beheld at Neufchatel, an object extremely agreeable, and perhaps the only one of its kind upon the face of the earth."[33] This, he continued, was "an entire mountain, covered with habitations, each of which forms the centre of the adjacent lands, so that these houses, at distances as equal as the fortunes of the proprietors, afford the numerous inhabitants of that mountain the tranquillity of retirement and the sweetness of society." The "fortunate peasants" of the region of Neufchatel paid no taxes or rents, and owned all the products of their land. But they were not simple cultivators. They employed all the hours that they could spare from tillage "in a thousand handicrafts, and in making a right use of that inventive genius with which nature has blessed them." In winter, in particular, they shut themselves away in their "neat wooden houses," and turned themselves to producing an astonishing array of homemade artefacts. "Never," Rousseau emphasised, "did carpenter, locksmith, glazier or turner by profession, enter that country; they all work for themselves, none for anybody else." The enforced winter leisure encouraged inventiveness, so that they also made "a thousand different instruments of steel, wood, paste-board, which they sell to foreigners, and a great many of which are sent as far as Paris, including those little wooden clocks, which have been seen there these past few years." They also made watches, including all the various tools usually produced by separate branches of the watchmaker's

---

[32] Jean-Jacques Rousseau, *A Discourse on the Origin of Inequality* [1755], trans. G.D.H. Cole, revised and augmented by J. H. Brumfitt and John C. Hall (London, J. M. Dent, 1973), p. 103.

[33] Jean-Jacques Rousseau, *A Letter from M. Rousseau of Geneva to M. d'Alembert of Paris, Concerning the Effects of Theatrical Entertainments on the Manners of Mankind* (London, 1759), p. 75. I have used this translation but have silently corrected it from the French when it strays too far from Rousseau's own vocabulary. For the original, see Jean-Jacques Rousseau, *Lettre à M. d'Alembert sur les spectacles*, ed. M. Fuchs (Geneva, Droz, 1948), p. 80. For background, see Madelyn Gutwirth, "The 'article Genève' Quarrel and the Reticence of French Enlightenment Discourse on Women in the Public Realm," *SVEC* 2001: 12, pp. 135–66.

business, so that even here they remained self-sufficient. Despite the scale
of their manufacturing industry, the inhabitants of the Neufchatel mountain slopes either consumed what they produced or exported it abroad, so
that domestic commercial transactions were based on reciprocal utility,
not necessity. Even this was not all. They made "cranes, loadstones, spectacles, pumps, barometers, camera obscuras," as well as tapestry, and all
the various implements that it required.

> They all understand something of designing; they know how to paint and to
> compute; most of them play upon the flute; and many are acquainted with
> the principles of music, and sing very justly. These arts are not taught them
> by masters, but delivered down to them by tradition. Of those whom I knew
> to understand music, one told me he had learnt it of his father, another of
> his aunt, another of his cousin, and some imagined they had learnt it without
> a master. One of their most frequent amusements is to sing psalms in four
> parts, with their wives and children, and you are amazed to find in those
> rustic huts, the strong and nervous harmony of Goudimel, so long forgotten
> by our learned artists.[34]

Looking back, Rousseau singled out this mixture of "finesse and simplicity" (his translator used the now archaic "cunning and simplicity"), which,
he added, "one would think almost incompatible," as the most memorable
feature of "those extraordinary people."[35] Joining culture to nature in this
setting was no oxymoron but something like a natural culture.

There was a point to the description that was more than simply didactic. In 1754, Rousseau was contemplating writing a history of the Valais,
a project to which he adverted again in 1756 in the context of a discussion
of the entry headed "Cretin" in the recently published third volume of
the *Encyclopaedia*. The article was, in fact, written by d'Alembert. As he
presented them, the physical deformities and moral imbecility exhibited
by the people of the Valais were a prime example of the real price to be
paid for self-sufficiency. With this as the background, Rousseau's description of the Valais in his *Letter to d'Alembert*, one that he repeated with
even more lyrical force in the famous twenty-third letter of his *Julie, or
the New Eloisa*, was a real settling of scores.[36] It was also a point-by-point
refutation of d'Alembert's assumption that isolation and cretinism were
simply two sides of the same coin. Everything about the culture of the

[34] Rousseau, *Letter*, pp. 76–7 (ed. Fuchs, pp. 81–2).

[35] Rousseau, *Letter*, p. 78 (ed. Fuchs, p. 83).

[36] For these factual details, see the editorial notes by Bernard Guyon to the edition of *Julie*
in Jean-Jacques Rousseau, *Oeuvres complètes*, ed. Bernard Gagnebin and Marcel Raymond,
vol. 2 (Paris, 1964), p. 1377, note to p. 60, and pp. 1386–90, note to p. 76. Surprisingly,
Guyon does not refer to Rousseau's description of the Valais in the *Letter to d'Alembert* in his
notes to Rousseau's later description in *Julie* (Rousseau, *Oeuvres complètes*, 2:76–84).

Valais that Rousseau described was designed to show that the opposite
was the case. The culture in question was based on a mixture of a rather
remote kind of equality (no one depended upon anyone else for any basic
necessity), social similarity (comparisons could not, therefore, become in-
vidious), technical independence (Rousseau was careful to highlight the
fact that even watchmakers made their own tools), and a flourishing export
trade (although Rousseau did not say so, the need to import materials for
making manufactured goods presumably blocked off the accumulation of
capital from trade surpluses). It was a real-life version of the second of
the three stages of human association that Rousseau was to describe in his
later *Letter to Christophe de Beaumont*, before individual interests came to
override common knowledge, and before comparisons, *amour-propre*, and
the wrong type of division of labour served to build inequality into the
social structure.[37]

As Rousseau repeatedly emphasised, the aim of a political society had
to be to try to re-create an artificial equivalent of this still largely natural
way of life, so that the physical and moral aspects of the two types of love
involved in *amour-de-soi* were still able to complement one another. Doing
so meant blocking desires and focusing on needs, and this, in turn, meant
establishing a set of social and political arrangements able to maintain a
clear distinction between the inner feeling of contentment involved in the
emotion of happiness, and the more volatile array of emotions involved
in the restless, and ultimately self-defeating, pursuit of pleasure.[38] Pleasure, Rousseau noted, was a sensation, while happiness was a sentiment, or
an opinion.[39] Enjoying the sensation entailed consuming its cause, while
having the feeling entailed indifference to the outside world. Given this
distinction, "the sweet sentiment of our existence" was all that was really
required to make life worth living. The model of the type of distinctly Epicurean emotional peace that happiness could entail was, Rousseau wrote
later, the two months that he had spent on the Island of Saint-Pierre in the
middle of Lake Bienne, near Geneva. There, he recalled, he had felt "self-
sufficient, like God," because, in this type of setting, "the soul can find a
resting-place secure enough to establish itself and concentrate its entire
being there, with no need to remember the past or reach into the future,
where time is nothing to it, where the present runs on indefinitely but this

---

[37] On the three stages of human association in Rousseau's thought, see above, pp. 112–4.

[38] For a helpful way into the distinction between happiness and pleasure in Rousseau's
thought, see Stephen G. Salkever, "Rousseau and the Concept of Happiness," *Polity* 11
(1978): 27–45. See, too, Victor Gourevitch, "Rousseau on Providence," in Todd Breyfogle,
ed., *Literary Imagination, Ancient and Modern* (Chicago, University of Chicago Press, 1999),
pp. 285–311 (especially pp. 293–5, 297–8).

[39] Jean-Jacques Rousseau, "Notes sur *De l'Esprit*," in Rousseau, *Oeuvres complètes*, 4:1121. See
also the fuller discussion of happiness in *Emile*, bk. 2, in Rousseau, *Oeuvres complètes*, 2:303–4.

duration goes unnoticed, with no sign of the passing of time, and no other feeling of deprivation or enjoyment, pleasure or pain, desire or fear than simply the feeling of existence, a feeling that fills our soul entirely, as long as this state lasts."[40] As one of Rousseau's critics commented, his idea of God was unusually Epicurean in character.[41]

The society of the Valais was one approximation of this ideal (Corsica, potentially, was another). In this sense, the arrangements that it housed were those that were most readily compatible with the feeling of equality that, Rousseau emphasised, was the hallmark of the general will.[42] As he noted, the community in the Valais was based on a system of individual property ownership that was fully compatible with commerce, but which was still entirely free of what, elsewhere in the *Letter*, he called "the impertinent prejudice of ranks and conditions."[43] Together, all these attributes amounted to something like the quintessence of what, in more recent times, has been called "flexible specialisation."[44] Two further features of the mixture of "finesse and simplicity" that Rousseau associated with the Valais were given particular prominence. The first was the strong emphasis that he placed on the value of the kind of matter-of-fact reasoning and practical, often technical, knowledge used by ordinary people in everyday life. It was the kind of knowledge that fitted Rousseau's lifelong interest in the works of the ancient natural historian Pliny, and not at all the type of

[40] Jean-Jacques Rousseau, *Reveries of a Solitary Walker* [1778], ed. and trans. Peter France (London, Penguin Books, 1979), pp. 88–9.

[41] Nathaniel Forster, *A Sermon Preached at the Visitation of the Rev. Dr. Moss, Archdeacon of Colchester at St. Peter's Colchester, May 20, 1765 and before the University of Oxford, May 24, 1767* (Oxford, 1767), p. 9, citing Rousseau's *Emile*: "la bonté est l'effet nécessaire d'une puissance sans borne et de l'amour de soi, essentiel à tout être qui sent. Celui qui peut tout étend, pour ainsi dire, son existence avec celle des êtres. Produire et conserver sont l'acte perpétuel de la puissance; elle n'agit point sur ce qui n'est pas; Dieu n'est pas le Dieu des morts, il ne pourrait être destructeur et méchant sans se nuire. Celui qui peut tout ne peut vouloir que ce qui est bien." For the passage, see Jean-Jacques Rousseau, *Emile, ou de l'éducation* [1762], ed. Michel Launay (Paris, Garnier Flammarion, 1966), bk. 4, p. 367.

[42] For helpful ways into this aspect of Rousseau's thought, but without quite the same emphasis on the connection between Rousseau's description of natural human attributes and his conception of political society as the way to re-create them in a collective setting, see Frederick Neuhouser, "Rousseau on the Relation between Reason and Self-Love," *International Yearbook of German Idealism* 1 (2003): 221–39; N.J.H. Dent, *Rousseau* (Oxford, Blackwell, 1988); and N.J.H. Dent and T. O'Hagan, "Rousseau on *Amour-Propre*," *Proceedings of the Aristotelian Society, Supplement* 72 (1998): 57–74. For a parallel discussion, without apparent awareness of this literature, see Géraldine Lepan, *Jean-Jacques Rousseau et le patriotisme* (Paris, Champion, 2007).

[43] Rousseau, *Letter*, pp. 22–3, note a (ed. Fuchs, pp. 30–1).

[44] See Charles Sabel and Jonathan Zeitlin, "Historical Alternatives to Mass Production," *Past & Present* 108 (1985): 133–76, and, more recently, Charles Sabel and Jonathan Zeitlin, *World of Possibilities: Flexibility and Mass Production in Western Industrialization* (Cambridge, CUP, 1997).

self-centredly speculative knowledge that he attacked in his first *Discourse* (according to one tradition, the mixture of astronomy, geography, history, chronology, medicine, botany, and agriculture contained in Pliny's *Natural History* was the reason why it had come to be called, notably by the seventeenth-century medical sceptic Guy Patin, *la bibliothèque des pauvres*, or "the library of the poor").[45] The second was the equally strong emphasis on the rather small number of emotions involved in this sort of practical, utility-oriented culture, and the threat to its stability that might be produced if a further array of emotions were allowed to be injected into established patterns of work, expenditure, and consumption. This, Rousseau argued, was exactly what erecting a theatre would do. Its first effect would be to supply an alternative source of diversion, and, by doing so, it would take the pleasure out of work. Once the people of the Valais had a theatre, "industry will no longer afford them the same leisure, nor the same inventions." Expenditure, however, would rise. Theatre tickets would, in the second place, have to be paid for, and more care and expense would go into dressing for theatrical occasions. Less work and more expenditure would, third, lead to higher prices for manufactured goods and the subsequent loss of export markets. In the fourth place, the theatre and its performers would also have to be maintained, and the lighting and road improvements that this entailed would require taxes. Finally, going to the theatre would lead to dressing for the sake of social appearance, by men as much as women, and this, Rousseau wrote, would signal the introduction of luxury. Luxury, in other words, occurred when it became desirable and feasible to appear to be what one was not (and ultimately, perhaps, to live like Rameau's nephew). By "exchanging reality for appearances," Rousseau warned, a people "who live at their ease, but who owe all their happiness to industry," would "hurry themselves to destruction from the moment that they seek to shine."[46]

---

[45] The description can be found in the editor's introduction to the French translation of Pliny, *Histoire naturelle*, 12 vols. (Paris, 1771–82), 1:xxv, but it was used earlier both by Guy Patin and by Daniel Georg Morhof in his frequently reprinted *Polyhistor* (Lubeck, 1688). On this translation, see Pierre Grosclaude, *Malesherbes, témoin et interprète de son temps* (Paris, Librairie Fischbacher, 1961), pp. 485–91, although it is not clear, in the light of the difference between the list of collaborators entrusted by Malesherbes with the translation (Grosclaude, p. 485, note 61) and those responsible for its final outcome (*Histoire naturelle*, 1:xix–xxi), whether it met with Malesherbes's approval, particularly given the strong editorial presence of one of the bugbears of Diderot's *Rameau's Nephew*, Louis Poinsinet de Sivry. Pliny, it is also worth noting, was a ferocious critic of luxury and the decorative arts: see the use to which he was put in the Huguenot minister David Durand's translation of his *Histoire naturelle de l'or et de l'argent* (London, 1729): "le crime le plus funeste à la société qui ait jamais été commis, c'est sans doute celui de cet homme vain qui s'avisa le premier de mettre de l'or autour de son doigt" (p. 4).

[46] Rousseau, *Letter*, pp. 80–1 (ed. Fuchs, pp. 83–5).

The same prognosis applied to Geneva. Here, Rousseau singled out the abbé Dubos by name to attack his argument about the relationship between the passions and the arts. In making it, Dubos had used the same opposition between *amour-de-soi* and *amour-propre* with which Rousseau is now more usually associated.[47] According to Dubos, the arts had the effect of neutralising the more divisive effects of *amour-propre* because of the purely artificial character of the passions that they produced, and the way that knowing that a passion was artificial made it possible to inject a level of self-control into what otherwise might have been brute feeling. Rousseau argued that exactly the opposite was the case. Artificial passions were intense and durable, with none of the intermittent rhythms of physical needs. Once awakened, they would become as much of a part of human nature as any purely physical need, and, unlike the need to eat, drink, or sleep, artificial passions had no physical limits because their power derived from memory and imagination, not from the more circumscribed properties of the senses themselves (Rousseau made this the key move in the argument of his *Essay on the Origin of Languages* by explaining how melody's existence in time gave it a double nature, and meant that it would work both as an immediate source of pleasure and, more powerfully, as an artificial sign of past or future feelings). On Rousseau's terms, natural emotions were weak and quickly forgotten, while artificial passions were strong and durable. This meant that Dubos's argument about the pleasure involved in knowing the artificial character of the painful emotions depicted on the stage could be turned against itself. The same mixture of feeling and knowing that, according to Dubos, favoured the kind of self-command involved in civility and decorum would, in fact, produce a flood of gratuitous emotion because the knowledge that the emotion in question had nothing to do with real life would simply magnify its intensity. The very ease with which a play could provoke the emotions was its real danger. Its cheap sentimentality, especially if it was any good, would create a kind of perpetual emotional rapture, where feeling everything would entail caring for nothing.[48]

The threat was more immediate to Geneva, Rousseau argued, than it was to the Valais. It was a real republic, not a small, rural community ruled from afar by a Prussian prince. Its population was also locked into a far more deep-seated division of labour than anything to be found in the Valais. In this sense, arrangements in Geneva corresponded to what, in his *Letter to Christophe de Beaumont*, Rousseau called "humanity's third, and

---

[47] See above, chapter 2.

[48] Rousseau, *Letter*, pp. 24–5 (ed. Fuchs, p. 33). "Thus the happiest impression of the very best tragedies is to reduce all the duties of humanity to a few barren affections; to make us extol our courage by commending that of others, our humanity by bewailing the miseries that we might relieve, and our charity by saying to a poor man, God bless you": p. 26 (ed. Fuchs, p. 34).

last state."[49] No Genevan could live in as self-sufficient a way as the psalm-singing peasant clockmakers of the mountain slopes adjoining Neufchatel. Geneva was rich and, although it did not have "those monstrous dispro-portions of fortunes that impoverish a whole country," it was still the case that "the affluence and ease of the greatest part is more owing to constant labour, to economy, and moderation, than to positive riches." Without "lands to support us," its people depended "entirely on our industry," supplying themselves with necessaries, "merely by denying themselves su-perfluities." "Go to the suburb of St Gervais," Rousseau wrote,

> and you imagine you see all the clockwork in Europe. Proceed thence to the Molard, and the low streets (*rues basses*), and you see such an appearance of wholesale trade, namely bales of goods in heaps, hogsheads scattered about confusedly, and the fragrant odour of spices, as to fancy yourself in a sea-port. At the pasture ground (*Pâquis*) and the springs (*Eaux-Vives*), the bustle and noise of the manufactures of printed calico and painted linen seem to transport you to Zurich.

Unlike the arcadia of the Valais, individual survival needs in Geneva were directly dependent on industry and trade. "Manual labour, employment of time, vigilance, and rigid parsimony," Rousseau concluded, "these are the treasures of the citizens of Geneva."[50]

Geneva was also a republic. Here, Rousseau simply followed Montes-quieu's typology of governments in arguing that establishing a theatre in the city would transform its nature. It would do so, he argued, by under-mining the broad social balance between the rich and the poor that was essential to the stability of the republic. "In monarchies," he wrote,

> where the several orders are intermediate between the prince and the common people, it may be very indifferent whether particular persons step from one to another, for as their place is soon supplied, this alteration does not break the chain. But in democracies, where the subjects and the sovereign are only the same men under different relations, as soon as the lesser number grow richer than the greater, the state must either be ruined or change its form.[51]

Rousseau's characterisation of Geneva as a democracy fitted the clear ana-lytical distinction between sovereignty and government that he made in the *Social Contract*. It meant not that Geneva had a democratic government, but that political sovereignty had to have a democratic foundation. "The

---

[49] See above, p. 114.

[50] Rousseau, *Letter*, pp. 123–4 (ed. Fuchs, pp. 124–5). On Geneva in Rousseau's political thought, see Herbert Lüthy, *Le passé présent. Combats d'idées de Calvin à Rousseau* (Monaco, Editions du Rocher, 1965), pp. 226–42.

[51] Rousseau, *Letter*, pp. 156–7 (ed. Fuchs, pp. 154–5).

democratical constitution hath been hitherto very superficially examined," Rousseau wrote in his *Letters Written from the Mountains* (a work designed to explain his differences with both sides in the conflict over the future of Geneva's system of government). "All those who have treated this subject were either ignorant of it, too little interested in it, or interested to misrepresent it. None them have sufficiently distinguished the sovereign from the government, the legislative power from the executive. There is no other mode of government in which these two powers are so separate, and in which they have been so much confounded, by the affectation of writers." Once the distinctions were recognised and established, Rousseau continued, the "democratical constitution is certainly the masterpiece of political art; but the more admirable the mechanism of it, the less are common eyes capable of inspecting into it."[52] Either sovereignty was democratic or it was illegitimate. It was a contractually based power to maintain public utility that had to rely upon every individual citizen's ability to feel the kind of equality produced by laws that applied to all, and, on the basis of this feeling, to be able to identify with a general will whose content could, with some governmental guidance, be recognised and internalised as their own. Government was another matter and, in the case of Geneva, consisted of a number of different decision-making councils. But if the city's government began to favour the interests of the rich because of their disproportionately large amount of wealth, either it would have to give up on democratic authorisation as its legitimating principle, and turn into a monarchy, or the state would simply die. Establishing a theatre, Rousseau argued, would bring that choice much nearer, because it would speed up the sequence of steps involved in bringing inequality to the tipping point that he had described in the *Discourse on the Origin of Inequality*. "What I know is this," Rousseau warned in the *Letter*, "that as things receive from time only a natural bias towards this inequality, and a successive progress towards its last term, it is highly imprudent to accelerate it by institutions tending that way."[53]

Rousseau, notoriously, singled out the new status of modern women as the most likely cause of this potentially accelerated slide towards the "last term." Here, the problem was not women's social exclusion but their all-too-visible social inclusion. "The ancients," Rousseau wrote, "in general had a great respect for the fair sex," which they usually expressed "by forbearing to expose them to the public eye," and in honouring "their modesty, by being silent on their other virtues."

> With us, on the contrary, the woman esteemed is she who makes the most racket and noise; who is most talked of; who is most seen in public; who

[52] Jean-Jacques Rousseau, *Letters Written from the Mountains*, in Rousseau, *Miscellaneous Works*, 4 vols. (Edinburgh, 1774), 3:226–7.

[53] Rousseau, *Letter*, p. 157 (ed. Fuchs, p. 155).

entertains most company at table; who gives herself the most insolent airs; who is the most positive; who pronounces and assigns the proper degrees and rewards to abilities, virtue and merit; in short, to whom the literati most humbly cringe for favour.[54]

It was almost a negative version of Marivaux's portrait of Mme de Tencin.[55] It is important to emphasise, however, that for Rousseau the problem was not really a problem about women but a problem about love, and about the way that the artificial passions that Dubos had praised had a basis in what, for Rousseau, was also an artificial passion. "Love," Rousseau wrote, "is the empire (*le règne*) of women. Here they must give the law because, in the order of nature, resistance belongs to them, and men cannot surmount this resistance, but at the expense of their liberty."[56] This, he continued, applied generally. "In all countries, and in all conditions of life, there is so strong and so natural a connection between the two sexes that the manners of the one ever determine those of the other." "If," he concluded, "you would therefore know the men, you must study the women." This, he added, was a "general maxim, and so far all the world will agree with me."[57] From this perspective, the maxim simply under-scored Voltaire's description of France in his 1732 tragedy *Zaïre* (Zara) as "that gay nation" where "men adore their wives, and woman's power draws reverence from a polished people's softness." Rousseau did not disagree with Voltaire's initial claim about women's power. But he disagreed very strongly with Voltaire's further claim that it entailed a way of life where women were "free without scandal, wise without restraint, their virtue due to nature, not to fear."[58] French-style familiarity between the

[54] Rousseau, *Letter*, pp. 58–9 (ed. Fuchs, pp. 64–5).

[55] See above, pp. 73–4.

[56] Rousseau, *Letter*, p. 57 (ed. Fuchs, p. 63). Rousseau's treatment of love baffled some of his warmest admirers. "Il est remarquable," wrote the Jacobin Pierre-Antoine Antonelle in an undated note, "que ce Jean-Jacques qui aime tant les sentiments innés, qui veut absolument que la conscience et la pudeur sont innées, se jette aussi dans l'excès contraire, et soutienne que l'amour de choix est une fantaisie entièrement factice, uniquement produite par l'application de ces idées de régularité et de proportion qui ne peuvent naître que des comparaisons insensibles et continuels que l'état social nous fait faire à notre insu, et que l'homme de la nature, toujours borné au simple discernement des sens, ne connaitrait pas les préférences": A. N., W 567ᵃ (Antonelle papers). For a more straightforward endorsement of Rousseau's characterisation of women's sexual power, see Henry Fuseli [Johann Heinrich Fuessli], *Remarks on the Writings and Conduct of J. J. Rousseau* (London, 1767), pp. 45–6: "A man has a character, and dares to do no more than what becomes a man; but women, they say have none, and therefore are never out of their sphere.... If a woman is bent on a purpose, swift as the thoughts of love, or lewdness, or fury, 'tis all one—she will throw herself headlong, and palpitate ecstasy on the bosom of perdition! She will break your heart, or have hers broken." See also pp. 36–7 for Fuseli's more famously erotic version of the same idea.

[57] Rousseau, *Letter*, p. 107 (ed. Fuchs, p. 109).

[58] Voltaire, *Zaïre* [1732], act 1, scene 1. I have used a London, 1791 translation, p. 1.

sexes, Rousseau argued, would produce exactly the opposite effect. This, he went on to claim, was because durably monogamous relationships were an effect of modesty, not familiarity.

Here, Rousseau parted company most decisively with Diogenes, and with the Cynic philosopher's notorious indifference to sex in the streets. According to the "new-fangled philosophy which has its rise and declension in the corner of a large city (Paris)," Rousseau wrote, "modesty has no foundation in nature; it is only a contrivance of society to secure the privileges of fathers and husbands and to maintain some order in families."

> Why should we blush at the wants we receive from nature? Why should we find reason to be ashamed of an act so indifferent in itself and so useful in its effects, as that which contributes to perpetuate the species? Since the desires are equal on both sides, why should there be any difference in disclosing them? Why should one sex be less ready than the other to comply with inclinations common to both? Why should man in this respect have any other laws than those of brutes?[59]

Shame about sex, Rousseau argued, was not an acquired contrivance. It was as natural as sleeping at night (when darkness helped to protect the helpless sleeper), or the solitude sought by a wounded animal (so that it could die in peace, beyond the range of the predators it could no longer resist). It was "the safeguard which nature has given to both sexes to protect them in a state of weakness and self-oblivion, when they are entirely at the mercy of the first comer."[60] It was also the bridge between the purely physical nature of the sexual act and the moral effects that it was able to produce. Sexual desire was undoubtedly as powerful in women as in men, but physical strength was another matter. If women were as physically able to satisfy their own desires as men certainly were, the effect of this reversal of roles would be to expose the very much more erratic character of male sexual prowess.

> The assailant might chance to pitch upon a time, when it would be impossible to succeed; the assailed would be let alone when it were proper for him to surrender, or continually harassed when he would be too weak to resist. In a word, power and will being ever at variance and never suffering the desires to be divided, love would no longer be the support, but the scourge and destroyer of nature.[61]

Modesty was nature's antidote to the physical differences between men and women, and more specifically to the difference between the continuous

[59] Rousseau, *Letter*, p. 108 (ed. Fuchs, p. 111).
[60] Rousseau, *Letter*, p. 109 (ed. Fuchs, p. 112).
[61] Rousseau, *Letter*, pp. 109–10 (ed. Fuchs, p. 112).

quality of female sexual availability, and the intermittent quality of male sexual capacity. As such, it was a natural obstacle to what might otherwise be potentially ferocious conflict among women for sexually potent males, and the real cause of durable monogamous relationships. Since women had to undergo the physical hardships of pregnancy and childbirth, it would be logical to expect them to be the more physically robust. But this, too, was to confuse cause and effect. As Rousseau put it bluntly, "to reduce them to this painful state, it was requisite that they should be so strong as not to yield without their own consent, and so weak, as to always have a pretext for yielding."[62] Modesty allowed them to do both. Even turtledoves, he added, seemed to know this.

The argument about the real social significance of women's modesty was still valid, Rousseau insisted, even if "the fear, modesty and shame by which their sex is so agreeably distinguished are human inventions."[63] As he had already pointed out, modesty and the way of life that it entailed were a feature of "all the ancient polished peoples." The modern condition of women was an effect of the decline of the Roman Empire. Then, "swarms of barbarians spread themselves like a torrent over Europe." Their wives were their camp followers. "This freedom," Rousseau observed (here, too, following Montesquieu), "a consequence in great measure of the natural coldness of northern climates, which require less reserve, introduced another way of life" into Europe. Chivalry reinforced the process, giving rise to "a notion of free converse between the sexes which was soon introduced into courts and great cities, where they pretend to most politeness; and this politeness, from the very nature of its progress, could not but degenerate at length into crudeness."[64] Women of quality, Rousseau commented puritanically, now had the manners of fishwives (*vivandières*).

Love, Rousseau emphasised, was a peculiarly powerful emotion. It did not "suit all men alike." It was "to be admitted rather as a supplement to virtuous affections than a virtuous affection itself." Although it was "commendable

---

[62] Rousseau, *Letter*, p. 113 (ed. Fuchs, p. 115).

[63] Rousseau, *Letter*, p. 115 (ed. Fuchs, p. 117).

[64] Rousseau, *Letter*, p. 118 (ed. Fuchs, pp. 119–20). Compare to the reply to Rousseau presented to the Manchester Literary and Philosophical Society in 1799 by the reverend George Walker: "This generous sympathy of our northern progenitors with the partners whom nature and God designed for them, happily coincided with the equal and liberal spirit of Christianity. And to these two powerful agents, which were nearly contemporary, we owe that wonderful revolution of social and moral sentiment which constitutes the distinction of later Europe. Woman has now been permitted to resume her proper rank in society, and to her we are greatly indebted for the present polish of ruder man; for that ease, propriety, grace, attention, and desire to please in the manner of every intercourse which offends the cynic eye of Rousseau": George Walker, "A Defence of Learning and the Arts, against some charges of Rousseau," *Memoirs of the Literary and Philosophical Society of Manchester*, 5 vols. (Warrington, 1785–1802), 5:450.

in its own nature, like every well-regulated passion," it was still the case that "its excess is dangerous and almost unavoidable." The "inordinate attachment" that it entailed cut across all the broader ties of affection towards relations, friends, one's country, or mankind. Affections like these did not, however, have the same type of political significance in monarchies as in republics. Monarchies (here, too, the idea came from Montesquieu) did not need them at all, and, since they did not, love could reign freely. This, Rousseau observed, was why the "French stage breathes nothing but love," and why a play like Voltaire's *Zaïre* was so seductively dangerous. No other tragedy displayed "the power of love and empire of beauty" with "greater charms." But its very power undermined the shallow grounds for believing in any kind of identifiable equality between men and women. In the last analysis, Rousseau insisted repeatedly, women ruled. "Paint the effects of love which way you please; it is a bewitching passion, or it is not love. If it be ill-painted, the play is bad; if it be well done, it renders us blind to every other consideration."[65] Love without the stabilising effects of virtue was simply incompatible with republican morality. Once the "love of human society and of our country" had been extinguished, "there remains only love, properly so called to supply their place because its attraction is most natural and is more difficult to eradicate than all the rest." "Upon this principle," Rousseau wrote, "I take upon me to affirm that there are countries where the morals of the people are so corrupt, that it would be happy for them could they reach so high as the passion of love." France was the most obvious example. In other countries, however, "it would be inconvenient to descend so low." This was the case with Geneva. As it was, the small republic was a "mansion of reason." But if Dubos's argument about the relationship between the artificial passions produced by the arts and the refinement of modern taste and civility were ever to be accepted, then plain common sense, or what Rousseau called "the solidity of reason," would begin to lose its hold.[66] Establishing a theatre would enhance the prestige of taste, and this, Rousseau argued, would mean the end of the republic.

> This requires we should live in great cities; it requires luxury and the polite arts; it requires intimate communication among fellow citizens and a close dependence upon one another; it requires gallantry, and even debauchery; in short it requires vices which we are forced to embellish in order to look for an agreeable side in everything, and to find it.[67]

It was Montesquieu's conception of monarchy, misliked. As Dubos (and Voltaire) had shown, taste and feeling went hand in hand, and, as Rousseau

[65] Rousseau, *Letter*, p. 68 (ed. Fuchs, p. 74).
[66] Rousseau, *Letter*, p. 162 (ed. Fuchs, p. 159).
[67] Rousseau, *Letter*, p. 162 (ed. Fuchs, pp. 159–60).

put it in his *Letter*, the "only instrument that serves to purge them is reason."[68] But this, on Dubos's own grounds, was exactly what the theatre
could not supply. "By favouring all our inclinations, it gives a new pre-
eminence to those that govern us. The continual emotion that it makes
us feel weakens and enervates us, making us even less able to resist our
passions; while the sterile interest in virtue which it gives us, serves only
to flatter our self-love."[69]

Rousseau's strong emphasis upon the extremely limited array of emotions
that were compatible with social and political stability in a republic like
Geneva picked up the major theme of his second *Discourse*. "For my part,"
Rousseau wrote in the *Letter*, "were I still to be treated as a knave for daring
to maintain that mankind are born good (his translator wrote "virtuous"),
I think and believe that I have proved it."[70] Goodness here was simply the
natural human capacity for self-preservation based on the information supplied by the physical senses, "the plain natural sensations," as Rousseau put
it in the *Letter*, "with which we are no longer affected."[71] As the example
of the Valais indicated, a good society was one that could rely as strongly
as possible upon this natural individual ability. "The immediate power of
the senses," Rousseau wrote—here, too, anticipating the argument of the
Essay on the Origin of Languages—"is weak and limited; it is by the aid of the
imagination that they do the greatest mischief. It is the imagination that
inflames the desires by representing things more charming than they are
really in themselves."[72] In themselves, things were either useful or useless.
Stripping them of their apparent qualities meant reinstating utility.

In a natural setting, utility was the only criterion of value. The difficulty
was to find a way to insulate it from all the culturally generated criteria
of value (itemised in detail in the *Discourse on the Origin of Inequality*) that
were part and parcel of the social state. Here, Rousseau argued, legislation
itself could never be a sufficient solution because "the force of laws has its
measure, and so has that of vice." "The knowledge of these two relations,"
he added, "constitutes the proper science of a legislator."[73] Giving force
to the law was more than a matter of applied drafting skills or sheer state
power. While it was easy enough to "draw up a moral code as pure as that
of Plato's republic," it was much more difficult to identify what would

---

[68] Rousseau, *Letter*, p. 19 (ed. Fuchs, p. 27).

[69] Rousseau, *Letter*, p. 71 (ed. Fuchs, p. 76).

[70] Rousseau, *Letter*, p. 22 (ed. Fuchs, p. 30).

[71] Rousseau, *Letter*, p. 56 (ed. Fuchs, p. 62).

[72] Rousseau, *Letter*, p. 186 (ed. Fuchs, p. 180). On the limited array of natural emotions in
Rousseau's political thought, see Patrick Coleman, "Rousseau's Quarrel with Gratitude," in
Victoria Kahn, Neil Saccamano, and Daniela Coli, eds., *Politics and the Passions, 1500–1850*
(Princeton, Princeton UP, 2006), pp. 151–74 (153).

[73] Rousseau, *Letter*, p. 83 (ed. Fuchs, p. 88).

make it work. This was not just a matter of the content of legislation, or the character of those responsible for its execution, but of the values of its designated targets who, in a republic, were both citizens and subjects. Legislation had to fit both sets of concerns. Here, Rousseau picked up the narrow definition of justice established by Grotius, Hobbes, and Pufendorf. "Another, and not less important consideration," he wrote, "is that matters of morality and universal justice are not regulated like those of particular justice and strict right, by laws and edicts." Strict right could be maintained by the force of the law (and the power of government), but morality would respond to legislation only if the laws in question already had something like the same moral content. In this case, Rousseau observed, the laws would "return that very force by a kind of reaction well known to true politicians." Since this was unlikely to occur particularly frequently "in the bosom of commerce and sordid gain" (Geneva was certainly not Sparta), the way that laws established by citizens could be made to affect their own behaviour as subjects had to come from public opinion.[74]

Rousseau seems to have been the first to have used the phrase "public opinion" in this deliberately nonsceptical sense (although the underlying idea has something in common with what Bernard Mandeville had written in *The Fable of the Bees* about how the abilities of a "skilful politician" could be used).[75] In contradistinction to more recent historiographical assumptions, he also emphasised that the power of public opinion was a feature of ancient, not modern, politics. It was, he wrote in *The Social Contract*, "a mechanism (*ressort*)" that had been "entirely lost by the moderns."[76] One example of its power, Rousseau suggested, could be found

[74] Rousseau, *Letter*, p. 84 (ed. Fuchs, p. 89). On the origins of the distinction between what Rousseau called "morality and universal justice" on the one hand, and "particular justice and strict right" on the other, see Richard Tuck, *Natural Rights Theories: Their Origin and Development* (Cambridge, CUP, 1979); and Istvan Hont and Michael Ignatieff, "Needs and Justice in the *Wealth of Nations*," now reprinted in Hont, *Jealousy of Trade*, pp. 389–443.

[75] The best, and most detailed, study of the subject can be found in Colette Ganochaud, *L'Opinion publique chez Jean-Jacques Rousseau* (Lille, Atelier de la Reproduction des Thèses, Université de Lille III, 1980). More generally, see Mona Ozouf, *L'homme régénéré. Essais sur la révolution française* (Paris, Gallimard, 1989), pp. 21–53; and Keith Michael Baker, *Inventing the French Revolution: Essays on French Political Culture in the Eighteenth Century* (Cambridge, CUP, 1990), pp. 167–99 (especially p. 189). A more recent discussion of the significance of Rousseau's usage, and the degree to which it can be distinguished from earlier, more standardly sceptical, uses of the idea of public opinion (notably by Montaigne) can be found in J.A.W. Gunn, "Queen of the World: Opinion in the Public Life of France from the Renaissance to the Revolution," *Studies on Voltaire and the Eighteenth Century* 285 (1995).

[76] Jean-Jacques Rousseau, *The Social Contract*, in Jean-Jacques Rousseau, *The Social Contract and Other Later Political Writings*, ed. Victor Gourevitch (Cambridge, CUP, 1997), bk. 4, ch. 7, p. 142 (a chapter that, as Rousseau noted, summarised the argument of his *Letter* to d'Alembert). Compare Rousseau's assertion to the claims about public opinion's modernity in the works listed in the previous note.

in the French prohibition on duelling. As things stood, the prohibition was totally ineffective. But, Rousseau argued, if the existing Tribunal of Marshals of France (whose military standing gave them the required status and authority in this kind of matter) were given a discretionary power to make some duels real trials by combat (as, according to Montesquieu, they had once actually been), then private duelling would begin to fall into disrepute. Once it was clear that some duels could, on public inspection, be deemed to be lawful, private duelling would start to lose its moral status and begin to look like any other case of premeditated murder. The way to get rid of duelling was, therefore, not to prohibit it, but to distinguish some duels from others, so that some looked honourable, while the rest looked shameful. The real trial would then no longer be between two duellists, but would instead be about the duel itself and would depend on the type of evaluation it was given by the military tribunal. Gradually, this new public source of honour and shame would eclipse private judgements, and, as the court began to apply increasingly strict criteria for defining an honourable duel, duelling itself would cease gradually to exist. If, Rousseau speculated, the Tribunal of Marshals of France were ever to become a real Court of Honour, then France, too, might begin to change into something other than an absolute monarchy. "Opinion," he wrote, "the sovereign of mankind, is not subject to the power of kings, but they themselves are her principal slaves."[77] It is easy to connect this idea to the creation, nearly fifty years later, of the French Legion of Honour.[78]

In the broadest sense, the science of the legislator amounted to finding ways to give public opinion a content that was compatible with the initial natural, utility-based sources of individual motivation. Without such means, Rousseau wrote, "neither reason, nor virtue, nor laws will prevail over public opinion so long as there is no contrivance to change it."[79] Although the case of French duelling was one example of "the choice of proper means for directing the public opinion," others were also available. Their key feature was the fact that they did not rely on laws or punishments, "nor any sort of coercive methods."[80] The most obvious, in Geneva, were the men's clubs or *cercles*, a new name, Rousseau noted, for a "very ancient" custom. When he was a boy, he wrote, they were called *sociétés* and were mainly the offshoots of the spring military exercises, the seasonal prize competitions with their accompanying banquets, and the Genevan passion for hunting. In those days, societies met solely for recreation,

[77] Rousseau, *Letter*, pp. 84–94 (ed. Fuchs, p. 89–98).
[78] On the origins of the Legion of Honour, see Michael Sonenscher, *Before the Deluge: Public Debt, Inequality, and the Intellectual Origins of the French Revolution* (Princeton, Princeton UP, 2007), pp. 15, 78–9, 81, 84, 86–7, 91, 96.
[79] Rousseau, *Letter*, p. 88 (ed. Fuchs, p. 93).
[80] Rousseau, *Letter*, p. 85 (ed. Fuchs, p. 90).

usually in an inn. But their character changed during the period of intense civil discord of the 1730s. Then, the need "to assemble oftener and to deliberate coolly" turned them into "more decent and regular assemblies," or circles, so that "from a very bad cause there arose very good effects."[81] They did have their drawbacks (smoking, drinking, and brawling), but they did, nonetheless, "preserve a faint image of the manners of antiquity"; because of this, "these virtuous and innocent institutions" served to form a series of centres for "everything that can anywise contribute to form the same men into friends, citizens, and soldiers, and of course whatever is best suited to a free people."[82] As Rousseau went on to argue in his *Social Contract*, a general will called for a combination of imaginative projection and individual abstentiveness. Its content had to be felt to be recognised, not simply understood as a set of reasoned arguments. Public opinion was not the general will, because it singled out particular types of behaviour for approval or disapproval. But the moral integration (or social conformism) that it produced helped to create conditions in which an individually internalised general will was feasible.

The same emphasis on institutions, as against laws and government, as the way to give public opinion a content consonant with individual evaluations of public utility, applied to gossip among women (the exclusively male character of the *cercles* meant that gossip confined to women would have an entirely different content from the gossip of the salon), to prize competitions for boating, hunting, and other types of physical ability, as well as to dances for the young (with the award of the title of queen of the ball to "the young lady who had behaved with the greatest decency and best deportment at the preceding dances," followed by a ceremonial procession back to her home, where her parents would be congratulated "for the excellent education given to their daughter," while she herself would be given a present, and "some mark of public distinction" when she came to marry).[83] Occasions like these, Rousseau observed, "would frequently be the means of reconciling families and of establishing peace, a thing so necessary in our republic."[84] Even the theatre, he emphasised, had once been a similar sort of institution. The Greek theatre had served mainly to keep local traditions alive, representing "some of their old national histories (*antiquités nationales*), which in all ages had been current among the common people," and which still had real significance to both actors and audience.[85] Nor, Rousseau pointed out, did the Greek theatre

---

[81] Rousseau, *Letter*, p. 132 (ed. Fuchs, p. 132).
[82] Rousseau, *Letter*, pp. 141, 142 (ed. Fuchs, pp. 140, 142).
[83] Rousseau, *Letter*, pp. 178–9 (ed. Fuchs, p. 174).
[84] Rousseau, *Letter*, p. 180 (ed. Fuchs, p. 175).
[85] Rousseau, *Letter*, pp. 36–7 (ed. Fuchs, p. 44).

ever actually have actors in anything like the modern sense. Its performers were rather more like priests or teachers, and sometimes really were
"the first men of the nation," so that its performances were more like
oratory (where an individual represented himself) than acting (where he
represented someone else).[86] As Plato had also famously argued, the way
to make the theatre moral was to eliminate the distinction between actors
and audience.[87] A vivid example of what he meant was Rousseau's memorable description of how, as a boy, he had seen a public dinner for the
regiment of the Genevan suburb of Saint-Gervais turn into a great torch-
lit procession of singers and dancers, all keeping time to the music of fifes
and drums, before dissolving into a rapturous and peaceful celebration of
joy and good feeling as the soldiers' wives and children came down from
their houses to join them on the streets below.[88]

ROUSSEAU AND HIS CYNIC CRITICS

It is tempting to think that much of the content of the many public festivities put on, not only during the period of the French Revolution, but
right up to the banqueting campaign that heralded the revolution of 1848,
can be traced back to Rousseau's *Letter to d'Alembert*.[89] In a weak sense,
this must be true. But Rousseau's interest in the causal relationships linking nonpolitical institutions like festivals or *cercles*, the content of public
opinion, and the real power of legitimate government overlapped with a
rather different and much older interest in the related subjects of singing,
dancing, morality, and government. This interest had little to do with the
strong analytical distinction between monarchies and republics that Rousseau took over from Montesquieu, or with the equally strong distinction
between "strict right" and "universal justice" that Rousseau adopted from
the natural jurisprudence of Grotius, Hobbes, Pufendorf, and Locke. Its
theoretical concerns were largely moral, not political, and its analytical
focus was communal, not individual. Here, too, the figure of Diogenes had
a kind of symbolic status. In this guise, however, Cynic philosophy stood
rather less for making true evaluations of real utility than for uncovering
those naturally human moral capacities that the unequal distribution of
wealth and power had come to obscure. In this sense, and whether or not

---

[86] Rousseau, *Letter*, pp. 100–2 (ed. Fuchs, pp. 103–5).

[87] Rousseau, *Letter*, pp. 163–4 (ed. Fuchs, pp. 160–1).

[88] Rousseau, *Letter*, pp. 187, note a (ed. Fuchs, p. 181, note 1).

[89] See, for example, Mona Ozouf, *La fête révolutionnaire* (Paris, Gallimard, 1976), and, for
one prerevolutionary example, Sarah Maza, *Private Lives and Public Affairs: The* Causes Célèbres *of Prerevolutionary France* (Berkeley and Los Angeles, University of California Press,
1993), pp. 72–3.

he was its intended target, Diderot's *Supplément au voyage de Bougainville* picked out something deeply ambiguous in Rousseau's thought ("Ah! Jean-Jacques," Diderot noted elsewhere, "how badly you defended the cause of the savage state against the social state. . . . Man forms societies the better to fight against his constant enemy, nature").[90] Much of the early criticism of both Montesquieu and Rousseau came from writers committed to less ambiguous types of moral theory than Rousseau or even Diderot himself. Here, the distinctions between monarchies and republics, and between "strict right" and "universal justice," took second place to a broader preoccupation with the moral foundations of political societies, and with the problematic relationship between internal goods like wisdom, courage, magnanimity, or generosity on the one hand, and external goods like property, wealth, office, or inherited privilege on the other. In this theoretical setting, monarchy was simply a species of the broader genus of res publica. But its unity and power could still be taken to be a measure of its unique ability to bring wealth and virtue into closer alignment.

This type of concern is now sometimes associated with the idea of a patriot king and with the kind of emblematic status given to France's King Henri IV by many more eighteenth-century writers than Voltaire.[91] But the range of historical and theological arguments in which both Voltaire and the best-known exponent of the idea of a patriot king, Henry Saint-John, viscount Bolingbroke, came to be recurrently embroiled is an indication of its older intellectual provenance. Much of the content of that older tradition was given a new salience by Montesquieu and Rousseau themselves and, in particular, by the severely truncated descriptions of human nature to be found at the beginning of *The Spirit of Laws* and, at far greater length, in the first part of the *Discourse on the Origin of Inequality*. But the frequent accusations of Epicureanism to which this kind of highly attenuated description of natural human attributes gave rise, and to which Rousseau, in particular, was subjected repeatedly, are an indication of the stronger preoccupation with morality and justice on which his critics relied. If Rousseau could be described as one kind of Cynic, so, too, could a strongly Christian critic of Epicurean worldliness. Although the charge of Epicureanism could, in the first instance, be applied most readily to the natural jurisprudence of Thomas Hobbes, it could also be applied more diffusely to any number of the many different moves made in both seventeenth-century Catholic and Protestant theology to find ways to escape from the baffling mixture of original sin, divine grace, and human redemption that were the hallmarks of both orthodox Calvinism and heterodox Jansenism in the century of

---

[90] Denis Diderot, *Réfutation suivie de l'ouvrage d' Helvétius intitulé "L'Homme"* [1775], in Denis Diderot, *Oeuvres*, 5 vols. (Paris, 1994–7), vol. 1, *Philosophie*, ed. Laurent Versini, pp. 902–3.

[91] For an overview, see Marcel Reinhard, *La légende de Henri IV* (Paris, 1935).

Louis XIV. The combination of knowing and feeling on which Dubos relied was one way of making Epicureanism more moral, one that chimed with much of the broader reevaluation of the passions associated with the works of Descartes, Gassendi, and Malebranche in the second half of the seventeenth century. But the Cartesian emphasis on the artificial passions associated with the arts left the arts themselves exposed to the same kind of charge. In this context, Epicureanism was simply the name given to what was taken to be a mistaken claim about the relationship between the divine and the human, or the spiritual and the physical. It may have been one that Voltaire, in *Le Mondain*, was prepared to accept, but the strong endorsement of the mixture of artifice, fashion, and display that it appeared to imply made it difficult to see how human culture could be reconciled with any particularly extensive idea of justice.

One way out was to reinstate natural passions in place of artificial passions, and to use these as the basis of a more comprehensive explanation of the part played by certain types of cultural acquisition in giving morality its grip on human behaviour. This type of move, and the way of thinking about society and its origins that it involved, has now been almost entirely forgotten, leaving the many works of the only one of its exponents now remembered by posterity, Giambattista Vico, marooned in a highly specialised subbranch of eighteenth-century historiography (which, in an older, now rather neglected, historiographical tradition was once known as "primitivism").[92] The type of concern with culture that it entailed grew

---

[92] On "primitivism," see Arthur O. Lovejoy and George Boas, *Primitivism and Related Ideas in Antiquity* [1935] (Baltimore, Johns Hopkins UP, 1997); George Boas, *Primitivism and Related Ideas in the Middle Ages* [1948] (Baltimore, Johns Hopkins UP, 1997); Lois Whitney, *Primitivism and the Idea of Progress in English Popular Literature of the Eighteenth Century* (Baltimore, Johns Hopkins UP, 1934). Edward Dudley and Maximillian E. Novak, eds., *The Wild Man Within: An Image in Western Thought from the Renaissance to Romanticism* (Pittsburgh, University of Pittsburgh Press, 1972). Its starting point was Lovejoy's classic 1923 article on the difference between "primitivism" and Rousseau: see "The Supposed Primitivism of Rousseau's *Discourse on Inequality*," reprinted in his *Essays in the History of Ideas* (Baltimore, Johns Hopkins UP, 1948), pp. 14–37. On Vico and the broader intellectual setting from which his works emerged, see Mark Lilla, *Gian Battista Vico: The Making of an Anti-Modern*, (Cambridge, Mass., Harvard UP, 1993); Arnoldo Momigliano, "Vico's *Scienza Nuova*: Roman '*Bestioni*' and Roman '*Eroi*,'" in Arnoldo Momigliano, *Essays in Ancient and Modern Historiography* (Oxford, OUP, 1977), pp. 259–76; Gilbert Chinard, *L'Amérique et le rêve exotique dans la littérature française du xviie et xviiie siècles* (Geneva, Droz, 1934); Frank Manuel, *The Eighteenth Century Confronts the Gods* (Cambridge, Mass., Harvard UP, 1959); Paolo Rossi, *I Segni del Tempo* (Milan, Feltrinelli, 1979), and, most recently, John Robertson, *The Case for the Enlightenment: Scotland and Naples 1680–1760* (Cambridge, CUP, 2005). For a recent discussion of the similarities and differences between Vico and Rousseau on music (as well as a fascinating description of the thought of an eighteenth-century Venetian historian of America, Lorenzo Boturini Benaduci), see Gary Tomlinson, "Vico's Songs: Detours at the Origins of (Ethno) Musicology," *Musical Quarterly* 83 (1999): 344–77.

out of a long-standing interest in the range of intellectual and moral resources that, particularly after the Flood, had once been available to both
the Jews and the Gentiles, and in the part that those resources might have
played before the Old Testament switched to the New, and both Jewish
and Gentile history could be projected forwards to meet the underlying
purposes of the whole Creation. The question of what those resources
might have been once formed part of the vast intellectual hinterland from
which both the famous quarrel between the ancients and the moderns,
and, more specifically, Vico's *New Science*, emerged, just as the gradual
disappearance of that hinterland took with it much of the more detailed
interest in explaining the origins and effects of the various types of cultural acquisition that gave this kind of historical speculation its content
and shape.[93] The focus on culture and cultural acquisition that this sort
of historical inquiry involved made it easier to build bridges between real
human societies and the more unverifiable aspects of Protestant or Catholic theology on the one hand, and between real human arrangements and

[93] For an anthology of texts, see Burton Feldman and Robert D. Richardson, eds., *The Rise
of Modern Mythology 1680–1860* (Bloomington, Indiana UP, 1972), and, for indications of its
intellectual resources, see Sam Smiles, *The Image of Antiquity: Ancient Britain and the Romantic
Imagination* (New Haven, Yale UP, 1994), pp. 113–28; Colin Kidd, *British Identities before Nationalism: Ethnicity and Nationhood in the Atlantic World 1600–1800* (Cambridge, CUP, 1999),
and his *The Forging of Races: Race and Scripture in the Protestant Atlantic World, 1600–2000*
(Cambridge, CUP, 2006), as well as Jonathan Sheehan, *The Enlightenment Bible: Translation,
Scholarship, Culture* (Princeton, Princeton UP, 2005). For an earlier (and still fascinating)
treatment of the same subject matter, see Robert R. Palmer, *Catholics and Unbelievers in
Eighteenth-Century France* (Princeton, Princeton UP, 1939), and, for indications of the polem-
ical uses to which these intellectual resources came to be put, see Leon Poliakov, *The Aryan
Myth: A History of Racist and Nationalist Ideas in Europe* (London, Chatto-Heinemann, 1974);
Bruce Lincoln, *Theorizing Myth: Narrative, Ideology, and Scholarship* (Chicago, University of
Chicago Press, 1999); Stefan Arvidsson, *Aryan Idols: Indo-European Mythology as Ideology and
Science* (Chicago, University of Chicago Press, 2006). None of these studies, however, pays
much attention to post-Grotian natural jurisprudence (here including Rousseau) as the intel-
lectual target at which much of this speculation was aimed. See also Richard H. Popkin, *Isaac
La Peyrère (1596–1676): His Life, Work and Influence* (Leiden, Brill, 1987); Jeremy D. Popkin
and Richard H. Popkin, eds., *The Abbé Grégoire and His World* (Dordrecht, Kluwer, 2000);
Ronald Schechter, *Obstinate Hebrews: Representations of Jews in France, 1715–1815* (Berkeley
and Los Angeles, University of California Press, 2003); Alyssa Goldstein Sepinwall, *The Abbé
Grégoire and the French Revolution: The Making of Modern Universalism* (Berkeley and Los
Angeles, University of California Press, 2005). For a contemporary overview of the bearing
of this type of scriptural history on the quarrel between the ancients and moderns, with a
bias towards the ancients, see Evrard Titon du Tillet, *Le parnasse français* (Paris, 1732), and,
for later examples of its continuing resonances, see James Parsons, *Remains of Japhet: Being
Historical Enquiries into the Affinity and Origin of the European Languages* (London, 1767), and
Jacob Bryant, *A New System, or An Analysis of Ancient Mythology*, 3 vols. (London, 1774). See,
too, Richard Popkin, "The Fifth Monarchy Redux," in Hans Blom, John Christian Laursen,
and Luisa Simonutti, eds., *Monarchisms in the Age of Enlightenment* (Toronto, University of
Toronto Press, 2007), pp. 162–72.

the more historically untenable or morally implausible aspects of social contract theory on the other, without, however, entirely undermining either. As with Vico, the broad aim of this type of historical speculation was to rescue morality from the scepticism of the heterodox French Protestant exile Pierre Bayle, on the one hand, and the state-centred natural jurisprudence of Grotius, Hobbes, Pufendorf, and Locke on the other, without, however, simply repeating dogma.

Many of its results now look rather strange. But their most important general feature is quite easy to see. This was the way that certain types of cultural acquisition could be used to explain social integration in terms of something other than necessity, expediency, or utility (Epicureanism), but still did not have to presuppose that humans were sociable right from the start. This type of move could be connected to Aristotle, and to the idea of a sequence of increasingly extensive social ties running from the family to the polis with which his thought could be associated. "Some writers, as Aristotle and a few moderns, implicit followers of his opinions," wrote the Presbyterian natural philosopher William Smellie towards the end of the eighteenth century, "deny that man is naturally a gregarious or associating animal." To reconcile this premise with the obvious fact of human society, "these authors," Smellie continued, "have had recourse to puerile conceits and to questionable facts, which it would be fruitless to relate."[94] The sort of "puerile conceits" and "questionable facts" involved in this now unfamiliar characterisation of Aristotle and his putative followers (one that Smellie shared with earlier Jansenist theologians) gave rise to many different versions of the capacious idea of sociability. Here, sociability was used to refer to something rather different from the mixture of knowledge and feeling involved in Ciceronian decorum, or the polite civility of salon society. In this sense, it joined up with Rousseau, against Voltaire. But in another sense, this way of explaining sociability parted company with them both, not only because of its more explicit reliance upon scripture, but also because of its much stronger emphasis upon natural passions as the real source of social cohesiveness and moral authority. In this intellectual setting, the arts were associated not with artificial passions, but with something much nearer to what, in the eighteenth century, it was usual to call "enthusiasm," or the strong feelings associated with awe, wonder, admiration, joy, or fear, and the intensely creative effects that this kind of emotion could sometimes be taken to have.

In some versions of this type of interest in the arts, the key ingredient was the discovery of fire (not only because of the socially cohesive effects of its awesomely attractive physical properties, but also, and more significantly, because of the prestige and power that its first, apparently

[94] William Smellie, *The Philosophy of Natural History*, 2 vols. (Edinburgh, 1790), 2:41.

Celtic, masters acquired).[95] In others, it was the change to the intensity of individual appetites that occurred when humans switched from herbivorous to carnivorous habits (an accidental effect of using teeth to tear the fleece from the flesh of a lamb for the more directly utilitarian purpose of keeping warm), and the transition from gathering to hunting that this entailed (as well, apparently, as the more intense quality of human sexuality that eating meat produced). In yet others, it was the stronger sense of self-awareness produced by the awakening of sexual desire at puberty, reinforced by the fact that human females were moved by sexual desire entirely independently of the short periods of fertility of the animal seasons.[96] Language, music, and painting could all be connected to this intensification of feeling, either because one or other of them could be connected to love (the first painting, an essay on the art of design suggested—citing what Montaigne had written in the sixteenth century—had been the work of lovers seeking to embellish one another's faces or bodies by imitating the colours of a salamander), or because of their association with birth or death (mothers might sing to babies, just as, in later life, feelings of grief or loss might lead children to make funeral monuments to commemorate their dead parents).[97] The same type of non–utility based move could be made by referring to the putatively unique human capacity for laughter, and to its connection to both popular revelry and the emergence of the art of comedy, with laughter taken here to be a "symbol of happiness," and "an apanage of joy," rather than, as with Thomas Hobbes, an indication of the natural human desire for vainglory.[98] Many of the works in which

[95] Louis Poinsinet de Sivry, *Origine des premières sociétés, des peuples, des sciences, des arts et des idiomes anciens et modernes* (Amsterdam and Paris, 1769), pp. 3–66.

[96] For these conjectures, see, on carnivorism, Augustin-Jean-François Chaillon de Jonville, *La vérité dévoilée* (Paris, 1789), p. 15; on puberty, sexual desire, and sociability, [Etienne-Gabriel Morelly], *Naufrage des isles flottantes, ou Basiliade du célèbre Pilpai. Poème héroïque* (Messina, 1742); and, on female sexual availability, François-René Richer d'Aube, *Essai sur les principes du droit et de la morale* (Paris, 1743). For variations on these latter ideas, but with more of an emphasis on jealousy, and this time explicitly presented as an alternative to Rousseau, see Jacques-Vincent Delacroix, *A Review of the Constitutions of the Principal States of Europe and of the United States of America*, 2 vols. (London, 1792), 1:i–xxvi. For a recent examination of vegetarianism (including its place in Rousseau's thought), see Tristram Stuart, *The Bloodless Revolution: Radical Vegetarians and the Discovery of India* (London, Harper Collins, 2006).

[97] [Henri-Claude Picardet *ainé*], "Considérations sur les écoles où l'on enseigne l'art du dessin et sur l'utilité d'un pareil établissement en faveur des métiers," *Mémoires de l'Académie de Dijon*, n.s., 2 (Paris and Dijon, 1774): 130–56 (on Montaigne's story, see p. 142, note 1). On this theme in early modern thought, see Robert Rosenblum, "The Origin of Painting: A Problem in the Iconography of Romantic Classicism," *Art Bulletin* 39 (1957): 279–90.

[98] This, too, can be found in the work of Louis Poinsinet de Sivry, this time in his introduction to the French translation of Pliny's *Natural History*. See Pliny, *Histoire naturelle*, 1:4, notes 4 and 5 by Poinsinet de Sivry, referring to his earlier *Traité des causes physiques et morales du rire* (Paris, 1768).

speculations like these occurred were published after the appearance of Rousseau's *Discourse on the Origin of Inequality* in 1755. Some were certainly intended to be replies to Rousseau. But it may be more historically accurate not only to position Rousseau's own historical conjectures against this older, and broader intellectual context, but also to describe Rousseau's conjectures as the intellectual stimulus that brought them back to life.

One example of the proximity between this type of concern with the mechanisms of cultural acquisition and Rousseau's own moral and political thought can be found in one of the first, and most hostile, reactions to the *Discourse on the Origin of Inequality*. This was a book entitled *L'homme moral opposé a l'homme physique de Monsieur R**** (The Moral Man Set against M. Rousseau's Physical Man) that was published in 1756 by the abbé de Saint-Pierre's friend Louis-Bertrand Castel, a French Jesuit. As its title indicates, it was intended to present a fuller and richer description of natural human morality as an alternative to the radically pared-down description of human nature that Rousseau had set out at the beginning of his second *Discourse*. According to Castel, the picture of human nature that Rousseau had presented amounted to an unsavoury mixture of Epicureanism, Hobbism, and Cynicism. But, as Voltaire noticed, there was something surprisingly similar to Rousseau in Castel's alternative version of natural morality. Although he was no admirer of Rousseau's second *Discourse*, Voltaire had no hesitation about deciding where his allegiances lay when faced with a choice between Rousseau and Castel. Castel, he wrote in a letter about *L'homme moral* to one of his Genevan correspondents, was "the Cynic of the Jesuits, just as that unhappy citizen is the Cynic of the philosophers." Unlike Castel, Voltaire observed, Rousseau had never said anything injurious about anyone and was also a much better writer, which, he added, were "two great merits."[99]

The Cynic parallel that Voltaire drew between Castel and Rousseau was quite well-judged. Despite their different treatment of the passions and the arts, it grew out of a shared aversion to inequality. Rousseau's solution was to turn *amour-propre* into patriotism by, as he indicated in his *Letter to d'Alembert*, devising ways to make public opinion turn what might seem honourable into something shameful and, by doing so, to make it easier for individual members of society to maintain a less emotionally clouded

---

[99] Voltaire to Pierre Pictet [February–March 1756], in Voltaire, *Correspondance*, ed. Theodore Besterman, 13 vols. (Paris, Pléiade, 1963–93), vol. 4 (Paris, 1978), no. 4385, p. 708. I have used the translation in Maurice Cranston, *The Noble Savage: Jean-Jacques Rousseau 1754–1762* (London, Allen Lane, 1991), p. 10, note (although Cranston mistakenly applies Voltaire's remark about Rousseau to Castel). For a generic version of the same claim, see Pierre-Paul Thiry, baron d'Holbach, *Système social* [1773], 2 vols. (Paris, 1795), 1:56: "Quelle différence réelle y a-t-il entre les vertus d'un Diogène, et celles d'un capucin ou d'un moine de la Trappe?"

evaluation of public utility. Once it had become clear that distinction was shameful, it would be easier to see, or feel, that what applied equally to all was the only real criterion for identifying the content of the general will. Castel's solution was to reinstate morality. As he proceeded to insinuate, much of the blame for what he took to be Rousseau's degrading characterisation of human nature fell upon Montesquieu. Castel had been one of Montesquieu's oldest acquaintances and had given Montesquieu's *Considerations on the Romans* a careful prepublication reading to ensure that it contained nothing that might offend the church.[100] He had, he wrote, been hurt when Montesquieu had not asked him to do the same for *The Spirit of Laws*, and had come to think that this might have had something to do with the highly attenuated description of human nature that Montesquieu had set out at the beginning of his book. Rousseau's second *Discourse* now appeared to confirm all his worst fears about the kind of intellectual monster that Montesquieu might, unwittingly, have helped to unleash. As Castel went on to argue in a long digression devoted to the shortcomings of *The Spirit of Laws*, the analysis of the three types of government (republican, monarchical, or despotic) that Montesquieu had described at the beginning of his book had been marred by his failure to start with a fourth type of government, "the first of them all and the rule and the basis of the three others." This, he wrote, was "the government of savages and the liberty, or rather the pure natural law, on which, uniquely, it was founded."[101]

Natural government, or what Castel called "naturalism" or "pure moralism," did not require kings or princes or magistrates, because the heads of families or tribal elders were the natural, but ad hoc, chiefs and governors of their communities.[102] Their authority was purely personal, and its application always temporary. Honour and shame, not fixed legal principles or formal codes of punishment, gave them moral authority, not political power, while tacit acceptance of communal values left every individual with the ability to do what the community might sanction, without having to take individual responsibility for the action itself. A woman might sleep with her lover, a miscreant might be murdered, or a peace treaty violated, but approval or disapproval of the act depended solely on the internalised norms of the whole community. Concepts like adultery, murder, or treason were, therefore, largely beside the point, since every particular evaluation was a product of shared feelings and common customs. This, Castel

[100] On Castel and Montesquieu, see Sonenscher, *Before the Deluge*, p. 132.

[101] Louis-Bertrand Castel, *L'homme moral opposé a l'homme physique de Monsieur R**** (Toulouse, 1756), p. 105. The text was later reprinted in the great folio edition of Rousseau's collected works published in Geneva in 1783; see *Supplément aux Oeuvres de J. J. Rousseau, citoyen de Genève* in Rousseau, *Oeuvres* (Geneva, 1783), 15:77–251.

[102] Castel, *L'homme moral*, p. 108.

wrote, was the form of government that he had suggested that Montesquieu should include in a revised edition of *The Spirit of Laws*, adding that he had also referred him to the works of the French missionaries in Canada for more detailed descriptions of how "naturalism" actually worked.

The arts could also be integrated into this version of "naturalism." Genesis, Castel noted, showed that the "liberal arts had been invented under the name of music by Jubal" and "the mechanical arts by Tubalcain, whose name was subsequently transformed by idolatry into Vulcan." But the very highest arts of all, namely, the arts of civil and political life, had more complex origins.[103] These were municipal in character and served to govern large concentrations of people. Towns, however, were the immediate product of the pathological behaviour of fallen man. As Castel pointed out, it had, after all, been Cain, the murderer of his brother, who had been responsible for the construction of Enochia, the very first town, and Romulus, also a fratricide, who had founded Rome. The episode of the Tower of Babel also revealed the dangerous moral effects of urban life, and the providential origins of the arts of civil and political life. These had really been given a proper foundation only with the Incarnation and the switch from the Old Testament to the New. In this sense, human history was also a progressive process of revelation, as humans became better equipped to make sense of the complexities of the whole providential system. Christian Europe was the work of the descendants of Japhet, whose wanderings through deserts and mountains had led them to fall entirely into barbarism, while the descendants of Ham and Shem had remained trapped in the urban idolatry that was to lead, in the case of the latter, to the Deicide that formed the bridge between the Old Testament and the New.[104] Gentile history was, therefore, also the history of how the barbarians who were descended from Japhet had become moral. The argument was similar to Vico's idea of history following a pattern of *corso* and *ricorso*. In morality, just as in later theories of economic development, there were advantages in backwardness.

Rousseau's mistake had been to adopt Montesquieu's starting point. "I agree," Castel wrote, "that orthodox theologians advert continually to the hypothesis (of the state of nature) and correct it of the philosophical excesses that you ascribe to it."

> They always make man in the state of pure nature a moral and sociable being, subject to natural duties towards God, his kin, and all of surrounding nature, whether physical or animal. You, on the other hand, reduce man to pure physicality and pure animality, which is purely deist and perhaps Epicurean.[105]

[103] Castel, *L'homme moral*, pp. 116–7.
[104] Castel, *L'homme moral*, pp. 117 et seq.
[105] Castel, *L'homme moral*, p. 31.

Rousseau's account of the purely self-centred drives produced by natural *amour-de-soi* implied what Castel called a condition of "negative innocence," while Adam's innocence had been "positive and meritorious." It might be thought, he continued, "that M. Rousseau had Hobbes very much in his sights, in order to refute what was impious in his system. Yet it is not clear that Hobbes's impiety revolts him greatly. If he refutes it, it is only to efface it or cover it over."

> Hobbes is impious only insofar as he assumes that man is capable of impiety. But man, for Rousseau, not having either virtues or vices, nor moral relations, nor known duties, can no more be impious, whatever he does, than can a brute beast.
>
> Hobbes's man is bestial to the point of impiety; Rousseau's is impious to the point of bestiality. He is not impious, but is not pious. He simply has no morality at all. He is merely gradually organised matter and, once animated and able at length to develop a mind, succeeds only in expiring and in reverting to nothingness by dint of refinement.[106]

As Castel acknowledged, he shared a measure of common ground with Rousseau in his reluctance to accept the strong distinction between the spiritual and the physical sides of both nature and human nature that he associated with the philosophies of Descartes and Newton. He had, he wrote, devoted his entire intellectual life to turning the dualism of their systems into something more comprehensively spiritual.[107]

This, in fact, had been the aim of his first book, a treatise on weight, that was published in 1724. The alternative system that Castel developed subsequently gave rise to a kind of thought experiment that was something like a mirror image of the one that Rousseau was later to develop in his *Discourse on the Origin of Inequality* (the young Rousseau, it is worth noting, was one of Castel's acquaintances). But where Rousseau began by trying to imagine what human nature might have been like before society and history had overlain its original properties, Castel began by trying to imagine what nature might have been like if it had not been overlain by human society and history. The basis of this conjecture was the rather strange physical system contained in his treatise on weight. There, Castel set out to reinstate a version of Aristotelian natural philosophy, against Descartes and Newton. Accordingly, matter consisted of earth, water, air, and fire, with different degrees of heaviness as their most basic physical properties. Left to themselves, he argued, the earth really would still be as it had been created, with all the earth concentrated at its centre, surrounded by a layer of water, which, in turn, would be surrounded by a

---

[106] Castel, *L'homme moral*, pp. 57–8.
[107] Castel, *L'homme moral*, p. 78.

layer of air. It would be genuinely timeless. The reason why it was not was that it also contained humans, and they had free will. This purely spiritual quality was, as Castel put it, what had stamped the seal of mortality on the otherwise unchanging features and uniform qualities of the earth. The huge array of apparently natural events that lay midway between miracles, on the one side, and genuinely natural events on the other were all, therefore, man-made. They occurred, Castel claimed, mainly because humans were responsible for mixing what would otherwise have been a very simple array of natural elements and, by doing so, for interfering with what otherwise would have been a very durable natural equilibrium. Mixing the elements led to disequilibria, which, in turn, produced the massive variety of apparently natural phenomena that humans were then able to exploit still further.

As with Rousseau, but unlike more strongly Augustinian Christians, Castel drew the line separating culture from nature quite a long way down, leaving very little on the side of nature and a great deal more on the side of culture. The combination of human free will and the mortality that human free will had brought in its wake was, therefore, the real cause of nature's enormous variety and abundance. "God," Castel concluded,

> placed man on earth to work it, and even to embellish it. But its beauties are fragile, and time harvests them, just as it harvests its authors. If we were not here, this, in a word, would be how the earth would look. Our houses, our palaces, our cities would soon revert to the level of the globe. The land that we have raised up to make fertile with so much care and effort by making it penetrable by the wind and the rain would dry out and harden, and then there would be no more corn, no more vines, fields, plants, trees, insects, or animals, and soon, perhaps, no more valleys, mountains, rivers, or seas, and, once the earth had dried out, it would go back to the centre, the waters would cover it, and the air would cover the water.[108]

It was something like the picture of the "first times" that Rousseau set out in his second *Discourse*, but seen here from a more obviously Christian point of view, where human freedom and human improvement complemented one another. Both, however, predicated their respective conjectures on human free will, and on the spiritual side of human nature that,

---

[108] Louis-Bertrand Castel, "De l'action des hommes sur la nature," originally published in the *Mémoires de Trévoux* and reprinted in the posthumously published *Esprit, saillies et singularités du père Castel* (Amsterdam, 1763), pp. 189–222 (pp. 220–1 for the passage cited). See, too, his "De la physique par rapport à la politique," in the same collection, pp. 155–83, with its discussion of the idea of circulation that is similar to that to be found in Richard Cantillon's *Essai sur la nature du commerce en général* (1755), as well as his "Lettre sur la politique adressée à Monsieur l'abbé de Saint-Pierre, par le P. Castel Jésuite," *Journal de Trévoux*, April 1725, pp. 698–729.

for both, set humans apart from animals. As one of Castel's less spiritually sanguine readers put it in the context of a satire on this distinctly non-Jansenist type of physicotheology, "our *erudite* philosopher was much taken to walking, being persuaded that man's movements help to move the sun and the whole *planetary senate*, and that all this helps the universal action of nature."[109] Castel's long, unsuccessful, search for a way to make a clavichord that would play colours instead of sounds was, it might be said, a strict application of theory to practice.[110]

To Castel, however, Rousseau had gone to the opposite extreme. Everything in his system, including the purely animal emotion of pity that Rousseau had made the anchor of his abstentive alternative to the golden rule, was a derivation of a physical principle, and this, for Castel, made him a Hobbist. The real alternative to Hobbes, Castel argued, had to be something far more spiritual than anything that Rousseau seemed to have found in Montesquieu. This, he went on to indicate, could be extrapolated from scripture and the mixture of Jewish and Gentile history that it contained. Contrary to Rousseau, he argued, separate civil societies did not begin with the first man to have said, "This is mine," but grew out of the vast providential system that God had designed to meet the purposes of the Creation. In the beginning, God had given the earth and all of its fruits to Adam and Eve, and had done so again to Noah and his descendants, commanding them, too, to go forth and multiply rather than remain together in a single place. Japhet and his descendants had wandered far and wide, while Ham, Shem, and their offspring had founded societies and developed flourishing empires in Asia. But two of their descendants, Nimrod and Asur, had tried to thwart the divine injunction to go forth and multiply by building the immense city of Babylon, with its Tower of Babel, in an attempt to keep the whole human race together. The result was the first empire, or the first claim to exclusive dominion over the earth. God, however, was not deceived and, by the Confusion of Tongues, had dissolved humanity into "three, or perhaps a hundred, or perhaps a thousand national societies" to fit the longer-term purposes of the Creation.[111] In contradistinction to what Rousseau had written, it was the human drive for empire, not the first acquisition of property, that lay behind the formation of separate political societies. This, Castel argued, meant that property was not an effect of imposture but the antidote to

[109] Pierre-François Guyot Desfontaines, *Dictionnaire néologique à l'usage des beaux esprits du siècle, avec l'éloge historique de Pantalon-Phoebus* (n.p., 1726), p. 117 (a footnote directed the reader to Castel's 1724 treatise on weight).

[110] On this aspect of Castel's intellectual career, see Donald S. Schier, *Louis-Bertrand Castel, Anti-Newtonian Scientist* (Cedar Rapids, Iowa, 1941), and Anne-Marie Chouillet-Roche, "Le Clavecin oculaire du père Castel," *Dix-Huitième Siècle* 8 (1976): 141–66.

[111] Castel, *L'homme moral*, p. 73.

empire. If human ambition made the original divine gift of the earth and all its goods to mankind in common unviable, then private property served to neutralise the abuse of common ownership that Nimrod and Asur had tried to secure. They were, moreover, not isolated individuals but the direct descendants of Shem and Ham and, in this guise, the leaders of a whole people. In this sense, it had been something like the whole human race that had been responsible for the construction of Babel and the imperial ambition on which that project was based.[112] The Confusion of Tongues and the privatisation of the whole earth had been God's solution to humanity's failure to keep to the divine injunction to disperse.

From this perspective, Castel conceded, Rousseau's hostility to the modern world of courts, capital cities, and great empires was right, even if it was based on the wrong reasons. Towns were, indeed, the usual source of the iniquities that, from time to time, had flooded the world. "The countryside is more usually the abode of innocence, and the pastoral life has, in all ages, won the suffrage of the poets and, in reality, of God himself."[113] Although towns were certainly part of the providential system, "great or excessively intimate societies were never to God's taste," as the dispersal after Babel showed. They were a "pure concession" rather than a positive institution, as was shown by God's permission to allow the Jews to inhabit Jerusalem and the other towns of Palestine. Towns occupied land, required private property, even if it belonged to the city itself, and entailed the construction of buildings that would outlast any individual life. Tents, or the tabernacles of the early Jewish patriarchs, on the other hand, were never finished houses that had been made to last forever, or at least for long periods of time. The truly moral life was, therefore, a pastoral and warrior life that was lived under tents, as was now exemplified by the Tartars. "The properly human and sociable life," Castel emphasised, was "the specifically Tartar, rural, tent-based, pastoral, and military life." Unlike urban life, "it has little to do with the land or, at least, is not rooted to it, but can instead be made and remade again and again and, like life itself, will always be ready to take wing, at the behest of the wind and our true needs."[114]

But although towns and idolatry went hand-in-hand, the arts that they housed were still a source of social cooperation and an obstacle to the more

---

[112] Castel, *L'homme moral*, pp. 73–4. Compare this account to the near contemporary Antoine-Yves Goguet, *De l'origine des loix, des arts, des sciences*, 3 vols. (Paris, 1758), as described by J.G.A. Pocock, *Barbarians, Savages and Empires* (Cambridge, CUP, 2005), pp. 42–64. Castel's text can be compared fruitfully to another critical reply to Rousseau, by Giovanni Francesco Mauro Melchiorre Salvemini di Castiglione, *Discours sur l'origine de l'inégalité parmi les hommes. Pour servir de réponse au discours que M. Rousseau a publié sur le même sujet* (Amsterdam, 1756).

[113] Castel, *L'homme moral*, p. 118.

[114] Castel, *L'homme moral*, pp. 126–7.

divisive effects of private property. Like many other more orthodox Catholics, Castel had no difficulty in accepting the vaguely Aristotelian idea (at least according to critics like William Smellie) of a gradual broadening of social ties as the first households came to be linked to others, and as these, in turn, came to form the more perfectly self-sufficient unit of the polis. In this framework, social specialisation and the division of labour had a more straightforwardly reciprocal character than it did in the more strongly self-centred version contained in Jansenist political theology. Charity itself, rather than the simulated charity produced by *amour-propre*, made the division of labour work. The famous example of the pin factory, which had already appeared in the Jansenist Noël-Antoine Pluche's *Spectacle de la nature* and in Diderot's *Encyclopaedia*, served to underline the point.

> Each trade and each art calls for thirty hands or thirty other arts and crafts to satisfy the least of our needs. A pin passes through thirty hands and thirty laboratories before becoming a pin that can be bought for one or two sols.[115]

Contrary to Rousseau, it was this kind of interdependence and the physical goods that it supplied that gave humans a genuine capacity for making choices. Without them, life really would be no more than an unremitting struggle for physical survival. Rousseau's indictment of the sort of political society that was now best exemplified by modern France was, therefore, both mistaken and presumptuous. He was in great danger of deserving the reproach of being a Cynic philosopher or "one of those who criticise everything, however appropriate or inappropriate that criticism might be."[116] Like the dogs who had given the ancient Cynics their name, and the real dogs to which Rousseau himself had referred in dedicating the second *Discourse* to the republic of Geneva, barking too often was likely to turn into no more than a public nuisance, effectively ensuring that a real warning would simply be ignored when it was actually needed. "Cynic pride," Castel warned, "is the capital sin of ordinary pride."

> The dishevelled Diogenes in his tub filled with dregs and filth showed more scorn towards Alexander, who had honoured him with a visit, as one might inspect the wild animal of the day (*la bête du jour*), than Alexander had scorned the whole universe, imposing silence upon its kings and peoples from the breast of his glory and in the brilliance of his victorious and conquering courage.[117]

It is not difficult to see where Castel's own loyalties lay.

---

[115] Castel, *L'homme moral*, p. 138. As indicated above, pp. 86, 168, strong Augustinians like Pluche and Smellie took the idea of a self-sufficient society forming out of a gradual broadening of social ties to be Aristotelian, rather than, as is usually thought now, Stoic.

[116] Castel, *L'homme moral*, p. 10.

[117] Castel, *L'homme moral*, pp. 190–1.

John Brown and the Progress of Civilisation

The Cynic parallel between Rousseau and the more moralistic side of Christian orthodoxy that Voltaire drew was repeated in a second book published fourteen years later. This time, however, the parallel was between Rousseau and a now rather obscure English political moralist and Anglican clergyman named John (or "Estimate") Brown. Here, both Brown and Rousseau were identified as Cynics. This characterisation was made by a former French Jesuit (the order was dissolved in 1763) named Jean-Louis Castilhon in a book entitled *Le Diogène moderne ou le désapprobateur* (The Modern Diogenes, or The Disapprover) that was published in 1770.[118] It was, ostensibly, a novel, consisting of an exchange of letters describing the life and ideas of an exiled Englishman named Sir Charles Wolban and, as the letters unfolded, an account of the sequence of events that led to Wolban's suicide. In reality, however, it was a quite skilful examination of the similarities and differences between Rousseau and Brown. Brown is now far less well known than Rousseau. But he did, in fact, gain a Europewide reputation thirteen years before Castilhon produced his novel with the publication in 1757 of his *Estimate of the Manners and Principles of the Times*. The *Estimate*, to which a second volume was added in 1758, was translated into almost every major European language and soon gave rise to a wide-ranging discussion of its grim examination of Britain's putative moral and social decline, and the strong claims about the combination of luxury, effeminacy, and inequality that, Brown argued, lay behind Britain's recent military failures and possible longer-term ruin. Even in 1807, it could still be cited in an article in The *Athenaeum* entitled "On the Effects of Heavy Taxation on the Morals of the People" for its warning about luxury, and the possibility that, under a new set of wartime conditions, "the question will shortly come to the issue which Dr Brown long ago predicted of 'who will not pay, but who will fight'" (and, by implication, the likelihood that luxury would sap the spirit of patriotism to the point at which neither would occur).[119]

---

[118] The best source of information on Brown can be found in Andrew Kippis, *Biographia Britannica: or The Lives of The Most Eminent Persons who have Flourished in Great Britain, From the Earliest Ages*, 5 vols. (London, 1778–93), 2:653–74, and the further entry on Brown in the *Corrigenda* to vol. 2, printed in vol. 3 (unnumbered pages). On the Rousseau-Brown pairing (but without reference to Castilhon's novel), see Henri Roddier, *J. J. Rousseau en Angleterre au xviiie siècle* (Paris, 1950), pp. 42–6, 119–24, 154–9, 232–5. For other examples of the Rousseau-Diogenes pairing (this one is not mentioned), see Monique and Bernard Cottret, *Jean-Jacques Rousseau en son temps* (Paris, Perrin, 2005), pp. 8, 334, 357; and, more generally, Herding, "Diogenes als Bürgerheld," 232–54.

[119] The *Athenaeum* (1807), p. 129.

The book's appearance, immediately after the early British disasters in the Seven Years War, played a part in generating the wave of patriotic enthusiasm that led to the elder Pitt's rise to the position of chief minister (Brown was also a passionate supporter of Pitt), and soon gave rise to a flurry of pamphlets, all offering various estimations of the estimator. As one of Brown's critics put it, "with all the ease and importance of an ancient oracle, he pronounced the whole kingdom a collection of scoundrels, cowards, gamesters, debauchees, without public or private virtue remaining." The English nonconformist Joseph Priestley was a fierce critic of Brown's theory of a state-controlled system of public education, and the intellectually stultifying conformism that, he argued, it was bound to produce. But, for the German philosopher Johann Gottfried Herder, Brown "the republican" was "a voice of patriotic wisdom and the reformer of his fatherland," while, towards the end of the eighteenth century, the British political reformer Vicesimus Knox could still single out Brown's *Estimate* as the best guide to the origins of what, as he indicated in the title of his own book, he called "the spirit of despotism" then prevailing under the younger Pitt's government of modern Britain.[120] Brown, "who dared to oppose Mr Hume, and died," wrote Henry Fuseli, one of Rousseau's most outspoken early supporters, would have endorsed the citizen of Geneva's distinction between the sovereign and the government (and, by implication, would also have proposed remodelling Britain's government along whatever Fuseli took to be Rousseau's lines).[121] In France, Brown's description of the French as, according to one summary, "more devout, more united, more bellicose, more attached to their principles, and less opulent than the English" played readily into the concurrent debate about the merits or demerits of a trading nobility, and helped to bolster the opposition to the campaign by Voltaire's disciple the abbé Gabriel-François Coyer, and his associates in the so-called Gournay group, to turn the younger sons of French nobles into an English-style landowning, but commercial, gentry.[122]

[120] See, for the passages in question, [Anon.], *The Contrast, with corrections and restorations. And an introductory dissertation on the origins of the feuds and animosities in the state* (London, 1765), p. 22; Joseph Priestley, *An Essay on a Course of Liberal Education for Civil and Active Life* (London, 1765), and Joseph Priestley, *Political Writings*, ed. Peter Miller (Cambridge, CUP, 1993), pp. 40–52, 108–18; Johann Gottfried Herder, *Selected Early Works, 1764–1767*, ed. Ernest A. Menze and Karl Menges (Pittsburgh, Penn State UP, 1992), p. 94; [Vicesimus Knox], *The Spirit of Despotism* (London, 1795), pp. 156–64.

[121] Fuseli, *Remarks on the Writings and Conduct of J. J. Rousseau*, preface (unnumbered pages). For Brown's attack on Hume, see John Brown, *An Estimate of the Manners and Principles of the Times*, 2 vols. (London, 1757–58), 1:54 et seq. and 2:86, as cited in Charles Moore, *A Full Inquiry into the Subject of Suicide* (London, 1790), p. 86.

[122] The summary of Brown's assessment of the French is cited from Jean-Pierre Grosley, *Londres*, 3 vols. (Neuchâtel, 1774), 3:336. On Coyer, and the debate about military reform

Brown's analysis of Britain's potential for ruin, with its easily generalis-
able claims about the dangers of inequality, luxury, and commerce, soon
earned him the nickname of "Estimate" Brown, encouraged the members
of the recently established Patriotic Society of Berne to invite him to address their own concerns with moral and political reform, and, in 1765,
resulted in an invitation from the Empress Catherine of Russia to travel to
Saint Petersburg to act as an advisor on the various civil, military, commercial, and educational reforms that she was planning to undertake (another
advisor was to be Denis Diderot). The prospect initially inspired Brown to
grandiose speculation. "This design," he wrote to a friend, "if in any degree successful, will realise many things in my principal work, *On Christian
Legislation*" (one that he never, in fact, seems to have completed).

> If you will indulge me in carrying my imagination into futurity, I can fancy
> that I see civilization and a rational system of Christianity extending them-
> selves quite across the immense continent, from Petersburg to Kamchatka.
> I can fancy that I see them striking farther into the more southern regions
> of Tartary and China, and spreading their influence even over the nations of
> Europe, which, though now polished, are far from being truly Christian or
> truly happy. Nay, I am sometimes fantastic enough to say with Pitt, that as
> America was conquered in Germany, so Great Britain may be reformed in
> Russia.[123]

But, whether it was because of the scale of expectations like these, or
because of the practical difficulties and health problems involved in the

---

in France, see below, chapter 5. See also the review (possibly by Georg-Ludwig Schmid
d'Auenstein) of a work entitled *Le luxe considéré relativement à la population et à l'économie*
(Lyon, 1762), in the *Journal du commerce et d'agriculture*, April 1762, pp. 72–88, describing
that work as a poor copy of Brown's. Schmid himself noticed the similarity, but emphasised
the difference, in the preface to the second edition of his *Essais sur divers sujets intéressants de
politique et de morale*, 2 vols. (n.p., 1761), 1:viii.

[123] Brown's never published *Principles of Christian Legislation, in Eight Books* was advertised in
his *A Dissertation on the Rise, Union, and Power, the Progressions, Separations, and Corruptions, of
Poetry and Music* (London, 1763). Both the *Dissertation* and the earlier *Estimate* were extracted
from this more ambitious project, which Brown described as "A History and Analysis of Manners and Principles in their Several Periods," in his *An Explanatory Defence of the Estimate and
Manners of the Principles of the Times* (London, 1758), pp. 3–7. The letter cited here is printed
in Kippis, *Biographia Britannica*, 2:667. On the background to Brown's aborted Russian expedition, see John H. Appleby, "Daniel Dumaresq D.D., F.R.S. (1712–1805) as a Promoter of
Anglo-Russian Science and Culture," *Notes and Records of the Royal Society of London* 44 (1990):
25–50; N. Hans, "Marginalia: Dumaresq, Brown and Some Early Educational Projects of
Catherine II," *Slavonic and East-European Review* 40 (1961): 229–35; and, on Diderot's involvement in the same project, Gianluigi Goggi, "Diderot et l'abbé Baudeau: les colonies de Saratov et la civilisation de la Russie," *Recherches sur Diderot et sur l'Encyclopédie* 14 (1993): 23–83, as
well as Marcus C. Levitt, "An Antidote to Nervous Juice: Catherine the Great's Debate with
Chappe d'Auteroche over Russian Culture," *Eighteenth-Century Studies* 32 (1998): 49–63.

undertaking, or because of the shame and humiliation that he felt when he finally decided that he could not make the journey, or simply because of the deeper compulsions of his own depressive character, the high early expectations turned into gloom, and Brown, like the character of Sir Charles Wolban in Castilhon's novel, committed suicide. On 23 September 1766 he cut his own throat.[124]

Both Rousseau and Brown could be identified with the figure of Diogenes because Cynic rhetoric could be taken to be either sceptical or dogmatic, especially where the subject of morality was concerned (the shock therapy might be sceptical, but its naturalistic outcome might still be dogmatic). In this context, Rousseau could be taken to be a sceptical Cynic, while Brown was a dogmatic Cynic. The pairing was quite well chosen, since (although it is unlikely that Castilhon could have known it) Brown had in fact published three sermons attacking the abstentive moral and educational theory that Rousseau had set out in *Emile*.[125] Yet there was still enough similarity between the two for the translator of a 1789 French version of Brown's 1765 pamphlet *On Civil Liberty and Factions* to highlight the compatibility between Brown's argument in favour of an egalitarian distribution of property and Rousseau's *Discourse on the Origin of Inequality*.[126] The point of the earlier parallel, however, was to show that the two kinds of Cynicism that Brown and Rousseau were taken to represent were fundamentally interchangeable. In Castilhon's novel, the Rousseau figure was Sir Charles Wolban (the name was similar to the Wolmar of Rousseau's *Julie, ou la nouvelle Héloïse*). Wolban was a sceptical Cynic, who criticised Brown (to whom he referred explicitly) as a dogmatic Cynic. The criticism centred not so much on the analysis of luxury underlying the *Estimate of the Manners and Principles of the Times* as on the underlying theory of sociability on which the analysis was based. This theory was not, in fact, particularly visible in the *Estimate* but was a prominent feature of one of Brown's later works, *A Dissertation on the Rise, Union and Power, the Progressions, Separations and Corruptions of Poetry and Music*, a work that was

---

[124] On Brown, see Roddier, *J.-J. Rousseau en Angleterre*; Hermann Flasdieck, *John Brown und seine Dissertation on Poetry and Music* (Halle, 1924); A. W. Evans, *Warburton and the Warburtonians: A Study in Some Eighteenth-Century Controversies* (Oxford, OUP, 1932), pp. 199–202; James Crimmins, *Secular Utilitarianism* (Oxford, OUP, 1990); Peter Miller, *Defining the Common Good: Empire, Religion and Philosophy in Eighteenth-Century Britain* (Cambridge, CUP, 1994), pp. 106–16, 333–6: William Roberts, *A Dawn of Imaginative Feeling: The Contribution of John Brown (1715–66) to Eighteenth-Century Thought and Literature* (Carlisle, Northern Academic Press, 1996); Nick Groom, "Celts, Goths, and the Nature of the Literary Source," in Alvaro Ribiero and James G. Basker, eds., *Tradition in Transition: Women Writers, Marginal Texts, and the Eighteenth-Century Canon* (Oxford, OUP, 1996), pp. 275–96.

[125] John Brown, *Sermons on Various Subjects* (London, 1764). Some of the content of Brown's criticism of Rousseau is reprinted in Roberts, *A Dawn of Imaginative Feeling*, pp. 227–37.

[126] [John Brown], *De la liberté civile et des factions* (n.p., 1789), pp. 3, 11.

published in 1763 and which then appeared in French translation as the *Histoire de l'origine et des progrès de la poésie dans ses différents genres* in 1768. The title of the book was a summary of the broader theory. As Castilhon presented it, it differed from Rousseau's only in that it was more dogmatic. But this did not mean that the sceptical Cynic had the advantage over the dogmatic Cynic. Like Brown, Wolban finally killed himself. So, too, the novel may have been intended to imply, would a sceptical Cynic like Rousseau.

Castilhon dedicated the novel to Voltaire. He was "a sage without ostentation, a philosopher without pride, a man of genius celebrated equally in every kind of literature, but one less dazzled by the glare of his own success than moved by the desire to make his country happier by arming his fellow citizens against the fires of fanaticism and the vile chains of superstition."[127] In the novel itself, Wolban (the Rousseau figure) was something like the opposite. He had inherited his own misanthropic disposition from a long line of Cynics. His father, who was Irish, had held high office but had lived as a recluse for thirty years before dying soon after the birth of his son. The son (Sir Charles Wolban) had been brought up by his great-uncle (another Cynic) and had been obliged to leave Ireland for London because the great-uncle (whose Cynicism may have been matched by Jacobite sympathies) was in the habit of speaking "so unguardedly about the most respectable families and useful citizens of Dublin and the enormous abuses of authority perpetrated by its magistrates."[128] London was no better. Wolban, accordingly, decided to try Paris. But Paris, too, failed to supply any relief for Wolban's restless dissatisfaction with himself and his hypersensitivity to others' shortcomings. One of his (few) friends advised him to take up agriculture. It was, he wrote, pointless to allow some people's wickedness or stupidity to become an obsession, when the important thing was simply not to be wicked oneself. This, he suggested, was why it was advisable for Wolban to turn to the life of a country gentleman and devote himself to improving his estates. Agriculture would not only supply solace. It was also a "beautiful art" and was "doubtless the most noble, the most august, and the first of them all."[129] The assertion gave Wolban his cue for setting out his own Cynic views.

---

[127] Jean-Louis Castilhon, *Le Diogène moderne, ou le désapprobateur*, 2 vols. (Bouillon, 1770), 1:vi. The same orientation is apparent in Castilhon's slightly earlier reworking of François-Ignace Espiard de la Borde's *Essai sur le génie et le caractère des nations* [1743] into his own, Voltaire-inspired, *Considérations sur les causes physiques et morales de la diversité du génie des moeurs, et du gouvernement des nations*, 2 vols. (Bouillon, 1769). On this (but without the Voltaire-inspired framework), see David A. Bell, *The Cult of the Nation in France: Inventing Nationalism, 1680–1800* (Cambridge, Mass., Harvard UP, 2001), pp. 10, 140–2.

[128] Castilhon, *Le Diogène moderne*, 1:15.

[129] Castilhon, *Le Diogène moderne*, 1:26.

It was quite simply false, he wrote, to say that the art of cultivating the land was the first of all the arts. It had, in fact, come to be seen as "the most useful kind of knowledge" only after "men, now reunited in society and enervated and weakened by their desires and the lassitude of satiety, ceased to set out to find their food in the simplicity of the various wild products of the vegetable kingdom."[130] Repeating (almost verbatim) what Rousseau had written in his second *Discourse*, Wolban went on to argue that a great deal of time would have had to pass before all the knowledge and technical capabilities needed for agriculture could have come into place. "Do you believe," he wrote, "that these observations and experiments could have been made before the formation of the first societies, an institution that is substantially later than the first age of the earth?"

> It would really be quite absurd or extremely foolish to think that men, in the state of pure nature, a state that probably lasted a great deal longer than is usually believed, and where men were isolated, fugitive, forest-dwelling wanderers, could have had the slightest idea of the art of making the land fertile, still less of daring to appropriate a piece of land, to settle on it and cultivate it.[131]

Humans were gatherers and cave- or forest-dwellers well before they acquired any capacity to plough the land or make their own fixed abodes. Yet they still had a range of human passions. These found expression in either articulated sounds, sudden gestures, or sharp or gentle cries, according to the kind of impression that the objects that moved them might make.

It followed, therefore, that "the most esteemed arts of our times, such as agriculture, sculpture, painting, geometry, and proud architecture," were all "new arts" and "the children of ignorance and corruption."[132] The first arts were actually "dancing, music, and poetry." These "three sciences" were "infinitely" prior in time to "all the other arts" and had preceded agriculture by "several thousands of centuries."[133] This insight, Wolban

---

[130] Castilhon, *Le Diogène moderne*, 1:39–40.

[131] Castilhon, *Le Diogène moderne*, 1:40.

[132] Castilhon, *Le Diogène moderne*, 1:44–5.

[133] Castilhon, *Le Diogène moderne*, 1:45–6. On the broader eighteenth-century interest in music and morality, see Cynthia Verba, *Music in the French Enlightenment* (Oxford, OUP, 1993), and, helpfully, Downing A. Thomas, *Music and the Origins of Language: Theories from the French Enlightenment* (Cambridge, CUP, 1995). Brown's theory was echoed by what came to be the better-known work by Robert Lowth, *Lectures on the Sacred Poems of the Hebrews* [1787]. As the editor of an 1815 edition of Lowth's book commented (Lowth, *Lectures*, p. 353), Lowth's description of Moses's ode followed Brown's treatment of poetry and religion. On the bearing of the subject on eighteenth-century discussions of the relationship between the arts and morality, see, despite its now dated style, the still fascinating analysis of Lessing's *Laocoon* in E. M. Butler, *The Tyranny of Greece over Germany* [1935] (Boston, Beacon Press, 1958), pp. 56–69.

wrote, was something that he had developed mainly by himself, but with some assistance from the "fictions and reasonings" of "Dr Brown."[134] Its starting point was the expressive character of the passions and the way that "pressing desires, lively sensations, or sharp feelings" would be given some kind of external expression. The type of expression that they were in fact given was shaped largely by human imitations of natural or animal sounds (the rustle of the reeds on the Nile, Wolban suggested, referring to the writings of Diodorus of Sicily and the seventeenth-century German Jesuit Athanasius Kircher, explained the Egyptian setting in which this capacity first emerged).[135] The origin of music was the easiest to explain in this way, but so, too, was poetry, which, in the beginning, was simply music performed by two or more individuals together. Dancing was also a product of the intensity and rhythms of the passions. It could be solemn or lively according to the emotion in question (the Greeks and Romans danced at funerals and on the tombs of their fellow citizens). Dancing for joy expressed an "inner cadence" that would be all the more pronounced "were we not held back by those laws of politeness and those social chains that polished peoples have had the imbecile feebleness to have forged."[136]

In all these ways, Castilhon took some care to ensure that Wolban's system avoided making the type of connection between the language of gestures and individual human needs that the abbé Etienne Bonnot de Condillac had made in his *Essai sur les origines des connaissances humaines* (An Essay on the Origins of Human Knowledge) of 1746 as a way of injecting a stronger moral theory into John Locke's *Essay on Human Understanding* (communities might sing together, but would not necessarily feel hungry or thirsty together).[137] Although the two sets of historical conjectures were somewhat similar, neither Condillac nor his brother, the abbé Gabriel Bonnot de Mably, made as much as Brown did of the parts played by music, poetry, and dance in producing the first forms of government. Together, as Wolban described them, the sounds and signs involved in music, poetry, and dance formed a poetic language that, in Egypt, Greece,

[134] Castilhon, *Le Diogène moderne*, 1:48. One reason for his interest in Brown may have been the very enthusiastic review of the French translation of Brown's book published in the *Journal des beaux arts et des sciences* 2 (April 1768): 113–27. Castilhon was one of its editors.

[135] Castilhon, *Le Diogène moderne*, 1:123. On Kircher, and this tradition in general, see, interestingly, Jan Assmann, *Moses the Egyptian: The Memory of Egypt in Western Monotheism* (Cambridge, Mass., Harvard UP, 1997).

[136] Castilhon, *Le Diogène moderne*, 1:51.

[137] On Condillac and eighteenth-century discussions of the origins of language, see Charles Porset, "*Grammatista philosophens*. Les sciences du langage de Port-Royal aux Idéologues (1660–1818). Bibliographie," in André Joly and Jean Stefanini, eds., *La Grammaire générale, des modistes aux idéologues* (Lille, Presses de l'Université de Lille, 1977), pp. 11–95; Hans Aarsleff, *From Locke to Saussure: Essays on the Study of Language and Intellectual History* (Minneapolis, University of Minnesota Press, 1982), pp. 146–209.

Persia, India, and Rome, had also formed the first philosophy (Rome, however, was a problematic case, because it had begun as a colony rather than in "the pure state of nature," which meant that such traces of a musical system of government as it had enjoyed were Greek imports that were soon subordinated to its own agricultural and martial values).[138] It was pointless, Wolban argued, to try now to determine whether it had been music, poetry, or dance that had come first, or to attempt to explain how one of the three might have brought the others into being. They were all copresent in the very earliest of times. Nor was it really essential to choose between the "aridity" of modern philosophy, with its undoubted utility, and the "beauties and fictions" of poetry and its rather different kind of utility. Poetry had become pernicious only after it had lost its ability to express feeling and had "renounced its primitive majesty."[139] It was this quality, however, that continued to justify its study, just as it did that of music and dance. It did not matter very much whether they once had been really united to form a single art both as the image of the various muses seemed to suggest and as "Dr Brown" had argued very strongly.[140] Even if, as seemed to be more likely, they had always been cultivated separately, they still had once possessed a dignity that had now been lost.

Wolban's objection to Brown's claim that music, dance, and poetry had once formed a single art was a product of his own religious scepticism. The point of Brown's insistence that the three arts had once been united was to highlight humanity's purely natural ability to recognise the sacred, and to emphasise the feelings of awe and reverence that this awareness of some sort of supernatural presence behind or beyond the natural world was likely to produce (Brown described the feelings in his poem *Night Scene in the Vale of Keswick*, where, as he put it, "this accumulation of beauty and immensity tends not only to excite rapture, but reverence").[141] The claim was similar to the better-known argument made by the young Edmund Burke in his *Philosophical Inquiry into the Origin of our Ideas of the Sublime and the Beautiful* of 1757. It meant, according to Brown, that the first of all art forms, and the synthesis of music, poetry, and dance, was the hymn. Such hymns were not the etiolated religious offerings of modern times but full-blown communal ceremonies in which dancing, singing, and chanted verse accompaniment served to give a unitary expression to the human recognition of the divine. The claim chimed well with the broader

---

[138] Castilhon, *Le Diogène moderne*, 1:242–7.

[139] Castilhon, *Le Diogène moderne*, 1:61.

[140] Castilhon, *Le Diogène moderne*, 1:61–2.

[141] The poem and the prose *Description of the Lake at Keswick* that accompanied it are reprinted in Roberts, *A Dawn of Imaginative Feeling*, pp. 237–43 (p. 241 for the passage cited here). See, too, Donald D. Eddy, "John Brown: 'The Columbus of Keswick,'" *Modern Philology* 73 (1976): S74–S84, for its possible date of composition.

theological arguments of Brown's mentor and patron, the High Anglican, but Whig, bishop of Gloucester, William Warburton, whose *Divine Legation of Moses* relied strongly on similar sorts of inference about the limited knowledge of the afterlife that God had first made available to the Jews, and the relationship that this naturalistic starting point was intended to have to the broader sequence of historical steps leading towards the final revelation of the full Christian dispensation that was built into the whole providential system.[142] For Brown, real evidence of this original human capacity could be seen in the ceremonies of the North American Indians, particularly as these had been described by the French Jesuit Joseph-François Lafitau, whose *Moeurs des sauvages américains comparées aux moeurs des premiers temps* (Customs of the American Indians Compared with the Customs of Primitive Times) had been published in 1724 (Lafitau's book was probably also the work that Castel had in mind when he referred to his attempts to persuade Montesquieu to examine what the "Canadian missionaries" had written about "naturalism").[143] As both Lafitau and Brown argued, the part played by music, dancing, and feasting among the American Indians indicated that sociability had its origins in natural religion, and that the first societies and the governments they housed were not the products of patriarchal authority, or human weakness, or the physical strength of a conqueror, or the reciprocal utility involved in exchange, or a social contract, but derived instead from the human ability to worship in common, and to admire the skills and prowess of those who took the lead in the ceremonial way of life that this entailed.

The first rulers were, therefore, singers and dancers. To illustrate the argument, Brown reproduced a long passage from Lafitau's book that gave a detailed description of this musical and ceremonial form of government as

---

[142] On Warburton, see Evans, *Warburton and the Warburtonians*; Brian W. Young, *Religion and Enlightenment in Eighteenth-Century England* (Oxford, OUP, 1998), pp. 167–212; and, on the bearing of his thought on English public art, Jerry D. Meyer, "Benjamin West's Chapel of Revealed Religion: A Study in Eighteenth-Century Protestant Religious Art," *Art Bulletin* 57 (1975): 247–65. For some older indications of the need for further study of the widespread French interest in Warburton's ideas and their bearing on the early thought of both Rousseau and Diderot, see Robert W. Rogers, "Critiques of the *Essay on Man* in France and Germany, 1736–1755," *English Literary History* 15 (1948): 176–93; James Doolittle, "Jaucourt's Use of Source Material in the *Encyclopédie*," *Modern Language Notes* 65 (1950): 387–92; Clifton Cherpack, "Warburton and the Encyclopédie," *Comparative Literature* 7 (1955): 226–39. On the broader moral and Christian context for Brown's views, see Ruth Smith, *Handel's Oratorios and Eighteenth-Century Thought* (Cambridge, CUP, 1995), pp. 52–140.

[143] On Lafitau, see Anthony Pagden, *The Fall of Natural Man: The American Indian and the Origins of Comparative Ethnology* [1982] (Cambridge, CUP, 1986), pp. 198–209; and David L. Blaney and Naeem Inayatullah, "The Savage Smith and the Temporal Walls of Capitalism," in Beate Jahn, ed., *Classical Theory in International Relations* (Cambridge, CUP, 2006), pp. 123–55.

it existed among the Iroquois people.[144] There, all the significant matters in Iroquois life were accompanied by ceremonial eating, singing, and dancing. "On the appointed day," Lafitau wrote, "early in the morning, they prepare the feast in the council-cabin, and there they dispose all things for the assembly." A public crier gave notice that the communal pot or kettle had been placed in a particular cabin, and "the common people and even the chiefs" gathered together, bringing their own kettles to the common meeting place. There was no "distinction of ranks among them," but the oldest men occupied "the foremost mats," while women, young men, and children watched the proceedings from afar (this, Lafitau noted, was a particularity of the Iroquois, since Brébeuf, in his early seventeenth-century *Relation of New France*, reported that he had seen a dispute for precedence in a Huron gathering). While the assembly was forming, "he who makes the feast, or he in whose name it is made, *sings alone*, like the person who chanted the theogony among the ancients, as if to entertain the company with things suitable for the subject which has called them together."[145] His song was intended to raise the subject of the assembly and establish its connection to "the fables of ancient times" and "the heroic deeds of their nation." Once the gathering was in place, its presiding speaker singled out the names of all those present and also entered "into particular detail of all that is in the pot." Each name, whether of a person or a thing, was echoed by a chorus of acclaim and approbation, as, too, was the subject matter of the assembly itself. Different subjects were introduced and addressed by different kinds of song, chorus, or dance, so that they formed the medium in which deliberation and decision making took place. As Lafitau also emphasised, the ceremonies had the same kind of format as those described by Homer in the *Iliad* or in descriptions of the pyrrhic dances of the ancients, or the Cretan dances that were still performed in Rome under the Caesars.[146] It followed, as the title of Lafitau's book could be taken to suggest, that music making and lawmaking were once indistinguishable, just as, according to Brown, the examples of the ancient bards and druids also served to show. The same sort of arrangements were, it was sometimes said, revealed by the "Ossian" poems that began to appear soon after Brown's death.[147]

[144] See Joseph-François Lafitau, *Customs of the American Indians Compared with the Customs of Primitive Times* [1724], ed. and trans. William N. Fenton and Elizabeth L. Moore, 2 vols. (Toronto, The Champlain Society, 1974), vol. 1, ch. 5, pp. 317–24. For the passage, see John Brown, *Histoire de l'origine et des progrès de la poésie dans ses différents genres* (Paris, 1768), pp. 8–20.

[145] Lafitau, *Customs*, ed. Fenton and Moore, vol. 1, ch. 5, p. 318, which is reproduced in Brown, *Dissertation*, pp. 29–36, and the further references to Lafitau in describing other forms of "savage enthusiasm" at pp. 51, 62, 75, 95, 119, 138.

[146] Lafitau, *Customs*, ed. Fenton ad Moore, vol. 1, ch. 5, pp. 319–21.

[147] For a helpful way in to both druids and "Ossian," see Philip C. Almond, "Druids, Patriarchs, and the Primordial Religion," *Journal of Contemporary Religion* 15 (2000): 379–94.

Wolban was not prepared to go so far as "the enthusiast" Brown.[148] Savage nations like the Iroquois and the Hottentots, he noted, did not have poetry or verse, but relied entirely on music, dance, and harmonious prose in their ceremonial life.[149] Both Plato and Clement of Alexandria also seemed to show that music was "the first of the sciences to have been cultivated in Egypt," and that Egypt's chief priest was "essentially a musician and dancer," but not a poet.[150] But Wolban still accepted the substantive claim about sociability and the origins of morality that Brown had made. This, he argued, could be separated off from the more problematic historical details about the union between music, dance, and poetry, and the part that hymns might have played at the very beginning of human society. The substantive point was that humans were sociable not because it was in their interest to be so, but because of their deep-seated imaginative ability to think of something beyond the realm of sense information, and their further ability, arising from feelings of awe, wonder, or fear, to identify themselves with its, not their own, aims and purposes. The results might, at first, be confused, and the effects of superstition might be perverse. But the bedrock of primary emotions, and the music and dance that they entailed, formed a robust alternative to claims about the origins of society in indigence, need, and utility, however they were couched.

The significance that both Rousseau and Brown attached to music and dancing in maintaining morality indicated another area of apparent common ground. Rousseau and Brown were both sentimentalists, but neither was a moral sense theorist in the style of the early eighteenth-century Anglophone moral philosophers Anthony Ashley Cooper, third earl of Shaftesbury, and Francis Hutcheson. Brown, in fact, first made his name by publishing a highly critical assessment of Shaftesbury's moral theory.[151] As one of Brown's admirers later explained, the major drawback of moral sense theory was its elitism. The "moral *taste* or *sense*," he wrote, "which in fact means no more than a certain *delicacy* of feeling" was not "given to all" but was, instead, peculiar to "a happy few, and even these do not

---

[148] Castilhon, *Le Diogène moderne*, 1:72 (see also p. 70).

[149] Castilhon, *Le Diogène moderne*, 1:131, 147.

[150] Castilhon, *Le Diogène moderne*, 1:142.

[151] John Brown, *Essays on the Characteristics* (London, 1751), a work that relied on the technique of parody to discredit Shaftesbury's moral sense theory. For helpful orientation on Shaftesbury and the broader subject of moral sense theory, see Stephen Darwall, *The British Moralists and the Internal 'Ought'* (Cambridge, CUP, 1995), and Michael B. Gill, *The British Moralists on Human Nature and the Birth of Secular Ethics* (Cambridge, CUP, 2006). On Brown's criticism of Shaftesbury, and on the similarities between the premises on which it was based and the thought of Edward Young, see Adam Potkay, *The Story of Joy: From the Bible to Late Romanticism* (Cambridge, CUP, 2007), pp. 105–6.

always turn it to the best advantage."[152] This, he continued, was because it lacked what was needed for the "formation of a *constant, uniform* and *general* principle." Here, as Brown had shown, the missing ingredient was religion. Unlike Shaftesbury's refined and high-flown moral sense, religion, as Brown had also shown, could be anchored to feelings that were available to everyone. "Why do we say that the generality of mankind are not capable of virtue on the terms of modern Platonism?" Brown's apologist asked.

> For this very obvious reason, that they can find no immediate pleasure, no charms in moral discipline, independently of its end and consequences. And why this again? Because the more general sources of pleasure in men are the senses, the imagination, and the passions.[153]

These natural capacities produced temper (meaning moderation) and character, without having to bring a moral sense into the picture, and they in turn governed most people's behaviour. As Brown had shown, this meant that moral sense theory was more likely than not to default into straightforward sensuality, simply because most people did not have the kind of capacity for discrimination that it presupposed. "In the gratifications of *sense* and *appetite*, such characters are sagacious and keen; but to a taste for the fine arts, *music, painting, architecture, poetry* etc, or the sublime feelings of *public* affection, they are utterly insensible." It also meant, as Brown himself had emphasised, that Shaftesbury's moral philosophy was likely to be self-defeating. "A more delicate frame awakens the powers of *fancy*; the taste runs into the more elegant refinements of the polite arts; or, in defect of this truer taste, on the false delicacies of dress, furniture, equipage, etc."[154] From this perspective, the passions themselves were all that was needed for the right kind of guidance to give hope and fear, candour or dissimulation, generosity or selfishness, and love or hatred a moral content. To bring the imagination and its fancies into the picture was actually a kind of Epicureanism masquerading as Platonism.

The argument paralleled Rousseau's more subtle demolition of moral sense theory and the entirely vacuous cosmopolitanism that, he argued, it entailed. Here, his target was Diderot and the Shaftesburyian argument that Diderot had used in his *Encyclopaedia* article on political right (*droit politique*) about how to counter "the violent reasoner" (or Thomas Hobbes's state-centred moral theory) by imaginatively projecting the universal rights

---

[152] [Laurence Nihell], *Rational Self-Love; or a* Philosophical and Moral Essay *on the Natural Principles of Happiness and Virtue: with Reflections on the various Systems of Philosophers, Ancient and Modern, on this Subject* [1770], (London, 1773), pp. 129–30.

[153] [Nihell], *Rational Self-Love,* p. 142.

[154] [Nihell], *Rational Self-Love,* pp. 142–3.

of the whole human race onto every more local setting.[155] As Rousseau pointed out in the *Letter to d'Alembert*, this still left a gap between theory and practice. Good feeling was never enough in the face of real human wickedness and, given the entirely imaginary foundations on which it was based, was more likely to weaken any more spontaneous ability to react. This, Rousseau argued, was why ordinary people were much better than philosophers at dealing with moral evil, and why, even if the theatre really did have a capacity for promoting virtue because of the gallery of moral examples that it could present, its effects were still likely to be self-defeating. The "knave" had every interest in promoting virtue, for everyone but himself.[156] Rousseau's scepticism towards moral sense theory fitted the broader endorsement of ordinary morality that was set out in Castilhon's portrait of the modern Diogenes. Wolban was entirely unimpressed by polished manners and urbane civility, either in Britain or in France, and was disgusted by the values and behaviour of the world of salons, theatres, and the opera. "What," he wrote, "is the class that essentially constitutes the state? It is not the clergy; it is not the nobility properly speaking. It is the people, the people alone."

> Now is the people, as the false and insulting opinion of nobles would have it, simply an assemblage of a large number of hardworking individuals called commoners (roturiers)? But who invents, who understands, who cultivates both the liberal and mechanical arts? Doubtless, all this is the work of these useful, enlightened, respectable, but all-too-little respected citizens to whom men who are infinitely less noble, because they are of absolutely no use, have scornfully given the name of commoner.[157]

The diatribe did not prevent Wolban, for reasons to do with the insuperable character of the human capacity for self-deception, from going on to defend the existence of social distinctions and the system of ranks. But it does indicate another of the similarities between Brown's and Rousseau's thought that Castilhon seems to have noticed. Diogenes may not have been a democrat. But the mockingly antielitist posture built into Cynic satire formed something of a bridge between Brown's and Rousseau's common hostility towards moral sense theory and its refined ability to imagine something like a society of the whole human race as the ultimate yardstick for making moral judgements. For Brown, the alternative to moral sense theory was religion. For Rousseau, it was politics. But music and language were central to both, either, in Brown's case, because they gave rise to integrated communities, or, in Rousseau's

---

[155] For the entry, see Diderot, *Political Writings*, pp. 17–21.
[156] Rousseau, *Letter*, pp. 23–4 (ed. Fuchs, p. 31).
[157] Castilhon, *Le Diogène moderne*, 2:361.

case, because they might, in the future, give rise to a multiplicity of self-sufficient political societies.

Brown was virtually the first English-language writer to use the French word "civilisation" in the context of describing what he took to be the attributes of a good society. (Interestingly, the very first appearance of the word in English seems to have occurred in one of the many replies to Brown's *Estimate*, entitled *A New Estimate of Manners and Principles*, which was published in 1760 by John Gordon, archdeacon of Lincoln. Gordon, like Castilhon, also associated Brown with Rousseau and devoted rather more of his text to attacking the latter than the former.)[158] Brown used the term in a way that matched the original concept to which the French word referred. Civilisation was something like the opposite of civility, because civility involved hypocrisy, politeness, and simulated morality, while civilisation itself was real.[159] In this usage, civilisation meant something nearer to the German word *Bildung*, with its emphasis upon the way that human culture could, progressively, enable more of what, spiritually, was inside human nature to come to be mirrored on the outside. Wolban's idea of civilisation was quite close to this view. It also involved a rather positive endorsement of enthusiasm. Every nation, he wrote, "in their first state of *civilisation*, had the same irregular, metaphorical, songs (*chants*), which were dictated by the enthusiasm that genius produces when heated by its own fire and, once abandoned to its enthusiasm, seeks to paint and express the poetical transports that move it so strongly."[160] Morality began with melody, but with no verse, and with music, but with no musicians.[161] Irrespective, moreover, of whether it had begun with music and dance, or had its own independent origins, the hymn, even among "enlightened peoples, long after their civilisation," was still the first form of poetry and

---

[158] On the initial usage, see John Gordon, *A New Estimate of Manners and Principles: Being a Comparison between Ancient and Modern Times* (Cambridge, 1760), pp. 55, 85, 87. The word "civilisation" is usually said to have made its first appearance in English in Adam Ferguson's *Essay on the History of Civil Society* in 1767, four years after its appearance in Brown's *Dissertation* and seven years after its appearance in Gordon's book. Ferguson's usage, it might be noted, grew out of the same interest as Brown's in the North American Indians as an original model of sociability. On the eighteenth-century concept of "civilisation," see, most recently, Bertrand Binoche, ed., *Les équivoques de la civilisation* (Seyssel, Champ Vallon, 2005), and, for Brown's use of the term, Georges Dulac, "Quelques exemples de transferts européens du concept de 'civilisation,'" in Binoche, pp. 105–35 (114–6). See, too, Jean Starobinski, *Blessings in Disguise; or the Morality of Evil* [1989], trans. Arthur Goldhammer (Cambridge, Polity Press, 1993), pp. 1–35, and the earlier secondary works referred to there.

[159] The word was coined by Victor Riqueti, marquis de Mirabeau, in his *L'Ami des hommes*, pt. 1 (Avignon, 1756), p. 136. Religion, he wrote there, "is the mainspring (*premier ressort*) of civilisation." The point of the neologism was to highlight the antithesis between civility and civilisation. Compare to Brown, *Histoire*, p. 21.

[160] Castilhon, *Le Diogène moderne*, 1:139 (the italics are in the original).

[161] Castilhon, *Le Diogène moderne*, 1:147–8.

192   CHAPTER THREE

had given rise to all the other poetic genres, "even the most licentious."[162] From Wolban's point of view, the Cynic's task was to try to find ways to recover the primary emotional purity that had once given the first arts their majesty and intensity in order to transform their debased modern counterparts, and put civilisation back on its proper moral foundations. As with Diogenes, the task was to deface the currency.

As Wolban acknowledged, the task was almost hopeless, although still not impossible.[163] This was because modern civilisation was based on a multiplicity of separate occupations and activities. Here, even poetry had an ambiguous status. If, like the Greek chorus, it had emerged as a separate component of what had once been an integrated musical system, then it had to be seen as the first step in the slow disintegration of unified human life. Once musical instruments came to be substituted for the human voice, the process was well under way. Musical instruments called for some sort of musical notation, and, with the beginning of written language, a door was open to the further cultivation of the sciences and the proliferation of even more specialised activities. Once music was cut off from its moorings in poetry and dance, so, too, was the whole system of moral authority and natural government that it had once supplied. The best dancers and singers could no longer be the natural leaders of whole peoples because they were, simply, musicians.[164] The process did not, however, run straightforwardly downhill. The addition of poetry to music led, initially, to the emergence of tragedy, and this, in turn, raised the status and authority of music and dance still higher. Here, myth and hymn could be combined to honour gods and heroes in epic public ceremonies in which the distinction between actors and spectators had not yet come into being. But if tragedy had been carried to its highest level by the ancient Greeks, it had been they, too, who had taken the process of social division another step further. This had occurred with the rise of gymnastics and the Olympic games, and the separation of dance from music that this had caused.[165] Once dance turned into gymnastics, music lost its prestige; as it did, it lost its unity with poetry, leaving poetry to become more ornate and corrupt once the technicalities of rhyme and metre began to replace the power and simplicity of earlier blank verse. The age of oracles, bards, auguries, and druids had begun to end.

[162] Castilhon, *Le Diogène moderne*, 1:70–1.
[163] Castilhon, *Le Diogène moderne*, 1:247.
[164] Castilhon, *Le Diogène moderne*, 1:73–6.
[165] Castilhon, *Le Diogène moderne*, 1:176. On Ossian, see Paul Van Tieghem, *Ossian en France*, 2 vols. (Paris, 1917); Howard Gaskill, ed., *Ossian Revisited* (Edinburgh, Edinburgh UP, 1991). For the parallel interest in both the Nibelungslied and the Edda myths, see Robert-Henri Blaser, *Un suisse J. H. Obereit, 1725–1798, médecin et philosophe, tire de l'oubli la chanson des Nibelungen* (Berne, Editions Berlincourt, 1965).

The views that Castilhon gave to the character of Wolban were not identical to Rousseau's. If Wolban was critical of Brown's theologically inspired views about the original union of music, dance, and poetry, he did not go very far towards the much more historically contingent set of claims about the origins of almost every human attribute that Rousseau set out in the first part of his *Discourse on the Origin of Inequality*. In some respects, Wolban's assertions about the poetic power of the primary emotions and the sublime metaphorical imagery that they could produce were rather similar in character to those made by another strong English religious and political moralist, the Anglican poet and clergyman Edward Young, whose *Night Thoughts* acquired an even broader following in France and Germany than Brown's works did (Mercier, for one, was a keen admirer of Young). Like Young, notably in his *Conjectures on Original Composition* of 1759, Wolban accepted that much of the genius of ancient poetry was still alive in Shakespeare and Milton (and had resurfaced more recently in the Ossian poems that had begun to emerge from Scotland). Common to both evaluations was the Platonic idea that creativity and frenzy (or enthusiasm) were closely connected.[166] Wolban's endorsement of this view ruled out the more subtle historical analysis of the origins of music's motivating power that, well before the appearance of his *Essay on the Origin of Languages*, could be pieced together from the entries to Rousseau's *Dictionary of Music*. He also made it clear that he did not agree with the claim made by "a polished savage in his absurd and very eloquent paradox on French music" (a fairly transparent reference to Rousseau) that the modern taste for musical harmony went along with the demise of any sense of local allegiance or patriotism.[167] Every nation, he replied, had a taste for its own music, irrespective of its harmonic or melodic character. But Wolban was still quite explicit in endorsing what Rousseau had written about the corrosive effects of the arts and the sciences. He

---

[166] Castilhon, *Le Diogène moderne*, 1:190–1. Although generally hostile to literature, Wolban was prepared to allow the daughter of one of his correspondents to read Richardson, some of Swift's works, and the *Spectator*, as well as "some few morsels of Pope, Dryden, and the sombre Young": 2:130. On the Platonic idea of creative frenzy, see Peter Kivy, *The Fine Art of Repetition* (Cambridge, CUP, 1993), pp. 35–74, and, on this aspect of Young's thought, see Patricia Phillips, *The Adventurous Muse: Theories of Originality in English Poetics 1650–1760* (Uppsala, 1984), pp. 95–110; Richard Bevis, *The Road to Egdon Heath: The Aesthetics of the Great in Nature* (Montreal and Kingston, McGill-Queen's UP, 1999), pp. 61–3; Shaun Irlam, *Elations: The Poetics of Enthusiasm in Eighteenth-Century Britain* (Stanford, Stanford UP, 1999), pp. 1–3, 171–200, 221–34; John Hope Mason, *The Value of Creativity: The Origins and Emergence of a Modern Belief* (Aldershot, Ashgate Press, 2003), pp. 103–4, 108–10, 140–2. On Young, see Walter Thomas, *Le poète Edward Young 1683–1765. Etude sur sa vie et ses oeuvres* (Paris, 1901), and Harold Forster, *Edward Young, the Poet of the Night Thoughts, 1683–1765* (Harleston, Erskine Press, 1986).

[167] Castilhon, *Le Diogène moderne*, 1:154.

did so by way of a comparison between what Rousseau had written in his first *Discourse*, and a long letter by the sixteenth-century Italian Platonist Lilio Gregorio Giraldi (an authority on the Gentile gods) to the better-known Platonist Pico della Mirandola. The letter was a diatribe, pouring scorn upon the vanity and pointless erudition of modern theologians and jurists, all compared unfavourably to the morality and simplicity of the Spartans, the ancient Egyptians, and the Scythians. The point of the comparison was partly to insinuate that Rousseau was not quite so original as he seemed (a common tactic adopted by Rousseau's critics, although, as a Cynic, Wolban went to some lengths to explain that the idea of plagiarism stood at odds with the fact that proper philosophers were bound to repeat the same natural truths).[168] Its main aim, however, was to highlight the Cynic pedigree of Rousseau's thought. "Not to approve of the opinions and system of the philosopher of Geneva," Wolban observed, "is also to condemn the letter or, if you will, the declamation of the all-too-little-known Cynic Lilio-Giraldi."[169]

Wolban's version of Cynic political thought also looked something like Rousseau's own. "An inner voice," he wrote,

> tells us perpetually that we were created to be independent, and this powerful voice is all the more cruel and disheartening (*accablante*) in that everything in society contradicts and proscribes that sweet and splendid liberty towards which we aspire so unremittingly, but always in vain. Men are born free and should be free, but they are slaves everywhere.[170]

But from Wolban's point of view, Rousseau's Geneva was simply off the theoretical map. To talk of political liberty or political virtue was simply to deal in conceptual oxymorons. Once there were societies, there were also power, constraint, subordination, and dependence, and only vanity and pride could make political societies and the inevitable social hierarchies that they housed bearable. Happily, however, people had an infinite capacity for self-deception. The Romans, Wolban observed, had been well advised to make a mere hat the symbol of liberty, instead of, as other ancient peoples had done, setting liberty alongside an array of goddesses or some other splendid symbols. In the curious civil ceremony that accompanied the emancipation of a slave, "the new citizen covered his head with the cap of liberty, a sort of woollen bonnet made of a very tightly matted tissue that was quite similar to our own [English] hats, and the unfortunate free man fell from domestic servitude into public slavery, because, as I have pointed out, which people was less free than that of

---

[168] Castilhon, *Le Diogène moderne*, 1:290–304, 359–81.
[169] Castilhon, *Le Diogène moderne*, 2:18–9.
[170] Castilhon, *Le Diogène moderne*, 2:427.

Rome?"[171] But, however much insight into the human condition Wolban imagined that he had, he had no insight at all into his own. Three unhappy love affairs finally led to the theft of all his wealth at the hands of the woman he imagined he was about to marry (Wolban's history was, in this sense, another examination of the problematic nature of the Cynic attitude to love). His suicide was a measure of the chasm between Cynic pride and the real simplemindedness that it served to disguise.

"THAT SUBTLE DIOGENES": IMMANUEL KANT AND ROUSSEAU'S DILEMMAS

It was Immanuel Kant who described the similarity between Rousseau's thought and more orthodox Christianity most succinctly. In a little essay entitled *Conjectures on the Beginning of Human History* that he published in the *Berlinische Monatsschrift* in 1786, and which he described as "no more than a pleasure trip," Kant presented Rousseau's *Discourse on the Origin of Inequality* as scriptural history without the scripture.[172] The setting that he used to rehearse Rousseau's story was supplied by Genesis 2–6 and its short version of Rousseau's longer account of the very first times. In the short version, the first humans could stand, walk, and talk. They could, therefore, think. All this, Kant emphasised, was still compatible with Rousseau's longer version of the story because these were all skills that could not have been innate, so that the full version of the story must indeed have taken a very long time. Even though, Kant continued, the first humans could think, they were still "guided solely by instinct, that *voice of God* which all animals obey."[173] This did not mean that they had any special faculty that had since been lost. All that it meant was that they were guided absolutely by sense information, knowing, for example, that the sense of smell in its affinity with the sense of taste was a reliable indicator of the type of food that was fit for consumption. It was, in short, *amour-de-soi*. The trouble began with the human use of reason. Reason could be used to compare information supplied by one of the senses to that supplied by another. Although smell might be all that was naturally required to distinguish between the edible and the inedible, once sight was

---

[171] Castilhon, *Le Diogène moderne*, 2:438.

[172] Immanuel Kant, *Conjectures on the Beginning of Human History*, in Kant, *Political Writings*, ed. Hans Reiss (Cambridge, CUP, 1991), pp. 221–34. For further examination of the Kant-Rousseau dialogue, see Richard L. Velkley, *Freedom and the End of Reason: On the Moral Foundations of Kant's Critical Philosophy* (Chicago, University of Chicago Press, 1989), and his *Being after Rousseau: Philosophy and Culture in Question* (Chicago, University of Chicago Press, 2002), pp. 1–61.

[173] Kant, *Conjectures*, ed. Reiss, p. 223.

used too, a new range of criteria about what might or might not be edible would be brought into play. It was, Kant observed, "a peculiarity of reason that it is able, with the help of the imagination, to invent desires which not only *lack* any corresponding natural impulse, but which are even *at variance* with the latter." These desires, Kant wrote puritanically, which were known primarily as "*lasciviousness*," might have been quite trivial (over an apple, for example), but their effects were still momentous. They led to a decision "to abandon natural impulses" and to a consciousness that reason was "a faculty which can extend beyond the limits to which all animals are confined." The result was "the first experiment in free choice," which did not turn out well. But that decision having been made, it was impossible "to return to a state of servitude under the rule of instinct."[174]

Once the instinct for food had been upset by reason, the next to go was the sexual instinct. "Man soon discovered that the sexual stimulus, which in the case of animals is based merely on a transient and largely periodic urge, could in his case be prolonged and even increased by means of the imagination." This was where the fig leaf came in. By making the object of the sexual instinct inaccessible to the senses, the fig leaf allowed memory and imagination to make inclination more intense, so that animal desire could become love, and "a feeling for the merely agreeable" could turn into "a taste for beauty." It also produced a "*sense of decency*" or "an inclination to inspire respect in others by good manners (i.e. by concealing all that might invite contempt)," which, Kant noted, was "the first incentive for man's development as a moral being." The result was "a whole new direction of thought," not only because it brought thinking about others into the picture, but also because it led to thinking about the future.[175] This was the third step that reason took. The huge range of possibilities presented by this vista was a source both of anticipation, because it went along with an ability to make preparations, and of apprehension, because it also went along with the knowledge that life would bring death. Both were powerful motivations for the first humans to think about maintaining the prospect of being able to live through their offspring. With this array of capacities, the fourth step could follow. This was the ability to differentiate human nature from animal nature and to see, first, that animals could be used to meet human purposes, but, second, that humans could not treat other humans as if they were animals.

The story of the Fall was, therefore, "nothing other" than man's "transition from a rude and purely animal existence to a state of humanity, from the leading strings of instinct to the guidance of reason—in a word, from the guardianship of nature to the state of freedom."[176] Seen thus, it

---

[174] Kant, *Conjectures*, ed. Reiss, pp. 223–4.
[175] Kant, *Conjectures*, ed. Reiss, pp. 224–5.
[176] Kant, *Conjectures*, ed. Reiss, p. 226.

was also the way "to reconcile with each other and with reason the often misunderstood and apparently contradictory pronouncements of the celebrated *J. J. Rousseau.*"

> In his essays *On the Influence of the Sciences* and *On the Inequality of Man*, he shows quite correctly that there is an inevitable conflict between culture and the nature of the human race as a *physical* species each of whose individual members is meant to fulfil his destiny completely. But in his *Emile*, his *Social Contract* and other writings, he attempts in turn to solve the more difficult problem of what course culture should take in order to ensure the proper development, in keeping with their destiny, of man's capacities as a *moral* species, so that this destiny will no longer conflict with his character as a natural species. Since culture has perhaps not yet really begun—let alone completed—its development in accordance with the true principles of man's *education* as a human being and citizen, the above conflict is the source of all the genuine evils which oppress human life, and of all the vices which dishonour it. At the same time, the very impulses which are blamed as the causes of vice are good in themselves, fulfilling their function as abilities implanted by nature. But since these abilities are adapted to the state of nature, they are undermined by the advance of culture and themselves undermine the latter in turn, until art, when it reaches perfection, once more becomes nature—and this is the ultimate goal of man's moral destiny.[177]

To show how "art" might once more become "nature," Kant continued to follow Rousseau's stadial history, still using Genesis as his guide. The gulf that reason opened up between human and animal nature led, first, to the domestication of wild animals and then to the development of agriculture and, with it, the replacement of "the age of leisure and peace" by "the age of *labour and discord*." Pastoral nomads could not live alongside farmers without conflicts over property and, on the side of the latter, efforts to protect their crops from the incursions of livestock. The first nucleated settlements began to take shape, and, as they did, exchange began to occur. This in turn entailed separate occupations and the beginnings of civil government and the public administration of justice. "This epoch," Kant noted, "also saw the beginning of human *inequality*, that abundant source of so much evil, but also of everything good."[178]

Inequality was, thus, the engine of history. Once there was inequality, there would be conflict, and, with conflict, there would be war. In the short term, the winners would be the inhabitants of the property-based world of the towns, and the settled societies and luxury that they housed. "In the course of time," Kant wrote, "the growing luxury of the town-dwellers

[177] Kant, *Conjectures*, ed. Reiss, pp. 227–8.
[178] Kant, *Conjectures*, ed. Reiss, pp. 229–30.

and in particular the seductive arts in which the women of the towns sur-
passed the unkempt wenches of the wilderness, must have been a powerful
temptation to the herdsmen to enter into relations with them."[179] The
seductions of town life would put an end to the antagonism between rural
nomads and property-based urbanity. But this new modus vivendi would
be the end of freedom. Just as Rousseau had ended his second *Discourse*,
so Kant ended his *Conjectures* with despotism. Generalised inequality "led
on the one hand to a despotism of powerful tyrants, and—since culture
had only just begun—to soulless extravagance and the most abject slavery,
combined with all the vices of the uncivilised state."[180] But the outcome
was still no reason to despair. As with Rousseau, what appeared to be an
evil could, at a deeper level, be seen to contain its own remedies. Here,
however, Kant began to superimpose rather more of his own philosophy
of history onto the apocalyptic end point of Rousseau's second *Discourse*.

The first and most obvious of the evils that inequality produced was
war. This was not just a matter of "actual wars in the past or present," but
of the "unremitting, indeed ever-increasing *preparation* for war" and the
massively wasteful consumption of resources that this involved. But it was
still the case that war and freedom went hand in hand. "We need only
look," Kant wrote, "at *China*, whose position may expose it to occasional
unforeseen incursions but not to attack by a powerful enemy, and we shall
find that, for this very reason, it has been stripped of every vestige of freedom." The grim conclusion was that "so long as human culture remains
at its present state, war is therefore an indispensable means of advancing it
further."[181] This, in the second place, meant that there was no alternative
to the jagged, often backward, course of human history. Although, Kant
suggested, it might seem desirable for humanity to be equipped with a
continuous collective memory of its own past existence, and a permanent
store of experience to draw on to avoid its earlier mistakes, the price of
this kind of agelessness was likely to be far too high. Every past wrong
would remain permanently alive, leaving no room at all for time and forgetting to do their work. This, too, was the message of Genesis, where
prediluvian humans had lived for eight hundred years. "Fathers would live
in mortal fear of their sons, brothers of brothers, and friends of friends,
and the vices of a human race of such longevity would necessarily reach
such a pitch that it would deserve no better a fate than to be wiped from
the face of the earth by a universal flood."[182] Nor, finally, was there any
point in wishing for a reversion to some "*golden age*," in which "we are,

[179] Kant, *Conjectures*, ed. Reiss, p. 231.
[180] Kant, *Conjectures*, ed. Reiss, p. 231.
[181] Kant, *Conjectures*, ed. Reiss, pp. 231–2.
[182] Kant, *Conjectures*, ed. Reiss, p. 233.

supposedly, relieved of all those imaginary needs with which luxury encumbers us" and "are content with the bare necessities of nature and there is complete equality and perpetual peace among men."[183] The problem with the golden age was that there had actually been one. But the first humans had found it to be unsatisfactory when they had made the discovery of choice. Even if it were possible to get back, it would simply be a new beginning, not the journey's end. There was, therefore, no alternative but to accept the fact that humans had got just the kind of history that they deserved.[184] And, since it really was *their* history, it would also have to be their future.

History, Kant concluded, did not "begin with good and then proceed to evil." Instead, it "develops gradually from the worse to the better."[185] As a rendition of Rousseau, it was entirely faithful to the historical dimension of his thought and, in particular, to the double-edged character of Rousseau's neologism *perfectibilité* and the combination of improvement and depravity that it implied. In other works, Kant used the term *unsocial sociability* to mean something similar. But the rather bleak theodicy that Kant drew out of Rousseau's thought relied quite heavily on two concepts that Rousseau himself did not use, at least in as positive a way. The first was "culture"; the second was "civilisation." These, when they were connected to the broader theological framework of Kant's thought, made his moral theory quite different from anything that could be pieced together from Rousseau's works. As Kant observed in his lectures on ethics, Rousseau was rather like a Cynic and, for this reason, could not escape the dilemmas built into Cynic philosophy.

> For Diogenes, the means of happiness were negative. He said that man is by nature content with little; because man, by nature, has no needs, he also does not feel the want of means, and under this want he enjoys his happiness. Diogenes has much in his favour, for the provision of means and gifts of nature increases our needs, since the more means we have, the more our needs are augmented, and the thoughts of man turn to greater satisfactions, so that the mind is always uneasy. Rousseau, that subtle Diogenes, also maintained that our will would be good by nature, only we always become corrupted; that nature would have provided us with everything, if we did not create new needs.[186]

If, as Kant observed, the Cynic concern with simplicity had much to commend it (it was, he commented, the shortest way to morality), the parallel

---

[183] Kant, *Conjectures*, ed. Reiss, p. 233.

[184] Kant, *Conjectures*, ed. Reiss, p. 233.

[185] Kant, *Conjectures*, ed. Reiss, p. 234.

[186] Immanuel Kant, *Lectures on Ethics*, ed. Peter Heath and J. B. Schneewind (Cambridge, CUP, 1997), p. 45.

also indicated the limitations of Rousseau's enterprise. "The perfect man of Diogenes," Kant noted, "is good without virtue."[187] This was because a real capacity for virtue called for a "concept of evil" and "the strength of soul to withstand, out of duty, the onset of evil." Goodness without virtue was simply innocence, and innocence, by definition, could not rely on wisdom or prudence when it was required to make a choice. It could not resist the most innocuous of desires (for an apple, perhaps); and, once there were desires and the means to meet them, innocence would be lost. "A man's desires keep on growing," Kant observed, "and without realizing it, he is out of his innocence. Rousseau has tried to bring it back again, but in vain."[188]

Kant's verdict was, in a sense, anticipated by Rousseau himself. Once there were political societies, there would have to be laws. But laws on their own could never be self-enforcing. There would have to be governments and institutions, and these, however well they might be arranged, would still require resources, if not of money, then at least of time. Even the most virtuous of societies would have to face these rival claims upon its allegiances, and the clash between individual interests and the public interest that they might entail. In a famous letter sent on 26 July 1767, Rousseau informed the marquis de Mirabeau, one of the founders of Physiocracy—the most intellectually ambitious attempt to conceive of a system of government that, according to its advocates, really could be compatible with both individual well-being and collective social life—trying to establish a government of laws, and to set the laws above both those responsible for enforcing them and those responsible for obeying them, was like trying to square the circle in geometry. Even a state with a sovereign general will would still have needs because no state could ever be entirely disembodied. The same applied to the Physiocratic idea of "legal despotism." However much the whole system might appear to be bound by the rule of nature's laws, there would still be a time when the needs of the state would have to come first, and when legal despotism might default into real despotism. There was no middle position, Rousseau wrote, between "the most austere democracy" and "the most perfect Hobbism," and, since democracy could not be expected to remain "austere," the only alternative was to set the sovereign so far above the laws that it would, in effect, be God.[189] Although it was originally private, Rousseau's letter was published

---

[187] Kant, *Lectures*, ed. Heath and Schneewind, p. 228. Although the subject of ancient moral philosophy and its eighteenth-century reverberations was not part of his brief, the remark suggests that the title of Patrice Higonnet's study of Jacobinism, *Goodness beyond Virtue* (Cambridge, Mass., Harvard UP, 1998), may have been more apt than he realised.

[188] Kant, *Lectures*, ed. Heath and Schneewind, p. 228.

[189] Rousseau to Mirabeau, 26 July 1767, in Jean-Jacques Rousseau, *Correspondance complète*, ed. R. A. Leigh, 52 vols. (Oxford, Voltaire Foundation, 1967–98), 33: 238–42 (p. 240 for the

in 1768 as part of a pamphlet entitled *Précis de l'ordre légal* (An Outline of the Legal Order) and reprinted in a second edition of Mirabeau's *Lettres sur la législation* (Letters on Legislation) published in Berne in 1775, as well as in several collections of Rousseau's own works.[190] Knowledge of its existence seems to have become quite widespread and seems, too, to have led to some interest in finding an answer to the questions that it raised. One answer, it might be said, was the system of representative government envisaged by Emmanuel-Joseph Sieyès. Another answer, however, was much nearer to the assessment of Rousseau that Louis-Sébastien Mercier published in 1791. Here, two aspects of Mercier's assessment were particularly widely shared. The first was the idea of society as a kind of living entity. The second was Mercier's endorsement of public credit. As Mercier had suggested in 1787, the two could go together remarkably well, particularly if a state could find a way to isolate itself. Together they looked like the way to give Rousseau's moral and political thought a real-world applicability and, by doing so, to deal with the vexed subjects of inequality, private property, and the property of the state that, in the last analysis, had brought Rousseau to a dead end.

---

phrases cited). One of the rare additions that could be made to that marvellous edition would be a publication history of this letter.

[190] Victor Riqueti, marquis de Mirabeau, *Précis de l'ordre légal* (Paris, 1768), and the note on it by Dupont de Nemours in the *Ephémérides du citoyen*, issue 8 (1769): 35, referring to "quelques objections" raised by "J.-J. R" that Mirabeau "repousse avec force." See also Victor Riqueti, marquis de Mirabeau, *Lettres sur la législation, ou l'ordre légal dépravé, rétabli et perpétué* [London, 1769], 2nd ed. (Berne, 1775), where the exchange was reprinted. Other copies of the letter can be found in Jean-Jacques Rousseau, *Oeuvres ... nouvelle édition* (Neufchâtel [Paris], n.d.), 5:358–63; Rousseau, *Collection complète des Oeuvres* (Geneva, 1782), 24:572–78; Rousseau, *Pièces diverses*, 4 vols. (London, P. Cazin, 1782). It was also reprinted in the *Bibliothèque de l'homme public* 10 (1791): 249–53.

⚜4⚜

PROPERTY, EQUALITY, AND THE PASSIONS

IN EIGHTEENTH-CENTURY

FRENCH THOUGHT

REFORM, REVOLUTION, AND THE PROBLEM OF STATE POWER

THE CYNIC label that was applied to both Rousseau and his more
orthodox Christian critics captured something common to their respective styles of moral and cultural criticism, but it also served to blur
what continued to divide them. For Rousseau, human history was made
up of three different states—solitary independence, self-sufficient families,
and socially interdependent households—with Geneva firmly in the third
(France, as he emphasised in his *Letter to d'Alembert*, was beyond the pale).
This radically unnatural state called for an equally radical, unnatural solution, which Rousseau set out in *The Social Contract*. For "Estimate" Brown,
however, the same three states pointed towards a more natural way out. In
a remote sense, the similarities and differences were connected to a way
of thinking about property, and its ability to neutralise the passions, that
originated in the late seventeenth century, and supplied a starting point
not only for modifying the strongly Augustinian views of fallen human nature of both orthodox Calvinists and heterodox Catholics like the French
Jansenists, but also for countering Thomas Hobbes's idea of representative political sovereignty on something like his own terms. This interest in
property arose from a new, theologically heterodox, interest in the human
body, and a different type of evaluation of the idea of human beings as
embodied souls. The first half of this chapter is an examination of its
origins, and its bearing on the moral and political thought of François de
Salignac de la Mothe Fénelon and his followers. Its aim is to present some
idea of the intellectual context that made it possible to align Rousseau's
moral and political thought either with Hobbes or with Fénelon, and,
ultimately, with both. With this established, it may then be easier to see
why the advocates of the ambitious programme of economic and social
reform that came to be known as Physiocracy were able to associate Rousseau, Hobbes, and Fénelon with something like the same, rather sober,

set of moral and political arrangements. Finally, it may then also be easier
to see why Physiocracy's practical failure did not, as is still sometimes assumed, discredit its broader moral concerns. These, instead, now came to
be linked to a new interest in the properties of public credit, and to the
possibility that modern public finance could be used to reach Physiocracy's goal, without recourse to Physiocratic means. Here, the common
ingredient was the idea that reform could be engineered indirectly, rather
than through direct reliance on royal legislation and state power. If this
really was the case, then, as the final part of this chapter is intended to
show, there was also a real alternative to the difficulties and dilemmas associated with the subject of reform that Montesquieu had been the first to
highlight, but which Rousseau had gone on largely to endorse.

In this context, the most immediate measure of both the similarities
and the differences between Rousseau and Brown lay in their respective
reactions to the typology of governments contained in Montesquieu's *The
Spirit of Laws*, and its bearing on the subject of reform. As Voltaire's admirer Jean-Louis Castilhon noticed, a sceptical Cynic like the Wolban-
Rousseau figure in his novel appeared to endorse Montesquieu's typology
but took it to indicate the unreformable character of absolute royal government, as Rousseau really did, while a dogmatic Cynic like "Estimate"
Brown appeared to reject Montesquieu's typology and, instead, to insist
upon the real compatibility between monarchy and the political virtue
that, in *The Spirit of Laws*, Montesquieu had consigned to republics.[1]
Brown set out his own views in a long memorandum to Catherine the
Great in 1766 describing the steps to be followed to correct the excessive enthusiasm of her predecessor, Peter the Great, for foreign trade and
urban industry by implementing what he called "a general and connected
plan of civilization."

> I call this [Brown wrote] a natural intervention, because it appears from the
> history of mankind that when the improvement and civilization of a king-
> dom proceeds by a more gradual and unforced progress of things—that is,
> when the sovereign engages his nobles and people, first in the practice and
> improvement of agriculture, by which the honest comforts of life are first ob-
> tained and a general spirit of industry is excited throughout the internal parts
> of the country; when to this is added an application to home manufactures,
> in order to make the best of what agriculture has produced; when population

---

[1] For an indication of the hostility provoked by Montesquieu's book, see Michael So-
nenscher, *Before the Deluge: Public Debt, Inequality, and the Intellectual Origins of the French
Revolution* (Princeton, Princeton UP, 2007), pp. 83–4, 95–7, 173–4; and, recently, Simone
Zurbuchen, "Theorizing Enlightened Absolutism: The Swiss Republican Origins of Prussian
Monarchism," in Hans Blom, John Christian Laursen, and Luisa Simonutti, eds., *Monarchisms
in the Age of Enlightenment* (Toronto, University of Toronto Press, 2007), pp. 240–66.

is thus naturally increased, and when these improved goods of nature are dispersed through such a country by the arts and contrivances of domestic commerce—when such is the natural and unforced progress of things, I believe your Imperial Majesty will find it a truth founded in the history of mankind, that among such a people, an honest simplicity of manners, with a concomitant regard to religious principles, and useful, though bounded knowledge, and if attended with a tolerable system of policy, almost spontaneously arise. And from thence the ascent is also easy and natural, nor yet dangerous, up to a higher state of elegance, arts, science and foreign emoluments, which may then be safely brought in by a guarded communication and commerce with foreign countries.[2]

Despite the similarity between "honest simplicity of manners" and "useful, though bounded knowledge" as the basis of their respective conceptions of a good society, Brown's projection was considerably more sanguine than anything that Rousseau envisaged, even, for example, in his *Considerations on the Government of Poland*. If it survived, Poland would be a large-scale version of the Valais, not Geneva. Rousseau's own view of "the natural and unforced progress of things" followed the logic of his *Discourse on the Origin of Inequality*. When (together with Brown) he was invited in 1762 by the Patriotic Society of the Swiss Republic of Berne to write an essay on the subject of how to reform the corrupted morals of a people, Rousseau flatly refused to take part. "Truth," he informed the society's secretary, Vincenz Bernhard Tscharner, "has almost never been effective in the world, because men are always guided more by their passions than by the light of reason, and do evil while approving the good. The century in which we live is one of the most enlightened, even in morality. Is it one of the best?"[3]

It was hard to overlook the tension between Rousseau's harsh indictment of the modern world and his stern refusal to engage with it. His concept of perfectibility appeared to supply a motivation for promoting human improvement, but his discouraging assessment of modern morality seemed to rule it out, leaving nothing beyond his corrosive indictment of modernity's pathologies, and of the state-centred selfishness that Machiavelli had apotheosised in *The Prince* (which, Rousseau wrote, was why it was a book for republicans). "Machiavellianism," wrote one of the most famous of his admirers and critics, Antoine de Caritat, marquis de

[2] Brown to Catherine the Great, 28 August 1766, in Andrew Kippis, *Biographia Britannica, or the Lives of the Most Eminent Persons who Have Flourished in Great Britain*, 5 vols. (London, 1778–93), 2:670.

[3] Rousseau to Tscharner, 29 April 1762, in Jean-Jacques Rousseau, *Correspondance complète*, ed. R. A. Leigh, 52 vols. (Oxford, Voltaire Foundation, 1967–98), vol. 10, letter 1761, pp. 225–6.

Condorcet, "is based on this single principle, that men are naturally stupid and wicked, and if the perfectibility of the human race were once to be proved, it (Machiavellianism) would fall back into nothingness, so that proving that perfectibility amounts to destroying every false system opposed to human well-being." It has now become clear how much time and effort Condorcet devoted to the task.[4] The immediate source of the difficulty, and of both Brown's and Rousseau's very different assessments of modernity's capacity for reform, was Montesquieu's *The Spirit of Laws*. The typology of governments that Montesquieu set out there made it difficult to think about reform without also having to think about the nature and limits of sovereign power, and about what, in the light of this, it was possible to change or necessary to keep. In a French setting, the subjects arose both because of the significance of what Montesquieu called subordinate, dependent, and intermediate powers in giving a monarchy its nature, and because of the risks to their existence that seemed to follow from reliance on centralised governmental power to promote economic or social reform. In this sense, Montesquieu's typology appeared to set firm limits on royal legislative power because it appeared to rule out any assimilation of monarchies to republics as species of the broader genus *res publica*. Both, he argued, had to be understood in the light of the properties of a third type of rule, despotism, and of the very different ways by which the members of both republics and monarchies were, in fact, shielded from the state's sovereign power. Failure to appreciate these differences, he warned, could lead to the wrong choice of one or other of the various types of law involved in all systems of rule, exposing either form of government to arrangements or judgements that were ultimately incompatible with their underlying norms. In this light, even the best-intentioned of reforms could have the worst of eventual outcomes. The real danger, according to Montesquieu, of failing to understand the despotic nature of sovereign power lay in the type of well-meaning application of republican principles to a monarchy that could be found in the idea of a "republican monarchy" contained in the as-yet-unpublished

---

[4] See the remarkable new edition of Marie-Jean-Antoine-Nicolas de Caritat, marquis de Condorcet, *Tableau historique des progrès de l'esprit humain. Projets, Esquisse, Fragments et Notes (1772–1794)*, ed. Jean-Pierre Schandeler and Pierre Crépel (Paris, Institut National des Etudes Démographiques, 2004), p. 174, for the passage translated here. As Condorcet emphasised in 1782 in his speech on his admission to the Académie française, it was "chimerical" to think that humans could be made to be more virtuous, but it was still possible to envisage "a system of laws" that would make "courage and virtue almost unnecessary," just as complicated machines allowed the least skilled worker to perform "masterpieces of human industry": *Recueil des harangues prononcées par Messieurs de l'Académie française dans leur réception*, 8 vols. (Paris, 1787), 8:413–49 (421–2). On Rousseau's characterisation of Machiavelli in *The Social Contract*, see Rousseau, *The Social Contract and Other Later Political Writings*, ed. Victor Gourevitch (Cambridge, CUP, 1997), bk. 3, ch. 6, p. 95.

Considerations on the Present and Former Government of France (written, to Voltaire's approval, by René-Louis de Voyer de Paulmy, marquis d'Argenson, towards the end of the third decade of the eighteenth century).[5] Instead of reducing injustice as d'Argenson hoped, trying to reform a monarchy along republican lines, Montesquieu suggested, might have the perverse effect of producing despotism.

Rousseau repeated Montesquieu's argument, but simply reversed his evaluations. Republics, as Montesquieu had shown, were a product of special conditions, as, too, were monarchies. But, Rousseau argued, the future still belonged to republics, not to monarchies, because, as he wrote repeatedly, the great territorial monarchies of modern Europe were soon likely to fall into a state of terminal crisis. All governments, he argued, became smaller and more powerful, the larger the number of people, and the greater the size of the territory that they were required to rule. As with Montesquieu, reforming a monarchy might simply accelerate the slide towards despotism and, as Rousseau predicted so frequently, result in revolution. The best-known of his predictions was the one that he published in his *Emile* of 1762, where he wrote, "[W]e are approaching the state of crisis and the century of revolutions," because, he added in a note, it was "impossible for the great monarchies of Europe to last much longer."[6] He repeated the claim in his *Considerations on the Government of Poland*, written in 1772 but published only posthumously in 1781. "I see," he wrote there, "all the states of Europe rushing to their ruin. Monarchies, republics, all those nations with all their magnificent institutions, all those fine and wisely balanced governments, have grown decrepit and threaten soon to die."[7] Here, the prediction applied as much to Britain as to the absolute monarchies of the European mainland, corroborating what he had written in 1761. "It is easy to foresee that in twenty years from this time, England, with all its glory, will be ruined and have lost the remainder of its liberty," he announced then.[8] The likely cause might come from within, as in the prediction of revolution made at the end of the *Discourse on the Origin of Inequality*, where, Rousseau wrote, the "uprising that finally strangles or

---

[5] On d'Argenson, see Sonenscher, *Before the Deluge*, pp. 159–65, and the secondary literature referred to there.

[6] Jean-Jacques Rousseau, *Emile, ou de l'éducation* [1762], ed. Michel Launay (Paris, Garnier Flammarion, 1966), bk. 3, p. 252. It may be worth noting that there is no entry on revolution in N.J.H. Dent, *A Rousseau Dictionary* (Oxford, Blackwell, 1992).

[7] Jean-Jacques Rousseau, *Considérations sur le gouvernement de Pologne* [1772], ed. Barbara de Negroni (Paris, Flammarion, 1990), p. 164. I have slightly modified the translation given in Rousseau, *The Social Contract and Other Political Writings*, ed. Gourevitch, p. 178.

[8] Jean-Jacques Rousseau, *A Project for Perpetual Peace* (London, 1761), p. 16 (see also Jean-Jacques Rousseau, *Oeuvres complètes*, ed. Louis-Sébastien Mercier, Gabriel Brizard, and Louis Le Tourneur, 38 vols. (Paris, 1788–93), 3:573, note).

dethrones a sultan is as lawful an action as those by which, the day before, he disposed of his subjects' goods and lives."[9] Or it might come from without, as in the Montesquieu-inspired prediction that Rousseau inserted into *The Social Contract*. "The Russian empire will try to subjugate Europe, and will itself be subjugated," he wrote there. "The Tartars, its subjects or neighbours, will become its masters and ours. This revolution seems to me inevitable. All the kings of Europe are working in concert to hasten it."[10]

These reiterated predictions matched Rousseau's pessimistic assessment of every political society's capacity for reform. "Nations, like men," he wrote in the *Social Contract*, "are teachable only in their youth; with age they become incorrigible." Those "violent epochs and revolutions in states" that had allowed some states, like Rome after the Tarquins, Sparta at the time of Lycurgus, or the Dutch and the Swiss in the sixteenth century, to leap "from the arms of death to regain the vigour of youth" were the exceptions that proved the rule.[11] Like Brown, most of Rousseau's contemporaries had a more confident view. Reform was the way to avoid political death, and monarchies were best equipped to make reform occur. The Cynic label that Voltaire applied to the Jesuit Louis-Bertrand Castel, and that Voltaire's admirer Jean-Louis Castilhon applied to "Estimate" Brown, simply highlighted something unusual in their version of this view, without, however, calling into question the broader set of presuppositions about the fundamental compatibility between morality and monarchy on which it was based or, in parallel, the underlying confidence in the power of a royal government to make reform occur. In this context, and in sharp contradistinction to the careful typology of cases and classes supplied by *The Spirit of Laws*, the economic, social, or moral advantages of reform could outweigh the potentially self-defeating character of reliance on centralised royal authority to bring reform about.

Rousseau's position on the line dividing monarchies from republics, and Montesquieu from his critics, was complicated, however, by his own, somewhat muted, endorsement of the eighteenth century's most famous programme of royal reform. This was to be found in *The Adventures of Telemachus, Son of Ulysses* by François de Salignac de la Mothe Fénelon, archbishop of Cambrai until his death in 1715, where the subject of how to reform a corrupt monarchy (named the kingdom of Salentum) was given a thorough examination by the goddess Minerva who, in the guise of Mentor to the young Telemachus, had taken on the task of guiding him on his

[9] Jean-Jacques Rousseau, *The Discourses and Other Early Political Writings*, ed. Victor Gourevitch (Cambridge, CUP, 1997), p. 186.

[10] Rousseau, *The Social Contract and Other Political Writings*, ed. Gourevitch, bk. 2, ch. 8, p. 73.

[11] Jean-Jacques Rousseau, *The Social Contract*, bk. 2, ch. 8 (London, Penguin, 1968), p. 89; see, too, Rousseau, *The Social Contract and Other Political Writings*, ed. Gourevitch, p. 72.

travels around the ancient world in search of his father, Ulysses, and, more literally, of teaching Fénelon's pupils, Louis XIV's grandsons, the range of qualities and considerations required for virtuous royal rule. Together with *Robinson Crusoe*, with its step-by-step description of the types of basic skill and essential goods required for self-sufficiency, *Telemachus* was one of the few modern books that, in *Emile*, Rousseau commended (Emile read Defoe, while Sophie read Fénelon).[12] The centrepiece of the programme of moral, economic, and political reform that it contained was an elaborate agrarian law. As Minerva explained, it was designed to maintain the stability of the seven different classes into which the reformed kingdom of Salentum would be divided, by limiting the amount of land that any family could own to no more than what was absolutely necessary for its subsistence. Limiting ownership in this way would serve to shield the manners of the people of Salentum from the corrupting effects of luxury.

> The laws we have made in relation to agriculture will render their lives laborious; and, notwithstanding their abundance, they will have nothing more than necessities, because we have proscribed all the arts that furnish superfluities. Even that abundance will be diminished by the encouragement it will give to marriage, and by the great increase of families. As each family will be numerous, and yet have but a small portion of land, they will be obliged to work it without ceasing. It is sloth and luxury that make men insolent and rebellious. Your people indeed will have bread in plenty, but they will have nothing but that and the produce of their own lands, earned with the sweat of their brows.[13]

This limitation applied to all the members of all the classes, so that no "one family, of what rank so ever" could "possess more land than is absolutely necessary to maintain the number of persons of which it shall consist."

By observing this rule inviolably, Fénelon wrote, "the nobles will not be able to aggrandise themselves at the expense of the poor; and every family will have land, but, as it will be of a very small extent, they will be obliged

---

[12] Jean-Jacques Rousseau, *Emile, ou de l'éducation* [1762], in Rousseau, *Oeuvres complets*, ed. Bernard Gagnebin and Marcel Raymond, 5 vols. (Paris, Pléiade, 1959–96), 4:454–60, 762, 775–6. On this aspect of Rousseau's thought, see Patrick Riley, "Rousseau, Fénelon and the Quarrel between the Ancients and the Moderns," in Patrick Riley, ed., *The Cambridge Companion to Rousseau* (Cambridge, CUP, 2001), pp. 78–93; and Patrick Riley, "Fénelon's Republican Monarchism in Telemachus," in Hans Blom, John Christian Laursen, and Luisa Simonutti, eds., *Monarchisms in the Age of Enlightenment* (Toronto, University of Toronto Press, 2007), pp. 78–100. On Fénelon and his impact, see Albert Chérel, *Fénelon au xviiie siècle en France* (Paris, 1917); Lionel Rothkrug, *Opposition to Louis XIV: The Political and Social Origins of the French Enlightenment* (Princeton, Princeton UP, 1965); Robert Granderoute, *Le Roman pédagogique de Fénelon à Rousseau*, 2 vols. (Geneva, Slatkine, 1985), vol. 1, pt. 1.

[13] François de Salignac de la Mothe Fénelon, *Telemachus* [1715], ed. Patrick Riley (Cambridge, CUP, 1994), p. 169.

to cultivate it with great care."[14] Since no surplus could be used to acquire more land, and since the available supply of manufactured goods would be limited to the acquisition of utilities, any agricultural surplus would have to be exported to other countries. Trade would be free, but no merchant would be allowed to risk more than half his assets or any part of anyone else's property in a single enterprise. Larger, more costly export undertakings would be handled by trading companies, while imports of foreign merchandise likely to promote "luxury and effeminacy" were prohibited. The resultant positive trade balance would be used to develop a substantial armaments programme, since "a state ought always to be prepared for war in order to avoid the disagreeable necessity of engaging in it."[15] The power and prosperity of the state would, therefore, be wholly independent of private commercial transactions, while the merit-based system of ranks would be entirely insulated from the vagaries of the rotation of property. The outcome was quite similar to Rousseau's later picture of the hardworking, but self-sufficient, clock-making peasant households of the Valais. In both cases, an egalitarian distribution of landed property ruled out dependence and made all social transactions entirely voluntary, while the hard work that was the price to be paid for real independence was the best antidote to imaginative flights of fancy. As Rousseau emphasised in his *Emile*, acquiring notions of property had to come before acquiring those of liberty.[16]

The picture of a just society that *Telemachus* presented soon acquired an aura that resonated far beyond the French and Catholic setting to which Fénelon belonged. The Swiss physiognomist Johann Caspar Lavater liked, so it was said, to be told that he might have been Fénelon's son, if Fénelon had not been an archbishop. The Quaker Josiah Martin published a version of Fénelon's *Dissertation on Pure Love*, while British Methodism's founder, John Wesley, was also an admirer of Fénelon, as, too, was the future Holy Roman Emperor Joseph II, whose speculations in 1761 about how "to humble and impoverish the grandees" were strongly redolent of the reform programme set out in *Telemachus*.[17] "That romance," Jeremy Bentham noted, in a rather neglected clue to his own moral and political thought, "may be regarded as the foundation-stone of my whole character,

[14] Fénelon, *Telemachus*, p. 169.

[15] Fénelon, *Telemachus*, pp. 162, 165.

[16] Jean-Jacques Rousseau, *Emile*, ed. and trans. Alan Bloom (New York, 1979), p. 99.

[17] On Lavater and Fénelon, see Fernand Baldensperger, "Les théories de Lavater dans la littérature française," in his *Etudes d'histoire littéraire*, 4 vols. (Paris, 1907–39), 2:51–91 (p. 58); on Martin, see François de Salignac de la Mothe Fénelon, *A Dissertation on Pure Love* (Dublin, 1739); on Wesley, see Jean Orcibal, *Etudes d'histoire et de littérature religieuses* (Paris, Klincksieck, 1997), pp. 163–232; and, on Joseph II, Derek Beales, "Joseph II's *Rêveries*," in his *Enlightenment and Reform in Eighteenth-Century Europe* (London, I. B. Tauris, 2005), pp. 157–81.

the starting point whence my career of life commenced. The first dawn-
ing of the principle of utility may be traced to it."[18] The resonance that
Telemachus acquired was not simply an effect of its stark warning about
the dangers associated with overcentralised government, and the twin social pathologies of luxury and inequality, or even a result of its unusually
detailed description of how they could all, systematically, be corrected,
but grew, more fundamentally, out of the underlying assumptions about
human nature (and, in contradistinction to Jansenist political theology,
the surmountable character of the Fall) that allowed Fénelon to argue that
the transition from social corruption to social health lay within political
reach. In the words of Fénelon's biographer, the Jacobite exile Andrew
Michael Ramsay, in the *Discourse on Epic Poetry* that was often published
as a preface or postscript to eighteenth-century editions of *Telemachus*,
"some philosophers, who in other respects have made fine discoveries in
philosophy" (the allusion, he later indicated, was to Grotius and Pufendorf), had still not made a sufficiently clear distinction between "the love
of order and the love of pleasure," or seen that "the will may be as strongly
moved by the clear view of truth as by the natural taste of pleasure."[19]
This, Ramsay wrote, was the moral theory on which *Telemachus* was based,
and the real source of the social cohesion at home, and the peace and
prosperity abroad, that Fénelon had sought to establish among the whole
human family.

Love of order was also, but with considerably diluted motivating power,
an important aspect of Rousseau's moral and political theory, where, notably in his *Letter to Christophe de Beaumont*, it appeared as one of what he
there called "the two principles" underlying the natural individual feeling
of *amour-de-soi*. The first of these applied to the body, and was connected
to the emotion of pity, while the second principle applied to the mind,
and, as Rousseau put it in the *Letter*, "expanded and become active, is
denominated conscience." Love of order, as he explained in *Julie*, also had
an aesthetic dimension that made it the source of the pleasure associated

---

[18] Jeremy Bentham, *Works*, 10 vols., ed. John Bowring (London, 1843), 10:10, as cited in
Frank E. Manuel and Fritzie P. Manuel, *Utopian Thought in the Western World* (Cambridge,
Mass., Harvard UP, 1979), p. 391. For an indication of the possible bearing of this type of
context on Bentham's thought, see Simon Schaffer, "States of Mind: Enlightenment and
Natural Philosophy," in G. S. Rousseau, ed., *The Languages of Psyche: Mind and Body in
Enlightenment Thought* (Berkeley and Los Angeles, University of California Press, 1990),
pp. 233–90.

[19] Andrew Michael Ramsay, "A Discourse on Epic Poetry" [1719], cited here in François
de Salignac de la Mothe Fénelon, *Telemachus* [1715] (Dublin, 1764), p. xxi. On the references to Grotius and Pufendorf, see also Andrew Michael Ramsay, "Discours de la poésie
épique et de l'excellence du poème Télémaque," in Fénelon, *Télémaque* (Amsterdam, 1725),
pp. xxxviii–xxxix, and (in English) Fénelon, *Telemachus*, 3rd ed., 2 vols. (London, 1720),
pp. xlii–xliv.

with neatness, symmetry, and tasteful harmony. In *The Social Contract* it was the basis of individuals' ability to distinguish sameness from difference in establishing what was general about the general will (the symmetry and neatness involved in sameness indicated equality, while the variety or heterogeneity involved in difference pointed towards distinction and, therefore, inequality).[20] There is no reason to think that Rousseau endorsed Fénelon's centrally driven programme of royal reform (his own idea of a legislator involved someone who was outside the political system), but there is still good reason to think that he did endorse its outcome. In large measure, this was because the outcome itself was quite compatible with his own political thought. Despite its unequivocal emphasis on royal authority as the means to push through the set of reforms that Fénelon envisaged, the resulting condition of political health that *Telemachus* described was not particularly like a monarchy, still less like the actually existing system of absolute government situated at Versailles. Once luxury had been eliminated, government decentralised, property redistributed, and merit ratified, the newly reformed society could be left largely to govern itself, relying mainly on individual respect, moral authority, and patriotic commitment rather than on reiterated legislation, state power, and a standing army to maintain domestic stability and external security. From the outside, it might still look like a monarchy, but from the inside it would work rather like a republic.

It is important, however, to emphasise that the ambiguity could go both ways, and that a monarchy based on the range of internal goods known collectively as the virtues (justice, wisdom, courage, and liberality, for example), and which could also ensure that external goods like office, wealth, or property were equally available to all, could also be taken to be a model of a *res publica*. Here, the relevant antithesis was not between monarchies and republics, but between both these forms of government and the feudal or Gothic system of government that had grown up all over Europe after the fall of the Roman Empire. This was the antithesis underlying the work that supplied Fénelon with much of the broader historical framework of the programme of reform contained in *Telemachus*, the abbé Claude Fleury's *Moeurs des Israelites* (Manners of the Israelites) of 1681 (the two men were personal friends and were both engaged by Louis XIV as tutors to his grandsons). Fleury's book was as much an endorsement of royal government (rightly understood) as it was a criticism of the legacy of injustice and inequality that, he argued, the modern European monarchies, and the French monarchy in particular, had inherited from Europe's feudal and Gothic past. Here, too, the relevant antithesis was not so much to the absolute government of Louis XIV as to the weak and divided government

---

[20] For these passages in Rousseau's writings, see above, pp. 113–9.

of the period of the Frondes. In this sense, Fleury's argument ran parallel to James Harrington's *Oceana* of 1656, with its ambitious attempt to establish a new basis for modern politics by bringing together the social and institutional lessons of Jewish, Spartan, and Roman history under the broad rubric of "ancient prudence" as the alternative to what Harrington took to be the bankrupt mixture of morality and politics built into Gothic government (Fleury also shared some of Harrington's more emphatic admiration of Machiavelli, endorsing the Florentine's claim that poor nations, not rich ones, were best equipped to be powerful and free).[21]

Fleury followed the same anti-Gothic line of argument as Harrington had done. The inequality and injustice of modern monarchies were, he argued, an effect of the conquest of the Roman Empire by the hunting peoples of the North, and the mixture of violence, slavery, and idleness that they had brought in their wake. The Israelites, like most of the other Southern nations, had first been shepherds, not hunters (horses, Fleury noted, were unknown in Palestine), and had initially followed a pastoral and nomadic way of life that involved no more than the purely temporary ownership of worldly goods that Rousseau's later critic Louis-Bertrand Castel was to associate with the Tartars. As Fleury put it, the pastoral life "has always passed as most perfect insofar as it attaches men least to the land" and, therefore, "corresponds most faithfully to the transient nature of earthly life."[22] Only after the exodus from Egypt did the Jews begin to cultivate the land (Fleury's descriptions of the two sets of arrangements, before and after the establishment of agriculture, supplied Fénelon with the template for his own descriptions of the communities that, in *Telemachus*, he called Betica and Salentum). As Fénelon was also to emphasise in his description of the reformed kingdom of Salentum, Fleury made a point of emphasising the care with which the Israelites managed their system of private property. Each Israelite, he wrote, "had his own field to cultivate, and the same one as that given by lot to his ancestors at the time of Joshua." It was, he continued, virtually impossible for the Jews "to change places, ruin themselves, or enrich themselves excessively," because the law of the Jubilee, revoking every alienation of land every fifty years, also made it illegal to call in debts either in the forty-ninth year or in every seventh year when the land lay fallow.[23] The small amounts of property that each household owned, and the absence of incentives to use credit and commerce, meant that the division of labour remained rudimentary. The Israelites prided themselves on their self-sufficiency, just as, Fleury

[21] Claude Fleury, *Réflexions sur les oeuvres de Machiavel*, reprinted in his *Oeuvres*, ed. Louis Aimé-Martin (Paris, 1837), p. 564.

[22] Claude Fleury, *Moeurs des Israélites* [1681], reprinted in his *Oeuvres*, ed. Louis Aimé-Martin (Paris, 1837), ch. 2, p. 130.

[23] Fleury, *Moeurs*, ed. Martin, ch. 4, p. 139.

noted, Ulysses had made and fitted out his own boat before embarking on his travels.

This pride in self-sufficiency was not, however, an effect of primitive ignorance. Fleury also made a point of emphasising the high level of development of the arts among the ancient Israelites, and its comparability to the proficiency displayed by the Egyptians and Greeks (the cherubim on the Ark of the Covenant, as well as the Golden Calf itself, served as evidence). But the Israelites' interest in the arts was limited to an admiration of the knowledge, imagination, and skill required to make something decorative or monumental, and did not involve any further interest in the utility, convenience, or advantages that the arts could supply. Although they knew a great deal about materials, and how to use them, they were still entirely indifferent to fashion and display. In terms of clothing, household furniture, or meals, the Israelites limited themselves to necessities, even though they could, and often did, have very large quantities of the types of necessity in question (this, too, Fleury noted, was a general feature of the ancient world, since, according to Horace, the Roman Lucullus owned five thousand military cloaks).[24] These substantial reserves not only enabled them to be liberal (it was usual, Fleury wrote, to give someone two tunics as a present so that there was always one to be worn while the other was being washed), to manage the vagaries of the seasons without undue difficulty, and to maintain supplies of provisions for wartime emergencies, but also enabled them to encourage population growth, and to maintain the very high level of population density that was a clear sign of the flourishing state of the ancient world. This, Fleury emphasised, "was the principal foundation of the politics of the ancients. *A multitude of people*, according to the wisdom of Solomon, *is the glory of a king, just as a small number of subjects is the shame of a prince*."[25]

The point was not lost either on Fénelon, or on several of Fénelon's later admirers. In this sense, the ideological origins of the French Revolution had as much to do with long-standing visions of royal reform as with opposition to absolute government, since the first were not necessarily seen to be at odds with the second. As will be shown in the following chapter, the political history of the French Revolution began only when it started to become clear that a Fénelonian-style reform programme might strengthen, not weaken, absolute government. "A powerful ruler in our time therefore made a very serious error of judgement," observed Immanuel Kant some time later, "when he tried to relieve himself of the embarrassment of large national debts by leaving it to the people to assume and

---

[24] Fleury, *Moeurs* (Lyon, 1808), p. 45.
[25] Fleury, *Moeurs* (Lyon, 1808), p. 31 (the words italicised by Fleury are a quotation from Proverbs 14.1).

distribute this burden at their own discretion."[26] Before then, however, the same emphasis on the high level of compatibility between monarchy, equality, and justice that could be found in Fleury's *Manners of the Israelites* became a feature of a sequence of books published over the course of the eighteenth century, beginning with *Telemachus*, continuing with the marquis d'Argenson's *Considerations on the Present and Former Government of France*, and culminating in Jacques-Henri Bernardin de Saint-Pierre's *Etudes de la Nature* (or *Studies of Nature* as the English translation was entitled) in 1781, where Rousseau's several, mainly rhetorical, gestures towards Fénelon were turned into a far more ambitious attempt to integrate their respective political visions into a single moral and political system. "He adopts almost all his [meaning Rousseau's] dislikes and paradoxes," wrote the ubiquitous Jean-Baptiste-Antoine Suard, dismissively. "But if it is sometimes with the energetic and passionate style of the citizen of Geneva, it is not with that profound dialectic that blends truth with error so artfully that even the best of minds have difficulty in distinguishing the one from the other."[27]

One indication of the difference was the emphasis that Bernardin de Saint-Pierre placed on d'Argenson's idea of *convenance* as the means both to bridge the gap between Fénelon and Rousseau, and to show what, he believed, Rousseau really did have in mind in describing "perfect Hobbism" as the way to reconcile the idea of a government of laws with the all too human reality of every actual system of government. In Bernardin de Saint-Pierre's hands, the idea of *convenance*, with its connotations of fitness, suitability, or decorum, became a providentially supplied moral principle underlying the whole Creation (the point of the *Studies of Nature* was to show how every detail played a part). Once identified, it could then be used by a reforming royal government to promote the mixture of real economic equality and genuine recognition of ability and merit that, Bernardin argued, were the hallmarks of both monarchies and republics at their best. The same absence of any real analytical distinction between

---

[26] Immanuel Kant, *The Metaphysics of Morals* [1797], in Immanuel Kant, *Practical Philosophy*, trans. and ed. Mary Gregor (Cambridge, CUP, 1996), p. 481. I have modified the translation slightly. On the potentially despotic effects of applying a patriotic and virtuous Fénelonian-style reform programme to public debt, as was highlighted in different ways by David Hume and Sir James Steuart, see Sonenscher, *Before the Deluge*, pp. 23–32.

[27] Jean-Baptiste-Antoine Suard, *Mélanges de littérature*, 2nd ed., 5 vols. (Paris, 1806), 1:359–60 (the review was published originally in the *Journal de Paris* in 1787). As another review published in the *Mercure de France* (20 August 1785): 102–25, put it, "il a de l'éloquent Rousseau, son ami, dont il célèbre souvent la mémoire, et qu'il associe partout à Fénelon, l'amour des paradoxes, et le talent de les faire gouter" (p. 113). On Bernardin de Saint-Pierre, see Richard H. Grove, *Green Imperialism: Colonial Expansion, Tropical Island Edens and the Origins of Environmentalism, 1600–1860* (Cambridge, CUP, 1995); and, most recently, Malcolm Cook, *Bernardin de Saint Pierre: A Life of Culture* (London, Legenda, 2006).

monarchies and republics also lay behind a further set of links between the moral and political ideas of Fénelon, d'Argenson, and James Harrington (as well as Rousseau) that came to be made in the early years of the French Revolution. As will be shown in the third part of this chapter, one of those who made them was the satirical critic of salon society, and Mme Geoffrin's self-appointed scourge, Jean-Jacques Rutledge, who for a brief period after 1789 was to become one of the leading figures in the Parisian Cordeliers club. For Rutledge, as for Louis-Sébastien Mercier, *The Spirit of Laws* was actually a disguised satire on monarchy.[28] Its real message, he argued, was to be found in the cryptic allusions to Harrington that Montesquieu had made, and the covert endorsement of a transformation of the existing property regime that they had really been intended to imply. Like Mercier, too, Routledge also argued that the modern system of public credit contained the means to effect the transformation peacefully.

The same focus on the underlying similarities between monarchies and republics and, in this context, on the Fénelonian origins of the analytical fusion, was also registered in the works of a number of now little-known eighteenth-century historians of republican Rome. The first was by an Anglo-Irish Catholic and Jacobite exile named Nathaniel Hooke (ca. 1690–1763), who was responsible for the translations of both Ramsay's biography of Fénelon and of Ramsay's own *The Travels of Cyrus* into English.[29] Hooke dedicated the first of his four-volume *Roman History* to another member of the same Catholic, Jacobite-leaning circle, Alexander Pope. He began it by excusing himself for seeming to be "too much biased to the popular side," justifying his position by arguing that "there is a sort of generosity in taking the part of the poor commons, who, in almost all their endeavours to free themselves from oppression, have been usually represented as an unreasonable, headstrong multitude, insolent, seditious and rebellious."[30] In the context of the history of the Roman republic, the charge applied particularly to the brothers Tiberius and Caius Gracchus, the most historically famous advocates of the full implementation of the Roman republic's agrarian laws. When Hooke came to write about the Gracchi, he made it clear that he was acting, as he put it, as "council for the accused."[31] Both

[28] [Jean-Jacques Rutledge], *Eloge de Montesquieu* (London, 1786).

[29] On Hooke, see Addison Ward, "The Tory View of Roman History," *Studies in English Literature* 4 (1964): 412–56; G. D. Henderson, ed., *Mystics of the North-East* (Aberdeen, 1934), pp. 59, 67, 177 note, 184, and 189; Mouza Raskolnikoff, *Histoire romaine et critique historique au siècle des lumières* Collection de l'Ecole française de Rome, 163 (Strasbourg and Rome, 1992) pp. 187–91, 437–8 and note 180. On Ramsay and his *Travels of Cyrus*, see Granderoute, *Le Roman pédagogique*, 1:227–300.

[30] Nathaniel Hooke, *The Roman History, from the Building of Rome to the Ruin of the Commonwealth*, 4 vols. (London, 1738–71), 1; (3rd ed., London, 1757), preface, p. iii.

[31] Hooke, *Roman History*, vol. 2 (2nd en., London, 1756), bk. 6, ch. 7, p. 530.

"the right of the people's claim," he wrote, and "the seasonableness of it at this time" exonerated Caius and Tiberius Gracchus of the charges levelled against them both by their relatively near contemporary Cicero, and by his modern followers, notably the British court Whig Conyers Middleton, who, in his very successful *Life of Cicero*, had repeated the accusation that the Gracchi had destroyed Rome's republican system of government.

Hooke replied by citing Middleton against himself. "Liberty and the Republic," he wrote, "are cant words where the bulk of a people have neither property, nor the privilege of living by their labour."

> Did our laws allow of any slavery in this island; and should the landed gentlemen, the proprietors of large estates, in order to make the most of them, take them out of the hands of their tenants, and import *Negroes* to cultivate the farms; so that the *British* husbandman and labourers, far from having any encouragement to marry, had no means to subsist: Would an universal practice of this sort be called *particular acts of injustice*? And could no public-spirited, popular man attempt a cure of this evil, without being seditious, because the *evil was far spread*, and he knew, that *the great and the rich were engaged in pride and interest to support it, and to oppose every remedy*? And the case in question was much stronger than what is here put; the lands, which the poor *Romans* were not suffered to cultivate, being of right their own, and detained from them by daring usurpers and oppressors.[32]

Tiberius Gracchus, Hooke concluded, "must appear the most accomplished patriot that ever Rome produced."[33]

Hooke's defence of the Gracchi was translated into French by his son, Luke-Joseph, a theology professor at the Sorbonne whose religious views were fairly similar in content to those that Pope, controversially, had set out in his *Essay on Man*, earning the younger Hooke some notoriety, first for his involvement in supervising the thesis by Denis Diderot's future protégé, the abbé de Prades (condemned as heretical, after Jansenist pressure, in 1752), and later, as retribution for his earlier mistake, for heading the committee of the Sorbonne that, under considerable political pressure, publicly condemned Claude-Adrien Helvétius's *De l'esprit* in 1758.[34] Nathaniel Hooke's attack upon the Roman Senate as a body of "daring usurpers and oppressors" was repeated in 1778 in the *Considérations sur l'origine et les révolutions du gouvernement des Romains* (Considerations on the Origin and Revolutions of the Roman Government), a substantially revised version

---

[32] Hooke, *Roman History*, vol. 2 (2nd ed., London, 1756), bk. 6, ch. 7, p. 536 (the italicised words were Middleton's).

[33] Hooke, *Roman History*, vol. 2 (2nd ed., London, 1756), bk. 6, ch. 7 p. 538.

[34] Thomas O'Connor, *An Irish Theologian in Enlightenment France: Luke Joseph Hooke, 1714–96* (Dublin, 1995). On the Prades affair, see Sonenscher, *Before the Deluge*, pp. 226–7, and the secondary literature referred to there.

of a history of Rome, first published in 1763, by the abbé Louis-Clair Le Beau du Bignon, grand-vicar of the dioceses of Bordeaux and then Cambrai during the reign of Louis XVI.[35] According to Bignon, the campaign by the Gracchi was the last of a long line of attempts by Rome's plebeians to break free of patrician domination by recovering the system of natural equality and common property that Rome had enjoyed at its origins.[36] But Bignon, like Hooke, made it clear that Rome's republican government was ultimately incapable of providing a genuine solution to the problem of patrician-plebeian conflict, because the plebians, despite the establishment of the office of tribune of the people, were no match for the economic and political power of Rome's patrician Senate. The unequal distribution of goods that accompanied the growth of the republic, he claimed (in an argument redolent of Montesquieu and Rousseau), necessarily generated dependence and political instability. But where Montesquieu and Rousseau had argued, respectively, that this state of affairs entailed either monarchy or revolution, Bignon opted for a more straightforward endorsement of reform. In the final analysis, he argued, real equality depended upon the existence of a powerful, but just, royal government, because only an absolute sovereign had the power to take on an aristocracy and win. Bignon repeated the argument early in 1789 in a pamphlet entitled *Qu'est-ce que la noblesse?* (What Is the Nobility?), a title modelled deliberately on Emmanuel-Joseph Sieyès's more famous *Qu'est ce que le tiers état?* (Bignon also chose to highlight what he took to be the close proximity between the two works by dedicating his pamphlet to Sieyès). From this perspective, the true hero of anti-Ciceronian Roman history, and the rightful heir to the mantle of the Gracchi, was Julius Caesar.

The absence of any particularly clear analytical distinction between monarchies and republics in Fénelon's moral and political thought, and the way that it allowed both to be subsumed under the broader genus *res publica*, continued to be registered well into the period of the French Revolution (helping, in this sense, to explain the moral, rather than the purely military, significance of the association between Bonaparte and Caesar).[37]

[35] It may be worth noting that a work entitled *Les Révolutions romaines* appears in the inventory of Robespierre's library made in 1794. The summary title may refer to Bignon's book or to the earlier history of Roman revolutions by the abbé Vertot. For the list, see Germain Bapst, "Inventaire des bibliothèques de quatre condamnés," *La Révolution française* 21 (1891): 532–6.

[36] On Le Beau du Bignon, see Franco Venturi, *Europe des lumières. Recherches sur le 18e siècle* (Paris, 1971), ch. 5, and, most recently, Raskolnikoff, *Histoire romaine*, pp. 456–72. For a similar argument, here applied to the United Provinces, and the need to neutralise the commercial interests of Amsterdam, see [Joseph Mandrillon], *Révolutions des provinces unies sous l'étendard des divers stadhouders*, 3 vols. (Nijmegen, 1788).

[37] For a recent examination of the association, see Peter Baehr and Melvin Richter, eds., *Dictatorship in History and Theory: Bonapartism, Caesarism, and Totalitarianism* (Cambridge, CUP, 2004).

There may have been a substantial measure of rhetorical opportunism in the association made by the Jacobin *Journal de la Montagne* (Journal of the Mountain) on 10 September 1793 between the recently murdered Jean-Paul Marat's drastic political views and a passage from *Telemachus* noting that "a great deal is saved" by "a little blood shed seasonably" (just when the embattled French republic's first law of suspects was about to come into force), but there is no reason to think that an earlier proposal, made on 4 October 1792, a month after France officially became a republic, to have Fénelon's remains transferred to the Pantheon, was anything but sincere. So, too, it might be added, was an even earlier proposal made by Tom Paine's friend Nicolas Bonneville in April 1791.[38] The author of the 1792 proposal, a now forgotten member of the French Convention named Armand-Benoît-Jules Guffroy (who, like Robespierre, was a barrister from Arras) had already signalled his own moral and political convictions in a series of pamphlets attacking the distinction between active and passive citizens established by the National Assembly in 1789. After Robespierre's fall in the summer of 1794, he went on to engage François-Noel, or "Gracchus," Babeuf to edit his *Journal de la liberté de la presse* (Journal of Press Freedom), thus setting in train the sequence of events that was to lead, three years later, to the Conspiracy of Equals that gave Babeuf his posthumous fame. "There are some people," Guffroy wrote in 1789, "who have claimed that it is necessary to own land to be elected. The idea seems vacuous to me, because it assumes that no one can be a citizen without owning land, and would lead one to believe that the assembly has already made up its mind about the need for agrarian laws." Whether this meant that the National Assembly had opted unwittingly in favour of an agrarian, or had deliberately ruled one out, Guffroy made it clear that, in his view, the only genuine property was the property owned by everyone (including women), namely, their property in their lives. Accordingly, everyone "judged as worthy (*digne*) by their co-citizens" was entitled to active involvement in the affairs of the nation.[39] Fénelon was certainly not an advocate of anything like this, even if the idea of a merit-based system of government was central to his own conception of political justice. But, as these episodes suggest, this does not mean that, during the

---

[38] See, for the passage in question, Fénelon, *Telemachus*, ed. Riley, bk. 10, p. 170, and, for the association between Fénelon and Marat, *Journal de la Montagne*, 10 September 1793, p. 694. Reference to the proposals to transfer Fénelon's remains to the Pantheon can be found in the vast study by Chérel, *Fénelon en France au xviiie siècle*, p. 443. On Guffroy, see Robert Legrand, *Babeuf et ses compagnons de route* (Paris, Clavreuil, 1981), pp. 149–52, 192–4; and, on Guffroy and Babeuf, see R. B. Rose, *Gracchus Babeuf: The First Revolutionary Communist* (London, Arnold, 1978), p. 157.

[39] Armand-Benoit-Joseph Guffroy, *Le Tocsin sur la permanence de la garde nationale, sur l'organisation des municipalités et des assemblées provinciales* (Paris, 1789), pp. 68–9.

French Revolution, the picture of what a republic might look like did not have a distinctly Fénelonian hue. As will be shown in the final chapter, it was one that was applied to Mably as much as Marat.

The tension between the Rousseau-Montesquieu pairing on the one side and the Rousseau-Fénelon pairing on the other, and their joint connection to Rousseau's treatment of the related subjects of revolution and reform, was played out comprehensively after 1789. In his Montesquieuian guise, Rousseau appeared to write off modern France. In his Fénelonian guise, he appeared to offer the prospect of salvation. The two pairings pointed towards two different types of historical and political possibility (revolution as the prelude to reform, or reform as the way to avert revolution), and towards a further set of questions, not only about whether either sequence could be managed politically, but also about whether either, or both, required the special conditions that the Montesquieuian Rousseau associated with republics, or the moral qualities that the Fénelonian Rousseau identified with every legitimate political regime. As the anonymous author of a pamphlet published in 1795 put it, Rousseau seemed to stand midway between systematic advocates of universal equality like Plato, Thomas More, and, surprisingly, Thomas Hobbes, and political relativists like Machiavelli and Montesquieu, with their concern with "the facts of history" and "the rules" that local circumstance appeared to offer for "mastering the future" by giving political institutions a capacity to balance various types of inequality and still have an ability to change. Both the alignment of Hobbes with Plato and More, and the comparison between thinkers like these on one side, and Machiavelli and Montesquieu on the other, were, in fact, made by Condorcet in his posthumous, and recently published, *Sketch for a Historical Picture of the Progress of the Human Mind*.[40] In this sense, Condorcet's sustained interest in the problems involved in collective decision making could be redescribed as an equally sustained attempt to come to terms with Rousseau's ambiguities, and to establish a real institutional foundation for the general will.

[40] "Les uns, imitant *Platon*, tels que *Morus* et *Hobbes*, déduisaient de quelques principes généraux le plan d'un système entier de l'ordre social, et présentaient le modèle dont il faillait que la pratique tendît sans cesse à rapprocher. Les autres, comme *Machiavel*, cherchaient dans l'examen approfondi des faits de l'histoire, les règles d'après lesquelles on pourrait se flatter de maîtriser l'avenir": B. L., F1107 (1), F. P. B***, *De l'équilibre des trois pouvoirs politiques, ou lettres au représentant du peuple Lanjuinais* (Paris, an III, 1795), p. 7 (see p. 13 for the remark that Plato, More, and Hobbes were all advocates of equality). Condorcet's words were identical: "Some philosophers like More and Hobbes imitated Plato, in deducing from certain general principles a plan for a whole system of social order and in constructing a model to which all practice was supposed to conform. Others, like Machiavelli, tried to find, after a profound scrutiny of the facts of history, general rules by means of which they could give themselves the illusion of mastering the future": Antoine de Caritat, marquis de Condorcet, *Sketch for a Historical Picture of the Progress of the Human Mind* [1795], ed. Stuart Hampshire (London, 1955), p. 112.

The ambiguities raised a range of questions about how and when reform could be implemented, and what its outcome might be. Implementation could be either direct or indirect, relying either on governmental power or on some extrapolitical agency, like public opinion, legal institutions, or economic processes. These differences in the causal mechanisms raised a further set of questions about both the properties of government and the significance of institutional design. Here, Fénelonian visions of virtuous royal reform could be counterposed to a range of alternative characterisations of monarchy, beginning with Montesquieu's anti-Fénelonian version, but going on to include his more famous description of the English system of government, and continuing further with the large number of other examinations of the English system's attributes and properties made by Montesquieu's assorted critics. In this third context, the key questions were whether, as Montesquieu had suggested, Britain after 1688 was simply a republic disguised as a monarchy; whether it was a genuinely limited monarchy, with a built-in capacity for reform supplied by the combination of its centralised, but complex, legislature and its decentralised system of elected political representation; or whether, in the final analysis, the modern British funding system had, in fact, so far eroded this combination that it had entirely lost its capacity for gradual and progressive change.[41] The range of different assessments of what was usually called the English system of government (described in more detail in the following chapter) was one reason why it turned out to be quite difficult to establish a consensus about reforming the French system of absolute government on British-style lines before and after 1789.

Other reasons, however, applied to the subject of outcomes, since these appeared to entail either more or less state power. This latter ambiguity was not, however, simply an effect of uncertainty about how the causation might work, or whether it might have potentially perverse effects; it was also a more deep-seated effect of the initial uncertainty about the subject of sociability that Rousseau had helped to create. If sociability was, in some way, natural, then the outcome of reform would, putatively, reinforce an already existing capacity for social cohesion. But if, as Rousseau argued, sociability was not natural, then the putative outcome of reform might be more, not less, state power. Rousseau's gestures, both in *The Social Contract* and in the *Considerations on the Government of Poland*, towards a federation of small, Montesquieuian-type, republics were one indication of how it might be possible to avoid the conundrum, but they did not alter the initial difficulties. According to the starting point, reform looked as if it had either to reduce the scale and scope of state sovereignty, or to increase it. From this perspective, the power of Rousseau's moral and

---

[41] On these assessments, see Sonenscher, *Before the Deluge*, pp. 41–57.

political criticism was rather easier to accept than his initial characterisation of the highly attenuated moral capacities built into human nature. As many of his critics argued, reform would look a great deal more attractive if it could rely on a more robustly altruistic moral theory. The question of what the content of this type of moral theory might be continued to preoccupy Diderot right up to the end of his life. As was recorded by Joseph Joubert—the Catholic mystic who, as a young man, worked as Diderot's amanuensis—his last, never completed, work was to have been an examination of the universal principles of morality.[42]

PROPERTY AND THE LIMITS OF STATE POWER

The difficulties applied with particular force to the subject of property. Here, too, Rousseau presented the problem most starkly. The most famous sentence of his *Discourse on the Origin of Inequality* ("The first man who, having enclosed a piece of ground, to whom it occurred to say *this is mine*, and found people sufficiently simple to believe him, was the true founder of civil society.") captured the real ambiguity of Rousseau's evaluation of political society and, in the light of his subsequent description of the steps leading to despotism and revolution, explained why their outcome would be revolution, not reform.[43] Once the property-based slide towards despotism was complete, he wrote, there would be "new revolutions" that would either "dissolve the government entirely" or "bring it closer to legitimate institution."[44] Before then, however, the political possibilities were more limited. Although property and legality gave civil society its nature, allowing an already existing system of private property to become the basis of legality amounted to starting the sequence of steps that would turn the strong and the weak first into the rich and the poor, and then into the powerful and the powerless. As Rousseau emphasised, civil society, or a state, had to come first. Legitimate ownership had to be state based, and the state itself had to have no reserved components (like a preexisting property system) as the

---

[42] On Diderot's last interest, see Rémy Tessonneau, *Joseph Joubert, éducateur, d'après des documents inédits, 1754–1824* (Paris, 1944), pp. 26–30; Joseph Joubert, *Essais 1779–1821*, ed. Rémy Tessonneau (Paris, Nizet, 1983); Joseph Joubert, *Carnets*, ed. David Kinloch and Philippe Mangeot (London, University of London Institute of Romance Studies, 1996). See also the Diderot-inspired work by Jacques-Henri Meister, *De la morale naturelle* (Paris, 1787), which reappeared as Jacques Necker, *De la morale naturelle, et du bonheur des sots* (Paris, 1788), with its discussion of the relationship between individual physical organs and social institutions, and the effect of the latter in neutralising the original influence of the former.

[43] Jean-Jacques Rousseau, *Discourse on the Origin and the Foundations of Inequality among Men* [1755], in Rousseau, *The Discourses and Other Early Political Writings*, ed. Victor Gourevitch (Cambridge, CUP, 1997), p. 161.

[44] Rousseau, *Discourse on Inequality*, ed. Gourevitch, p. 182.

basis of its legitimate authority. Nor, since the state was a general will, would the state itself own any more property than its own territory. It would, instead, turn individual occupation into private property by requiring all individuals to respect what was not their own. As Rousseau put it at the end of the chapter dealing with the subject of real property in *The Social Contract*, "the fundamental pact, rather than destroying natural equality, on the contrary substitutes a moral and legitimate equality for whatever physical inequality may have placed between men, so that while they may be unequal in force and genius, they all become equal by convention and by right." This comment, which he described as "the basis of the entire social system," meant, he added in a note, that "the social state is advantageous for men only insofar as all have something and none has too much of anything."[45]

The vagueness of the words "something" and "anything" lent themselves to a multiplicity of later interpretations, with land and industry jostling for first place on the side of "something," and the hazy lines separating necessities, conveniences, and luxuries variously determining what could be ruled in or out on the side of "anything." If, in the first instance, Rousseau's strong emphasis on a contractually based general will as the sole source of legitimate ownership eliminated a large number of earlier justifications of private property, it also placed a huge onus on his moral theory to explain how the very sparse assortment of natural sentiments on which it was based (with pity and love of order supplying the motivation for individuals to do their own good with the least possible harm to others) might be able to carry the full weight of the type of social state that he had in mind. As the German philosopher Johann Gottlieb Fichte complained in his 1794 course of lectures *On the Vocation of the Scholar*, "Rousseau consistently depicts reason *at peace*, not *in battle*. Instead of *reinforcing reason, he weakens sensibility*."[46] Thinking through the possible implications of a property-based political system, Fichte implied, had to involve working out much stronger theoretical and practical connections between rational institutional design and individual emotional motivation than Rousseau's self-centred, largely abstentive moral and political system could supply. Sieyès's verdict was similar. Emotions, he noted, were essentially indeterminate and could be caused by, or associated with, a broad range of different objects. Reason, however, had a built-in self-limiting capacity because

[45] Rousseau, *The Social Contract*, ed. Gourevitch, bk. 1, ch. 9, p. 56.

[46] "Rousseau dépeint sans trêve la raison *en repos* et non *au combat*; *il affaiblit la sensibilité au lieu de renforcer la raison*": Johann Gottlieb Fichte, *Conférences sur la destination du savant*, trans. J. L. Vieillard-Baron (Paris, Vrin, 1980), p. 88, here translated by Alexis Philonenko, "Rousseau et Fichte," in Ives Radrizzani, ed., *Fichte et la France* (Paris, Beauchesne, 1997), pp. 63–82 (p. 78 for the passage in question). I have slightly modified the translation in *Fichte: Early Philosophical Writings*, trans. and ed. Daniel Breazeale (Ithaca, Cornell UP, 1988), p. 184.

it worked sequentially on one object at a time.[47] It could, in principle, work out a set of arrangements capable of accommodating private property in ways that went beyond emotion's analytical range. For Sieyès, trying to design a state on the basis of simple natural sentiments was like using the rudimentary technical knowledge involved in making a canoe to design a ship of war. However inventively placid humans might be when left to their own devices (as in the Valais), and however much the type of political society that Rousseau had in mind aimed at just that sort of natural placidity, it was hard to have much confidence in its motivational power.

The assessments paralleled Kant's characterisation of Rousseau as "that subtle Diogenes."[48] Ultimately, the subtlety of the historical and psychological insights could not outweigh the limitations of their real-world applicability. Without a stronger moral starting point, it was hard to avoid the self-centred premises of Rousseau's version of social contract theory, and the very particular set of conditions that could still make it collectively viable in a property-based social setting. Rousseau himself made this clear. "The precept of never doing harm to others," he wrote in a note to his *Emile*, "carries with it that of having the least possible to do with human society, because in the social state, the good of the one necessarily makes for the evil of the other. That relationship is of the essence of the thing, and nothing can change it." An "illustrious author," he continued, aiming directly at Diderot, "says that only the wicked are alone, while I say that only the good are alone, and if this proposition is less contentious, it is truer and better thought-through than the other." Solitude for the wicked would simply nullify their ability to do harm. Solitude for the good, however, would require an almost superhuman forbearance in an interdependent social setting, since, as Rousseau put in the text, "the most sublime virtues are negative; they are also the most difficult, because they are without ostentation, and are even above that pleasure that is so sweet to the human heart, namely, to send someone away content with us."[49]

One way out of Rousseau pointed towards the various theories of the political state associated with Sieyès, Kant, and Hegel. Another, however, pointed towards a more morally rich natural state and, by extension, towards further versions of the idea of sociability, and the natural, rather than the contractual, origins of private property. These could be fed quite easily into the type of vitalist explanations of natural society that, for example, Louis-Sébastien Mercier found in the works of Charles Bonnet and

[47] A. N., 284 AP 5, dossier 1; see also Emmanuel-Joseph Sieyès, *Political Writings*, ed. Michael Sonenscher (Indianapolis, Hackett, 2003), pp. lvi–lvii, and Christine Fauré, "Sieyès, lecteur problématique des lumières," *Dix-Huitième Siècle* 37 (2005): 225–41.

[48] Immanuel Kant, *Lectures on Ethics*, ed. Peter Heath and J. B. Schneewind (Cambridge, CUP, 1997), p. 45.

[49] Jean-Jacques Rousseau, *Emile*, 4 vols. (London, 1762), 1:121, and note 13.

Johann Caspar Lavater. Many earlier justifications of private property also had a significantly richer emotional content than anything to be found in Rousseau. In broad terms, those that did were more likely to be found in Catholic than in Protestant Europe. One reason for this was that Protestant theology was able to rely more heavily on the idea of utility (or necessity) to explain the formation of private property, because it could also rely on the idea of a covenant between God and mankind (represented first by Adam, and then by the second Adam, Jesus Christ) to keep utility and justice aligned.[50] Covenant, or "federal," theology, and the prominence that it gave to a scripturally based idea of a covenant between God and Adam (a covenant of works), which (as a covenant of grace) had been renewed between God and Christ, supplied a broad normative framework that could accommodate both Genesis 1:26, with its description of God's gift of the earth and all its fruits to all mankind, and the real existence of both national territories and private property.

A very comprehensive examination of how both types of covenant could be integrated into an explanation of both property formation and the emergence of separate, contractually based, political societies could be found in the works of the great seventeenth-century German natural jurist Samuel Pufendorf. As Pufendorf presented it, the ultimate legitimating principle of both property and states was what he called the "divine feudal law."[51] It was divine because it came from God, and feudal because the original relationship between God and Adam was analogous to the reciprocal relationship involved in the two different ways of owning the same property (known, technically, as owning either the direct or the useful domains) that was the hallmark of the feudal system. In this quasi-feudal sense, Adam, as the representative of mankind, was given the earth for his use, while God remained its ultimate owner. In the second covenant, or covenant of grace, Christ, as the representative of God on the one side and humanity on the other, renewed the original covenant of works on terms that were compatible with humanity's fallen state (requiring the virtues of "patience, mercy," and "beneficence to the poor" that were not necessary before the Fall, when human misery did not exist).[52] The normative

---

[50] On covenant, or federal, theology, see David A. Weir, *The Origins of the Federal Theology in Sixteenth-Century Reformation Thought* (Oxford, Clarendon Press, 1990); Edward Vallance, "'A Holy and Sacramentall Paction': Federal Theology and the Solemn League and Covenant in England," *English Historical Review* 116 (2001): 50–75; and Willem J. Van Asselt, *The Federal Theology of Johannes Cocceius (1603–1669)* (Leiden, Brill, 2001).

[51] See now Samuel Pufendorf, *The Divine Feudal Law: or Covenants with Mankind, Represented* [1695], ed. Simone Zurbuchen (Indianapolis, Liberty Fund, 2002). See, for Pufendorf's version of covenant theology, pp. 88, 92–103, 106–7, 108–77, in the London, 1703, translation on which this edition is based.

[52] Pufendorf, *The Divine Feudal Law* (London, 1703), pp. 172–3 (ed. Zurbuchen, p. 116).

framework that the sequence of covenants supplied left room for a utility-based justification of private property, and for property's continuing subordination to a higher moral authority, as well as, in exceptional cases of grave necessity, for recourse to the idea of the originally common character of property to justify everyone's ultimate right to live. Both sides of Pufendorf's argument were repeated in the first half of the eighteenth century, first (but without the Lutheran theology) in 1743 in the *Essai sur les principes du droit et de la morale* (Essay on the Principles of Law and Morality) by Montesquieu's self-important rival François-René Richer d'Aube, and then in 1748 in the *Principles of Natural and Politic Law*, written by the Swiss professor of natural jurisprudence Jean-Jacques Burlamaqui. Richer d'Aube simply reproduced Pufendorf's argument. "Before the establishment of property," he wrote, "everything for men was in a negative community, meaning that nothing belonged to one, any more than to the other." Ownership arose from first occupation, and, since there were families and clans, the first positive forms of ownership were communal, rather than individual, with possession and use continuing to apply to goods located within the community. Only gradually, as population grew and resources became more scarce, did individual households begin to subtract land from the common stock, to form, eventually, a contractually based property system.[53] The book's debt to Pufendorf seems to have been well known. "I have not read it," the comte de Sade (father of the marquis) informed his brother, "but the book is said to be no more than a compilation of Pufendorf, and looks as miserable as its author" (Richer d'Aube was famously hideous).[54] Burlamaqui's argument was quite similar. As he presented it, there was no original difference between "the gifts of nature" and "the fruits of industry." In the original "state of primitive community of goods," anyone who cultivated "a field or a garden" had no more of a right to its products "than a stranger," just as anyone who "makes a spade, mattock, or any other implement of husbandry" had no exclusive right to its use.[55] Gradually, however, more extensive communities formed and,

[53] François-René Richer d'Aube, *Essai sur les principes du droit et de la morale* (Paris, 1743), pp. 221–6. For the same, Pufendorf-derived, account of the original "negative community" in which goods were available, see Gaspard de Réal de Curban, *La science du gouvernement: ouvrage de morale, de droit, et de politique*, 8 vols. (Aix-la-Chapelle and Paris, 1761–65), 1:42–3, 3:317–21 (a work that also, without signalling it, relied quite heavily on the ideas of Pierre Nicole: see, for example, 1:136–7).

[54] Maurice Lever, ed., *Bibliothèque Sade (I). Papiers de famille. Le règne du père 1721–1760* (Paris, Fayard, 1993), p. 142.

[55] On Burlamaqui and Pufendorf, see the editorial annotations in the recent edition of Jean-Jacques Burlamaqui, *The Principles of Natural and Political Law* [1763], ed. Petter Korkman (Indianapolis, Liberty Fund, 2006), and, for a critical eighteenth-century discussion of Burlamaqui's theory of property formation, see Henry Dagge, *Considerations on Criminal Law*, 3rd ed., 3 vols. (London, 1774), 3:118–9 (referring to Burlamaqui, *Principes de Droit Naturel*

as they did, separate national territories came into being. Once territorial ownership had been established, real private property could develop under the dual aegis of a contractually based society and a contractually secured system of government. The contractual underpinnings of both society and government could then be relied upon to set limits to the scale and scope of individual ownership and moderate its capacity to generate inequality, by replacing primogeniture by partible inheritance. Together, the combination of individual ownership and collective responsibility for the distribution of property that Burlamaqui described came to form the basis of the property theories of the "common sense" philosophers of late eighteenth-century Scotland (developed to correct Hume and Smith), and of Thomas Jefferson's well-known objection to hereditary property, as well as his famous claim in a letter to James Madison on 6 September 1789, written in the context of the French National Assembly's Declaration of the Rights of Man, that "the earth belongs always to the living generation."[56]

In Catholic theology, the idea of a covenant did not exist (the nearest eighteenth-century approximation was the idea of Adam as the *syndic*, rather than the representative, of the whole human race, an idea that also entailed a rather stronger emphasis on humanity's indivisibility, and continuing right to common property, than covenant theology implied).[57] This made it more difficult to reconcile the potentially competing claims of individual and general utility. One way of reconciling the two was to do as the Jansenists did, and adopt a very purposeful and direct idea of Divine Providence as the ultimate legitimating principle underlying the unequal distribution of goods, combining it with a very strong emphasis on human depravity as the mechanism binding the members of human society together. The greed and fear that were the hallmarks of the fallen state would keep society together in ordinary circumstances, but the divine rights built into sovereign power would maintain society in the exceptional circumstances created by famine or war. As the seventeenth-century Jansenist jurist Jean Domat emphasised in his frequently reprinted *Traité des lois* (*A Treatise of Laws*), human societies were as much a matter of

---

[Geneva, 1748], 1:128). For a recent examination of the resonances of Burlamaqui's property theory in the United States of America before and after 1776, see Peter Garnsey, *Thinking about Property: From Antiquity to the Age of Revolution* (Cambridge, CUP, 2007), pp. 222–5.

[56] The full text, with all its variants, is printed in *The Papers of Thomas Jefferson*, ed. Julian Boyd et al., 33 vols. to date (Princeton, Princeton UP, 1950–), 15 (1958): 384–98; see, more generally, Adrienne Koch, *Jefferson and Madison: The Great Collaboration* (New York, 1964), pp. 62–96.

[57] On the idea of Adam as humanity's *syndic*, see Pierre Cuppé, *Le ciel ouvert à tous les hommes* [1743], ed. and trans. Paolo Cristofolini as *Il cielo aperto di Pierre Cuppé* (Florence, Olschki, 1981).

involuntary as of voluntary obligations, which, in turn, meant that the claims of charity had, ultimately, to outweigh those of utility.

> Thus [he wrote], the condition of those who are members of society, who are destitute of the means of subsistence, and unable to work for their livelihood, lays an obligation on all their fellow members to exercise towards them mutual love, by imparting to them a share of those goods which they have a right to. For every man being a member of the society has a right to live in it: and that which is necessary to those who have nothing, and who are not able to gain their livelihood, is by consequence in the hands of the other members; from whence it follows, that they cannot without injustice detain it from them. And it is because of this engagement, that in publick necessities private persons are obliged, even by constraint, to assist the poor according to their wants.[58]

The argument could be aligned both with Genesis and with claims about the ultimate responsibilities of states to enforce the fact that necessity trumped rights of individual ownership in conditions of scarcity or famine. "As far as necessities are concerned," announced a seventeenth-century compilation on the natural principles of law and politics, reissued in 1765 during the great French debate on the grain trade, "men remain in the right in which they were placed by nature, namely, that these things belong no more to some than to others, and anyone is in the right to take them where he can, so that if men refuse one another, we will have reverted to that state of war which we wish to avoid."[59] This emphasis upon utility, necessity, and, ultimately, reasons of state as the real basis of both the legitimacy and limitations of private property formed much of the framework for the recurrent conflicts between Jansenist magistrates and royal ministers over taxation that took place during the eighteenth century, fuelling the rival claims about political necessity and property rights on which so many of these conflicts were based. As events were to prove, both at the time of the Maupeou coup in 1771 (the event that gave the poet Gilbert his cue for his satire on the eighteenth century), and in 1789, the difficulty of deciding who, on Jansenist premises, had the right to define a case of necessity led to the disintegration of Jansenism as a political force.[60]

---

[58] Jean Domat, *A Treatise of Laws* [Paris, 1689], trans. William Strahan (London, 1722), ch. 4, §4, p. xi.

[59] [Louis Desbans], *Les principes naturels du droit et de la politique*, ed. J. F. Dreux du Radier (Paris, 1765), pp. 66–7.

[60] On the various political trajectories of prominent Jansenists in 1789 and afterwards, see Michael Sonenscher, "The Nation's Debt and the Birth of the Modern Republic: The French Fiscal Deficit and the Politics of the Revolution of 1789," *History of Political Thought* 18 (1997): 64–103, 267–325.

One way of avoiding these difficulties was to drop the initial connection between property, utility, and necessity altogether, and shift the explanatory focus on to the passions. Taking utility and necessity out of the equation made it easier both to justify private property and, at the same time, to explain why, in cases of real physical necessity, its entitlements still had to be limited. Here, justifications of private property had much the same kind of content, and followed much the same type of logic, as those used to explain how music, dance, and poetry had first given rise to authority and government, so that sociability was taken to be synonymous with what Rousseau's critic Louis-Bertrand Castel called "naturalism" or "pure morality."[61] Applying the same type of argument to the case of property allowed individual ownership to be given the same sort of natural emotional origin. The results may now look rather odd. In some renditions, private property began with shame, because shame had driven fallen humanity to cover its nakedness, and clothes once worn could not, without repugnance or impropriety, be worn by anyone else. In others, it began with death, mourning, and the need to set land aside for ancestral graves, or with migration, nostalgia for a now-forsaken territory, and the desire to re-create what, with hindsight and folk memory, had once been a golden age. In others, property began with marriage, because without this union between men and women, the world would have had to be made up of two different types of things, some for men, and others for women. In yet others, it began with pride, the invention of proper names, and the association among persons, their progeny, and the things they used, or with cave paintings and their testimony to the human propensity to embellish and decorate what otherwise would have been no more than temporary shelter. In still others, it began with the digging of wells for livestock to water, or, more speculatively, with the prestige and the special vocation of the first custodians of fire and, in return, their right to be kept by the whole community.[62]

---

[61] For these arguments, see above, pp. 168–70.

[62] For these various explanations of the origins of private property, see, on clothes and property, Réal de Curban, *La science du gouvernement*, 1:46–50 (the work, it should be noted, was published posthumously; it was written some two decades earlier); on proper names and property, Charles de Brosses, *Histoire de la république romaine dans le cours du vii*ᵉ *siècle par Salluste*, 3 vols. (Dijon, 1777), 1:xxxi–xxxvi; on marriage and property, [P. G. Michaux], *Les coutumes, considérées comme loi de la nation* (Paris, 1783); on wells, William Blackstone, *Commentaries on the Laws of England* [1765–9], ed. A. W. Brian Simpson, 4 vols. (Chicago, University of Chicago Press, 1979), vol. 2, bk. 2, ch. 1, pp. 5–6; on funerals, Giambattista Vico, *New Science* [1744], ed. Anthony Grafton, trans. David Marsh (London, Penguin Books, 1999), pp. 223–5; on migration as the source of the idea of a golden age, which, in turn, was the basis of the first property system, Jean-Antoine Roucher, *Les Mois* (Paris, 1779), canto 1, note 14 (as Roucher noted, the idea was actually Jean-Silvain Bailly's); and, on fire, Louis Poinsinet de Sivry, *Origine des premières sociétés, des peuples, des sciences, des arts, et des idiomes anciens et modernes* (Amsterdam and Paris, 1769), pp. 37–44.

Individual or collective utility had little to do with this type of explanation of the origins of private property. Nor, according to the type of emotion in question, did the explanation have to point unequivocally to private
property at all (wells, or the territory nostalgically associated with a golden
age, were more likely to be commonly, rather than individually, owned).
At its most pronounced—as in the *Code de la nature, ou du véritable esprit
de ses lois* (Nature's Code, or the True Spirit of Her Laws), an anonymous
work published in 1755, partly, as its subtitle suggests, as a somewhat op-
portunistic reply to Montesquieu, but mainly as a reply to Jansenist political theology—this way of explaining how the emotions were connected to
property could still be used to make an elaborate, but entirely naturalistic,
justification of common ownership. The *Code de la nature* was often attributed to Denis Diderot, mainly because it appeared in at least two of the editions of Diderot's collected works published during his lifetime, but it was
actually written by an obscure tax official named, it would seem, Etienne-
Gabriel Morelly.[63] It was designed to show how its author's earlier claim
that sexual love was the real basis of both individual personality and human
association (and its extremely graphic descriptions of sexual pleasure had
very little to do with the moral value of procreation) also had to entail a
comprehensive system of collective ownership, production, and distribution that would be kept in place by a decentralised system of government
in which offices would rotate on the basis of age and seniority (the model,
as is well known, appealed strongly to Gracchus Babeuf).[64] The *Code de
la nature* may have imposed a rather unusual conclusion upon the idea of
giving property an emotional foundation, but it still belonged to the same
type of concern with explaining property formation in terms of something
other than utility or necessity (a rather similar set of ideas were developed
later in the eighteenth century by the librarian, and self-styled *homme sans
Dieu*, or godless man, Sylvain Maréchal, whose own mixture of religious
scepticism and moral realism gave rise to the same type of anti-Rousseauian
endorsement of the arts and sciences as Morelly himself made).[65] Nor did

[63] For the most recent speculations on the identity of the mysterious Morelly, see Guy
Antonetti, "Etienne-Gabriel Morelly, l'homme et sa famille," *Revue d'histoire littéraire de la
France* 83 (1983): 390–402; Guy Antonetti, "Etienne-Gabriel Morelly: l'écrivain et ses pro-
tecteurs," *Revue d'histoire littéraire de la France* 84 (1984): 19–52.

[64] See Michael Sonenscher, "Property, Community and Citizenship," in Mark Goldie and
Robert Wokler, eds., *The Cambridge History of Eighteenth-Century Political Thought* (Cambridge, CUP, 2006), pp. 465–94. For a contemporary attack on Babeuf's idea of common
ownership, with its emphasis on the army as a model of a non-property-based system of
distribution, see Etienne-Géry Lenglet, *De la propriété et de ses rapports avec les droits et avec la
dette du citoyen* (Paris, an VI/1797), pp. 40–4.

[65] On Maréchal, and his endorsement of the very distinguished set of noble patrons of the
society of the arts and sciences established in 1781 by Pahin de la Blancherie, see *Courier de
l'Europe* 9, no. 49 (19 June 1781). For a similar argument by a member of the "point central

explanations of this type have to involve the kind of complicated, and widely criticised, claims about labour and mixing involved in John Locke's explanation of the origins of private property.[66] Instead, they took what, for one reason or another, could be said to be natural human emotions as their starting point and used these to explain how both national and individual ownership could have come into being.

The connection between property and the emotions could, however, be given a very different type of evaluation. Here, the outcome could look like something like Rousseau's account of the interaction between property and *amour-propre*, but it was, in fact, based on very different premises. One version of this type of claim was to be found in the many works published by the abbé Gabriel Bonnot de Mably in the third quarter of the eighteenth century. As Mably presented it, it was not the case that the emotions gave rise to property, but rather that property gave rise to a range of pathological human emotions, notably avarice and ambition, that had no natural basis. Humans, Mably argued in his *De la législation* (On Legislation) of 1776, were sociable creatures because they were naturally equipped with a mixture of intelligence and emotions that made society their natural habitat (here Mably was following the criticism of Rousseau made by his friend the abbé François-André-Adrien Pluquet in his *De la sociabilité*, or *Of Sociability*, of 1767).[67] These natural endowments, he

---

des arts et métiers séant au Louvre" during the period of the Revolution, with recognition of individual talents as the basis of private property, but of "common necessity" as its limiting principle, see [Claude Romieux], *Les éléments du contrat social, ou le développement du droit naturel de l'homme sur la propriété* (Paris, 1792).

[66] See, most fully, the criticisms of Locke set out by the Cambridge law professor Thomas Rutherforth in his *Institutes of Natural Law* in 1754 (a course of lectures on Grotius's *De Jure belli ac pacis*): "If I knowingly employ myself, in working upon the materials of my neighbour, however I may have mixed a personal act, which is my own, with his property; this will never give me a reasonable claim to his materials." The same argument applied to the case in which the materials in question "are not the property of any one" but belonged to the whole human race. If "mixing my labour with the materials of an individual will not make these materials mine, in opposition to his exclusive right, I know not how any act of the same kind, or the mixing of my labour with materials, which belong to all mankind, should make them mine in opposition to their common right": Thomas Rutherforth, *Institutes of Natural Law. Being the substance of a course of lectures on "Grotius de Jure Belli et Pacis" read in St John's College Cambridge*, 2 vols. (Cambridge, 1754), vol. 1, bk. 1, ch. 3, pp. 51–2.

[67] On Pluquet, see Patrick Coleman, "The Enlightened Orthodoxy of the Abbé Pluquet," in John Christian Laursen, ed., *Histories of Heresy in Early Modern Europe: For, against, and beyond Persecution and Toleration* (New York, Palgrave, 2002), pp. 223–38; Gisela Schlüter, "Exporting Heresiology: Translations and Revisions of Pluquet's *Dictionnaire des hérésies*," in Ian Hunter, John Christian Laursen, and Cary J. Nederman, eds., *Heresy in Transition: Transforming Ideas of Heresy in Medieval and Early Modern Europe* (Aldershot, Ashgate, 2005), pp. 169–80. For a similar argument, see Jean-Jacques de Barrett, *De la loi naturelle*, 2 vols. (Paris, 1790).

went on to argue, had been the basis of a real system of common property, in which production and distribution were coordinated by a natural
magistracy produced by age, wisdom, and the authority they entailed. Private property began only with the gradual breakdown of this system of
common ownership, caused either by the partiality of some magistrates
towards their own kin, or by the propensity of some members of the
community to free ride on others' industry and application. Before then,
however, the idea of being able to have what was not one's own, or to have
the status that accompanied the ownership of different types of goods, did
not exist. Natural human pride, Mably suggested, allowed all individuals
to believe that they were as good as everyone else. With the privatisation
of property, however, a space began to open up for a more viciously self-
serving range of human emotions, and, once they were ignited, there was
no way back. The only solution was to be found in constitutional design,
and in the ability of a well-constituted republican government to keep the
passions in check. Mably's emotionally austere solution to the problem
of private property could look a little like Rousseau's. But the very much
more drastic way of neutralising the passions that he was prepared to
contemplate was very un-Rousseau-like, as, too, was his conviction that
these measures really could produce a stable political outcome. As one of
Mably's obituarists noted, if Rousseau's hero was Fénelon, Mably's was
the Roman republican Cato.[68]

The Fénelonian aspect of Rousseau's interest in property as the antidote
to the emotions could also be connected to the theory of human nature
underlying Fénelon's own political theology. By piecing together its intellectual origins, it is possible to throw further light on the common ground
shared by both Rousseau and his critics. That theory was also strongly
grounded in emotion, most obviously in the idea of "pure love" that was
to earn Fénelon his theological notoriety. But the idea itself was actually
Protestant, not Catholic, in origin and was first set out in what is now a
largely Dutch and Belgian context, in reaction both to the strong Calvinist ideas about predestination and divine justice to be found in orthodox
Dutch Protestantism, and to the much weaker versions of Calvinism that
came to be known as Arminianism and Socinianism. According to Pierre
Poiret, the heterodox Protestant theologian who was largely responsible

---

[68] Gabriel Brizard, "Eloge historique de l'abbé Mably," in Gabriel Bonnot de Mably, *Oeuvres*, 13 vols. (London, 1789–90), 1:85. The original passage reads: "L'homme que Jean-
Jacques a le plus loué, c'est Fénelon. Celui qui obtint tous les hommages de Mably, c'est
Caton; et le gouvernement qu'il loua le plus, c'est Lacédémone." As the editor of an edition
of Mably's *De la législation* put it in 1790, "he was an austere Spartan, transported to live
within the walls of Paris": Gabriel Bonnot de Mably, *De la législation*, reprinted in the *Bibliothèque de l'homme public*, 12 vols. (Paris, 1790), 7:304–5. For the further, political, implications of Mably's thought, see below, chapter 6.

for first developing the mystical idea of pure love, orthodox Calvinist ideas about predestination could not avoid appearing to make God the author of evil (thus inadvertently opening a door to atheism), while the modified version of covenant theology used by the Arminians and the Socinians attributed too much power to human reason to be compatible with the idea of the divinity of Christ as the one true cause of human redemption (thus opening a different type of door to atheism).[69] The way to God had to be more spiritual in character, as, according to Poiret, had been exemplified by the mystic Jacob Boehme, as well as by the meditations and spiritual exercises of two French Catholics, Antoinette Bourignon and Fénelon's disciple, Jeanne Guyon, whose biography Poiret also wrote. As Poiret explained in the general preface to his vast *The Divine Oeconomy, or an Universal System of the Works and Purposes of God towards Men, Demonstrated*, his initial target had been the subject of predestination, but his polemical focus had shifted towards the version of covenant theology that he associated with what he called "the Cocceian system," meaning the theology of Johannes Cocceius, a Dutch theologian and his followers, who were often described as Socinian.[70] "I am not ignorant," Poiret fulminated, "that that system is grounded upon that famous *covenant of works*, which, say they, God entered into with Adam as with a *hired servant*." According to Poiret, however, the idea of a covenant was "a mere fiction and human invention," since "God did not create men for any such mercenary purpose as to put them upon seeking after a communion with him by way of wages or rewards as their just purpose and right."[71] Predestination and Socinianism degraded both God and man. The idea of pure love was an alternative to both.

Its starting point was a somewhat unorthodox version of the Fall, in which the first sinner was not Adam but the Devil. The idea, which went back to the theology of the third-century biblical scholar Origen, was

---

[69] On this still relatively unexplored network of individuals and ideas, see Marjolaine Chevallier, *Pierre Poiret (1646–1719), du protestantisme à la mystique* (Geneva, Labor et Fides, 1994), and her articles "La réponse de Poiret à Fénelon," *Revue d'histoire de la spiritualité* 53 (1977): 129–64, and "Deux réactions protestantes à la condamnation de Fénelon," in François-Xavier Cuche and Jacques Le Brun, eds., *Fénelon, Mystique et Politique* (Paris, Champion, 2004), pp. 147–161.

[70] On Cocceius, see Van Asselt, *The Federal Theology of Johannes Cocceius*.

[71] Pierre Poiret, *The Divine Oeconomy: or An Universal System of the Works and Purposes of God towards Men, Demonstrated*, 6 vols. (London, 1713), vol. 1, general preface, secs. 1 (on predestination) and 4 (on Cocceius), pages unnumbered, and vol. 3, pp. vii–viii. See also vol. 6 and Poiret's *Letter* to the Socinian Jean Le Clerc, published, on separately numbered pages, there. On Le Clerc, see Annie Barnes, *Jean Le Clerc (1657–1736)* (Geneva, Droz, 1938). On Cocceius and Socinianism, see the chapter entitled "The Cocceians," in Louis Maimbourg, *The History of Arianism*, 2 vols. (London, 1728–9), 1:149–60, and Hannah Adams, *An Alphabetical Compendium of the Various Sects which have Appeared in the World from the Beginning of the Christian Era to the Present Day* (Boston, 1784), pp. 50–2.

based on an initial set of claims about the existence of a long, purely spiritual history, populated entirely by angels and devils, that had occurred well before the beginning of the history described in Genesis.[72] Here, the first sinner was an angel, not a human, and, since the angel in question was by nature a purely spiritual being, its corruption had no relationship to a body. Being a devil, it could adopt any guise, but being a purely spiritual creature, it could not have a truly embodied nature, as was the case with humans, which was why it could simulate any number of natural beings. For Poiret, the serpent that had tempted Eve was not like any actual snake. It could imitate human behaviour by walking upright, could speak a human language, and could also use hands to offer the apple to Eve. It was, in short, just like Descartes's description of the purely mechanical parts of the human body.[73] Its soul, however, was entirely evil. Humans, Poiret argued, were more complicated, because of their embodied nature. The Fall described in Genesis had left them with a residual knowledge of the abilities that had once been part of their own first nature, but with a highly limited ability to internalise its implications into moral behaviour. "The nature of size, quantity, and numbers," Poiret wrote, "not having been corrupted by sin and having always remained the same, these cannot be mistaken and nothing falsifies the idea and truth of them." The same, however, did not apply to less abstract entities. "[T]he nature of created beauty, of power, goodness, and the light available to created beings having been perverted and entirely violated by sin, it is difficult to recognise its primitive state and see what, in its original, it is."[74] This, however, did not mean that humans were entirely dependent on God as the occasional cause of almost everything that they could know and choose (according to Poiret, this was the mistake that had been made by the Oratorian theologian Nicolas Malebranche), because they could themselves, he argued, cause the kind of knowledge and behaviour that, among other things, could enable them to cooperate freely with divine grace.

This idea was usually taken to be what, in theological language, was called a semi-Pelagian heresy, meaning that it transferred too much causal weight to human agency (or spiritual pride) for the merit and justice that,

[72] For helpful ways into the subject, see D. P. Walker, *The Decline of Hell* (London, Routledge, 1962), especially pp. 11–8, and Philip C. Almond, *Heaven and Hell in Enlightenment England* (Cambridge, CUP, 1994).

[73] Pierre Poiret, *L'oeconomie divine, ou système universel et démontré des oeuvres et des desseins de Dieu envers les hommes. Ou l'on explique et prouve d'origine, avec une évidence et une certitude métaphysique, les principes et les vérités de la nature et de la grâce, de la philosophie et de la théologie, de la raison et de la foi, de la morale naturelle et de la religion chrétienne, et ou l'on résout entièrement les grandes et épineuses difficultés sur la prédestination, sur la liberté, sur l'universalité de la rédemption et sur la providence, etc.*, 7 vols. (Amsterdam, 1687), 3:213–5.

[74] Poiret, *L'oeconomie divine*, vol. 1, preface, §22.

in the fullness of time, would be responsible for individual salvation. Poiret denied that there was anything heretical in the idea. The alternatives, he argued, pointed either towards the materialism that he took to be implicit in Malebranche's theology (a view that Fénelon was to share) or to the even more heretical idea that God was the author of evil, which, Poiret argued, was bound to come out of orthodox Calvinism.[75] God, he wrote, created man in the light of the sinful behaviour of angels. Knowing that humans would also sin, he set out to arm them against the fate of the angels, and to equip them with all the means that he had in his wisdom and power. This was why he had made man with a body and given the soul a connection to the body that angels did not have. Thus, when man fell, he did indeed turn away from God, but, unlike a fallen angel, did not turn inwards towards himself. Instead, humans turned outwards towards the abundance of objects that made so great an impression on their physical senses. The result was that they were caught up in a world of external objects that, in turn, would have a direct impact on their senses, well before they began to reflect upon themselves. Rather like Rousseau's later remark about a thinking animal being a depraved animal, fallen humans were not as radically impaired as the Devil itself, because their reliance on their senses for information meant that they did not have to think in self-reflective ways.[76] As a result, the original divine faculties were not directly violated (which was why humans still had an ability to know the truth of sizes, quantities, and numbers), and God was not directly rejected because, unlike a fallen angel, a human could put something other than him- or herself in place of the divinity. This meant that the type of impairment to which a purely spiritual creature like an angel might be subject was far more final than the impairment that would affect an embodied creature like a human being. Since it was the soul, with its capacity for making moral choices, that was both the agent and patient of the corruption of human nature, the body gave humans a layer of moral protection that angels (or devils) simply did not have. The link between the soul and the body also meant that some of the inferior and sensual faculties were, in some measure, equipped with an ability to enjoy God himself, while God could in some measure communicate bodily with humans. This, Poiret explained, was why it was possible for God to channel human faculties towards himself by limiting the appeal of other sensual goods. The way to do so had been established when God became a human and, by way of the example of Christ and the precepts of

---

[75] Poiret, *L'oeconomie divine*, vol. 1, ch. 6, §9, pp. 121–2; vol. 1, ch. 3, §14, pp. 64–73; vol. 1, ch. 12, §2, pp. 306–8; vol. 2, ch. 24, §18, pp. 632–3, 644–5, 662, 664–5; vol. 6, ch. 2, §1, pp. 32–3.

[76] Poiret, *L'oeconomie divine*, vol. 3, ch. 11, §§12–14, pp. 185–9. For an indication of the wider intellectual context, see Roger Mercier, *La réhabilitation de la nature humaine, 1700–1750* (Villemomble, 1960).

the Christian Gospel, had shown humans how to relegate other sources of sensual pleasure to their proper place.[77]

This reassessment of the relationship between the physical and the spiritual gave a new value to the purely physical side of human nature. It turned the body into the vehicle responsible for protecting the soul from the dangers to which both its spiritual nature and its capacity for volition left it exposed. As Poiret put it, "the members of the mystical body of Jesus Christ each have, for as long as they are on earth, a natural and infirm body that has need to be relieved, either ordinarily in the form of food and clothing, or extraordinarily, in cases of illness and perilous encounters."[78] This was the justification of the golden rule, and the love and charity on which it was based. It also entailed the further idea that humans were able to achieve a capacity for "pure love," or an entirely disinterested love of God. Fénelon was later to call the techniques involved in the development of this kind of capacity "disappropriation," in opposition to the "appropriation" that was the hallmark of the ordinary behaviour of fallen mankind.[79] If humans really did have this capacity, it meant that the body and its assorted physical or psychological needs were not as all-consuming as the idea of concupiscence presupposed. This, in turn, left the status of the passions more open. Some were certainly evil, but those that simply helped the body to work had a more positive moral quality. They could be taken to mean that humans were naturally good in the straightforwardly physical sense of Rousseau's later usage (although Poiret was not, of course, as sceptical as Rousseau about the reality of original sin).

Nor, since the body seemed able to perform all the functions required to preserve the soul without any apparent volition, was it clear why the passions had to exercise as much power over human behaviour as they appeared to have (much of the eighteenth-century interest in reflex action, muscular contraction, and the other, mainly involuntary, aspects of human physiology thus had a strongly spiritual dimension, as can be seen from the work of Poiret's contemporary Francis Mercurius Van Helmont, and from the subsequent bearing that this kind of vitalist physiology was to have on Charles Bonnet's spiritualised version of natural philosophy and on Johann Gottfried Herder's striking claim that humans were not embodied souls, but ensouled bodies).[80] Putting the soul ahead of the body in this way, thus making the body an increasingly complicated derivation of the soul's striving for eternity, was to lead to the strange combination of

[77] Poiret, *L'oeconomie divine*, vol. 3, ch. 11, §14, pp. 188–9.

[78] Poiret, *L'oeconomie divine*, vol. 5, ch. 6, §4, pp. 155–7.

[79] On the Origenist dimensions of Van Helmont's thought, see Almond, *Heaven and Hell in Enlightenment England*, pp. 17–22; and, on this aspect of Fénelon's thought, see Jean Deprun, *La philosophie de l'inquiétude en France au xviiie siècle* (Paris, Vrin, 1979).

[80] See above, p. 121.

metempsychosis and universal salvation that was to be described in great
detail in the posthumously published *Philosophical Principles of Natural and
Revealed Religion* (1748) by Fénelon's disciple the chevalier Andrew Michael Ramsay.[81] Ramsay's ideas, with their very literal interpretation of
God's general will to save everyone, soon acquired a significant following,
particularly in British Methodist and other heterodox Protestant circles,
where they also came to play a part in the late eighteenth- and early nineteenth-century American Universalist Movement, one of whose founders,
Elhanan Winchester, was a great admirer of Ramsay's philosophy (in an
English setting, Ramsay's ideas may also have had a bearing on the equally
strange ideas of William Blake). "After I had preached this sermon," Winchester recorded, "I had the Chevalier Ramsay's *Philosophical Principles of
Natural and Revealed Religion* put into my hands. I read the same with
great pleasure and advantage, and I must acknowledge it to be a work of
great merit, and I have reason to bless God that ever I had an opportunity
of reading it."[82] According to the American republican Benjamin Rush,
the egalitarian implications of the idea of "God's universal love to all his
creatures" was a "polar truth," leading to truths upon all subjects, "but
especially upon the subject of government."[83] In the later words of the
poet Samuel Taylor Coleridge, whose youthful interest in establishing
a self-governing community under the name of Pantisocracy also had a
rather Fénelonian hue, "almost all the followers of Fénelon" subscribed to
the idea of metempsychosis.[84]

---

[81] On this aspect of Ramsay's thought, see the fine study by Marialuisa Baldi, *Verisimile,
non Vero. Filosofia e politica in Andrew Michael Ramsay* (Milan, FrancoAngeli, 2002), as well as
her earlier "Nature and Man Restored: Mysticism and Millenarianism in Andrew Michael
Ramsay," *Anglophonia* 3 (1998): 89–102, and "Tra Giacobiti e Massoni. La Libertà secondo
Ramsay," in Luisa Simonutti, ed., *Dal necessario al possibile. Determinismo e libertà nel pensiero
anglo-olandese del xvii secolo* (Milan, FrancoAngeli, 2001), pp. 265–80.

[82] Elhanan Winchester, *The Universal Restoration examined in Four Dialogues between a Minister and his Friend* (Boston, 1831), p. xxvi. On the Methodist interest in Fénelon and Ramsay,
see Jean Orcibal, "Les spirituels français et espagnols chez Jean Wesley et ses contemporains," and his "L'influence spirituelle de Fénelon dans les pays anglo-saxons au xviiie siècle,"
both reprinted in his *Etudes d'histoire et de littérature religieuses* (Paris, Klincksieck, 1997), pp.
163–220, 221–32.

[83] Cited in Ann Lee Bressler, *The Universalist Movement in America, 1770–1880* (Oxford,
OUP, 2001), p. 19.

[84] Irene H. Chayes, "Coleridge, Metempsychosis, and 'Almost All the Followers of Fénelon,'" *English Literary History* 25 (1958): 290–315. On Pantisocracy, see Christopher
J. P. Smith, *A Quest for Home: Reading Robert Southey* (Liverpool, Liverpool UP, 1997), pp.
41–83, and W. A. Speck, *Robert Southey, Entire Man of Letters* (New Haven, Yale UP, 2006),
pp. 42–61, and the further bibliographical guidance supplied there. For a parallel project
for establishing an "agricultural society, or society of friends" (*société agricole ou d'amis*) that
circulated among Brissot and his friends in 1790, see Claude Perroud, "Un projet de Brissot
pour une association agricole," *La Révolution française* 42 (1902): 260–65.

Poiret himself had no illusions about the difficulties involved in the human capacity for pure love (Origen, it was said, had actually castrated himself). Some, he observed, claimed that humans were naturally good, or could be made good by political establishments, a claim that led to chimeras like "Plato's republic." Others, "like Hobbes," assumed that "all men are wicked and, taking this wickedness for a principle of justice and natural law, spin fables about fear bringing men together and leading them to divest themselves of this first detestable right, to invest it in another, making him, according to his fancy, the rule of the just and unjust."[85] Interestingly, Poiret opted for a modified version of the latter point of view, without, however, accepting Hobbes's idea of a representative sovereign state as the solution to the problem (Poiret seems to have understood Hobbes fairly well). He endorsed what he called "the natural state of the politicians (*MM. les politiques*), where all are against all and everything is allowed to everyone and those who are strongest," but argued that God had ruled out the politicians' solution.

> God, seeking to prevent this infernal upheaval and to place a measure of order in this disorder, did not allow that all should transfer this so-called diabolical right to one person to dispose of according to his corrupt fantasy or that this should be the principle of justice, even according to God, as published to the world on behalf of Hell by the unseeing Hobbes.[86]

He had, instead, made provision for a number of different obstacles (*barrières*) to human corruption, so that these would form "a system for a corrupt world, or a system of police" to protect humanity's better parts and help its more wicked elements to abandon their malice, if they had a will to do so.[87]

Although Poiret did not go into any detail about the type of obstacles in question, he made it clear that their purpose was to limit the power of both church and state, so that men and women would be left free to find their own way to God. Nor, he emphasised, would these obstacles be designed to promote virtue in any strong sense of the term. To assume that they should have this purpose, he argued, would lead directly towards the error of the Pharisees and the blindness of spirit involved in trying to cast out the eyes of every putative sinner. There was, Poiret emphasised, "a great difference" between "real wickedness" and "political wickedness," "real vices" and "political vices," and between "real virtue" and "political virtue." In terms of good politics, "one can be (and many in effect are) virtuous, honourable, just, and chaste, without in fact having a thread of

[85] Poiret, *L'oeconomie divine*, vol. 7, ch. 9, §7, pp. 231–2.
[86] Poiret, *L'oeconomie divine*, vol. 7, ch. 9, §3, p. 226.
[87] Poiret, *L'oeconomie divine*, vol. 7, ch. 9, §3, p. 226.

virtue, honour, justice, or chastity before God."[88] This was simply the human condition. However "politically well-covered and finely ornamented the old Adam might be," the "diabolical corruption" of human nature still remained. But true human wickedness was God's affair. Provided that it had no external consequences, it was possible for someone to be wicked within and still be "a politician with honour" or "virtuous in a political way." It was also possible that the type of external restraint ("for political and human reasons") that this would involve might make "one more disposed to listen to the voice of God within."[89]

This emphasis on policy (or *police*), rather than state power, as the way to calm the passions and enable individuals to find their own ways to God was quite compatible with the reform programme that Fénelon described in *Telemachus*, and, in particular, with his claim about the way that property could be used both to neutralise "sloth and luxury" and to force individuals to lead their own lives without—in contradistinction to feudal or Gothic arrangements—having to depend on anyone else. It could also be fitted into the broader moral theory on which Fénelon seems to have drawn as part of his responsibilities as a royal tutor. The moral theory itself was set out in a compilation entitled *The Lives and Most Remarkable Maxims of the Ancient Philosophers* (as the almost simultaneous English translation was entitled) that was published in 1725, ten years after Fénelon's death. Its appearance provoked a complaint by Fénelon's biographer and literary executor, the chevalier Ramsay, on the grounds that the publication was not something that Fénelon himself would have authorised, since it had never appeared in print in his own lifetime (and, Ramsay suggested, it was also possible that it had not actually been written by Fénelon himself).[90] The related questions of authenticity and author's rights may well have been all that was at issue in Ramsay's complaint, but the content of the text itself may also have played a part. Instead of the Platonism with which Fénelon is often associated, *The Lives and Most Remarkable Maxims of the Ancient Philosophers* was an apparently eclectic mixture of mainly Cynic, Epicurean, Stoic, and Aristotelian philosophy, with a surprisingly positive treatment of the first two schools. Plato was certainly one of the twenty-six philosophers whose lives and maxims Fénelon chose to describe (relying, it seems, on standard sources like Plutarch, Cicero, Juvenal, and Diogenes Laertes). But he was described mainly as a rather unreliable guide to the thought of his teacher, Socrates (Xenophon was more trustworthy), and as an unsuccessful courtier whose taste for high living and pageantry was the cause of

[88] Poiret, *L'oeconomie divine*, vol. 7, ch. 9, §12, pp. 236–7.

[89] Poiret, *L'oeconomie divine*, vol. 7, ch. 9, §12, pp. 237–8.

[90] Ramsay's objections were reprinted in the early nineteenth-century edition of Fénelon's *Oeuvres*, ed. Aimé Martin, 3 vols. (Paris, 1835), 3:264–7.

his stormy relationship with his protector, Dionysius, the tyrant of Sicily (a character trait that Fénelon also chose to emphasise by rehearsing the story about Diogenes the Cynic and Plato's purple carpets). His ideas about the gods (consisting of the higher gods who were beyond human comprehension; the middle gods, or daemons, who ministered to humans; and the demigods, like sylphs, salamanders, water-nymphs and gnomes, who were the authors of dreams and miracles), as well as his endorsement of metempsychosis, and his theory of ideas, matter, and forms, had all been "transmitted to us after a very perplexed manner," Fénelon wrote, testily, but had still been enough to earn him "the title of divine."[91]

Fénelon made rather more of another of Socrates' pupils, Antisthenes, "the chief of the Cynics." He had been "the first to adopt the Cynic attire" and, in keeping with what he had been taught by Socrates, "the founder of moral philosophy among the Greeks," had made moral philosophy his exclusive preoccupation. The "most useful science," according to Antisthenes, "was to unlearn that which is evil." The starting point of this type of self-analysis was his belief about the nature of the gods that all the Cynics subsequently came to share. Their "usual saying" was "that the property of the gods was to want nothing, and those whose wants were least approached nearest to the divine state." This was why the Cynics "valued themselves for their contempt of riches, nobility, and all other gifts of nature and fortune," but also why "they were men void of modesty, who were ashamed of nothing, not even of the most infamous of actions, having no respect to persons, nor regard to decency." It also explained why the Cynics believed that "the wise were not obliged to live according to the laws, but according to the rules of virtue," and, by extension, why "nobility and wisdom were the same thing," so that "nobody was noble who was not wise." This combination of austerity and self-analysis was, Fénelon wrote, the only way to approach the gods. No being, according to Antisthenes, resembled the divine nature, which was why it was "foolish to form a notion of it by any representation subject to the senses."[92]

This fairly sympathetic treatment of Cynic philosophy was matched by a number of further entries on several of the more notable later Cynics (specifically on Diogenes, whose life and ideas were given the longest treatment of the whole book, and on Crates and Bion, although the latter later dropped Cynic philosophy and died of debauchery). Even Zeno, the founder of the Stoics, was treated as a kind of Cynic. As Fénelon noted,

---

[91] François de Salignac de la Mothe Fénelon, *The Lives and Most Remarkable Maxims of the Ancient Philosophers* [1726] (London, 1726), pp. 129 (on Xenophon as more reliable than Plato on Socrates), 154 (on Plato's admiration for pageantry and grandeur), 199 (on Plato and his purple carpets), 143–6 (on Plato on the gods).

[92] Fénelon, *Lives*, pp. 147–55.

Juvenal had written that "the Stoics and Cynics differed only in dress, but their doctrine was the same."[93] But Fénelon also went on to describe certain Stoic ideas that did not appear in the entries on the Cynics. Alongside the Stoic preoccupation with virtue (which was indistinguishable from its Cynic counterpart), he also highlighted Zeno's examination of "things that were neither good nor evil, though they had the power to move our appetites and incline us to choose the one preferably to the other." These included "life and health, beauty and strength, riches and nobility, pleasure and glory," as well as their opposites, "death and sickness, ugliness and weakness, poverty and meanness, pain and reproach." These "indifferent things" had no power to make anyone truly happy or unhappy, since things that could be used for good or evil could not be good or evil in themselves.[94] In other respects, however, the Stoics were quite similar to the Cynics. Like them (and like Pythagoras too), they believed that "all things belonged to the gods and that, amongst friends, all things (including women) were in common."[95]

Fénelon, however, also made a point of singling out Epicurus's view that friendship and common property were not, in fact, different sides of the same coin. The result was a more positive evaluation of private property. Epicurus, he wrote (in what was also one of the longest entries in the book), "would never suffer his followers to make a common bank as the scholars of Pythagoras did, it being the mark of distrust rather than friendship."[96] Nor, Fénelon emphasised, was Epicurus anything like the voluptuary of philosophical folklore (the truth was actually nearer to the remark by Cicero in his *Tusculan Questions*: "O good gods; how great was the abstinence of Epicurus").[97] The posthumous reputation that he had acquired, Fénelon wrote, owed a great deal to Stoic character assassination, a rather characteristic feature of a sect "who make profession of a severe and rigid virtue, but, at the bottom are full of vanity." The real Epicurus was "a glorious and eminent example of temperance and sobriety, and his morals were pure and uncorrupted."[98] This moral integrity went along with an idea of a supreme being who "had a right to be adored for the excellency of his nature," and "not out of fear of punishment or the hope of a reward." This, however, was as far as any human relationship to the gods could go. Since the gods were utterly unlike humans, no human image of divinity could be at all appropriate, just as there was no point to

---

[93] Fénelon, *Lives*, p. 272. It is unlikely that modern scholarship would agree.
[94] Fénelon, *Lives*, pp. 274–5.
[95] Fénelon, *Lives*, pp. 82 (on Pythagoras), 276–7 (on Stoic and Cynic property theory).
[96] Fénelon, *Lives*, p. 246.
[97] Fénelon, *Lives*, p. 245.
[98] Fénelon, *Lives*, p. 264.

any human emotion about the gods and their attributes. For Epicurus, stories about hell and eternal punishments were simply allegories of our real and violent passions.[99] The mixture of Epicurean and Cynic philosophy that Fénelon presented amounted to something quite similar to the balance between human faculties and needs that Rousseau was later to call happiness.[100]

Intriguingly, Fénelon also supplied a fairly detailed summary (based on the Roman poet Lucretius's *De rerum natura*) of Epicurus's account of the origins of life, and the formation of the very first human societies, beginning with the way that the heat of the sun had begun to warm the earth, causing little mushroom-like tumours to burst into life, leaving "little rivulets of milk" for the first living creatures to feed upon.[101] The bodies of many of these creatures were ill-adapted to life, so that only those "whose bodies were perfectly framed" came to form any existing species. The first humans were solitary animals, who lived by foraging and gathering, associating initially to protect themselves from wild animals, and clothing themselves with the pelts of the animals that they managed to kill. Society began with the formation of monogamous families, and language emerged from gestures and cries. Property accompanied the building of "cities," but it was divided very unequally, with the largest share going to those who "excelled in strength and policy." These individuals "made themselves kings and constrained the rest of mankind to obey them." The discovery of fire and its ability to melt metals led to the first weapons, and to the further discovery that one material, iron, could be used to make several different things, including the tools required for agriculture. But the character of these now largely agricultural societies was transformed "as soon as gold began to be esteemed and everyone was charmed by the beauty of the metal." Until then, kings could rely on "force and policy." But once gold had revealed its charms, the people deserted their kings and transferred their allegiance to the rich. Kings were assassinated and "the government became popular," with laws and popularly designated magistrates "to take care of the commonwealth." These new forms of association were more peaceful at home, with convivial gatherings, communal feasts, and the first use of music, but were also more bellicose abroad, with

---

[99] Fénelon, *Lives*, pp. 250–2.

[100] On Rousseau's concept of happiness, see above, p. 150.

[101] Fénelon, *Lives*, p. 256. On the eighteenth-century interest in Lucretius, see Eric Baker, "Lucretius in the European Enlightenment," in Stuart Gillespie and Philip Hardie, eds., *The Cambridge Companion to Lucretius* (Cambridge, CUP, 2007), pp. 274–88. On the relevance of Lucretius to Rousseau's thought, but without the possible bearing of Fénelon's text on the subject, see Victor Gourevitch, "Rousseau on Providence," cited above, chapter 3, note 38, and the version of the same article in *Review of Metaphysics* 53 (2000): 565–611 (with the further bibliography on Rousseau and Lucretius supplied in his note 83).

wars arising for "no other motive than to make themselves masters of each other's estate." War gave rise to painting and poetry to commemorate heroic deeds and their authors, while periods of peace allowed the arts, which had originated in necessity, to be carried to perfection.[102]

This, for didactic purposes, was as far as Lucretius could be taken. Fuller treatment of political societies was supplied by Aristotle. According to Fénelon, Aristotle "maintains in his politicks that the monarchical state is the most perfect of any, because all other governments are managed by several persons" (the best example of this sort of unity was an army, where one leader was more effective than several). Republics were always vulnerable to the potential for division caused by the large number of different decision-makers. Nor, according to Aristotle, did any of the members of a republic have good reason to prevent its possible ruin, "provided they can enrich themselves elsewhere." This inbuilt risk of faction did not exist in monarchies, where "the interest of the prince and the state are inseparable and must consequently flourish."[103] But, as Fénelon described it, Aristotle's conception of monarchy also added a new dimension to the broad emphasis on virtue as the real source of happiness that was a common theme of Cynic, Epicurean, and Stoic philosophy. In some respects, they all shared a substantial measure of common ground. Physical pleasure, according to Aristotle, had nothing to do with happiness, because it could produce loathing and weaken the body, just as much as it could produce enjoyment and health. Nor did honour and happiness go together, because what really had to be honoured was the virtue, not the person. The same judgement applied to riches, because riches had to be laid out and distributed to be useful, but the mere fact of having them gave rise to the fear to use them. Unlike wealth and its uses, happiness was "something fixed, which is to be preserved and kept." But the connection between wealth, liberality, and generosity that Fénelon associated with Aristotle introduced an aspect of morality that was not present in his descriptions of Epicurean, Stoic, or Cynic philosophy. For Aristotle, happiness was not only connected to "the endowments of the mind"; it was also connected to "the advantages of the body, as beauty, strength and health, and the gifts of fortune, as riches and nobility."[104]

This shift of emphasis was given a stronger inflection by the custodian of Fénelon's historical legacy, the chevalier Andrew Michael Ramsay. Ramsay's *Travels of Cyrus* was a modified version of *Telemachus*, and a further move away from the largely Cynic, Stoic, and Epicurean moral themes of the *Lives and Most Remarkable Maxims of the Ancient Philosophers*

---

[102] Fénelon, *Lives*, pp. 256–61.
[103] Fénelon, *Lives*, pp. 183–4.
[104] Fénelon, *Lives*, pp. 181–2.

towards the more liberal (in its old sense) conception of monarchy that Fénelon associated with Aristotle (someone who was "liberal," noted a work published at around the same time, "did not have *l'esprit propriétaire*," or a proprietary spirit).[105] Its starting point, however, was a reaffirmation of the claim "that the earliest opinions of the most knowing and civilized nations come nearer to the truth than those of later ages" that was a common feature of the moral and political thought of Harrington, Fleury, and Fénelon.[106] Ramsay's version of the claim was rather nearer to Poiret's than to Fénelon himself, both because of its more explicit emphasis on the type of purely spiritual history that, according to Origen, had preceded the story described in Genesis, and because of its bearing on the fact that, as Ramsay put it, "the world could not come out of the hands of a wise, good and powerful Creator in its present ignorance, disorder and corruption."[107] Part of the point of the *Travels of Cyrus* was, therefore, to highlight the compatibility between some of the findings of modern science, notably those made by Isaac Newton, John Woodward, and Hermann Boerhaave, and the kind of nonphysically mediated knowledge that had once been available to purely spiritual beings.[108] Another part of the same argument was to emphasise the connection between knowledge that had once been perfect, and the moral principles that it entailed. The knowledge that the youthful Cyrus was to acquire on his travels, before he released the Jews from the Babylonian captivity, would enable him to see, as Ramsay put it, "that the duties of religion, morality, and good policy flow from the same source, conspire to the same end, and mutually support and fortify each other; and, in a word, that all the civil and human virtues, the laws of nature and nations are, so to speak, but consequences of *the love of order*, which is the eternal and universal law of all intelligences."[109]

Humans, however, were not simple "intelligences" but embodied creatures living in a material environment (which was why Ramsay attached such significance to the natural philosophy of Newton and Boerhaave). The substance of *The Travels of Cyrus* consisted, accordingly, of an examination of the various sets of social and political arrangements that were most compatible both with the original moral principle and with humanity's embodied nature. Egypt supplied the first model. It was, in fact, rather like Britain after the Glorious Revolution because it was ruled by a usurper, named Amasis. He had proclaimed that "all authority originally resides in

[105] Pierre-François Guyot Desfontaines, *Dictionnaire néologique à l'usage des beaux esprits, avec l'éloge historique de Pantalon-Phoebus* (n.p., 1726), p. 126.
[106] Andrew Michael Ramsay, *The Travels of Cyrus* [1726]. I have used an Edinburgh, 1800, edition of the same work, here citing the preface, p. xiii.
[107] Ramsay, *Travels*, p. xvi.
[108] Ramsay, *Travels*, pp. 63, 66–7, 90, note.
[109] Ramsay, *Travels*, p. xvii.

the people," and that they were "the absolute arbiters of religion and of royalty, and create both your Gods and your Kings." Amasis had presented himself as a liberator, saying, "I set you free from the idle fears both of the one and of the other by letting you know of your just rights," namely, that "all men are born equal," and that "it is your will alone which makes a distinction."[110] In practice, however, this demagogic flattery masked a real tyranny. It also indicated the cause of Egypt's present misfortunes. As Cyrus came to learn, "great cities and magnificent courts have only served too much to corrupt the manners and sentiments of mankind; and that by uniting a multitude of men in the same place, they often do but unite and multiply their passions."[111] But, for all these defects and its current ruler's political illegitimacy, Egypt housed a fundamentally healthy society. "Agriculture, the mechanic arts and commerce, which are the three supports of a state, flourished everywhere, and proclaimed a laborious and rich people as well as a prudent, steady and mild government."[112]

Cyrus soon reconquered Egypt (a scenario denied to Ramsay himself) and began to learn of its ancient wisdom. Egyptian history was made up of three ages. The first was an age of shepherd kings in which Egypt had been divided among several different dynasties. There was then no foreign trade and a largely pastoral way of life, where shepherds were heroes, and kings were philosophers (the description matched Fénelon's account of Betica). Conquest by Arab invaders brought this golden age to an end. The invaders were "uncivilized" and despised "the sublime and occult sciences," preferring instead to value "sculpture, painting and poetry," with the result that these sense-based sources of information "obscured all pure ideas and transformed them into sensible images."[113] The way was now open to the "conquests and luxury" of the age of Sesostris, whose crumbling empire was conquered in turn by the Babylonian king Nebuchadnezzar. All that remained was the memory of Egypt's ancient laws and the lessons from them that Cyrus could learn. The laws in question applied to kings, polity, and civil justice. The first concerned the duties of kingship and the moral qualities required for virtuous rule. The second related "to polity and the subordination of ranks." Here, Ramsay echoed Fénelon's description of the reformed kingdom of Salentum. The land was divided into three parts, with one part forming the royal domain, a second belonging to the chief priests, and the third to the "military men." The "common people" were also divided into three classes, consisting of husbandmen, shepherds, and artisans. The transmission of knowledge from one generation to the next was maintained by laws

[110] Ramsay, *Travels*, bk. 3, pp. 84–5.
[111] Ramsay, *Travels*, bk. 3, p. 92.
[112] Ramsay, *Travels*, bk. 3, p. 94.
[113] Ramsay, *Travels*, bk. 3, pp. 98–9.

preventing anyone from abandoning his father's profession. In this way, "the arts were cultivated and brought to a great perfection, and the disturbances occasioned by the ambition of those who seek to rise above the rank in which they were born were prevented." To ensure that "no-one would be ashamed of the lowness of his state and degree," the mechanical arts were "held in honour," so that "a due subordination of ranks" was preserved, "without exposing the noble to envy or the meaner to contempt." The third set of laws, concerning civil justice, was designed to complement these arrangements. These provided for a supreme council of thirty judges, drawn from all the principal cities, to administer justice throughout the entire kingdom.[114]

Cyrus was favourably impressed by almost everything about Egypt's laws, apart, however, from the legal obligation for children to follow their father's occupation. The requirement violated the rights of justice and merit. As Cyrus observed, "we see in almost all countries, and all ages, that the greatest men have not always had the advantage of an high birth." Superior ability could be wasted by being confined to hereditary occupation. "In political establishments," he commented, "we should avoid everything whereby nature may be constrained and genius cramped. The noblest prerogative of a king is to be able to repair the injustice of fortune by doing justice to merit."[115] Greece helped to confirm this view. The Spartan regime, for all its institutional and social merits, was equally noteworthy for its "savage fierceness," and its inability to find a way to reconcile "military virtues and tender passions," particularly because the latter were vital for family life. Even worse was the reliance upon the helots for agriculture and manufacture. "Agriculture and the mechanic arts," Cyrus commented, "appear to me absolutely necessary to preserve the people from idleness, which begets discord, effeminacy and all the evils destructive of society. Lycurgus seems to depart a little too much from nature in all his laws."[116] Athens was a significant improvement. There, Solon had succeeded in modifying the "excessive power of the people" by attacking those "who taught that all men are born equal," and "that merit alone ought to regulate ranks." Although it was certainly true, Solon conceded, that merit "essentially distinguished men and ought solely to determine ranks," ignorance and the passions made it hard to maintain any stable criteria defining merit's real nature. "Disputes, discord and illusion would be endless, if there was not some rule more fixed, certain, and palpable than merit alone, whereby to settle ranks and degrees." In "small republics" ranks could be regulated by election, but in "great monarchies" the criterion had to be birth. It was certainly "an evil," but it was "a necessary evil."[117]

[114] Ramsay, *Travels*, bk. 3, pp. 101–3.
[115] Ramsay, *Travels*, bk. 4, p. 116.
[116] Ramsay, *Travels*, bk. 4, p. 122.
[117] Ramsay, *Travels*, bk. 5, pp. 145–6.

The same argument applied to property. All men were certainly brethren, "and each man has a right to whatever he has need of." But "if there were not laws established to settle ranks and property among men, the avarice and ambition of the strongest would invade all." The laws in question might not be "what is best in itself" but could still be "what is least mischievous to society." Unless Astraea were to return, Solon concluded, "merit alone" could never "determine the fortunes of men."[118] The same policy applied to the problem of the "excessive riches of some" and the "extreme poverty of others." Here, the solution was not a Spartan-style "community of goods" but recurrent debt reprieves, so that the inequality of ranks and property could not be inflamed by excessive personal dependence. The outcome of these reforms was the moderate monarchy of the archon Pisistratus, whose status was rather similar to that of a Dutch Stadthouder or a Venetian doge. Pisistratus was the architect of Athenian naval power, which was based on the way that the city's merchant navy was adapted to military purposes in times of war. Apart from the additional resources supplied by this flexibility, it also had desirable moral effects. As Pisistratus explained to Cyrus, "whenever a people carry on commerce only to increase their wealth, the state is no longer a republic but a society of merchants, who have no other kind of union but the desire of gain." Dual use added patriotism to naval power.[119] The laws of Minos supplied a further perspective because they seemed to present a synthesis of all that Cyrus had been able to observe. Looking back, he decided that Egypt's government was too despotic, while the Athenian government remained too favourable to its people's inclination towards liberty, luxury, and pleasure, and the Spartan regime was "too contrary to nature," since "equality of ranks and community of goods cannot subsist long."[120] The laws of Minos appeared to combine the best elements of all three: the stable property regime of the Egyptians, the opportunities for merit to shine supplied by the laws of the Athenians, and the fierce military patriotism of the Spartans. It was not surprising, he concluded, that they had been adopted by the Romans, or that the combination had made the Romans "fit to conquer the whole world."[121]

The final part of the journey took Cyrus to Tyre, which (after the first city of Tyre had been razed by the Babylonians) had been reconstructed on an island and was ruled by a king who had been restored to his throne. In this sense, Tyre was a Jacobite vision of Britain's future. Unlike Rome, its greatness was based on commerce, not conquest. But its commerce

[118] Ramsay, *Travels*, bk. 5, pp. 147–8.
[119] Ramsay, *Travels*, bk. 5, pp. 148, 152–8.
[120] Ramsay, *Travels*, bk. 6, p. 191.
[121] Ramsay, *Travels*, bk. 6, p. 193.

was, in turn, based on a well-managed system of money and credit, making it somewhat more stable than Athens. As Cyrus went on to learn, "wherever commerce flourishes under the protection of wise laws, plenty becomes universal and magnificence costs the state nothing."[122] The key to this condition was, in part, free trade. It was also, however, to be found in Phoenician monetary and financial policy. Bahal, the kingdom's ruler, had encouraged the principal merchants to advance substantial amounts of credit to Tyre's artisans, and also to deal with one another mainly on the basis of credit. These credit-based manufacturing and commercial sectors made it easier to maintain a cash-based consumer sector. Coin was left to circulate among the people, "because they have need of it to secure themselves against the corruption of ministers, the oppression of the rich, and even the ill usage that kings might make of their authority."[123] Inventions were encouraged and "great workhouses for manufactures" established, where all those "eminent in their respective arts" were housed and fed. All tariffs were abolished and monopolies were outlawed. The result was a booming trading economy.[124]

As Cyrus was warned, however, the trading interest still had to be regulated. "In a city like Tyre, where commerce is the only support of the state, all the principal citizens are traders; the merchants are the princes of the republic, but in great empires, where military virtue and subordination of ranks are absolutely necessary, commerce ought to be encouraged, without being universal."[125] This was why trading companies were required. They would be responsible both for trade and for foreign settlements, as well as for the upkeep of the naval forces required for protection against piracy. Those not directly involved in trade would still be encouraged to invest in these public companies. The funds, "thus united, will produce an hundred fold" and would work in tandem with a flourishing agriculture. Cyrus then proceeded to draw out the broader message by summarising the stages of economic development that it implied. "In a kingdom that is fruitful, spacious, populous and abounding with seaports, if the people is laborious they may draw from the bosom of the earth immense treasures, which would be lost by the negligence and sloth of its inhabitants." Manufacture would then improve the productions of nature, and add still further to national riches. The result would be that "a solid commerce is established in a great empire." It would be based on the export of superfluities and the import of anything that could be covered by the sale of those superfluities. The state would then have no debts abroad and a stable balance of trade.

---

[122] Ramsay, *Travels*, bk. 7, p. 203.
[123] Ramsay, *Travels*, bk. 7, p. 205.
[124] Ramsay, *Travels*, bk. 7, pp. 205–6.
[125] Ramsay, *Travels*, bk. 7, p. 206.

On this basis, "great advantages will be reaped from commerce, without destroying the distinction of ranks or weakening military virtue."[126]

Ramsay's modifications to Fénelon gave the subject of the relationship between morality, culture, and wealth a real-world salience. The type of examination of women, salons, fashion, and the arts that could be found in Marivaux, Dubos, or Voltaire was one way of thinking about how culture and morality were connected. Here, the causal weight fell most strongly on culture, with civility and morality as its derivative effects. Reversing the causal relationship was more difficult. It was easy enough to connect morality to a very simple culture. But, as Ramsay's cautious treatment of the relationship between wealth and culture in Athens and Tyre indicated, it was more difficult to see how morality could survive exposure to the full glare of culture at its most ostentatiously ornate. The point was driven home by Montesquieu in *The Spirit of Laws*. The difficulty was not simply a matter of deciding where, for example, to draw a line separating luxury from magnificence, but, more fundamentally, of identifying a culturally independent standard of morality that could be used to give the line separating good from bad forms of culture a real discriminatory power. Religion was one obvious candidate. But religion itself was so culture bound that, except to the faithful, it was not clear whether it really could be used as an independently defined source of morality. Rousseau's contractual alternative was no better. Its focus on equality certainly supplied a moral dimension for politics. But, to its critics, it did not have enough of a moral starting point to get political morality off the ground. The need was to identify something that was like religion, but still not religion. It had to have something like the disinterested love of order that, for Ramsay, had once been possible for the purely intelligent beings of the time before the human state, but it still had to be suitable for real human life. Whatever it was, it had to be capable of explaining morality and, at the same time, sufficiently robust to deal with the wealth and culture of the modern world with a real measure of discrimination. One way of solving the problem appeared to lie in the programme of economic and political reform that came to be called Physiocracy.

PHYSIOCRACY, REFORM, AND THE FRUITS OF THE TREE OF LIFE

There was a significant measure of continuity between Ramsay's historical and theological speculations, and Physiocracy. The marquis de Mirabeau, its cofounder along with François Quesnay, took *The Travels of Cyrus* to be one of its intellectual precursors, along with *Telemachus*. One reason for

---

[126] Ramsay, *Travels*, bk. 7, p. 207.

the initial impact of Physiocracy—or the idea of a system of government based, according to the group of individuals usually known in the eighteenth century as the French economists, on the naturally contractual relationship between humans and nature—was the prospect that it appeared to offer of the possibility of having modernity's wealth, culture, and potential for morality, without having its inequality, injustice, and war.[127] The deliberate oxymoron "legal despotism" that its advocates used to refer to the type of government responsible for its implementation captured much of the sense of how Physiocracy was designed both to use sovereign power and to use it in a highly limited way. The legal part of the phrase referred to its respect for property and legality. The despotic part referred to the state's role in maintaining the combination of free trade and a single tax that would allow Physiocracy to work. The mixture of direct and indirect mechanisms implied by the idea of legal despotism added up to a relatively limited amount of state involvement in the process of reform. In sharp contrast to the punitive taxation, trade prohibitions, property limitations, sumptuary laws, and population resettlements of Fénelon's reform programme, implementing Physiocracy involved no more than two state-supported causal mechanisms, free trade and a single tax. The others, its supporters argued, would be produced simply by the cumulative and indirect effects of individual choice. It is important to stress, however, that although this emphasis on changing the structure and content of social arrangements mainly by way of indirect, rather than direct, mechanisms was considerably different from Fénelon's emphasis on the virtuous use of royal power, it still pointed towards a rather similar outcome. The goal, in both cases, was something like the picture of the reformed kingdom of Salentum that Fénelon described in *Telemachus*, with its hard work, flourishing agriculture, equitable property distribution, public opulence, social stability, and external security. The key difference was not so much that Physiocracy entailed less reliance on centralised royal power, as that it involved a gradual process of levelling up, rather than, as with Fénelon, a more abrupt process of levelling down.

The way to level up was built into Physiocracy. The system relied on a single tax on the net product (effectively a tax on rental income) to set a ceiling on the wealth of the landowners, the first of the three analytical classes into which the French economists divided society. Since neither of the two other classes, the producers of agricultural goods and the members of

---

[127] For this characterisation of Physiocracy, see Sonenscher, *Before the Deluge*, pp. 189–222. Mirabeau planned to publish a book called *Hommes à célébrer*, based on the courses of public lectures that he gave in Paris, mainly during the last years of the reign of Louis XV. Only a small part of its content, dealing with Sully, came into print before he died in 1789, but manuscript versions of other parts survive, both among Mirabeau's surviving papers in the A. N., and in the Belgian Bibliothèque royale, Brussels, Mss. 20797 et seq.

the "sterile," manufacturing sector, would pay any taxes at all, they would enjoy a larger share of the additional wealth generated by the productivity gains arising from investment in agricultural production. The incentive to invest would, in turn, be supplied, first, by price stability and, second, by the leads and lags involved in the periodic adjustments of rents to prevailing levels of prices and taxation. Over time, the relative distribution of wealth among the three classes would change as the effects of rising returns to agriculture pushed up the income of the productive class, and as its rising expenditure on both capital and consumer goods pushed up the income of the sterile, or manufacturing, class. The virtuous circle would be kept in place by the continuous fiscal pressure on the landowners and the incentive that it gave them to push up rents. The leads and lags involved in rent adjustments, particularly if these were fixed for relatively long periods of time, would supply an equally powerful incentive to the productive class to raise its output and push up its own tax-free income before the next cycle of rent adjustments took place. Higher agricultural productivity would have the effect of lowering the unit costs of wage goods, leading, in turn, to a rise in the living standards of the manufacturing class, both because of the relative fall in the real price of subsistence goods and because of the growing competitiveness of the export trade. Over time, therefore, the broad distribution of wealth would move in an upward direction towards equality, but at a much higher level of opulence than there had ever been before.

Physiocracy was also grounded on a strong set of claims about human social capacities. "The manner by which man is organised proves that he is destined by nature to live in society," announced the first sentence of the first chapter of one of the economists' manifesto texts, Pierre-Paul Le Mercier de la Rivière's *L'ordre naturel et essentiel des sociétés politiques* (The Natural and Essential Order of Political Societies) of 1767. One indication of this was the range of emotions that humans were capable of feeling, and their obvious impossibility or pointlessness outside society. "It is evident," Le Mercier de la Rivière continued, "that man, being capable of compassion, pity, friendship, benevolence, glory, emulation, and of a multitude of affections that can be experienced only in society, was destined by nature to live in society."[128] The same argument applied to human intelligence. Its utility developed only in society. Left to themselves, humans would have remained in a condition that, in several respects, would have been lower than that of a brute. Intelligence was a common human patrimony whose value depended on the part that everyone played in developing its resources. It was the link connecting the past to the present

---

[128] Pierre-Paul Lemercier de la Rivière, *L'ordre naturel et essentiel des sociétés politiques* [1767], ed. Edgard Depitre (Paris, 1910), p. 2.

and the antidote to the natural indigence of isolated individuals. Although the emotions were sense based, this did not mean that the human appetite for pleasure and aversion to pain were a purely physical matter. The appetite for pleasure included "what we might call the delectation of the soul, or those lively and gentle affections that penetrate it so deliciously," while the aversion to pain encompassed "all those unbearable, boring, or shameful situations in which the soul can find itself only because of our existence in society." Feelings like these had the power to override even the most cherished sensations, indicating a range of purely "social affections" that, Le Mercier de la Rivière wrote, "we obey when we seem to renounce ourselves to live only in others, enjoying only others' joy, and knowing pleasure only insofar as it passes through them before it reaches us." These "social affections" were what lay behind the human ability to set aside wealth or even life itself, and to prefer physical pain, or even death, to the feeling of dishonour or other sources of "chagrin" that could arise only from living in society.[129]

The implicit criticism of Rousseau was made more explicit in a much bigger book that began to appear six years later. This was the vast *Le monde primitif, analysé et comparé avec le monde moderne* (The Primitive World, Analysed and Compared to the Modern World) that started to come out in 1773 and, eight volumes later, was still in progress at the time of its author's death in 1783. The individual in question, a Franco-Swiss Protestant named Antoine Court de Gebelin (whose father, Antoine Court, had been a Protestant minister) made a point of emphasising the inbuilt, divinely given, human capacity for improvement based on the physiological structure of the mouth and the tongue, and the way that they enabled humans to use vowel and consonant sounds to communicate emotions and ideas (animals, he argued, were not equipped with this dual capacity and were, therefore, unable to produce the multiple combinations of differentiated sounds that human physiology made possible). The language instinct built into human nature was, therefore, the physiologically grounded key to the human capacity for improvement. The word that Court de Gebelin used to describe this capacity was Rousseau's neologism "perfectibility." "According to whether one accepts or rejects this perfectibility," Court de Gebelin wrote, "the history of peoples either becomes clear or turns into an absurd fable. Man must either have shown himself to be what he is, a creature that is very superior to all the others and, guided

---

[129] Lemercier de la Rivière, *L'ordre naturel et essentiel des sociétés politiques*, ed. Depitre, pp. 2–4. See also his *L'intérêt général de l'état ou la liberté du commerce des grains* (Amsterdam and Paris, 1770), where he argued that Physiocracy involved counting on the passions (p. xi), as the basis of preserving the unity of the common interest (something that, p. 18, he was careful to distinguish from the interest of the majority). The whole system, he went on to argue (pp. 190–1), was the only way to avoid state bankruptcy and social dissolution.

by a higher light, must have worked without interruption to perfect himself, or, indistinguishable from the animals, must have crawled like them over the face of the earth, and been enlightened only by causally weak and chronologically infrequent accidents."[130] He repeated the claim in the general view of the primitive world that he set out at the beginning of the eighth volume of *Le monde primitif*. It was contrary to truth, he wrote, to subscribe to "those bizarre opinions" in which "each word was the effect of chance," and "speech and grammar were no more than the effects of chance, agreement, or caprice." It was also a mistake to imagine "that the arts that applied to primary needs had been discovered only after repeated efforts, and the most painful and inconclusive trials over several thousands of centuries, as if man began by being a true savage, in the fullest sense of the word."[131] Although he did not mention Rousseau by name, it is hard not to believe that the passages were aimed at Rousseau's *Discourse on the Origin of Inequality* (this, certainly, was how they were construed in a pair of more orthodox Catholic examinations of their works, published in 1785 and 1786).[132]

Court de Gebelin made a point of highlighting the convergence between his own research on language formation and the agriculturally driven model of human improvement that was the centrepiece of Physiocracy. He had, he wrote, begun his own investigations independently, but had then been surprised and pleased to see how well his naturalistic explanation of the origins of language fitted the economists' system. The key to the convergence was the concept of a great providential order that, once understood and internalised, could supply the rules of human conduct required by every complex political society. Part of the human ability to understand and internalise the norms built into this great order was supplied by the physiological basis of language acquisition. The other part, however, was supplied by agriculture and the temporal continuities and differences that it involved. Unlike hunting, gathering, or fishing on the one hand, and the nomadic existence of shepherds and pastoral peoples

---

[130] Antoine Court de Gebelin, *Le monde primitif, analysé et comparé avec le monde moderne*, 9 vols. (Paris, 1773–83), 1:78–9. Although Court de Gebelin made a point of highlighting the convergence between his researches and Physiocracy, this aspect of his thought is not apparent in the secondary literature: see, for example, Robert Darnton, *Mesmerism and the End of the Enlightenment in France* (Cambridge, Mass., Harvard UP, 1968), pp. 116–7; and, most recently, Anne-Marie Mercier-Faivre, *Un supplément à l'Encyclopédie: Le Monde primitif d'Antoine Court de Gebelin* (Paris, Champion, 1999), where the connection is indicated but its linguistic basis is not described.

[131] Court de Gebelin, *Monde primitif*, 8:xxiii–xxiv.

[132] [Jean-Charles-François Le Gros], *Analyse des ouvrages de J. J. Rousseau de Genève, et de M. Court de Gebelin, auteur du Monde primitif, par un solitaire* (Paris, 1785), p. 221; and his *Examen des systèmes de J. J. Rousseau de Genève, et de M. Court de Gebelin, auteur du Monde primitif, par un solitaire* (Paris, 1786), p. 61.

on the other, agriculture relied on measurement and comparison not only between one season and another, but between one year and many others. It did so because the fixed settlements of agricultural societies ruled out the possibility of simply setting off for new pastures when local resources began to dry up. Agriculture, with its need for abstract knowledge, was, therefore, what had switched on the language instinct, turning humans into natural communicators and equipping them with the ability to begin to understand the vast providential order to which the seasons and their associated array of activities, occupations, and knowledge all, ultimately, belonged. The point of Court de Gebelin's vast research programme into the allegorical meanings of ancient language and artefacts (funded, in part, by Physiocracy's cofounder, the marquis de Mirabeau, and conducted with the help of a small army of research assistants, including the future founder of the American Philological Society, Peter Stephen Duponceau, and the Swiss pastor, Pierre de Joux) was to show how every early language housed identifiable traces of this original human insight.[133]

A further piece in the moral jigsaw was supplied by the astronomer and future mayor of Paris after 1789, Jean-Silvain Bailly.[134] In his *Histoire de l'astronomie ancienne* (History of Ancient Astronomy) of 1775, Bailly gave the idea of a great providential order an astronomical content by arguing that Court de Gebelin's claim about the connection between agriculture and the language instinct could be supported by astronomical evidence. His starting point was the curious chronological coincidence of the surviving record of astronomical observations by Egyptian, Chaldean, Persian, Indian, Chinese, and Tartar astronomers, all of which seemed to date

[133] On Peter Stephen Duponceau, and his early involvement with Court de Gebelin, see Joan Leopold, ed., *The Prix Volney: Its History and Significance for the Development of Linguistic Research*, 3 vols. (Dordrecht, Kluwer, 1999), and, on Pierre de Joux (who, like his compatriot, Carl Ludwig von Haller, converted later from Protestantism to Catholicism), and his five-year collaboration with Court de Gebelin, see the autobiographical "avant-propos" to his *Lettres sur l'Italie*, 2 vols. (Paris, 1825), 1:li.

[134] On Bailly, see, helpfully, Edwin Burrows Smith, "Jean-Sylvain Bailly: Astronomer, Mystic, Revolutionary, 1736–1793," *Transactions of the American Philosophical Society*, n.s., 44 (1954): 427–538 (see pp. 427, 453–5, 463–8, 473–4 for Bailly's sympathetic interest in Court de Gebelin). Smith's work is more reliable on the science and astronomy than on the other aspects of Bailly's intellectual life, mainly because it conflates Bailly's interest in Court de Gebelin with Freemasonry rather than with Physiocracy (which does not, of course, mean that the two interests were mutually exclusive). The whole vast subject has become entangled with the historiography of Orientalism, leaving much of the detailed history still to be recovered. See, for the starting point, Raymond Schwab, *The Oriental Renaissance* [1950] (New York, Columbia UP, 1972), with a generous introduction by Edward W. Said, and, more recently, Philip C. Almond, *The British Discovery of Buddhism* (Cambridge, CUP, 1988); Thomas R. Trautmann, *Aryans and British India* (Berkeley and Los Angeles, University of California Press, 1997); J. J. Clarke, *Oriental Enlightenment: The Encounter between Asian and Western Thought* (London, Routledge, 1997).

from within a century of the year 3000 BCE. According to Bailly, the detail, sophistication, and common features of these observations all seemed
to indicate that they were based on a much larger number of earlier observations, reaching back a further fifteen hundred years. Most of these apparently discrete astronomical traditions referred to seven known planets,
used the same periods of time to predict eclipses, divided the year into 360
+ 5 days, with one extra day every four years, used the sexagesimal system to measure the number of degrees in a circle, or minutes in an hour,
and referred to the stars of the zodiac in terms of twelve basic signs and
twenty-eight constellations—all this, Bailly argued, was evidence of the
existence of an antediluvian, agricultural civilisation that had once really
been the Atlantis of mythology. The type of civilisation that would have
been able to make these observations must, he suggested, have been situated in a particular geographical location to have been able to do so, and
must also have had sufficient reason for wanting to make them. By relying
on Buffon's theory about the original heat of the earth, Bailly went on to
argue that the uninhabitable nature of most of the globe in prehistoric
times would have restricted the first human habitats to the then temperate
polar regions, which, because of the long periods of day and night that
they contained, were ideally suited to the type of detailed astronomical observations that only an agricultural people was likely to have made. This,
he concluded, meant that Court de Gebelin's speculations could be nar-
rowed down to an agricultural civilisation located in Kamchatka. Recent
archaeological discoveries, Bailly went on to suggest, seemed to indicate
that Selinginskoe in Siberia was, in fact, the cradle of civilisation.

The ingenuity of this mixture of science and conjecture had an immediate intellectual impact. It supplied much of the conceptual architecture
for the huge didactic poem entitled *Les Mois* (The Months) published in
1779 by the Montpellier poet Jean-Antoine Roucher, partly as a reply to
the earlier *Seasons* by Voltaire's friend Jean-François, marquis de Saint-
Lambert. It also supplied the starting point of the multivolume *Origine de
tous les cultes* (The Origin of All Forms of Worship) by Charles-François
Dupuis, a professor of rhetoric at the college of Lisieux, that began to appear a decade later, but was prefigured in a series of publications and contributions to the proceedings of the French Academy of Sciences between
1778 and 1786.[135] According to Dupuis, all forms of worship originated in

---

[135] On Dupuis, see Claude Rétat, "Lumières et ténèbres du citoyen Dupuis," *Chroniques
d'histoire maçonnique* 50 (1999): 5–68 (thanks to Edward Castleton for bringing this article
to my attention). On contemporary interest in Dupuis, see Albert J. Kuhn, "English Deism
and the Development of Romantic Mythological Syncretism," *PMLA* 71 (1956): 1094–116;
Frank Manuel, *The Eighteenth Century Confronts the Gods* (Cambridge, Mass., Harvard UP,
1959), pp. 259–70; P. J. Marshall, ed., *The British Discovery of Hinduism in the Eighteenth Century* (Cambridge, CUP, 1970), pp. 1–44; Martin Bernal, *Black Athena*, 3 vols. (London, Free

the emotions of gratitude, expectation, anxiety, and reverence that the first sun worshippers felt for the sun, because its daily, and seasonal, movements were the basis of their own understanding not only of the passage of time, or the recurrent availability or scarcity of natural resources, but of the deeper power of generation that it seemed to possess. Bailly himself, however, seems to have abandoned his interest in the idea of an antediluvian civilisation, perhaps because of the attacks that it earned him from some of Physiocracy's original supporters, like the abbé Baudeau, or because of the jibes that it attracted from his great rival, the marquis de Condorcet ("only brother illuminist Bailly knows about these things," Condorcet informed Voltaire in 1777, dismissively), or because of the ammunition supplied to sceptics by Court de Gebelin's memorably ridiculous death, in the middle of a mesmerist cure in 1782, or, most plausibly, simply because additional astronomical and linguistic research, notably by the brilliant English Orientalist Sir William Jones, made it clear that his own chronological speculations were untenable. Jones's arguments, in favour of a chronology that, as he announced in his contributions to the Bombay-based periodical *Asiatic Researches*, went back no more than fifteen or sixteen hundred years before the birth of Christ, in conjunction, perhaps, with Bailly's own wish to maintain his growing stature as the public face of French science, made further conjecture seem pointless.[136] Roucher, too, seems to have abandoned his earlier interest, partly perhaps because of the catastrophic reception given to his poem (see, for a very gleeful description of the catastrophe, the entry on Roucher in Jean-François Laharpe's *Cours de Littérature*), but also perhaps because of his own responsiveness to the same scientific and linguistic developments.[137]

Association Books, 1987–2006), 1:182–4, 250–2; and, for broader background, Nigel Leask, *British Romantic Writers and the East: Anxieties of Empire* (Cambridge, CUP, 1992); Martin Priestman, *Romantic Atheism: Poetry and Freethought, 1780–1830* (Cambridge, CUP, 1999).

[136] The results of this research appeared in Sir William Jones, "Dissertation on the Antiquity of the Indian Zodiac," and "Dissertation on the Chronology of the Hindus," in his *Dissertations and Miscellaneous Pieces Relating to the History and Antiquities, the Arts, Sciences, and Literature of Asia*, 2 vols. (London, 1792). For a helpful survey of subsequent research, notably by Jones, and its devastating impact on Bailly's system, see the French translation of the work of the Swedish astronomer and philologer C. G. Schwarz, *Le zodiaque expliqué, ou recherches sur l'origine et la signification des constellations de la sphère grecque*, 2nd ed. (Paris, 1809), with summaries of, and quotations from, Jones's contributions to the *Asiatic Researches*. See, too, Victor de Dalmas, *Mémoire sur le zodiaque en faveur de la religion chrétienne* (Paris, 1823), for a more emphatically Christian reply to Bailly's chronological claims. On Jones, see Garland Hampton Cannon, *The Life and Mind of Oriental Jones* (Cambridge, CUP, 1990); Trautmann, *Aryans and British India*, pp. 28–98; Bruce Lincoln, *Theorizing Myth: Narrative, Ideology, and Scholarship* (Chicago, University of Chicago Press, 1999), pp. 76–95.

[137] For Laharpe's vengeful demolition of Roucher's poem, see Jean-François Laharpe, *Lycée*, 16 vols. (Paris, 1799–1805), 8:335–472.

His last work, before his execution during the Terror, was to translate Adam Smith's *Wealth of Nations*.

Bailly, however, was given a public reminder of his earlier interest in an antediluvian agricultural civilisation in a series of letters (modelled on those setting out the Siberian Atlantis hypothesis that Bailly himself had written to Voltaire), published in 1787 by the Protestant pastor and future Girondin leader Jean-Paul Rabaut Saint-Etienne. Rabaut's *Lettres à M. Bailly sur l'histoire primitive de la Grèce* (Letters to M. Bailly on the Primitive History of Greece) were quite a skilful synthesis of the causal claims connecting agriculture, language, and astronomy to the idea of a great providential order that Court de Gebelin and Bailly had made.[138] These made it easier to adopt something like "Estimate" Brown's description of the original union between music, poetry, and dance (which was what Rabaut proceeded to do), but to avoid offering the same type of opening to religious scepticism as Brown had done by giving a clearer set of identifiable causes to the natural moral system that music, dance, and poetry had once expressed. As Rabaut also emphasised, this made it easier to put more morality into Rousseau. Rousseau, he wrote, had been right to observe that it was hard not to laugh at scholarly efforts "to explain the fantasies (*rêveries*) of mythology," but had been wrong to conclude that mythology itself was devoid of interest. Euhemerist speculation about the real people represented by fabulous creatures had put mythology on the wrong track, allowing Rousseau to think that its subject matter was no more than "the chatter of a frivolous people," both in the ancient past and in more recent erudition. Rightly understood, however, as Court de Gebelin and Bailly had begun to show, it was the key to recovering what the seventeenth-century English statesman Francis Bacon had called "the wisdom of the ancients," and, by extension, was the way to make a connection between that wisdom and the predicaments of more recent times.[139]

Getting mythology right, Rabaut argued, meant dropping every assumption about its meaning that could be described in alphabetical language. As Court de Gebelin had shown, mythology was allegorical, but the allegories themselves had once existed in a purely figurative or imagistic written language that preceded the use of the alphabet (still, of course, to be found in Chinese writing). Once it was clear that the allegories were images, not narratives, it was easier to see that they were images of physical phenomena or geographical locations, and had nothing to do

---

[138] For Rabaut's indications of his indebtedness to Court de Gebelin and Bailly, see Jean-Paul Rabaut Saint-Etienne, *Lettres à M. Bailly sur l'histoire primitive de la Grèce* (Paris, 1787), pp. 7, 15, 24, 30, 47–8, 51.

[139] Rabaut Saint-Etienne, *Lettres à M. Bailly*, pp. 51, 66 (for the phrase cited).

with people at all. "Mythological history," Rabaut emphasised, "is natural history set in images."[140] It was a vast and rich body of knowledge that, as Bailly had begun to show, connected the heavens to the earth to form a comprehensive, monotheistic, natural religion that catered to the real needs of agricultural peoples.[141] This, Rabaut argued, meant (in contradistinction to what Voltaire had suggested) that emotions like curiosity and wonder, or, still less, the practice of embellishing leisure time with tales of fabulous creatures, were either entirely irrelevant to explanations of the origins and nature of ancient myths, or, more probably, were derivations of the more continuously pressing imperatives of the agricultural cycle.[142] It also meant that the chronologies that had been established by making connections between Greek myths and astronomical events (as, for example, Isaac Newton had done) were largely false.[143] As Rabaut announced, a more detailed examination of the real content of ancient myths would be supplied by Charles-François Dupuis in his forthcoming *Origine de tous les cultes*. In this sense, he wrote, his own book was simply a foretaste of Dupuis's more ample investigations, with rather more of an emphasis on simply clearing the ground for the correct approach to the study of ancient mythology.[144] But their joint message was still the same. Before the Flood, there really had been "an age of enlightenment" (*une époque de lumière*), but the nature of that early civilisation had, literally, been overwritten by the alphabetically based form of writing that the Phoenicians had passed on to the Greeks.[145] The "brilliant reign of the imagination

[140] Rabaut Saint-Etienne, *Lettres à M. Bailly*, p. 194. Or, as he put it earlier, "the physics of the first times has, for us, become history" (p. 50), so that "physics became history and physical beings became personages" (p. 118).

[141] Rabaut Saint-Etienne, *Lettres à M. Bailly*, p. 37.

[142] Rabaut Saint-Etienne, *Lettres à M. Bailly*, pp. 48–9, 55–6, 80, 217.

[143] Rabaut Saint-Etienne, *Lettres à M. Bailly*, pp. 50, 294–303.

[144] Rabaut Saint-Etienne, *Lettres à M. Bailly*, pp. 47–8, note 1, 210, note 1. For an indication of the convergence between Rabaut's theory and the works of Court de Gebelin, Bailly, and Dupuis, see the review of the *Lettres à M. Bailly* in the *Mercure de France*, 10 February 1787, pp. 56–73. Dupuis outlined his system in a series of articles in the *Journal des savants* in June, October, and December 1778, and February 1781, which were published as a *Mémoire sur l'origine des constellations et sur l'explication de la fable par le moyen de l'astronomie* (Paris, 1781). See, too, the comment on Dupuis in Pierre-Jean-Baptiste (Publicola) Chaussard, *Fêtes et courtisanes de la Grèce*, 4 vols. (Paris, 1801), 1:32: "Ce professeur illustre a présidé en quelque sorte à deux écoles: de sa classe d'éloquence sont sortis les talents brillants et aimables de Colin d'Harleville, Demoustier, Richard, Cauchy, Legouvé. On l'a vu réunir à l'école philosophique dont il est le fondateur, les chefs même de la philosophie, Volney, Rabaut Saint-Etienne, Delaunay, l'auteur du Polythéisme analysé etc. Ils ont développé le système de l'auteur de l'origine des cultes, et leurs écrits ont répandu les principes qu'il eut le double gloire de signaler et de développer." See also 2:395 for Chaussard's summary of Dupuis's system and its claim that all religions originated in the difference between night and day, or darkness and light.

[145] Rabaut Saint-Etienne, *Lettres à M. Bailly*, p. 82.

disappeared, and, in place of that naïve age, of that age of allegory, came the age of reason."[146]

Rabaut Saint-Etienne's agricultural and astronomical interpretation of Greek myth, and its reliance on retranslating the alphabetically based histories of human events that the Greeks had produced back into the allegorical images of physical occurrences that they had originally been, was designed to supply what he took to be a more securely factual foundation for speculation about the earliest times. The analytical and historical framework that he used to get behind alphabetical writing, to recover the allegorical meaning of image-based writing (which meant that a monument like Stonehenge could be seen as a form of writing), was also designed to indicate something of the real contours of human history and mankind's possible future. Together, they can be taken as evidence of how much of the moral and historical dimensions of Physiocracy continued to resonate long after its more explicitly political and administrative features had been called into question. As the marquis de Mirabeau put it at the very beginning of the preface to the economists' manifesto text, the *Philosophie rurale* (Rural Philosophy) of 1763, Physiocracy was a synthesis of very ancient and very modern wisdom. "One man," he wrote (alluding to Physiocracy's founder, François Quesnay), "has imagined and explained the table that depicts the source, direction, and effects of *circulation* and made it the summary and basis of economic science, and the compass of the government of states." Another "had examined the fruit of the tree of life and presented it to humans," inviting them to assist him in his work by saying, "[L]et them make a trial; let them try to explain it in their way."[147] As Mirabeau presented it, "rural philosophy" involved applying the lessons of Quesnay's economic table to restore the knowledge of the tree of life to its rightful place (later interpreters of scripture associated the existence of the tree of life, described mainly in the biblical book of Solomon, with the fact that Adam and Eve were not naturally immortal, but were equipped with knowledge of where to find, and how to use, the fruits of the tree of life so that they would never die).[148] The synthesis, with its gesture towards Solomon's now hidden wisdom, captures something of the Baconian and

[146] Rabaut Saint-Etienne, *Lettres à M. Bailly*, p. 110.

[147] Victor Riqueti, marquis de Mirabeau, *Philosophie rurale, ou économie générale et politique de l'agriculture* [1763] (Amsterdam, 1764), p. iii.

[148] See also Revelations 22.1–2, with its description of the tree of life "which bare twelve manner of fruits, and yielded her fruit every month: and the leaves of the tree were for the healing of nations." On speculation about the properties and location of the tree of life, see Benjamin Kennicott, *Two Dissertations: The First on the Tree of Life in Paradise ... The Second on the Oblations of Cain and Abel* (Oxford, 1747), and Richard Gifford, *Remarks on Mr. Kennicott's Dissertation upon the Tree of Life in Paradise* (London, 1748), as well as the earlier discussion in Pufendorf, *The Divine Feudal Law*, p. 71.

Masonic themes with which Physiocracy, like so much else in the second half of the eighteenth century, was associated (very literally, according to some of its critics).[149] It also suggests something of the similarity between Physiocracy and Rousseau's thought. Both took a limited set of features of human nature as their starting point, but then set out to explain how the same set of features could be replicated at a higher level of social and political integration once a way had been found to remove the wrong sort of political and social arrangements. As the exchange between Rousseau and Mirabeau indicated, the difference between them was largely a matter of their respective assessments of whether, in a context like that formed by the French system of absolute government, the process of removal was possible without a real revolution.

Rabaut Saint-Etienne's treatment of the theme of simple natural origins and richer social outcomes was broadly similar. Here, however, it was Leibniz who supplied the framework for thinking about its shape and direction.[150] Just as the transition from speech to image-based writing was the first step in "the passage from the state of nature to civilisation," and the means by which the "robust children" of the original human state had become the natural image makers still to be found in so many areas of modern popular culture, so the later transition from imagery to alphabetical writing was a further step in the process of cultural acquisition.[151] Imagery had had disadvantages (idolatry and superstition) that alphabetical language had begun to cure (by way of science and the modern critical spirit), and there was no reason to think that the process could not continue. In the future, Rabaut suggested, Leibniz's idea of a far more highly differentiated and technically precise written language was likely to be the next big step in the progress of civilisation, leaving alphabetical script looking as mysterious and as hard to interpret as figurative language had now become. In this sense, going back to recover what had been lost was the way to reveal how much further there might still be to go.[152] From this perspective, the broadly Physiocratic position that Rabaut Saint-Etienne took over from Court de Gebelin and the early works of Jean-Silvain Bailly (coupled with the pared-down version of Protestantism that he had acquired from his Socinian education in Geneva) looked like the way to add

---

[149] On this aspect of Physiocracy, see Paolo Bianchini, "Le annotazioni manoscritti di Augustin Barruel ai *Mémoires pour servir à l'histoire du Jacobinisme*," *Annali della Fondazione Luigi Einaudi* 33 (1999): 367–444 (pp. 381–3), and, for a helpfully compatible characterisation of Freemasonry, see Pierre-Yves Beaurepaire, *L'Europe des francs-maçons, xviiie–xxie siècles* (Paris, Belin, 2002).

[150] Rabaut Saint-Etienne, *Lettres à M. Bailly*, pp. 70–1, and note 1.

[151] Rabaut Saint-Etienne, *Lettres à M. Bailly*, pp. 58 (for the second quoted phrase) and 80 (for the first).

[152] Rabaut Saint-Etienne, *Lettres à M. Bailly*, pp. 70–1, note 1.

a more practical dimension to Rousseau's moral and political criticism. As Charles Grivel, one of the marquis de Mirabeau's many protégés, put it in a *Lettre sur les économistes* (Letter on the Economists), published in the political economy section of the *Encyclopédie méthodique* in 1786, the economists had unlocked the secret of a new system of "morality and politics" that, once implemented, would supply an answer to Rousseau's description of the double bind produced by the way that "the progress of the sciences entails the progress of corruption."[153] To its supporters, Physiocracy not only had a stronger moral starting point but also had a real implementation strategy. Once implemented, Grivel wrote, it would fulfil the hopes of "the illustrious author of *Telemachus*," and the "honourable abbé de Saint-Pierre," as well as the original progenitor of the idea of a peaceful and prosperous world order in which every "polished nation" would form part of a "single family," namely, France's king, Henri IV.[154] But, as events had served to show during Turgot's short ministry between 1775 and 1777, its only, but fatal, drawback was that it would take a long time to work. From the perspective contained in Rabaut Saint-Etienne's synthesis of Court de Gebelin and Jean-Sylvain Bailly, however, Physiocracy appeared to be based on enough of a moral theory to rule out the need for some of the more draconian aspects of its reform programme, notably the single tax on the owners of land. A different implementation strategy appeared to offer better prospects of success.

JOHN LAW'S LEGACY AND THE AFTERMATH OF PHYSIOCRACY

The new implementation strategy was based on a number of claims about the reforming power of public credit (unlike Physiocracy, this type of reform programme was not given a name until the nineteenth century, when it came to be called "socialism" in its new, modern guise). The largely indirect mechanisms involved in relying on a public debt to promote reform were, at least in this respect, similar to those advocated by the French economists. In an immediate sense, this type of claim was a product of the widespread sense of Physiocracy's practical failure after the short ministerial career of Louis XVI's best-known controller general of finance, Anne-Robert-Jacques Turgot, and the intense political difficulties involved in the idea of imposing a single tax on the owners of landed property, not only because of their status and power, but also because of the highly volatile character of cereal prices themselves and their propensity to respond suddenly

---

[153] Charles Grivel, "Lettre sur les économistes," in *Encyclopédie Méthodique. Economie Politique*, 4 vols. (Paris, 1784–91), 2:186–96 (here, p. 189).

[154] Grivel, "Lettre," p. 196.

and violently to rumour and panic as much as to real changes in supply. In a less immediate sense, however, this type of claim was also a reversion to some of the arguments about the properties of public credit that had been made much earlier in the eighteenth century by the Scottish financier John Law.[155] Law's system, put simply, amounted to inflating the value of a state-owned asset to eliminate a state-owned liability. If the value of the asset could be made to grow, it could be used to eliminate the liability and still leave the original value of the asset in place. The asset that Law used was foreign trade (henceforth incorporated into a trading company). The liability was the backlog of debt left over from Louis XIV's wars (hence-forth consolidated into a public debt). The ingenious part of Law's system was the way that it was designed to use the liability to inflate the asset, so that, over time, the one would eliminate the other. The causal mechanism built into the system was based on two giant institutions, the trading company, which would own the asset, and the public bank, which would own the liability. The trading company would issue shares, and would have a monopoly of the most lucrative branches of foreign trade, while the bank would buy all the outstanding debt and, to do so, would issue banknotes to an equivalent amount. Shares in the trading company would be purchasable only with banknotes, but taxes would still have to be paid in gold and silver coin. The former debt holders would, therefore, be forced to use banknotes to buy shares in order to get hold of the cash needed to pay taxes. The initial boost to share prices produced by this surge in demand would set up a virtuous circle, in which the rising price of shares would bring more and more cash into circulation (both to buy banknotes and to use speculative returns from investments in the trading company to go back into cash to pay taxes more easily). The long-term result would be the elimination of the debt and a far more highly monetised trading economy.

Law's system failed spectacularly. But the idea of using a liability to in-flate an asset, and of then using the inflated asset to eliminate the liability itself, lived on (it still does). The difficulty was to find an asset that could be guaranteed not only to inflate but also not to deflate in as devastating a way as Law's bubble had done. Law's system showed that trading com-panies were far too volatile. Land was an obvious alternative, and a land bank was one way to get the causal sequence going, and to make the kinds of causal mechanism involved in Law's system more feasible. A privately funded but state-backed bank could take over a state's debt and issue notes to the same amount. The notes, issued either to former debt owners or to a network of local banks, would bear a relatively low rate of interest, and this in turn would encourage their owners to lend them to others at somewhat higher rates to fund the costs of land purchases or agricultural

[155] For a more detailed description, see Sonenscher, "The Nation's Debt," 64–103, 267–325.

improvements. The higher returns either from the land itself or from the widening circle of prosperity generated by rising agricultural productivity and the growth of disposable incomes would broaden and deepen the tax base, so that even without any change in the rate of taxation, part of the larger flow of tax revenue could be used to manage the money supply and limit further cycles of debt. This sort of variation on Law's system lay behind the speculations about using public credit in an Irish context that were made by the Anglican bishop of Cloyne George Berkeley, in the series of questions and answers that he published in 1735 in *The Querist* and, at far greater length, in the former Jacobite Sir James Steuart's *Inquiry into the Principles of Political Oeconomy* of 1767, as well as in the publications of two of Steuart's admirers, the Anglo-Swiss political economist Jean-Frédéric Herrenschwand and the Anglo-Welsh political reformer, and close friend of Jacques-Pierre Brissot, David Williams.[156]

In all these works, the emphasis fell on the idea of using public credit to level up, instead of relying on agrarian laws to level down. "The patrons of agrarian laws and of universal equality, instead of crying down luxury and superfluous consumption," Steuart commented, "ought rather to be contriving methods for rendering them both more universal."[157] As his now better-known admirer, the Anglo-American republican Tom Paine, was to indicate in the title of one of his late pamphlets, modern public finance (typified in his case by the continental currency that had been used to fund the costs of America's War for Independence) allowed agrarian laws to give way to what he was to call "agrarian justice." The same idea attracted the attention of the Franco-Prussian noble Anacharsis Cloots, later to be famous as the self-styled "orator of the human race" during the early years of the French Revolution. "A French king," Cloots wrote in 1786, "who developed all the economic resources of his kingdom and freed the industry of a thousand idle hands, or the coins buried in forgotten cloisters through ignorance of true principles, would easily be able to impose a project that, harming no one, and setting France in her true place, would leave him with nothing more than the desire and the capacity to see Europe flourish in perpetual peace."[158] An even more radical variation

---

[156] On Berkeley and public credit, see, most recently, Patrick Kelly, "Berkeley's Economic Writings," in Kenneth P. Winkler, ed., *The Cambridge Companion to Berkeley* (Cambridge, CUP, 2005), pp. 339–68; Joseph Johnston, ed., *Bishop Berkeley's Querist in Historical Perspective* (Dundalk, Dundalgan Press, 1970); Jean-Fréderic Herrenschwand, *De l'économie politique moderne. Discours fondamental sur la population* (London, 1786). See, on the latter figures, Sonenscher, *Before the Deluge*, pp. 255, 327.

[157] Sir James Steuart, *An Enquiry into the Principles of Political Oeconomy* [1767], ed. Andrew Skinner, 2 vols. (Edinburgh, 1967), vol. 1, bk. 2, ch. 26, pp. 315–6.

[158] Jean-Baptiste, baron de Cloots du Val-de-Grace, *Voeux d'un Gallophile*, new ed. (Amsterdam, 1786), reprinted in Anacharsis Cloots, *Oeuvres*, ed. Albert Soboul, 3 vols. (Munich,

on the same idea of using an inflated asset to eliminate an existing liability was to focus on the value of subsistence goods. Since cereals were the basic components of everyday expenditure, borrowing against a tax on subsistence goods looked like a guaranteed way not only to get an asset to inflate but to ensure that it would never deflate. In France, this type of scheme was promoted energetically by the marquis Charles de Casaux in a series of publications in the dozen or so years that preceded 1789.[159] The highly unfavourable comparison between Jacques Necker and John Law made (to Law's advantage) by Louis-Sébastien Mercier in 1791 was one indication of what, by then, had become a more widely shared recognition of the possibility that public credit could be used to reach something like a Physiocratic outcome without reliance on Physiocratic means.[160]

One example of this way of thinking could be found in a book that was sent to Jacques-Pierre Brissot in November 1791 by an English friend of liberty named Sir George Staunton, an acquaintance of Tom Paine who was later to accompany Lord Macartney on his famous expedition to China.[161] The book itself was entitled *An Essay on the Right of Property in Land*; it had been published in 1781 by William Ogilvie, Professor of Humanity (as his professorial chair was called) at King's College, Aberdeen University, mainly as a call for reform in the light of the impending British defeat in the American War of Independence.[162] In the letter that Staunton wrote to Brissot to accompany the book (which he entrusted to Brissot's friend, the soon-to-be elected mayor of Paris, Jerome Pétion, who was in London at the time), he gave some indication of its content by emphasising the way that Ogilvie's property theory imposed limits on hereditary rights of a rather Jeffersonian kind. "I trust something will be

---

1980), 2:53–4. On Cloots, see, most recently, François Labbé, *Anacharsis Cloots le Prussien francophile. Un philosophe au service de la révolution française et universelle* (Paris, L'Harmattan, 1999).

[159] See [Charles de Casaux], *Considérations sur les principes politiques de mon siècle* (London, 1776), and, on Casaux, see Philippe de Roux, "Le marquis de Casaux. Un planteur des Antilles inspirateur de Mirabeau" (Paris, Société d'histoire des colonies françaises, 1951).

[160] On Mercier's positive assessment of Law, and negative assessment of Necker, see above, p. 129.

[161] On Staunton's acquaintanceship with Paine, see Philip S. Foner, ed., *The Complete Writings of Thomas Paine*, 2 vols. (New York, 1945), 2:1040, 1301.

[162] On Ogilvie, see D. C. Macdonald, *Birthright in Land* (London, 1891), which reprints Ogilvie's *Essay on the Right of Property in Land with Respect to its Foundation in the Law of Nature; Its Present Establishment by the Municipal Laws of Europe and the Regulations by which It Might be Rendered more Beneficial to the Lower Ranks of Mankind* [1781] (London, 1782), with a biographical introduction. For the wider context, see Stephen Conrad, *Citizenship and Common Sense: The Problem of Authority in the Social Background and Social Philosophy of the Wise Club of Aberdeen* (New York, Garland, 1987); Paul B. Wood, *The Aberdeen Enlightenment: The Arts Curriculum in the Eighteenth Century* (Aberdeen, Aberdeen UP, 1993).

done to check, by degrees, if not to destroy, the mischiefs of hereditary property, as well as of hereditary titles," Staunton told Brissot. "Mr Mirabeau's last work upon wills," he continued (referring to the great French Revolutionary orator's call, shortly before his death in April 1791, to make equal, partible inheritance a part of the new French civil code), "contains great truths, but either he did not know or chose to keep back at that time a truth of equal importance, that the acquisition of property is justly and naturally limited by the life of him who made it, after which it should revert to society, to be fairly divided among those who want it."[163]

Ogilvie's work was based upon two premises. The first of these asserted that

> [a]ll right of property is founded either in occupancy or labour. The earth having been given to mankind in common occupancy, each individual seems to have by nature a right to possess and cultivate an equal share. This right is little different from that which he has to the free use of the open air and running water; though not so indispensably requisite at short intervals for his actual existence, it is not less essential to the welfare and right state of his life through all its progressive stages.[164]

The second premise, which was the starting point of the argument of the whole work, was that "every state or community ought in justice to reserve for all its citizens, the opportunities of entering upon, or returning to, and resuming this their birthright and natural employment, whenever they are inclined to do so."[165] This goal, he wrote (using a phrase that may also indicate something of Jeremy Bentham's own concerns), was "wholly consonant with natural justice and favourable to the greatest happiness of the greatest number of citizens."[166] As Ogilvie presented it, "occupancy" was not only the original title to property; it also modified the entitlements of labour. "Whatever has been advanced by Mr. Locke and his followers," he wrote,

> concerning the right of property in land, as independent of the laws of a higher original than they, and of a nature almost similar to that divine right of kings, which their antagonists had maintained, can only be referred to this original right of equal property in land, founded on that general right of occupancy, which the whole community has, to the territory of the State.[167]

Acquisition by labour was an individual right, sanctioned by positive law. As such, it was "natural and just." But it could not negate the community's

---

[163] A. N. 446 AP 6, dossier 2, George Staunton to Jacques Pierre Brissot, 7 November 1791.

[164] Ogilvie, *Essay*, p. 11.

[165] Ogilvie, *Essay*, p. 13.

[166] Ogilvie, *Essay*, pp. 92–3.

[167] Ogilvie, *Essay*, pp. 10–1.

"general right of occupancy" to the territory of the state. The need now, Ogilvie argued, was for the law "to pay equal regard" to both types of entitlement in order to bring "the freedom and prosperity of the lower ranks" into closer alignment with "the improvement of the common stock and wealth of the community."[168]

Three developments, he claimed, made this a real possibility. The first was the rise of the modern state and its capacity for general legislation. The second was the emergence of ever-larger standing armies and the progressive erosion of the distinction between civil and military life that it entailed. The third was the growth of the modern, debt-financed, funding system and the potential it housed, beyond its immediate function of meeting the costs of war, for promoting the rotation of property by way of its impact upon relative asset prices over different periods of time. In addition, public credit could be used to make funds available to enable those without property to acquire land by legislating for the enclosure of under-exploited common land or for the breakup of large, hereditary landed estates. Together, Ogilvie argued in the body of his work, the combination of legislative power and public credit amounted to a powerful set of levers available to any reforming government to use the financial resources of the modern state to bring occupancy and labour, the two original sources of the right to property, into the sort of balance that earlier ages had been unable to achieve. He was open-minded about what the constitution of such a reforming government should be. "Princes of heroic minds, born to absolute monarchy, might," he wrote, "establish a complete reformation in their whole dominions at once." But so, too, might "conquering princes" or "the candidates for disputed thrones," or "the collective body of the whole people, if at any time their power shall predominate."[169] The circumstances favouring reform were equally varied. "Bodies of men oppressed in other respects," like the English Dissenters or the Irish Catholics, "ought to claim this right also," and "it might become the ministers of religion to support it." "Public calamities" might "induce the rulers of a state to think of renovating the vigour of the community by a just regulation of property in land." So, too, might "imminent and continual dangers," and so, too, he concluded, should "the accumulation of public debts."[170] Ogilvie maintained this position all his life. "I even build some hopes on the transcendent talents of Buonaparte," he wrote in a letter to his former pupil Sir James Mackintosh, in 1805, long after the latter had abandoned the highly favourable view of liberty's French prospects that he had put forward in his *Vindiciae Gallicae* of 1791.[171] "It is impossible for me

---

[168] Ogilvie, *Essay*, p. 12.

[169] Ogilvie, *Essay*, §§46, 49, 57, 58.

[170] Ogilvie, *Essay*, §§59–62.

[171] For Mackintosh's early affinities with Ogilvie, see Sonenscher, *Before the Deluge*, pp. 50–1.

to believe that this child and champion of popular rights, so endowed by nature, formed, as we are told, on the best ancient models, and tinctured with the sublime melancholy of Ossian, can prove ultimately unfaithful to the glorious cause, the idol of his youth."[172]

This interest in the equalising effects of modern, debt-based, public finance was given more extended treatment in a pamphlet entitled *J. J. Rousseau à l'Assemblée Nationale* published late in 1789 (despite the ambiguity of the preposition, its content makes it clear that the English translation should be "J. J. Rousseau in, or at, the National Assembly"). The title was intended to indicate the bearing of Rousseau's thought on the future policies of the French National Assembly and, more specifically, to explain why a peaceful transition to a more egalitarian society had to precede increased popular involvement in political decision making. Getting the sequence wrong, argued the pamphlet's author (a twenty-four-year-old admirer of Bernardin de Saint-Pierre named François-Jean-Philibert Aubert de Vitry), was a formula for promoting violent political conflict between the rich and the poor. Public credit, he went on to claim, in a way that was quite similar to the views of William Ogilvie, supplied the means to effect the transition to economic and social equality, obviating draconian political measures. To support the argument, Aubert de Vitry summarised the works of some forty individuals whose ideas about morality, politics, and public credit all had a bearing on the related subjects of revolution and reform (he gestured, too, towards the poet Nicolas Gilbert, here associated with the "unfortunate" English poet Thomas Chatterton, as well as the French historian Louis Chabrit, as suicides whose deaths could be taken to be testimony to the "despair caused by atrocious tyranny").[173] As a result, the pamphlet is an unusually broad overview of a range of late eighteenth-century publications, mainly written after Rousseau's death in 1778, and after the first flush of enthusiasm for Physiocracy had passed.

It was also, however, motivated by a strong endorsement of the characterisation of Rousseau's thought made by the self-appointed keeper of Rousseau's flame, Jacques-Henri Bernardin de Saint-Pierre. Accordingly, the Rousseau whom Aubert de Vitry commended to the National Assembly was the theorist of the "republican monarchy" that Bernardin de Saint-Pierre, with the help of the ideas of Fénelon and the marquis d'Argenson, had extrapolated from Rousseau's works. Here, Rousseau's letter to the marquis de Mirabeau, and the phrase about "perfect Hobbism" that it contained, were taken to be evidence of Rousseau's final approval of the idea of a "royal democracy" that the marquis d'Argenson had described.[174]

---

[172] Macdonald, *Birthright in Land*, p. 301.

[173] [François-Jean-Philibert Aubert de Vitry], *J. J. Rousseau à l'Assemblée nationale* (Paris, 1789), pp. 167–8.

[174] [Aubert de Vitry], *J. J. Rousseau*, p. 270.

It was also taken to be compatible with the combination of strong royal government and modern public finance that could be found in Sir James Steuart's *Inquiry into the Principle of Political Oeconomy* of 1767. As Steuart wrote there, "modern liberty" was postfeudal and had developed out of competition among the European monarchies for wealth and power. The rise of industry and trade, he argued, was a product of "the ambition of princes, who supported and favoured the plan in the beginning, principally with a view to enrich themselves, and thereby to become formidable to their neighbours." But, to do so, they had been compelled to turn to those who were "fertile in expedients for establishing public credit and for drawing money from the coffers of the rich, by the imposition of taxes." The outcome, Steuart argued, was a new kind of monarchy. "Formerly," he wrote, "the power of princes was employed to destroy liberty, and to establish arbitrary subordination; but in our days, we have seen those who have best comprehended the true principles, or the new plan of politics, arbitrarily limiting the power of the higher classes, and thereby applying their authority towards the extension of public liberty, by extinguishing every subordination other than that due to the established laws."[175]

Aubert de Vitry's idea of monarchy was identical. As he presented the subject, Steuart's credit-centred interest in political economy could be combined with d'Argenson's idea of a "democratic monarchy" and Bernardin de Saint-Pierre's moral theory to produce a more just society. Somewhat surprisingly, the individual whom Aubert de Vitry singled out for writing most interestingly about the subject of a reforming royal government was the critic of salon society James Rutledge. Here, however, it was not the satirical playwright whose ideas were commended, but the disciple of the seventeenth-century English republican James Harrington. In this context, the vaguely Jacobite milieu to which both Rutledge and Steuart belonged can be taken to be indicative of quite a significant current in eighteenth-century thought, one whose focus fell less on finding a dynastic solution to the problem of Anglo-French relations (by continuing to give precedence to the old Jacobite fixation on engineering a Stuart restoration), than on finding ways to make the dynastic problem less contentious. Through analysis of the underlying causes of Anglo-French rivalry, and through the demonstration of how these could be overcome, the dynastic question could, it could be argued, be divested of much of its explosiveness. Rutledge's publications shared this kind of concern. According to Aubert de Vitry, he had explained not only how public credit could be used to avert the threat of violent social conflict, but also how it

---

[175] Steuart, *Enquiry*, bk. 2, ch. 13, pp. 240, 245, 248. For an interesting set of critical reactions to the argument, see Arthur Young, *Political Essays Concerning the Present State of the British Empire* (London, 1772), essay 2, pp. 70–3.

could lay the foundations of a more stable international system than the eighteenth century had been able to have. From this perspective, public credit and a republican monarchy were not only the antidotes to inequality and injustice at home; they were also the means to bring the age of Machiavellian power politics to an end.

The starting point of the whole argument was an assumption about the fundamentally healthy condition of French society. Aubert de Vitry began the pamphlet by describing an imaginary conversation, set in the Elysian Fields, among an assortment of "French patriots" (including Suger, Joan of Arc, Fénelon, Voltaire, D'Argenson, Mably, Turgot, and Rousseau) and virtuous royal rulers (including Louis the Fat, Louis IX, Louis XII, and Henri IV) about the "happy revolution" that was in train. The French, they had learned, were "tired of living in the degradation of slavery and amidst the disorders of anarchy," and had begun to turn to the means to recover "liberty and happiness." A "citizen king" had convoked his "faithful subjects" to discover "the wish of the nation" and "dislodge the yoke of the aristocracy."[176] The gathering was joined by one of Physiocracy's founders, the marquis de Mirabeau, who had, in fact, died on 14 July 1789, and who, he said, "had reached the end of his life amidst the clamour of the aristocracy at bay"; his "last vision" had been "the sight of the tyrants in flight." Fénelon welcomed the news with pleasure, reminding Henri IV of his wish that one day "every peasant" would have a chicken in his pot, and telling him that it looked as if Louis XVI would make his wish come true. Mably commented that the news showed that he had been right "to say that it was sometimes worth purchasing liberty with blood." Rousseau objected, saying that the endorsement of civil war that could be found in Mably's *Des droits et des devoirs du citoyen* (On the Rights and Duties of Citizens) was not the reason why Mably had been admitted to the Elysian Fields. "Your male virtues and charity," he told Mably, "made it possible to overlook the inhumanity of some of your principles and the immorality of some of your lessons" (the allusion was not only to Mably's endorsement of civil war, but to his even more bloodcurdling condemnation of Brutus for his refusal to recommend the trial and execution of anyone who might have been sympathetic, even in thought, to the aims of the Cataline conspirators).[177] His own principles, he continued, were less violent and more compatible with those to be found in the works of Fénelon and "the eloquent and virtuous" Bernardin de Saint-Pierre.[178] Having said

---

[176] [Aubert de Vitry], *J. J. Rousseau*, pp. 1–2.

[177] [Aubert de Vitry], *J. J. Rousseau*, pp. 4–8 (in the text, Rousseau's remark to Mably contains an obvious typographical mistake, with "immortalité" printed instead of "immoralité"). For a further examination of Mably's political thought, see below, chapter 6.

[178] [Aubert de Vitry], *J. J. Rousseau*, p. 13, note 1.

this, Rousseau decided to return to France "to offer some useful ideas that
might have escaped the wisdom of an assembly concerned with so many
great issues and interests."

His first intervention in French political life was to attack what Aubert
de Vitry called "the abbé Sieyès's and Brissot de Warville's system on the
constituting power."[179] It was certainly true, the reincarnated Rousseau
acknowledged, that a "constituting power" could not be conflated with a
"constituted power," and equally true that the first of these powers "resides
in essence in the people, who cannot alienate it." What Sieyès had called
a constituting power derived from the nature of the social contract itself
and was, therefore, the basis of "the natural and essential order of political
societies."[180] The association between Sieyès, Rousseau, and Physiocracy
that Aubert de Vitry made here is quite an interesting example of the
broader eighteenth-century awareness of their fundamental compatibility,
indicating, as Le Mercier de La Rivière (the author of the text to which
Aubert de Vitry alluded) also seems to have assumed, that Physiocracy
was, put crudely, Rousseau plus morality. At this point, however, Aubert
de Vitry began to break into his own voice. The power to draw up a
constitution, he argued against Sieyès, was not a constituting, but a constituted, power. Although the Americans, when ratifying the constitution
of their republic, had treated it as if it were a constituting power, which
was why they had presented it for ratification to the members of all the
states, the same policy was both unnecessary and inappropriate in France.
It was unnecessary for the first reason. It was also inappropriate because
France not only was not a federal republic like the United States, but was
also far more economically and socially divided. In a federal system, nonratification would simply entail the secession of one or more states from
the union.[181] But in a unitary political system, particularly one as socially
divided as late eighteenth-century France, nonratification was a formula
for civil war. It followed, Aubert argued, that the constitution had to be
drafted by the National Assembly without any reference back to a putatively ratifying constituting power, and, more important, that a great deal
more had to be done first to promote economic and social equality. Unless
this sequence was given priority, he warned, France would be faced with
the "terrible" prospect of the war that "its enemies" hoped to inflict upon
it, namely, the war "of poverty against wealth."[182]

Establishing the right sequence, Aubert argued, required making use of
public credit to correct the massive amount of inequality presently to be

[179] [Aubert de Vitry], *J. J. Rousseau*, p. 17.
[180] [Aubert de Vitry], *J. J. Rousseau*, pp. 17–8.
[181] [Aubert de Vitry], *J. J. Rousseau*, pp. 20–40.
[182] [Aubert de Vitry], *J. J. Rousseau*, pp. 64–5.

found in France. This was why he singled out Rutledge's works for their immediate political relevance. According to Aubert, Rutledge had spent the past twenty years composing a work entitled *On Civilisation* based on James Harrington's writings (it was never, in fact, published). Present French circumstances now made its publication particularly apposite. As Aubert put it, "we are now happily disposed to benefit from the ideas and the sublime plan of the friend of the unfortunate Charles I, who will always be regarded by those who know him, as the most virtuous of political writers because he knew how to make his life conform to his principles."[183] That "friend of the unfortunate Charles I" was Harrington, and his "sublime plan" was the *Oceana* (the characterisation of Harrington as a supporter of monarchy may now seem rather unusual, but it does suggest the compatibility between Harrington's ideas and the more overtly Fénelonian concerns of writers like the marquis d'Argenson or Bernardin de Saint-Pierre). To bridge the gap until the publication of Rutledge's book, Aubert referred his readers to two discussions of Harrington published in Rutledge's journal *Calypso* and, more particularly, to the 1784, London edition of Rutledge's three-volume *Essais politiques sur l'état actuel de quelques puissances* (Political Essays on the Present State of Several Powers), which, Aubert de Vitry stated, was a work to be read in its entirety, since, he added hyperbolically, Rutledge was "the most really universal man who exists and who perhaps has ever existed."[184]

There is no trace of the edition of Rutledge's work to which Aubert de Vitry referred. The only existing edition was published (in one volume) in 1777 on the eve of French intervention in the Anglo-American war. Its aim was to show how the impending conflict (which Rutledge expected Britain to lose) might lead to the formation of new world order to supersede the system based on the treaties of Westphalia and Utrecht of 1648 and 1715. These, Rutledge wrote, were the quintessence of "all political ideas inspired by the notion of self-preservation."[185] Since they simply ratified inequalities between states established by force of arms, they had become the basis of "the so-called balance of power, the chimera and idol of vulgar politics, which, by filling all Europe with alarm, suspicion, and anxieties, foments eternal leagues, awakens rather than curbs ambition, and, by flooding her with immense armies, perpetuates misery and slavery among her impoverished peoples."[186] The lynchpin of the new system would be an Anglo-French common market designed to protect Europe

---

[183] [Aubert de Vitry], *J. J. Rousseau*, p. 232.

[184] [Aubert de Vitry], *J. J. Rousseau*, p. 231.

[185] [Jacques Rutledge], *Essais politiques sur l'état actuel de quelques puissances* (London, 1777), p. 210.

[186] [Rutledge], *Essais politiques*, p. 25.

from the long-term threat to civilisation represented by Russia in the East and the emergence of the New World in the West. But its emergence depended, Rutledge argued, upon the French embarking upon a gradual programme of reform to bring their nation's economy up to a level to match Britain's.

Rutledge emphasised that such a programme had to be implemented gradually, singling out the early eighteenth-century British prime minister Sir Robert Walpole and the French Cardinal Fleury as models of the type of reforming statesmen he had in mind.[187] The problem was that the French political system did not favour such caution. The French system of government, he wrote, was "a real despotism" whose hasty and ill-considered decisions had earlier overwhelmed "the wise system of the Scot, Law," and could now, at best, offer no more than the hope of a rare "shepherd king" (an allusion to Louis XVI) willing to transform his kingdom into a prosperous agricultural and commercial nation.[188] France was internally weak and in need of a long period of convalescence, as, according to Rutledge, Turgot's rash decision to free the grain trade in 1775 had shown. That "precipitate operation" had revealed the vulnerability of "the multitude of industrious people" to sharp increases in the price of basic necessities, and had underlined the underdeveloped state of domestic trade and "vivification." The result had been that an attempt to enrich the agricultural class had caused an outcry from all the rest because they were simply unable to bear the disproportionately high level of prices. The first step, Rutledge argued, should have been to establish price stability before any further moves were undertaken.[189] There were, he wrote, two possible ways to do so. The first was to force down grain prices in France by coercive ordinances; the second was to increase the means available to the nonagricultural class to enable it to carry the higher costs of free trade. The first, he wrote, was unjust and an attack on property, which meant that public credit had to be used to overcome the potential clash of interests. Like the plan proposed by the marquis de Casaux, Rutledge's solution involved using the funding system to promote a virtuous circle of rising demand and increasing output based upon the credit made available, in this instance, by a land bank. Using public credit in this way was, like Law's original system, designed to eliminate the state's debt. Of the five classes into which France was divided—the landowners, tenants, agricultural labourers, artisans, and *rentiers*—the interests of the last had to be sacrificed to the interests of the rest. It was, Rutledge wrote, "the most idle class and the only one, according to our principles, exposed to a

---

[187] [Rutledge], *Essais politiques*, p. 195.
[188] [Rutledge], *Essais politiques*, pp. 26–7, 29.
[189] [Rutledge], *Essais politiques*, pp. 42–3.

diminution of its comforts, which is no great evil."[190] Increasing the means available to the propertyless by establishing a land bank would (as Ogilvie argued a few years later) make property and tenancy more profitable. "It will cause land to be subdivided. More extensive division will multiply and enrich both the agricultural class and those accessory to it, which amounts to the whole political body, whose nurture and support it supplies."[191]

The French, according to Rutledge, were becoming tired of "a misery propagated from one generation to the next, first under a great number of feudal tyrants and then under a single despot."[192]

> The contrast between peoples to whom nature has granted no more than slight relative advantages and who, under the auspices of a civil liberty engraved in more stable and popular constitutions, have been able to procure abundance and previously unknown facilities for themselves, has awakened individual self-interest and has removed the infatuation with public prosperity. This disposition will mean that rulers will be forced to show more care for men and property.[193]

It was Steuart's argument in another form. The examples set by the Dutch and the British could, if combined with the moderation of a more popular constitution (similar to d'Argenson's royal democracy), allow the potential of the French economy to be gradually realised, and, as the burden of England's public debt set increasingly severe limits upon her imperial ambitions, the two peoples would be able, finally, to establish a more realistic foundation for perpetual peace than the one put forward by the abbé de Saint-Pierre in his "chimerical" early eighteenth-century peace plan. An Anglo-French common market would equip both powers to withstand the possible threats to their long-term survival from either the East or the West. By, "so to speak, sharing sovereignty over the other peoples" of the world, they might arrive at something more realistic.[194] It was clear, Rutledge wrote, that the British and French territorial and commercial systems were intrinsically different and did not need to clash. Modern public finance and its ability to stimulate manufacturing industry also ruled out the need to place as much initial emphasis on agricultural productivity as the supporters of Physiocracy had done. Once both Britain and France had developed fully, their economic power would rule the world. "The ambition

---

[190] [Rutledge], *Essais politiques*, pp. 126–7.

[191] [Rutledge], *Essais politiques*, p. 125.

[192] [Rutledge], *Essais politiques*, p. 201.

[193] [Rutledge], *Essais politiques*, p. 202.

[194] [Rutledge], *Essais politiques*, p. 205. For an earlier version of the same argument, and a possible source of some of Rutledge's ideas, see [Jacques Accarias de Sérionne], *Les intérêts des nations de l'Europe développés relativement au commerce*, 4 vols. (Paris, 1767), 1:373–410 (on the British public debt and the possibility of Anglo-French commercial cooperation).

of these two great peoples can no longer be anything other than that of enriching themselves, despite the view of certain economists who deal only with population and foodstuffs without ever considering how much symbolic wealth (*richesses significatives*) draws in ordinary wealth (*richesses usuelles*) from every side."[195] The outcome of the entire process, Rutledge argued, would be a system of government based on merit, not property, and an international system based upon commercial cooperation rather than the present sordid scramble for commercial advantage.

Both Rutledge and Aubert de Vitry seem to have kept to this view throughout the period of the French Revolution.[196] When, on 8 July 1793, Louis-Antoine Saint-Just gave a report to the Convention on behalf of the Committee of Public Safety describing the events that had led to its decision to order the expulsion and arrest of Brissot and his allies on 31 May, one episode to which he referred was the appearance of a poster in Paris some weeks previously, in March, calling upon "republicans" to "unite with the industrious people and the bourgeois" to wage "an implacable war on the brigands seducing and misleading you" (meaning, in this context, Robespierre and his Jacobin allies). "Bourgeois, industrious people, *sans-culottes*," the poster announced, "unite; arm yourselves"; "leave your work for a moment, and go back to it only after expelling the brigands from the clubs, the sections, and the national convention, to leave it made up entirely of true republicans, and of the friends of concord and virtue." According to Saint-Just, the poster was signed "Harrington," and its author was someone named "Aubert."[197]

Dominique-Joseph Garat, the Modern Idea of Happiness, and the Dilemmas of Reform

The difficulties involved in implementing any of these various reform programmes were captured very well early in the reign of Louis XVI by a writer named Dominique-Joseph Garat. Garat is now remembered mainly as Georges Danton's successor as minister of justice of the first French republic, where he was responsible for trying (largely unsuccessfully) to manage the acrimonious aftermath of the prison massacres of September 1792, and for overseeing the trial and execution of Louis XVI in January 1793.

---

[195] [Rutledge], *Essais politiques*, p. 115.

[196] On Rutledge's later career, see Rachel Hammersley, *French Revolutionaries and English Republicans: The Cordeliers Club, 1790–1794* (Woodbridge, Suffolk, The Royal Historical Society and The Boydell Press, 2005).

[197] Louis-Antoine Saint-Just, *Oeuvres*, ed. Anne Kupiec and Miguel Abensour (Paris, Gallimard, 2004), pp. 606–7 (an editorial note, p. 1202, identifies the "Aubert" in question as Aubert de Vitry but gives his first name simply as "François" rather than François-Jean-Philibert).

He went on to become one of the high dignitaries of Napoleon's empire
and, after the Restoration, to publish an intriguingly opaque biography of
the ubiquitous Jean-Baptiste-Antoine Suard (as several of his contemporaries pointed out, opacity was one of the more characteristic features of
Garat's works).[198] But the opacity can, to some degree, be taken to be a
real measure of the tension between Garat's reach and his grasp in trying
to deal with some of the difficult moral and political questions of the last
decades of the eighteenth century. He was trained as a lawyer and, before
1789, was one of a small group of individuals (others were Jean-Baptiste-
Antoine Suard, Pierre-Louis Lacretelle, Jacques-Pierre Mallet Du Pan,
André Morellet, and Pierre-Louis Roederer) who wrote regularly for the
Mercure de France and the *Journal de Paris*, the two periodicals of real intellectual calibre published during the reign of Louis XVI.[199] He was the

---

[198] "Il pourrait sans doute faire de grandes choses, s'il voulait mettre plus d'ordre, de préci-
sion, et de méthode dans ses pensées, éloigner du sujet principal des épisodes étrangères, ne
point prendre pour modèle des écrivains qui ont corrompu le goût de la littérature, et sur-
tout arrêter ou suspendre les mouvements d'une imagination qui, dans son délire, multiplie
les erreurs, les faux jugements, et les contradictions": [Jean Chas], *Réponse aux réflexions de
M. Garat insérées dans le Mercure du 14 mai 1785* (London, 1785), p. 5.

[199] A list of Garat's signed contributions to the *Mercure de France* includes the following:
15 February 1779, pp. 172–90 (Garat's famous description of his meeting with Diderot);
review of Lacretelle, *Mélanges philosophiques de jurisprudence*, *Mercure de France*, 25 March
1779, pp. 277–89; review of [Liquier], *Discours qui a remporté le prix de l'académie de Marseille
sur cette question, Quelle a été dans tous les temps l'influence du commerce sur l'esprit et les moeurs
des peuples?*, *Mercure de France*, 15 April 1779, pp. 149–63; account of Chamfort's reception
speech of 19 July 1781 to the Académie française, *Mercure de France*, 1 September 1781,
pp. 14–34; account of Condorcet's reception speech of 21 February 1782 to the Académie
française, *Mercure de France*, 6 April 1782, pp. 9–36; review of abbé Robin, *Nouveau voyage
dans l'Amérique septentrionale en l'année 1781*, *Mercure de France*, 1 March 1783, pp. 55–73;
review of M.P.D.L.C., *Lettres sur l'état primitif de l'homme jusqu' à la naissance de l'esclavage*,
Mercure de France, 19 July 1783, pp. 103–21, 151–77; review of Pierre Chabrit, *De la monarchie française*, *Mercure de France*, 6 March 1784, pp. 9–27; 10 April 1784, pp. 58–80; review of
[Anon.], *Loix municipales et économiques du Languedoc*, *Mercure de France*, 12 December 1785,
pp. 54–68; 19 February 1785, pp. 103–32 (this gave rise to a pamphlet by Jean-François Berthelot entitled *Réponse à quelques propositions hasardées par M. Garat contre le droit romain dans le
Mercure de France du 19 février 1785*, reviewed in the *Mercure*, 3 September 1785); "Réponse
de M. Garat à une lettre du docteur du province à un docteur de Paris sur un article du
Mercure," *Mercure de France*, August 1785, pp. 155–85; review of Rivarol, *De l'universalité de
la langue française*, *Mercure de France*, 6 August 1785, pp. 10–34; account of Morellet's reception speech to the Académie française, *Mercure de France*, 16 June 1785, pp. 114–36; review
of d'Albisson, *Discours sur l'origine des municipalités de Languedoc*, *Mercure de France*, 9 June
1787, pp. 55–69. Two further reviews, signed simply by "G," of Letrosne, *De l'administration
provinciale*, and of Etienne Clavière, *De la foi publique*, appeared in the *Mercure de France*, 7
February 1789, p. 8, and 27 June 1789, p. 170. According to Stella Lovering, *L'activité intellectuelle de l'Angleterre d'après l'ancien "Mercure de France" (1672–1778)* (Paris, 1930), Garat
published a review of Winckelmann's *History of ancient art* in the *Mercure* of January 1783,
pp. 63 et seq. and 104 et seq.

author of a quite penetrating critical assessment of Rousseau's thought, published in the *Mercure* in 1783. Like Kant, but also like Condorcet, he focused on Rousseau's concept of *perfectibilité*. But where Kant highlighted the connection between perfectibility and his own idea of unsocial sociability, and Condorcet highlighted its connection to the moral, epistemological, and rational problems that, he began to show, could be treated by way of the calculus of probabilities and a correspondingly broadly based system of political representation, Garat highlighted its connection to the passions, and to the accounts of human improvement and the progress of civilisation to be found in Adam Ferguson's *Essay on the History of Civil Society* and John Millar's *Origin of the Distinction of Ranks*.[200] This focus on the passions, and their ability to give civilisation a real moral foundation, was the main theme of almost everything that he wrote. It informed the long note on the subject of divorce that he contributed to Roucher's poem *Les Mois*, as well as a number of entries, including one on sovereignty, to the new multivolume legal dictionary, the *Répertoire universel et raisonné de jurisprudence* (The Universal Reasoned Repertory of Jurisprudence) edited by Joseph-Nicolas Guyot, that began to appear in 1781 (many years later, he recycled several of these publications in his biography of Suard). It was, however, particularly visible in his very first publication. Like Aubert de Vitry's pamphlet, the range of works to which it referred makes it a helpful guide to French moral and political thought in the decade that followed Rousseau's death and Physiocracy's practical failure.

The publication in question was an *éloge* of the sixteenth-century French chancellor Michel de l'Hôpital. It appeared in 1778, two years after Turgot's dismissal, an event that supplied it with much of its real subject matter, which was an assessment of the various aims and achievements of the legislator, in the light, as Garat put it, of "the various epochs of society in which nature placed his birth."[201] The content of the essay, as well as its copious notes, was shaped by the idea that Europe's retrograde historical development, with trade and industry running ahead of agriculture, had, somewhat counterintuitively, supplied modern legislators with an unparalleled ability to make law compatible with purely natural principles. This, Garat argued, anticipating the more famous assertion made by Saint-Just in 1794, was because taking the notion of happiness as the primary goal of legislation was a peculiarly modern idea, one that had emerged out of the conquest and slavery of the feudal epoch. Ancient constitutions, Garat wrote, "were the work of free men." Political allegiance in the ancient world thus required further motivation. This, Garat argued, was

---

[200] Dominique-Joseph Garat, review of M.P.D.L.C., *Lettres sur l'état primitif de l'homme jusqu'à la naissance de l'esclavage*, *Mercure de France*, 19 July 1783, pp. 103–21, 151–77.

[201] Dominique-Joseph Garat, *Eloge de Michel de l'Hôpital, chancelier de France* (Paris, 1778), p. 4.

why the dominant value of all the most famous societies of antiquity had been glory. The value itself had no particularly determinate content, since glory was something that could be acquired by different means, as was illustrated by the moderation of the Spartans, the trade and industry of Tyre, the arts of Athens, the dominion of the seas of the Carthaginians, or the liberty and empire of the Romans. But whatever its content, glory, as Garat put it, was "the luxury of human nature," not its most basic need. It was a purely relative quality and, as a result, could not be assigned any definable limit.[202] It could, for that reason, turn out to be self-defeating.

The desire for happiness, on the other hand, was more straightforwardly natural. It was "the first natural law of all sensible beings" because it was "the only desire that precedes any reflective will."[203] It led to association before there were political societies, and gave the virtues a physical basis to go along with their moral basis in conscience. This, Garat claimed, meant that the desire for happiness was naturally self-correcting, since too much of a good thing really could do actual physical harm. Nor, since it was primary and individual in origin, did the desire for happiness have any initial connection to politics. This was why it could still survive in the conditions of servitude that had arisen after the fall of the Roman Empire and the rise of feudal tyranny. The "primary origin of all the present governments of Europe," Garat wrote, "goes back to an age when every people still bore the chains of feudalism." Here, "the only question was how to soften the evils of servitude," and the first impulse was "to believe that one might not be unhappy, even without ceasing to be a slave." Far from experiencing "those generous sentiments that exaggerate man's strength and destiny," the inhabitants of the post-Roman world did not dare even to aspire to "the so natural and almost indestructible feeling of liberty" but were prepared simply to accept the right to complain about oppression, "almost as a grace." As a result, "happiness" had become the object and principle of the "manners, laws, and opinion" of the moderns. It meant, Garat concluded, that "from the shame and misfortune of slavery, modern peoples have derived a principle of legislation that is much more in keeping with human nature and is also much more able to secure the peace, prosperity, and duration of empires."[204]

This difference between the principles underlying ancient and modern political societies had several implications. The first had to do with modern forms of government. "One can," Garat wrote, "entrust the care for one's happiness to another, but to obtain glory one has to deserve it oneself. Almost all the ancient peoples governed themselves, while almost

[202] Garat, *Éloge de l'Hôpital*, pp. 41, 76–9, note 8.
[203] Garat, *Éloge de l'Hôpital*, p. 78.
[204] Garat, *Éloge de l'Hôpital*, p. 78.

all modern peoples are governed by monarchs." This, in the second place, had implications for how ancient and modern governments worked. "The desire for glory," Garat continued, "if it becomes the sentiment of a whole nation, necessarily joins into a single interest those wills that the desire for happiness divides among a multiplicity of different objects."[205] This meant that ancient governments could work by relatively simple means, since particular acts could encompass the whole national interest, and that it would usually be a matter of indifference as to whether the act in question was the work of the legislature or the executive. The diversity and incommensurability of modern ideas of happiness, however, ruled out this simple type of legislation by command. The range of possible connotations that individual happiness could have was responsible, in the first instance, for the scale, complexity, and frequently pointless character of modern legal systems. But the very proliferation of legislation supplied a self-correcting mechanism. The variety of different purposes that modern legislation had to serve meant that legal reform had to be general in character and would also have to be enforced by a more complicated distribution of the legislative, executive, and judicial powers. This interest in constitutional propriety would, in the third place, be reinforced very powerfully by the fact that modern legislation was not the work of the whole people. "One is much more prepared to put up with the evils that one inflicts upon oneself," Garat wrote, "than with those that one receives from others. The laws must, therefore, have more perfection among modern peoples because what we admire in them is not our own work, and we always judge them with rigour or even suspicion." This, in the fourth place, meant that "the rights of man must have a larger extent and more independence, because the less liberty there is in the political laws, the more there has to be in the civil and criminal laws." Some European governments, Garat concluded, "whose power is almost unlimited, finally seem to want to understand a little of this."[206]

Understanding the rights of man presupposed a knowledge of human nature. This, Garat wrote, called for a "a good theory" of all those sensations that are converted into feelings, in order to distinguish those able to produce social affections from those likely to produce passions that were harmful to society, as well as "a good theory" of all those sensations that are converted into ideas, in order to distinguish true from false ideas. The latter, he noted, could be found in the work of Etienne Bonnot de Condillac. The former, however, was less well developed, but, Garat observed, the notes to the poem entitled *The Seasons*, by Voltaire's friend the marquis de Saint-Lambert, were "the best" of this type to be found (it is

[205] Garat, *Éloge de l'Hôpital*, p. 78.
[206] Garat, *Éloge de l'Hôpital*, p. 79.

likely that this interest was superseded by Garat's later involvement with
Roucher's didactic poem *Les Mois*).[207] More broadly, however, they were
to be found in "the true principles of the laws, the arts, and morality" that
could be extracted from Plato's *Republic*, Aristotle's *Politics*, Rousseau's
Emile, Adam Ferguson's *History of Civil Society* (which, in 1778, had not
yet been published in French), and Montesquieu's *The Spirit of Laws*.[208]
Alongside these, however, were the fruits of the progress of the arts and
sciences. "From the most necessary arts to those that are most superfluous," Garat wrote, "everything bears the imprint of perfection."

> Mechanics has, so to speak, created new beings who ought to be our only
> slaves. At each step, one can come across machines working for man and
> sparing him from everything that is most painful in his work. The fine arts
> have several temples within the walls of a single city. Men with their clothes,
> women with their finery, all society with its decorations, everything strikes
> the eye with a dazzling luxury that seems to celebrate man's triumph over the
> needs to which nature sought to subject him.[209]

But this glittering display concealed the more pernicious effects of inequality. "Revolted, above all, by the unjust distribution made by luxury
of all the work for some and all the delights of society for others," an
observer might well regret the age when barbarism could, at least, ensure
that everyone had the same lot. The point looked like Rousseau's, but, for
Garat, there were still grounds for hope. The "long cultivation of the arts
and reason" had given rise to a capacity for intellectual correctness, and
an emotional gentleness (*douceur*) and pity "that often produces the same
effects as virtue." The shock produced by others' misfortune could lead to
a desire to help others, "if only to avoid exposure to a spectacle that might
introduce some discomfort into pleasure."[210]

Appearances notwithstanding, this meant that the modern world had
an unrivalled capacity for reform and justice. This, Garat argued, was why
the Machiavellian emphasis on reverting to first principles, and on trying
to revive the politics of the ancient world, was deeply misguided. Despite
the attempt made by Rousseau, among others, to distinguish between the
messages contained in Machiavelli's republican *Discourses* and his tyranni-
cal *Prince*, both works, Garat argued, relied on the same moral theory. In
both cases, "he very often believes that perfidy, murder, and all the crimes
of that form of politics known by his name are as necessary and as useful to
liberty as to tyranny, and as advisable for republics as for tyrants."[211] The

[207] Garat, *Éloge de l'Hôpital*, pp. 52, 81, note 10.
[208] Garat, *Éloge de l'Hôpital*, p. 88.
[209] Garat, *Éloge de l'Hôpital*, p. 88.
[210] Garat, *Éloge de l'Hôpital*, p. 88.
[211] Garat, *Éloge de l'Hôpital*, pp. 6, 55, note 2.

"odious system" associated with Machiavelli still, "after two hundred years of the disasters that he caused, reigns over the greatest part of Europe." This type of condemnation of Machiavellianism did not have any particularly determinate political content. It formed the starting point of the political speculations that led the marquis de Mirabeau to publish *L'Ami des hommes* (The Friend of Mankind) in 1756. Half a century later, it could still be found as the basis of the now forgotten *Celtic Researches* published by the Welsh cleric Edward Davies in 1804 (one of the authorities listed by Davies among his intellectual predecessors was Mirabeau's protégé Court de Gebelin). "Perhaps," Davies wrote, "there is no topic, upon which the moderns have shown less of their accustomed liberality or candour."

> They have taken *their* sketch of primitive man as they found him, at the dawn of profane history, in the *middle ages* of the world; that is when the little states of Greece or Italy, and of the adjacent regions, began to want *elbow room*; when ambition had violated the good faith of prior establishment or compact, and before the *law of nations* had rooted *their* principles of mutual forbearance between the rights of the belligerent parties at the end of their conflict. These were consequently times of confusion, which degraded the human character into a pestilent and brutal spirit of rapine. But earlier, and sacred history of that same noble creature, *man*, proves, to the most incredulous, that *savage life* is the *child of accident*, and has no filial marks of nature as her parent.[212]

Garat's earlier version of the same idea relied much less on sacred history but still followed the same logic of reform leading to the recovery of something natural.

For Garat, this did not mean that every aspect of Machiavellian politics had to be dropped. The real way out had, instead, to be something like its mirror image. Just as Machiavellian politics relied on sharp, but often criminal, action, so the modern legislator had to adopt the same kind of decisive policies to bring about reform. The real mistake, Garat argued, was to adopt a policy based upon the words of Solon, the ancient Athenian legislator who, famously, had said, "I have given the Athenians, not the best laws, but the best laws possible for the Athenians." Instead of following Solon, the modern legislator should imitate Lycurgus, "who appeared armed on the public square and who established laws in exactly the same way as one overturns them, by a conspiracy." Cicero's "clemency," Garat noted, had been unable to achieve what Cato's "rigour" had done.[213] "This revolution," Garat concluded, "would be entirely worthy of the enlightened government under which we live, and the confidence

---

[212] Edward Davies, *Celtic Researches, on the Origin, Traditions and Language of the Ancient Britons, with some Introductory Sketches on Primitive Society* (London, 1804), pp. ix, xi–xii.

[213] Garat, *Éloge de l'Hôpital*, p. 93.

with which people have been calling for and expecting it is certainly the most flattering homage that they can offer it." But, he warned, "time is short, and if another century were to pass without producing any renewal of things, it can be predicted that all will be lost irretrievably."[214]

Garat was less certain about what the content of that "all" might be. Early in 1779, he outlined a set of questions in the *Mercure de France* about Rousseau's as yet unpublished *Considerations on the Government of Poland* in the final section of a review of a prize essay on the influence of commerce on the spirit and manners of peoples in all ages. The questions were occasioned by the obvious parallel between the essay's emphatic conclusion that trade and the arts were incompatible with "all the great virtues" and had "always weakened the spirit and corrupted the manners of every nation," and the way that the same subject had, as Garat put it, "established the reputation of the celebrated citizen of Geneva." The subject, Garat continued, formed something like Rousseau's life's work, as was now apparent in the *Considerations on the Government of Poland*, with its prime injunction to the Poles "to break off almost all communication with the rest of Europe." This, Rousseau had emphasised, was not a matter of establishing import duties or trade embargoes, or even of doing something analogous to building the Great Wall that the Chinese had constructed in a vain attempt to keep the Tartars at bay. For Rousseau, as Garat put it, "national character would be the barrier." Once the Poles were truly Poles, their national character would be an invincible obstacle to the loss of their independence, even if they were conquered by Russia. As Rousseau himself had written, however much the Russians might swallow them up, they would still be unable to digest them.

Garat summarised Rousseau's argument sympathetically, listing all the details of the public festivities, generalised military service, graduated promotion, national honours, monetary frugality, and the carefully calibrated way of electing a monarch that, according to Rousseau, would allow Poland to become a nation apart. But he remained unpersuaded. He set out his doubts in the form of six questions about the implications of Rousseau's Polish solution to modernity's problems. The first suggested that the invention of the compass, printing, and gunpowder, as well as the discovery of the New World, had produced such fundamental changes in the human mind (*l'esprit humain*) as to prevent "modern peoples" from drawing on "the models of ancient legislation" as the basis of their laws. The second drew out the implication of this difference by asking whether it was really feasible now to think that it might be possible to eliminate the ambition for both wealth and glory from the modern world. Eliminating the first, Garat suggested, might simply turn "man's restless activity" towards even

---

[214] Garat, *Éloge de l'Hôpital*, p. 94.

more harmful objectives. This, in turn, raised a further question about the desirability of erecting barriers between nations. These, Garat warned, were as likely to ignite "national hatreds" that would soon spill beyond the barriers themselves, as had been the case with the Persians and Spartans in the ancient past. It was not obvious, therefore, that Europe should, as Rousseau had argued, consist of the English, the Russians, or the French, rather than mere Europeans. "If all these national characters were effaced," Garat asked, "is it not more likely that the pure, original features of human nature would be more apparent among the men of every country and age?" What was called "national character," he suggested, was as likely to be the product of "prejudice, defects, and vices" as the outcome of "virtue and enlightenment." In addition, since wars and conquests were "inevitable," it was possible to think that people with similar manners would be assimilated more readily with one another in the wake of the realignments that conquests would produce. These questions all raised a final question about Rousseau's endorsement of small republics. Although it was certainly true that "a single, isolated" state would be better governed, smallness of scale necessarily meant that there would be many states, and, with many states, there would also be many possible internal or external causes of conflict. Liberty in "great empires," however, could be established only if representatives made up the legislature. This, Garat concluded, meant that it was an open question as to whether Rousseau had been right in claiming that liberty was lost whenever it was entrusted to representatives, or whether, in fact, his Genevan critic Jean-Louis Delolme had been more correct in saying that liberty was more secure in the hands of representatives than in those of the people themselves.[215]

It followed that the type of revolution that, in contradistinction to Rousseau, Garat envisaged would be the work of a reforming royal government, not the more open-ended outcome of a catastrophic political crisis. He was certainly not unusual in calling for this type of revolution. An even more emphatic version of the same sort of appeal was made by Maximilien Robespierre early in 1789. Here, too, revolution was, in the first instance, bound up with the idea of virtuous royal reform. "Another sovereign," Robespierre wrote, "might limit his ambition to reviving and restoring those ancient and sacred maxims that protect the ownership of our goods. He might believe that he had accomplished everything by succeeding in reopening all the sources of national wealth and by reassuring the alarms of trade and a languishing agriculture."

But the glory of procuring all the treasures of abundance for us, of embellishing your reign with all the finery and pleasures of luxury, success of that

[215] Garat, review of [Liquier], *Discours* (see pp. 161–3 for Garat's questions).

kind, which to the vulgar politician seems the most admirable masterpiece of human wisdom, is not the most interesting part of the august mission appointed to you by both heaven and your own soul. To guide men to happiness by means of virtue, and to virtue by means of a system of legislation based upon the immutable principles of immutable morality that are designed to restore human nature to all its rights and all its original dignity; to rebind the immortal chain linking man to God and to his fellows by destroying all the causes of oppression and tyranny, and the fear, suspicion, pride, servility, egoism, hatred, cupidity, and all those vices they sow in their wake, and which take man far from that end to which the eternal legislator assigned society, this, Sire, is the glorious vocation to which he has called you.[216]

Louis XVI, Robespierre continued, was in position "to carry out a revolution attempted by Henri IV and Charlemagne, but which was not yet possible in the times in which they lived." Times, however, had changed, and the moment to act was now at hand. But, Robespierre warned, "if we are to let it slip, it may perhaps be decreed that the only glimmer of light left to us will be one that reveals nothing more than days of trouble, desolation, and calamity! Ah, Sire, hasten to seize it; take pity on an illustrious nation that loves you well, and ensure that there is at least one happy people on this earth."[217] If, as Garat had argued, the principle of happiness was modern, then the revolution that Robespierre advocated would be a modern revolution. Apart from its rather stronger emphasis on divine providence, it was not particularly different from the one that Louis-Sébastien Mercier envisaged when the new reign began.

[216] Maximilien Robespierre, "Mémoire pour le Sieur Louis-Marie-Hyacinthe Dupond" [1789], in *Oeuvres complètes de Maximilien Robespierre*, 10 vols. (Paris, 1910–67), vol. 1, ed. Victor Barbier and Charles Vellay, 573–682 (pp. 661–5, 669–70, 672–3).

[217] Robespierre, "Mémoire pour Dupond," in *Oeuvres*, 1:672–3.

⊰ 5 ⊱

THE ENTITLEMENTS OF MERIT

VISIONS OF PATRIOTISM

THERE IS an intriguing textual variant in reports of the great speech made by Maximilien Robespierre to the French republican Convention on 10 April 1793, attacking what he called "a powerful faction," headed by Jacques-Pierre Brissot, for "conspiring with the tyrants of Europe to give us a king and a kind of aristocratic constitution."[1] In the authorised version of the speech, published in the tenth number of his own *Lettres à ses commettants* (Letters to his Constituents), Robespierre accused the Brissotins of hiding their ambition under a mask of moderation and a spurious love of order.

> They called all the friends of the fatherland agitators and anarchists; even inciting real agitators and anarchists to make that calumny seem true. They showed themselves skilled in the art of covering up their criminal enterprises by imputing them to the people. Early on, they horrified citizens by raising the spectre of an agrarian law. They separated the interests of the rich from those of the poor; they presented themselves to the former as their protectors against the *sans-culottes*; they attracted all the enemies of equality to their party.[2]

Here, by implication, it was Robespierre and his Jacobin allies who were the true protectors of the *sans-culottes*, while it was Brissot and his allies who were the protectors of the rich. But in the version of the speech published by the *Logotachigraphe* (which, as its name implies, was meant to be a verbatim record of speeches to the Convention), Robespierre was reported to have said exactly the opposite, namely, that Brissot and his supporters had presented themselves not as the protectors of the rich against the *sans-culottes* but, instead, as "the protectors of the *sans-culottes*" against the rich.[3] This curious discrepancy is a clue to the real sequence of events that lay behind the transformation of the salon society joke from an emblem of urbanity into an emblem of virtue.

[1] Maximilien Robespierre, *Oeuvres*, vol. 9, ed. Marc Bouloiseau, Jean Dautry, Georges Lefebvre, and Albert Soboul (Paris, 1958), pp. 376–416 (p. 376).

[2] Robespierre, *Oeuvres*, 9:377–8.

[3] Robespierre, *Oeuvres*, 9:401.

That sequence began well before the Bastille fell, because, right from the start, the subjects of wealth and poverty were central to royal justifications of reform. "Enough others," wrote Charles-Alexandre de Calonne, Louis XVI's controller general of finance, to the poet Pons-Denis Ecouchard Lebrun, on the eve of the first assembly of notables in the spring of 1787, "have sung the praises of the bloody exploits of the conquerors of the earth." Lebrun's task, however, was to be different. His "heroic lyre" was to praise "the useful virtues of a benevolent king," and to mobilise "the astonishing effects" that patriotism could produce. "Divine patriotism," Calonne suggested, had, therefore, to be "the muse of my Pindar" (Ecouchard Lebrun's admirers, it should be explained, had renamed him "Pindar" Lebrun, after the ancient Greek founder of lyric poetry). Patriotism would certainly flee "those unfortunate countries that slavery oppresses," and might still languish in those in which "a more temperate authority governs, but governs alone"; but, Calonne emphasised, it could not even exist "unless a nation also exists." The poet's assignment was, therefore, to show how the forthcoming assembly—"formed," the minister noted, "by a more enlightened choice" than those once made in elections to the old estates-general—promised France a future that would match the image of her present king. Where Louis XIV's "fatal ambition" and "thirst for glory" had necessarily produced "despotism as its offspring" during the reign of Louis XV, France now had a ruler of a different type. Louis XVI's destiny was to "give the nation back its existence," thus allowing it, "more than ever," to identify itself with its reigning king. The "most discordant constitution" would be "restored to the most desirable unity," and the "odious empire of arbitrariness" would be annihilated. Taxation would be lightened by a better distribution of the burden, and, once it was, complaints would begin to die down, along with the demise of "the exceptions" that produced them. Agriculture would be revived by the growing value of its products. Commerce would increase by way of the liberty "that is its element," while "those strange barriers separating different parts of the same empire," and "those cruel rights" that both subjected "the commodity most necessary to life" to "an excessive dearness" and condemned its consumers "to the most barbarous of vexations," would all disappear. This, Calonne ended, was how "nature's bard (*chantre*)," by becoming "the bard of the fatherland," might celebrate "the most memorable epoch of the monarchy" (Lebrun, it should also be explained, was famous for an unfinished poem entitled "Nature, or Rural and Philosophical Happiness" that he had begun in 1760).[4]

Lebrun duly obliged. His *Discours en vers, à l'occasion de l'assemblée des notables* (Discourse in Verse, on the Occasion of the Assembly of Notables)

[4] Calonne to Lebrun [late 1786, or early 1787], in Pons-Denis Ecouchard Lebrun, *Oeuvres*, 4 vols. (Paris, 1811), 4:273–9.

faithfully followed the minister's script. Contrary to malign rumour, the modern Pindar began, the forthcoming assembly was not a sign of some secret political disorder, since France, as the recent victorious war against Britain showed, was still a "colossus." But France was also a "confused collection of discordant principles and ancient abuse." Error piled on error, over thirteen centuries of assorted kings, had left the nation without the laws it needed to secure its well-being, so that "wisdom and genius" were now required to produce "harmony as their offspring." A state, Lebrun observed, could still languish "in the midst of its glory." The "weaknesses of a king" and the "errors of a minister," joined to "the sinister legacy" of the succeeding reign (the allusions echoed Calonne's advice on what to say about Louis XIV and Louis XV), could erode the foundations of the finest throne if "cruel subsidy's erratic system" were to dry up the sources of public wealth. Now, however, hope was at hand. The "days of horror and alarm," when "desperate eyes" could see nothing in the state but "misery coupled to luxury," and when "the sons of Plutus dared to drink the tears of the fatherland from gilded cups," while "pale, feeble wretches fought their frightened flocks for the grass on the ground," would, Lebrun announced, soon belong to the past. Like a "wise cultivator" improving his fields, "a wise king" had begun the work of reform. Wealth, he knew, was to be found not "in the mines of Golconda," but in those "smiling fields made fertile by labour." Spain testified all too well to the sterility of "gold-driven indigence." Gold ran out, but the land itself was "inexhaustible." Properly encouraged, France would soon shine again with renewed splendour. Abundance, the arts, and trade would flourish; credit would be healed of its ancient wounds; and gold would flow safely along broad highways, allowing the humble "cabin" to escape, finally, from its crushing burden. It was hard not to see, Lebrun concluded, that the bloodline running from France's virtuous king Henri IV to her present ruler was a sign that Louis XVI would, in fact, be his reincarnation.[5]

Events, of course, proved otherwise. But Lebrun's rehearsal of so many of the bromides of the eighteenth century should still be taken seriously (Robespierre, in his encomium of Louis XVI on the eve of the estates-general cited at the end of the previous chapter, certainly seems to have done, since it looks rather like a reply to Lebrun's Calonne-inspired ode).[6] At the limit, as many royalist pamphleteers were to point out after the Bastille fell, there was no constitutional reason to prevent Louis XVI from simply adopting the scenario as his own, and acting unilaterally as a patriot king. In 1787, and again in 1788, more than one voice, including

[5] Pons-Denis Ecouchard Lebrun, "Discours en vers, à l'occasion de l'assemblée des notables," in his Oeuvres, 2:237–41.

[6] See above, pp. 281–2.

Simon Linguet's, was also quite willing to suggest that this type of unilateral action meant reviving Henry St John, viscount Bolingbroke's advice on how to deal patriotically with a public debt, with Henri IV and his virtuous minister Sully as the models.[7] The fact that nothing like this happened may well have had something to do with Louis XVI's character, together with ministerial infighting, as well as the fear of the political reaction that a voluntary bankruptcy might have provoked (timidity tends to be overdetermined).[8] But it also had quite a lot to do with the concurrent subject of army reform, and with the political obstacles to implementing a patriotic royal solution to the government's financial problems that were created by a growing argument over the subject of promotion within the royal army. That argument ran alongside the more prominently public conflict between the royal government and the parlements of France between 1787 and 1788, recurrently nullifying royal attempts to use military force to bring the parlements to heel.[9] By the late summer of 1788, it was clear that a forceful, royal solution to the problem of the deficit was unavailable, and that the government would have to try to reach an accommodation with its political opponents by convening an assembly of the kingdom's estates-general.

As Jacques Mallet du Pan, one of the group of political journalists who, like Dominique-Joseph Garat, were associated with the *Mercure de France*, pointed out in a letter to one of his Genevan compatriots in late August 1788, patriotic political coups had always been the way that the French monarchy had solved its problems. Garat, in his homage to Michel de l'Hôpital in 1778, had advocated just that. But Mallet du Pan was far less sanguine than Garat may have been about the prospect that was now unfolding in France. "History informs us," he wrote, "that, beginning with Sully, the ministers of that monarchy have always managed to pull it out of distress only by means of operations equivalent to bankruptcies."

> Reflection easily offers an explanation of this conduct. It derives from the nature of the government and a national character that is incapable of order,

---

[7] For examples, see B. L. 910. b. 1 (2), [Anon.], *Idées à communiquer aux états-généraux* (n.p., 1789); and Jacques-Louis de la Tocnaye, *Les causes de la révolution de France et les efforts de la noblesse pour en arrêter les progrès* (Edinburgh, 1797). For others, see Michael Sonenscher, "The Nation's Debt and the Birth of the Modern Republic: The French Fiscal Deficit and the Politics of the Revolution of 1789," *History of Political Thought* 18 (1997): 64–103, 267–325.

[8] On the high politics of the French monarchy, see, helpfully, Munro Price, *The Fall of the French Monarchy* (London, Macmillan, 2002).

[9] The fullest account of these attempts, notably in the Dauphiné and Brittany in June 1788, remains L. Hartmann, *Les officiers de l'armée royale et la révolution* (Paris, 1910), pp. 57–70, 77–8. More generally, see Bailey Stone, *The French Parlements and the Crisis of the Old Regime* (Chapel Hill, University of North Carolina Press, 1986).

thrift, and patience, as well as the almost insurmountable difficulty of righting wrongs in a great empire without producing great convulsions. You, sir, have been able to see the progress of the disorder and, in the light of what I have said [presumably in an earlier letter], will be able to put your finger on the palpable reasons obstructing these remedies. The king needed authority, but the kingdom is in anarchy; he needed concerted action, but discord (*trouble*) has been created everywhere; he needed great consideration and tact, but, steel in hand, national confidence has been cut off at its roots. Sovereign power has been compromised, just when it needed all its energy. It was believed that fine prologues to ridiculously paternalistic edicts were the way to govern the state and opinion (*l'état et les esprits*), and that the resources to be sought were the very ones that are bound to produce an upheaval. This is the first time, I think, that a sovereign, with no money, can be seen trying to carry out a revolution that will overturn the civil and judicial order of a kingdom of thirty thousand square leagues.

"In any case," Mallet warned, "expect this crisis to be very long, unless it is aggravated (*brusqué*) by operations of even greater violence than those yet tried."[10]

The details of the internal disaffection, bordering on mutiny, caused by the royal government's attempts to reform the army in the period before the estates-general assembled have been described very fully.[11] The moral dimension of the subject is, however, rather less well known.[12] In one sense, it was connected to the monarchy's financial problems because, as was the case with every eighteenth-century state, French military expenditure accounted for by far the largest proportion (well over two-thirds) of government spending.[13] In this sense, and independently of its bearing on the composition or proficiency of the French army, military reform

[10] Mallet du Pan to Aubert de Tournes, banker of Geneva, 25 August 1788, in "Deux lettres inédites de Mallet du Pan," *Mémoires et documents de la société d'histoire et d'archéologie de Genève* 22 (Geneva, 1886): 9–11.

[11] See Hartmann, *Les officiers*. As the historian who has paid the sharpest attention to this aspect of the French Revolution has put it, "it could be argued that the French Revolution was in part a military putsch": see T.C.M. Blanning, *The French Revolution; Aristocrats versus Bourgeois?* (London, Macmillan, 1987), pp. 15, 37–8 (p. 38).

[12] The recent work of a number of historians has, however, begun to change this. See Rafe Blaufarb, *The French Army 1750–1820: Careers, Talent, Merit* (Manchester, Manchester UP, 2002); Jay M. Smith, *The Culture of Merit: Nobility, Royal Service, and the Making of Absolute Monarchy in France, 1600–1789* (Ann Arbor, University of Michigan Press, 1996); Jay M. Smith, *Nobility Reimagined: The Patriotic Nation in Eighteenth-Century France* (Ithaca, Cornell UP, 2005); Jay M. Smith, ed., *The French Nobility in the Eighteenth Century: Reassessments and New Approaches* (University Park, Penn State UP, 2006); John Shovlin, *The Political Economy of Virtue: Luxury, Patriotism and the Origins of the French Revolution* (Ithaca, Cornell UP, 2006).

[13] For an overview, see Charles Tilly, *Coercion, Capital, and European States, A.D. 900–1990* (Oxford, Blackwell, 1990).

complemented the broader objective of reducing the amount, and changing the distribution, of the tax burden. But in another sense, the subject
of army reform introduced a new and different element into the relatively
familiar standoff between ministers and magistrates that began to unfold
in France after the failure of Calonne's assembly of notables in 1787.[14]
The unusual way that the question of promotion within the army came
to be handled, especially in 1788, not only made it hard for Louis XVI to
adopt the mantle of a patriot king, but also played a part in turning the
related subjects of justice, civil equality, and individual merit into political
issues that were to remain alive in the months and years that followed the
fall of the Bastille. Establishing a constitution and establishing financial
stability were not simple tasks. Rewarding merit, and reconciling several,
potentially different, concepts of justice, not only raised the threshold of
expectation somewhat higher but also added to the difficulties facing the
self-proclaimed French National and Constituent Assembly. The failure
of the royal government to carry through the type of reform programme
that "Pindar" Lebrun was instructed to extol left the French National Assembly with the problem of finding a way to implement a programme of
patriotic reform, without a patriot king.

The Army and Its Problems in the Eighteenth Century

The moral and social dimensions of the subject of army reform grew out
of the range of questions that it generated about property and inheritance,
as against merit and distinction, in determining both the composition of
the French nobility and its relationship to the French royal government.
In the eighteenth century, the complicated historical arguments that
Montesquieu used in his *The Spirit of Laws* of 1748 to answer these questions were not widely endorsed.[15] For the intellectual mainstream, and in
contradistinction to Montesquieu's characterisation of monarchy, nobility
could be a virtue, but it could also be a privilege, and, if it was, then, under
some conditions, privilege could be a real obstacle to truly merited distinction. As Jacques-Henri Bernardin de Saint-Pierre put it in his *Etudes de la
nature* (Studies of Nature) of 1784, "every government, whatever it might
be, is happy at home and powerful abroad when it gives all its subjects

---

[14] On earlier conflict between ministers and magistrates, see particularly Julian Swann,
Politics and the Parlement of Paris under Louis XV, 1754–1774 (Cambridge, CUP, 1995).

[15] On Montesquieu, property, and inheritance, see Michael Sonenscher, *Before the Deluge:
Public Debt, Inequality, and the Intellectual Origins of the French Revolution* (Princeton, Princeton UP, 2007), pp. 95–172. For a recently published example of this type of criticism of
Montesquieu, see Jean-Pierre-François Ripert de Monclar, *Les commentaires sur l' "Esprit des
lois" de Montesquieu* (Paris, Institut Michel Villey, 2006).

the natural right to aspire to honours and fortune, and the opposite occurs if it reserves for a particular class of citizens goods that should be
common to all." The same "community of hope and fortune available to
all conditions," he emphasised, was as available in the Prussian monarchy
as in the Dutch republic, and even among the Ottoman Turks.[16] What
was less clear, however, particularly after the Ségur ordinance of 22 May
1781 (named after Philippe-Henri, marquis de Ségur, the incumbent war
minister), was whether anything like the "community of hope and fortune
available to all conditions" that Bernardin de Saint-Pierre singled out as
the hallmark of good government was still to be found in France.

The Ségur ordinance included a stipulation—first made at the time of
the foundation of the French Royal Military School in 1751, and subsequently reiterated both in the ordinance itself and in a later ordinance of
17 March 1788—that every army officer above the rank of sublieutenant
was obliged, to be eligible for promotion, to prove that he came from
a family having four degrees of nobility (meaning that the individual in
question had to be able to present proof of nobility going back at least
four generations). The strong moral outcry that the ordinance provoked
had less to do with this requirement per se than with the way that it was
applied. Once, the requirement was taken to be evidence of a prerevolutionary "aristocratic reaction" that was designed to prevent members
of the Third Estate from rising to positions of status and power. More
recently, however, it has become clear that it was part of a broader reforming strategy whose aim was to establish a clearer distinction between
what might be called the dignified and efficient parts of the French army
by filtering out unsuitable candidates, often the sons of the recently ennobled whose titles derived from the purchase of venal offices, to leave
what its advocates hoped would be a more homogenously effective officer
corps.[17] What was at issue in this attempt to separate the dignified from
the efficient parts of the French army was not the question of entry into,
but of promotion within, its massively top-heavy officer corps. Here, what
mattered was not the social origins of the individuals in question, or even
the number of degrees of nobility that different types of nobles were able
to invoke, but the rival claims of service and merit, as against wealth and

[16] Jacques-Henri Bernardin de Saint-Pierre, *Etudes de la nature* [1784], ed. Napoléon
Chaix, 2 vols. (Paris, 1865), 1:252, 255–6.
[17] See particularly Blaufarb, *The French Army*, which, by focusing more clearly on promotion within, rather than entry to, the French army, clarifies the classic articles by David
D. Bien, "La réaction aristocratique avant 1789: l'exemple de l'armée," *Annales E. S. C.* 29
(1974): 23–48, 505–34; and his "The Army in the French Enlightenment: Reform, Reaction,
and Revolution," *Past & Present* 85 (1979): 68–98. I have borrowed the distinction between
dignified and efficient parts from Walter Bagehot, *The English Constitution* [1867], ed. Paul
Smith (Cambridge, CUP, 2001), p. 5.

connection, in determining the grounds for promotion to offices higher up the scale of what, in the second half of the eighteenth century, had become an increasingly tangled chain of military command.

The broad aims of the subject of army reform went back to the middle of the eighteenth century and to a more extensive range of arguments about the nature and status of the French nobility. From one perspective, the French nobility continued to embody the values of service, above all military service, that were the hallmark of either its Roman and imperial, or its German and feudal origins. From another perspective, however, the more recent combination of absolute government, venal office, and the growth of the monarchy's own legal, fiscal, military, and administrative systems had changed its character completely. From this latter perspective, highlighting the nobility's unitary character amounted to opting for an illusion, leaving France increasingly mired in the court-centred government, backward agriculture, rural poverty, and unproductive industry that, it could be claimed, were the most conspicuous features of the kingdom's present state. According to this argument, failing to address the many questions raised by absolute government about the compatibility between nobility as a moral quality, nobility as an estate of the realm, and nobility as an inherited privilege amounted to jeopardising French domestic prosperity and external power not only because of the urgent need to raise the productivity of the large amount of landed property that the French nobility owned, but also because of the many fiscal, legal, and administrative problems involved in maintaining the illusion that the nobility was, in any real sense, a single entity. From this point of view, the way out had to be a more highly differentiated nobility, with some nobles involved in trade, as in Britain, but with others involved in the army, as in Prussia, and with, perhaps, a higher order of nobility as a reward for service in either civil or military life.

The idea was a particular feature of the works of the assortment of mid-eighteenth-century political reformers loosely known as the Gournay group, whose reform proposals amounted to the next generation's continuation of the ideas associated earlier in the eighteenth century with the figures of Voltaire, Jean-François Melon, and Charles-Irénée Castel, abbé de Saint-Pierre (in addition to a trading nobility, Saint-Pierre also proposed establishing a system of military promotion based on an initial ballot among the members of each level of the officer corps).[18] Here, the most prominent expression of the Gournay group's views was set out in the abbé

---

[18] On Saint-Pierre's advocacy of a trading nobility, see Charles-Irénée Castel de Saint-Pierre, *Les rêves d'un homme de bien, qui peuvent être réalisés* (Paris, 1775), p. 217: "Or, nous pouvons, par l'augmentation de notre commerce maritime, donner, comme les anglais, cette ressource à notre pauvre noblesse." On his idea of a system of military promotion and its endorsement by Mably, see note 20 below.

Gabriel-François Coyer's *Noblesse commerçante* (A Commercial Nobility), a work that, despite its title, was as much an argument in favour of a military as a commercial nobility, because, as Coyer stressed, a more highly differentiated nobility was the way to eliminate the royal favour, backstairs intrigue, and unnecessary proliferation of military offices that were the most glaring effects of impecunious noble status. "Instead of having recourse to commerce, that all too abundant stream of resources (*fleuve si abondant*) for the nobility that does not fight," he wrote in reply to his critics, "everything comes to be solicited: new establishments, renewed favours, the abolition of venality in military posts, the restoration of offices of second-in-command, the creation of crowds of others, and finally of whole bodies of gentlemen soldiers."[19] Although they did not seem to realise it, he added, he was as able as his critics to see the merits of the military estate. The real question was how to make it effective.

Many of the subsequent reform projects, particularly those associated with Louis XV's penultimate principal minister, the duc de Choiseul, as well as the Ségur ordinance itself, took their cue from this idea of a reformed nobility (the abbé Gabriel Bonnot de Mably, for example, was an advocate of Saint-Pierre's idea of a ballot-based system of military promotion).[20] In the high political world of the last years of the reign of Louis XV, and the beginning of the reign of Louis XVI, the Choiseul party, as it was sometimes called, was charged quite often with this type of plan to transform the nobility. To its supporters, reform of this kind looked like the way to bring trade, taxation, and a more fully professional military establishment into closer alignment and, by doing so, to give France a social and political structure that would be able to match its British counterpart on something like similar terms. But to its opponents, it looked more like

[19] Gabriel-François Coyer, *Développement et défense du système de la noblesse commerçante*, 2 vols. (Amsterdam, 1757), pp. 196–7. On Coyer, the Gournay group, and military reform, see Jay M. Smith, "Social Categories, the Language of Patriotism, and the Origins of the French Revolution: The Debate over *noblesse commerçante*," *Journal of Modern History* 27 (2000): 339–74; Ulrich Adam, "Nobility and Modern Monarchy—J. G. G. Justi and the French Debate on Commercial Nobility at the Beginning of the Seven Years War," *History of European Ideas* 29 (2003): 141–57, and his *The Political Economy of J. H. G. Justi* (Berne, Peter Lang, 2006), pp. 96–109. According to Diderot, Coyer's call for a commercial nobility was written to a ministerial brief: see Elie Carcassonne, *Montesquieu et le problème de la constitution française au xviiie siècle* (Paris, 1927), p. 223. For a clear indication of military reform as the aim of Coyer's proposal, see the discussion of his ideas in the context of a critical review of Mirabeau's *L'Ami des hommes* in the January 1759 issue of the Gournay group's organ, the *Journal de Commerce* (Brussels, 1759), pp. 177–79. See also the critical discussion of Coyer in [Georg-Ludwig Schmid d'Auenstein], *Essais sur divers sujets intéressants de politique et de morale*, 2 vols. (n.p., 1761), 1:347–51.

[20] On Mably's endorsement of Saint-Pierre's idea, see Gabriel Bonnot de Mably, *Des droits et des devoirs du citoyen* [1789], ed. Jean-Louis Lecercle (Paris, Marcel Didier, 1972), pp. 204–7.

a new effort to revive earlier attempts by the French dukes and peers to turn themselves into a sort of separate supernobility, with all the rewards of royal favour and court patronage at their command. This, according to Louis-Sébastien Mercier, writing in 1792, had been the underlying aim of Choiseul's interest in military reform and the real reason for the emergence of what he called "that impertinent aristocracy that pullulated and infected our armies with gangrene."[21]

Suspicions like these played some part in making it difficult to implement the strategy. But the difficulties were also a product of the many entrenched interests that it was bound to affect, as well as the wider questions about property, legality, and the legitimate use of royal power that it raised. The problem of implementation was most acute in the case of incumbent army officers, not only because of the more considerable legal, financial, or political problems involved in dislodging those already in place, but also because of the relatively straitened financial circumstances of the French monarchy in the aftermath of the American War of Independence.[22] These legal and financial constraints may have been the reason why the implementation strategy, particularly in 1788, came to rely on the use of a certain amount of smoke and mirrors to meet the requirement to prove possession of four degrees of nobility. Instead of buying out incumbents, or risking the howls of complaint that were likely to follow from simply abolishing some offices and expelling those incumbent officers who fell foul of the genealogical test, the strategy consisted of establishing a twin-track system of military promotion, with both tracks nominally being subject to the requirement to prove four degrees of nobility, but with one set of largely supernumerary offices serving to siphon off unqualified candidates with no identifiable military ability, leaving the other set reserved for those with both a real military pedigree and an established record of command. As article 14 of the ordinance of 17 March 1788 specified, the king retained the right to make promotions directly to some military offices in order, according to the rather artful wording of the article, "to secure outlets for that portion of his nobility that is called on more particularly to command his regiments."[23] This entailed creating

---

[21] Louis-Sébastien Mercier, "Portrait de Choiseul," *Chronique du mois*, September 1792, 49–60 (58–9). On Choiseul's plans to establish a chamber of peers, see Carcassonne, *Montesquieu*, p. 553, and, on the so-called Choiseul party in the politics of the reign of Louis XVI, see Munro Price, *Preserving the Monarchy: The Comte de Vergennes, 1774–1787* (Cambridge, CUP, 1995), and John Hardman, *French Politics 1774–1789* (London, Longman, 1995).

[22] On these, see, still helpfully, John Bosher, *French Finances 1770–1795: From Business to Bureaucracy* (Cambridge, CUP, 1970), and, for more recent literature, see Sonenscher, *Before the Deluge*, p. 38.

[23] For a hostile reaction to the article, see [Anon.], *L'armée française au conseil de la guerre* (n.p., n.d., but early 1789 from the content), p. 1.

a number of largely dignified offices, with titles like sublieutenant, second-captain, deputy-major, adjutant-colonel, or aide-major-general, to complement the efficient part of the military establishment. Promotion to these offices could be fast-tracked, making it easier to weed out the wrong type of noble without actually having to purge the army, thus leaving the right type of putatively more competent army officer more securely in place.

This, at any rate, was the aim, but it backfired spectacularly. Instead of being seen as an attempt to entrench ability, experience, and an established military pedigree, it came to be seen as an attempt to reward insiders, court favourites, and exactly those recently ennobled individuals that it was designed to weed out, with the inflated supply of dignified offices, and the concurrent relative fall in the number of efficient offices, leading to a further scramble for positions of influence and power with every oscillation in the status of one or other of the components of the new military hierarchy. Instead of favouring ancient military lineage, as it was intended to do, army reform came to look like a reward for parvenus. "Nobility is merited, not bought," thundered one pamphlet published in 1789.[24] "Intrigue, under the specious name of talent," announced another, "stole (*ravit*) positions that were due to merit."[25] "Only in France," proclaimed a third, "could aristocrats blinded by the abuse of their credit come to adopt so unreasonable a system."[26] Army reform, noted a fourth, "tended and still tends towards maintaining an aristocratic hierarchy"—one, it continued, that was radically incompatible with "the principle of honour characteristic of the French nation," not, however, as described by Montesquieu in *The Spirit of Laws*, but as delineated by John Brown in his "excellent" *Estimate of the Manners and Principles of the Times* of 1757.[27] "One of our most recent acts of delirium," wrote Charles-François Lebrun in 1789, "has been to turn our militia into a German chapter and make the duty of every citizen the pride and property of a single order." Lebrun, a former secretary of Louis XV's chancellor Maupeou, who went on to become a high dignitary of Napoleon's empire, was a strong advocate of the type of patriotic programme of royal reform that Calonne had commended to his namesake in 1787. By early 1789, however, it looked like a forlorn hope.[28] It was simply

[24] [Anon.] *Observations sur le règlement de 22 May 1782* [sic] *concernant les preuves de noblesse exigées pour entrer au service* (London, 1789), p. 21.

[25] [Anon.], *Voeux d'un citoyen pour le militaire français* (n.p., n.d., but spring 1789 from the content), p. 9.

[26] [Anon.], *L'armée française au conseil de la guerre*, p. 9.

[27] [Antoine-Joseph-Michel Servan], *La seconde aux grands* (n.p., n.d., but 1789 from the content), pp. 7–11. On the same subject, see also the translator's notes to the French translation of Gilbert Stuart, *Tableau des progrès de la société en Europe*, 2 vols. (Paris, 1789), 1:i–vi; 2:187.

[28] Charles-François Lebrun, *La voix du citoyen* [n.p., 1789] (Paris, 1814), p. 22. On Lebrun's alternative prognosis, see Sonenscher, *Before the Deluge*, pp. 31–2.

"revolting," the marquis de Toulangeon concluded, "to see favour put so often in place of merit, and long-serving officers commanded by the most inexperienced youth."[29]

The outcry had no particularly determinate political content, beyond the mixture of venal office, court society, and royal favour that, it could be claimed, absolute government had spawned. Instead of merit and ability it rewarded wealth, connection, and intrigue, and added a further gloss to the veneer of status and old-established distinction that, all too rapidly, they were able to acquire. "At the end of the eighteenth century," noted another of the keepers of Rousseau's flame, the abbé Gabriel Brizard, in an edition of Rousseau's collected works that, in collaboration with Louis-Sébastien Mercier, he began to produce between 1788 and 1793, "the most violent champions of the feudal aristocracy were two-day-old nobles (*nobles de deux jours*), gentlemen who had arrived a few centuries too late."[30] As Brizard emphasised in another note in the same edition, this sort of parody of real distinction was relatively recent in origin. "Bodin," he wrote in a comment on Rousseau's *Social Contract*, referring to what the sixteenth-century jurist Jean Bodin had written about citizenship, "was writing in an age when the rights of the people and the value of liberty were still known in France, and when the name 'citizen' had not yet become an empty word."[31] Oddly, but rather aptly, Brizard (who was an avid collector of Rousseau relics, as well as an equally strong admirer of the moral and political thought of the abbé Gabriel Bonnot de Mably) was employed in the office of the royal genealogist, Gabriel Chérin, the man responsible for vetting the noble titles on which eligibility for military promotion had come to be based. Brizard went on to become a strong Jacobin supporter. So, equally aptly, did Chérin's own son.[32]

---

[29] Thomas Vernier, *Éléments de finances* (Paris, 1789), p. 83. For a further example, coupled with a call to establish "une armée nationale," see the loosely Bolingbroke-inspired pamphlet by Toussaint Guiraudet, *Qu'est-ce que la nation et qu'est-ce que la France?* (n.p., 1789), pp. 27–32. See also the attack on the Ségur ordinance in Jacques-Henri Bernardin de Saint-Pierre, *Voeux d'un solitaire* (Paris, 1793), p. 23; and, on the broader subject of army reform, [Jean-André Perreau], *Le bon politique, ou le sage à la cour* (London, 1789), pp. 82–90 (Perreau was a Physiocrat and a protégé of the marquis de Mirabeau; the work itself was a reprint of his earlier, Fénelonian, *Misrim, ou le sage à la cour*). For a parallel discussion of the technology of fortification, and its bearing on a more merit-based political system, see *Première collection de pétitions, d'écrits et de mémoires présentés à la nation française et à ses représentants aux états-généraux* (Paris, 1789).

[30] Jean-Jacques Rousseau, *Oeuvres complètes*, ed. Louis-Sébastien Mercier, Gabriel Brizard, Louis Le Tourneur, 38 vols. (Paris, 1788–93), 8 (Paris, 1790): 20, note (initialled by Brizard).

[31] Rousseau, *Oeuvres complètes*, 8 (Paris, 1790): 31, note (initialled by Brizard).

[32] Blaufarb, *The French Army*, pp. 1–2. For further information on both Brizard and Chérin, see Jean-Jacques Rousseau, *Correspondance complète*, ed. R. A. Leigh, 52 vols. (Oxford, Voltaire Foundation, 1967–98), 32:290–1, 45:163–225, 52:44, 61; and Bibliothèque de l'Arsenal, Mss. 6101, and 6103.

A more wide-ranging example of the same, mainly moral set of terms in which the outcry was couched can be found in a pamphlet entitled *L'écho de l'Elisée, ou dialogues de quelques morts célèbres sur les états-généraux de la nation et des provinces*, or *An Echo from Elysium*, that was published in October 1788. Its author, a man named Antoine Dingé, was one of the small circle associated with Bernardin de Saint-Pierre, and librarian of the prince de Condé. As its subtitle indicated, the pamphlet was an imaginary conversation among several famous dead men over the forthcoming meeting of the French estates-general. Its protagonists were Lewis Clary, viscount Falkland, secretary of state of England's King Charles I at the beginning of the English Civil War; John Hampden, the leader of the English parliamentary party in 1641; Louis the Fat, the twelfth-century French king, and his later successor, Louis XII; as well as two figures from the eighteenth century, René-Louis de Voyer de Paulmy, marquis d'Argenson, minister of foreign affairs during the period of the War of the Austrian Succession, and Valentin Jaméry-Duval, the self-taught peasant's son who became a distinguished historian, as well as librarian of the duke of Lorraine and keeper of the imperial medal collection in Vienna. The point of the pamphlet was to highlight the need to establish an alternative to the rival positions represented by the twin aristocracies of the royal court on the one side and the magistrates of the French parlements on the other. Both embodied privilege, making neither compatible with justice. This, as this conversation was intended to show, meant reconstituting the estates-general to include proper representation of the peasants, as the Swedish constitution provided. It also meant reconstituting the ministry and every other public office to make it easier for careers to be open to talent. As the d'Argenson character put it, the nobility had taken hold of everything, including, as illustrated by the Ségur ordinance of 1781, the army, as well as the church, the embassies, and the most lucrative royal services, so that there was now no hope that the magistracy would include a distinguished commoner like Michel de l'Hôpital, the sixteenth-century French chancellor, or that the episcopacy would have a Fléchier, the navy a Duguay-Trouin, or the army a Chevert. Bringing merit and distinction back to their proper, complementary relationship meant, above all, breaking the hold of money and inheritance over French public life. Calling the people the Third Estate, the pamphlet concluded, quoting a passage from Rousseau's *Social Contract*, amounted to relegating the public interest to no more than the third rank. Inversely, calling some land "noble land" was a moral affront, unless, the pamphlet noted, this time quoting Louis-Sébastien Mercier, it meant that the land in question was ploughed by noble horses, furrowed by a noble plough, and fertilised by noble manure. The pamphlet ended by quoting a fable, published by the abbé Jean-Louis Aubert earlier in the eighteenth century, called "The Eagle and the

Assembly of the Birds," whose point was to show why the eagle was right to force the peacocks to pay their share, as the sparrows did.[33]

CONSTITUTIONAL GOVERNMENT, TAXATION, AND EQUALITY

Getting the peacocks to pay raised a number of political dilemmas. These, in turn, helped to rule out the old vision of a powerful reforming monarch as the solution to absolute government's financial problems. The political history of the French Revolution began with the unavailability of this alternative. Irrespective of the damage done by the argument over military reform to any plausible prospect of relying on Louis XVI to be a patriot king, the model itself pulled strongly against both the realities of modern war finance and the more urgent political need to consolidate, not abolish, the royal debt. Once, in October 1787, there were real fears that the government would opt for a bankruptcy. By August 1788, when the government suspended interest payments on its outstanding debt, but after it had already announced its decision to summon an assembly of the estates-general, those fears shifted towards the future and the possibility that the estates-general themselves might be persuaded to sanction a royal debt default. Some pamphlets did recommend this course of action, but a broad consensus, including Sieyès's privately circulated *Views on the Executive Means Available to the Representatives of France in 1789*, came out strongly against any type of voluntary state bankruptcy. As Sieyès argued at length, the deficit had to be used as a political lever to impose a system of constitutional government on its absolute counterpart.[34] Although a patriotic political coup might look like the high road to justice and equality (which was the message of Aubert's fable), it could also look far more like the beginning of the eighteenth-century's widely predicted slide into despotism.[35] Scything through the tangle of office and privilege might

[33] [Antoine Dingé], *L'écho de l'Elysée, ou dialogues de quelques morts célèbres sur les etats-généraux de la nation et des provinces* (n.p., October 1788), pp. 29–36, 54–5, 103–7.

[34] See Emmanuel-Joseph Sieyès, *Political Writings*, ed. Michael Sonenscher (Indianapolis: Hackett, 2003), pp. 21–3, 29, 45–8, 56–8, 111–2; and, on the broader political and intellectual context militating against a patriotic royal coup, Sonenscher, *Before the Deluge*, pp. 22–67.

[35] On these predictions, see Sonenscher, *Before the Deluge*, pp. 1–9, 23–32. The same argument in favour of a programme of patriotic royal reform can be found in [François-Antoine-Etienne de Gourcy], *Des droits et des devoirs du citoyen dans les circonstances présentes, avec un jugement impartial sur l'ouvrage de M. l'abbé Mably* (n.p., 1789), an attack, as its title indicates, on Mably's *Des droits et des devoirs du citoyen*: "N'est-ce donc pas aux talents éminents, aux vertus sublimes qu'appartiennent les premières places et les honneurs les plus distingués? L'auteur de la nature, aussi indépendant que magnifique dans ses dons, ne les a point circonscrits dans le cercle étroit qu'ont tracé la vanité et la politique" (pp. 25–6).

bring merit and justice into closer alignment, but eliminating undeserved inequality would also reinforce royal power just when the problem of the French royal deficit appeared to call for less drastic action. In this context, acting as a patriot king could well tap absolute government's unique capacity for unilateral action, but the prospect that it appeared to offer was less a bright new dawn than a menacing nightmare.

But if the ambiguities in the model itself ruled out a patriotic royal coup (or helped to push it back until it really was too late), the constitutional alternatives to absolute government were no more clear-cut. Opting for a British- or American-style mixed or balanced system of government not only required a strong initial assertion of the nation's sovereignty, but also required an equally strong measure of patriotic self-sacrifice by the nobility, the clergy, and the commoners to enable their future analogues in any newly constituted system of government to establish their political legitimacy. In itself, the sequence from national unity to national self-differentiation was quite demanding. Under the conditions created by the royal deficit, it increased the need for patriotic self-sacrifice still further. Bridging the financial gap appeared, at least in the first instance, to call for more tax revenue. But, however they were distributed, higher taxes could easily give rise to higher prices, particularly if the bulk of the additional tax burden was to fall on the owners of landed property. Since the demand for cereals was constant and inelastic, higher taxes could simply be passed on as higher grain prices, leading, in the longer term, to more, rather than less, inequality.[36] Blocking that outcome required either more patriotism or what, a generation earlier, the French Physiocrats had called a legal despot. But the arguments that applied to the model of the patriot king applied even more forcefully here. Physiocracy was simply not intended to be compatible with a national debt. This left an initial broad consensus in favour of a constitutional alternative that could be compatible both with modern public finance and with the broader range of concerns about justice, equality, merit, and distinction that the content of the debate about military reform had helped to bring out into the open.[37] The difficulty, however, was to find a way to combine the two. Opting for a British-style alternative ran the risk of increasing, not reducing, inequality. Opting for something new was a leap into the unknown.

These uncertainties go some way towards explaining the failure of the two most prominent alternatives to absolute government discussed by

[36] On cereal production and price movements in eighteenth-century France, see the still apposite remarks in David S. Landes, "The Statistical Study of French Crises," *Journal of Economic History* 10 (1951): 195–211.

[37] See Kenneth Margerison, *Pamphlets and Public Opinion: The Campaign for a Union of Orders in the Early French Revolution* (West Lafayette, Purdue UP, 1998), pp. 46, 49.

the National Assembly between July and December 1789. The two
alternatives—the first associated with a lawyer from Grenoble named Jean-
Joseph Mounier, and the second with the more famous political pam-
phleteer Emmanuel-Joseph Sieyès—were discussed in parallel but can be
presented more easily in sequence.[38] Both alternatives were the product of
critical assessments of Montesquieu's concept of monarchy, but the first
placed rather more weight on patriotic self-sacrifice as the way to make
representative government work, while the second relied more heavily on
the idea of representation itself as the way to avoid having to depend too
strongly on patriotism. To their critics, however, both sets of constitutional proposals appeared to make too many concessions to inequality. For
Mounier, to begin with, creating a system of constitutional government,
particularly the type of British-style mixed or balanced system of government that he himself had in mind, called for a high initial level of political
agreement, and, in the context of the meeting of the French estates-
general in 1789, a willingness to turn its three separate orders into a single
deliberative body to secure a broadly acceptable constitutional outcome.
Maintaining this type of constitutional government, on the other hand,
called for a correspondingly high level of willingness to accept the different degrees of status and power that made mixed or balanced government
work, with a multiple legislature, a royal veto, and a clearly specified separation of legislative, executive, and judicial powers. The process thus required a two-step sequence. The nation first had to assert its determination
to establish a constitution, but then had to accept the separation of powers
and the different types of political, legal, or administrative distinction that
constitutional government would bring in its wake.[39] As Mounier recognised, switching from the first to the second step was unlikely to be easy,
because the broad political consensus required for creating a constitution

[38] On Mounier, see Jean Egret, *La révolution des notables. Mounier et les Monarchiens* (Paris,
Armand Colin, 1950); Robert Griffiths, *Le centre perdu. Malouet et les 'monarchiens' dans la
révolution française* (Grenoble, Presses universitaires de Grenoble, 1988); François Furet
and Mona Ozouf, eds., *Terminer la révolution. Mounier et Barnave dans la révolution française*
(Grenoble, Presses Universitaires de Grenoble, 1990). On the large literature on Sieyès, see
the bibliography in Sieyès, *Political Writings,*, pp. 181–2.

[39] Jean-Joseph Mounier, *Nouvelles observations sur les états-généraux de France* (n.p., 1789),
pp. 246–7. See also the passage in his later *Considérations sur les gouvernements, et principalement sur celui qui convient à la France* (Versailles, 1789), p. 40: "Personne n' a été plus
convaincu que moi de la nécessité de délibérer par tête et en un seul corps, dans les Etats-
Généraux de 1789. Pour donner une constitution à un peuple, il faut nécessairement adopter
des moyens qui triomphent de tous les obstacles et qui facilitent la destruction des abus.
Mais j'ai pensé, et je pense encore, que les mêmes moyens mis en usage après la constitution
la rendraient incertaine, favoriseraient les changements, ne permettraient jamais une bonne
législation, et auraient une force irrésistible qui pourrait entrainer la France dans les plus
grands malheurs."

could easily become an obstacle to establishing the more highly differentiated array of legislative, executive, legal, or administrative institutions required for constitutional and political stability. This, he argued, was why patriotism was vital for the transition to go smoothly.

The need for patriotism was also, Mounier argued, the reason why Montesquieu's concept of monarchy was utterly inappropriate to the task at hand. "What, above all," he wrote in 1789, "makes this author so dangerous is that he has not been understood. His distinction between monarchy and despotism is absolutely chimerical. Montesquieu's monarchy is not one tempered by laws. It is a real despotism that is quite willing to observe formalities (*formes*) and usages when its interest does not call for violence, but will scorn them with impunity whenever it wishes." It was "a detestable government," whose "intermediary bodies, separate ecclesiastical jurisdiction, luxury, venal offices, and proliferating laws" served simply to sustain that "false honour" that Montesquieu himself had singled out as the underlying principle of the morally tainted political system that he had called monarchy. Those, Mounier concluded, who "despise false honour, who love your country, who respect truth and frankness, who feel able to sacrifice your dearest interests to the public good, and who have no wish to be counted as a courtier, nor crawl beneath them, ought to abhor Montesquieu's monarchy, and ought never to cite his odious principles."[40] True monarchy, for Mounier, was something more like the system of government that had been established in Britain and whose real nature had been described by one of Montesquieu's most forceful critics, the Genevan political exile Jean-Louis Delolme. As Delolme had shown in his *Constitution of England* of 1775, the modern British monarchy owed nothing to the famous German woods that Montesquieu had associated with Europe's post-Roman system of rule. It was, instead, the product of conquest, and of the protracted resistance by both lords and commons to the unitary system of despotic power that England's Norman invaders had established. For all its initial brutality, however, the Norman conquest had also had benefits that were still unavailable in the rest of Europe. Conquest had produced a unitary sovereign state, with a single legislative capacity. Time, and political conflict, had since given it the constitutional structure that it had come to acquire, and it was this postfeudal model of limited government that was now available for adoption in France. For Mounier, France in 1789 had a chance to make a peaceful transition to a system of government that it had taken generations of "blood," "tears," and "the furies of civil wars" to establish in Britain.[41]

[40] Mounier, *Nouvelles observations*, pp. 211, 214–5, 216, 217–8.
[41] Mounier, *Nouvelles observations*, p. 250. For Mounier's reliance on what, in that work, he called Delolme's "ouvrage profond" (p. 26), see also his *Considérations sur les gouvernements,*

As Mounier emphasised, patriotism was simply the name for those actions and achievements that gave rise to merit and distinction on a coun-
trywide scale. Nor, he also emphasised, was wealth itself an obstacle to
acquiring this kind of recognition. Modernity's misfortune was, rather,
the way that the European mainland's history of feudal government and
its absolute successor had led to the formation of clusters of both central
and local power that, in turn, had allowed inherited advantage, personal
connection, and local privilege to override personal merit and real distinction. As Delolme's examination of the English constitution showed,
the peculiarities of English history had allowed Britain to escape from
this mixture of privileged institutions, separate orders, and ancient local
entitlements, with their continuing capacity to fracture the unity of the
European monarchies. In Britain, the purely political character of the
peerage, the uniform nature of British legislation, and the ties of kinship
that ran from the peerage to the gentry and commoners, ruled out the
self-contained pockets of wealth, privilege, and power that prevailed elsewhere in Europe. In this sense, modern Britain, despite its often corrupt
politics, was a genuine example of the principles of public service and real
merit that, for Mounier, could also be found in the two basic components
of the system of rule that France had initially inherited from its German
and Roman pasts, but which had then disappeared under Gothic and absolute rule.

The first of these two components, Mounier wrote, rehearsing the standard passage from Tacitus's *Germania* (*de minoribus principes consultant, de
majoribus omnes*) to make the point, were the "general assemblies" that,
like the modern North American Indians, the assorted Frankish "barbarians" had held from time to time to deliberate on important affairs.[42] The
second comprised the distinctions and dignities of imperial Rome. According to Mounier, the idea that the French nobility had its origins in the
distinctions established by the Germanic "barbarians" after their invasion
of Roman Gaul was an idea whose "falsehood is now well-established."
"The conquest of China by the Tartars," he wrote, "simply retraced the

pp. 17, 29, 34–5, 46, and his *Réflexions politiques sur les circonstances présentes* (Geneva, 1790),
p. 64. According to a letter from Huet de Foberville, secretary of the Academy of Orléans,
published in the *Chronique de Paris*, no. 19 (11 September 1789), Mounier's constitutional
theory was "un plagiat, presque à la lettre" of Delolme. For helpful guidance both to Delolme's political thought and to the wider range of eighteenth-century constitutional theories,
see David Wootton, "Liberty, Metaphor, and Mechanism: '*Checks and Balances' and the Origins of Modern Constitutionalism*," in David Womersley, ed., *Liberty and American Experience in
the Eighteenth Century* (Indianapolis, Liberty Fund, 2006), pp. 209–74.

[42] Mounier, *Nouvelles observations*, p. 7. The passage from Tacitus is usually translated as
"on minor affairs, they consulted the principal members of the community, and on major
affairs, they consulted everyone."

revolution that occurred in Europe after the barbarian invasions." As in China, Gaul's Germanic conquerors "were tamed by the arts, the religion, and the luxury of the conquered country." They were captivated by "the honour of being clad in Roman dignities, and several of their princes gloried in being the officials, tributaries, or servants of the emperors of Constantinople." One reason, Mounier added, why these distinctions appealed so readily to the invading Germanic peoples was that they already had a rudimentary nobility of their own. Here, too, a well-known passage from Tacitus's *Germania* (*reges ex nobilitate, duces ex virtute fumunt*) supported the claim.[43] Like the Tartars, Mounier argued, the Germanic peoples had simply adapted their own more primitive social hierarchy to an already-established set of distinctions that had emerged much earlier in Rome, when, as he put it, "the patricians and plebeians no longer formed two distinct classes and when possession of public office became open indiscriminately to all indigenous citizens." Then, he wrote, the words *nobilis* and *gentilis* came to be used to refer, in the case of the first, to families who had produced illustrious individuals, and, in the case of the second, to families whose origins were free, as against those who were simply the descendants of emancipated slaves. "A noble family," he explained, "was a distinguished, or remarkable, family," while a *gentilis*, or gentleman, "was a man who had a *race*," because, unlike the descendant of an emancipated slave, he had a real lineage, while "slaves had no family since they usually knew no more than their mothers and were owned by her master." The two types of distinction were, Mounier wrote, largely personal. Although they did entail exemption from some forms of punishment, they did not carry any right to public office or any legal entitlement to influence public affairs. The "illustration" (meaning "distinction") that accompanied nobility, he emphasised, "had no other foundation and no other proof than opinion, so that this type of nobility was more likely to favour than to obstruct emulation."[44] This old, but potentially new, form of distinction was, Mounier argued, now a political possibility in France.

Sieyès may, or may not, have been a major political theorist, at least as the term has been applied to some of his German or British contemporaries.[45] But his unusually acute sense of the political possibilities and

[43] Mounier, *Nouvelles observations*, p. 16. The passage is usually translated as "they chose their kings from distinguished families and consulted virtue alone in choosing their other leaders."

[44] Mounier, *Nouvelles observations*, pp. 12, 14–15.

[45] In this and the following two paragraphs, I have summarised the longer description of Sieyès's thought in Sonenscher, *Before the Deluge*, pp. 10–18, 67–94. It may also be worth pointing out that, as noted by the future *doctrinaire* Pierre-Claude-François Daunou in his *Vues rapides sur l'organisation de la république française* (Paris, 1793), p. 12, Sieyès's idea of a representative system could encompass full political rights for women.

constraints supplied by the emergence, during the eighteenth century, of the peculiarly modern combination of sovereign states, permanent military establishments, and public debts entailed a different type of move away from Montesquieu. Instead of the stress on patriotic self-sacrifice that was so marked a feature of the constitutional arrangements advocated by Mounier and his political allies, Sieyès's alternative to absolute government relied more heavily on the mechanisms of representation. In this sense, instead of simply turning away from Montesquieu, it involved turning Montesquieu's own idea of representation to radically different ends. In some respects, the idea of representation in question chimed very readily with the emphasis on service and merit that had been highlighted by the opposition to military reform. Instead of direct elections to a new national legislature, this system of "graduated promotion," as Sieyès's political allies called it, consisted of a step-by-step process of election, beginning at the bottom, and continuing up a hierarchy of elected offices all the way, in some cases, to the very top. In this sense, it was rather like promotion in the army, but with the addition of an electoral mechanism. The real aim of the new system, however, was to try to avoid the political dangers built into the nation's seizure of sovereign power. That, Sieyès acknowledged, had been unavoidable and, by the summer of 1789, had become highly desirable (although he had, in 1788, initially advocated a royally sponsored election of something like an American-style constitutional convention to give France a system of representative government by purely legal means). But the difficulties involved in making the same assembly responsible for exercising the nation's constituting power on the one hand, and for dealing with events as they arose on the other, was bound to create a tension between the high level of agreement required for the first task, and the real differences of interests and opinions that events might produce.

From this point of view, the rather precarious mixture of sovereignty and government that was now in the hands of the National Assembly (but also still, in some measure, in those of the royal ministry) meant that the most urgent political requirement was to prevent divisions and conflicts within the assembly, or between the assembly and the ministry, from wrecking the opportunity to establish a new system of representative government. These were most likely to arise, Sieyès seems to have thought, from a misapplication of the spirit of patriotism to the problem of the deficit. He took no part in the famous night of 4 August 1789 that culminated in the abolition of feudalism. He also publicly opposed the National Assembly's decision to abolish the clerical tithe and, following Talleyrand's proposal on 14 October 1789, its decision to nationalise church property on 2 November 1789. Although his critics took this to be a sign of clerical self-interest, and posterity has sometimes taken it to reveal the conceptual limits of the rhetoric of bourgeois revolution, Sieyès's own concerns were focused more fully on the difficulties involved in establishing a strong fiscal system, both to restore and maintain financial stability under probable future conditions of war and debt, and, in the longer term, to rebalance the distribution of property away from its bias towards landownership.[46] The strong patriotic drive to reinforce national unity by abolishing feudal rights and privileges, as well as by bringing the church and its property under the nation's ownership, amounted, he argued, not only to giving the landowners a tax-free windfall (with the abolition of the tithe), but also to magnifying the problems of funding the deficit (by turning church expenditure into national expenditure).[47] Uniting the nation in this way was, in this sense, radically self-defeating. It added to public spending, while reducing public income, stripping future governments of the leverage that they might need to maintain security abroad and justice at home. The real source of national unity, Sieyès argued, had to be a strong fiscal state, equipped with all the authority that only a legitimate system of representative government was able to supply.

The alternative that Sieyès envisaged involved placing less stress on the spirit of patriotism. The first step was to divide the kingdom into a new set of administrative and electoral units. The second was to use these as the basis of a new system of political representation that would be built up gradually, beginning from the bottom. Elections to municipal office (based on a smaller number of cantonal municipalities than the actually existing forty-four thousand municipal units) would not only supply an initial cadre of local representatives but would also form a second political electorate. It would elect representatives to departmental administrations, and they, in turn, would form the electorate from which the membership of the new national legislature would be drawn. Elections would be staggered, with a third of the national legislature leaving office at two-yearly intervals. All the members of every legislature would, therefore, have been subjected to three sets of elections and two periods of trial in office before they took their seats. They would be well known, with established reputations, and this, in turn, would give them the legitimacy and authority required to make a fiscal state work. Political decision making would also be based on a functional, rather than a British- or American-style, separation of powers, with separate branches of the legislature responsible for initiating, discussing, and approving future laws, and separate branches of the executive forming a collectively responsible ministry, appointed by an individually irresponsible, purely symbolic, head of state. Sieyès toyed with many variations on these themes, including the further

[46] On Sieyès as a prisoner of bourgeois ideology, see William H. Sewell, *A Rhetoric of Bourgeois Revolution: The Abbé Sieyès and "What Is the Third Estate?"* (Durham, Duke UP, 1994).
[47] Emmanuel-Joseph Sieyès, *Observations sommaires sur les biens ecclésiastiques* (Paris, 1789), p. 1.

idea that this system of political representation would produce a new, nonpolitical moral elite, or what, some years later, was to become the original version of the French Legion of Honour, with the same idea of graduated promotion, rather than nomination from above, as its informing principle. But despite (or perhaps because of) the strong support that Sieyès's proposed electoral mechanism received from the dominant figure in the National Assembly, the comte de Mirabeau, as well as the parallel that its supporters drew between this system of graduated promotion and Rousseau's idea of an "elective aristocracy," Sieyès's alternative to absolute government never got off the ground. To its critics, the long period of time that would elapse before a new national legislature came into being, coupled with the extended sequence of steps required to rise from municipal to national office, and the likelihood that these could all be taken only by those endowed with substantial financial resources, added up to what, from their point of view, looked less like an "elective aristocracy" than like a self-sustaining oligarchy. As Sieyès recalled with some bitterness nearly ten years later, Antoine-Joseph Barnave, one of the leading figures in both the National Assembly and the recently established Jacobin club, warned in a speech on 10 December 1789 that if the system of gradual election were put into effect, the revolution would last for ten more years. Barnave's political ally, the former magistrate in the Paris parlement Adrien Duport, was equally scathing in March 1790 about Sieyès's proposals for a new, more specialised, legal system ("they are the greatest proof," he told the National Assembly, "that those who conceived of them have no acquaintance with, or even knowledge of, the subject").[48] For both Barnave and Duport, political legitimacy and legal authority required something else.

---

[48] For discussion of the idea of gradual promotion, and Barnave's hostility towards it, see *Courier de Provence* 72 (9–10 December 1789): 10–26, and Sonenscher, *Before the Deluge*, pp. 15, 76–7, 83, 237, 266, 279, 314–7, 319, 334. On Sieyès's recollection of Barnave's warning, see [Anon.], *Exposé historique des écrits de Sieyès* (n.p., an VIII/1799), p. 40, note 10. I am grateful to Pierre-Yves Quiviger for passing on an electronic version of the text (which was probably written by Sieyès's admirer Konrad Engelbert Oelsner). The claim is a slightly distorted recollection of Barnave's statement that he could not conceive of how, in light of Mirabeau's proposal to establish a system of gradual promotion, "on peut proposer une loi qui ne pourra être exécuté que dans dix ans": *Archives parlementaires*, ed. M. J. Mavidal, E. Laurent, and E. Clavel, 82 vols. (Paris, 1872–1913), 10 (10 December 1789): 497. For Duport's assessment of Sieyès's planned legal reforms, see *Archives parlementaires* 12 (29 March 1790): 434. According to Joseph Lanjuinais, one of Duport's critics, adopting an English-style jury system, as Duport recommended, would bring along with it English-style legal chicanery. Lanjuinais spoke in favour of Sieyès's proposals, commending them as the work of "un homme auquel vous ne refusez pas le titre de penseur philosophique profond": *Archives parlementaires* 12 (31 March 1790): 487. For Sieyès's reply, with support from another Breton deputy, Isaac Le Chapelier, see *Archives parlementaires* 12 (8 April 1790): 582–4.

POLITICAL LIBERTY, PUBLIC FINANCE, AND PUBLIC WORSHIP

This hostility towards Sieyès's political proposals was a product of a rather different conception of France's future. In historiographical terms, the politics of the group of individuals (headed by Barnave, Duport, and the Lameth brothers) who, after the summer of 1791, came to be known as the Feuillants have been somewhat overshadowed by those of their better-known contemporaries Sieyès, Condorcet, Brissot, and Robespierre.[49] But, by late 1790, they had come to be associated with a body of policies and opinions that, retrospectively, helped to make them look like the most consistent advocates of almost all the measures taken by the French National Assembly to bring the old regime to an end. They played a major part in igniting the debate of the night of 4 August 1789 that culminated in the proclamation abolishing feudalism in France. They strongly opposed giving the king a royal veto in subsequent discussion of the new French constitution, but strongly supported the nationalisation of the property of the French church on 2 November 1789, as well as the suspension of the thirteen French parlements a day later.[50] They promoted the National Assembly's decision on 21 December 1789 to issue government bonds, or *assignats*, as the means to buy nationalised church property, and then, on 29 September 1790, to turn the *assignat* into a circulating paper currency.[51] They argued in favour of transferring the right to declare war and peace from the king to the legislature and, as a corollary, supported the new, militia-based system of national defence initially established alongside the still nominally royal army. In addition to the potential savings produced by reducing the size of the standing army, the new National Guard appeared to offer a solution to the questions of merit and distinction raised by the bitter conflict over army reform and, at the same time, to supply a real institutional mechanism for local involvement in the public life of the reformed monarchy. Finally, in a departure from the order of subjects listed for debate on 19 June 1790, and in a clearly coordinated set of speeches, they bounced the National Assembly into abolishing all noble titles.[52] The

---

[49] For an overview, see Furet and Ozouf (eds.), *Terminer la révolution* (above note 38).

[50] During the debate on the royal veto in September 1789, Barnave insisted that no decision should be taken on giving the king even a suspensive veto until Louis XVI had given his assent to the abolition of feudalism on 4 August 1789: see *Courier de Provence* 41 (11–14 September 1789): 23.

[51] On the *assignat*, see, particularly, François Crouzet, *La grande inflation. La monnaie en France de Louis XVI à Napoléon* (Paris, Fayard, 1993), and Ferenc Feher, *The Frozen Revolution: An Essay on Jacobinism* (Cambridge, CUP, 1987), pp. 30–48.

[52] On the future Feuillants' role in preparing the events of the night of 4 August 1789, see Georges Michon, *Essai sur l'histoire du parti feuillant. Adrien Duport* (Paris, 1924), pp. 59–61;

measure effectively confirmed the fact that, as the assembly's committee on feudal rights put it in February 1790 in its official report on the situation created by their abolition, "the lords (*seigneurs*) have descended to the rank of simple creditors."[53] Henceforth, there was simply property and all the attendant transactions involved in a property-based society.

It may, perhaps, seem surprising to find policies like these described as "republican." But this, certainly, was how they were described by a writer named Joseph Fauchet (later one of the first French republic's diplomats in the United States) in a pamphlet published towards the end of 1790. There, Fauchet presented those whom he called "the eloquent Barnave," "the courageous and unshakeable Lameth," and the "patriot d'Aiguillon," along with those "austere Romans, Menou, Robespierre, Biauzat, Camus, and Dubois de Crancé," as "incorruptible friends of the people" whose "love of true liberty" matched his own republican political views.[54] Robespierre's friend Camille Desmoulins made an amalgamation of the same type. "Live," he wrote in September 1790, "in ways that are above suspicion, like Phocion, Cato, Barnave, Lameth, Pétion, and Robespierre" (Duport, perhaps because of his prerevolutionary status as a magistrate in the parlement of Paris, or his earlier friendship with Sieyès, never seems to have been given the same treatment).[55] In the light of subsequent political divisions, the lists now look somewhat incongruous. But they are no more incongruous than the poet Michel de Cubières-Palmézeaux's decision in the summer of 1791 (taken, he wrote, in the light of his friend Jean-Baptiste Cloots's decision to call himself "Anacharsis" Cloots) to rename some of the leading political figures of the day as "Tullius" Bailly, "Scipio" Lafayette,

and, on the abolition of noble titles, see most helpfully, Blaufarb, *The French Army*, pp. 62–3; Timothy Tackett, *Becoming a Revolutionary: The Deputies of the French National Assembly and the Emergence of a Revolutionary Culture* (Princeton, Princeton UP, 1996), pp. 292–6; and William Doyle, "The French Revolution and the Abolition of Nobility," in Hamish Scott and Brendan Simms, eds., *Cultures of Power in Europe during the Long Eighteenth Century* (Cambridge, CUP, 2007), pp. 289–303.

[53] On the report, see Philippe-Antoine Merlin de Douai, *Rapport fait à l'assemblée nationale au nom du comité de féodalité, le 8 février 1790* (Paris, 1790), p. 7, and, more generally, James Q. Whitman, "The Seigneurs Descend to the Rank of Creditors: The Abolition of Respect," *Yale Journal of Law and Humanities* 6 (1994): 249–83.

[54] [Joseph Fauchet], *Le despotisme décrété par l'assemblée nationale* (London, 1790), pp. 60–1. On Menou, see below, p. 331. On the part played by these individuals in the early leadership of the Jacobin club, see Tackett, *Becoming a Revolutionary*, pp. 252–3.

[55] Camille Desmoulins, "Eloge de M. Loustallot" [September 1790], reprinted in Alphonse Aulard, *La société des Jacobins. Recueil de documents pour l'histoire du club des Jacobins de Paris*, 6 vols. (Paris, 1889–97), 1:294. Desmoulins had not changed his evaluations even by late May 1791, when he was involved in a public argument with Brissot over what, he claimed, was Brissot's unwarranted hostility towards Barnave and Charles Lameth, and his excessive sympathy towards Mirabeau and La Fayette: see *Patriote français*, issues 656, 657, 659 (26, 27, and 29 May 1791).

"Plato" Sieyès, "Brutus" Robespierre, and, memorably, "Fénelon" Talleyrand. As Cubières-Palmézeaux also noted, several of the individuals on whom he chose to bestow these names were his personal acquaintances because, well before 1789, some of them had frequented the salon kept by his patron, Marie-Anne-Françoise, or Fanny, de Beauharnais.[56] There, he wrote, it had been possible to meet not only Jean-Sylvain Bailly, Jean-Paul Rabaut Saint-Etienne, François-Antoine Boissy d'Anglas, and Pierre-Paul Gudin de la Brenellerie, but also Gabriel Brizard, Louis-Sébastien Mercier, Jean Dusaulx, and Nicolas-Anne-Edme Restif de la Bretonne, as well as the now self-styled "orator of the human race" Anacharsis Cloots.[57]

There is no reason to think that there were not real intellectual differences among these individuals, but there is also no reason to think that they were matched by any correspondingly strong political divisions. Rabaut Saint-Etienne was rather more committed than Bailly had become to Court de Gebelin's idea of an agriculturally generated natural religion (Rabaut's friend Constantin-François Volney was later to use much of the argument of Rabaut's *Letters to Bailly* as the basis of his own examination of religion in his *Ruins of Empire* of 1791).[58] Brizard and Mercier (as well as the translator of Edward Young's *Night Thoughts*, Louis Le Tourneur) collaborated on a sympathetic edition of Rousseau's collected works, while Cloots, after his pilgrimage with Brizard to Rousseau's tomb at Ermenonville in the summer of 1783, became one of Rousseau's more outspoken critics. "His political works," he wrote in 1791, "are inexhaustible sources of aristocracy and anarchy. Were anyone with a sound mind to read the *Social Contract* and the treatise on Poland with any attention, they would

[56] On Fanny de Beauharnais, see F. K. Turgeon, "Fanny de Beauharnais: Biographical Notes and a Bibliography," *Modern Philology* 30 (1932): 61–80, and his unpublished Ph.D. dissertation, "Fanny de Beauharnais" (Harvard, 1931).

[57] Michel de Cubières-Palmézeaux, *Les états-généraux du Parnasse, de l'Europe, de l'église, et de Cythère, ou les quatre poèmes politiques* (Paris, 1791), pp. 13, 16. For corroboration of Cloots's friendship with Rabaut Saint-Etienne, see the latter's "Réflexions politiques sur les circonstances présentes," in Jean-Paul Rabaut Saint-Etienne, *Précis de l'histoire de la révolution française*, ed. François-Antoine Boissy d'Anglas (Paris, 1827), p. 333. Cloots may have stood out for his hyperbole, but his moral and political thought can be aligned readily with Rabaut Saint-Etienne's *Lettres à M Bailly sur l'histoire primitive de la Grèce* (described above, pp. 256–60). See, too, Christine Le Bozec, *Boissy d'Anglas. Un grand notable libéral* (Privas, Fédération des Oeuvres Laïques de l'Ardèche, 1995), pp. 100–7.

[58] Constantin-François Volney, *Les ruines* [1791], in Volney, *Oeuvres*, 3 vols. (Paris, Fayard, 1989–98), 1:315–23. Interestingly, despite his copious notes, Volney did not refer to Rabaut's book, possibly because of its author's controversial political reputation after the conflicts between Catholics and Protestants in Nîmes in 1790, and the civil constitution of the French clergy of the same year. For a contemporary indication of the two works' common provenance in the ideas of Charles-François Dupuis, see the passage from Pierre-Jean-Baptiste (Publicola) Chaussard, *Fêtes et courtisanes de la Grèce*, 4 vols. (Paris, 1801), 1:32, cited above, p. 257, note 144.

no longer be surprised to see so many priests, so many nobles, as well as the members of the late 1789 club and other assorted round- or flat-heads come out so warmly for him."[59] But, before 1791, these differences remained largely intellectual or personal, and do not seem to have interfered with the assemblies presided over by Fanny de Beauharnais. "Your little blue and silver salon," wrote Cubières-Palmézeaux, looking back from the late summer of that year, was "the National Assembly's egg."[60]

From Cubières-Palmézeaux's point of view, the new regime now emerging from that egg would still be based on what he called "Aristotle's systems," since, he wrote, it was Aristotle who "had studied the advantages and disadvantages of popular government most closely," and who had been the first to produce "the plan of those composite governments that, up to now, only the English have been able to revive and put into practice."[61] But this rather vague gesture still pointed towards a rather different version of British-style "composite government" from the one advocated by Mounier and the Monarchiens. In one sense, it did place more stress on Aristotle's idea of the "middle classes" as the broad ballast of political society than was apparent in Mounier's more meritocratic constitutional proposals. But, in another sense, it also relied heavily on the distinctly un-Aristotelian idea of the politically stabilising effects of public debt. This type of claim about public credit as a source of political stability paralleled the types of argument about the compatibility between public credit and social justice made by the assortment of writers referred to in Aubert de Vitry's pamphlet *J. J. Rousseau à l'assemblée nationale*. It also threw a different light on the nature of the so-called English system of government from those to be found in either Montesquieu or Delolme. It was first made in a British context, initially in the late seventeenth century, and then during the wars of the mid-eighteenth century, often in reply to some of the more lurid predictions of impending British ruin made both by patriotic political moralists like "Estimate" Brown and by supporters of the popular English politician John Wilkes. Here, the version of the argument that came to have the most direct bearing on subsequent claims about postrevolutionary France's political future first appeared in an anonymous

---

[59] Anacharsis Cloots, *L'Orateur du genre humain, ou dépêche du Prussien Cloots au Prussien Herzberg* (Paris, 1791), reprinted in Anacharsis Cloots, *Oeuvres*, ed. Albert Soboul, 3 vols. (Munich, 1980), 1:120–1, note 1 (the pagination reproduces that of the original pamphlet). On Cloots's friendship with both Fanny de Beauharnais and Gabriel Brizard, see his earlier *Voeux d'un Gallophile*, new ed. (Amsterdam, 1786), reprinted in Cloots, *Oeuvres*, 2:68–76, 243, 250–2, as well as Rousseau, *Correspondance complète*, ed. Leigh, 45:163–225; and Joseph Clarke, *Commemorating the Dead in Revolutionary France* (Cambridge, CUP, 2007), p. 19.

[60] Cubières-Palmézeaux, *Les états-généraux du Parnasse*, p. 14.

[61] Cubières-Palmézeaux, *Les états-généraux du Parnasse*, p. 68.

pamphlet entitled *An Essay on the Constitution of England* that was published in London in 1765. The pamphlet was then republished in 1789 in two separate French translations by a lawyer named Jean Chas, who subsequently became a prominent pro-Feuillant political journalist, and, in later life, an energetic Bonapartist propagandist.[62] In this new context, it set out a way of thinking about the political advantages of public debt, and the relationship between the church and the state in France, that was considerably different from anything available in either Mounier or Sieyès.

In a foreword to one of the two editions of his translation, Chas attributed the pamphlet's authorship to either Sir William Temple or Sir Edward King. Other possible candidates have been the painter Allan Ramsay, Jean-Louis Delolme, and Edward Gibbon. The French-domiciled Portuguese political economist Isaac de Pinto, a critic of both David Hume's and the marquis de Mirabeau's assessments of public debt, claimed that part of its argument (and text) was based on his own *Essay on Circulation and Credit*, published in English only in 1774, but, he wrote, written and circulated widely in French in 1761.[63] Pinto's comment, in the preface to what at the time was a widely read book, probably explains the later French interest in the pamphlet, and in its author's identity. Whoever he (or she) might have been, the author in question, according to an early

---

[62] The translation was published anonymously, first under the title of *Réflexions sur la constitution de l'Angleterre* (London, 1789), and then under the more didactic title of *A l'assemblée des états-généraux, ou coup d'oeil sur la constitution, sur le prêt et l'emprunt* (London, 1789). Chas seems to have had an early interest in Rousseau's life and thought that, among other things, resulted in a public argument with Dominique-Joseph Garat: see [Jean Chas], *Réponse aux réflexions de M. Garat insérées dans le Mercure du 14 mai 1785* (London, 1785), pp. 26–7. On his later political views, see his *Sur la souveraineté* (Paris, 1810), with its justification of Napoleon's imperial sovereignty on the grounds that "sovereignty resides in the government, is inherent to it, and cannot be separated from it" (p. 29), as well as his earlier *A la nation française* (Paris, 1805), and his *Principes élémentaires des constitutions et des gouvernements* (Paris, 1807). The two latter works are eclectic compilations of received ideas (partly taken from Montesquieu and Rousseau) written to justify prevailing French political arrangements and French policy towards Britain.

[63] [Jean Chas], "Avertissement" (unpaginated) to his translation of the *Réflexions* (attributing the pamphlet's authorship to Temple or King, who both did publish works with similar titles); Francis Blackburne, *Memoirs of Thomas Hollis*, 2 vols. (London, 1780), 2:803 (attributing it to Allan Ramsay, who published a work with a similar title); Delolme's *Constitution of England* was registered with the Company of Booksellers in 1776 under the same title as the 1765 pamphlet, which gave rise to this attribution, while the "advertisement" to a reprint of the 1765 edition of the pamphlet (two others appeared, in 1766 and 1793), in John Palmer, ed., *Tracts on Law, Government and Other Political Subjects* (London, 1836), attributed its authorship to Gibbon, but with a question mark. On Pinto's claim that the pamphlet was based on the argument of his own work, see Isaac de Pinto, *An Essay on Circulation and Credit in Four Parts, and A Letter on the Jealousy of Commerce* (London, 1774), p. xiii. See, too, I.J.A. Nijenhuis, *Ein Joodse Philosophe. Isaac de Pinto (1717–1787)* (Amsterdam, 1992), pp. 50–1, 146, note 265, where authorship of the pamphlet is also attributed to Ramsay.

nineteenth-century commentator, "was, I suspect, a courtier who, in the early years of the last reign [of George III], not unmarked by popular discontents, would counteract the growing opinion that the former times were better than the present, and thus recover the declining national attachment to the person and government of his 'truly British and patriotic sovereign.' " The characterisation captures part of the pamphlet's purpose and content quite successfully. The "strenuous Whig" Thomas Hollis disagreed very violently with its contents but had no difficulty at all in seeing what, for him, was the unpalatable point of the pamphlet's scepticism about the ancient foundations of Britain's free constitution. As another later commentator noted, "the author, whoever he was, appears to have been a person of enlarged mind; he has expressed himself with much freedom, both on political and religious subjects; and seems to have been quite exempt from party bias, though great political agitation then prevailed, and the popular cry was 'Wilkes and Liberty.' "[64] A short set of extracts from the pamphlet were published in the 8–10 January 1765 issue of *The London Chronicle*, where they came to the attention of the philosopher David Hume. As Hume wrote with some irritation to his publisher William Strahan on 26 January 1765, the extracts from the "treatise" (as he called it) indicated that it "seems to be nothing but an abridgement of my *History*," even though, he continued, "I shall engage that the author has not named me from the beginning to the end of his performance."[65] But, despite his suspicions, the argument on which the pamphlet was based was not really Humean. It relied, instead, on the idea, famously associated with the seventeenth-century English Commonwealthman James Harrington, that the balance of political power followed the balance of property. But the vocabulary in which this version of Harrington's idea was couched also chimed very readily with the political and constitutional debates that arose in France before and after 1789.

The first step of the pamphlet's argument was summarised concisely in *The London Chronicle*; it consisted of the proposition that "the commonly defined modes of government are merely nugatory, and that wherever the *major vis* [or superior power] of the constitution resides, it will be despotic."[66] This, the pamphlet itself emphasised, did not mean that all

[64] Thomas Burton, *Parliamentary Diary*, ed. John Towill Rutt (London 1828), p. 407, note (for the first characterisation); Palmer, *Tracts*, advertisement (for the second). For Hollis's assessment, see the letter he sent to *The London Chronicle* on 31 January 1765, reprinted in Blackburne, *Memoirs of Thomas Hollis*, 2:803–5.

[65] Hume to Strahan, Paris, 26 January 1765, in *The Letters of David Hume*, ed. J.Y.T. Greig [1932], 2 vols. (Oxford, OUP, 1969), 1:492. For the notice publicising the pamphlet and the extracts from it, see *The London Chronicle*, 3–5 January 1765, p. 23; 8–10 January 1765, pp. 36–7.

[66] *The London Chronicle*, 8–10 January 1765, p. 36.

governments really were despotic, but simply that the sovereign power exercised by them all, irrespective of whether they were aristocracies, democracies, or monarchies, still was. It was unitary and indivisible because it amounted to the whole power of the nation, and was still located somewhere in every political society, whatever the name that its government happened to have. Ascertaining how, in practice, the power of that "autocrator," or "chief magistrate," actually was exercised depended on finding out "in what set of hands the power of that nation happens at the time to be lodged": so that, with "an exact knowledge of these constituents, arises an exact knowledge of the constitution of each country, and the just application of all the general maxims of government, which, however wise they may be in themselves, may, by misapplication, produce the very reverse of what is expected from them."[67] One illustration of this more general point was the maxim "The well being of the people is the supreme law" (*Salus populi suprema lex esto*). Its truth, the pamphlet noted, was indisputable, but to be applied properly, "it must be understood by the word *people* that part only which is constituent of the supreme magistrate, and to whose interests and opinions he must ever pay a religious regard."[68] Putting this "simple truth" into practice was not, however, quite as simple as it seemed, because it was "by no means easy to find out at all times, with precision, who those constituents are, and the most learned and experienced rulers have brought themselves into difficulties by mistaking them."[69] Here, the pamphlet argued, appearances were deceptive. The common opinion was that constitutions, and the rights of rulers and ruled, were established and maintained by laws and customs. In fact, however, exactly the opposite was the case, because, as the pamphlet put it, "the laws being not the makers, but the creatures of the constitution and of the constituents of government, who either make or abolish, alter or explain, as best pleases them."[70]

The key to constitutional theory was, therefore, to identify the location of what the author of the *Essay* called "the constituent power," since it, not the laws themselves, was the basis of "the general principle, *that the constitution of every country constantly changes with its constituent powers*."[71] With this as a guide, it was not difficult to explain the changes that had occurred to the English constitution along loosely Harringtonian lines. Once, according to the pamphlet's anonymous author, "the constituents of the English government were a few great land-holders, called barons."[72] During the reign of Henry VII, however, "the lands, which at that time, were

---

[67] [Anon.], *An Essay on the Constitution of England* (London, 1765), pp. 4–5.

[68] [Anon.], *Essay*, p. 5.

[69] [Anon.], *Essay*, p. 6.

[70] [Anon.], *Essay*, pp. 7–8.

[71] [Anon.], *Essay*, pp. 10, 23 (the latter passage is italicised in the original).

[72] [Anon.], *Essay*, p. 11.

the only valuable property of the nation, began to be parcelled out into a great number of hands," so that "the constituents, by this splitting of lands, became so numerous and so dispersed, that it was no longer possible for them to unite their forces against the crown." Subsequently, trade, "which had taken root" during the reign of Elizabeth I, "now sprang up under the pacific influence of James, in a most luxuriant manner, and put a considerable share of riches into a set of men utterly unknown to Old England." This "new monied interest" lay behind the rising power of the commons and the events of the seventeenth-century English revolutions. But it also formed the basis of the further set of changes that had begun to occur during the period of the Wars of the League of Augsburg and the Spanish Succession of the late seventeenth and early eighteenth centuries. "War, in England," the pamphlet continued, "became advantageous to almost every rank of men. The poor wished for it, as the greater demand for labourers increased the price of labour. The rich wished for it, as the greater the demand for money, the greater the advantage to those who were possessed of it, while those in the administration of government were easily persuaded into a measure which, with such universal approbation put such unlimited power into their hands." As war came to be funded by debt, an entirely new constituent power began to arise. "With the debt of the nation, so grew, in proportion to its credit, and by degrees produced a new set of constituents who, without being necessarily connected with the land, with the trade, with either of the Houses of Parliament, or with any corporation or regular body of men in the kingdom, became no less formidable than they were useful to the government."[73] These, the pamphlet claimed, were now the real underlying source of British political stability.

Running alongside these changes in the composition of the constitution's constituent powers were a parallel set of changes to the interests associated with religion. In this part of the argument, the pamphlet took the subject of the worldly nature of property in a different direction. In the beginning, its author wrote, the early Christian church had owned no property, and this simplicity, when set against the luxury and corruption of imperial Rome, had been one of the sources of its initial appeal. But, as the church and the empire began to merge, property and religion began to fuse, giving the church an extra set of reasons for maintaining its dogmas. For as long as the two remained entangled, no religious toleration had been possible, especially after the decline and fall of the Roman Empire, when the church itself had become feudal Europe's most substantial property owner. The Reformation had, initially, simply magnified the problem, by adding the clash between different sets of ecclesiastical proprietors to arguments over dogma. Only as states had begun to emancipate

---

[73] [Anon.], *Essay*, pp. 13, 17–8, 22, 70–1.

themselves from ecclesiastical sources of public revenue had politics begun to break free of religious opinion. This, the pamphlet argued, was why what it called "the religion of the magistrate," or the civil toleration produced by confessional pluralism, was a recent development in modern Britain. In this context, the phrase "the religion of the magistrate" meant something like the opposite of a state religion. Its content was, instead, supplied by a strong distinction between judgements that applied to this life and those that would have a bearing on an individual's afterlife. The magistrate was responsible for the former, while God was responsible for the latter. Since most religious observances had more to do with the next life than with this, they were for God, not the civil magistrate, to judge. In this sense, the pamphlet took the phrase "the religion of the magistrate" to mean something like what it had meant for John Locke in his *Letter concerning Toleration* and his often misinterpreted *The Reasonableness of Christianity*. As Locke argued consistently, the mysteries of the revealed Christian religion were beyond reason's grasp, which was why no religious dogma could be sanctioned by the state.[74] This was also the view adopted by the pamphlet's author. "No religion," it emphasised, "which requires an assent to any particular opinion can ever become a religion for the magistrate." The polytheism of the Romans had made this possible in republican Rome, just as the new relationship between the church and the state established in Britain after the Hanoverian succession now promised to make the same nondogmatic "religion of the magistrate" the antidote to the use of religion as a tool of faction.[75]

The two main subjects of the *Essay on the Constitution of England* complemented one another fairly fully. Public debt was a source of political stability, while the "religion of the magistrate" removed most of the content of different types of religious belief from public life. Together, they helped to explain British political stability without having to refer either to the intricacies of the English constitution itself, or to the post–Norman Conquest British state's capacity for general legislation, or to

[74] As Locke put it, "those that are averse to the religion of the magistrate," meaning all non-Anglicans, "will think themselves so much more bound to maintain the peace of the commonwealth" if "the partiality that is used towards them in matters of common right" were removed. "Those whose doctrine is peaceable," he continued, "and whose manners are pure and blameless, ought to be on equal terms with their fellow-subjects," so that "neither *pagan*, nor *mahometan*, nor *jew*, ought to be excluded from the civil rights of the commonwealth because of his religion": John Locke, *A Letter Concerning Toleration* [1689] (London, 1765), pp. 61–3. Compare to the distinction between "the religion of the ruler" and "the ruling religion" made by Samuel Pufendorf in his *The Divine Feudal Law: or Covenants with Mankind, Represented* [1695], ed. Simone Surbuchen (Indianapolis, Liberty Fund, 2002), p. 17.

[75] [Anon.], *Essay*, pp. 37, 48, 75. For a concurrent discussion, see Colin Kidd, "Civil Theology and Church Establishment in Revolutionary America," *Historical Journal* 42 (1999): 1007–26.

the rather implausible idea of an unusually developed British capacity
for moral and political forbearance. Although it is not clear whether the
pamphlet's translator actually endorsed its argument (early in 1788 Chas
seems to have coauthored a vigorous defence of ecclesiastical immunities
that, at first sight, is not obviously compatible with the idea of a religion
of the magistrate), the two subjects addressed by the English pamphlet
lent themselves readily to circumstances in postrevolutionary France.[76]
This was not simply because of the need to restore stability to French
public finances, or even because of the compatibility between the nondogmatic content of the idea of a "religion of the magistrate" and the new
status of the Catholic Church after November 1789, but primarily because
of the way that the newly nationalised church property could be seen as a
bridge between the two subjects, with the means to promote both social
equality and religious liberty. In this context, the type of interest in the
power of public credit that, well before the French Revolution began,
could be found in the works of individuals like Sir James Steuart, William
Ogilvie, James Rutledge, David Williams, Jean-Frédéric Herrenschwand,
or the marquis de Casaux came to be associated with a land-based version
of the Scottish financier John Law's original system. The first collected
edition of Law's works was published in Paris in the autumn of 1790, and
its editor, Etienne de Sénovert, made a point of highlighting its current

[76] The defence of ecclesiastical immunities appeared as [Jean Chas and Henri de Mon-
tignot], *Réflexions sur les immunités ecclésiastiques, considérées dans leurs rapports avec les maximes du droit public et l'intérêt national* (Paris, 1788). Its argument (particularly its insistence,
pp. 116–7, that "money" was now "the universal agent") can be aligned with that of the English pamphlet, although its Fénelonian moral tone was quite different. One of its targets was
an earlier, six-volume, *Traité des droits de l'état et du prince sur les biens possédés par le clergé* by
Etienne Mignot (Amsterdam, 1755–7), a work that can be taken as an indication of the fact
that discussion of church property did not begin with the French Revolution. The pamphlet
was attacked in a *Lettre à M. D. par M. L., ou examen d'un ouvrage intitulé "Réflexions sur les immunités ecclésiastiques"* (Paris, 1788), whose author (as indicated in the pamphlet) was also responsible for a large earlier work, *Les coutumes, considérées comme loi de la nation* (Paris, 1783),
which, on the basis of the sacred character of marriage and the profane character of worldly
goods, argued that the nation, not the church, had to be the legitimate owner of clerical
property (this latter work is attributed by library catalogues to an obscure *procureur* named
P.-G. Michaux, but the name does not fit the initials used in the later pamphlet's title). As
this exchange suggests, hostility to ecclesiastical privilege could be based on spiritual, as
much as secular, grounds, and on a long-standing, but still underresearched, form of devout
anticlericalism that had nothing to do with Voltaire. For another example, see the discussion of *L'esprit et les principes du droit canonique* in Nicolas-Silvestre Bergier, *Traité historique
et dogmatique de la vraie religion*, 12 vols. (Paris, 1780), 9:219–62. Chas is also taken to be the
author of a *Nouvelle vie de M. François de Salignac de la Mothe Fénelon* (Paris, 1788), and of a
later *Exposition de quelques principes politiques et quelques opinions religieuses* (n.p., n.d.), a piece
of anti-British war propaganda, published, from its content, in 1798 or 1799. It is not clear
that all these works really were by the same individual, because there were at least three men
named Chas (Jean, Pierre, and Castor) who published pamphlets at this time.

relevance. "Credit," he wrote at the beginning of his introduction to the edition, citing Steuart for corroboration, "plays so considerable a role in the political economy of modern nations, and is connected so intimately to their prosperity, and even to their existence, that it could be said that the science of government is nothing but the science of credit itself."[77] Sénovert's assessment of Law was, however, judiciously neutral. As he went on to emphasise, both in the rest of his introduction and in the notes that he added to Law's own works, it was difficult to decide whether Law's system was a real example or a dreadful warning.

Etienne Clavière, Law's System, and French Liberty

The revival of interest in Law's system was the product of an emerging consensus over the desirability of using some type of deficit finance to maintain the political stability of the new regime. Here, the most immediate obstacle to doing so was the reputation of the system itself. Memories of the trail of destruction that it had left in its wake were rehearsed very graphically during the spring and summer of 1790 by a banker named Nicolas Bergasse who had been elected to the National Assembly from the city of Lyon. In some respects, Bergasse's doubts about using public credit in the way that the French National Assembly decided to do in April 1790 were similar to Sieyès's own, even if the aim of Bergasse's alternative proposal was rather more spiritual in character.[78] Without an adequate tax base, Bergasse warned in a pamphlet dated 1 May 1790, an initially small gesture towards deficit finance would spiral out of control, just as Law's system had done. A more stable solution, he argued, would have been to rely on the church's tax-gathering capacity, and to have borrowed money against the revenue that the clerical tithe would have supplied, thus, as Bergasse would also have preferred, making a reformed Catholic Church one of the pillars of the new regime.[79] Sieyès's alternative was similar, although it presupposed the liquidation, rather than the continued existence, of the tithe. He, too, argued that financial stability was best achieved through the use of church revenue as security for government borrowing. The plan that he envisaged involved a new loan, whose subscribers would receive their income from revenue generated by individuals

---

[77] [Gabriel-Etienne de Sénovert, ed.], *Oeuvres de J. Law* (Paris, 1790), pp. i–ii. An editorial note (p. 127), referring to a "small treatise" on the *Théorie et pratique des assignats* that Sénovert read to the 1789 society on 5 and 6 September 1790, indicates that this edition was published after that date.

[78] On Sieyès's views, see the introduction to Sieyès, *Political Writings*, ed. Sonenscher, p. xliv.

[79] Nicolas Bergasse, *Lettre de M. Bergasse, député de la sénéchaussée de Lyon à ses commettants, au sujet de sa protestation contre les assignats monnaie* (Paris, 1790).

buying out their existing obligation to pay the tithe. The church itself would be radically reorganised, with a tiny number of bishops (Sieyès seems to have envisaged no more than four) and enough property of its own to maintain a more austerely Christian clerical establishment without needing to rely on public funds.

By the early winter of 1789, however, a broader consensus had begun to emerge in favour of using church property in more ambitious ways. As it did, Law's ideas became a more prominent feature of public debate. The individual who played the major part in giving them their prominence, although he was always careful to emphasise the difference between his own proposals and Law's system, was Jacques-Pierre Brissot's friend and political ally the Genevan banker Etienne Clavière.[80] As Mirabeau wrote in a secret note to the royal court in September 1790, Clavière was "the *assignats*' author" (which was why, he suggested with characteristic brutality, the king should put him in charge of liquidating the public debt, leaving him to be "a victim without consequences" if the plan were to fail).[81] Although events were to do a great deal to compromise his later reputation, there is no reason to disassociate Clavière's financial speculations from his broader moral concerns. "Would you like an image of what the rich are like everywhere?" he wrote to Rousseau's Calvinist critic Jean-André Deluc in 1774.

> Look at the countryside, where there are never enough walls to protect them from losing a flower. The rich eat up the very air that the poor are able to enjoy only on the high roads, since they cannot enjoy the ownership of land. It is said that the poor need the rich; other more gentle souls say that the need is reciprocal. According to my observations, it is the rich who have great need of the poor, while the latter can do very well without the rich. Happiness has a great deal to do with opinion. Who, however, drives opinion, if not the rich? Banish them from a country and the poor will soon see how to base their opinions on their own condition (*état*), and be the happier for it. Where are the rich in Lapland? You may not want to be a Laplander, but I, at least, would like to remove as much as possible from the domination of the rich.[82]

[80] On Clavière and his milieu, see, most recently, Richard Whatmore, "Etienne Dumont, the British Constitution, and the French Revolution," *Historical Journal* 50 (2007): 23–47.

[81] Guy Chaussinand-Nogaret, *Mirabeau entre le roi et la révolution* (Paris, Hachette, 1986), p. 92.

[82] Etienne Clavière to Jean André Deluc, 17 April 1774. Geneva, BPU, Mss. 2463. Cited in André Gür, "Quête de la richesse et critique des riches chez Etienne Clavière," in Jacques Berchtold and Michel Porret, eds., *Etre riche au siècle de Voltaire* (Geneva, Droz, 1996), pp. 97–115 (104–5). For more pro-commercial interpretations of Clavière's thought, see Richard Whatmore, *Republicanism in the French Revolution: An Intellectual History of Jean-Baptiste Say's Political Economy* (Oxford, OUP, 2000), pp. 10–2, 77–82, 86–93; James Livesey, *Making Democracy in the French Revolution* (Cambridge, Mass., Harvard UP, 2001), pp. 25–31, 70.

The debt reduction scheme that Clavière imported to France grew out of this vision. He settled in the kingdom in 1784, following an initial spell in England and Ireland after his flight from Geneva in 1782, when French military force put an end to attempts by the Genevan *représentants* to change the republic's constitution, a conflict in which Clavière himself played a major part.

Clavière's subsequent career as a financial speculator cannot be divorced from Genevan politics, since the primary aim of his speculative activities over the next four or five years was to wreck Genevan investments in French debt by using secondary markets either to buy long, or to sell short, in the hope that the sudden lurches in prices that this might produce would set off a chain of bankruptcies among his patrician enemies in Geneva. After 1789, however, the new situation in France offered a different opportunity, and, accordingly, a different strategy. While Clavière's earlier speculations centred on using the markets to free Geneva, his later proposals centred on using the markets to free France, but with Geneva still in the background. They amounted to trying to realise Rousseau's moral and political vision, using modern financial means. It was an idea that he shared not only with Louis-Sébastien Mercier but with Jacques-Pierre Brissot. In a review of two English works on public credit published in his *Journal du lycée de Londres* in 1784, Brissot argued that speculation on the public funds was not necessarily an evil. The facts, he wrote, showed that England and Holland, two countries in which playing the markets had existed for a long time, and had been raised to a high level of technical sophistication, housed "a great number of political geniuses, citizens distinguished by their public benefactions, and all that characterises the soul of a patriot."[83] There was, he suggested, no reason to be amazed that patriotically playing the markets could be combined with "pure manners and the public virtues" if one remembered that the reason for doing so was interest. "The benefactor of humanity is interested and speculates for others; the egoist is interested in himself and speculates for his own benefit."[84]

Here, too, public credit was given the same type of positive evaluation that it was given by Sir James Steuart and by Brissot's friend David Williams (and, too, by another of Brissot's prerevolutionary acquaintances, Jeremy Bentham).[85] At its most ambitious, the future that both Brissot and Clavière envisaged would be a world that could accommodate trade, but one in which trade would be based on a more clearly differentiated set of natural economic endowments, and, more importantly, where trade would be free, not simply in the negative sense of being unimpeded, but

[83] Jacques Pierre Brissot, *Journal du lycée de Londres* 3 (1784): 330.
[84] Brissot, *Journal du lycée de Londres* 3 (1784): 332.
[85] On Brissot and Williams, see above, pp. 42–5.

in the stronger sense of being voluntary and reciprocal, rather than simply necessary and competitive. From this point of view, Law's idea of inflating an asset to eliminate a liability had the merit of indicating a peaceful way to remove the distortions generated by France's overreliance on industry, trade, and public debt. France, as Clavière viewed it, was both an agricultural and a trading nation.[86] With these as the basic features of its economy, it could rely more heavily on the skill-intensive manufacturing industries of the Swiss or Dutch republics for its imports of manufactured goods, and, in the longer term, on the additional resources supplied by a further, westward, extension of the whole, now economically rebalanced, international system, as the American economy came to complement its European counterpart. Then, as he wrote with Brissot in their coauthored book on France and the United States, American agriculture would underpin the growth of French manufacturing industry, to form an alliance based on real common interests.[87] Although there is no direct evidence of Clavière's familiarity with David Williams's financial and political speculations, there is also no reason to think that both he and Brissot did not endorse Williams's idea of a debt-based, socially just, republican system. As the pieces fell gradually into place, so, too, all three believed, would Britain revert to a position more compatible with its size, population, and real economic resources.[88]

The first version of the debt reduction scheme that Clavière began to develop was published in a letter to Mirabeau's journal, the *Courier de Provence*, on 1 October 1789, a month before the National Assembly decided to confiscate the property of the church. In this initial version, funding the deficit was to be achieved by a mixture of Roman-style republican patriotism and Law's idea of inflating the value of an asset to eliminate a liability. The patriotism, as Clavière had argued already in two earlier pamphlets, would consist of voluntary donations of gold and silverware to the royal treasury.[89] Instead of being turned into coin, however, the gold and silver supplied by these patriotic gifts, or *dons patriotiques*, would be used as security to borrow an initial sum of between 300 and 400 million

---

[86] The description can be found in Etienne Clavière, *Dissection du projet de M. l'évêque d'Autun. Sur l'échange universel et direct des créances de l'état contre les biens nationaux* (Paris, 3 July 1790), p. 75.

[87] Etienne Clavière and Jacques-Pierre Brissot, *De la France et des Etats-Unis* [1787], ed. Marcel Dorigny (Paris, Editions du C.T.H.S., 1996), pp. 45–70.

[88] On Brissot's view of Britain's future, see Jacques-Pierre Brissot, *Testament politique de l'Angleterre* (London, 1782).

[89] On Clavière's earlier calls to imitate the Romans and melt down gold and silverware, see his *De la foi publique envers les créanciers de l'état* (London, 1788), p. 119, and his *Opinions d'un créancier de l'état sur quelques matières de finance importantes dans le moment actuel* (Paris, 1789), pp. 119–20.

livres. This cash reserve would then act as security for a larger loan that would be funded through the issuance of a billion livres' worth of interest-bearing state bills, to be used solely to buy out the obligation to pay the clerical tithe. The initial cash reserve would be used to pay interest on the bills, while the bills themselves would fall gradually out of circulation when they were purchased and used by private individuals to buy out future tithe payments. The church would end up owning the bills, leaving the question of their future redemption open, while the tithe would be consolidated into private property; since private property would no longer be subject to tithe payments, the capital value of land would rise, and this, in turn, would boost the security of private credit, setting up a virtuous circle of more agricultural investment, more domestic trade, and more tax revenue.[90]

It was more difficult, however, to apply this type of mechanism to the scaled-up version of the same idea. As Clavière emphasised in a further letter to the *Courier de Provence* in early November 1789, the broad aim of the system that he envisaged was to break the hold of Parisian banking and financial institutions over the nation's economic life by eliminating the tangle of public and private credit that, in its current form, was threatening France with economic ruin. The royal government had issued many different types of paper to fund its debts. Some circulated at, or near, par, while others fell into the category of what would now be called junk, or distressed debt. Both types of paper had been used as security for many different types of further private transactions, creating a huge mass of public and private credit that was extremely vulnerable to any interruption of circulation. Paris was the hub of these multiple chains, consuming some 600 million livres' worth of goods a year, and supporting a financial turnover amounting to many times more, because of the massively over-centralised systems of finance and government of the old regime. Money had to be injected into the machine, both to keep the economy alive and, in the longer term, to reduce its dependence on Paris.[91] The letter coincided unusually precisely with Talleyrand's proposal to the National Assembly to confiscate the property of the church, and the warning that the letter contained soon became the justification of Clavière's further pamphlet campaign to tie the newly nationalised church property to a paper instrument that could be used both to buy land and as a currency. Using the same financial instrument for both purposes, he argued, was the only way to meet the twin goals of reducing the debt and increasing prosperity,

---

[90] Etienne Clavière, "Lettre aux rédacteurs du Courier de Provence," *Courier de Provence* 48 (29 September–1 October 1789): 18–24.

[91] Etienne Clavière, "Sur les rapports des provinces et de Paris, relativement à la dette publique," *Courier de Provence* 61 (2–3 November 1789): 34–43.

without either setting off further rounds of financial speculation or igniting a chain of bankruptcies that would bring economic activity to a halt.

But this variation on Law's idea was, in some respects, as difficult to implement as Law's original system had been. The original version relied on the potential returns from foreign trade to boost the value of the shares that, by way of the paper currency required to buy them, would then be used to liquidate the backlog of debt. Clavière stressed repeatedly that applying the idea to the land would give the new version a more solid foundation. But it also brought in uncertainty from another direction, not only because of lingering questions about the stability and durability of the new property settlement (a subject to be taken up in chapter 6), but also because of the decentralised and piecemeal nature of land sales, and the unavoidably slow rates of return from agricultural improvement. Nothing could raise the productivity of the land overnight. And, even when it did become more productive, further delays were bound to be involved both in generalising rising rural prosperity across the whole society and in establishing the stable flow of public income required for debt liquidation. The difficulties were compounded further by the way that the fiscal system came to be entangled with the new regime's electoral system, with the potentially perverse result that changes to taxation could have the effect of changing the system of political representation. In the end, trying to manage these problems, and the various, potentially clashing, time horizons attached to each of them, turned out to be too difficult, as it did with Law's original system.

The initial appeal of the idea lay in both its political character and its general nature. It kept responsibility for evaluating the entitlements of different types of creditor, and for managing the sequence of payments involved in debt liquidation, in the hands of the royal government, or its future successor. It did not entail the creation of a public bank with a special responsibility for debt liquidation, as Jacques Necker and a prestigious body of financial opinion proposed. Nor did it entail limiting the monetary use of the *assignat* to the purchase of a new set of annuities to be issued to the owners of unfunded debt, as the marquis de Montesquiou-Fezensac, the head of the National Assembly's finance committee, proposed. Finally, it did not transfer the initiative for liquidating the debt to the creditors themselves by giving them first call on the distribution of *assignats* and, by extension, a prior claim on nationalised church property, as, in June 1790, Talleyrand proposed. Clavière was particularly scathing towards this third proposal and its argument that, since local administrators would have to come from the countryside, issuing *assignats* directly to the owners of outstanding debt would, as Talleyrand put it, be "an additional reason to give it an influx of men whose ease and education will have equipped them with a taste for study, an aptitude for work, and enlightenment (*lumières*)

THE ENTITLEMENTS OF MERIT

to spread." This, Clavière replied, simply served to show how, "despite the most generous of sentiments, aristocracy continues to reveal itself, with its proud pretensions." What, he wrote, the countryside needed most was "more common sense than wit, more experience than recondite knowledge (*science*), more straightforwardness than urbanity, and more solidity than finesse (*plus de rondeur que de finesse*)."[92] Although Clavière did not say so, what it really required was something like a rural Socrates, or Hirzel's model peasant farmer Kliyogg.[93]

As Clavière acknowledged, liquidating the debt in the way that he proposed was likely to mean that prices would rise. But, he argued, the inflation produced by an increase in the money supply would not affect the large mass of urban consumers because, he explained, "the people works and, under a good constitution, the price of labour is not entirely at the mercy of the rich." It was a claim that would be put to the test in the spring of 1791, when a wave of disputes in the Parisian trades helped to raise a more general question about the right to associate and to petition collectively that applied as much to political clubs as it did to people who worked. The connection formed the context in which the famous Le Chapelier law came to be passed.[94] In 1790, however, Clavière's argument, as Talleyrand had also shown, applied to both the landowners and the owners of manufacturing industry (*le propriétaire industriel*), since they, too, were able to raise the prices of the products they sold. The only real victims of the *assignat* were likely to be the *rentiers*. Their interest, Clavière wrote, "is certainly a respectable one, but they have chosen repose, even though everything that man needs exists only by way of work. Whatever their disadvantages, would they be wise to want to be the moderators of work, by demanding that the amount of money in circulation should be set according to their own convenience?"[95] Putting the question like this made the answer entirely self-evident. So, too, according to Clavière, was the need to make the *assignat* a fiat currency. As he pointed out in an article in Brissot's *Patriote français* in late March 1790, it was a mistake "in a revolution proceeding from despotism to liberty, to count on capitalists, credit, and loans." Under the old regime, the power of the royal government gave private financiers the confidence to advance funds because they were also likely to be secure in the knowledge that force would be used to raise taxes should the need arise. Since this was no longer the case, options

92 Clavière, *Dissection*, pp. 11–2.

93 On the rural Socrates, see above, p. 111.

94 On these disputes, see Michael Sonenscher, *Work and Wages: Natural Law, Politics, and the Eighteenth-Century French Trades* (Cambridge, CUP, 1989), pp. 346–52 (although the surrounding claims about the connection between these disputes and the *sans-culottes* require revision).

95 Clavière, *Dissection*, pp. 72–3, 74.

were more limited.[96] The inherited legacy of debt now left no margin for manoeuvre between a forcibly introduced currency and a forcibly imposed debt reduction. The question was simply which kind of force would do least damage to liberty. In some circumstance, Clavière wrote in April 1790, "a despotic will can be more reassuring than the practices (*usages*) of liberty." Turning the *assignat* into a fiat currency was not only "a result of reason"; it would also increase its stability. "Since no one can refuse them, everyone will fear their depreciation," giving everyone a real interest in maintaining their parity.[97]

The only real objections to these claims came from applying Clavière's own arguments to the subject of foreign trade. Here, as the chemist and former royal tax farmer Antoine Lavoisier pointed out in a paper presented to the Parisian 1789 Society on 29 August 1790, the thought experiment of quintupling the amount of money in circulation that David Hume had set out in his essay *Of Commerce* of 1752 was an indication of the problems that the *assignat* might create.[98] If Clavière was right, and prices and wages simply adjusted to the growth of the money supply, then France would soon lose its export markets, leaving the debt problem no nearer a solution, and the nation even more dependent on the expenditure of rich *rentiers* than Clavière had seen. Lavoisier's warning did not, however, affect the broad consensus. When Turgot's disciple Pierre-Samuel Dupont de Nemours rehearsed Lavoisier's Hume-inspired objections during the National Assembly's debate in late September 1790 on whether to implement its earlier decision to use the *assignat* as a currency, and to issue up to 1.2 billion livres' worth of the new paper money, both Adrien Duport and

[96] *Patriote français* 226 (21 March 1790): 4, summarising Clavière's *Observations nécessaires sur la partie du mémoire du premier ministre des finances, relative aux subsides qu'exige le déficit de 1790, et sur la convenance d'une prompte émission d'assignats monnaie* (Paris, 1790).

[97] Etienne Clavière, "Seconde suite des observations sur le mémoire de M. Necker," *Courier de Provence* 128 (1790): 303–34 (319–20). See, too, the parallel argument in Joseph-Joachim Cerutti, *Idées simples et précises sur le papier monnaie, les assignats forcés, et les biens ecclésiastiques* (Paris, 1790), pp. 20–1: requiring everyone to use the currency, he argued, would create a common interest against the interest of the clergy.

[98] Antoine Lavoisier, *Réflexions sur les assignats et sur la liquidation de la dette exigible ou arriérée, lue à la société de 1789, le 29 août 1790* (Paris, 1790). On this aspect of Hume's thought and its wider reverberations, see Istvan Hont, "The 'Rich Country–Poor Country' Debate in the Scottish Enlightenment," in his *Jealousy of Trade: International Competition and the Nation-State in Historical Perspective* (Cambridge, Mass., Belknap Press, 2005), pp. 267–322, and, most recently, "The 'Rich Country–Poor Country' Debate Revisited: The Irish Origins and French Reception of Hume's 'Paradox,'" in Margaret Schabas and Carl Wennerlind, eds., *David Hume's Political Economy* (London, Routledge, 2008). A parallel argument was made in an essay written in 1779, but published in December 1791, by James Madison, who followed Hume's thought experiment and made its connection to public credit explicit. See James Madison, "Essay on Money" [1791], in *Selected Writings of James Madison*, ed. with an introduction by Ralph Ketcham (Indianapolis, Hackett, 2006), pp. 4–11.

Antoine-Joseph Barnave spoke up in support of Clavière's idea.[99] For Duport, the new system amounted to relying on a "real Mississippi," rather than the "chimerical Mississippi" on which Law's gamble had been based. "If the Mississippi could have been transported to France," one of Duport's allies told the Parisian Jacobin club on 13 August 1790, citing Duport's analogy, "Law's bills would have been excellent. But we do, in fact, have the Mississippi."[100] For Barnave, Adam Smith had dealt successfully with Hume's anxieties. It was, Barnave told the assembly, "a veritable absurdity, and sovereign ignorance of the principles of circulation, to believe and say that the *assignats* will be used mainly to buy consumer goods. In citing the authority of Smith [as both Lavoisier and Dupont de Nemours had done], whose arguments are consistently travestied, it ought to have been possible to set out his true principles, which are entirely to the advantage of my own view."[101] As Smith had shown, Barnave argued, the stimulus to capital investment, not consumption, that would be supplied by the *assignat* meant that productivity gains would override projected losses in price competitiveness. Painful adjustments in the composition of the economy might still be required, but rising domestic prices and wages were not, in themselves, real obstacles to the long-term survival of foreign trade. The argument amplified on what Clavière himself had already written, in a section on what he called "Smith's opinion of paper money," published at the end of a pamphlet dated 15 September 1790, as well as in an article published at the same time in the *Courier de Provence*. "Sir James Steuart," Clavière wrote there, "had completely refuted" Hume, as, too, had Smith. As he went on to assert in the pamphlet itself, Smith "would have been unusually (*singulièrement*) approving of using national land (*biens nationaux*) to extinguish part of the debt," since he himself had written in favour

[99] For Dupont de Nemours's use of Lavoisier (and Hume) in his speech of 25 September 1790, see *Archives parlementaires* 19 (Paris, 1884): 228.

[100] Maurice Gouget-Deslandres, *Sérieux et dernier examen sur le rachat de la chose publique* (Paris, 1790), reprinted in Alphonse Aulard, *La société des Jacobins. Recueil de documents pour l'histoire du club des Jacobins de Paris*, vol. 1 (Paris, 1889), 204–25 (p. 225 for the phrase cited). It is worth noting that this pamphlet is dated 13 August 1790 and refers back to Duport's phrase (cited above, p. 41), even though Duport used it only in his speech to the National Assembly on 29 September 1790. It is not clear whether this means that Deslandres incorporated it into his pamphlet at a later date (since it appears as a postscript), or whether Duport used it in an earlier speech to the Jacobins that has not survived (a rather faint manuscript note on the B. N.'s copy of the published version of Duport's speech appears to date it to 16 April 1790, during the earlier debate on the *assignat*). For further examples of the broad early consensus that had emerged by the late summer of 1790 in favour of the *assignat* as a more solid version of Law's system, see Rebecca L. Spang, "The Ghost of Law: Speculating on Money, Memory and Mississippi in the French Constituent Assembly," *Historical Reflections* 31 (2005): 3–25 (especially pp. 14, 20–21, 23–24).

[101] For Barnave's speech of 28 September 1790, see *Archives parlementaires* 19:306.

of using crown property to prevent a possible future British state bank-ruptcy. Smith's well-attested hostility towards the Ayr Bank scheme was a different matter, because that project relied on the issue of bank paper, not paper representing the real value of land. As the example of the crown lands indicated, Clavière claimed, Smith would have had no qualms about using the *assignat* both as a debt reduction mechanism and as a paper cur-rency. Even if, he emphasised, the *assignat* were entirely the same as the American continental currency (and its security in land meant that it was not), this was still no reason not to follow their example, "since a paper currency saved them; nothing is more certain."[102]

FEUILLANTS AND BRISSOTINS

Clavière's identification of both Steuart and Smith with the *assignat* cap-tured something more deeply ambiguous about the objectives that could be attributed to Law's system. In the immediate aftermath of the system's fail-ure, Montesquieu had associated Law with Fénelon, describing the Scot-tish financier in his *Persian Letters* as a bagpipe-playing charlatan who had enchanted the inhabitants of Fénelon's Betica into turning their gold into air. Voltaire, on the other hand, had described Law as France's saviour, and the system as the means by which, despite the costs of Louis XIV's wars, French commercial and manufacturing prosperity had been carried through from the age of Colbert to more recent times.[103] Both pairings—either between Law and Fénelon, or between Law and Colbert—had a measure of truth. From the first point of view, the system appeared to equip France with a capacity to eliminate the backlog of interest payments due on the plethora of financial instruments accumulated during Louis XIV's reign without requiring either a state bankruptcy or a deeper commitment to trade, taxation, and price competitiveness as the only available alternative means to restore financial stability. In this sense, the system would make France more self-sufficient. From the second point of view, however, the system appeared to give France a new ability to tap the mass of largely un-used productive resources tied up in existing property arrangements. In this second sense, the system would make France more competitive, because it would force the owners of interest-bearing assets to become traders. For as long as wealth was available simply from land rent or interest payments,

---

[102] Etienne Clavière, *Réponse au mémoire de M. Necker concernant les assignats* (Paris, 15 September 1790), pp. 135 (on the American continental currency), 150–7 (on Steuart and Smith). See also his "Réflexions nouvelles sur les assignats," *Courier de Provence* 197 (1790): 413–30 (p. 428, for the claim about Steuart's refutation of Hume).

[103] For these characterisations, see Sonenscher, *Before the Deluge*, pp. 116–8.

property was likely to be used in ways that fell far short of its productive capacity and general utility (this, it might be noted, was the main reason why, before it collapsed, Ernst Ludwig Carl, the German advocate of the French system of fashion-based trade, strongly endorsed Law's system).[104] Using wealth to fund production rather than consumption, or as capital rather than as income, could point towards more, not less, involvement in foreign trade.

The tension between these two objectives resurfaced during the French Revolution as the underlying reason for the disintegration of the early patriot consensus over France's future that emerged after the fall of the Bastille. Here, the two different ways of endorsing deficit finance were no longer represented by Fénelon and Colbert, but by Sir James Steuart and Adam Smith. On Steuart's terms, public credit offered the prospect of autarchy, and an escape from the competitive pressures produced by trade and payments balances. On Smith's, it was the engine of productivity. The two goals were certainly not incompatible, but they assigned different values to different parts of the combined process of debt liquidation and economic regeneration. From the first point of view, public credit continued to be the means to eliminate a backlog of unpaid debt and, by doing so, to reduce the economic and social distortions produced by existing property arrangements. From the second, it was the means to boost the productive capacity of hitherto undeveloped economic resources, and by doing so, to reach the same long-term outcome. The difference lay in where in the sequence justice was most likely to be secured. After 1789, four subjects gave this tension a political dimension. The first was the question of the identity of the putative purchasers of nationalised property, and its bearing on the different types of social and political arrangements that might arise if those purchasers were either largely institutional (such as a municipality, department, or hospital) or individual in character. The second was the issue of the future relationship between France and its colonial empire. The third was the problem of the growing stream of noble and clerical emigrants who began to leave France after 1789. The fourth was the connection between the fiscal and electoral systems established by the National Assembly in 1790. Together, they raised an increasingly intractable set of questions about whether civil and political liberty could be established and maintained without collective, as well as individual, property ownership, and, in parallel, whether both types of liberty could survive without either an empire or the tax revenue supplied by *émigré* expenditure.

The fourth subject was to give rise to the most glaring political problems. This was the system of political representation established by the National Assembly early in 1790. As is well known, the new electoral

---

[104] On Carl, see above, pp. 92–7.

system based both the right to vote and eligibility to stand for election on direct tax payments, with tax payments equivalent to the local level of three days' wages distinguishing full, or active, citizens (in practice most adult men) from passive citizens (women, domestic servants, and temporary residents), and with a further requirement to pay taxes equivalent to the value of a silver marc establishing eligibility for election to national office. One reaction to the new system was to object to its partiality. "There is, however, a class of men," complained the *Chronique de Paris* in early November 1789, "who, thanks to the shapeless (*informe*) organisation of our societies, cannot be called upon to represent the nation. They are the *proletarians* of our age."[105] Rousseau, it was also pointed out, would have been ineligible for election and might even have had to struggle to be able to vote (in fact, as is now clear, most adult men were able to qualify for active citizenship). A more considered reaction arose from the link now established between the electoral system and the fiscal system. By tying political rights to tax payments, the National Assembly had, inadvertently, closed off its room for manoeuvre on fiscal reform. As Condorcet pointed out in June 1790, an abrupt switch from direct to indirect taxation would effectively disenfranchise the whole nation. "You have," he informed the National Assembly, "made the title of active citizen depend on direct taxation, and, by doing so, tied financial laws to constitutional laws. A change in the former could alter the constitution, that precious benefaction (*bienfait*) that we owe to your wisdom." Converting "some direct taxes into indirect taxes" could, he warned, change "a free constitution into an aristocracy."[106] This scenario was unlikely. But a less immediate, though more real, threat to the stability of the electoral system came from the possibility of a gradual erosion of its tax base. If foreign trade were to dry up because of the disintegration of the French colonial empire, and if the depreciation of the paper currency meant that a larger proportion of popular expenditure would have to be allocated to both the payment of rent and the purchase of basic subsistence goods, then the number of active citizens would begin to fall, and political power would fall into the hands of a smaller and smaller number of prosperous citizens. The result was a rather awkward political dilemma. Indirect taxation of discretionary expenditure might maintain the stability of the prices of subsistence goods, but threaten the stability of the size of the electorate. Direct taxation of landed revenue might maintain the stability of the size of the electorate,

---

[105] *Chronique de Paris* 71 (2 November 1789). The word "proletarians" (referring, of course, to their original Roman counterparts) was italicised in the original.

[106] Marie-Jean-Antoine-Nicolas de Caritat, marquis de Condorcet, *Adresse à l'assemblée nationale sur les conditions d'éligibilité. 5 juin 1790*, reprinted in Condorcet, *Oeuvres*, ed. A. Condorcet O'Connor and F. Arago, 12 vols. [1847] (Hamburg, 1968), 10:77–91 (79–80 for the passages cited).

but threaten the stability of living standards. Both appeared to raise a question mark against the long-term prospects for liberty. In circumstances like these, Rousseau's bleak assessment of the despotic propensity built into every political society could begin to look less reassuringly remote.[107] Nor was there an obvious solution. One way out was to try to preserve the tax base by maintaining currency stability and popular purchasing power, even if this meant trying to hold on to the empire, and to bring the *émigrés* back. Another, however, was to change the electoral system itself.

The political history of the French Revolution began with the realisation that Louis XVI could not be a patriot king. It was followed by the emergence of a broad patriot consensus in favour of trying to reach the same egalitarian objectives, against the inegalitarianism that could be imputed to Mounier and Sieyès. That broad early patriot consensus began to fall apart during the spring of 1791, and then collapsed completely after Louis XVI's flight from Paris on 20 June 1791 and his arrest at Varennes a day later. By April 1791, Barnave, Duport, and the Lameth brothers had begun to discuss political strategy secretly with the queen, continuing the clandestine negotiations that Mirabeau had been pursuing until his death on 2 April 1791.[108] These negotiations had first started on 3 July 1790, prompted either by the king's hostility towards the National Assembly's plan to establish a civil constitution for the French clergy or, more probably, by the assembly's earlier decision, on 20 June 1790, to abolish the French nobility.[109] From Mirabeau's point of view, the latter reason may well have outweighed the former (as with Sieyès, the fate of the church was not, in itself, a high priority). As he put it in a graphic note to the court that he wrote on 23 December 1790, the gradual erosion of royal power that the events of the previous six months had produced was likely to turn the monarchy into "a phantom that it might be easy to believe could be done without." The danger, he added, would be all the more

[107] On the idea of modern (post-Rousseauian) historical awareness as a secularised eschatology, see, classically, Reinhart Koselleck, *Critique and Crisis: Enlightenment and the Pathogenesis of the Modern Society* (Cambridge, Mass., MIT Press; Leamington Spa, Berg Press, 1988); and, more particularly, his *Futures Past: On the Semantics of Historical Time* (Cambridge, Mass., MIT Press, 1985), as well as his *The Practice of Conceptual History* (Stanford, California, Stanford UP, 2002).

[108] The fullest account of these discussions is still to be found in Michon, *Essai sur l'histoire du parti feuillant*, pp. 182–98; see also Alma Söderhjelm, *Marie-Antoinette et Barnave. Correspondance secrète (Juillet 1791–Janvier 1792* (Paris, 1934), and Timothy Tackett, *When the King Took Flight* (Cambridge, Mass., Harvard UP, 2003), pp. 124, 237, note 6. See, too, Mona Ozouf, *Varennes: la mort du royauté, 21 juin 1791* (Paris, Gallimard, 2005).

[109] The first possibility can be found in Munro Price, "Mirabeau and the Court: Some New Evidence," *French Historical Studies* 29 (2006): 37–75 (p. 59), although the civil constitution had not, as yet, been given final approval by the National Assembly (it did so on 11 July), which suggests that the second possibility also had a bearing.

pronounced "if the authors of the majority of the republican forms that have been adopted had also had some sort of underlying idea (*arrière-pensée*) in laying the foundations of their work, and had actually believed in the possibility of a great democracy."[110] In fact, he implied, they had not, and had simply done so inadvertently. The remark may have been designed merely to boost Mirabeau's alternative strategy in the eyes of his royal readers, but it can also be taken to be an indication of the real political problems that Barnave and his allies now began to face. From one point of view, generalising credit across a whole society may have looked like the way to entrench political stability. With a strong set of common interests attached to the new French regime, there would be no room for anything other than ability and merit to determine election to office. But from another point of view, relying on credit in this way opened up a space for a further set of claims about the need to take further corrective action to prevent the backlog of economic and social inequality from turning the new regime into a self-perpetuating oligarchy. Injecting additional currency into the money supply was not, in itself, a guarantee of its general availability.

The first example of this tension between the supply and distribution of money served, however, to reinforce the initial consensus. It arose early in 1790, when, on 10 March of that year, a deputation from the municipality of Paris headed by its mayor, Jean-Sylvain Bailly, presented a memorandum to the National Assembly offering to buy up half the whole amount of *assignats* (or 200 million of the total of 400 million livres) that, on 19 December 1789, the assembly had decided to issue to enable future purchasers of national property to subscribe for the first instalment. As Bailly argued, there was a contradiction between the widely accepted need to raise revenue as quickly as possible and the likely slump in land prices that would be caused by the arrival of so large a supply of property onto the market. This, accordingly, was why he proposed that the municipality of Paris should buy all the former church property in its jurisdiction and acquire half the total issue of *assignats* to do so. It would pay for the *assignats* in fifteen instalments of ten million livres a year, funding the first payment by way of a loan, with the returns from subsequent sales paying for the rest. The same procedure, he suggested, could be applied to the remaining *assignats* by the larger municipalities of provincial France. To cover the cost of the initial purchase, both the Parisian and provincial municipalities would issue interest-bearing bills in relatively small denominations (of between two hundred and one thousand livres) to be used to give additional security to private transactions and prevent a credit crunch from bringing economic life to a halt. The fifty million livres' profit on the

---

[110] Chaussinand-Nogaret, *Mirabeau*, pp. 174–5.

whole transaction that would go to the municipality of Paris would, Bailly emphasised, be used to fund the cost of public works, including the construction of "a palace" to house the National Assembly.[111] As he explained in a further speech, on 16 March 1790, "Paris made the revolution; Paris secured the revolution; but the whole burden of the revolution, and all its evils, fell on Paris." For six months, he added, the people of Paris had relied on alms. They were now, he concluded, entitled to demand that "Paris, whose fate is inseparable from that of the provinces; Paris, which is the centre of the kingdom; Paris, which is the abode of a great people, made up of all the peoples of France, should not be crushed by the effects of a revolution in which it has both played so great a part, and borne the whole burden."[112]

The proposal followed hard on the heels of a grim description of the state of the nation's finances presented to the National Assembly by Jacques Necker on 6 March 1790, and was soon given the assembly's approval. Disagreement was confined to the largely clerical and noble opponents of the whole idea of confiscating church property, and a small number of other voices. One was Brissot's friend Jérôme Pétion, who argued against both the projected sale of church property to the municipalities alone and the initial recourse to private finance to underwrite what he called this "fictitious sale." The real way to avert a credit crunch, he told the assembly, was to monetise the *assignat* and make the acquisition of former church land available to everyone, as was the case with every other type of purchasable good.[113] Although Pétion did not mention his name, this was also the argument that Clavière was presenting in a number of concurrent articles in Brissot's newspaper, the *Patriot français* (Pétion, in fact, went rather further, lending his weight to a scheme for the creation of a decentralised land bank, advocated intermittently between 1789 and the date of its eventual foundation in 1798 by a man named Jacques-Annibal Ferrières, that was also supported by, among others, James Rutledge and the Parisian Cordeliers club).[114] But, on 18 March 1790, the assembly

---

[111] *Archives parlementaires* 12 (10 March 1790): 112–5. The episode is mentioned briefly in Bernard Bodinier and Eric Teyssier, *"L'événement le plus important de la révolution": La vente des biens nationaux (1789–1867) en France et dans les territoires annexes* (Paris, Société des études robespierristes, 2000), pp. 387–8, but without consideration of the wider context.

[112] *Archives parlementaires* 12 (16 March 1790): 195–6.

[113] *Archives parlementaires* 12 (17 March 1790): 207–8.

[114] On this scheme, see Jacques-Annibal Ferrières, *Plan d'un nouveau banque nationale et territoriale* (Paris, 1789); B. L. F213 (3), [Anon.], *Rapport du 22 janvier 1790 fait par MM les commissaires pour l'examen du plan de M. Ferrières au comité générale du district de Henri IV* (Paris, 1790). The plan was similar to those proposed by Constantin-François Volney: see his *Moyen très simple pour vendre en moins de deux ans, et sans dépréciation, tous les biens appartenant ci-devant au clergé et au domaine* [1790], in Constantin-François Volney, *Oeuvres*, 3 vols. (Paris, Fayard, 1989–98), 1:151–5; and to an earlier land bank proposal, explicitly modelled

decided to back Bailly's proposal and authorised the sale of the full 400 million livres' worth of *assignats* to the municipalities of both Paris and the rest of the kingdom.[115]

Some two months later, however, it began to have second thoughts. It did so partly in response to a speech on 13 May 1790 by Jacques-François Menou, the man whom Joseph Fauchet, six months later, named the "austere" Menou (and who, later still, became a member of the Feuillant club, and, subsequently, the general who led the French army into the *faubourg* Saint-Antoine to crush the last popular Parisian insurrection in the spring of 1795). It did so mainly, however, because of the furious reaction in Paris that Menou's speech provoked. In the speech, Menou told the assembly that he had been offered a bribe during the negotiations between the Parisian municipality and the financiers whose credit was to be used to underwrite its initial payment for the nationalised church property. The speech served to discredit the scheme overnight. The future Feuillant leaders Duport and Lameth now joined Pétion in opposing Bailly's proposal. For Duport, it amounted to giving "a present of three million livres to the capitalists of Paris." For Charles Lameth, "it was a mistake to think that the security offered by capitalists was required to give the *assignats* credit. If anything is likely to discredit the *assignats*, it is to involve capitalists in the acquisition and sale of these assets. Underwriting would have been shameful even under Calonne. The National Assembly cannot countenance an operation like this."[116] The episode played into the already difficult relationship between Bailly, the Parisian municipality, and the sixty districts (soon to become forty-eight sections) into which the capital was divided. The municipality's communal assembly, then presided over by Sieyès's critic the future Girondin bishop Claude Fauchet, had already criticised Bailly's proposal, arguing instead that the Parisian districts should deal directly with the National Assembly over the future fate of church property, and Menou's speech helped to reinforce its hostility.[117] On 20 May a public *Lettre adressée par les représentants de la commune à leurs commettants* (Letter from the Representatives of the Commune to

on the Ayr bank scheme: see *Le fonds des dîmes ecclésiastiques mis en circulation, ou création d'un crédit territorial pour la liquidation de la dette de l'état* (n.p., 18 September 1789), and *Les jetons. Apologue politico-économique* (Paris, 1789).

[115] *Archives parlementaires* 12 (18 March 1790): 212.

[116] The only detailed account of the episode is to be found in Sigismond Lacroix, *Actes de la commune de Paris pendant la révolution*, première série, 7 vols. (Paris, 1894–8), 5:375–489 (the remarks by Lameth and Duport, as well as Pétion's earlier speech, are quoted on pp. 378, 381). See also *Archives parlementaires* 15 (13 May 1790): 501–2.

[117] See, for the wider context, Gary Kates, *The Cercle Social, the Girondins, and the French Revolution* (Princeton, Princeton UP, 1985), pp. 33–66 (pp. 59, 64–5 for this episode), and Maurice Genty, *L'apprentissage de la citoyenneté. Paris 1789–1795* (Paris, Messidor, 1987), pp. 35–62 (p. 50 for a passing mention of this episode).

Their Constituents) amplified on what Menou had said, and called for the scheme to be dropped. Although Bailly replied in kind, and refused to attend a meeting with the representatives of the commune, the scheme was effectively dead.

In a superficial sense, the episode has some of the hallmarks of a post-Soviet scramble for spoils. But in a real sense, it was an indication of the difficulties involved in reconciling debt reduction on the one side with promoting justice and prosperity on the other. To its critics, opting for Bailly's proposal amounted to cementing the relationship between Paris and the rest of France into the political future. Opting against it not only implied rearranging the longer-term relationship between the kingdom and its capital, but, in the short term, paying less attention to the need to focus on the deficit. A further reason for doing so had arisen on 12 April 1790, when, mainly to neutralise clerical claims that the sale of church property was, as the bishop of Nancy put it, designed purely to appease a few "capitalists," a piously patriotic Carthusian monk named Dom Gerle had proposed that Catholicism should be declared the state religion. If it were, he suggested, then clerical opposition to the confiscation of church property could be exposed more easily as the self-interested policy that it really was. The proposal polarised the assembly and set in train the sequence of events that led, on 12 July 1790, to the civil constitution of the French clergy. On 13 April 1790, the same Jacques-François Menou successfully proposed a countermotion, predicated on his argument that the National Assembly had no power to turn any religion into a state religion. As the motion put it, "the National Assembly declares that, out of respect for the Supreme Being and the Catholic, Apostolic and Roman religion, the only religion maintained at the expense of the state, it does not believe that it can pronounce on the question."[118] It was a commitment to something like what the anonymous English author of the *Essay on the Constitution of England* had called the religion of the magistrate, but at public expense.

This additional commitment, followed a month later by Menou's revelation of an attempted "capitalist" bribe, led the National Assembly to drop its initial support for the Necker-Bailly scheme. On 17 May 1790, it reversed its earlier approval of Bailly's proposal and opted instead for using former church property for more redistributive and egalitarian purposes. In doing so, it decided to adopt a system of sale that fitted the views of Duport, Lameth, and Pétion within the assembly, as well as those advocated by Brissot and Clavière from the outside. Municipalities were now

[118] *Archives parlementaires* 12 (13 April 1790): 715–6. On the broader sequence, see Nigel Aston, *The End of an Elite: The French Bishops and the Coming of the Revolution 1786–1790* (Oxford, OUP, 1992), pp. 231–42; and Tackett, *Becoming a Revolutionary*, pp. 265–71.

required to fix land prices at a multiple of twelve times their annual yield, and to offer units for sale for a down payment of 20 percent, with the remainder to be paid off over a period of twelve years. This, in the wake of the establishment of the civil constitution of the clergy, remained the policy when, on 2 November 1790, the former duc de la Rochefoucauld, in his capacity as head of the National Assembly's combined committees of finance and the alienation of national property, set out their joint recommendations for the final implementation of the property sales. Anyone who bought property before 15 May 1791 would be entitled to pay for it over a period of twelve years, while purchasers after that date would be required to pay a fifth of the sale price a month after the purchase, together with a further fifth in the course of the same year, with the balance to be paid at six-monthly intervals over the following four years. There would be no loss to the state for what de la Rochefoucauld called "this political measure," not only because deferred payments would be subject to an annual interest rate of 5 percent, but also, he emphasised, because the new implementation strategy was likely to lead to an acceleration of sales.[119]

Under these conditions, more sales did not necessarily mean more revenue. The deliberate shift to deficit finance that occurred during the summer of 1790 magnified the tension between the short-term debt problem and the longer-term problem of inequality. Failure to deal with the first was likely to make it harder, not easier, to deal with the second. This was one reason for Mirabeau's willingness to respond to the overtures from the court, and it also became the reason for the joint decision by Barnave, Duport, and the Lameth brothers to join the negotiations in the autumn of 1790. They were parties to Mirabeau's not entirely secret dealings with the king and queen well before he died on 2 April 1791. To the growing number of their enemies, the move was motivated by political ambition, a charge voiced most powerfully by Robespierre when, on 16 May 1791, he launched his famous (and successful) proposal to bar members of the National Assembly from standing for reelection to the next legislature.[120] But to Barnave, Duport, and the Lameth brothers, their success in turning the *assignat* into a fiat currency, and in promoting the sale of national property

---

[119] The details of the legislation, but without a description of the accompanying arguments, are described in Marcel Garaud, *Histoire générale du droit privé de 1789 à 1804*, 2 vols. (Paris, Sirey, 1953–8), vol. 2, *La Révolution et la propriété foncière*, pp. 305–6, 313–6. For La Rochefoucauld's speech, see *Archives parlementaires* 20 (2 November 1790): 196. In broader terms, French revolutionary fiscal policy has not been studied as fully as French revolutionary fiscal performance. For a clear overview of the latter, see Donald M. G. Sutherland, "Taxation, Representation and Dictatorship in France, 1789–1830," in W. M. Ormrod, Margaret Bonney, and Richard Bonney, eds., *Crises, Revolutions, and Self-Sustained Growth: Essays in European Fiscal History, 1130–1830* (Stamford, Shaun Tyas, 1999), pp. 414–26.

[120] Robespierre, *Oeuvres*, 7:377–402, followed, pp. 403–23, by his reply to Duport.

to real individuals on relatively long credit terms, now meant that financial stability had to be the first priority. Robespierre's proposal was supported by Pétion (as well as by Dominique-Joseph Garat) but was opposed by Adrien Duport in an apocalyptic speech to the National Assembly on the following day. "Degree by degree," he told his audience, "you have been led towards a veritable and complete disorganisation of society." This, in the first instance, was an effect of the way that, as he put it, "some men" were sensible of only "one type of danger," namely, "popular movements." These, he said, were certainly excusable, at least in terms of their causes, but their effects were incompatible with legal and political stability. "One more step," he warned, "and the government will no longer be able to exist, or will be concentrated totally in the executive power." The ban on reelection, coupled with the two-year life span of each legislature, would give the members of every forthcoming legislature a built-in incentive to cater very heavily to the interests of the departments that had elected them, since these would be where their political futures would lie. Irrespective of the additional effects of the loss of continuity and experience that the ban would entail, it would leave the political initiative in the hands of the executive. "It has sometimes been said, doubtless as a joke," Duport informed the assembly, "that the king is useless for our constitution." But, he warned, it was far more likely to be the legislature that was useless. "Everything will be there, with a king, and some departments; the first for the general interest, and the rest for local interests." Famously, as Duport put it, "what has been called the revolution is finished (*la révolution est faite*)." But this did not mean that liberty, as some claimed, was now secure. Man, he explained, lives in no more than three states (*il n'y a que trois états pour l'homme*). These followed a clear sequence, running from independence to slavery, and then to liberty. But the sequence could also be circular, since too much liberty could lead to independence, and independence (or what Duport called "individuality") would, in turn, lead to a reversion to slavery. Without a real government, Duport warned, and deputies elected to play an active part in administration by taking responsibility for following a clear plan of taxation and finance, for liquidating and amortising the public debt, and for dealing with questions of war and peace, the colonies, and commercial treaties, liberty would be lost.[121] It was an argument about government's tendency towards despotism that met Robespierre (and Pétion) on something like their own Rousseauian terms.

As the argument indicates, it is important not to assume that there was any intrinsic affinity between Rousseau's thought and the policies advocated by any particular political faction. Underlying the warning that Duport issued were two potentially urgent problems. The first was the

---

[121] *Archives parlementaires* 26 (17 May 1791): 149–53.

growing stream of emigrants. Not only did they take wealth with them, leaving land neglected and property unattended, but their gradual disappearance also threatened to undermine the one source of tax revenue that was less likely to have a direct impact on the price of subsistence goods and the consumption of the poor. This was the income produced by indirect taxes on colonial or manufactured goods (in many cases, as with printed cotton fabrics, or *indiennes*, the two overlapped). Here, differences in tax policy were an indication of wider differences in political orientation. Where Clavière was not at all committed to indirect taxation, preferring, in the long run, to consolidate all taxes into a single tax, based on the rental value of property (thus removing small property owners from the tax base), Barnave and his political allies preferred to see taxes fall largely on nonessential items of consumption.[122] This divergence was connected to the second, more immediately urgent, problem. This was the question of the nature and future of the French colonial empire. As Barnave began to warn from the spring of 1790 onwards, the possibility that trade and the colonial sources of tax revenue might dry up ruled out dismantling the slave-based French empire anywhere nearly as fast as the supporters of the French Society of Friends of the Blacks, headed by Brissot and Clavière, would have liked (Duport, it is worth remembering, as well as Sieyès and Mirabeau, had also been members). In 1790—despite the public argument, mainly between Brissot and Barnave, over the subject—the question of the empire and the status of its black population did not interfere with the broader consensus over church property and the *assignat*. By 1791, it did. While both sides in the argument over the empire acknowledged that slavery and liberty seemed able to coexist, however provisionally, within the federal structure of the United States of America, the mixture of a unitary government with a unitary debt, but with a fragile fiscal system, made the problem more intractable in France. As Barnave told the National Assembly bluntly on 12 May 1791, "the national interest and reason of state (*raison d'état*) cannot permit 600,000 men in a state of slavery to receive their liberty."[123] One increasingly urgent reason was that the growing stream of *émigrés* threatened to bring back the same problem from another direction. Losing the colonies could cut off the supply of tax revenue from nonessential items of consumption, but so, too, could losing the tax base itself. Either prospect pointed towards greater reliance on tax revenue generated directly by landed property, and a vicious circle

---

[122] For Clavière's views, see Etienne Clavière, *Réflexions sur les formes et les principes auxquels une nation libre doit assujettir l'administration des finances* (Paris, 1791), *avant-propos*, pp. 10–1, and pp. 43–8.

[123] *Archives parlementaires* 26 (12 May 1791): 14. On the membership of the Société des amis des noirs, see Marcel Dorigny and Bernard Gainot, *La société des amis des noirs 1788–1799: contribution à l'histoire de l'abolition de l'esclavage* (Paris, Editions UNESCO, 1998).

of higher taxation, rising cereal prices, and growing dependence by mainly poor urban consumers on largely rich rural landowners. If the British example showed that the balance of political power followed the balance of property, then the subjects of empire and emigration were two sides of the same coin. As Barnave began to insist, keeping the first and stopping the second really were reasons of state.

The problems generated by these subjects led to two drastic changes in political orientation. These were already beginning to become apparent by 28 February 1791, when the presiding head of the National Assembly's constitutional committee, a man named Isaac-René-Guy Le Chapelier, gave the assembly a report on a decree on emigration that the committee had discussed. Le Chapelier (who six months later became a member of the Feuillant club) was reluctant to read the actual text of the decree because, he informed the assembly, the committee had been divided over whether or not its provisions were constitutional. It soon became clear that the source of the division could be found in the second of its three, short articles. This stipulated that, were the decree to come into force, the National Assembly would appoint a three-man council to exercise, as the article in question put it, "dictatorial power over the right to leave, and the obligation to return to, the kingdom." Although Le Chapelier did not express his own views, it soon became clear that he, as well as Mirabeau, who spoke eloquently against it, did not support the proposal. Mirabeau recommended dropping it altogether and proposed that the assembly should pass on to the order of the day. There was noisy opposition, and the assembly decided finally to adjourn, rather than drop, the subject. By the time that it came back, Mirabeau was dead, and, on 20 June 1791, Louis XVI had tried, if not to emigrate, at least to move the royal government to somewhere outside Paris. When the new legislature took up the subject, in October 1791, positions began to shift. The discussion that began on 2 October 1791, almost as soon as the Legislative Assembly started to sit, continued into the second week of November. On 20 October, Mathieu Dumas, a member of the five-man committee that had taken over Mirabeau's secret negotiations with the king and queen (the others were Barnave, Duport, Lameth, and Antoine-Joseph, formerly baron, d'André) proposed a decree ordering a court-martial for any soldier who left his post without having first submitted his resignation. "It is often said in this tribunal, where Montesquieu's shade is so often and so rightly remembered," Dumas told the assembly, "that it may be necessary to draw a veil for a while over liberty, as it was customary to veil the statues of the gods."[124]

---

[124] *Archives parlementaires* 34 (20 October 1791): 320. The phrase appears in Charles-Louis de Secondat, baron de Montesquieu, *The Spirit of Laws* [1748], trans. Thomas Nugent (New York, Hafner Publishing Company, 1949), bk. 12, ch. 19.

But, he continued, harking back to Mirabeau's earlier opposition to the proposed use of "dictatorial power" to put a stop to emigration, prevailing constitutional stability and political principle ruled out any more literal application of Montesquieu's metaphor.

Five days later, however, the metaphor reappeared, but this time in a rather different sense. The speaker now was another prominent Feuillant, Charles-Emmanuel-Joseph-Pierre Pastoret (but an ally of Lafayette, rather than of Duport, Barnave, and Lameth). "On some occasions," he said, rehearsing Montesquieu's metaphor, "it may be necessary to draw a veil for a while over liberty, as it was customary to veil the statues of the gods." This time, however, Pastoret endorsed Montesquieu's recommendation. Rousseau, he added, citing book 3, chapter 18, of *The Social Contract*, had explicitly equated emigration designed to avoid serving one's country with desertion. Accordingly, Pastoret proposed a decree made up of six articles. The first two ordered the king's brothers, the comte de Provence and the comte d'Artois, to return to France within six weeks. Any soldier or public officer who had left his post after the king's acceptance of the constitution was to be deprived of his citizenship, but all other *émigrés* were to be invited to return to France within two months under the safeguard of the law. This carrot was accompanied by the threat of a future stick, since the sixth article of the projected decree left it open to the assembly to decide, on 1 January 1792, what to do with anyone who failed to obey its requirements.[125]

This shift of emphasis can probably best be explained by the tactics that Barnave and his allies had come to adopt. The public record of their negotiations with the queen began immediately after the flight to Varennes. According to the notes made by Marie Antoinette, their first demand was to get the *émigrés* to come back. "The king," she was told early in July 1791, "can keep the throne with dignity, and obtain confidence and respect, only by obtaining great advantages for the nation." These would consist, first, of the return of the princes and the *émigrés*, or at least some of them, and, second, of a declaration by the Holy Roman Emperor recognising the new French constitution and expressing his friendly and peaceful intentions towards the French nation.[126] By late October, particularly after the Pilnitz Declaration by the rulers of the empire and Prussia of 27 August 1791, it is likely that the prospects of the delivery of these advantages were beginning to look like a forlorn hope. Barnave and his allies seem accordingly to have decided to switch tactics, and to rely on threats, rather than promises, to get the *émigrés* back. Where, in February 1791, it had been the Jacobin component of the French National Assembly that had been prepared to take Montesquieu's

[125] *Archives parlementaires* 34 (25 October 1791): 404–7.
[126] Söderhjelm, *Marie-Antoinette et Barnave*, p. 42.

metaphor to heart and draw a veil over liberty, by October 1791 Barnave and his allies had decided that it was they who would have to draw the veil. From their point of view, getting the *émigrés* back, with or without a further declaration of peaceful intent by the Holy Roman Emperor, was the key to maintaining domestic political stability. Without them, the economy would continue to go backwards, the deficit would grow, the *assignat* would fall, and public and private credit would be strangled. Necessity, from this perspective, meant adopting Jacobin means to achieve constitutional ends.

This switch produced a second switch, this time on what, by the autumn of 1791, had become the Jacobin side. Until the autumn of 1791, the strongest supporters of the *assignat* were Brissot, Clavière, and their political allies. Irrespective of its potential long-term benefits, they argued repeatedly, its most immediate advantage was its capacity to prevent a catastrophic debt default and the economic disaster that a bankruptcy was likely to cause. By late 1791, however, the emphasis changed. Where Barnave and his allies began to try very hard to bring the *émigrés* back, Brissot and his allies began to try equally hard to keep the *émigrés* out. Bringing them back meant trying to maintain the financial stability that, among other things, would give them something to come back to. Keeping them out, on the other hand, meant removing the financial enticements that might bring them back. Clavière, accordingly, began to describe the nation's debt in a new and rather different way. Instead of arguing, as he had done earlier, that using the *assignat* was the best way to manage all the many different types of financial obligation owed by the nation to its assorted creditors, he began, in an article dated 25 November 1791, to revive the distinction between what he called the "constituted" and the "demandable" (*exigible*) debts. The first, consisting of perpetual or life annuities, remained a real obligation, but the second, consisting of debt arising from the abolition of venal offices, the suppression of feudal dues, the arrears of interest payments, and anticipations of tax revenue, was no longer a matter of public faith. Trying to cover both sets of obligations, Clavière now argued, would lead to a massive rise in the issue of *assignats* and a further, more pronounced, devaluation of the currency. There was no alternative, he stated, to suspending payments on the *dette exigible*.

As the Feuillant *Journal de Paris* commented, this amounted to calling for a partial state bankruptcy.[127] In one sense, it could be said, it was

---

[127] Etienne Clavière, "De ce qu'il faut faire dans l'état actuel des finances," *Chronique du mois* 2 (December 1791): 4–30 (pp. 10–3, 18, 28–30). The description (rejected by Clavière) of his proposal as a national bankruptcy was published in issue 329, p. 1335, of the 1791 volume of the *Journal de Paris*. For a similar characterisation of Clavière's proposal, see the commentary in the pro-Feuillant *Ami des patriotes* described in Odette Dossios-Pralat, *Michel Regnaud de Saint-Jean-d'Angély, serviteur fidèle de Napoléon* (Paris, Editions Historiques Teissèdre, 2007), p. 89.

simply a capitulation to reality and, as Clavière himself wrote, a recognition that the spiralling prices that continuing deficit finance was likely to produce would destroy political stability. But in another sense, it was also a very public indication that there would be no financial carrots available to returning *émigrés*. For Clavière, finally, keeping the public faith took second place to politics, and, by late 1791, politics required widening, not reducing, the breach with Barnave and the Feuillants. If this ruled out any further gestures towards trying to maintain urban expenditure on colonial and manufactured goods, it also eliminated any further need to try to use a mixture of inducements and intimidation to bring the *émigrés* back. With this breach in place, the only available constituency to which Brissot, Clavière, and their allies could turn to was a popular one. Without the resources of empire, or the expenditure of the *émigrés*, the one remaining pillar of the new regime had to be the people.

ANTOINE-JOSEPH GORSAS AND THE POLITICS
OF REVOLUTIONARY SATIRE

These switches in orientation are a measure of what had come to be at stake by the autumn of 1791. As Robespierre may really have said, the transformation of the joke about breeches into the political emblem that the words *sans culottes* became was largely the work of Jacques-Pierre Brissot and his Girondin, or Brissotin, political allies. It occurred during the autumn and winter of 1791–2 in the aftermath of Louis XVI's unsuccessful flight to Varennes on 21 June 1791 and the final split in the Parisian Jacobin club that the king's flight precipitated. The immediate result of the king's flight was a campaign in Paris organised by a minority of the members of the Jacobin club, together with members of the Cordeliers club and the looser moral and political association known as the Social Circle, calling, somewhat ambiguously, for the proclamation of a republic. The question of the fate of the monarchy split the Jacobin club completely; three weeks after the king's flight, the majority of its members seceded and, on 15 July 1791, established another political society meeting in a former Feuillant convent. The effect of the split was magnified two days later by what came to be known as the massacre of the Champ-de-Mars, when a crowd that had been called together there to sign a petition protesting against the National Assembly's decision to reinstate the king (the site had been used, three days earlier, to commemorate the second anniversary of the fall of the Bastille) was dispersed violently by the Parisian National Guard, leaving up to fifty people dead.[128] The events of 17 July 1791 left the tiny

---

[128] On these events, see, classically, George Rudé, *The Crowd in the French Revolution* (Oxford, OUP, 1959), and, more recently, David Andress, *Massacre at the Champ de Mars*

Jacobin rump exposed both to the threat of prosecution for having insti-gated the petition campaign (earlier legislation, including the famous Le Chapelier law of 14 June 1791, had made collective petitioning illegal) and to the broader charge of bearing a moral and political responsibility for the massacre of the Champ-de-Mars.[129] This was the context in which the salon society joke was turned into a substantive noun.

The neologism was used, as the version of Robespierre's speech printed in the *Logotachigraphe* later implied, to present Brissot and his political allies as friends of the poor and enemies of the rich, mainly to prevent a possible pro-Feuillant vote in the Parisian elections to the new French Legislative Assembly in September 1791 and to block the threat of pros-ecution for the events on the Champ-de-Mars. The strategy certainly worked. Between July and November 1791, the Jacobin rump enjoyed an extraordinary political renaissance. Not only did Brissot and his al-lies win the Parisian elections to the Legislative Assembly and have one of their leaders, Jérôme Pétion, elected to the office of mayor of Paris in November 1791, but, by March 1792, they had become the king's min-isters. This, in fact, was the ministry that Louis XVI dismissed in June 1792, precipitating the Parisian insurrection that first saw the banner *libres et sans-culottes* on display. To its enemies, this Brissotin ministry (though Brissot himself was not actually one of its members) was once known as the *ministère sans-culotte*.[130]

There were many reasons for the Jacobin revival, not all of them con-fined to Paris, or even entirely to France.[131] The reaction to the Pilnitz Declaration by the rulers of Prussia and the Holy Roman Empire of 27 August 1791, the hostile clusters of *émigrés* on France's northern and eastern borders, the violence in Avignon after the more or less legal an-nexation of the papal enclave, the slave insurrection in San-Domingo, the sugar shortage that it produced, and the inflationary spike in prices that the collapse in the supply of colonial goods entailed—all played their part. So, too, however, did the neologism that the name *sans-culotte* became. It did so because it played into the political situation produced both by the conflict between the Jacobins and the Feuillants that developed after the

---

(London, The Royal Historical Society, Boydell Press, 2000), and his "Order, Respectability and the Sans-Culottes," *The French Historian: Bulletin of the Society for the Study of French History* 10, no. 1 (Autumn 1995). For a clear overview, see William Doyle, *The Oxford History of the French Revolution* (Oxford, OUP, 1989), pp. 152–5.

[129] On the background to the Le Chapelier law, which, in the first instance, was as much concerned with collective petitioning by political clubs as with trade associations, see Sonen-scher, *Work and Wages*, pp. 350–2.

[130] M. Touchard-Lafosse, *Souvenirs d'un demi-siècle*, 6 vols. (Brussels, 1836), 2:262.

[131] On the wider international setting, see T.C.M. Blanning, *The Origins of the French Revolutionary Wars* (London, Arnold, 1986).

massacre of the Champ-de-Mars, and by the perceived threat to French external security represented as much by the alarming longer-term military implications of the depreciation of the *assignat* as by anything actually done by the rulers of Prussia and the Empire. The rush to war in the winter of 1791–2 owed less to military delusion than to a bleaker (but still possibly ill-judged) assessment that the longer a war might be postponed, the more unstable French public finances might become, and, as a result, the more difficult it might be to win a war later, rather than sooner, particularly in the absence of the Franco-British alliance that, almost to the last, Brissot and his supporters hoped for.[132] In this sense, the war was not so much a gamble on the pro-French sympathies of the Belgians, or even on the patriotism of the French army command, as a gamble on the future, where the risks seemed to pile up the further ahead it stretched. This formed the context of the Brissotin campaign for war and the appeal to the *sans-culottes*. The details of how the new emblem caught on can be reconstructed quite fully, and this, in turn, helps to throw fresh light on the kinds of concern that it was intended to catch. Although this is not so apparent now, it was the least obviously republican (or even recognisably political) of a number of different emblems that, at one time or another between July 1791 and May 1792, began to be used by supporters of the initially tiny Jacobin rump to win back a popular following. In the beginning, there was no established connection between the salon society joke and the emblem that it became.

Two other emblems had a more recognisable historical and political pedigree. Both lent themselves readily to the type of metonymy involved in using the name of a thing or a condition (like being without breeches) for the name of a person. The first was the pike, with its well-established patriotic and republican connotations, while the second was the Phrygian cap or bonnet, which, as Castilhon's character Wolban observed, the Romans had once given to an emancipated slave (the Romans called it a *pileus*).[133] Both were to be seen on the day that Voltaire's remains were transferred to the Pantheon—Monday, 11 July 1791—when, according to one observer, the procession included contingents from the political clubs, fraternal societies, and the pike-carrying inhabitants of the Parisian suburbs,

---

[132] On these hopes and the background to them, see A. N. F⁷ 4774⁷⁰, dossier Pétion; Marcel Reinhard, "Le voyage de Pétion à Londres, 24 Octobre–11 Novembre 1791," *Revue d'histoire diplomatique* (1970): 1–60; and Albert Goodwin, *The Friends of Liberty: The English Democratic Movement in the Age of the French Revolution* (London, 1979), pp. 186–8.

[133] For Wolban's remark, see above, pp. 194–5. On its eighteenth-century currency as a republican emblem, see, too, the description of the library of the English republican Thomas Hollis, in Caroline Robbins, "The Strenuous Whig, Thomas Hollis of Lincoln's Inn" [1950], reprinted in her *Absolute Liberty*, ed. Barbara Taft (Hamden, Conn., Archon Books, 1982), pp. 168–205 (p. 182).

"newly called," he noted, *"bonnets de laine."*[134] This, now largely forgotten, metonym initially had a far wider currency than the better-known *sans-culotte*, if only because its direct association with the Roman republic made it a more immediately obvious political symbol. The use to which it was put was made mainly by a journalist named Louis-Marie Prudhomme, the proprietor of a newspaper called *Les Révolutions de Paris*, and one of the leaders of a Parisian political club called the Society of Indigents that he, among others, had founded in 1790. Prudhomme gave the sort of people that the Society of Indigents was intended to represent the name of *bonnets-de-laine*, meaning woollen caps, and, between the summer of 1791 and the spring of 1792, embarked on a serious press campaign to turn it into the name of a real political force. As Prudhomme presented them, they were intended to embody a set of moral and political qualities that were not to be found among what, in an earlier article, he had associated with the *bourgeoisie*. The article, headed *Des bourgeois de Paris et autres* (On the Parisian and other Bourgeois), which was published in the 5–12 March 1791 issue of the *Révolutions de Paris*, painted a largely unsympathetic picture of what Prudhomme called "a class of citizens that had not done much to be talked about during the Revolution." The *bourgeois*, he wrote, was rather like the rat of Lafontaine's fable, happy to hide in its hole and nibble at its Dutch cheese when war was raging around. If the noise got too loud, it would withdraw even further; and, once the noise died down, it would stick out its nose to see which way the wind was blowing, before venturing out. And if a *bourgeois* was not a rat, then the same *bourgeois* was just as likely to be a sheep. In either case, Prudhomme observed, a *bourgeois* "is not a democrat."[135]

By implication, a *bonnet de laine*, or a *sans-culotte*, was. For a time, the two terms were used interchangeably, as is indicated by a letter published in late March 1792, and written by a self-styled police commissioner (*commissaire de police*) of the *bonnets de laine* and *sans-culottes* of the *faubourg* Saint-Antoine, the suburb located to the east of the site of the Bastille.[136] The overlap was particularly marked in the spring of 1792 during the Parisian campaign to free the Swiss soldiers of the Chateauvieux regiment who had been imprisoned for mutiny in 1790, and whose release had become a Jacobin cause célèbre.[137] It was still visible at an open-air banquet

---

[134] Charles de Villette, *Lettres choisies sur les principaux évènements de la révolution* (Paris, 1792), p. 186.

[135] *Révolutions de Paris* 87 (5–12 March 1791): 453–7 (pp. 453–4 for the phrases cited). Compare to Sarah C. Maza, *The Myth of the French Bourgeoisie: An Essay on the Social Imaginary* (Cambridge, Mass., Harvard UP, 2003). See also *Révolutions de Paris* 82 (February 1791): 169–75 for an earlier discussion of the rich and the poor.

[136] *Courrier des LXXXIII Départements*, 27 March 1792, pp. 425–6.

[137] *Courrier des LXXXIII Départements*, 17 March 1792, pp. 265–7.

on the Champs-Elysées organised by the Parisian market porters for some four to five hundred people on Sunday 25 March 1792 to commemorate the laying of a stone from the Bastille as the foundation of the new Parisian central market building. The banquet, presided over by Santerre, the new commander of the Parisian National Guard, and attended by Pétion and Claude Fauchet, the bishop of the department of the Calvados and the leading figure in the Parisian Cercle Social, set the seal on the earlier emblem's brief popularity. The toasts—to the soldiers of the Chateauvieux regiment, to the free blacks of San-Domingo, to the conquerors of the Bastille, to the *bonnets de laine* and *sans-culottes*—captured the contours of a political force that had begun to emerge. The high point of the ceremony was the baptism, by Fauchet, of a little girl named Pétion-Nationale-Pique who was then escorted, via the Jacobin club, to the *faubourg* Saint-Antoine where her father was a drummer in the National Guard.[138] The whole affair was rather like Rousseau's description of the ceremony that he had seen in the Genevan suburb of Saint-Gervais nearly eighty years earlier, as, too, was the mixture of military and civil service symbolised by the liberty cap, with its Roman republican connotations. Despite considerable variations in its size, shape, and colour, the Phrygian cap was widely adopted (most famously on 20 June 1792, when Louis XVI was forced to put one on).[139] But for all its undoubted popularity, it never came to be turned into a name given to, and used by, real people in the way that the words *sans culottes* did. As Prudhomme himself later acknowledged, by *bonnets-de-laine* he had really meant *sans-culottes*.[140]

While the *bonnets-de-laine* gradually disappeared from history, the *sans-culottes* did not. The neologism caught on quite slowly, between September 1791 and May 1792, and, as it did, what began as a joke turned, gradually, into a symbol of class conflict (the classes in question were "the bourgeoisie," "the mercantile class," or "the property owners" on the one side, and "the people," "the class of workers," "the indigent, useful, and laborious class," or "the industrious class" on the other).[141] If, in the longer term (and in French Revolutionary terms, that meant a year), the new name was to set the seal on its authors' political fate, in the short term it proved to be their political making. As Mercier later wrote, the noun that the joke became really had been used as a term of abuse ("there has been an insurrection at the Champ-de-Mars by people without breeches [*de gens sans*

---

[138] *Courrier des LXXXIII Départements*, 28 and 29 March 1792, pp. 440–3, 455–61. See also *Gazette universelle*, 28 March 1792.

[139] On the Phrygian cap, see Richard Wrigley, *The Politics of Appearances: Representation of Dress in Revolutionary France* (Oxford, Berg, 2002), pp. 135–86.

[140] Louis-Marie Prudhomme, *Louis Prudhomme aux patriotes, le 13 juin 1793* (Paris, 1793).

[141] See, for example, Antoine-Joseph Gorsas, *Le Courrier des LXXXIII Départements*, 1 May 1792, p. 7; 2 May 1792, pp. 26–9; 15 May 1792, p. 237.

culottes] and others who do not want a king," one Parisian supporter of the monarchy wrote to a provincial friend on the day of the Champ-de-Mars massacre itself).[142] As he also indicated, the neologism simply turned the joke against its authors. But as Mercier did not indicate, it did so in a way that was redolent of the Cynic-style cultural criticism that he himself had practised many years before the events of 1791. Here, the main exponent of this mixture of satire and strong moral criticism was not actually Mercier himself but a man of letters and journalist named Antoine-Joseph Gorsas, because it was Gorsas, not Mercier, who was largely responsible for turning the words *sans culottes* into an emblem of the differences between the Jacobins and the Feuillants, and the moral and political gulf that now lay between them.

Before 1789, Gorsas had followed a career that was rather similar to those that Rutledge and Mercier had also followed, but, unlike them, he had specialised in art criticism rather than the theatre, and theatre criticism, in which they were both involved. He was the son of a shoemaker from Limoges who, after an education at the former Jesuit Du Plessis college in Paris, had become the head of a private military school at Versailles (where, according to his enemies, he had run afoul of the authorities for darkly unspecified reasons).[143] Gorsas published his first work of art criticism, the *Promenades de Critès au salon* (A Stroll at the Salon with Critès), in 1785. Despite its apparently neutral title (Critès

---

[142] Pierre de Vaissière, *Lettres d' 'aristocrates'. La révolution racontée par des correspondances privées* (Paris, 1907), pp. 247–8. As Mercier wrote, this usage was quite common. The prominent part played by women in the march on Versailles in October 1789, for example, allowed royalist pamphleteers to play (nastily) upon the sexual connotations of the word *culotte*. Thus Théroigne de Méricourt, one of the woman who led the crowd, was said, in a pamphlet published in 1790, to have "excited the fury of the famous *sans-culotte* [*sic*] and, braving sabres, muskets, pistols, and halberds, single-handedly buried a whole squadron of guards": B. L. F 399 [4]. [Anon.], *Théroigne et Populus, ou le triomphe de la démocratie. Drame nationale en vers civiques* (London, 1790). It can also be found in the title of an undated pamphlet entitled *La Nation Sans Culotte* (B. L. F 388 [10], Paris, n.d.), an imaginary conversation in an inn in the Champagne whose purpose was to alert the local citizenry to the politics of the Jacobin club of Chalons-sur-Marne. From its allusions to the districts (rather than the sections) of Paris, it must have been written early in 1790.

[143] See his own note on his earlier life in *Le Courrier de Paris dans les provinces et des provinces à Paris* 10 (23 November 1789): 139. The fullest account of Gorsas's life and political career, but one that does not say much about the part he played in giving the words *sans culottes* their now familiar political connotations, is in Antoine de Baecque, *Les éclats du rire. La culture des rieurs au xviiie siècle* (Paris, Calmann-Lévy, 2000), pp. 235–87. On the newspapers (like the *Chant du Coq* and the *Babillard*) that were the targets of Gorsas's press campaign, see David Andress, "Press and Public in the French Revolution: A Parisian Case-Study from 1791," *European History Quarterly* 28 (1998): 51–80. Further information on Gorsas can be found in Richard Wrigley, *The Origins of French Art Criticism: From the Ancien Regime to the Restoration* (Oxford, OUP, 1993), pp. 187–8.

was simply a Greek-like word for critic), the pamphlet was actually an extended exercise in Cynic satire. The Crites in question was given the guise of a cobbler from the Limousin named Chrysostomus Crites, a name borrowed from a once very famous early eighteenth-century satire on antiquarianism called *Le Chef d'oeuvre d'un inconnu* (An Unknown Artist's Masterpiece), by Claude Thémiseul de Saint-Hyacinthe, or, less grandly, Hyacinthe Cordonnier, a name that made him a shoemaker (*cordonnier*) to Gorsas's cobbler (*savetier*).[144] This performance was followed by another, equally Cynic sequel, a description of the next year's salon that Gorsas published in 1787 under the title of *La Plume du coq de Micille* (Mycillus's Cockerel's Feather).

Here, Gorsas used the trick of treating the paintings and sculptures at the salon as if they were real people. He also gave himself the persona of another cobbler, this time named Mycillus, who had managed to get into the salon because he owned a cockerel's feather that made him invisible (the idea came from Pythagoras, who believed that, in a previous life, he had been a cockerel belonging to Mycillus).[145] Once inside the salon, Mycillus was made welcome by the busts of Cassandra, Racine, Bayard, Molière, Marshal de Luxemburg, and Saint Vincent de Paul before he got on with making his assessments of the paintings and sculptures on display. These, it turned out, had views of their own, allowing Mycillus not only to describe what they had said, but to add his own comments on their often rather curious pronouncements. In doing so, and just as Mycillus was in the process of returning a tiny lamb to the portrait of Mlle Dugazon by Mlle Vigée-Lebrun that was hanging next to her own self-portrait, he came across the statues of Racine, by Boizot, and Molière, by Caffieri, who, to the consternation of their neighbour, Saint Vincent de Paul, were in the middle of a furious argument (which, Mycillus reported, was why Saint Vincent's posture in the bust by Stouf was said to look rather uncertain). The argument, he continued, would certainly have shocked the ladies on the wall nearby because it was about a pair of breeches (*une paire de culottes*). "Give me back my breeches," Racine was saying. "You can't have them," Molière said back.

> Be informed that the *History of the Royal Academy* and, moreover, the guide to this year's exhibition positively says, on page 46, line 6, word 7, including the comma and at the twelfth character of the line, that *Molière had a fine leg* and that Mme Geoffrin had some fashionable breeches (*des canons à la mode*) made for me, simply to be able to show off my fine . . .

---

[144] For a recent edition, see Claude Thémiseul de Saint-Hyacinthe, *Le chef d'oeuvre d'un inconnu*, ed. Henri Duranton (Paris, Editions du CNRS, 1991).

[145] For a version of the story, see François de Salignac de la Mothe Fénelon, *The Lives and Most Remarkable Maxims of the Ancient Philosophers* [1726] (London, 1726), pp. 84–5.

At that point, however, Molière suddenly fell silent. On closer inspection, it turned out that Caffieri had simply forgotten to add the key anatomical detail.[146]

Gorsas was an unusually imaginative satirist (and, as this passage indicates, someone who was familiar both with the joke about breeches and with the use to which it had been put by Rutledge in his rather less successful satire on Mme Geoffrin and her salon). He had already revealed his ability in another, longer, satire published in 1786. This satire, entitled *L'âne promeneur, ou Critès promené par son âne* (The Strolling Ass, or Crites Borne by His Ass), was, as Gorsas indicated, a parody of Fénelon's *Telemachus*, with Chrysostomus Crites, the cobbler-*cum*-art critic from the Limousin, here appearing as the "new Telemachus" and a Cochin-Chinese donkey named Gu-Tien-Gu as his "long-eared Minerva" and Mentor.[147] In this incarnation, instead of travelling around the ancient world, the new Telemachus travelled in both time and space, mainly back to the chaos that had preceded the Creation, and, in the process of writing the text itself, through an introduction, preface, pre-preface, disquisition on the origin of the preface, printer's announcement, author's admonition, lawyer's advice, and a further range of interruptions and diversions that, in the end, meant that the narrative finally went nowhere (or simply to *utopia*). But, in the course of this Menippean exercise, Gorsas did indicate his targets quite clearly. These had nothing to do with Fénelon but were instead two much more recent comic dramatists: a playwright named Louis Archambault Dorvigny, whose very successful comedy *Janot, ou les battus paient l'amende* (which, in a more modern idiom, might be translated as "Janot, or Punishing the Victim") was first performed in 1779; and his more famous contemporary Pierre-Auguste Caron de Beaumarchais, whose satirical comedy, *The Marriage of Figaro*, was first performed publicly in 1784. Gorsas called their achievement "Jeannoto-Figarotism" (which, with the addition of the donkey's insights, would then become "Jeannoto-Figaroto-Gu-Tien-Gutism").

It has often been said that satire played some part in undermining the old regime, and *Figaro*, in particular, has sometimes been singled out as an example of how it did.[148] Gorsas's *Âne promeneur* throws a rather different

[146] Antoine-Joseph Gorsas, *La Plume du coq de Micille, ou aventures de Critès au salon, pour servir de suites aux Promenades de 1785* [1787], in René Démoris and Florence Ferran, eds., *La peinture en procès. L'invention de la critique de l'art au siècle des lumières* (Paris, Presses de la Sorbonne Nouvelle, 2004), pp. 285–369 (pp. 332–3 for this episode). Thanks to Katie Scott for bringing this edition to my notice.

[147] Antoine-Joseph Gorsas, *L'âne promeneur, ou Critès promené par son âne* (Paris, 1786), pp. 10–1.

[148] For a recent example, see Colin Jones, *The Great Nation: France from Louis XV to Napoleon* (London, 2002), pp. 322–6, 334–5. For a critical edition of the play, and a discussion of the reactions to it (but not those described here), see Gerard Kahn, ed., *Beaumarchais,*

light upon the subject because it was a satire on a satire, with a strong moral point. As Gorsas noted, this aligned him with the satirical poet Nicolas-Joseph-Laurent Gilbert, although he preferred mockery to Gilbert's "extreme" and "venomous" satires.[149] If its immediate targets were Beaumarchais and Dorvigny, its broader aim was directed at the sort of society in which their type of humour could flourish (one example could be found in a satirical royalist pamphlet published early in 1791, where both Janot and Diogenes appeared as paid hirelings of Jacobin demagoguery).[150] Crites' "Cynic rhymes" (as, at one point, Gorsas called them, noting, too, that Crites was actually a corruption of the name Crates, one of Diogenes' pupils) were meant to highlight the scale of moral corruption needed to make figures like Janot (a victim of legal chicanery) or Figaro (a witty, but artful, lackey) seem captivating.[151] Gorsas underlined the point in the poem that he wrote as an epigraph to the whole satire. "Among a people who were friends of talent," he began, "*wisdom* established games of every sort, where wit, grace, nobility and praise of the virtues, tender feelings, and the arts triumphed together in enchanting pomp." But *folly* (*sottise*) soon arose to destroy those games and their entrancing quality. "A day came when a number of *apes* (*singes*) made an appearance on the stage, and, almost at once, the whole people had its eyes fixed on them." Although a few objected, the "contagion" was irresistible. "A ridiculous clown, an ape, a Figaro, triumphed over wit, nobility, and the graces." Since that was the case, the poem concluded, there was no alternative but to do the same. "I, too," Gorsas wrote, "know how to make faces" (which was the point of the whole subsequent performance).[152]

The strong contrast between real culture and the superficial sophistication of the modern French theatre, typified by the witticisms of Beaumarchais and Dorvigny, that was the underlying message of the satire was a view that Gorsas shared with both Louis-Sébastien Mercier and Jacques-Pierre Brissot. *Figaro*, wrote Mercier in his *Tableau de Paris*, sent off "a stench of moral corruption."[153] According to Brissot, the play's

---

"*Le mariage de Figaro*", *SVEC* 2002: 12. For helpful discussions of the play's reception, see W. D. Howarth, "Beaumarchais homme de théâtre et la révolution française," in Philip Robinson, ed., *Beaumarchais, homme de lettres, homme de société* (Berne, Peter Lang, 2000–2), pp. 69–89; and Gregory S. Brown, "Beaumarchais, Social Experience and Literary Figures in Eighteenth-Century Public Life," *SVEC* 2005: 04, pp. 143–70.

[149] Gorsas, *L'âne promeneur*, pp. 61–2 and note 3.

[150] B. L. F 453 (3), *Jeannot et Diogène à Paris* (n.p., n.d., but spring 1791 from internal evidence).

[151] Gorsas, *L'âne promeneur*, pp. 66, 231, note 1.

[152] Gorsas, *L'âne promeneur*, epigraph.

[153] Louis-Sébastien Mercier, *Tableau de Paris* [1781], 12 vols. (Amsterdam, 1782–88), vol. 9, ch. 698, "Le mariage de Figaro."

popularity confirmed the shortcomings of the system of royal censorship, and the way that it tended to "suppress truths" but to sanction "scandalous productions, wherein reason is sacrificed to sarcasms and severe morality to amiable vices." *Figaro*, he wrote, "under the appearance of defending morality, turned it into ridicule." Its aim, he added, seemed to have been "to parody the greatest writers of the age, by giving their language to a rascally valet; to encourage oppression, by bringing the people to laugh at their degradation and to applaud themselves for this mad laughter; and, finally, to give the whole nation, by culpable imposture, that character of negligence and levity which belongs only to her capital."[154] Gorsas also wrote enough, in *L'âne promeneur*, to indicate that his own moral and political views were quite similar to those of both Mercier and Brissot.

He did so in the course of describing a dream by Crites' cousin Jocrisse, which, although it was interrupted when Jocrisse sneezed, was something like a parable of the human condition. It began in the chaos that existed before the Creation. But then, in rough keeping with its scriptural counterpart, a mighty Jehovah brought light, warmth, and life into being, and millions of globes covered with millions of different types of being came into existence. The globes were rather like monads (although Gorsas did not use the word). One of these "imperceptible globules" was inhabited by "a tiny atom with two legs." Infatuated with its own reason, it proclaimed itself king of all the other globes and of the whole universe. But its reach outstretched its grasp, and it lost the little parcel of reason that it had been given. It became, if not an ensouled body, an embodied soul. "The atom could no longer reason," Jocrisse dreamt, "and began instead to feel. No duty tied it any longer to the other atoms; no desires arose in the midst of its pleasures (*jouissances*); its only remaining desires were those indicated by need." Need now governed all its behaviour, and necessity became its sole guide. The atom now lived in an eternal present, stirred into action only when hunger or the need for sex made their demands felt. In this entirely self-centred state, the needs of any other atom were entirely alien to its limited consciousness. Even love was a sheer physical fact, since a female atom had "enough charm" for a male simply by having "the one organ required for the only brutal sensation that it could seek and have."[155] It was Rousseau's original state of nature in another guise.

When (after the sneeze), the dream resumed, the atom was given a second chance. The Master of the World placed it (now called "man") between two columns, one bearing a sign marked "good" and the other

---

[154] Jacques-Pierre Brissot and Etienne Clavière, *The Commerce of America with Europe, particularly with France and Great-Britain, comparatively stated and explained* (London, 1794), pp. 6–7, and note.

[155] Gorsas, *L'âne promeneur*, pp. 187–91.

"evil." The good column stood at the top of an apparently inaccessible cliff, which became easier to approach the higher one climbed. The bad column stood in a verdant, flower-covered meadow, but the terrain became increasingly harsh the nearer to it one moved. The point of the columns, the God explained, was to enable humans to make choices, while the rewards and punishments lying along the way to the one or the other were designed to help them to make the right choices. This knowledge of their new ability produced a moral awakening among the no longer atomlike humans. They began to associate, and to share both good and evil, good so that it could be distributed more widely, and evil so that it could be borne more lightly (Gorsas later used the same idea in the more politically charged context of 1792).[156] "They covered themselves with simple and modest clothes. Wealth, rank, fortune, and vain dignities were all unknown among them. If the fields that they cultivated produced more or better fruits, they were quick to share them with their friends, and their friends were all mankind."[157] But this golden age did not last. Population grew; new, hitherto unknown, needs arose, and these in turn gave rise to ideas of property. Once these new feelings had been experienced, it became apparent that the means to satisfy them were inadequate. "The so-called useful arts were invented, as well as some of those named agreeable. Social commerce took on a new form; hordes gathered; industry and cultivation began to lend one another their mutual help, and soon it became necessary to establish laws of decorum (*des lois de convenance*)."[158]

This was the first social contract. Men, Jocrisse dreamt, "would never have stopped being happy if they had not diverged from it. But ambition, the thirst for wealth, the envy to dominate by some of the members of those first associations, gradually inverted that precious legislation's system." Men who were "more adroit than the others" proposed reforms; since they did so in ways that were so intellectually seductive, wit (*esprit*) finally triumphed over reason (*raison*), silenced the voice of "modest prudence," and became "the first to welcome the dangerous innovations of these ambitious men." From then on, it was downhill all the way. The only beneficiaries of reform were its advocates, and, having established the way to overturn existing laws, they soon had imitators, who, in their turn, set out to reform the reforms, and put yet newer laws in place of the old.

The chain of society was broken; mistrust and odious suspicion were born; the principles of equality were destroyed; dissension grew; and hypocrisy

[156] "Le bonheur de tous ne peut se trouver que dans une égale répartition de maux et de biens": Antoine-Joseph Gorsas, *Courrier des LXXXIII Départements*, 10 May 1792, p. 153.
[157] Gorsas, *L'âne promeneur*, pp. 205–6.
[158] Gorsas, *L'âne promeneur*, pp. 208–9.

took on virtue's blindfold in order to suffocate virtue herself. Equity and the social system were turned into no more than empty idols, honoured in the morning for convenience, only to be violated at night to satisfy ambition and its pleasures. The rich man could now fall asleep in the bosom of opulence since the cries of the wretched could no longer be heard, and could awaken again simply to oppress the weak as they stretched out their imploring hands towards him. Man had become man's murderer.[159]

At this point a huge, three-headed monster burst into the dream and blocked off the route leading towards the column marked with the word "good" by disgorging three hydras on whose heads, "written in letters of fire," were the words "irreligion." "impudence," and "bad taste." The uproar caused Jocrisse to wake up. How, he wondered, could he have had a dream like that, especially one that was so far out of place in a book about a cobbler and a donkey?[160]

Gorsas certainly knew his Fénelon. For all its broad similarity to Rousseau's second *Discourse*, the dream also owed as much to *Telemachus*, but without the programme of royal reform. The first social state was like the community of Betica, while the second, post–social contract state showed what Salentum would have become if Idomeneus had not taken Minerva's advice (in this sense, Jocrisse's dream was also a continuation of Montesquieu's Fénelon-inspired *History of the Troglodytes*). But Gorsas was not quite so committed to the ancients as Fénelon had been, nor, perhaps, to the Quietist idea of pure love. Throughout the satire, the contrast fell not so much between ancient morality and the type of society that could have produced a Figaro, as between many of the more grotesque features of the modern age, with its mesmerism and balloons, as well as its Janots and Figaros, and an eclectic mixture of ages that, as the satire's epigraph announced, really did display "wit, nobility, and the graces." Here, Gorsas's knowledge of art also had a moral and political significance. In a long note towards the end of the satire, he made a point of highlighting the achievements of Raphael (for his *Transfiguration of St Peter*), Rubens, and the Carracci, not only for what they had painted, but also for what they had written.[161] The point of the note was to emphasise the absurdity of having academies and, even more so, of having one academy for the fine arts and another for literature. Real culture, Gorsas implied, did not need either (in the same note he also made it clear, as he had written in *Crites' Apotheosis*, another satirical pamphlet on the Royal Academy salon, that he was a supporter of the painter Vien and his pupils David, Vincent, and Taillasson in their hostility to the academy).

[159] Gorsas, *L'âne promeneur*, p. 210.
[160] Gorsas, *L'âne promeneur*, p. 211.
[161] Gorsas, *L'âne promeneur*, p. 249, note.

In this sense, Gorsas's cultural theory, with its emphasis upon the integration of the arts, was quite similar to the one that Voltaire's admirer, Jean-Louis Castilhon, attributed to the "modern Diogenes," Wolban. It is important to bear this aspect of cultural criticism in mind in explaining republican hostility towards the French academies in 1793. Real culture involved all the graces. It also required real morality. Later, Gorsas had no hesitation in recommending a very Christian plan of educational reform, written by one his acquaintances, the abbé Pierre-Nicolas-Joseph Hazard, who was the director of the National Military School at Nanterre. He also went to the trouble of publishing and reviewing a *Discourse on the Immortality of the Soul* by the abbé Jean-André Michel. Michel, Gorsas noted in his highly favourable review, appeared to have given "deep consideration" to the *Lectures* (*Discours*) published by the moderate Scottish Presbyterian minister Hugh Blair, a figure whose international fame owed as much to his championship of the apocryphal poems of the ancient Celtic bard Ossian as it did to his criticism of the religious and moral scepticism of David Hume and Adam Smith.[162] The idea of the soul's immortality, Michel wrote, was the real source of morality. "The forest-dwelling savage, as much as the inhabitant of populous cities, can both, in the depths of their hearts, tell themselves, we are immortal!" Even "the unfortunate African, torn by fraud and violence from his native land, and transported to a foreign soil," could still rely on the consoling idea of the soul's immortality, when "putting himself to death, not to end his life, but to end his suffering."[163] It was the one idea that transcended time and place, binding rich and poor together by reinforcing the feelings involved in compassion, and by neutralising those that might otherwise lead to despair. By doing both, the idea of the immortality of the soul supplied something like the true measure of human dignity and gave a real foundation to humanity's obligations.

The alternative to the intrigue and deception that lay at the core of the sort of society that could produce a Figaro was something like its polar opposite. Here, as with his art criticism, Gorsas looked back to a more integrated society, one that he associated with the Renaissance and the residue of feudal chivalry, real piety, popular theatre, wholehearted revelry, and honourable gallantry that he, like so many others, identified both with Rabelais in the early sixteenth century and with the age of Henri IV.

[162] Gorsas, *Le Courrier de Paris dans les provinces et des provinces à Paris* 12 (25 November 1789): 187; 11 (16 March 1790): 167–72 (the work in question was published by Gorsas himself; see p. 172, for the reference to Blair). On Blair and the Ossian controversy, see Richard B. Sher, *Church and University in the Scottish Enlightenment: The Moderate Literati of Edinburgh* (Princeton UP, 1985); Howard Gaskill, ed., *Ossian Revisited* (Edinburgh, Edinburgh UP, 1991); and Jeffrey M. Suderman, *Orthodoxy and Enlightenment: George Campbell in the Eighteenth Century* (Montreal and Kingston, McGill-Queen's UP, 2001).

[163] Jean-André Michel, *Discours sur l'immortalité de l'âme* (Paris, 1790), pp. 7–8.

Something of the qualities of those times, Gorsas suggested, was the hall-mark of a good society. So, he also indicated, were the age of Racine and Molière, along with Greece in its glory, as well as the more earthy idiom of modern English opposition politics. Lapsing into pidgin English, Gor-sas proceeded to introduce two "foreigners" into the plot. "Do you know what's the matter, my dear Baronet?" one of them asked. "It is the whole band of the French Figarotins Monkeys, produced by the *vis comica* of the grand Figaro."

> They all dance as they speak. They call it *Antipoder* at Paris. Well! my dear. Let us be *Antipodes* too in England and call it *vis inversa*, *vis inversa*, or the silly production of the most silly father. I wish to God, our dear Country may be preserved from such idle trash's; methinks a literary impertinence crowned with success is the most fatal thing in political world [*sic*].[164]

The observation (provoked by a new French dance style) was made during a dance in the Parisian Palais Royal that had begun as a celebration of the values that Gorsas himself endorsed. There, in a palace garlanded with flowers, jewels, and cascading water, and with music supplied by a troop of donkeys (singing surprisingly melodiously), all the books in the book-sellers' arcades began to dance. As they danced, "the eloquent Fénelon" could be seen alongside "the decent Rollin, the Cynic Jean-Jacques, and the wise Montesquieu," dancing a *contredanse* with "the gracious Sévigné, the tender Deshoulières, the lovely Bourdic, and the sparkling Duboc-cage."[165] The mixture may have been eclectic, but it was definitely not Beaumarchais.

Gorsas carried much of the style (and some of the content) of this kind of satire into the campaign that, in the winter of 1791, he launched against the Feuillants. The context in which it took place was formed by the pro-tracted sequence of elections that occurred in Paris, first to the Legislative Assembly, which began sitting on 1 October 1791, then to the adminis-tration of the department of the Seine in which Paris was situated, and finally to the municipal administration of Paris itself. This long period of elections (running from mid-September to mid-November) meant that many of the members of the legislature who were also members of either the Feuillant or the Jacobin club (the first initially had 345 deputies among its members, while the second had 135) came to be caught up in Parisian politics, just as, from the other side, Parisian politics leaked into the work of the Legislative Assembly, particularly because electing a new mayor of Paris overlapped with the early sittings of the new legislature. The elec-tions in Paris were fought in an organised way, with two semipermanent

---

[164] Gorsas, *L'âne promeneur*, p. 262.
[165] Gorsas, *L'âne promeneur*, p. 257.

organisations—meeting, respectively, in the chapel of the former parlement of Paris and in a room in the Cathedral of Notre-Dame—forming
slates of candidates and supplying information about how to vote. The first
organisation, or *club de la sainte-chapelle*, supported the Feuillants, while the
second, or *club de l'évêché*, supported the Jacobins. The *évêché* club carried
the day in the elections to the legislature, just as the *sainte-chapelle* club
(whose president was the poet and future translator of Adam Smith Jean-
Antoine Roucher) dominated the elections to the departmental administration.[166] This left the municipality at stake.

Here the contest was between the former commander of the national
guard General Lafayette, the man whose troops had been responsible for
the massacre of the Champ-de-Mars, and Jérôme Pétion, who, with Brissot and Robespierre, had been one of the few Jacobins to remain a member of the club after the Feuillant secession. Pétion, in addition, was one
of Brissot's closest political allies (both were natives of Chartres, and the
two men had been friends for many years). His early views on the subjects
of property, equality, and legitimate government were quite similar to
Brissot's, and, it can be assumed, to those of the Anglo-Welsh political
reformer David Williams, parts of whose *Letters on Political Liberty* Pétion
incorporated (using a translation by Brissot) into his own *Avis aux François*
(Advice to the French), in 1789. Like Brissot and Robespierre, he was a
lawyer, and, like them too, he first broached these subjects in a number
of entries to academic prize competitions before 1789. One was an essay
on marriage, and its disorders, that he submitted to the prize competition
held by the Academy of Châlons-sur-Marne in 1784. "I have sought to
find the causes of these disorders," he wrote there, "and I seem to have
discovered them in the dangerous systems and abuses that reduce men's
means of subsistence; in the excessive inequality of fortunes; in the unjust
distribution of property; in luxury; in the laws that undermine citizens'
security and liberty; in the obstacles placed in the way of the naturalisation
of foreigners, and the marriage of French Protestants; in the corruption of
manners, and the indissolubility of the marriage bond; in the difficulties
experienced by some in being able to marry; in the monetary advantages
that women bring as dowries to their husbands, and in the absence of
protection given to married couples; and in the quantity of citizens of
both sexes who remain celibate by estate, by taste, or by necessity, etc. etc.
etc."[167] It was a fairly comprehensive indictment. As Pétion argued in an

[166] On these organisations, see [François Boissel], *Adresse à la nation française. Peuple français, voici ta constitution* (n.p., n.d., but late 1791 from the content), pp. 25–6.

[167] Jérôme Pétion de Villeneuve, *Essai sur le mariage considéré sous des rapports naturels,
moraux et politiques* (Geneva, 1785), pp. 6–7. On Pétion's use of Williams, see his *Avis aux
français sur le salut de la patrie* (Paris, 1789), pp. 76–88.

earlier work dealing with the more general subject of the need to reform the civil law, property necessarily gave rise to domination (either by men over women, adults over children, or the rich over the poor). But if the resultant distinctions were "indispensable," they could be legitimate only if they were based upon utility, which meant that all those distinctions inherited from the feudal past that, according to Pétion, Montesquieu had celebrated, had to be abolished.[168] It would have been an impressive moral pedigree, even if Lafayette, who was not a writer, had something more to show than the massacre of the Champ-de-Mars.

Pétion's electoral success did not, however, put an end to the conflict. As Gorsas reported on 24 November 1791, the Feuillants now opted for a press campaign to undermine Pétion's authority, and the charges and countercharges soon turned into a press war.[169] Gorsas used the newspaper that he published, now named the *Courrier des LXXXIII Départements*, as a battering ram to discredit the pro-Feuillant journals, the *Gazette universelle*, the *Journal de Paris*, the *Chant du coq*, the *Spectateur*, and the *Feuille du jour*, and their contributors, including the lawyer Jean Chas, the poets André Chénier and Jean-Antoine Roucher, Roucher's fellow economist Pierre-Samuel Dupont de Nemours and Sieyès's later admirer, Pierre-Louis de Lacretelle (as well as "the daughter of the baron de Coppet," meaning Germaine de Staël).[170] The campaign gradually broadened into a drive to destroy Feuillant influence altogether by bringing a genuinely popular ministry to power to defend a revolution that, according to Gorsas, was now threatened by the rich and their protectors, the fabled "Austrian committee" that, he claimed, was dominated by the queen and her client Antoine-Joseph Barnave. Here, the old joke about breeches now had a more obvious political point. If Barnave was a client of the queen (with all that this implied about gifts and breeches), then his political opponents were *sans culottes*. At the outset, however, the tone of the campaign was mainly satirical, and the neologism that the word *sans-culotte* became took some time to acquire its now familiar connotations. Gorsas had, in fact, been one of the first to use the pike and the Phrygian cap as metaphors for real people. Both made an appearance in an apocryphal letter signed by "General Pike, commander of the *bonnets de laine* of the *faubourgs St-Antoine, St-Marcel, halles et marchés de Paris*," reporting rumours of an impending royal flight, which Gorsas published in the 24 April 1791 issue of his newspaper.[171] Six months passed before he began to

[168] Jérôme Pétion de Villeneuve, *Les loix civiles et l'administration de la justice ramenées à un ordre simple et uniforme* [1782], reprinted in his *Fragments d'un ouvrage sur les loix civiles* (Paris, 1789), pp. 13, 54–61.
[169] Gorsas, *Le Courrier des LXXXIII départements*, 24 November 1791, p. 379.
[170] Gorsas, *Le Courrier des LXXXIII Départements*, 19 May 1792, p. 298.
[171] Gorsas, *Le Courrier de Paris dans les provinces et des provinces à Paris*, 24 April 1791, p. 377.

use the new buzzword. In a report on 18 October 1791, dealing with the reopening of the Parisian churches, the *Courrier* noted that the authorities had taken elaborate precautions to ensure that no worshipper, as had been threatened, had had her bottom smacked. There would have been very many fewer deaths on the Champ-de-Mars, Gorsas observed, if the authorities had taken as much care then as they had shown now to prevent a few fanatical bottoms from being smacked. The royalist view, he wrote, was rather different. A member of the monarchist Impartial Society, the *Courrier* claimed, had been heard to say, when talking about the massacre of the Champ-de-Mars, that "the only people who had been killed had been *sans culottes*, and that it was far better for a hundred rogues of that sort to lose their lives than for an aristocratic skirt to have been lifted."[172] In the 30 November 1791 issue of the *Courrier*, Gorsas put the figure of a *sans-culotte* into an extract from the sixteenth-century monarchomach François Hotman's *De jure Regni Galliae* to make a more immediately relevant political point (made by the apocryphal sixteenth-century *sans-culotte*) about the limits of royal inviolability and the fact that not all attacks on royal misdemeanours were the work of "factions" and "republicanism," as the Feuillants claimed.[173]

Gorsas kept up the satirical tone during a campaign to force the Feuillants to open their meetings to the public in December 1791. On 13 December the *Courrier* reported that four hundred citizens had gathered outside the Feuillant club on the rue de Richelieu to demand entry. One of its members was said to have told its presiding officer that "he had to get rid of these *sans-culottes*." Nonetheless, Gorsas wrote, the *sans-culottes* were given the honour of the meeting and, through their orator, politely suggested to the Feuillants that they open their meetings to the public.[174] The same issue contained a report headed, ironically, "Great Victory over the *sans-culottes* of Strasbourg by the Heralds from beyond the Rhine" (*Grande victoire remportée sur les sans-culottes de Strasbourg par les Héraults d'Outre-Rhin*), describing how a thousand-strong *émigré* force headed by the cardinal de Rohan and the viscount de Mirabeau (the brother of the more famous orator) had succeeded in capturing three boatmen near Strasbourg.[175] The irony was followed by a hint of what was to come. On 18 December Gorsas reported that "the people of Paris" had turned the insulting epithet used by "MM. les Richelieus-Feuillants" into a term of honour and, as evidence, quoted a petition to the Legislative Assembly by the "*sans-culottes*" and pikemen (*hommes à piques*) of the *Quinze-Vingts*

---

[172] Gorsas, *Courrier des LXXXIII Départements*, 18 October 1791, p. 263.
[173] *Courrier des LXXXIII Départements*, 30 November 1791, pp. 472–4.
[174] *Courrier des LXXXIII Départements*, 13 December 1791.
[175] *Courrier des LXXXIII Départements*, 13 December 1791.

section attacking the Feuillant-dominated departmental directory.[176] But the burlesque character of the campaign continued when a second deputation of *sans-culottes* gathered outside the Feuillants on 20 December with the intention of presenting a petition to the club. According to Gorsas, the petition had been by a man wearing the garb of a cobbler (clearly intended to be a reincarnation of Chrysostomus Crites) who solemnly addressed the assembled Feuillants and persuaded them to have the *sans-culotte* petition printed in the Feuillant newspaper, the *Gazette universelle*.[177]

In the next instalment Gorsas revived the Cynic cobbler-*cum*-art critic Mycillus and his cockerel's feather (although this time, he was described as the cobbler's great-nephew). Reports of the activities of the Feuillants were now presented by this invisible eyewitness or, when he was away repairing the *sans-culottes'* shoes, by another "valiant *sans-culotte*," an equally fictitious joiner. According to Mycillus, a Feuillant had been heard to say that "for as long as three to four hundred thousand *sans-culottes* had not been killed, things will go badly."[178] Gorsas rounded off the performance by printing a poem in honour of Jesus for Christmas:

I took nothing with me,
Expelled from my ancient asylum
And forced to descend below,
Without breeches (*sans culottes*), a shirt or stockings,
And without a civil list.[179]

By 1792 Gorsas had begun to turn the word *sans-culotte* into a synonym for the ordinary people of Paris, noting, for example, how a meeting of the Jacobin club early in January had approved of a proposal by the Legislative Assembly's committee on legislation concerning the distribution of money to provide relief to the *sans-culottes* and, early in February, commending the *sans-culottes* of Versailles for calling for public sessions of a club suspected of "aristocratic" sympathies.[180]

The shortages of sugar and other goods produced by the slave insurrection in San-Domingo and the price-fixing riots that occurred in Paris in January and February 1792 added a new dimension to the term. In late

[176] *Courrier des LXXXIII Départements*, 18 December 1791.
[177] *Courrier des LXXXIII Départements*, 22 December 1791, p. 346.
[178] *Courrier des LXXXIII Départements*, 24, 25, and 29 December 1791, pp. 375, 392–5, 456.
[179] *Courrier des LXXXIII Départements*, 26 December 1791, p. 398: "Je n'ai rien emporté. Je me suis vu chassé de mon antique asile. Forcé de descendre ici-bas, sans-culotte, chemise et bas, et sans liste-civile." For other, later, examples of Christ as a *sans-culotte*, see Frank Paul Bowman, *Le Christ romantique* (Geneva, Droz, 1973), pp. 14–20. The *chemise* in the poem was an allusion to an earlier joke, where Gorsas had claimed that the reason for the royal princesses' hurried departure from Paris in March 1791 was that they had stolen one of his shirts.
[180] *Courrier des LXXXIII Départements*, 9 January and 4 February 1792.

January 1792 Gorsas printed a letter from François-Xavier Lanthénas (the man who, six months later, was to describe the archetype of a *sans-culotte* as the virtuous market porter, Quatorze-oignons), reporting that the price of materials in the hatting trade had rocketed by 30 percent after a dozen or so major manufacturers in Lyon had combined to buy up supplies in Paris, Rouen, and Marseille.[181] The letter was a clear hint about what the real cause of the Parisian grocery riots might have been (Brissot, in the *Patriote français*, published a letter explicitly stating that the sharp rise in sugar prices was the work, among others, of the pro-Feuillant deputy d'André who had bought up 400,000 livres' worth of sugar in Lille).[182] The subject grew into a major controversy when the mayor of Paris, Pétion, published an analysis of the riots' causes and possible political implications. In an open letter published in several newspapers, he claimed that the riots had been provoked to generate division within the popular cause. The "numerous and prosperous class of the bourgeoisie," Pétion wrote, had "made a scission with the people," opening up a breach whose only beneficiaries would be the enemies of liberty. There had, therefore, to be a revival of that union "between the bourgeoisie and the people" that had once formed the "union of the Third Estate against the privileged" or, as Gorsas himself put it, the union between the "honourable artisan" and the "honourable bourgeois" that had been the making of the revolution.[183] The letter produced a hostile Feuillant response. The poet André Chénier, in an article published in the *Journal de Paris*, argued that if Pétion's diagnosis was right, then this should be a reason for giving the Jacobins pause for thought, since "that class that he refers to as the bourgeoisie" stood midway between "the vices of opulence and misery" or "the prodigality of luxury and the most extreme need" and was, therefore, the real source of political stability.[184] According to the Feuillant *Gazette universelle*, Pétion's letter seemed to be calling covertly for the enfranchisement of passive citizens. It attacked his implicit assertion that the bourgeoisie could be distinguished from the people, noting that the distinction could be made only if the term *bourgeois* were used to mean something different from that part of society that was legally entitled to take part in popular elections. If, the *Gazette* stated, Pétion meant that "the people" was

[181] *Courrier des LXXXIII Départements*, 26 January 1792.
[182] See the reply to it in the *Journal de Paris*, supplement 13 (9 February 1792): 165.
[183] *Courrier des LXXXIII Départements*, 13 February 1792, pp. 193–4.
[184] *Journal de Paris*, supplement 19 (26 February 1792): 3–4. On Chénier, see Paul Dimoff, *La vie et l'oeuvre d'André Chénier jusqu'à la révolution française*, 2 vols. (Geneva, 1936), which, as its title indicates, stops short of his political career. On the idea of the "classe mitoyenne" as the ballast of the new regime, see also Philippe-Antoine Grouvelle, *De l'autorité de Montesquieu dans la révolution présente*, reprinted in the *Bibliothèque de l'homme public*, 12 vols. (Paris, 1790), 7:60–5.

something other than those who enjoyed political rights by dint of their "honest industry," and who, as members of the National Guard, were responsible for maintaining law and order, then he was engaging in the kind of dangerous demagoguery used by the Roman republican and advocate of an agrarian law Caius Gracchus (whose fate, it noted, was presently available for inspection in the tragedy of the same name).

Gorsas was quick to defend Pétion. It was difficult, he commented on 13 February 1792, to accept the assumption made by the *Gazette universelle* that passive citizens were the sole threat to law and order unless it was also assumed that "it is the *sans-culottes* who engross metal coin, insult magistrates, commit arbitrary acts, protect ministerial corruption, favour the party of Coblenz, or send articles ready-made to the *Gazette universelle*."[185] He returned to the subject in the 22 February issue of the *Courrier* in the context of the campaign to free the soldiers of the Chateauvieux regiment. Here, he accompanied a story about a deaf-mute who had donated six sols to the soldiers' cause with a none-too-subtle modification of Pétion's examination of the relationship between the bourgeoisie and the people in the context of a further attack on the Feuillant-backed *Gazette universelle*. The Feuillants, Gorsas wrote, had made it look like a crime for the "virtuous Pétion" to have said that "it was necessary to distinguish the bourgeoisie from the people." But Pétion had been right. The bourgeoisie, Gorsas continued, were "a pile of financiers, legal bigwigs (*robins*), wholesale merchants, bankers, money-dealers, annuitants, and the majordomos (*intendants*) and dressing-room valets of former seigneurs."[186] The people, on the other hand, consisted of "men of letters, retailers, artists, craftsmen (*fabricants*), in short of all those whom the once-privileged caste called the *populace* and whom they now style as barefooted rustics (*va-nu-pieds*), *sans-culottes*, etc."[187] The contrast between honest industry and *honnêtes gens* was sharp. It was matched, Gorsas emphasised, by two quite different visions of politics. While the people was wholeheartedly committed to the revolution, the bourgeoisie favoured "a mixed government" where, "with a little money and a talent for intrigue, they can be really *free*, namely, the masters of every position, and where, through corruption, disposing of all the favours of the court and the nation, they will be in a position to lead both."[188]

Gorsas's claim that political differences were the expression of conflicting social interests provoked a hostile reply in the form of a letter from a *bourgeois de Paris*, published as a *Supplement* to the pro-Feuillant *Journal*

---

[185] *Courrier des LXXXIII Départements*, 13 February 1792, pp. 194–6.
[186] *Courrier des LXXXIII Départements*, 22 February 1792, p. 348.
[187] *Courrier des LXXXIII Départements*, 22 February 1792, p. 348.
[188] *Courrier des LXXXIII Départements*, 22 February 1792, pp. 348–9.

de Paris on 1 March 1792. After noting that Gorsas had placed men of
letters at the head of his list of the component parts of the people, the
anonymous *bourgeois* pointed out how apt his choice had been. While, he
wrote, some men of letters might imagine that they were likely to find a
place in any society in which honesty and ability were honoured, Gorsas
had had the peculiar insight to recognise that his talents were of a higher
order. Here, the anonymous Parisian burgher turned the neologism that
the word *sans-culotte* had become back to its original meaning. Gorsas,
he wrote, was simply a hack writer who fitted all the specifications of
Voltaire's earlier caricature in *Le pauvre diable* and, "superior to the good
Lafontaine, who received his breeches from Mme de la Sablière, you receive none from anyone, and walk out, proud of your nakedness."[189] His
claim that merchants belonged to an aristocracy of the rich, the author of
the letter concluded, was both false and divisive (he himself, he emphasised, was a patriotic wholesale merchant), sanctioning exactly the kind of
violation of property rights that had occurred during the Parisian grocery
riots of January and February 1792.

The impact of Gorsas's campaign was also registered in a further article
headed "on the abuse of words," written by the Feuillant Regnault de
Saint-Jean-d'Angély and published (anonymously) in the *Journal de Paris*
of 21 April 1792 (shortly after the public reception put on by the municipality of Paris on 15 April 1792 to welcome the now-free soldiers of the
Chateauvieux regiment). The abuse in question applied not only to the
word *sans-culotte*, but also to the words *aristocrate* and *patriote* because,
Regnault claimed, the neologism had also caused their respective meanings to change. When the word *sans-culotte* "was introduced into conversation," he wrote, "several men began to use it cleverly to capture the
compassion and interest attached to poverty for their party, and to load
all those who are not poor with all the hatred justly deserved by proud
and merciless opulence." But, he continued, it was not necessary to be a
Jacobin to recognise, as the Christian maxim put it, that misery was a sacred thing (*res est sacra miseria*), or to agree that legislation was needed to
reduce inequality. There were limits, however, to what the law could do
to eliminate what was "an incurable disease of industrious and commercial societies." In the last analysis, commerce and industry had to be left
to their own devices to correct opulence and inequality. This, Regnault
continued, meant that it was even more of a political mistake to collude
with those affecting the rags of poverty to acquire positions of power and
wealth for themselves and their followers. Those, he wrote, who now
called themselves *sans-culottes* did not lack any essential item of clothing. Their aim, rather, was no more than the crude despoliation of other

---

[189] *Journal de Paris* 61, supplement 19 (1 March 1792): 2.

people's property, while their method was merely to use the courtier's age-old strategy of flattery to manipulate the people for their own unsavoury purposes. This, in turn, meant that the word *aristocrate* had come to be used to refer to the rich, rather than to those who, in 1789, had claimed a privileged right to exercise authority. The effect of this abusive usage had been to imply that a patriot was an enemy of the rich. By setting one class against another in this way, Regnault concluded, and by "embittering classes on whom fortune had been distributed unequally," those who called themselves *sans-culottes* had created a travesty of patriotism, one that would force free men "to fawn under the ignoble yoke of terror or the yet more shameful yoke of fanaticism and party spirit."[190]

Gorsas countered the charge of inciting social envy by accusing his opponents of inciting social hatred. He did so in an article about the words *populace* and *canaille* that he published in the *Courrier des LXXXIII Départements* of 2 May 1792. The former term, he wrote, had been applied abusively to any individual who, "born into an obscure estate, disdaining favour and intrigue, remains industrious and poor, offering no more than manual strength and virtues to society, but who still remains a man and, at the least, a good citizen." The latter term (usually translated as "rabble" or "scum") was used to refer to the "most indigent part of the populace." Those who used such language, Gorsas asserted, firmly believed that the Declaration of the Rights of Man of August 1789 existed solely for the rich. This, he concluded, meant that the true meaning of the terms was self-evident. The real *populace française* was to be found at Coblenz and, Gorsas asserted, within the secret council forming the "*parti autrichien.*" The true *canaille* consisted of those so-called men of goodwill who were paid to speak, write, and act on its behalf. A *sans-culotte* would therefore be able to recognise a Roucher, a Chénier (two of the Feuillants' leaders), or the authors of "certain supplements" to the *Journal de Paris* as the real social and political scum.[191] The effect of this further round of insults was to turn the new buzzword, *sans-culotte*, into the name of one side of the political and economic divide. By the spring of 1792, it had acquired all the connotations now more usually associated with 1793 and the politics of the Year II of the first French republic.

According to a note written in 1793 in answer to "the impertinent question," what is a *sans-culotte*?, a *sans-culotte* was "a man who goes everywhere on his own two feet, who has none of the millions you're all after, no mansions, no lackeys to wait on him, and who lives quite simply with his wife and children, if he has any, on the fourth or fifth floor. He is useful, because he knows how to plough a field, handle a forge, a saw, a file, to

[190] *Journal de Paris* supplement 52 (21 April 1792): 2–3.
[191] Gorsas, *Courrier des LXXXIII Départements*, 2 May 1792, pp. 26–9.

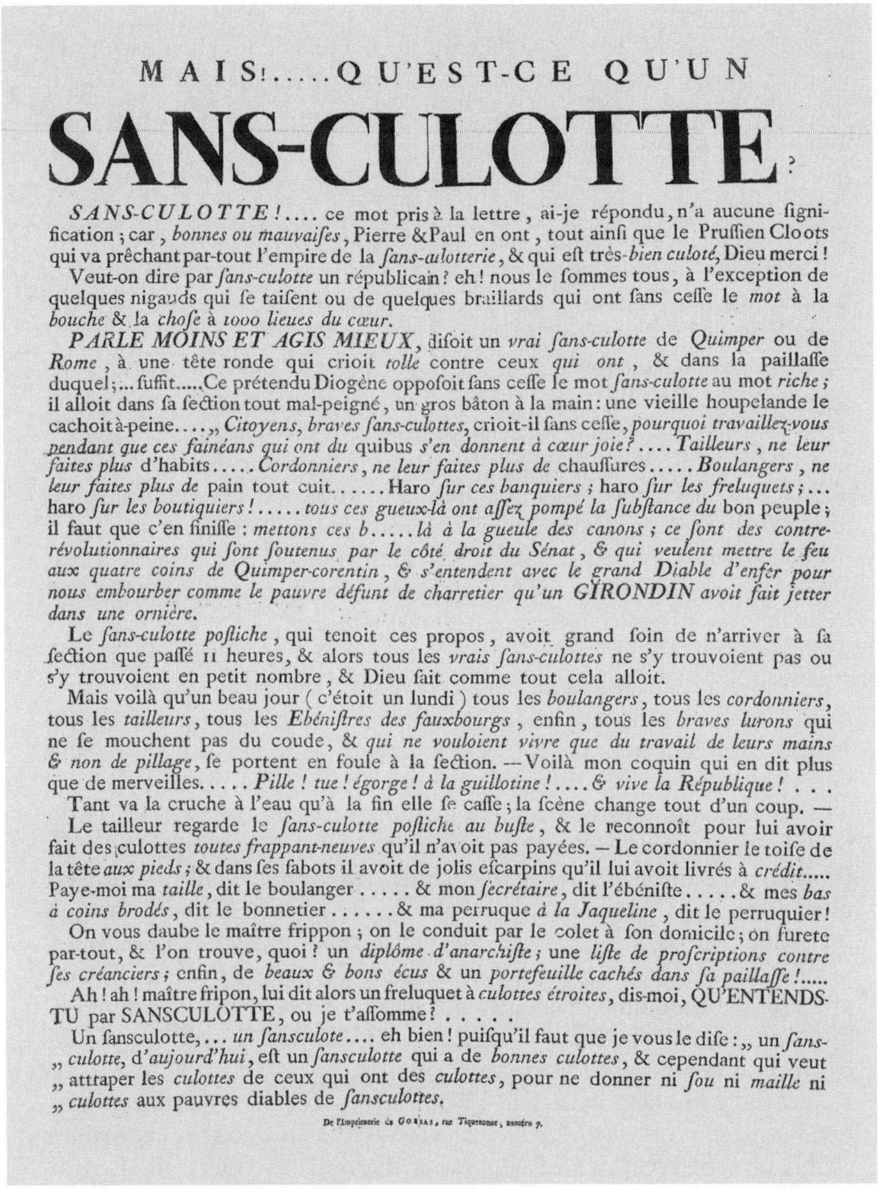

MAIS!.....QU'EST-CE QU'UN

SANS-CULOTTE?

SANS-CULOTTE!.... ce mot pris à la lettre, ai-je répondu, n'a aucune signification; car, *bonnes ou mauvaises*, Pierre & Paul en ont, tout ainsi que le Prussien Cloots qui va prêchant par-tout l'empire de la *sans-culotterie*, & qui est très-*bien culoté*, Dieu merci!

Veut-on dire par *sans-culotte* un républicain? eh! nous le sommes tous, à l'exception de quelques nigauds qui se taisent ou de quelques braillards qui ont sans cesse le *mot* à la *bouche* & la *chose* à *1000 lieues du cœur*.

PARLE MOINS ET AGIS MIEUX, disoit un vrai *sans-culotte* de *Quimper* ou de *Rome*, à une tête ronde qui crioit *tolle* contre ceux *qui ont*, & dans la paillasse duquel;...suffit.....Ce prétendu Diogène opposoit sans cesse le mot *sans-culotte* au mot *riche*; il alloit dans sa section tout mal-peigné, un gros bâton à la main: une vieille houpelande le cachoit à-peine...., „ *Citoyens, braves sans-culottes*, crioit-il sans cesse, *pourquoi travaillez-vous pendant que ces fainéans qui ont du quibus s'en donnent à cœur joie?* .... *Tailleurs, ne leur faites plus* d'habits..... *Cordonniers, ne leur faites plus de chaussures* .... *Boulangers, ne leur faites plus de pain tout cuit*.....Haro *sur ces banquiers*; haro *sur les freluquets*;... haro *sur les boutiquiers!* ..... *tous ces gueux-là ont assez pompé la substance du* bon peuple; il faut que c'en finisse : mettons ces b.....là à la gueule des canons; ce sont des contre-révolutionnaires qui font soutenus par le côté droit du Sénat, & qui veulent mettre le feu aux quatre coins de Quimper-corentin, & s'entendent avec le grand Diable d'enfer pour nous embourber comme le pauvre défunt de charretier qu'un GIRONDIN avoit fait jetter dans une ornière.

Le *sans-culotte postiche*, qui tenoit ces propos, avoit grand soin de n'arriver à sa section que passé 11 heures, & alors tous les *vrais sans-culottes* ne s'y trouvoient pas ou s'y trouvoient en petit nombre, & Dieu sait comme tout cela alloit.

Mais voilà qu'un beau jour (c'étoit un lundi) tous les *boulangers*, tous les *cordonniers*, tous les *tailleurs*, tous les *Ebénistres des fauxbourgs*, enfin, tous les *braves lurons* qui ne se mouchent pas du coude, & *qui ne vouloient vivre que du travail de leurs mains & non de pillage*, se portent en foule à la section. —Voilà mon coquin qui en dit plus que de merveilles.....*Pille! tue! égorge! à la guillotine!....& vive la République!* ...

Tant va la cruche à l'eau qu'à la fin elle se casse; la scène change tout d'un coup. — Le tailleur regarde le *sans-culotte postiche au buste*, & le reconnoît pour lui avoir fait des culottes *toutes frappant-neuves* qu'il n'avoit pas payées. — Le cordonnier le toise de la tête *aux pieds*; & dans ses sabots il avoit de jolis escarpins qu'il lui avoit livrés à *crédit*..... Paye-moi ma *taille*, dit le boulanger .....& mon *sécrétaire*, dit l'ébéniste.....& mes *bas à coins brodés*, dit le bonnetier......& ma perruque *à la Jaqueline*, dit le perruquier!

On vous daube le maître frippon; on le conduit par le colet à son domicile; on furete par-tout, & l'on trouve, quoi? un *diplôme d'anarchiste*; une *liste de proscriptions contre ses créanciers*; enfin, de *beaux & bons écus* & un *portefeuille cachés dans sa paillasse!*.....

Ah! ah! maître fripon, lui dit alors un freluquet à *culottes étroites*, dis-moi, QU'ENTENDS-TU par SANSCULOTTE, ou je t'assomme? .....

Un sansculotte,... *un sansculote*.... eh bien! puisqu'il faut que je vous le dise: „ un *sans-culotte, d'aujourd'hui*, est un *sansculotte* qui a de *bonnes culottes*, & cependant qui veut „ attraper les *culottes* de ceux qui ont des *culottes*, pour ne donner ni *sou* ni *maille* ni „ *culottes* aux pauvres diables de *sansculottes*.

De l'imprimerie de GORSAS, rue Tiquetonne, numéro 7.

Figure 6. Antoine-Joseph Gorsas, *Mais ... qu'est-ce qu'un sans-culotte?* Bibliothèque nationale de France, Paris.

cover a roof, how to make shoes, and to shed his blood to the last drop
to save the republic." As in Gorsas's earlier Cynic, anti-Janoto-Figarotin
diatribe, he could lapse readily into demotic English. "*God save the People!
God-dam the Aristocrates!* . . . Brethren and Friends, will you to assure the
revolution? Knock down the Snake Brissot, the Viper Guadet, the reptile
Vergniaud . . . etca, etca, and that'll do!"[192] By then, however, Gorsas had
been hoist with his own petard. When, early in 1793, he published a wall
poster containing his own definition of a *sans-culotte* (see figure 6), the
political alignments had switched. "A sans-culotte, a *sans-culotte*," Gorsas
ended his reply to the same question about what a *sans-culotte* might be,
"well, since I have to tell you, today's *sans-culotte* is a *sans-culotte* who has
fine breeches, but who still wants to get hold of the breeches of those
who do have breeches, so as not to give a thread or a penny, or even any
breeches, to those poor devils who have no breeches, the *sans-culottes*."
Whatever a *sans-culotte* might have been in 1791, a *sans-culotte* in 1793 had,
as Gorsas put it in his poster, become a "*sans-culotte postiche*," a fake *sans-
culotte*, and a "pseudo-Diogenes," whose demagogic rise to revolutionary
prominence was likely to hide a very shady past.[193] The political message
of the poster was similar in content to the later poster signed by "Harrington," with its call to "the bourgeois, the industrious people, and the
sans-culottes" to unite against the Jacobin "brigands" that Saint-Just was
to describe in July 1793.[194] The problem for Gorsas was that by 1793 he
was not the only judge of what a *sans-culotte* might be.

[192] I have used the translation in Gwyn A. Williams, *Artisans and Sans-Culottes* [1968], 2nd
ed. (London, Libris, 1989), pp. 19, 57. For the original French document, see Walter Markov and Albert Soboul, *Die Sansculotten von Paris* (Berlin, Akademie Verlag, 1957), p. 2.

[193] [Antoine-Joseph Gorsas], *Mais! . . . Qu'est-ce qu'un sans-culotte?* (Paris, Imprimerie Gorsas, n.d.). It is possible that the better-known definition of a *sans-culotte* referred to in the
previous note was actually a manuscript reply to Gorsas's poster.

[194] On this poster, see above, p. 273. Brissot, in May 1793, made a similar claim, accusing
the Jacobins "of dividing society into two classes, those who have, and those who do not, or
the *sans-culottes*, and the property owners," in order, as he put it, "to perpetuate their power,
and in needing to perpetuate disorder" to be able to do so: Jacques-Pierre Brissot, *A ses commettants sur la situation de la Convention nationale* (Paris, 22 May 1793), p. 22.

❦6❧

CONCLUSION: DEMOCRACY AND TERROR

POLITICS AND HISTORY IN JACOBIN THOUGHT

BY THE beginning of 1793, when Gorsas published his poster, the old set of evaluations involved in having, or not having, breeches had lost much of their earlier, salon-related, connotations. From then on, the name *sans-culottes* was a republican emblem, as, at least in historical terms, it still is. There was nothing preordained in this outcome, or in the ramifying sequence of conflicts in which Gorsas, like so many others, was engulfed. As has been shown, the emergence of the *sans-culottes* in their now familiar guise was a relatively sudden political response to the disintegration of a broad consensus in favour of using the resources of modern public finance to make property generally available, and, once property had lost its socially charged status, to give merit and distinction their proper place in social and political life. The very particular setting in which the switch occurred goes some way towards explaining why the mixture of descriptive and causal claims built into the old master concepts of class or sovereignty of French Revolutionary historiography have never been able to provide much of an explanation of either its content or course, at least without the more complicated assumptions supplied by an assortment of nineteenth-century philosophies of history.[1] Reconstructing that setting, on the other hand, does go some way towards explaining what led to the fusion between high politics and popular politics that occurred in France in the winter of 1791–2. Here, the cumulative sequence of decisions that came to form a real set of connections between the initially separate subjects of the entitlements of French citizens, the stability of the French national debt, the constitution of the French church, the composition of the French army, the future of the French nobility, the status of the French colonial empire, and the legitimacy of the French monarchy tells its own story. One way of writing about the French Revolution would be to tell the story on those terms. As these initially separate subjects came, progressively, to be locked

---

[1] The same objection applies to the more recent mutation of both concepts into "culture," used largely, and for much the same deliberately fuzzy reasons, as a synonym for the eighteenth-century concept of "commerce," as in commerce between the sexes, or polite, public, or private, commerce: see, classically, Jürgen Habermas, *The Structural Transformation of the Public Sphere* [1959] (Cambridge, Mass., MIT Press, 1991).

together as parts of a single political problem, politics itself turned into an increasingly simple choice between supporting and opposing what had previously been done.[2]

In another sense, however, even this sequence of steps, and the many possible alternatives that arose along the way, still do not add up to the whole story; nor do they help to explain the final switch from the initial Brissotin drive to win the support of the newly named *sans-culottes* in 1791–2 to the better known association between Robespierre, Saint-Just, and the *sans-culottes* that emerged in 1793. Circumstances, particularly the war, may have played their part, but so, too, did the intellectual resources of the array of historical and political investigations that Rousseau's conjectures helped to ignite. Pushing nineteenth-century philosophies of history out of the historiography of the French Revolution does not mean that there were simply *no* philosophies of history available before or after 1789. Here, the themes of progress and corruption, decline and fall, ruin and recovery, or barbarism and civilisation, could be fitted into as rich and as varied a range of conceptual matrices as anything that the nineteenth century was able later to supply. But, largely because of what happened during the period of the French Revolution, the conceptual matrices in question were not quite the same. In the context of what, by the end of the eighteenth century, could be called post-, or anti-, Rousseauian civilisation theories, both the sequence of steps that occurred between 1789 and 1793, and the many possible alternatives that arose along the way, were informed by different ways of thinking about history, and by different assessments and evaluations of the possibilities and constraints that the present appeared to house. If, in the last analysis, the concepts of class or sovereignty seem to have so little purchase on the events of the French Revolution, this may be less a matter of their lack of fit with empirical reality than with the different assessments and evaluations of empirical reality that eighteenth-century conceptual usage implied.

One example of these differences is the subject of an agrarian, the noun to which the phrase "agrarian law" was often reduced. It is well known that, on 18 March 1793, the French Convention passed, to acclaim, a decree imposing the death penalty on anyone proposing "an agrarian, or any other, law, subversive of territorial, commercial, or industrial property." It is still sometimes assumed that the measure can be taken to be an indication either of Jacobin hostility towards *sans-culotte* redistributive aspirations, or of a more pragmatic Jacobin political balancing act (*politique*

---

[2] On the links between these subjects and the historiographical gaps that remain to be filled in examining them, see, helpfully, Claude Langlois, "Religion, culte ou opinion religieuse: la politique des révolutionnaires," *Revue française de sociologie* 30 (1989): 471–96 (particularly, p. 484, note 16).

d'équilibre) between popular demands for real equality and the need to maintain political stability, or of the political eclipse of the Parisian Cercle Social and the demise of the earlier interest in an agrarian displayed by some of its leading members, including, as has been shown, Louis-Sébastien Mercier, or, finally, of the tension between a long-standing, Greek-inspired republican tradition and short-term political realities.[3] But, as the decree's advocate Bertrand Barère, speaking in his capacity as head of the Convention's committees of defence and general security, pointed out in his speech to the assembly, the reason for this draconian measure was straightforwardly Ciceronian, because the French republic now faced a state of affairs comparable to those that had once faced the Roman republic. "Cato, too, in the midst of Rome's agitations," Barère informed the Convention, referring to the Roman republican's behaviour at the time of Catalina's conspiracy against the Roman republic, "always wanted only to follow laws made for peaceful times; he was not a revolutionary. This is what Cicero told him: 'Cato, your wisdom and your virtue make you forget that we are not in ordinary times. When the ship is battered by a storm, you have to save yourself however you can (*on se sauve comme on peut*).' "[4] In the modern equivalent of those extraordinary times, the threat to the republic came, Barère said, from a combination of *émigrés*, nonjuring priests, and the inaction of those simply waiting to see what would happen next. As he presented it, the recent attempt in the town of Orléans on the life of a member of the Convention named Léonard Bourdon was an indication of the broader threat to political stability that the republic now faced.[5] Insurrections were already afoot in the Vendée and Brittany, and while part of the Convention was quite right to believe that it really was fully in a revolution (*en pleine révolution*), the other did not. As Cicero's conduct during Catalina's conspiracy indicated, Barère argued, the Convention could either follow events, and fail, or act decisively, and save the republic.

Barère's attack on the advocates of an agrarian (meaning here, the agents of what he called, unequivocally, "counterrevolution" and their putative plans to reverse the earlier transfer of property from the church to the

[3] For examples, see R. B. Rose, "The 'Red Scare' of the 1790s: The French Revolution and the 'Agrarian Law,' " *Past & Present* 103 (1984): 113–30, and his *Gracchus Babeuf, the First Revolutionary Communist* (London, Arnold, 1978), pp. 131–38; Peter Jones, "The 'Agrarian Law': Schemes for Land Redistribution during the French Revolution," *Past & Present* 133 (1991): 96–133; Gareth Stedman Jones, introduction to Karl Marx and Frederick Engels, *The Communist Manifesto* (London, Penguin, 2002), p. 149; Eric Nelson, *The Greek Tradition in Republican Thought* (Cambridge, CUP, 2004), p. 193, note 166. On Mercier's advocacy of an agrarian, see above, p. 109.

[4] *Archives parlementaires*, vol. 60, ed. M. Mavidal, E. Laurent, et al (Paris, 1901), p. 292.

[5] On this murky episode, see Michael J. Sydenham, *Léonard Bourdon: The Career of a Revolutionary 1754–1807* (Waterloo, Ont., Wilfred Laurier UP, 1999), pp. 149–61.

nation) echoed a long-established Machiavellian theme in the historiography of republican Rome. Here the focus fell less on an agrarian as a counterpart to justice than on the demagogic abuse of the idea under conditions of social inequality and political faction, at the times of both Catalina's conspiracy and that of the brothers Tiberius and Caius Gracchus. Under these conditions, it was widely claimed, popular misery and political demagoguery had combined to destroy the Roman republic, just as, Barère argued in 1793, a combination of refractory priests and *émigré* agents now threatened to destroy the French republic by raising the prospect of a transfer of recently nationalised church and *émigré* property back to its original owners. These were the terms in which Cicero had described the demagogic abuse of the idea of an agrarian law in his attack upon the Gracchi (whose turbulent political careers spanned the decade 133–121 BC). According to him, the two brothers belonged to a class of "enthusiastic" politicians who, "by bringing forward bills providing for the distribution of land," threatened to undermine "the very foundations on which our commonwealth depends." Politicians with such intentions, he wrote, "are aiming a fatal blow at the whole principle of justice; for once rights of property are infringed, this principle is totally undermined."[6] Machiavelli modified Cicero's assessment in one respect, noting that the intentions of the Gracchi "were more praiseworthy than their prudence," but still concluded that, by trying to revive the agrarian law, they "wholly destroyed the Roman republic."[7] James Harrington, despite his insistence that "the equality of a commonwealth consist in the equality first of the agrarian, and next of the rotation," followed Machiavelli. By the time that Tiberius Gracchus tried to revive the Roman agrarian, he wrote, "the remedy being too late, and too vehemently applied, that commonwealth was ruined."[8]

The same view continued into the eighteenth century, forming a counterpoint to the more positive endorsement of the Gracchi visible in the works of Fénelonian advocates of comprehensive programmes of royal reform, like the Roman historians Nathaniel Hooke and Louis-Clair Le Beau du Bignon.[9] "I would rather see many abuses subsist, than a Cromwell, a Pisistratus, a Caesar, or (if you will) a Gracchus, assuming lawless power to redress them," wrote the English Commonwealthman Thomas Gordon in his *Political Discourses on Sallust* (a work first published in 1744, and which the French republican Camille Desmoulins later drew upon

---

[6] Cicero, *On Duties* (Harmondsworth, Penguin, 1971), bk. 2, p. 164.

[7] Niccolò Machiavelli, *Discourses*, introd. Max Lerner (New York, 1950), ch. 37, pp. 210, 212.

[8] James Harrington, *The Commonwealth of Oceana* [1656], ed. J.G.A. Pocock (Cambridge, CUP, 1977), p. 184.

[9] On these historians, see above, pp. 215–7.

heavily in the unsuccessful campaign against Robespierre and the revolutionary government of the Year II that he launched in his newspaper, *Le Vieux Cordelier*, during the winter of 1793–4).[10] When, earlier in 1793, an obscure Picard land surveyor decided to change his name from François-Noël to "Gracchus" Babeuf, he was also opting, deliberately or inadvertently, against a long-standing republican way of thinking about agrarian laws and the risks involved in their promotion, either by overenthusiastic reformers or by more sinister political demagogues.[11] Both types of political actor raised the spectre of a Caesar and the end of the republic at the hands of popularly supported military force (Babeuf, it might be noted, was not only an advocate of the redistributive effects of public credit; he was also fascinated by the way that an army could provide for the needs of its members, although they themselves owned no property).[12] For Barère, there was no contradiction at all between advocating the death penalty for royalist demagogues and, on exactly the same occasion, urging the Convention to "devote all its concerns towards multiplying the number of proprietors by as much as possible, since when a man is attached to the soil, he defends it." This meant reviving an earlier decree to sell off confiscated *émigré* property in small units, and demolishing abandoned seigneurial *chateaux* so that the materials could be used "to build homes for less fortunate agriculturalists (*agriculteurs*)." Outlawing the advocates of an agrarian, and promoting the redistribution of property, followed the same principle. "You will not exist," Barère told the Convention in a phrase that earned him lasting notoriety; "the republic cannot have any

[10] Thomas Gordon, *The Works of Sallust Translated into English, with Political Discourses on that Author* (London, 1744), p. 79.

[11] On Babeuf, see Michael Sonenscher, "Property, Community and Citizenship," in Mark Goldie and Robert Wokler, eds., *The Cambridge History of Eighteenth-Century Political Thought* (Cambridge, CUP, 2006), pp. 489–91.

[12] For a critical discussion of this model, with a particular focus on Babeuf, see Etienne-Géry Lenglet, *De la propriété et de ses rapports avec les droits et avec la dette du citoyen* (Paris, an VI/1797), pp. 40–51. For a further example of this mixture of Fénelonian and more conventional republican themes, see the painting entitled *The Death of Caius Gracchus* by Babeuf's friend and coconspirator François-Jean-Baptiste Topino-Lebrun, exhibited at the Parisian *Salon* of 1798. On Topino-Lebrun's painting, see James Henry Rubin, "Painting and Politics II: J. L. David's Patriotism, or The Conspiracy of Gracchus Babeuf and the Legacy of Topino-Lebrun," *Art Bulletin: A Quarterly Published by the College Art Association of America* 58 (1976): 547–68. On the Gracchi, see, most recently, Luciano Perelli, *I Gracchi* (Rome, Salerno Editrice, 1993), and, for a collection of the main sources, Claude Nicolet, *Les Gracques* (Paris, Gallimard, 1980). For their subsequent reputation, see Marta Sordi, "La tradizione storiografica su Tiberio Gracco e la propaganda contemporanea," *Sesta Miscellanea Greca e Romana* (Rome, Istituto Italiano di Storia Antica, 1978), pp. 299–330; and, on Caesar as the solution to patrician-plebeian conflict, see, most recently, Peter Baehr and Melvin Richter, eds., *Dictatorship in History and Theory: Bonapartism, Caesarism, and Totalitarianism* (Cambridge, CUP, 2004).

other basis than *biens nationaux*," or the property of both the church and the *émigrés* that the nation now owned.[13]

ROUSSEAU AND REVOLUTION

This type of assessment of past circumstances and present possibilities cuts across more familiar characterisations of different sides in the French Revolution as either left or right, revolutionary or counterrevolutionary, or popular and bourgeois, in the various senses in which these terms came to be used in the more philosophically and ideologically charged histories of the nineteenth and twentieth centuries. During the French Revolution itself, different types of historical and political assessment were brought into play. These applied most immediately to the subject of war. As Etienne Clavière presented it in early January 1792, war with the Holy Roman Empire was the least bad of the options available to France. If, he wrote, it was decided that peace was preferable to war, so that not a single French soldier crossed the frontier, then there should be no hesitation in adopting what he called a "completely different system of political economy." But, he warned, the implications of that alternative were grave.

> Would we be able to close the kingdom with such exactness and so much severity that no one will be able to leave for as long as the crisis lasts? Will no one be allowed to enter unless they have enough in hand to allow them to make common cause with us, without being a burden? Will no merchandise be allowed to leave unless it has been paid for in advance? Will we know how to reduce the salaries of every public official to a level compatible with the most basic needs? Will the king give up his expenditure on himself, and his household, however different it may be from that of the simple citizen, with no luxury or superfluity? Will we know how to arrange things as if in a city under siege, and ensure that what may be superfluous for some will be distributed equitably to those lacking necessities? Will sufficiently severe measures be taken against avarice, greed, bad faith, and idleness to ensure that what we need for food and clothing is not exposed to those sudden moments of dearness that trouble all harmony, causing open warfare between different types of property, and filling the social body with anxieties and animosities? Will we, after stopping the import of all foreign goods, and the export of all metal coin, know how to remove every opportunity for those

[13] *Archives parlementaires* vol. 60 (Paris, 1901), pp. 290–94. For a guardedly sympathetic reaction to Barère's speech, and a further example of Montesquieu's metaphor of casting a veil, this time over the statue of justice, not liberty, in times of crisis, see Pierre-Toussaint Durand-Maillane, *Examen critique du projet de constitution présenté à la Convention nationale* (Paris, 1793), pp. 10–1, and note.

abominable speculations that, through the artifice and falsehoods of scoundrels, are destroying everything essential to the public fortune? Finally, will
those austere friends of liberty be numerous enough, and firm enough, to be
able to withstand the sophisms and sarcasms that will be used every day to
attack the severity of their measures?[14]

If all this were the case, and if the French really could revive the virtues of
Sparta (*les vertus de Lacédémone*), then there would be no reason not to opt
for peace. But, Clavière warned, "our Asiatic habits, our terror of sarcasm,
and our fickle loyalties do not lend themselves to such harsh courage."[15]
There was, therefore, no reason to hesitate. Attack was the only serious
option. It was the least dangerous choice for liberty itself.

It was a bleak justification of war. It was also clearly intended to be a reply
to Robespierre's equally bleak justification of peace, with its insistence on
the divided character of French society, the lack of patriotic public spirit,
the fragility of the postrevolutionary constitutional settlement, the implau-
sibility of expecting old-style Flemish political and religious fundamental-
ists to welcome proselytising French "armed missionaries," and the dangers
of entrusting what, he argued, was likely to be a long war to an army that,
from top to bottom, was still the last social bastion of the old regime. Here,
it was also the Roman republic, with its civil wars, that supplied the salient
example. War, Robespierre warned on 10 February 1792 (in a reply to Brissot and Clavière), was likely to lead to civil war, but, unlike Mercier, he had
no confidence at all in its putatively positive political effects. The threat of
political dissolution, he argued, could be averted only by raising a conscript
army from the whole armed nation, coupled with measures to restore common land usurped by noble landowners to their original peasant owners,
as well as with the additional impetus to patriotism supplied by permanent
political mobilisation and great civic festivals.[16] Both sets of assessments
were also redolent of Rousseau's frequent predictions of the future await-
ing the modern world. All roads, Rousseau argued, led either to despotism
or to social breakdown (and, in a more extended sense, to both).[17] At best,
he appeared to suggest, all that the impending age of crisis and revolution
would be likely to leave would be a small number of largely agricultural,
self-sufficient political societies, like Corsica, and, possibly, Poland, beyond
the silent, empty ruins of Europe's once great modern states.

---

[14] Etienne Clavière, "De la conjuration contre les finances, et des moyens d'en arrêter les
effets," *Chronique du mois* 3 (January 1792): 127–8.

[15] Clavière, "De la conjuration contre les finances," p. 129.

[16] On Robespierre and war, see, most fully, Georges Michon, *Robespierre et la guerre révolutionnaire, 1791–92* (Paris, 1937), pp. 34–44, 51–4, 76–8, and the content of his speeches of
18 December 1791, 2 January 1792, and 10 February 1792 cited there.

[17] See above, pp. 206–7.

The best-known monument to this kind of concern—since it makes most sense in this Rousseau-inspired context—was Constantin-François Volney's *Les Ruines, ou méditations sur les révolutions des empires* of 1791 (or *The Ruins, or A Survey of the Revolutions of Empires*, as the near contemporary English translation was entitled). It was a reply to Rousseau, based largely on the characterisation of human nature and history that, in a remote sense, Volney took over from the works of Claude-Adrien Helvétius, and, in a more immediate sense, from Rabaut Saint-Etienne's *Letters to M. Bailly on the Primitive History of Greece* (along with that work's intellectual debt to those of Bailly himself, Court de Gebelin, and Charles Dupuis).[18] The book began memorably. Looking at the ruins of Palmyra, Volney recalled, he began to think of France.

> I recalled her fields so richly cultivated, her roads so admirably constructed, her cities inhabited by a countless people, her fleets spread over every sea, her ports filled with the produce of both the Indies: and then comparing the activity of her commerce, the extent of her navigation, the magnificence of her buildings, the arts and industry of her inhabitants, with what Egypt and Syria had once possessed, I was gratified to find in modern Europe the departed splendour of Asia; but the charm of my reverie was soon dissolved by a last term of comparison. Reflecting that such had once been the activity of the places I was then contemplating, who knows, said I, but such may one day be the abandonment of our countries? Who knows if on the banks of the Seine, the Thames, the Zuyder-Zee, where now, in the tumult of so many employments,

[18] According to a review in the English *Analytical Review* 12 (1792): 36–8, however, its "great and leading idea"—namely, that "national, as well as individual evils are owing, ultimately, to ignorance and cupidity"—was "taken from" the preliminary discourse to Louis-Mathieu Langlès, *Fables et contes indiens nouvellement traduits avec un discours préliminaire sur la religion, la littérature, les moeurs, etc. des Hindous* (Paris, 1790). The remark may, or may not, be consistent with Volney's gift of a copy of the third edition of his book to Langlès, who, in the introductory essay to his *Fables*, argued that Christianity was a derivation of an earlier natural religion whose first incarnation was Indian and Hindu (pp. xv–xvi), an argument that, he wrote, was compatible with the earlier publications by Voltaire, Bailly, and Goguet (p. xxi). On this characterisation of Hinduism as a natural religion, see Wilhelm Halbfass, *India and Europe: An Essay in Understanding* [1981] (New York, State University of New York Press, 1988), pp. 56–68. On Volney's intellectual debts to Bailly, Dupuis, and Rabaut Saint-Etienne, see above, p. 257.

According to the more orthodox Orientalist Thomas Maurice, in his *Indian Antiquities*, 5 vols. (London, 1793–4), 4:viii–ix, "Voltaire first, and afterwards Bailly and Volney, have principally founded those false and impious systems which have plunged a great nation in the abyss of atheism, and all its consequent excesses and miseries." More generally, see Jean Gaulmier, *L'idéologue Volney 1757–1820. Contribution à l'histoire de l'orientalisme en France* [1951] (Geneva, Slatkine, 1980); Nigel Leask, *British Romantic Writers and the East: Anxieties of Empire* (Cambridge, CUP, 1992); Robert M. Ryan, *The Romantic Reformation: Religious Politics in English Literature 1789–1824* (Cambridge, CUP, 1997); Martin Priestman, *Romantic Atheism: Poetry and Freethought, 1780–1830* (Cambridge, CUP, 1999).

the heart and the eye suffice not for the multitude of sensations,—who knows
if some traveller, like myself, shall not one day sit on their silent ruins, and
weep in solitude over the ashes of their inhabitants, and the memory of their
former greatness?[19]

Equally memorable was its fifteenth chapter, with its dramatised characterisation of the events of 1789, based, at least in part, on a personified
version of Sieyès's *Essay on Privileges*, but with hindsight allowing Volney
to bring the drama to a more harmoniously triumphant conclusion. The
book's ending was, however, oddly inconclusive. After a debate on the true
principles of morality among personifications of all the major religions of
the world, the protagonists agreed to go back to basics. "Upon this," the
first part of the *Ruins* ended, "the legislators resuming their inquiry into
the physical and constituent attributes of man, and the motives and affections which govern him in his individual and social capacity, unfolded
on the following terms the laws on which nature herself has founded his
felicity."[20] The terms themselves, however, were not supplied.

The second part of *The Ruins* did not appear until the summer of 1793,
when Volney published his *Laws of Nature, or Principles of Morality, deduced
from the physical constitution of mankind and the universe* (as the English version of his *La loi naturelle* was entitled). It is not clear what the cause of
the delay might have been, or how, in the light of its occurrence, Volney
intended the two works to be connected. The easiest explanation is simply
that events intervened (in the interim, Volney became a government official in Corsica), and that when he went back to the book, the principles set
out in the second part followed on straightforwardly from the first. A more
narrowly historical explanation, however, might be that Volney really did
intend to end the *Ruins* as a kind of warning. In this sense, its inconclusive
ending could be taken to be a deliberate indication of the type of turning
point that the revolution appeared to have reached by the early autumn of
1791, after the flight to Varennes and the final split in the patriot party that
it brought in its wake. From this point of view, *The Laws of Nature* might
also be taken to be a more deliberately political resumption of the earlier
work, undertaken in the summer of 1793 only when, after the discussion
of the fundamental principles underlying the new French republic, Volney
decided that there was now an opportunity (or, at least, a responsibility) to
set out what he took these to be. It continued to rehearse the same kind
of naturalistic moral and political theory that Volney had taken over from
Rabaut Saint-Etienne's *Letters to M. Bailly on the Primitive History of Greece*,
but made no reference at all to Rabaut's earlier, more confident, assessment

[19] Constantin-François Volney, *The Ruins, or A Survey of the Revolutions of Empires* [1791]
(London, 1795), pp. 7–8.
[20] Volney, *Ruins*, p. 138.

of the conceptually refined, and linguistically streamlined, prospects that the future seemed likely to hold. Instead, Volney warned, unless political societies consumed less than they produced, they faced the threat of dissolution and despotism. The warning appeared in a vivid description of the effects of luxury that, somewhat surprisingly, introduced the final recapitulation of the broad principle of reciprocal utility underlying the argument of the whole short book. Luxury was simply unproductive consumption, and, as public expenditure swallowed up larger and larger amounts of available wealth, falling private production and rising taxation would lead to social divisions, and then to despotism, and, as Volney had written in his earlier *Travels in Egypt and Syria*, "with barbarous and brutal despotism, there is no tomorrow" (*il n'y a point de lendemain*).[21] Here, too, Volney may have intended to make a political point that, by the summer of 1793, was not too hard to see. It followed the logic of Clavière's earlier warning about the way of life prevailing in modern political societies, and the limits to ancient republican politics that this way of life entailed, but it was now a warning that applied to wartime conditions themselves, not just to the initial reasons for going to war. Without self-imposed patriotic austerity, Volney warned, getting consumption to fall below production was likely to require despotic political power.

The phrase that Volney associated with despotism resurfaced some years later as the title (*Point de lendemain*) of one of the French Revolution's most famous novels, and as a verdict on more than a decade of political conflict. Even by 1791, however, when Volney published the first part of his examination of the historical themes of ruin and recovery, Rousseau's predictions could begin to look more eerily prescient. For Adrien Duport in the spring of that year, the excessive sensibility towards popular dangers to which, he argued, his political opponents had succumbed, amounted inadvertently to opening a door towards executive despotism. As the Franco-Portuguese political economist Isaac de Pinto had emphasised in a note in his *Essay on Circulation and Credit* of 1774—quoting Rousseau's remark that if Rome and Sparta had perished, no state could hope to last forever—it was wrong "to attempt to govern a corrupted people by the same laws which suit a virtuous people."[22] For Antoine-Joseph Barnave, the erosion of the tax base caused by the combination of emigration and imperial collapse threatened to leave France exposed to the revived economic power of the landowners, and to despotism from a different route. For Brissot, Clavière,

[21] Constantin-François Volney, *La loi naturelle, ou catéchisme du citoyen français* [1793], in Volney, *Oeuvres*, 3 vols. (Paris, Fayard, 1989–98), 1:497–99. On Volney's characterisation of despotism, see his *Voyage en Egypte et en Syrie* [1785], 6th ed., 3 vols. (Paris, 1823), vol. 1, ch. 1, p. 8.

[22] Isaac de Pinto, *An Essay on Circulation and Credit in Four Parts, and A Letter on the Jealousy of Commerce* (London, 1774), p. 106, note.

and their assorted allies, luxury, and its hugely distorted legacy of urban industry and propertyless producers, left no room for manoeuvre between maintaining popular purchasing power and avoiding social dissolution.[23] In one sense, the disagreement between the increasingly polarised sides of the political argument turned on differences over the timing, speed, and practicalities of implementing reform. In a deeper sense, however, it also turned on different evaluations of the underlying causes of modern social and political stability, and different assessments of how weak, or strong, these were likely to be. On Rousseau's premises, however, both sets of assessments pointed towards the same disastrous outcome. Either the government would become the sovereign, as Duport and Barnave feared, or the sovereign would simply disintegrate, as, in different ways, both Robespierre and Clavière feared. The two sets of arguments could look like two sides of the same coin. Rousseau himself, moreover, supplied little guidance about what to do, either to prevent disaster, or to promote reform. In the end, he wrote in book 3, chapter 11, of *The Social Contract*, every state was doomed to die.

MABLY, ROUSSEAU, AND ROBESPIERRE

Rather more guidance could, instead, be found in the works of the abbé Gabriel Bonnot de Mably.[24] "The most eloquent writer of our times has supported this paradox," Mably wrote in 1775 in his *De l'étude de l'histoire* (Of the Study of History), referring explicitly to the same chapter in the *Social Contract* where Rousseau had asked, "[I]f Rome and Sparta perished, what state can hope to last forever?"[25] While Rousseau made it clear that the answer would always be negative, Mably disagreed. Real people certainly died, since time alone wore out all the organs and springs of life, but the same was not true of "the body of society, whose parts are all renewed ceaselessly by new generations." The old were always available to deliberate, just as the young would always be there to act. It was true, Mably wrote, "that we are born with passions that incline us towards vice, and that, consequently, every state has a tendency towards corruption, and

---

[23] On Duport and Barnave, see above, pp. 333–5. The same, Rousseau-inspired, idea of revolution can also be found in the slightly later publications of Gracchus Babeuf: see Sonenscher, "Property, Community and Citizenship," pp. 489–91.

[24] On Mably, see Keith Michael Baker, *Inventing the French Revolution: Essays on French Political Thought in the Eighteenth-Century* (Cambridge, CUP, 1990), pp. 86–106; Johnson Kent Wright, *A Classical Republican in Eighteenth-Century France: The Political Thought of Mably* (Stanford, Stanford UP, 1997); and, recently, Nelson, *The Greek Tradition*, pp. 176–83.

[25] Jean-Jacques Rousseau, *The Social Contract and Other Later Political Writings*, ed. Victor Gourevitch (Cambridge, CUP, 1997), p. 109.

its final end." No people, he acknowledged, had yet been able to resist it, but this did not mean that no people ever would. It was not nature's fault that the passions were diverted from their natural purposes. Provided that they were confined to certain limits, they gave virtue activity and could lead people to happiness. "A state that is wise enough to content itself with a modest sufficiency (*médiocrité*) for its fortune," Mably concluded, "is a state that can, and should, live eternally, provided, Monseigneur, that it keeps to the rules that I have had the honour of discussing with you" (the "Monseigneur" to whom the remark was addressed was the young prince of Parma, whose education was primarily the responsibility of his brother, the abbé Etienne Bonnot de Condillac, with Mably supplying historiographical assistance).[26]

The rules in question, as Mably outlined them, were derived almost entirely from ancient Greek or Roman thought and practice. First, there had to be laws and magistrates. Second, the laws in question had to be just, and to be just, they had to be impartial, which meant that there also had to be a broad equality of fortune and dignity among citizens. One important effect of this equality, Mably emphasised, was that it would neutralise the passions, since the passions' more pernicious motivating power flourished under conditions of inequality. The third rule was that obedience to the law had to apply as much to magistrates as to citizens. This meant that the magistracy not only had to be given a permanent existence, but also had to be prevented from abusing its power. The executive had to be separated from the legislature, and the people had to have its own magistracy, like the Roman tribunes or the Spartan ephors, to propose legislation, while executive magistrates were to play no part at all in any legislative deliberation. Additionally, no magistrate was ever to be allowed to be renewed in office, and, as again with the Romans, the whole magistracy was to be divided into as many separate functional agencies as were required. The fourth rule was to avoid unnecessary involvement with the outside world. Although, Mably wrote, it was impossible for nations to isolate themselves, it was essential for them to avoid becoming rich enough to tempt their neighbours' cupidity. This meant a wholehearted adoption of the anticommercial morality of the ancients in general, and the Spartans in particular. With this in place, the absence of the self-defeating pursuit of wealth and power would then make it easier to follow the moral foreign policy, based on the identification of a durable set of natural allies and enemies, that, Mably wrote, he had described already in his earlier *Phocion's Conversations* and *Principles of Negotiations*. "If Persia could be subjugated by the Macedonians; if Carthage was vanquished by the Romans," he

---

[26] Gabriel Bonnot de Mably, *De l'étude de l'histoire* [1775], ed. Barbara de Negroni (Paris, Fayard, 1988), pt. 1, ch. 6, pp. 61–7.

warned, "providence did not intend wealth to be a means used by policy to make society flourish."[27] This pointed towards the fifth and final rule, namely, that states should not aim at any other happiness than the modest sufficiency (*médiocrité*) that nature intended each of them to have.

Like Rousseau, Mably also had a reputation for political prescience. "He loved to repeat Leibniz's adage, *the present age is big with the future*," wrote one of his obituarists, the abbé Jean-Jacques Barthélémy, in the posthumous edition of Mably's collected works that was published in 1790. He had predicted "the American revolution" in the revised edition of his treatise on European public law, the *Droit public de l'Europe*, published in 1764. He had anticipated the French invasion of Geneva in 1782, as well as the conflicts in the Dutch republic that were still under way when the French Revolution began. His friends sometimes called him "the prophet of doom" (*prophète de malheur*), and it was true, he was said to have replied, "that I know enough about men not readily to hope for their good."[28] In one sense, his views on Europe's future anticipated Rousseau's. "At present," he wrote in his *Observations on the Romans* in 1751, "should one of the powers of Europe possess superior forces to any other particular state, and even surpass them all in the knowledge of military discipline; suppose this power to be always guided by the same principles, to be neither dazzled by prosperity nor dejected by adversity, to possess such firmness as never to give over its enterprises, and to be so intrepid as even to prefer utter ruin to an inglorious peace; were there such a power in being, we should soon see these leagues, confederacies, and alliances vanish, whereby the independence of each state is maintained." Modern international politics, he continued, was driven solely by two passions. The first was "the jealous fear" produced by "some ambitious people." The second was the hope of being able to resist them, based on the knowledge that no people appeared to have "all the qualities or resources necessary to raise them to universal empire." But, he warned, if any state looked as if it might be able to extinguish the hope, then fear would be "the only passion remaining, and then Europe would soon lose its liberty."[29] Yet, despite this prognosis, Mably was not actually as bleak a political thinker as Rousseau. Nor, despite his frequent attacks on modern luxury and the self-defeating politics of commercial competition on which it was based, was he as insistent as Rousseau about the special character of the political arrangements required

[27] Gabriel Bonnot de Mably, *De l'étude de l'histoire* [1775], in his *Oeuvres*, 13 vols. (London, 1789–90), vol. 12, ch. 5, p. 67.

[28] Jean-Jacques Barthélémy, "Vie privée de l'abbé de Mably," in Gabriel Bonnot de Mably, *Oeuvres*, 13 vols. (London, 1789–90), 13:248–9.

[29] Gabriel Bonnot de Mably, *Observations on the Romans* [1751] (London, 1751), pp. 147–8. It is possible that this was the passage that Edmund Burke had in mind nearly fifty years later in his *Letters on a Regicide Peace*.

to secure the compatibility between a subsistence-based social and technical division of labour and individual liberty. For Mably, altruism did not require Rousseau's imaginative emotional acrobatics. "As for myself," he wrote in one his late works, "while bemoaning all our miseries, I am persuaded along with Leibniz, that man is as perfect as he can be, since he is made up of two substances as different as the soul and the body." In this characterisation of human nature, and "to know the fate of our captive reason," he was, he explained a little earlier in the same work, also relying on "my brother's philosophy that I am simply applying to moral and political matters."[30]

After a long lapse of time in which Mably's brother, Condillac, was usually taken to be a French populariser of John Locke's epistemological theories, it has now begun to become clear, as it was in the eighteenth century, that Condillac was, in fact, a very careful and thorough student of Leibniz.[31] Of all "the metaphysicians," wrote one late eighteenth-century commentator, "he is the one who penetrated Leibniz's ideas most deeply," quoting Condillac's own endorsement of "the system of monads" in support ("There is nothing that it cannot account for, while the insurmountable difficulties of every other system are here explained in the most intelligible way. It should therefore be regarded as something better than a hypothesis").[32] Here, the Leibniz in question was the original theorist of windowless monads, and of a preestablished harmony between these two entirely different types of spiritual and physical entity, rather than the posthumous Leibniz of the vitalism of the second half of the eighteenth century. Mably left the metaphysical side of Leibniz to his brother. But, as he indicated, Condillac's Leibnitzian philosophy had a real bearing on moral and political matters. It did so mainly because it opened up a way

[30] Gabriel Bonnot de Mably, "Du développement, des progrès, et des bornes de la raison," in Mably, *Oeuvres* [1797], 15 vols. (Ahlen, Scientia Verlag, 1986), 15:42, 26.

[31] See, particularly, Etienne Bonnot de Condillac, *Les Monades*, ed. Laurence L. Bongie, *Studies on Voltaire and the Eighteenth Century* 187 (1980). It may be worth noting that the Jesuit Nicolas-Silvestre Bergier took the ideas about the acquired character of the notion of justice to be found in the controversial theology thesis produced in the mid-eighteenth century by the abbé de Prades to be derived from Locke: Nicolas-Silvestre Bergier, *Traité historique et dogmatique de la vraie religion*, 12 vols. (Paris, 1780), 3:484–90.

[32] [Paul Abeille], introduction to Chrétien-Guillaume Lamoignon de Malesherbes, *Observations sur l'histoire naturelle générale et particulière de Buffon et Daubenton*, 2 vols. (Paris, an VI/1798), 1:xxx–xxxi. For an earlier discussion of the Leibniz-Condillac relationship, see Johann Bernhard Merian, "Parallèle de deux principes de psychologie," in *Histoire de l'Académie Royale des Sciences et Belles Lettres, année 1757* (Berlin, 1759), pp. 375–91. For a suggestive indication of how the emphasis on self-mastery in Leibniz's moral theory may have played into both Condillac's and Mably's later interest in neutralising the passions, see Donald Rutherford, "Leibniz on Spontaneity," in Donald Rutherford and J. A. Cover, eds., *Leibniz: Nature and Freedom* (Oxford, OUP, 2005), pp. 156–80.

to restore the part played by reason and rationality in moral or political choice, and, by doing so, to correct the various types of eighteenth-century moral philosophy that, from his point of view, had succumbed too comprehensively either to moral sense theory, to sentimentalism, or to the moral scepticism that, in different ways, could be imputed to Hobbes, Locke, Montesquieu, and Rousseau (in this sense, Condillac was not so much a follower as a philosophical critic of Locke). In doing so, it also offered a more morally unambiguous picture of human dignity and human improvement than Rousseau's deliberately slippery concept of perfectibility, with its equally deliberate intention of avoiding exposure to Jansenist objections to Jesuit "pelagianism" and Leibnitzian "optimism" (both, because of the controversies about Montesquieu, Pope, and the abbé de Prades, were hot topics when Rousseau wrote his second *Discourse*).[33] In the use to which Condillac put Leibniz's concern with language, logic, and concept formation, rationality and morality were integrated analytically into a developing process of conceptual and moral clarification. In contradistinction to Rousseau, this type of rational moral theory did not have to rely on debatable claims about the presocial feelings of pity or justice, because it took the passions to be no more than simple natural products of the physical side of human nature. This, very obviously, meant that the passions came first, both in individuals, and in human history. The more spiritual, rational, side of human nature not only came later but then had to be used to revise and correct the accumulated legacy of error and misfortune that the passions themselves had produced.

As Mably presented it, this meant that it was possible to think about politics without having to subscribe either to the fear-based, state-centred, political theory usually associated with Thomas Hobbes, or to the benevolence-driven, community-centred, political theory that he associated with the ideas of the seventeenth-century Anglican divine Richard Cumberland (although, Mably wrote approvingly, Hobbes's philosophy had the merit of ruling out the "terrors of a second life").[34] Both types of political theory, he argued, overlooked the cumulatively progressive character of human rationality, and its growing potential to guide and manage the passions towards their properly subordinate role in a well-designed social setting. This type of setting, he argued, was not hard to identify, since most of its features were already visible in the ancient world, notably in Sparta and republican Rome. But ancient morality was necessarily local

---

[33] On the background to the second *Discourse*, see Michael Sonenscher, *Before the Deluge: Public Debt, Inequality, and the Intellectual Origins of the French Revolution* (Princeton, Princeton UP, 2007), pp. 226–7, and the further bibliographical guidance indicated there.

[34] Mably, "Du développement, des progrès, et des bornes de la raison," in Mably, *Oeuvres* [1797], 15:2–5, 17, 27.

and partial, with none of the modern awareness of humanity and its rights. Here, as with Leibniz, it was the Christian revelation that supplied the prime difference. "Human policy," Mably wrote, "is wavering and subject to error. It requires support to guide it constantly towards justice and virtue, and religion alone can supply it." "Never forget," he added, "that the dogmas of Epicurus alone, after corrupting and overturning all the states of Greece, caused the ruin of the Roman republic."[35]

Unlike many of his contemporaries, Mably showed no interest at all in trying to find out about any putatively monotheistic natural religion that could be used to give Rousseau's political thought both a real historical foundation and a fuller moral content. Privately, he condemned Rousseau's religious views. "I commiserate most sincerely with Rousseau," he informed one of his Swiss correspondents in 1765, "but I would commiserate with him a great deal more if I could persuade myself that he is in good faith. His mixture of Christianity and deism revolts me. Why isn't he straightforwardly deist? Then, the priests and the devout would not torment him so much, and he himself would not be forced to contradict himself, and often garble his reasoning (*il ne se verrait pas forcé de se contredire et de déraisonner souvent*)."[36] This muted religious orthodoxy set Mably apart from several of Rousseau's more intellectually ambitious critics. Here, a brief set of descriptions may help to clarify the differences and, at the same time, may make it easier to position both Mably and Condillac among the many different types of moral and political reformers of late eighteenth-century France. Both, it is worth emphasising, were held in high regard, at least in some loosely political circles. Mably was talked about as a possible tutor for Louis XV's son, the dauphin of France, who died in 1765. His, and Condillac's, subsequent appointment to be tutors to the duke of Parma was the work of the same loosely political circles, with their connections to Louis XV's queen, Maria Leczinska (Mably seems to have been on good terms with several members of this

[35] Gabriel Bonnot de Mably, *Le Destin de la France* [1781], in Mably, *Oeuvres*, 13:154–5, 155–6.

[36] Mably to Daniel Fellenberg, 5 December 1765, in Jean-Luc Malvache, ed., "Correspondance inédit de Mably à Fellenberg 1763–1778," *Francia* 19 (1992): 47–93 (55–6). Mably's objections to Rousseau's civil religion paralleled the stronger criticism made by the Jansenist magistrate Louis-René de Caradeuc de la Chalotais, in his *Essai d'éducation nationale* (1763). As La Chalotais argued there, the minimalist content of Rousseau's civil religion presupposed too many of the precepts of the gospel (notably an afterlife, with its future rewards and punishments) to be able to stand up in its own right. Nor, he argued too, was it easy to see how "une religion purement philosophique" could be "nationale" without a real system of public worship. In its absence, it would either "abolish itself" or "infallibly bring the multitude back to idolatry." La Chalotais's criticisms of Rousseau were cited approvingly by the Swiss theologian Jacob Vernet: see his *Réflexions sur les moeurs, sur la religion, et sur le culte* (Geneva, 1769), pp. 69, 76–7.

circle, like the abbé Jean-Marie-Bernard Clement and the abbé Antoine
Sabatier de Castres). Here, one of Mably's patrons was a noblewoman
named Mme de Vassé, who was also a friend of Condillac's muse Mme
Ferrand (Mme Ferrand made Mme de Vassé her heir when she died in
1752, leaving Condillac six thousand livres "to enable him to have books,"
and Mably a chest of drawers and her small lacquer writing table, while
Mme de Vassé, in turn, left one of her diamonds, worth six thousand
livres, to Condillac when she died in 1768). Another member of the same
circle was the most prolific contributor to Diderot's and d'Alembert's
Encyclopaedia, the Protestant chevalier de Jaucourt, whose relative the
marquis de Jaucourt was named by Mme de Vassé as the executor of her
will. Another of her friends and protégés was the comte d'Angiviller, the
director of royal buildings during the latter part of Louis XV's reign, and
a strong advocate of a patriotic royal coup against the nation's creditors in
1787 and 1788.[37] At the least, Mably's moral and political theories were
not an obstacle to patronage, nor, it would seem, were his dealings with
the rich and powerful as tortured as Rousseau's (in later life, patronage

[37] Mably's acquaintance with Mme Ferrand and Mme de Vassé may have begun in the
1740s, when he was a diplomatic official and they were protecting Charles Edward Stuart,
the young Pretender: see Laurence L. Bongie, *The Love of a Prince: Bonnie Prince Charlie
in France* (Vancouver, University of British Columbia Press, 1986), pp. 273, 315, note. On
these circles (which, according to d'Angiviller, also included Turgot, and are not usually
mentioned in biographies of Mably), see Louis Theodor Alfred Bobé, ed., *Efterladte Papirer
fra den Reventlowske Familiekreds I Tidsrummet 1770–1827*, 10 vols. (Copenhagen, 1895–
1931), 7:186–8, and his edition of the *Mémoires de Charles-Claude Flahaut comte de la Billarderie d'Angiviller, avec des notes sur les "Mémoires" de Marmontel, publiés d'après le manuscrit*
(Copenhagen, 1933). See also Claude-François Lezarde de Radonvilliers, *Oeuvres diverses*,
3 vols. (Paris, 1807); Jacques Silvestre de Sacy, *Le comte d'Angiviller, dernier directeur général
des bâtiments du roi* (Paris, 1953); and Henry A. Stavan, *Gabriel Sénac de Meilhan, 1736–1806.
Moraliste, romancier, homme de lettres* (Paris, Lettres modernes, 1968). On Mably and the abbé
Antoine Sabatier de Castres, see the latter's obituary notice on Mably in the *Journal Encyclopédique*, June 1785, pp. 504–8; and, on the abbé Jean-Marie-Bernard Clément, see Mably's
enthusiastic comments on his criticisms of the marquis de Saint-Lambert's poem *Les saisons*
in Malvache, "Correspondance inédit de Mably à Fellenberg." On the relationship between
Mme Ferrand and Mme de Vassé, and among the Jaucourt brothers, Mably, Condillac, and
Mme de Vassé, see A. N., Paris, Minutier central, LXCVIII, 417 (20 May 1765); XCII, 575,
8 February 1752 (testament de Mme Ferrand); XCII, 715, 30 May 1768 (testament de Mme
de Vassé); XCII, 717, 1 August 1768 (dépôt mortuaire des effets de Mme la comtesse de
Vassé); XCII, 719 (10 December 1768). See also Mably's account of Mme de Vassé's death
in his letters to Fellenberg of 13 January, 29 March, and 1 July 1768, in Malvache, "Correspondance inédit de Mably à Fellenberg." It needs to be said, too, that the same circles also
included both Helvétius (before the publication of *De l'esprit* in 1758) and, via d'Angiviller's
lover, Mme de Marchais, the founders of Physiocracy, François Quesnay and Victor Riqueti,
marquis de Mirabeau. For a recent, and timely, corrective to the question-begging image
of these circles as simply "devout" (which does not, of course, preclude both conventional
and unconventional styles of political theology), see Bernard Hours, *La vertu et le secret. Le
dauphin, fils de Louis XV* (Paris, Champion, 2006).

also came from Turgot's friend the duchesse d'Enville and the broader La Rochefoucauld clan).[38]

Where the focus of Mably's own moral and political theories fell largely on modernity's potential to revive the principles of ancient politics, but in a more comprehensively rational moral and political setting, many of Rousseau's other critics focused more firmly on the future. Some continued to develop the loosely Origenist historical speculations underlying the earlier works of Pierre Poiret and the chevalier Ramsay. One example of what this type of intellectual undertaking could look like can be found in the rather strange extrapolation from Rousseau's *Discourse on the Origin of Inequality* made by the self-styled "unknown philosopher" Louis-Claude de Saint-Martin in his *Des erreurs et de la vérité* (Of Truth and Error) of 1775, with its reworking of Rousseau's conjectural history of inequality into a more spiritually driven account of mankind's fall, recovery, and rise towards a military-style, but morally just, theocracy.[39] A different version of the same idea lay behind the crisp theological slogan *Et plus bas, et plus haut* (The further you fall, the higher you rise) underlying the moral and historical speculations of the late eighteenth-century Protestant pastor of Waldbach Jean-Frédéric Oberlin, whose ideas, it has been shown, played an important part in the intellectual formation of the Catholic bishop of Blois Henri Grégoire. Oberlin's slogan was the basis of the millennial expectations underlying Grégoire's own political theology. It also throws a clearer, more obviously theologically inspired light on Grégoire's remark, mentioned earlier, that "true genius is almost always *sans-culotte*."[40] Here, history and providence (as well as a different type of Freemasonry from Saint-Martin's own) went together to form a sequence of steps that, as with other prominent French Catholics—like Claude Fauchet (who, during the Revolution, became bishop of Calvados), or Adrien-Antoine Lamourette (who became bishop of Lyon)—took their starting point in revised versions of Rousseau's *Discourse on the Origin of Inequality* to arrive at an end point that did not have to fit the Geneva-oriented specifications of the *Social Contract*, and could, instead, form the basis of a more morally integrated French nation, and a reformed French church.

[38] See Joseph Ruwet, ed., *Lettres de Turgot à la duchesse d'Enville* (Louvain, 1976).

[39] On Saint-Martin, see Nicole Jacques-Lefèvre, *Louis-Claude de Saint-Martin, le philosophe inconnu (1743–1803)* (Paris, Editions Dervy, 2003).

[40] On Oberlin, see *Memoirs of John Frederick Oberlin, Pastor of Waldbach in the Ban de la Roche*, 2nd ed. (London, 1833), and, on Grégoire, see Alyssa Goldstein Sepinwall, *The Abbé Grégoire and the French Revolution: The Making of Modern Universalism* (Berkeley and Los Angeles, University of California Press, 2005). On Grégoire's remark about "true genius," see above, p. 62. Oberlin is perhaps better known now from the nineteenth-century novella *Lenz* by Georg Büchner describing Oberlin's treatment of the writer J.M.R. Lenz after Lenz had his first nervous breakdown.

A further variation on same theme of ruin and recovery can be found in the works of the heterodox Benedictine monk Dom Léger-Marie Deschamps.[41] Where Origenist-inspired reworkings of Rousseau involved the recovery of a lost human dignity, Deschamps's version of the same exercise called for the elimination of an all-too-visible catalogue of human error, notably, as he argued in detail in his *Vrai système de la nature* (The True System of Nature), the many misconceived ideas of religion produced by thinking of the divinity as a person. For Deschamps, Rousseau's second *Discourse* opened up a way to rethink the idea of the Fall as a widely used metaphor that had arisen in humanity's original savage state (*état sauvage*). The ubiquity of the metaphor was, he argued, evidence of humanity's natural inability to see itself as the real author of its own misfortunes, and its propensity, instead, to transfer responsibility to complicated providential systems, and to the many unverifiable personifications and imaginary agencies that they housed (gods, states, and laws, to name the most pervasive). In a more modern idiom, human history was driven by ideological delusion, in the strong sense of what ideology can mean. According to Deschamps, Rousseau's account of the transition from the savage state to a legal state (*état de loix*) fitted the broad contours of human history but, because of its asocial starting point, failed to present an indication of the further transition that lay ahead. This, he wrote, would be a "state of union without disunion, which is the state of manners (*état de moeurs*), the social state without laws."[42] In this purely moral community, there would be no laws, no private property, no family, no government, and no state (animals, Deschamps emphasised, were incapable of this type of community, since they had no capacity for morality, and were de facto atheists). Although, in his *Lettres sur l'esprit du siècle* (Letters on the Spirit of the Age), a short work, published in 1769 under the fictitious imprint of "Edward Young, London," Deschamps endorsed Rousseau's attack on the arts and sciences, and what he took to be its call for "men to have manners as simple as the religion he would like them to have," the second *Discourse* was still "useless and demoralising (*affligeant*)," because of the conundrum that Rousseau appeared to have presented between a lost savage state and the impossibility of getting back to it.[43] The solution, instead, had to come from the future. Every actually existing society,

[41] On Deschamps, see, most recently, the bibliographical guidance and editor's introduction in Léger-Marie Deschamps, *Correspondance générale établie à partir des archives d'Argenson*, ed. Bernard Delhaume (Paris, Champion, 2006), pp. 17–35.

[42] Léger-Marie Deschamps, *Le Vrai système de la nature*, in Léger-Marie Deschamps, *Oeuvres philosophiques*, ed. Bernard Delhaume, 2 vols. (Paris, Vrin, 1993), 1:111, 279–90 (on Rousseau).

[43] Léger-Marie Deschamps, *Lettres sur l'esprit du siècle* (London, 1769), pp. 23–4. On it, see Viola Recchia, "La via segreta alla rivoluzione. Le *Lettres sur l'esprit du siècle* di Dom Deschamps," *Studi Settecenteschi* 21 (2001): 85–110.

Deschamps claimed, was testimony to the human incapacity to disentangle moral principles from metaphysical claims about God. Separating the two (by understanding the divinity in purely negative terms, leading to what Deschamps called "nothingism," or *riénisme*) was the way out. Progress, he argued, had begun with the kind of radical religious scepticism initiated by Hobbes, which Rousseau had continued but had failed to carry through to a clear conclusion. For all its apparent "Spinozism," Deschamps's *True System* was a kind of heterodox Catholic counterpart to William Godwin's later, equally heterodox, Protestant speculations.[44]

"Spinozism" was often the name given to this use of religious, or epistemological, scepticism to revise and correct Rousseau's moral scepticism. In the late eighteenth century, the label was used most frequently in the German-speaking world, but it also applied to the same sort of mixture of religious scepticism and moral realism developed by one of Rousseau's many enemies, Pierre-Paul Thiry, baron de Holbach (whose intellectual debts to the "Spinozism" of the German-speaking world remain to be explored).[45] For the English Unitarian John Jebb, there was no contradiction at all between the moral principles set out in Holbach's materialistic *Système de la nature* and his own "theopathetic" conception of morality. Jebb certainly subscribed, for theological, moral, and historical reasons, to a view of the afterlife that Holbach denied ("To have revealed a future state too soon," he noted, "would have put men under the power of priests too soon; but the almighty kept back that knowledge till men had improved their laws etc. so as to be able the better to bear it"), but, as far as this life was concerned, "Mirabaud" (the pseudonymous author of Holbach's book) had expressed "my idea of the religion of nature, so far as it relates to our duty to our neighbour. He conceives this to be the voice of nature.

[44] On Godwin, and the wider context of his thought, see, Knud Haakonssen, ed., *Enlightenment and Religion: Rational Dissent in Eighteenth-Century Britain* (Cambridge, CUP, 1996).
[45] For an example of this type of combination of religious scepticism and moral realism, see Jean-André Naigeon, *Adresse à l'assemblée nationale sur la liberté des opinions, sur celle de la presse, etc.* (Paris, 1790), pp. 16–20, with its objection to Henri Grégoire's proposal to include the subject of God in the Declaration of the Rights of Man, on the grounds that scepticism about God would give rise to scepticism about morality. On the subject, see Friedrich Heinrich Jacobi, *The Main Philosophical Writings and the Novel "Allwill"*, ed. George di Giovanni (Montreal, McGill-Queen's UP, 1994), and the very helpful introduction by its editor. See, too, Frederick Beiser, *The Fate of Reason: German Philosophy from Kant to Fichte* (Cambridge, Mass., Harvard UP, 1987), and his *Enlightenment, Revolution, and Romanticism: The Genesis of Modern German Political Thought 1790–1800* (Cambridge, Mass., Harvard UP, 1992). The only scholar who, to my knowledge, seems to have noticed the French, and Protestant Dissenting, dimensions of the subject is Seamus Deane, *The French Revolution and Enlightenment in England, 1789–1832* (Cambridge, Mass., Harvard UP, 1988). For a different rendition of Spinozism, see Jonathan Israel, *Enlightenment Contested: Philosophy, Modernity, and the Emancipation of Man 1670–1752* (Oxford, OUP, 2006).

I only differ from him in thinking it the voice of God. He is right in thus founding morality on fact." The only fact that he had forgotten was that of the Resurrection, and the way that "it gives to religion its perfection, and confirms piety as a moral duty." All that was needed, Jebb wrote, to make "Mirabaud's" materialist language compatible with "the language of Berkeley and Malebranche" was the earlier argument made by another English Dissenter, David Hartley, about the purely spiritual nature of the divine intelligence, and the purely sense-based character of human knowledge.[46] Once the distinction was accepted, Holbach's morality, and its strong claims about human rationality and capacity for improvement, made perfect sense.

The same sort of mixture of religious scepticism and moral realism re-surfaced during the period of the French Revolution in the work of the Moravian financier Moses Dobruška (also known as Franz Thomas von Schönfeld and, when he wrote this, as the French Jacobin Junius Frey) in his *Philosophie sociale* (Social Philosophy) in 1793, a work that was headed by an epigraph from Alexander Pope's *Essay on Man*, and began with a foreword reproducing the first chapter of Thomas Hobbes's *Of Human Nature*.[47] "We can say in general," Frey wrote, "that all the governments that have established two personalities (*deux moi*) in society, the general *moi* of the state and the individual *moi* of the government . . . might be, and are, in effect, the result of a very skilful political combination." It was, however, a combination "that was entirely in favour of the rulers against the ruled." Humanity, Frey continued, "is certainly one indivisible whole, because all that it contains is man. Only tyrants and short-sighted legisla-tors, by establishing various different *moi* in the great *moi* of society, could have divided mankind into different classes."[48] The vocabulary came from Rousseau, but, as Frey emphasised, the positive argument could not be found in any of the Genevan citizen's works. Rousseau, he wrote, "had certainly made people feel the necessity of disorganising the old order of things." But he had supplied no more than "some artificial and very complicated remedies, none in truth," to the problem of preventing the

---

[46] John Jebb, *The Works*, 3 vols. (London, 1787), 2:161, 163, 168, 174 (it should be men-tioned that these were private notes, made in 1773, and published posthumously).

[47] On Junius Frey, see the fascinating study by Gershom Scholem, *Du Frankisme au Ja-cobinisme. La vie de Moses Dobruška alias Thomas von Schönfeld alias Junius Frey* (Paris, Ecole des Hautes Etudes en Sciences Sociales, 1981), and, for a helpful way in both to the type of Masonic circles to which Frey belonged and to the same type of interest in injecting more morality into Rousseau's thought, see Pierre-André Bois, *Adolph Freiherr Knigge (1752–1796). De la "nouvelle religion" aux Droits de l'Homme* (Wiesbaden, Wolfenbütteler Forschun-gen, Band 50, 1990). For an earlier example of the same type of use of Hobbes, see Naigeon, *Adresse à l'assemblée nationale*.

[48] [Junius Frey], *Philosophie sociale. Dédiée au peuple françois* (Paris, 1793), pp. 28–9.

interests of some from becoming the state's interest (*intérêt d'état*).[49] One part of the solution, Frey claimed, could be found in the religion of Christ. This was not because of its applicability to the affairs of this world, but, on the contrary, because of its rigorous lack of applicability (only in its degenerate modern form, Frey commented, had the doctrine of the gospel been turned into an appendix to the works of Hugo Grotius).[50] A second could be found in the works of "a new revolutionary giant in philosophy, the destroyer of the two principal columns of scepticism and dogmatism, the disorganiser of every philosophical system, Immanuel Kant." Armed with this combination, and after so much idolatry and so many idols, Frey wrote, humanity was at last in a position to enjoy its own "*divinity.*"[51]

Mably avoided this type of speculation. At most, he argued, the anthropomorphism of the pagan gods of Greece and Rome, and the human effects that their behaviour was believed to have caused, had a social utility that undermined modern claims about the viability of a society of atheists. There was, he agreed, an atheism that might be found among "savages who still live, sheltering from hunger, misery, and nakedness, in the manner of brutes," but this was a matter of sheer ignorance. A community of enlightened atheists was a moral oxymoron. It was better to raise altars to a Jupiter, a Venus, or an Apollo, or even "the vegetables in our gardens" or the "poultry in our courtyards." In the end, reason could turn even "the most absurd theology into the religion of Aristides, Socrates, and Plato."[52] In this sense, Mably's religious views were rather like Leibniz's but without the spiritualised physiology of later, neo-Leibnizian natural philosophy.[53] Revealed religion, with its focus on the afterlife, was simply a more rational version of the many peculiarities of natural religion. This ruled out the need to try to identify some primary form of natural monotheism to counter Rousseau's moral scepticism. Scriptural history, as Mably indicated at the beginning of The Study of History, was an adequate guide to human beginnings.[54] What came next, however, fell outside scriptural and Jewish history, because Gentile history was largely a matter of the mixture of practical philosophy, error, and superstition

---

[49] [Frey], *Philosophie sociale*, p. 27.

[50] [Frey], *Philosophie sociale*, p. 44.

[51] [Frey], *Philosophie sociale*, pp. 48–9, 50.

[52] Gabriel Bonnot de Mably, *De la législation, ou principes des loix* [1776], in Mably, *Oeuvres*, 9:328–30; and in the Amsterdam, 1777, edition of the same work, pp. 146 (on reason's ability to correct "the most absurd theology"), 148–9 (on the difference between ignorant and enlightened atheism), 168 (on altars to "the vegetables in our gardens").

[53] On Leibniz and revealed religion as a rational step up from natural religion, see Patrick Riley, *Leibniz' Universal Jurisprudence: Justice as the Charity of the Wise* (Cambridge, Mass., Harvard UP, 1996), pp. 120–4, 176–8.

[54] Mably, *De l'étude de l'histoire*, ed. Negroni, p. 7.

that had begun in the great Asian empires of Assyria, Babylon, and Egypt. As with his brother, Gentile religion began with polytheism and idolatry, moving towards monotheism only as scepticism began to raise questions about how purely physical occurrences, like thunder or lightening, could have spiritual properties.[55] In this sense, Christianity really was a religion for sceptics, because, as Mably emphasised repeatedly, its kingdom was, literally, not of this world (Polish translations of the works of Fleury, Nicole, and Bossuet were advisable, he suggested to the Poles, to dispel the mistaken beliefs they might have on this subject, and its bearing on their misconceived ideas of secular papal authority).[56] But Christianity's gospel of love, and its rejection of any moral differences among the whole human family, were the key to the difference between the ancient and modern worlds. This was the theme of his most successful work, *Phocion's Conversations*, and, as Gabriel Brizard noted in the biography attached to several editions of Mably's collected works, the only sign that it was "the work of a modern." It also, as one of Mably's critics pointed out, made his moral and political thought look surprisingly like Fénelon's.[57] As Mably himself argued, love of humanity added a modern, moral, foundation to ancient politics in a way that complemented the ultimately providentially grounded idea of human improvement.[58]

This real, but still limited, capacity for improvement was, Mably argued, the reason why arguments about selfishness or benevolence as fundamental attributes of human nature, and as the basis of the putative content of natural law, were largely beside the point. So, by extension, were unverifiable claims about original sin, or original innocence. As the

---

[55] Etienne Bonnot de Condillac, *Traité des animaux* [1755], ed. M. Malherbe (Paris, Vrin, 2004), pp. 171–2 (a text that, as Bongie has shown, reproduces a passage from his earlier *Monades*, ed. Bongie, pp. 200–1). For a recent study of Condillac's moral and political thought (but without discussion of Mably), see Gianni Paganini, " 'Everything Must Be Redone': Condillac as Critic of Despotism and Defender of Toleration," in Hans Blom and John Christian Laursen, eds., *Monarchisms in the Age of Enlightenment* (Toronto, University of Toronto Press, 2007), pp. 144–61, and the further bibliography cited there.

[56] Gabriel Bonnot de Mably, *Du gouvernement et des loix de la Pologne* [1770], in Mably, *Oeuvres*, 8:152–3. For a later (and more rigorous) version of the same argument, see Alasdair Macintyre, "The Logical Status of Religious Belief," in Stephen Toulmin, Ronald W. Hepburn, and Alasdair Macintyre, *Metaphysical Beliefs: Three Essays* (London, SCM Press, 1957), pp. 167–211.

[57] Mably, *Oeuvres*, 1:104. On claims about the similarity between Mably and Fénelon, see below, p. 411.

[58] As Mably wrote in his *De la législation, ou principes des loix* of 1776, legislators "devaient se regarder comme des coopérateurs de la providence; ils devaient penser qu'elle ne nous invite à nous unir en société que pour donner plus d'énergie à nos qualités sociales, et empêcher qu'elles ne se détournent de la fin pour laquelle elles nous ont été données. Les loix devaient nous guider selon les vues de la nature, et les magistrats devaient nous faire respecter ces guides": Mably, *Oeuvres*, 9:25.

character "Cleophon" in one of Mably's pseudo-Socratic conversations put it, "our soul, hampered by our senses, rises as far as it can to reach its dignity, but, for perfect instruction, one has to go to the trouble of dying" ("Cleophon," Mably wrote, "was always accompanied by his Leibniz and his Condillac").[59] In the beginning, natural law was simply an injunction to self-preservation, and, since human needs were simple and passions were few, self-preservation was not, initially, self-defeating. But altruism was still an acquired capacity. "How could it have been possible, without contradicting itself," Mably pointed out, "for nature to have ordered me to love myself preferably to all else and, relying on this bond to bind me to my fellows, to have prescribed a law to prefer the public good to my own good?" Concern for others could not have come first. Neither, therefore, could love of humanity, or even patriotism. It followed, Mably continued, that the public good was not a law of nature "but a real law of politics that, using to advantage our needs, social qualities, weakness, passions, and tastes, serves to teach the love we have of ourselves, by a wise distribution of rewards and punishments, that it is useful to moderate itself, to hide and forget itself, and to manage our fellows' self-love (*amour-propre*) to make them the instruments of our own well-being." The human materials were already there, but it was "up to politics, or human reason, to put them in place and arrange them to form a solid and regular edifice."[60]

This focus on politics aligned Mably with Rousseau. But where Rousseau's critics (like Garat, Brissot, Rabaut Saint-Etienne, or Mercier) objected to what they took to be the moral void at the heart of his political thought, Mably's critics (in many cases, the same individuals) objected to what they took to be his excessive political moralism. "When one has been through the abbé de Mably's works with any attention," Dominique-Joseph Garat wrote in 1784 in a highly critical review of Mably's *Observations on the Government and the Laws of the United States*,

> one can see that, in the whole history of the human race, he has been struck by a single thing, the constitutions of empires. With every people, whether ancient or modern, he looks for their constitution. All the authors he talks of are to be admired or dismissed in terms of what they had to say of constitutions. According to him, there is only one sort of genius, the one that conceives of and executes a fine constitution. There is only one sort of happiness, which is to live and die in a free constitution.[61]

[59] Gabriel Bonnet de Mably, "Des talents," in Mably, *Collection complète des Oeuvres*, ed. Peter Friedemann, 15 vols. [Paris, 1794–5] (Aalen, Scientia Verlag, 1977), 14:88.
[60] Mably, "Du développement, des progrès, et des bornes de la raison," in Mably, *Oeuvres* [1797], 15:30–31.
[61] Dominique-Joseph Garat, *Mercure de France*, 6 March 1784, pp. 22–3. As another of Mably's critics noted (referring to his *Observations on the Government of the United States*), "the

Brissot was equally critical. In a short notice on Mably's *Of the Study of History*, he described Mably's ideas as one of the "last embers" of the great vogue for antiquity that had flourished for the past two hundred years.[62] He continued the discussion in a review of Mably's *Observations on the Government and the Laws of the United States*, along with the Anglo-Welsh dissenting minister Richard Price's *Observations on the Importance of the American Revolution*. He agreed with both Mably and Price that the greatest danger facing the Americans was the "baneful mania for overly extensive trade" and the risk of entanglement in the European system of luxury that it was likely to cause, but still argued that neither of them had identified a way to "restrain trade within such limits as to prevent the alteration of the virtues and simple tastes of these republicans." Price, Brissot wrote, had failed to address the part played by the passions in any political society, while Mably, on the other hand, displayed an unwarranted hostility to the people, overlooking the fact that an aristocracy (even the elected aristocracy provided for by the constitution of Massachusetts that Mably commended) had "a hundred times stronger passions" than a democracy.[63]

In the book itself, Mably highlighted the similarity between his own ideas and those in John Brown's *Estimate of the Manners and Principles of the Times*. "If those at the head of American affairs seek further enlightenment," Mably wrote, "they will find it in the excellent work published by Doctor Brown some twenty-five or twenty-six years ago." "I do not know," he continued, "of any more profound work in politics. The author, in the manner of the ancients, considers the present moment for the future that it announces." For that reason, Mably emphasised, Brown, in his *Estimate*, had been able to predict the breach that had subsequently occurred between Britain and what was now the United States.[64] The real point of Mably's advice, however, occurred some twenty pages later, where he turned to the subject of American commercial policy. Plato, he wrote, might have been bold enough to say that "those savages who rove

abbé has the idea that every law is or should be in the state constitutions": Filippo Mazzei, *Historical and Political Researches on the United States* [1788] (Charlottesville, University of Virginia Press, 1976), p. 141, note 1.

[62] Jacques Pierre Brissot, *Journal du lycée de Londres* 3 (1784): 228.

[63] Brissot, *Journal du lycée de Londres* 3 (1784): 270, 276, 279, 283. The assessments were modified slightly during the period of the revolution, with Garat, in issue 151 of the *Journal de Paris* of 1791, repeating what he had written earlier, but with Brissot, in issue 672 of the *Patriote français* (11 June 1791), writing that if "enlightened reason, a firm will, and independence of opinion" were the hallmarks of a "great character," then the term could be applied to Mably, even if his works contained "blemishes" and "his system had its weak sides."

[64] Gabriel Bonnot de Mably, *Observations sur le gouvernement et les loix des Etats-Unis* (Amsterdam, 1784), pp. 359–60.

around your frontiers are less removed from the principles of wholesome civilisation than the people who cultivate commerce and cherish riches."[65] Savages, however, were nomads, with no fixed property. Once settled societies had been established, they would, initially, own property in common. But the clan-based character of communal government would lead to the gradual decay of common ownership. Magistrates would neglect their responsibilities, or favour their kin, and, to restore justice, privatisation would occur.[66] Savage society would turn into barbarous society, and here trade was not only unavoidable but desirable. The transition from common to private property was also a transition from the purely personal qualities underlying the fluid distinctions of savage society to the more stable distinctions of barbarous society, and, once the latter were in existence, Plato's maxims required modification.

Mably had already made the same argument in the earlier advice that he had given to the Poles. Once individual property ownership had been established, he argued there, it had to become as widely available as possible, and this, in turn, made trade essential. It was vital, he wrote at the very end of his two-hundred-page book of policy recommendations to the Poles, to emancipate the Polish serfs and to encourage the emergence of a Polish Third Estate. This meant entrenching both private property and trade. "You will not fail to tell me," Mably wrote to his Polish interlocutors, "that you are highly astonished by the doctrine that I am preaching, since you have been accustomed to hearing me condemn trade, and often in a very harsh manner.

> I have the honour to reply that trade is necessary for all those peoples that are not savage, and who seek to come out of their barbarism. I will praise trade when, without ostentation or luxury, it serves simple needs and does not irritate our passions. Trade, which needs to be encouraged to reach a certain praiseworthy term, then needs to be stopped in its progress, as soon as, having passed that term, it is fit only to loosen the bonds of society because of the corruption to manners that it introduces. If it is not then stopped, all its subsequent progress will become no more than greater and greater vices, which will then precipitate the ruin of the state.[67]

The argument dovetailed with Brown's own evaluation of the relationship between trade and civilisation in both his *Estimate* and his correspondence with Catherine the Great, and Mably had no hesitation in rehearsing

[65] Mably, *Observations*, p. 375. I have used the English translation, published as *Remarks concerning the Government and the Laws of the United States of America* (London, 1784), p. 187.

[66] For this account of the origins of private property, see Mably, *De la législation ou principes des lois*, reprinted in his *Oeuvres*, vol. 9, bk. 1, ch. 3, pp. 69–78.

[67] Mably, *Du gouvernement et des loix de la Pologne*, in Mably, *Oeuvres*, 8:203.

388 CHAPTER SIX

Brown's version to his American readers (perhaps, too, simply because it was also more readily available to his Anglophone readers).[68] Trade in its beginnings, and during its mediocrity, the Anglican estimator had written (here Mably quoted Brown) was "very advantageous" to a nation, but having reached "a higher period in its subsequent progress, it becomes really harmful and dangerous." In the first stage, it provided for the mutual necessities of trading nations, anticipated their needs, increased their knowledge, cured them of their prejudices, and extended their sentiments of humanity. In the second stage, it supplied agreements, increased the number of citizens, led to money, produced the sciences and the arts, gave rise to equitable laws, and spread abundance and prosperity far and wide. But in the third stage, it changed its nature and produced quite different effects. With opulence came superfluities, and with these came avarice, luxury, and a refinement of delicacy among people of the highest rank, serving only to soften them and corrupt the principles of the whole nation. From then on, Brown and Mably agreed, it was downhill all the way.[69]

After this summary of Brown, Mably went on immediately to write that "to so grave an authority, I could join that of Cantillon, a man of the most penetrating and extensive genius."[70] Richard Cantillon's *Essai sur la nature du commerce en général* of 1755 (or *The Analysis of Trade, Commerce, Bullion, Banks and Foreign Exchanges* as it was called in English in 1759) was also the work of an earlier generation, and one that Mably had made use of in three of his previous works, first in his *Phocion's Conversations*, then in his *Principles of Negotiations*, and, most fully, in the revised edition of his *Droit public de l'Europe* of 1764. In the context of his advice to the Americans, Mably simply summarised these earlier arguments to buttress Brown's three-stage model of the advantages and disadvantages of foreign trade. According to Cantillon, foreign trade first promoted prosperity, but the gains that it produced then turned into losses as the rising costs of trade-based prosperity began to allow poor nations with lower costs to capture the markets occupied by rich countries. Public credit and paper money might then appear to be the solutions, but they, too, would fail, leaving only the ultimately wasteful expenditure of war as the last available, finally self-defeating, resource to support external trade. This, Mably argued, was why the state of Massachusetts had been unwise to encourage private and public societies to promote trade, industry, and finance. "The belief," he commented, "seems to be that, as with Dr Brown, mediocre trade produces some advantages

[68] On Brown's letter to Catherine the Great, see above, pp. 203–4.

[69] Mably, *Observations*, pp. 376–8. On Brown's version, see, in addition to his letter to Catherine of Russia cited above, his *Estimate of the Manners and Principles of the Times*, 4th ed. (London, 1757), pp. 183–4.

[70] Mably, *Observations*, p. 378.

to society and, overlooking the rest of his doctrine, the conclusion seems to have been that even more trade would have even greater benefits." But, Mably warned, "it was also, on the contrary, necessary to see, with Plato, that this mediocre trade, by reawakening untameable passions, was the germ of a crowd of vices that are stronger than politics and laws."[71]

In this sense, the historical perspective supplied by what Mably took to be both Plato's and Brown's characterisations of the differences between savage and barbarous societies helped to reinforce Cantillon's insights into the destructive progress of foreign trade. This made Mably less sanguine than Cantillon had been about the possibility of managing the recurrent switches in the competitive positions of rich countries and poor countries. "Trade," he wrote at the beginning of his discussion of Cantillon's analysis, "is a kind of monster that destroys itself with its own hands." For Cantillon, "skilful magistrates" could bring the economy back up from its luxury-generated low point by using the advantages of a newly acquired backwardness to turn the deflationary effects of the loss of external markets and the lower level of economic activity into a new competitive capacity. For Mably, however, this type of policy was both unfeasible and self-defeating. It was unfeasible, he argued, because it would be difficult to bring down levels of government expenditure and taxation to match the reduced level of economic activity. The range of vested interests committed to prevailing levels of taxing and spending were more likely to produce a fiscal squeeze and divert even more resources into unproductive consumption. It was also likely to be self-defeating, not only because of the obvious lack of real stability involved in the perpetual process of oscillation, but also because it was simply wrong to imagine that a switch from luxury to poverty could, in itself, produce a recovery in competitive capacity. "Nothing," Mably wrote, "could be more ridiculous or more unfortunate for a people than to have the vices of wealth in a state of poverty." If, he continued, Cantillon had written an essay on the nature of government, rather than the nature of trade, "he would doubtless have shown that the prosperity of a state derives solely from its attentiveness to conforming to nature's views." Doing so meant "considering men's needs in their natural order, and maintaining so clear a harmony, and proportion between the springs of politics, that one branch of society, despite attaining all the growth of which it might be capable, can never grow at the expense of the rest."[72]

---

[71] Mably, *Observations*, p. 381.

[72] Mably's most extensive discussion of Cantillon is in Gabriel Bonnot de Mably, *Le droit public de l'Europe fondé sur les traités*, in Mably, *Oeuvres complètes*, 13 vols. (London, 1789–90), 6:311–28 (pp. 315–8 for the passages cited in this paragraph). Compare to the long earlier note on Cantillon in *Les Entretiens de Phocion*, in Mably, *Oeuvres*, 10:164–7.

Despite the rather Physiocratic appearance of the phrase about considering men's needs in their natural order, Mably, it is well known, was a harsh
critic of the French economists (he published a large book to explain why he
was). Physiocracy was a system of government that was designed to manage
the transformation of desires into needs, and the higher levels of prosperity
and culture that the process entailed.[73] Much of the later interest, typified
by Mercier's evaluation of Law, in using public credit to give economic
prosperity and political stability a secure social foundation followed the
same logic, however much it entailed using substantially different means.
Mably's idea of government was the opposite. Good government served to
block the way that, over time, desires turned into needs. It was designed,
instead, to establish a durable balance between what Mably took to be real
human needs and the relatively limited array of additional resources that
government and laws required. The author of a discourse published in
1785, on whether luxury corrupts manners and destroys empires, expressed
this idea by using a passage from Mably's *Phocion's Conversation* as his epigraph: "[O]ur fathers, with ten talents, were rich; we, with two thousand,
are poor."[74] Superficially, this made Mably look rather like Rousseau. But
he was much less of a moral sceptic than Rousseau; he did not, therefore,
have to adopt the Genevan's strong distinction between the lack of morality in the natural condition of individual independence on the one side, and
a common morality in the social condition produced by interdependence,
the power of public opinion, and the sovereignty of the general will on the
other (with a second, intermediate, stage, like the nucleated community of
the Valais, representing either a past golden age or, possibly, Europe's only
viable future).[75] For Mably, as for Brown, with his three-stage theory of
civilisation, individual needs and social interdependence were entirely compatible, provided that political societies were based solely on real needs,
and that civilisation remained at its non-luxury-based second stage.

[73] On Physiocracy, see Sonenscher, *Before the Deluge*, pp. 189–222, 260–1, 287–8, 290–1.

[74] [Antoine-Prosper Lottin, but published under the pseudonym of Saint-Haippy], *Discours
sur ce sujet: le luxe corrompt les moeurs et détruit les empires*, 2nd ed. (Amsterdam/Paris, 1785).

[75] Here, the clearest indications of the differences are likely to be found in their respective
assessments of events in Poland and Geneva. Mably, as indicated, urged the Poles to promote trade based on agriculture, while Rousseau insisted on autarchy. The differences were
also visible on Geneva. As the translator of Mably's *Observations sur le gouvernement et les loix
des États-Unis* noted, Rousseau's position on the *représentants*' attempts to reform the government of Geneva put him at odds with "those who cherished, loved and honoured him. This
zealous champion of political equality describes the citizens of Geneva as having perpetually
sacrificed too much to appearances and too little to essentials; as having suffered their over-
anxious solicitude in favour of a general council to damp and diminish a necessary zeal in
their attachment to its members; and as having looked rather to the maintenance of authority
than the immovable establishment of freedom!" Mably, *Remarks*, p. 242, note. Mably, on the
other hand, was closer to the *représentants*.

This, less morally sceptical, starting point, made Mably a different type of admirer of the Cynic philosopher Diogenes from Rousseau. Where Rousseau singled out Diogenes' fruitless quest for a man as a symbol of the gulf between the ways of life of ancient and modern societies, Mably singled out Diogenes' extreme material simplicity as an illustration of the array of virtues that, both at home and abroad, political societies required. Temperance, he wrote in his *Principes de morale* (Principles of Morality) of 1784, was the one virtue that could never become harmful because it was possibly the only virtue that could never be carried to excess. The two cardinal virtues, prudence and justice (in that order), were both susceptible to abuse. Prudence could turn into calculation, while justice, precisely because it was an idea that was so readily available to everyone, was always exposed to partiality. Temperance was required to give both their true content. This, Mably continued, was why it was so important "to banish both great poverty and great wealth from a state," and, by extension, why the figure of Diogenes could be taken to symbolise "the perfection" of temperance. Here, it was the moral, not the satirical, side of Cynic philosophy that Mably singled out. "It is not," he wrote, "the bizarre and capricious man who always scorned public manners so ostentatiously and who often made wisdom itself ridiculous whom I wish to praise." Instead, it was the courage of a man who preferred a barrel to a palace, and who, because of his knowledge of the vanity (*misère*) of human affairs, could set himself above Alexander the Great. Above all, it was the moral example of a man who could break his own drinking cup when he saw a child drinking from the palm of its hand. As Diogenes in this guise showed, temperance was a hard virtue to acquire and preserve, which was why, Mably continued, the fourth of the cardinal virtues had to be courage. Together, the combination of prudence, justice, temperance, and courage amounted to the way to reconcile individual and common well-being. Without them, Mably argued, all the other virtues would turn into their opposites. Frugality, generosity, leniency, and patience would turn into avarice, prodigality, laziness, and resignation, while love of country, love of glory, or love of the public good would be cut off from their moral foundations and, as a result, fall hostage to the vagaries of public opinion.[76]

For Rousseau, public opinion really was the queen of the modern world. For Mably, however, the evaluation was a product of a mistaken diagnosis of modernity's pathology. "A very eloquent writer," he wrote, "but who often neglects to pay enough attention to his own opinions (*qui souvent néglige trop l'examen de ses opinions*), has said that whoever invented clogs

---

[76] Gabriel Bonnot de Mably, *Principes de morale* [1784], in Mably, *Oeuvres complètes*, 14 vols. (Paris, 1797), 10:232–9.

(*sabots*) deserved to be put to death."[77] Rousseau never seems to have written anything quite like that (by the time that Mably published his work, he had been dead for six years, and well before then the two men had broken off all relations). It helped, however, to reinforce Mably's assertion that the idea was "ridiculous and unsociable (*farouche*)." "How," he continued, "could I be so hard as to condemn as something harmful to mankind an art that everyone can practise easily, and, as a result, that establishes no difference among them, does not offend their natural equality, and cannot excite any violent commotion of rivalry, jealousy, hatred, or vanity in the soul?" It followed that "the necessary and crude arts unite citizens," while only "the superfluous and overly perfected arts make them enemies of one another" (the antithesis elided Rousseau's emphasis on the intermediate set of arrangements based on self-sufficient households).[78] As Mably had written earlier in his *Droit public de l'Europe*, the first of these "necessary and crude arts" was agriculture, as, more generally, were all those arts related to domestic production and consumption. The simpler but more solid their products were, Mably emphasised, the less frequently they would need to be replaced. This, in turn, would not only eliminate the seductions of fashion but would also reduce the volume of goods in circulation and the attendant need for money. A state, he argued, was rich enough when it had enough money to maintain its domestic circulation. According to Cantillon, this amounted to a quantity of money equal in value to a third of the annual rent received by the landowners. This was all that was required to secure the condition of "honest mediocrity" that was the basis of long-term social and political stability. It meant, too, Mably concluded, after some initial hesitation, that "foreign trade is not necessary in any state and is always harmful."[79]

This did not prevent him, rather later in the same book, from writing that it was to be hoped "that, instructed by a thousand experiences and the writings of philosophers, Europe would one day finally succeed in giving trade the place that it should occupy in society, and manage it on the basis of the principles that suit it." If that day were ever to come, trade would no longer be "a source of corruption, calamities, quarrels, and wars" but would serve as "a bond among all nations and would make them love peace."[80] From this, more future-oriented perspective, trade could be a positive good. Within the framework of the large, federal system of republican government that Mably envisaged as the real alternative to Europe's

[77] Mably, *Principes de morale*, p. 208.
[78] Mably, *Principes de morale*, p. 208.
[79] Mably, *Le droit public*, pp. 324 (on foreign trade), 327 (on Cantillon and the quantity of money).
[80] Mably, *Le droit public*, p. 298.

modern state system, it would also be mainly domestic.[81] A large federal state entailed a common market with interprovincial trade, and an end to the problems produced by trade and payments imbalances. A decentralised system of sumptuary laws, a rigidly enforced agrarian, and a frequently rotating system of magistracies could then be relied upon to prevent trade in its natural form from acquiring its more self-defeating modern properties (all these arguments, it is worth noting, were also set out in a 1776 work by his brother, Etienne Bonnot de Condillac, *Commerce and Government Considered in Relation to One Another*, which was why, three years later, Jean Dusaulx, the author of a study of gambling and its vicious effects, could describe the two as "worthy brothers" whose "salutary maxims" were now to be found in what he called the "Philadelphia manifestos," or the American Declaration of Independence).[82] With arrangements like these in place, there would be no further need to interfere with trade because it would be fair trade as well as free trade. Here, Mably emphasised repeatedly, the morality of the gospel continued to mark the difference between the ancients and the moderns. Ancient politics, for all their perfections, applied to single states, leaving them with a choice between autarchy (Sparta) and conquest (Rome). Modern politics, with its different moral foundations, had a potential third way available. The problem, however, was that it had become available only after history and the passions had already done their work (had it been available for the Romans, Mably suggested, Cato would not have advocated the destruction of Carthage, and Rome would have avoided its subsequent history).[83] This explained the ultimate failure of even the best of republics that the ancient world had been able to establish, but it also offered grounds for thinking that the moderns really did have a larger array of conceptual and strategic resources at their disposal.

Mably, it is well known, endorsed civil war. Although Mercier's endorsement was the first to appear in print, Mably's preceded it, either by a year or two, if he composed his *Des droits et des devoirs du citoyen* (On the Rights and Duties of the Citizen) towards the end of the reign of Louis XV, or, as is more likely, a dozen years earlier, in 1758.[84] Mably's

[81] For a fuller description, see Sonenscher, *Before the Deluge*, pp. 239–53.

[82] Jean Dusaulx, *Motion faite à la convention nationale, après la pétition des exécuteurs testamentaires de Mably, pour demander en faveur de ce grand homme, les honneurs du Panthéon française* (Paris, 1795), p. 11, citing his earlier *De la passion du jeu depuis les temps anciens jusqu'à nos jours* (Paris, 1779), p. 190.

[83] Mably, "Du développement, des progrès, et des bornes de la raison," p. 63. For other examples (Europe at the time of the Renaissance; France in the age of Louis XI; and Venice after the doge was dispossessed of sovereignty), see *Principes des négociations*, in Mably, *Oeuvres*, 5: 23–34; *De l'étude de l'histoire*, in Mably, *Oeuvres*, 12:111–3.

[84] Gabriel Bonnot de Mably, *Des droits et des devoirs du citoyen* [1789], ed. Jean-Louis Lecercle (Paris, Marcel Didier, 1972). See pp. 62–3, 68 for the endorsement of civil war. According

endorsement, however, became publicly available only in 1788 when *Des droits et des devoirs du citoyen* was published for the first time. Its treatment of the subject of civil war was, however, significantly different from the way that Mably had dealt with it in his examination of political conflict in the ancient world. There, particularly in his observations of the history of the Roman republic, the *Observations sur les Romains* of 1751, he had emphasised the ultimate futility of political violence. As the republic stumbled towards its final crisis, he wrote in that book, the Romans simply did not have the conceptual resources needed to identify the underlying causes of the divisions and conflicts driving it towards its fall. Among the many causes of the republic's ruin, all that the Romans could perceive was inequality, along with the corruption of manners that it had brought in its wake. Accordingly, they could do no more than echo Cato the Censor's lament about the corrosive effects of luxury, imagining that the impotent example of the virtue of a few honourable men might be enough to stem the flood. But all that this moralistic declamation served to do was to create conditions for ambitious demagogues like the Gracchi to exploit popular misery. By the time of Caesar, Mably wrote, the only way to preserve the republic would have been to jettison the rule of law and do whatever was necessary to enable the republic to survive. Brutus, he observed, had been right to assassinate Caesar as a tyrant, but wrong to spare his allies and clients. His legalistic argument that, as Roman citizens, Caesar's allies were entitled to the benefits of the rule of law because, although they were planning to commit acts of tyranny, they had not actually done so, was, Mably argued, incompatible with the survival of the republic. In some desperate circumstances, he wrote, politics calls for the punishment of intentions, or even of the mere power to do harm. Yet, he warned, even if this more prudent policy had been followed, the republic would probably still have fallen. There was no liberty left for the Romans to aspire to, unless some citizen, after making himself master of them all, were to change the form of the state from top to bottom and, by giving up all of Rome's conquests, were then to go on to compel the Romans to readopt the manners and poverty of their ancestors. Even if such a reform had been practicable, Mably commented, it was unlikely that any Roman citizen would have been virtuous enough to usurp sovereign power and use it in this way.[85]

Despite the corruption of the modern world, the possibility of implementing a comprehensive programme of moral and social reform was,

---

to a note among Brizard's papers, the book was published at the time of the second assembly of notables, late in 1788: Bibliothèque de l'Arsenal, Mss. 6076, fol. 13.

[85] Gabriel Bonnot de Mably, *Observations sur les Romains* [1751], reprinted in his *Oeuvres*, 12 vols. (Paris, 1794–5), 4:314–24, 356–8, and, in the thirteen-volume (London, 1789–90) ed., 4:275–6, 302, 314–6, 317.

paradoxically, more readily available to the moderns than to the ancients. Here, civil conflict could turn into what, in *Des droits et des devoirs du citoyen*, Mably called a "managed revolution." In part, this was an effect of the rise of modern monarchy. "When," Mably noted in his parallel *Observations on the Greeks*, "a free people is once corrupted, they grow familiar with their vices; they love them, they cherish them, and it is very scarce to find that a private citizen has courage enough to struggle against the prejudices, passions, and customs which reign imperiously in the breast of the undocile multitude, or has credit enough to persuade his degenerate countrymen to make an effort upon themselves in order to recover the point of happiness from whence they are fallen." Monarchies, however, had a real capacity for reform. "The history of monarchies," he continued, "is, on the contrary, full of those kinds of revolutions so scarce in republics. As the citizen there is not his own legislator; as he is obliged to obey and to receive whatever impression his sovereign is pleased to impose, a great prince has it always in his power to form a new people. The subject awakes from his lethargy, quits his vices, and without hardly perceiving it, assumes a new character, and the portion of virtue which one chooses to give him."[86] Unsurprisingly, Fénelon's *Telemachus* was one of the set books included in the course of study that Mably and his brother devised for the prince of Parma. Even without a "great prince," however, reform was still possible, at least in a French context. This was not simply a product of respect for the virtues of the ancients but was also an effect of the surviving residue of the passions created during France's feudal past. Absolute government and court society had not entirely eradicated the values of clerical piety, noble honour, and bourgeois probity underpinning the old system of estates, and, as Mably went into considerable detail to show, their remaining embers could still be used by a resolute magistracy to build up enough popular support to force the royal government to revive the French estates-general, so that it, rather than a patriot king, would then have the initiative for reform. "If," the English reformer of Mably's *Des droits et des devoirs du citoyen* asked his French interlocutor, "there were to be a reign when everything went wrong, where each individual trembled for his domestic fortune, where the nation was even more wretched than usual at home, and dishonoured abroad, I ask you, are your souls really so besotted and depraved as to be insensible to this situation?"[87] As it has been described, it was something like a script for the beginning of the French Revolution.[88]

[86] Gabriel Bonnot de Mably, *Observations sur les Grecs* [Geneva, 1749], revised as *Observations sur l'histoire de la Grèce* [Geneva, 1766], and, for this passage, see the translation published as *Observations on the Manners, Government, and Policy of the Greeks* (Oxford, 1784), pp. 151–2.

[87] Mably, *Des droits et des devoirs du citoyen*, ed. Lecercle, p. 183.

[88] Keith Michael Baker, "A Script for a French Revolution: The Political Consciousness of the Abbé Mably," in his *Inventing the French Revolution* (Cambridge, CUP, 1990), pp. 86–106.

It was also, however, an entirely different script of its content and course. This was not simply a product of a failure to foresee the future, but, more accurately, of a very different assessment of prevailing political possibilities and constraints. It set Mably's political vision apart, not only from Sieyès's more daring political speculations, but also from the broader political mainstream that emerged after 1789. The long-term goals of them all may have been quite similar (long-term goals often are), but, from Mably's disenchanted point of view, the obstacles to establishing civil and political liberty were far greater. Once in existence, he wrote in *Des droits et des devoirs du citoyen*, the estates-general had, certainly, to establish its own permanence and ensure that it would be able to meet regularly every two or three years. To do so, it would have to assert its fiscal supremacy and strip the monarchy of its power to tax. It would have to have its own treasury and appoint its own, publicly accountable, officials to manage tax revenue and public expenditure; with these agencies in place, it would be able to publish a clearly itemised, regular statement of public accounts. It would then also have to establish a clear separation between the legislative and executive powers, and to divide the executive into as many councils or committees as its different functions required.[89] The king himself would become head of a council of foreign affairs (although decisions on war and peace would be the responsibility of the legislature) and would also be the inspector and censor of the army (although real command would be transferred to a six-man council of war, with two further field commanders). But any precipitate move towards real equality, Mably argued, would be entirely self-defeating. This meant that the estates-general had, instead, to work with the grain of the accumulated legacy of corrupt interests and the mass of potentially explosive passions that they had brought in their wake. This, he emphasised, meant that the Third Estate alone would have to shoulder the burden of royal indebtedness. It also meant that the nobility should be given more status, not less, in order to disarm its suspicion of future reform. The army would be turned into a genuinely noble career, with the selection of eligible candidates for promotion based on the abbé de Saint-Pierre's idea of a ballot by each grade of the military hierarchy, but with the final decision on promotion transferred from the king to the estates-general. The standing of the parlements would be magnified through the abolition of appeals to the king's council, and through the elimination of the appeal functions of the lower courts, leaving the parlements as the only high courts of appeal. Provincial assemblies would meet in the years in which the estates-general was not sitting. They would elect the members of subsequent meetings of the estates-general; they would

---

[89] Mably commended the same type of conciliar executive to the Poles in his *Du gouvernement et des loix de la Pologne*, p. 140.

also elect the members of a network of provincial tribunals with responsibility for overseeing manners by acting as censors, enforcing sumptuary laws, supervising public education, and drafting policy recommendations for consideration by future meetings of the estates-general.[90]

In the light of this conception of a "managed revolution," unwinding the effects of the past would be a slow process. As Mably's criticism of Cantillon implied, managing the transition from a luxury-based to a needs-based society had to involve providing temporary support to the wrong sort of institutions and economic activities (like privileged trading companies or guilds), if only because abolishing them too quickly was likely to be self-defeating.[91] The whole transition process, he emphasised, was certain to be highly dangerous. If, he wrote in the concluding section of *Des droits et des devoirs du citoyen*, "the progress of evil (*les progrès du mal*) is such that ordinary magistrates cannot correct it effectively, have recourse to an extraordinary magistracy, whose time will be short, and whose power is considerable. The imagination of citizens will need then to be struck in a new way, and history has shown you how useful a dictatorship was to the Romans." Mably later gave the same advice to the Americans, highlighting the need for the leaders of the new republic to use extraordinary, and draconian, powers to force it entirely out of Europe's luxury-based system of trade and industry.[92] Here, however, he emphasised its particular relevance to the situation produced by war. "A republic, even if governed with the greatest wisdom," he wrote, "sometimes experiences great evils in a war with its neighbours."

> Rome encountered a Pyrrhus and a Hannibal. Finding itself at a hair's breadth
> (*à deux doigts*) from ruin, and to avoid it, it could find no other rule than the

[90] Mably, *Des droits et des devoirs du citoyen*, ed. Lecercle, pp. 175–81, 187–209.

[91] For the same emphasis on the "long convalescence" involved in reform, and the need to avoid "too high a perfection," see, too, Mably's advice to the Poles, in his *Du gouvernement et des loix de la Pologne*, pp. 43, 46. The implications of the radically different policies required by needs-based and luxury-based trade were spelled out in detail by an admirer of Condillac's "excellent" *Le commerce et le gouvernement considérés relativement l'un à l'autre*, the Orientalist Abraham-Hyacinthe Anquetil-Duperron, in his *Dignité du commerce et de l'état commerçant* (Paris, 1789)—see p. 8 for the remark on Condillac—and, at greater length, in his *L'Inde en rapport avec l'Europe*, 2 vols. (Hamburg, 1798), a work that was to have been published in 1782, but was prohibited by the royal government. As Anquetil-Duperron emphasised, needs-based trade might be open and reciprocal, but once nonnecessities were involved, then all the economies of scale associated with privileged trading companies and debt-based private finance were unavoidable. The best study of Anquetil-Duperron remains Raymond Schwab, *Vie d'Anquetil-Duperron* (Paris, 1934).

[92] On this, see Michael Sonenscher, "Republicanism, State Finances and the Emergence of Commercial Society in Eighteenth-Century France—or from Royal to Ancient Republicanism, and Back," in Martin Van Gelderen and Quentin Skinner, eds., *Republicanism: A Shared European Heritage*, 2 vols. (Cambridge, CUP, 2002), 2:275–91.

law that says that the safety of the people has to be the supreme law. After trying to force all the mechanisms of government, but with no success, one is sometimes obliged to have recourse to extraordinary means, often even to means contrary to the constitution of the state.[93]

This, too, had its dangers. It was "extremely rare," Mably continued, for peoples who adopted such means not to become "inebriated with joy," and to lose the "calm (*sang froid*)" required to appreciate the shock applied to "the whole political edifice." Emergency government ran the risk of turning into permanent dictatorship. This was why it was also necessary for there to be a "fundamental law" stipulating that there should be a general review of the system of government at the end of each war. This was particularly necessary if the war was victorious. Without this rigorous process of constitutional scrutiny, the huge boost to pride and confidence produced by military success would turn out to be no more than the prelude to later decline and fall, as both Greek and Roman history showed. This final provision, Mably suggested, could be adopted as a principle for peacetime as well. At periodical intervals, he wrote at the very end of his book, there should be "a year of reform." It would have the merit of neutralising the "lack of solidity" in the French character, with its propensity to give up on its resolutions and fall back on routine and haphazard policies. It would also have the final merit of forestalling further cycles of conflict or, as Mably put it more graphically, would "prevent us from going back to our vomit."[94]

It is important to emphasise the availability of this type of prognosis once the French Revolution began, as well as the fact that Mably's "script" was published only in late in 1788, because it provides a way to avoid the rather overheated argument over the putatively ideological or circumstantial origins of the Terror.[95] From the perspective supplied by Mably's political thought, both types of origin could apply, because, on its terms, the French Revolution could look quite easily as if it was turning into the wrong kind of revolution. This, in turn, makes it easier to understand the otherwise rather mysterious political resonance of the pronouncements of the revolution's most famously bloodcurdling figure, Jean-Paul Marat, and his repeated calls for a more comprehensively physical liquidation of the old regime. If its harsh political realism made it redolent of Machiavelli

---

[93] Mably, *Des droits et des devoirs du citoyen*, ed. Lecercle, pp. 218–9.

[94] Mably, *Des droits et des devoirs du citoyen*, ed. Lecercle, pp. 220–2. The idea of a revising constitutional convention was not, of course, peculiar to Mably. It is now associated mainly with Thomas Jefferson, but, as Jérôme Pétion noted, it could also be found in Solon, Locke, and Condorcet, as well as in Mably (and, it could be added, Sieyès): see Jérôme Pétion de Villeneuve, "Discours sur les conventions nationales," in his *Oeuvres*, 3 vols. (Paris, 1792), 2:328–30.

[95] For a recent overview, see Peter Davies, *The Debate on the French Revolution* (Manchester, Manchester UP, 2006).

(all of Marat, according to Pierre-Louis Roederer, was to be found in Machiavelli), it also fitted this aspect of Mably's political thought.[96] Strong democracy belonged to the past, which was why, for Mably, only an unacceptably strong version of dictatorship could bring it back, and, by extension, why the most considered political prudence had to be the real alternative to well-meaning programmes of moral and political reform. What Mably called political "inebriation" might be an unavoidable feature of a political emergency, but it would still have to be managed with unusual political skill. "In revolutions, the sage Mably remarks," the English political radical Daniel Eaton wrote in 1794, "enthusiasts are necessary, who in transgressing all bounds, may enable the wise and temperate to attain their ends. Had it not been for the Puritans, whose aim was equally to destroy both episcopacy and royalty, the English would never have attained that portion of civil and religious liberty which they enjoy."[97]

A further indication of the implications of this type of disabused political realism can be found in another of the reactions to the lawyer Simon Linguet's account of his imprisonment in the Bastille in 1780. This one, however, was not at all satirical. It was a pamphlet entitled *Observations sur l'histoire de la Bastille publiée par Monsieur Linguet* (Observations on the *History of the Bastille* by M. Linguet) published in 1783 by a friend of Mably named Jean Dusaulx (who, in 1795, proposed that Mably's remains should be transferred to the Pantheon, not only because of the part that his works had played in the French Revolution, but also, he said, because they were the source of the American Declaration of Independence of 1776).[98] Dusaulx made a point of singling out the bathos of Linguet's story about his breeches by setting it against the harsh realities of modern political power, as he took Montesquieu to have described them. "There is no word," he began, quoting Montesquieu, "that admits of more various significations, and has made more varied impressions on the human mind, than that of liberty."

> Some have taken it as a means of deposing a person on whom they had conferred a tyrannical authority; others for the power of choosing a superior

[96] On Roederer's association of Marat with Machiavelli (made in the context of a review of a new translation of Machiavelli's works published in 1797), see A. N. 29 AP 110, fol. 465, and Pierre-Louis Roederer, *Oeuvres*, ed. A.-M. Roederer, 7 vols. (Paris, 1851–8), 5:316–9. Roederer recognised the uses to which Mably's thought was put during the period of the Terror, but argued that it was absurd to claim that it had causal properties of its own. See Roederer, *Oeuvres*, 4:512: "Il est ridicule d'attribuer à trois pages de Mably un pouvoir que n'eurent jamais l'Evangile ni l'Alcoran. Ce qui a enfanté les crimes de la Terreur, je le répète, c'est la souffrance populaire poussée jusqu'à la frénésie par des scélérats qui avaient le besoin du crime et une grande autorité politique."
[97] Daniel Eaton, *Politics for the People; or a salmagundi for swine*, 2 vols. (London, 1794–5), 1:152.
[98] Dusaulx, *Motion faite à la convention nationale*, pp. 8–9, 11.

whom they are obliged to obey; others for the right of bearing arms, and of being thereby enabled to use violence; others, in fine, for the privilege of being governed by a native of their own country, or by their own laws. A certain nation for a long time thought liberty consisted in the privilege of wearing a long beard. Some have annexed this name to one form of government exclusive of others. Those who had a republican taste applied it to this species of polity; those who liked a monarchical state gave it to monarchy. Thus they have all applied the name of liberty to the government most suitable to their own customs and inclinations; and as in republics the people have not so constant and so present a view of the causes of their misery, and as the magistrates seem to act only in conformity to the laws, hence liberty is generally said to reside in republics, and to be banished from monarchies.

"This," Dusaulx continued, smuggling in a sentence of his own to the passage from Montesquieu, "has been the chimerical idea on which so many books have been written and so many political systems based."[99]

His own definition of liberty was actually much more unequivocal than Montesquieu's sceptical itemisation of its various historical meanings. For Dusaulx liberty was, in fact, a synonym for democracy. This, he explained, was why Linguet's histrionics about his imprisonment and, a fortiori, his diatribe about his breeches were so hopelessly misplaced.[100] "Democracies," he pointed out, "made up of legislators and sovereigns, had no need of state prisons, since their members were themselves the state. Then, what was to be feared were the virtues of citizens, not their vices. Ostracism was the only known punishment, and, to deserve it, one had to be covered in glory. Then, in contradistinction to our modern age, one was punished for what, today, would be rewarded."[101] Times, however, had changed. "Since democracy no longer exists, peoples have no other character than the one given them. They do not act, but are made to act; they do not think, but are made to think. It is from this principle that they derive all their virtues, as well as all their vices. Open the history of the universe from the decline of the Roman Empire, or read the annals of all the nations of the world, and you will find that men derive their ways of thinking from the fundamental constitution."[102] This was the theme of

---

[99] [Jean Dusaulx], *Observations sur l'histoire de la Bastille publiée par Monsieur Linguet* (London, 1784), pp. 18–9. The passage, without the final sentence, was cited from Charles Louis de Secondat, baron de Montesquieu, *The Spirit of Laws* [1748], trans. Thomas Nugent (New York, Hafner Publishing Company, 1949), bk. 11, ch. 2, pp. 149–50. Biographical information on Dusaulx can be found in the entry under his name in Louis-Gabriel Michaud, ed., *Biographie universelle ancienne et moderne*, 45 vols. (Paris, 1843–65), and in Gary Kates, *The* Cercle Social, *the Girondins, and the French Revolution* (Princeton, Princeton UP, 1985), pp. 28–9, 190, 207.

[100] [Dusaulx], *Observations*, pp. 103–4.

[101] [Dusaulx], *Observations*, p. 107.

[102] [Dusaulx], *Observations*, p. 4.

all of Mably's many political works. It was also why, as Dusaulx argued, it was wrong to imagine, as Linguet seemed to assume, that a people might be gentle and affable, while its administration could be hard, austere, and cruel. "In matters of character, government is the cause, and national genius, the effect."[103] Complaining about the Bastille in modern France was as pointless as complaining about night and day.

"By a fatality attached to human nature," Dusaulx wrote, "one cannot refine the mind without spoiling the heart. The evil is in the thing itself." Rousseau, he added immediately, "in defending the cause of the goodness (*bonhomie*) and simplicity of men in the first times," had said so. But he had not said it enough, even though he had written a big book (the *Discourse on the Arts and Sciences*) to say it. If, Dusaulx wrote, Rousseau had simply compared the reign of Attila the Hun to that of the Roman emperor Augustus, and the reign of Louis XIV to France's first king Clovis, then his case against the arts would have been unanswerable. It was a sad thing to think, but it was even sadder to accept that it was true. "If one compares the arts to manners, it will be found that, in every age, corruption entered the soul (if the expression is allowed) by way of the mind (*esprit*)."[104] As Dusaulx also knew, Montesquieu's remarks about liberty had appeared as an introduction to his celebrated examination of "the constitution of England," where, as Montesquieu put it, "liberty will appear in its highest perfection."[105] Here, too, Dusaulx took a different tack, one informed by more than the fact that, in 1783, Britain and France were still at war. "Ever since the corruption of the great republics," he wrote, "an epidemic disease has been forming in Europe, whose seat is in England, the source of all the vagaries (*égarements*) of the human mind." That disease was liberty, "a foreign divinity in our climates, whose short, fleeting empire began with the first Greek republic, and ended with the Roman Empire."[106] There might once, Dusaulx conceded, have been "an atmosphere of liberty" in Britain, when, as he put it, the "dawn light of that island could have enlightened citizens who preferred the public good to their personal interest, and who could see the republic before seeing themselves." But that time was now gone. Modern Britain was entirely corrupt. "Ever since a prodigious luxury, an immeasurable love of riches, a violent desire to be distinguished, to grow great, to acquire, to possess, to enjoy, to see no more than oneself, to know no more than oneself, to love no more than oneself, have taken hold of every heart, that atmosphere has been much obscured."[107] The English might still say fine things about political

---

103 [Dusaulx], *Observations*, p. 4.
104 [Dusaulx], *Observations*, p. 7.
105 Montesquieu, *The Spirit of Laws*, bk. 11, ch. 5, p. 151.
106 [Dusaulx], *Observations*, pp. 17–8.
107 [Dusaulx], *Observations*, pp. 98–9.

liberty, write books about it, and cite Montesquieu complacently, but even there, Dusaulx concluded, liberty would never be more than a word. This grim assessment of the compatibility between liberty and modernity meant that people who complained about the Bastille were simply making a category mistake. The modern world was long past its meridian.

The same bleak view was expressed a few years later by Mably's literary executors. "Are we not allowed to hope that one day every political society will no longer be left to the brigandage of tyranny," they wrote to Thomas Jefferson, in the spring of 1791, enclosing two volumes of Mably's posthumous works. "To do so," they continued, "it would be necessary to extinguish men's love of riches and domination, and enlighten them on justice, the only basis of happiness. It would be necessary to make them see agriculture as the source of all civil, moral, and political prosperity, and the arts as corrupting principles unless they are kept within just limits. We do not wish to condemn men solely to the use of the axe and the scythe. Austerity of that kind was fit only for Spartans. But we would wish only that a less immoderate luxury might restrain our desires." The history of every age, however, did not seem to justify such hopes. "Societies become corrupt as they grow old and torrents of blood have to be spilled to regenerate them."[108] The prognosis may have looked like Edmund Burke, but, in the winter of 1791–2, it also fitted Robespierre's assessment of the risks of going to war to, as Brissot and his supporters argued, defend liberty.

On Mably's terms, the authors of the French Revolution were trying to do too much too soon, and with modern financial, not ancient prudential, means. By doing so, they were running the risk of promoting ruin, rather than recovery, leaving the French republic exposed to the fate of republican Rome. The slip about the Brissotins as the friends of the *sans-culottes* that Robespierre may have made in his speech in April 1793 captures the force of the claim quite well.[109] Nor is there any need to set Mably's political thought against Robespierre's own more familiar endorsement of Rousseau, because Mably's politics of crisis management lent themselves readily both to Rousseau's own, more lurid, predictions of crisis and to the more generic features of his democratic conception of political sovereignty (in itself, the claim that sovereignty began from below was a theoretically trivial aspect of Rousseau's thought). In the wake of the fall of the French monarchy on 10 August 1792, and the resulting de facto existence of the first French republic, Mably's politics formed a practical counterpart to whatever Rousseau's theory was taken to be. Rousseau was well aware of Mably's robust endorsement of the politics of necessity, and,

<hr/>

[108] Chalut and Arnoux to Jefferson, 20 May 1791, in Thomas Jefferson, *The Papers of Thomas Jefferson*, ed. Julian Boyd et al., 33 vols. to date (Princeton, Princeton UP, 1950–), 20:428.
[109] On this, see above, p. 283.

privately, condemned it.[110] But, until the time of the discussion of the fundamental principles underlying the republic in the spring of 1793, when Sieyès's political ally Pierre-Louis Roederer made a determined effort to explain the difference between Mably and Rousseau (and to suggest that Robespierre's views about property and the rights of humanity were actually Mably's, not Rousseau's), it was quite common to amalgamate their respective political theories.[111] It was not difficult, after the overthrow of the French monarchy in 1792, to apply Mably's politics to fill the empty space left by Rousseau's own concept of revolution.

There was also, however, something available in Rousseau. After the overthrow of the monarchy, there was a republic but no constitutional system of republican government. Here, one aspect of Rousseau's political thought filled a real practical gap and, as happened so frequently in the late eighteenth century, could be used to turn an argument that really did derive from his own thought into something different. As Rousseau indicated, even if a republic did not have a constitution, there could still be a de facto system of rule to keep sovereignty alive, because the name of a government that allowed a sovereign to act as a government was democracy. Democracy, Rousseau wrote, had the ability to enable a sovereign to do what, in the light of his sharp distinction between sovereignty and government, only a government was normally entitled to do. Just as, he commented in his *Social Contract*, the English House of Commons could turn itself into a committee of the whole House when it wanted to discuss legislation before actually legislating, so, "by one of those astonishing properties of the body politic," a sovereign could turn itself into a democracy to make the acts of selection and discrimination that only a government could make. With a democracy, as Rousseau put it, "the people who are but sovereign and subject can become prince or magistrate on certain occasions." "It is," he concluded, "the distinctive advantage of a democratic government that it can be established by a simple act of the general will. After which this provisional government either remains as it is, or establishes in the name of the sovereign the government prescribed by law according to the regulation determined on, and everything is conformable to the rule in both."[112] Rousseau's own text may well have been intended to refer to the latter, but, after 1792, it was the first option that was most immediately relevant. In the conditions of war, soon followed by civil war, that had come into being by the spring of 1793, democracy became the

---

[110] See Sonenscher, *Before the Deluge*, pp. 243, 246–7, 252–3.

[111] On Roederer's argument, see Sonenscher, *Before the Deluge*, pp. 323–4.

[112] I have combined most of the translation in Rousseau, *Social Contract*, ed. Gourevitch, pp. 117–8, with some phrases in the (less reliable) eighteenth-century translation, Jean-Jacques Rousseau, *An Inquiry into the Nature of the Social Contract, or Principles of Political Right* (London, 1791), bk. 3, ch. 17, pp. 277–8.

system of provisional government that, among other things, was called upon to manage the political force of the *sans-culottes* that Brissot and his political allies had helped to unleash.

In a democracy, every citizen was potentially a magistrate, just as every magistrate would revert to the status of a citizen, provided, however, that the rotation of office and the real opportunity for public scrutiny involved in what Robespierre called "*l'économie populaire*" remained operational, so that, as he put it in his famous speech on the republic's constitution of 10 May 1793, "the virtue of the people, and the authority of the sovereign," would be "the necessary counterweight to the passions of the magistrate, and government's tendency towards tyranny."[113] The argument still applied even after the French Convention established a republican constitution similar to the one that he and his close political ally Louis-Antoine Saint-Just had recommended. This, in the first instance, meant bringing price inflation under control, and establishing a general maximum on the prices of both basic subsistence goods and a broader range of now essential commodities. But, as Saint-Just pointed out in a major speech to the Convention on 10 October 1793 calling on it to declare the government to be "revolutionary" until peace was won, establishing a maximum was no more than an unavoidable necessity. Putting a ceiling on prices would, in itself, simply benefit the rich, because they would have an already existing range of accumulated financial sources at their disposal to take advantage of the price freeze. It would also have the perverse effect of increasing the purchasing power of the agencies responsible for acquiring provisions for the war effort, making it easier for them to buy up supplies, and to put an even tighter squeeze on popular consumer needs.[114] In this sense, the effects of imposing a maximum on prices pulled very strongly against the need both to maintain the unity of the democracy and to prevent the potentially fatal abuse of power by those responsible for exercising any of the republic's many magistracies. In itself, the maximum would magnify, not reduce, economic and political divisions.

The argument dovetailed with Robespierre's idea of "popular economy" as the real alternative to representative government. This was why the same conception of democracy as magistracy was the premise of Saint-Just's call to make the republic's "provisional government" revolutionary until an eventual peace settlement. "The laws are revolutionary," Saint-Just said; "those executing them are not." This, he continued, meant that "government is a perpetual plot (*une conjuration perpétuelle*) against the

---

[113] Maximilien Robespierre, *Oeuvres*, vol. 9, ed. Marc Bouloiseau, Jean Dautry, Georges Lefebvre, and Albert Soboul (Paris, 1958), p. 507.

[114] Louis-Antoine Saint-Just, *Oeuvres complètes*, ed. Michèle Duval (Paris, Editions Gérard Lebovici, 1984), p. 523.

present order of things." Ministers made appointments to posts (*emplois*), and their appointees did the same. The result was that government had become "a hierarchy of errors and outrages." If, Saint-Just asserted, "one were to examine with severity the men administering the state, remarkably few perhaps of the thirty thousand individuals employed would be among those for whom the people would vote." The present state of the government, he argued, precluded constitutional rule. "In the circumstances in which the republic finds itself, the constitution cannot be established. It would be turned to ashes by itself. It would become the guarantee of outrages on liberty because it would lack the violence needed to repress them." This, Saint-Just concluded, was why "you cannot hope for prosperity unless you establish a government that, restrained (*doux*) and moderate towards the people, will be terrible towards itself, because of the energy of its own internal relationships. It must press down (*peser*) on itself, not the people."[115] In a democracy, if the magistracy went wrong, everything went wrong. A great deal of what turned into the Terror followed from this very simple analysis of democracy's pathology. Treating it required applying Mably's political practice to Rousseau's political theory. This in turn required a command structure able, in a positive way, to ensure that every citizen was supplied with necessities and, in a more ferociously negative way, able, too, to root out all the possible sources of civic corruption. Both ways closed the moral and political circle.

Much of what followed was designed to keep it closed, either against those, like Robespierre's former political ally Camille Desmoulins, who argued that the revolutionary government was, for republican reasons, a travesty of anything republican, or against those, like Robespierre's other former political ally Anacharsis Cloots, who made the same argument from a different side, claiming that the *sans-culotte* militia, with its vanguard in the Parisian revolutionary army, not the eighteen-month-old French Convention, was now the real source of republican political stability. The Committee of Public Safety, Desmoulins wrote, quoting the French translation of the *Discourses on Sallust*, by the eighteenth-century English Commonwealthman Thomas Gordon, had adopted the despotic maxim that "it was better that some who were innocent died, than one who was guilty escaped."[116] Robespierre, for equally republican reasons,

---

[115] Saint-Just, speech to the Convention of 10 October 1793, also in *Archives parlementaires*, vol. 76, ed. M. Mavidal and E. Laurent (Paris, 1910), pp. 313, 315. For a similar, earlier, argument by the future *babouviste* Pierre-Antoine Antonelle, see his *Lettre au citoyen S . . . rédacteur de l'article "Paris" dans le journal dit "Annales patriotiques, littéraires"* (Rochefort, 18 April 1793). On Robespierre's concept of *l'économie populaire* as the real alternative to representative government, see above, p. 54.

[116] Camille Desmoulins, *Le Vieux Cordelier* [no. 3, 15 December 1793], ed. Henri Calvet (Paris, 1936), p. 89.

amalgamated them all. But there are enough clues to suggest that Robespierre was not as straightforward a republican as either Desmoulins or Cloots (one of the points of this book has been to suggest that there is actually nothing at all straightforward about republicanism). He may, or may not, have been an admirer of Edward Young, as Young's German translator insinuated, just as he may, or may not, have been an admirer of John Brown, as has also been suggested.[117] His extended panegyric of Louis XVI early in 1789 was recognisably Fénelonian.[118] The remarks that he made about the very devout Catholic bishop of Amiens Louis-François-Gabriel d'Orléans de La Motte (the individual responsible for the trial and execution for blasphemy of the nineteen-year-old chevalier de la Barre in 1766), in his eulogy of the poet Jean-Baptiste-Louis Gresset (*Eloge de Gresset*) of 1786, displayed the same sort of moral concerns. According to Robespierre, Gresset himself was distinguished for the way he had given up the literary life that made him famous in favour of pious obscurity (the initial fame was a result of a poem about a convent and a parrot named *Ververt*, and the insight into human vanity revealed, in a gentle way, by the pride that even a nun could feel if her cell were graced by a parrot that could recite the *Pater*). The bishop, however, was an even more admirable example. "Thanks to your virtues," Robespierre wrote, "we might have believed that one of those saintly bishops who once gave lustre to Christianity in its cradle had come back to life to console an exhausted religion and reaffirm a tottering piety" (in the manuscript version the praise was even more extended, with a stronger emphasis on the bishop's charity and unremitting concern for the poor).[119] Robespierre may have been a sincere admirer of Rousseau, and, as he said himself, "had been a poor sort of Catholic," but his own ideas may also have had something in common with those of Rousseau's Catholic critic Louis-Bertrand Castel, and with the mixture of "spiritualism" and "naturalism" underlying Castel's less well-known thought experiment of a world without humans (rather than, as with Rousseau, of humans without the world), and the rich cultural life that, in the light of the experiment, it could be shown that human spirituality supplied. Both, according to Voltaire, were Cynics, but Rousseau, according to the same source, never set out to write anything injurious.[120]

---

[117] I am grateful to Hilary Mantel, the author of *A Place of Greater Safety* (London, Viking, 1992), for an enjoyable electronic correspondence on the subject.

[118] On this, see above, pp. 281–2.

[119] Robespierre, *Oeuvres*, 1:79–152 (p. 139 for the passage on d'Orléans de La Motte, and pp. 107–8 for the manuscript version). For some information on the earlier career of the bishop of Amiens, see John Rogister, *Louis XV and the Parlement of Paris* (Cambridge, CUP, 1995), pp. 52–8.

[120] For all its emphasis on nature as "the legislator of the universe," it is also worth noting the scriptural resonances of the final article of the draft Declaration of the Rights of

EPILOGUE

Robespierre's fall did not bring the arguments over Rousseau's ambiguous legacy to an end. Nor did it entirely efface the earlier idea of what a *sans-culotte* might be. According to a former member of the Rhino-Germanic Convention named Georg Christian Gottlieb Wedekind, the idea of a revolutionary state, "where abandoning justice and principles to necessity was itself turned into a principle," was something to be abhorred. So, too, however, was unlimited commercial freedom. "If," Wedekind wrote, "it was possible to change man's nature, and make him entirely wicked and blinkered, it would be by means of commerce." Both, he argued, were derivations of the assumption that "happiness" was the underlying principle of human action, rather than, as Kant had shown, justice, duty, and cosmopolitan right. Both, too, he added, but Jacobinism in particular, had destroyed "the just and advantageous maxims of *sans-culottisme*."[121] But by 1795, when Wedekind published his pamphlet, Mercier's and Gorsas's use of the term no longer applied in a French context.

Rousseau's ambiguities, however, still remained alive. For some of the supporters of new republican constitution of 1795, his reservations about democracy helped to justify the balanced system of government made up of a two-chamber legislature and a five-man executive directory that replaced the French Convention. For "Gracchus" Babeuf, in the final peroration of his five-day speech for the defence at his trial at Vendôme in May 1797, Rousseau, along with those "other levellers," Diderot, Helvétius, and Mably, was one of the inspirations of the system of common property that his failed conspiracy of the equals had sought to achieve.[122] Somewhat later, in the aftermath of the coup d'état of the 18 Brumaire of the Year VIII, Sieyès's political ally Pierre-Louis Roederer could assert that "the elective aristocracy that Rousseau spoke about over fifty years ago is what today we call *representative democracy*." The ideas contained by

---

Man that Robespierre presented to the Convention on 24 April 1793: "Kings, aristocrats, tyrants, whoever they may be, are slaves rebelling against the sovereign of the earth, which is the human race, and against the legislator of the universe, which is nature" (Robespierre, *Oeuvres*, 9:463). As Eric Nelson has established, this association of the origins of monarchy with a state of rebellion (by the Jewish people against God) was a feature of a heterodox seventeenth-century reading of scripture: see Eric Nelson, " 'Talmudical Commonwealthsmen' and the Rise of Republican Exclusivism," *Historical Journal* 50 (2007): 809–35. On Robespierre's description of himself as a "poor sort of Catholic," see J. M. Thompson, *Robespierre* (Oxford, Blackwell, 1939), p. 430; and on Castel as a Cynic, see above, p. 170.

[121] [Georg Christian Gottlieb Wedekind], *Idées d'un allemand sur les rapports extérieurs de la république française, adressées au peuple français et à ses représentants* (n.p., 1795), pp. 1, 29–32.

[122] Victor Advielle, *Histoire de Gracchus Babeuf et du babouvisme*, 2 vols. (Paris, 1884), 2:316.

the two sets of terms were, he claimed, identical. "*Elective aristocracy* and *representative democracy* are therefore one and the same thing."[123] For several of the surviving members of the Jacobin Committee of Public Safety of 1793–4, however, it was Mably, not Rousseau, who remained the more authoritative point of reference for republican political morality. Here, the related subjects of the use and abuse of private property, the price and availability of basic subsistence goods, and the ability of the now almost totally worthless *assignat* to protect popular purchasing power and, by extension, insulate the whole French republic from the price-driven vagaries of markets and foreign trade continued to give Mably's thought its more immediate political salience.

One indication of the continuing appeal of Mably's thought, particularly to those who had been involved in Robespierre's revolutionary government of 1793–4, can be found in an argument conducted between the autumn of 1795 and the spring of 1796 on the pages of *L'Ami des loix* (The Friend of the Laws), a Jacobin-leaning newspaper published by a man named François Poultier, and *L'Historien* (The Historian), a newspaper published by the former Physiocrat Pierre-Samuel Dupont de Nemours. The argument was a product of the French Convention's decision to abolish the maximum on cereal prices that had first been set in the summer of 1793, and the subsequent discussion, under the new French Directory, of the future of the *assignat*. The two subjects were connected very closely, because of their joint impact on the workings of markets and, by extension, on popular purchasing power and living standards. For Robert Lindet, one of the surviving former members of the Committee of Public Safety, who began to publish a series of articles in *L'Ami des loix* in the autumn of 1795, free trade had to be fair trade. It was, therefore, right to require that the sale and purchase of cereals should be carried out publicly at marketplaces and fairs, but wrong to authorise cereal producers to sell their grain either directly to merchants or to officials of the republic. Open, public transactions, Lindet argued in November 1795, were necessary for every citizen to have bread, "that faculty that the laws and the government ought to guarantee."[124] Free trade, the newspaper itself editorialised,

---

[123] *Moniteur*, no. 165 (15 Ventôse an 9): 689. The text is reprinted in Pierre-Louis Roederer, *Oeuvres*, 7:135–45. For Roederer's long-standing, and very hostile, assessment of Mably—"un prolixe amplificateur, et un sectateur outré de quelques propositions de Rousseau qu'il a très-mal entendues"—see his "De la propriété. De quelques philosophes qui l'ont attaqué et des hommes qui accusent de ses attaques tous les philosophes et la philosophie," *Journal d'économie publique* 3 (Paris, 1795): 113–32, as well as A. N. 29 AP 87 (Roederer papers), containing the text of a "Discours sur le droit de la propriété lu au lycée le 19 Frimaire an 9" that develops the content of the earlier journal article. The texts are reprinted in Roederer, *Oeuvres*, 5:523–39.

[124] *L'Ami des lois* 95 (2 Frimaire an IV, 23 November 1796).

amounted to adopting "that fatal chimera of transforming an agricultural, warrior nation into a people of merchants." Trade was "doubtless useful and necessary," but it was still possible to ask "how far it was suitable for the French people to be commercial (*commerçant*).[125]

The issue overlapped with discussions of the future of the *assignat*, and of the republic's policy of requisitioning grain to supply the armies. Withdrawing the *assignat* from circulation, as the Directory proposed to do, amounted, Lindet wrote on 1 December 1795, to sacrificing the "twenty million" who now had no metal coin to the interests of "several thousand well-to-do citizens," while imposing a flat, 20 percent, requisition on harvested cereals would penalise small producers with little left over to sell and fuel the speculations of the rich.[126] Two weeks later, Jean-Bon Saint-André, Lindet's former colleague on the Committee of Public Safety, argued that the *assignat* should be replaced by a currency that was "fixed, invariable, and independent of human wills, so that error and crime cannot debase it." Gold and silver were unsuitable, since they were subject to "traffic" and appropriate only to "the genius of cosmopolitans (*cosmopolites*)," while "republicans" required "a system that should make them independent of the rest of the world." For Saint-André, the alternative to the paper currency had to be one whose value was based on the quantity of cereals in domestic circulation. Once this cereal-based currency was in existence, the *assignat* could then revert to its original purpose, as the means to buy nationalised land.[127] The arguments were all largely replies to the parallel campaign conducted on the pages of *L'Historien* in favour of demonetising the *assignat*, and of replacing the policy of debt finance by transferring the costs of funding the war to a combination of private banks and private military contractors. Here, the arguments were largely a replay of those that had been made against the initial monetisation of the *assignat*. As Necker and Bailly had argued in 1790, and as the Feuillants came to see in 1791, debt finance was sustainable only if it could be offset either by privately supplied funds or by a continuing flow of tax revenue. From the point of view of *L'Historien*, however, subsidising Parisian consumption, as Lindet also proposed, was likely to be equally self-defeating. "All the great cities have their *proletarians*," the newspaper warned, "and those of every great city will proudly demand to be treated like the capital."[128] The argument ran on into the following spring, but, by March 1796, a compromise began to emerge with the Directory's decision

---

[125] *L'Ami des lois* 99 (6 Frimaire an IV, 27 November 1796).

[126] *L'Ami des lois* 103 (10 Frimaire an IV, 1 December 1796), 104 (11 Frimaire an IV, 2 December 1796), 105 (12 Frimaire an IV, 3 December 1796).

[127] *L'Ami des lois* 118 (25 Frimaire an IV, 16 December 1795).

[128] *L'Historien* 88 (28 Pluviôse an IV, 17 February 1796).

to replace the *assignat* with a new paper currency to be called *mandats-territoriaux* (territorial mandates), but to drop the broader programme of privatisation of public finance and military contracting recommended by Dupont de Nemours and his political allies. This, in the short term, brought the argument to an end.

The decision was welcomed by a satirical editorial in *L'Ami des loix*. "How wrong it was to praise Mably," the newspaper announced. "We are too old to be reformed. We need the rich to give alms, the poor to receive them, hoarders to ruin us, docile stomachs ready to die of hunger, very arrogant traders, and very humble workers, banks that make their directors' fortunes, and shareholders who speculate in their shares." What need, it commented, was there to relieve the indigent by restoring the credit of the *assignat*, when all those remaining in circulation were now in the hands of the poor, the rich having got rid of them a long time ago. Mably, the newspaper concluded, "was not a man to be cited, still less to be read." It followed this up, however, by printing a letter from the republican *Journal des hommes libres* (Journal of Free Men) calling, as Jean Dusaulx had done nearly a year earlier, for Mably's remains to be transferred to the Pantheon. The letter was followed by an editorial comment explaining why Mably's thought did, in fact, deserve to be both cited and read (a point that it reinforced by printing a copious set of extracts from Mably's *De la législation*). "We might wish," the editorial began, "that man could be independent, and doubtless his happiness would be the more pure, and his virtues would receive no obstacles."

> But we are not hunters or shepherds, or even simple farmers. Our population exceeds our production, and the rich are a necessary evil when territorial harvests cannot supply enough to meet all individual needs. Then, they are to political bodies what mountains are to the universe. These inequalities are the principle of fountains that give life, and of metals that give wealth. But their height can become monstrous were they to be formed by volcanic explosions, and were they also to deprive the plains of the beneficent influence of the sun, and if nothing other than bitter, poisoned water were to fall from their slopes. Then, instead of gold and iron, they would produce no more than arsenic, and it would then be the responsibility of the legislator to sap them and change these dangerous massifs into useful hills.[129]

It may have been rather florid, but it still conveys something of the difference between Mably and Rousseau. However ferocious some of his solutions may now look, Mably really was a reformer (Henri Grégoire, the Jacobin-leaning bishop of Blois, published several articles in his *Annales de la religion* in 1795 that presented a similarly positive view of Mably's

---

[129] *L'Ami des lois* 223 (1 Germinal an IV, 20 March 1796).

thought, this time on religion, just as Lindet and Jean-Bon Saint-André were to do with his views on the grain trade).[130] Rousseau, even in his posthumous *Considerations on the Government of Poland*, was more guardedly bleak.

The argument was given a broader airing in a speech to mark the opening of the republic's system of state schools (*écoles centrales*) that was given in 1796 by Louis de Fontanes, Napoleon's future university grand master, as his official title ran. In it, Fontanes explicitly associated the Jacobin politics of the immediate past with both Mably and Fénelon. "The solemn opening of these sanctuaries (*asiles*) of letters and the sciences," Fontanes began, "promises us that the blasphemies made against them by the ignorance of the end of the eighteenth century will no longer be renewed." "Narrow minds," he continued, "will no longer seek to apply the laws of Crete and Lacedaemonia to that immense republic that has no model, and which has to possess the warrior virtues of Rome, the arts of Athens, and the trade of Carthage at one and the same time." This, he asserted, meant that it would no longer be possible to rely on the authority of a man (identified in a note as Mably), who had been forgiven for sullying names greater than his own solely because he had spread maxims of virtue and liberty in his works, despite the "prejudices and sour spirit (*humeur chagrine*)" that all too often clouded his judgement. "I doubt," Fontanes concluded dismissively, "whether great modern states can usefully find enlightenment in a political writer who never raised his views higher than the republic of Salentum, and never embellished them with Fénelon's style. The arts and civilisation have made great progress since the plans devised by Mentor and Phocion. It is necessary to recognise, not delay, the successive and inevitable developments of the human mind, and guide them towards a laudable goal, rather than accuse them of the evils of society. If they have produced some, have they not also produced those indubitable goods that the detractors of perfected societies enjoy ungratefully every day?"[131] Fontanes's idea of a perfected society was certainly not

---

[130] *Annales de la Religion* 1, nos. 5, 12 (30 May, 18 July 1795). For an earlier, very positive, evaluation of Mably's thought, see Philippe-Antoine Grouvelle, *De l'autorité de Montesquieu dans la révolution présente*, reprinted in the *Bibliothèque de l'homme public*, 12 vols. (Paris, 1790), 7:38. For the continuing interest in the two, see the theses printed in 1812, and supervised by a philosophy professor named J. B. Maugras, in the B. N., under the call marks 4° R. Pièce 1773, and 4° R. Pièce 1783. On Mably, too, see Lenglet, *De la propriété*, a work whose criticism of Mably, and its broader argument, are similar to Pierre-Louis Roederer's *Cours d'organisation sociale* delivered in the spring of 1793, but published only posthumously (on it, see Sonenscher, *Before the Deluge*, pp. 322–34).

[131] Louis de Fontanes, "Discours prononcé au nom des professeurs des écoles centrales," *Magasin encyclopédique* 7 (1796): 508–17 (513–4 for the passages cited here). On Fontanes, and for part of the text cited here, see Norbert Savarian, *Louis de Fontanes. Belles-lettres et enseignement de la fin de l'ancien régime à l'Empire*, SVEC 2002: 8, pp. 166–7.

Rousseau's, but on the terms of his speech, Rousseau's concept of perfect-ibility served to counter Mably's less subtle attack on modern civilisation.

The more philosophical aspects of Rousseau's legacy also resurfaced in a number of different settings. Two, to end with, are worth singling out. The first was already in place before the French Revolution began, but remained a subject of discussion until well into the nineteenth century. This was the subject of music and its bearing on the broader question of the underlying mechanisms of human association. The putative connec-tion between music, the passions, the origins of language, and the primary mechanisms of social integration formed the major area of overlap between Rousseau and his critics. In the context of this initial common ground, Rousseau's moral and political thought amounted to an application of Montesquieu's radical historical vision to a number of long-established traditions of Christian speculation about the natural origins of society, morality, and government. This, to his dismay, was what the Jesuit Louis-Bertrand Castel recognised. In place of the type of passion-based natural history of music, society, and government that was the hallmark of a body of thought that stretched far beyond the confines of Castel's own works, Rousseau substituted a more historically contingent "genealogy" (as he called it) of the passions to produce a more state-centred outcome. The result was a Hobbes-like theory of political society, but, in what Rous-seau called the "third stage" of human association, with interdependent individual survival needs making political sovereignty unavoidably demo-cratic, and with what Emmanuel-Joseph Sieyès was to call "electicism," the necessary corollary of representative government.[132] Events, not only in France, and not only after 1789, have shown how difficult it can some-times be to combine the two.

One response was to try to broaden and deepen the common ground that Rousseau and his critics appeared to share. This was the enterprise that, after 1789, came to form the intellectual, moral, and political con-text from which the *sans-culottes* emerged. Another, however, was to try to undermine the common ground itself. This entailed rejecting the initial, largely natural emotional premise of the links between music, language, and society that Rousseau appeared to share with his critics. The first move in this direction came in an essay entitled *De l'expression en musique et de l'imitation dans les arts* (On Expression in Music and on Imitation in the Arts) that was published in the *Mercure de France* in November 1771 by the abbé André Morellet, a man now better known as the political economist responsible for the first, never finished, translation of Adam Smith's *Wealth of Nations*. Morellet began with what appeared to be a quite

[132] On Sieyès and "electicism" (or the electoral system), see Emmanuel-Joseph Sieyès, *Political Writings*, ed. Michael Sonenscher (Indianapolis, Hackett, 2003, pp. ix–x).

naturalistic explanation of music's power. Musical sounds, he suggested, were imitations of natural sounds. But, he went on to argue, the imitation in question was more metaphorical than literal. Just as a mnemonic does not need to have anything in common with its subject matter for memory to be able to work, so, Morellet suggested, musical sounds do not need to have anything in common with natural sounds for feelings to occur. Even the most radically unnatural sounds, he argued, could still produce quite natural emotional effects, while a purely natural sound, like, he wrote, one made by a whistle able to imitate the sounds of a nightingale, could have no emotional effect at all. This, Morellet continued, seemed to indicate that whatever it was that gave music its power owed more to metaphor and the imagination than to the natural properties of sound, or even to melody itself. It followed that it was the artificial, not the natural, element in music that was the real source of its power. This, in turn, placed music on the same ground as the other arts. As was more intuitively apparent with painting or sculpture, Morellet concluded, artifice, not nature, was the real explanation of the relationship between music and the passions.[133]

The argument may have been aimed at Rousseau (or, at least, at his published claims about melody, not harmony, as the key component of music, since the *Essay on the Origin of Languages* was not yet known). But it was, in fact, rather more compatible with Rousseau's conjectures about melody, the imagination, and the passions than with the older, more strongly naturalistic, explanation of the relationship between music, language, and morality that John Brown took over from Joseph-François Lafitau, and the broader tradition of Christian speculation to which Lafitau's work belonged. The breach between the two ways of thinking about the subject—the one relying on signs, memory, and the imagination; the other on the feelings of awe, wonder, and reverence—was sealed with the publication in 1779 of Michel-Paul-Guy de Chabanon's *Observations sur la musique, et principalement sur la métaphysique de l'art* (Observations on Music, and Principally on the Metaphysics of the Art), followed, in 1785, by his programmatically entitled *De la musique considérée en elle-même et dans ses rapports avec la parole, les langues, la poésie et le théâtre* (On Music Considered in Itself, and in its Relationship to Speech, Languages, Poetry, and the Theatre). Chabanon took his cue explicitly from Morellet's essay.[134]

[133] André Morellet, *De l'expression en musique et de l'imitation dans les arts* [*Mercure de France*, November 1771, pp. 113–43], reprinted in André Morellet, *Mélanges de littérature et de philosophie du 18ᵉ siècle*, 2 vols. (Paris, 1818), 2:366–413. An English translation can be found in Edward A. Lippman, ed., *Musical Aesthetics: A Historical Reader*, 3 vols. (New York, Pendragon Press, 1986–90), 1:269–84.

[134] Michel-Paul-Guy de Chabanon, *Observations sur la musique, et principalement sur la métaphysique de l'art* (Paris, 1779), pp. x, 25–9. Part of the text is translated in Lippman, *Musical Aesthetics*, 1:295–318.

But he also reinforced Morellet's argument about the artificial character of music's effects by emphasising the closed quality of metaphorical language. Metaphors, he argued, did not have to refer to anything natural to produce emotional effects. There was, therefore, no reason to continue the discussion of the putative relationship between music and language because there was simply no intrinsic connection between them at all. For Chabanon, musical effects were simply a product of music's properties; they did not require nonmusical categories like language, morality, or society for these effects to be explained. The argument (summarised very crudely here) really did consign the old, largely scripturally based, set of claims about music, morality, and language that Jean-Louis Castilhon satirised in his *Modern Diogenes* to the history of ideas. But it also brought back many of the problems raised by Rousseau's more morally sceptical historical conjectures from another direction. As his first critics had claimed, it was hard to see how morality could be anything other than local or conventional if it did not have some sort of natural starting point. Unsurprisingly, the argument continued—both in more specialised studies of music like the self-explanatorily entitled *Recherches sur l'analogie de la musique avec les arts qui ont pour objet l'imitation du langage, pour servir d'introduction à l'étude des principes naturels de cet art* (Researches into the Analogy between Music and the Arts Whose Object Is the Imitation of Language, Serving as an Introduction to the Study of the Natural Principles of That Art) published by a man named Guillaume-André Villoteau in 1807, and in the broader subjects of what, in the early nineteenth century, came to be known as ideology and social science. The French Revolution may have been the proximate cause of the emergence of both, but they really began with Rousseau.

The second, and related, aspect of Rousseau's legacy was also in place before the French Revolution began. It can be found in a large didactic poem called simply *Le Mal* (Evil) that was published in Berne in 1789, but which had first appeared, under a different title, in 1784, and was then republished, with significant revisions, in Lausanne in 1813.[135] It was, in its way, a recapitulation of many of the eighteenth-century discussions of morality, history, and politics that lay behind the transformation of the

---

[135] Emmanuel Salchli, *Le mal, poème philosophique en quatre chants, suivi de remarques et dissertations relatives au sujet* (Berne, 1789), and *Le mal, poème philosophique en neuf chants* (Lausanne, 1813). All references in the following footnotes are to the 1789 edition (those to that of 1813 will be indicated). That edition was, in some sense, a successor to an earlier poem entitled *Les causes finales et la direction du mal* (Berne, 1784), but Salchli went to some lengths in his preface to the 1789 poem (p. iii) to indicate that the two poems had "absolutely nothing in common with one another, other than part of their plan." For the purposes of what follows, comparison to the 1784 poem is unnecessary. On Salchli himself, see the short entry under his name in Michaud, *Biographie universelle*.

salon society joke into a republican emblem, and, in the light of the differences between the versions of the poem published in 1789 and 1813, an indication of one of their possible outcomes. Although it was published in Switzerland, the poem was, in fact, aimed primarily at a French readership. This was apparent not only from the dedication of the version published in 1789 to the former minister of state, and future defender of Louis XVI, Guillaume-François-Chrétien de Lamoignon de Malesherbes, but also from the critical comments in the poem's preface about the state of modern French poetry, and the need, as its author put it, to give it "that grand manner, that audacity, that originality, and that naturalness" that were the characteristics of "true poetry." These qualities, he wrote, borrowing a phrase from Louis-Sébastien Mercier, would make the poems produced by the French "a hundred times more admirable" than the effect of "vernal frost" produced by the "factitious polish" they standardly received. Rather than in the imitation of others, proper guidance for poetic composition was to be found in the disdain for formal rules advocated by Edward Young in his *Essay on Original Composition*, which, to his regret, the author of the poem itself had read only when he was two-thirds of the way through his own composition.[136] The individual in question was a man named Emmanuel Salchli, a professor of Greek and Roman literature, and later of universal history and statistics, at the Political Institute of Berne, who went on to become a pastor of the German, or Lutheran, church at Stettlen, near Berne. The poem was a theodicy, but, as Salchli went to some lengths to explain in the copious notes that he attached to its text, it was intended to expand upon, and modify, the arguments contained in Gottfried Wilhelm Leibniz's own, much earlier *Essays on Theodicy* of 1709.

The broad framework of the poem was still, however, supplied by Leibniz; it consisted of an examination of the various types of evil that Leibniz had set out to explain, in order, as his Catholic follower Alexander Pope put it in his *Essay on Man*, to justify God's ways to man (Pope, Salchli noted, had fallen rather short of the goal, because, unlike Edward Young in his *Night Thoughts*, his poem was too full of universal assessments, leaving it bereft of any examination of the real human condition and its future state).[137] For Salchli, evil could be categorised as metaphysical, moral, or physical. Metaphysical evil was an effect of the finite quality of the creation. Unlike moral or physical evil, it was unavoidable, because it was rationally impossible for something endowed with all the attributes of a

---

[136] Salchli, *Le mal*, pp. v (on Young), xvi (on Mercier).

[137] Salchli, *Le mal* (1813 ed.), p. xxii. For an overview of these earlier discussions, see Pierre-Alexandre Alès de Corbet, *De l'origine du mal, ou examen des principales difficultés de Bayle sur cette matière*, 2 vols. (Paris, 1758), which contains, pp. 47–8, a discussion of Pope, and the similarities between his theodicy and that set out in Louis-Jean Levesque de Pouilly, *Théorie des sentiments agréables* (Dublin, 1749).

divinity to create something identical to itself (omnipotence, for example, could not, without self-contradiction, create omnipotence). Moral evil was also, in the first instance, an effect of the finite character of created beings. To be themselves, they had to have their own properties; and to remain themselves, they had to maintain those properties that made them different from all the rest. In purely natural terms, this meant that the world could be envisaged as a harmonious whole, with the imperfections and collisions of created beings forming a system of natural laws that was consonant with the idea of a just and omniscient deity. Divine wisdom, Salchli suggested, implied a creation governed by general laws, not miracles, and with a positive natural balance of good over evil in the ordinary processes of life and death.[138]

In more narrowly human terms, however, moral evil had a more open-ended status, which, in turn, made the relationship between good and evil more finely balanced. The mixture of the spiritual and the physical built into human nature meant, Salchli wrote, that the passions were the mechanisms that led either to God, or, once entangled with the material world, to evil.[139] In this latter case, human freedom, and its capacity to make the wrong moral choices, pulled against the general, law-bound character of the creation to produce the physical evils that were the most obvious hallmark of the human condition. But the grim record of human history, and the difficulties that it created for deciding whether, on balance, good really did outweigh evil, were also, Salchli argued, part of the broader providential system. The equivocal quality of the balance gave the whole system a capacity for self-correction, not only because physical evils sometimes really did have the effect of destroying their moral causes, but also because the very uncertainty built into human assessments of aggregate good and evil would always supply some people with real grounds for hope (a less unequivocal answer would entail either complacent indifference or resigned despair). From this perspective, human causation could work against itself in a genuinely positive way. As the whole didactic poem was designed to show, real physical evils (war, destruction, and death) had led and could still lead mankind to find ways to eliminate the moral evils that were the cause of its own misfortunes. Effects, in this way, would destroy their causes.

From one point of view, this made the subject matter of Salchli's poem the history of mankind. As he emphasised, however, it was not quite the same type of history as could be found in the works of Rousseau, Adam Ferguson, or his Scots compatriot Henry Home, Lord Kames.[140] It was, instead, much nearer in content to the more recent history of mankind

---

[138] Salchli, *Le mal*, pp. 301–3.
[139] Salchli, *Le mal*, pp. 433–5.
[140] Salchli, *Le mal*, p. 290.

CONCLUSION 417

produced by Johann Gottfried Herder, and to the "sublime idea" of the great chain of being on which Herder's history was based. Herder's typology of an organic chain, made up of beings distinguished from one another either by their fibres, informed by the vital principle of "elasticity" (plants), or by their muscles, informed by "irritability" (animals), or by their nerves, informed by "sensibility" (humans) made it possible to recast Leibniz's theodicy in more naturalistic terms.[141] It also made it easier to align Rousseau with this type of natural philosophy (and to substitute a paean of praise for the peasant community of the Emmenthal region of Switzerland for Rousseau's description of the Valais).[142] Here, the key text that Salchli used to make the point was Rousseau's letter to Voltaire about the Lisbon earthquake of 1755. "You draw a distinction between events that have effects and those that do not," Rousseau had written in the seventeenth part of his letter.

> I doubt the distinction is sound. Every event seems to me necessarily to have some effect, moral or physical, or a combination of the two, but which is not always perceived because the filiation of events is even more difficult to follow than that of men. In general, since one should not look for effects more considerable than the events that they produce, the minuteness of causes frequently makes inquiry ridiculous, although the effects are certain, just as several almost imperceptible effects frequently combine to produce a considerable event.

"In a word," he concluded, "recalling the grain of sand mentioned by Pascal, I am in some respects of your Brahmin's opinion, and regardless of how one views things, it seems to me indisputable that while all events may not have sensible effects, they all have real effects, of which the human mind easily loses the thread, but which nature never confuses."[143] Here, for the final time, a line of thought that could be derived from Rousseau was turned into something different. From Salchli's point of view, Rousseau's argument was one that could be reconciled quite easily with Herder's organically interdependent and spiritually charged concept of nature (as well, Salchli argued, as making it easier to come to a more positive view of the arts and sciences than Rousseau himself had done).[144] So, too, but in a different sense, could Buffon's uniformly molecular concept

[141] Salchli, *Le mal*, p. 295.
[142] Salchli, *Le mal*, pp. 431–3.
[143] Salchli, *Le mal*, pp. 297–8. For the original, see Jean-Jacques Rousseau, *Letter from J. J. Rousseau to M. de Voltaire* [1756], in Rousseau, *The Discourses and Other Early Political Writings*, ed. Victor Gourevitch (Cambridge, CUP, 1997), pp. 232–46 (238).
[144] Salchli, *Le mal*, pp. 401–3 (a long note on Zinga, the seventeenth-century African queen, and the famously evil people of Jaggas whom she ruled, an example that Salchli used to refute Rousseau's claim about the relationship between moral evil and the refinement of the arts and sciences).

of nature. Instead of molecules, Salchli wrote, the system "most generally adopted today" was one that took living "germs" to be the most basic natural units, but the "organic forces" that they housed might still be said to attract those molecules that were most analogous to their nature to produce the same type of ascent from the physical to the spiritual involved in Herder's idea of the soul's striving towards perfection.[145] The result was a more physically individuated way of thinking about nature that, for Salchli, had a real moral bearing.

Here, like so many others before him, he took Cicero as his starting point. The moral problems laid out in Cicero's *On Duties*, reexamined recently in the annotated translation by the German popular philosopher Christian Garve, arose, Salchli wrote, largely from the multiple sets of relationships and the various types of character, or *personae*, that every adult was obliged to adopt. An individual could be a human, and a doctor, and a mother, and could also be materially fortunate or unfortunate in several other ways (richer, more beautiful, or more athletic, for example). The difficulty, as always, was to find a way to reconcile these different roles, and the various types of obligation that they might entail, or, as Salchli said that the French philosopher Claude-Adrien Helvétius had put it, to find a way to avoid paying lip service to doing good wholesale, while behaving like a scoundrel (*fripon*) retail. For Salchli, the type of natural philosophy that he associated with Herder (and with the Genevan Charles Bonnet) appeared to offer a solution and "a new science" that might one day allow morality to be adapted to "all the collisions, and all the particular cases, in which someone might be found."[146] It did so, not because of any strongly positive moral principles that it was likely to be able to offer, but because of the real scientific grounding for natural human diversity and individuality that it already appeared to have established. Seeing people in this more naturally individuated sense gave more value to respect for others, and for the various roles that physiology, history, and circumstance had assigned to them. From this point of view, natural philosophy not only appeared to have opened up a way to reinstate the value of private judgement, in a secular rather than a purely religious sense, but also appeared to indicate real, physiological reasons for setting limits on how far private judgement was entitled to go. "The effect of a deeper morality," Salchli wrote, "would be to make men more circumspect in the judgements that they make of others. It may then become easier to understand why, strictly speaking, no man can be a judge of anyone other than himself." Actions, and their consequences, would still be subject to laws and government, but the broader array of everyday human qualities and activities would be

---

[145] Salchli, *Le mal*, pp. 298–9.
[146] Salchli, *Le mal*, pp. 319 (on Helvétius), 320, 435 (on Bonnet).

subject to a real, rationally, but also aesthetically, grounded, measure of individual human respect. "A morality like that," Salchli observed, "would certainly be the first of all the sciences."[147] It was something like the moral basis of the more recent politics of cultural diversity.

This affirmation of individuality, together with the idea of effects counteracting their causes, made it easier to think of the history of mankind in terms of a reversion to first principles, but on the basis of a higher level of knowledge and understanding. Well-founded private judgement, Salchli wrote, was possible only in the primitive state, or one in which man was "entirely enlightened." There was simply "no middle position." If, he continued, "civil man does not have the knowledge that his moral and political relationships require, he stands below the savages of Louisiana and Canada who, though ignorant of what is foreign to their state, still, as Ferguson showed, have a very good knowledge of their national interests." The knowledge available to "polished peoples" was biased in favour of "the arts, trade, war, the agreements and commodities of life, and objects and speculations of pure curiosity," leaving no room at all for "the moral and political state" (here, the relevant authority was the Diderot of Guillaume-Thomas Raynal's *Philosophical History of the European Settlements in the Two Indies*, rather than Adam Ferguson). It followed that a "polished people" could become "good and happy" only when its reason was "entirely developed," and when it had acquired "all the knowledge that its moral, civil, and political state requires." There was no other way available, Salchli concluded, "to repress and abolish the despotism that, by suffocating the generous moral instincts engraved by nature on every human heart, degrades them and forces them to become wicked."[148] This was not a matter of turning everyone into scholars (*savants*), but of "enlightening" them, according to the requirements of their various conditions and ways of life. To this end, they had to be given the means to find out truth, and to distinguish the good from the beautiful. Three "essential works" were required for this purpose. The first was "a practical logic," the second "a considered moral theory (*une morale approfondie*)," and the third "a general theory of the beautiful" (a starting point was available in Edmund Burke's *Philosophical Inquiry into the Origin of our Ideas of the Sublime and the Beautiful*). With these, and when "love of the true, the good, and the beautiful" had become "the principle" of mankind's actions, then, as Salchli put it in the poem itself, "the arts and simplicity would be united," and it would be possible to see "the state of liberty in the state of culture," and "natural man in civil man."[149]

[147] Salchli, *Le mal*, p. 321.
[148] Salchli, *Le mal*, p. 325.
[149] Salchli, *Le mal*, pp. 325–6. Full discussion of the subject would involve comparison between Salchli's gestures towards aesthetic theory and Friedrich Schiller's *On the Aesthetic*

In the version of the poem that he published in 1789, Salchli made it clear that events, in both America and France, heralded an imminent transformation. "Philosophers and superior writers," he wrote, could now "dispose of public opinion, and force sovereigns and their ministers to submit to the empire of truth." They had already been able to impose limits on arbitrary power, extinguish "the torch of fanaticism," and promote the spirit of humanity and toleration that now obtained among peoples of different religious persuasions. They had made it clear how necessary it was to reform education, laws, criminal jurisprudence, and governments, as well as to guide the sciences and talents towards public utility. But these, Salchli continued, were no more than harbingers of "new, yet greater revolutions." Soon, princes would no longer embark on wars without their subjects' consent; "hierarchical power" would be confined to just limits; the spirit of religion, "more widespread than it is at present," would banish superstition and theological quarrels; and "the breath of genius" would overturn "the Gothic edifice of our barbarous laws and institutions." Then, politics and morality would no longer be separate. The civil law would no longer be opposed to natural laws. Agriculture would become the state's prime concern, while agricultural producers (*laboureurs*) would no longer be trampled underfoot by the great and powerful. Moderate taxes would be distributed fairly. Standing armies, "the instrument of despotism, and the prime source of financial disorder and poverty," would be abolished or reduced. There would no longer be "that huge inequality in fortunes that makes the poor the slave of the rich." The various ranks would become closer, and the "absurd prejudices of nobility" would evaporate. Love of beauty, nature, and the countryside would expel, or at least weaken, love of luxury, display, and magnificence. And all these changes, Salchli concluded, would "certainly" happen, "well before 2440."[150]

When the poem reappeared in 1813, it was no longer the 450-page octavo of the edition of 1789, but a smaller, 268-page book, with a radically truncated set of notes, and with nine cantos instead of four. This, however, was more of an effect of what seems to have been a change (for the worse) in its author's circumstances than a change in his convictions, because the broad message of the poem, and its underlying philosophical system of effects counteracting their causes, remained largely the same. Readers of the later edition were referred recurrently to the notes in the earlier edition for amplification or clarification of its more philosophical arguments, even though, as Salchli indicated, the poem itself contained two entirely new sections, dealing, respectively, with "the development of beings according

---

Education of Man (1801), with its more critical assessment of both Burke and the aesthetic theories to which Mercier subscribed.

[150] Salchli, *Le mal*, pp. 387–8.

to Herder's system" and with "the present situation of Europe."[151] The first of these new sections in fact simply transferred some of the content of the earlier notes to the poem itself, so that much of Herder's system, with its focus on an organic force common to the whole natural world, and on virtue as a capacity produced by the finer physiological structure imparted by the soul to the body in its ascent towards spiritual perfection, now reappeared in metrical form.[152] The second section, however, was necessarily new. Here, the insertions and changes that Salchli introduced were both a register of the impact of the French Revolution and a transformation of his earlier conjectures about mankind's future into a more settled, and now more firmly retrospective, point of view.

The effects of this transformation were most apparent in Salchli's treatment of France, where the earlier projections of the poem's first incarnation gave way to a different assessment of France's present state. Where, in 1789, the chief obstacles to reform had been despotic governments, corrupt ministers, religious obscurantism, unjust privilege, and excessive inequality, these, in 1813, were replaced by a different cast of characters. Although the broad outlines of the story of ruin and recovery remained the same, the opposition to reform was no longer to be found, hypocritically, in "the republican air of a grave aristocrat," but, still hypocritically, in the same "republican air," now assumed by an "ardent democrat" (*démocrate fougueux*). Liberty's "proud partisans" were now "malcontents," while "barriers against the pride of kings" had become barriers against "every oppressor." "Whole nations" were no longer condemned to "shake with despair under murderous laws." Nor, "subject to the yoke of a cruel despot," were they condemned to "tremble in exposing themselves to his mortal aspect." Peoples were no longer "the innocent victims" of their bellicose kings, nor were they required "to dig their own graves to feed their kings' despotic pride," while nature's design was no longer "the happiness of the world" but, more ethereally, "the happiness of spirits (*esprits*)."[153] It is easy to assume that the changes were indicative of a political disenchantment that was widely shared. But that was not actually Salchli's point.

The point, in fact, was the opposite. The modifications that Salchli made to his poem were not at all the product of disappointment over an unrealised future, but of satisfaction with a more fully, and magnificently, achieved present. Looking back from the vantage point of 1813, it now seemed clear that France had come to a real resting place, under the rule of Napoleon Bonaparte. In a France that, Salchli now wrote, had "fallen

[151] Salchli, *Le mal* (1813 ed.), p. xxxiii.
[152] Salchli, *Le mal* (1813 ed.), pp. 77–86.
[153] The phrases cited were all either cut or changed as indicated in the first two cantos of the 1813 edition.

prey to anarchy," the "marvellous exploits" of "the greatest of Caesars" had succeeded in "repressing the furies of divided parties" and "by wise laws" had allowed "reason to triumph." Napoleon, "that hero, the model prince," had given Europe "a new face, in which legality and a civil code stood in place of both divisive privilege and viciously partisan popular politics." It was, his panegyrist continued, as if he had been sent from heaven to earth to calm a universe "shattered by the shock of ardent passions," not only because he had been able to repress "the people's frenetic rage," but also because he had confounded "the dark (*sombre*) politics" of kings. Under his sons, the seat of the new empire would be transferred to Rome, and, once the freedom of the seas had been wrested from "Albion's insulting arrogance," this prince, one "greater even than Charlemagne," would inaugurate "a new reign of peace in the universe"; there, stripped of imperial ambition, even British "arts and industry" would give new life to a world that, one day, would have no more than one god and one fatherland (*patrie*).[154] This time, however, Salchli dropped the reference to the year 2440. He did so, presumably, not because it was an embarrassment, but because it was now simply redundant. Louis-Sébastien Mercier was still alive in 1813 when Salchli published the revised version of his poem (he died the following year). The regime that came to be headed by Napoleon Bonaparte may not have been quite what Mercier had had in mind when, some forty years earlier, he wrote his book, or even when, some two decades later, he and Antoine-Joseph Gorsas began to give a different sense to an old joke about salons and breeches, but it is still possible that they might have agreed.

This, of course, is conjecture. But the differences between the two versions of Salchli's poem still have a real historiographical significance. They show how much of the moral and political thought of the period before 1789 was blotted out by the events of the French Revolution, and how difficult it still is to get behind the wall of retrospective evaluation that it left in its wake. The point applies with particular force to the phrase *sans culottes*. The joke that gave the phrase its initial significance made it an emblem of urbanity, intelligible only in the context of salons, cities, and cultivated women. A great deal was required to make it a name used to refer to artisans, crowds, and popular politics. Taking what the name became as a guide to its original connotations amounts to opting inadvertently for a historical and historiographical blind alley, with no way in to such subjects as Ciceronian decorum, Cynic moralism, Rousseau's cultural

---

[154] Salchli, *Le mal* (1813 ed.), pp. 209, 211, 214. For another quasi-naturalistic justification of the first empire, based on the concept of what its author called *l'homme pouvoir*, see Charles His, *Théorie du monde politique, ou de la science du gouvernement considérée comme science exacte* (Paris, 1806).

and political criticism, Fénelon's vision of a flourishing society, Ogilvie's property theory, Bonnet's and Lavater's vitalism, Edward Young's enthusiasm, John Brown's civilisation theory, Law's and Leibniz's intellectual legacies, or Mably's disabused moral and political realism, to list some of those that this book has traversed. All of them had a bearing on what the *sans-culottes* became. They did so, however, in ways that were almost entirely unforeseen and unintended, and, when they did become more purposeful and deliberate, as they did in Mercier's and Gorsas's hands in 1791–2, they were soon forgotten or deliberately disowned. Putting them back in place has the effect of making the French Revolution look different, with a broader and thicker array of conceptual resources, historical assessments, and moral evaluations involved in the often intensely uncertain moments of political decision making and choice that arose in France after 1789. This, in turn, makes it easier to see how much we have lost, both historically and historiographically, by taking later evaluations of the French Revolution at their face value, and how much we may still gain by trying to piece together its political history from its protagonists' points of view. The suggestion applies not only to what occurred in France after 1789 but also to what happened after the French Revolution itself was over, when the combination of democracy and public debt became, in the hands of individuals like Louis Blanc or Pierre-Joseph Proudhon, the major republican alternative to constitutional monarchy in almost every European state in the thirty-three-year period that led up to the 1848 revolutions. The story set out here has been largely a story about property, and about the way that an early eighteenth-century set of claims about how fashion and fashion's empire could neutralise property's divisive effects came, at the hands of its critics, to look radically self-defeating ("the masterpiece of politics of our century," in Rousseau's sarcastic phrase). So, too, by 1793, did the scientist, debt-driven, teleologically oriented alternatives developed not so much by Rousseau as by his assorted admirers or critics to reach a more socially comprehensive version of the same goal, with a less morally tainted array of the arts available generally, and an authentically natural culture in place of the spurious polish of a privileged few. From this perspective, there may not have been as much of a conceptual gulf between the archetypical *sans-culotte* Quatorze-oignons and Napoleon Bonaparte, at least in his Ossianic guise, as there may now seem. But whichever of the two was the real archetype, the *sans-culottes* are still history. It is less clear, however, whether the subjects and questions with which they were once associated are too, at least in the same demotic sense. There may, therefore, still be quite a lot to find out about how these subjects and questions came to be treated, after the *sans-culottes* had gone.

BIBLIOGRAPHY

Manuscript Sources

Archives nationales, Paris. 284 AP—Sieyès papers.
Archives nationales, Paris. 446 AP—Brissot papers.
Archives nationales, Paris, Minutier central des notaires, LXCVIII, 417 (20 May 1765); XCII, 575, 8 February 1752 (testament de Mme Ferrand); XCII, 715, 30 May 1768 (testament de Mme de Vassé); XCII, 717, 1 August 1768 (dépôt mortuaire des effets de Mme la comtesse de Vassé); XCII, 719 (10 December 1768).
Archives nationales, Paris, W 567^a (Antonelle papers).
Bibliothèque de l'Arsenal, Mss. 6076, 6101, and 6103—Brizard papers.
Bibliothèque nationale de France, Collection Joly de Fleury, Mss. 1426.

Eighteenth- and Early Nineteenth-Century Journals and Newspapers

L'Ami des lois. Paris, 1795–97.
Analytical Review. 22 vols. London, 1788–98.
Annales de la Religion. 18 vols. Paris, 1795–1803.
The Athenaeum. London, 1807.
Le Catholique. Paris, 1826–30.
Chronique de Paris. Paris, 1789–93.
Courier de l'Europe. London, 1777–88.
Courier de Provence. 17 vols. Paris, 1789–91.
Ephémérides du citoyen. 62 vols. Paris, 1767–72.
Gazette universelle. 3 vols. Paris, 1789–92.
L'Historien. Paris, 1795–7.
Journal de commerce et d'agriculture. 20 vols. Brussels, 1759–62.
Journal de la Montagne. 8 vols. Paris, 1793–4.
Journal de Paris. Paris, 1778–1800.
Journal des beaux arts et des sciences. 36 vols. Bouillon and Paris, 1768–75
Journal des Révolutions de l'Europe en 1789 et 1790. 14 vols. Strasbourg, 1789.
Journal des savants. Paris, 1665–.
Journal encyclopédique. Liège, 1756–93.
The London Chronicle. London, 1757–.
Magasin encyclopédique. Paris, 1795–.
Mercure de France. Paris, 1710–91.
Moniteur Universel. Paris, 1789–99.
Morning Post. London, 1772–.
Nouvelles politiques nationales et étrangères. Paris, 1792–7.
Patriote français. Paris, 1789–93.
Révolutions de Paris. Paris, 1789–93.

PRIMARY TEXTS

A l'assemblée des états-généraux, ou coup d'oeil sur la constitution, sur le prêt et l'emprunt. Translated by Jean Chas. London, 1789.

L'abeille, ou recueil de philosophie, de littérature et d'histoire. The Hague, 1755.

Abeille, Paul. Introduction to Chrétien-Guillaume de Lamoignon de Malesherbes, *Observations sur l'histoire naturelle et générale et particulière de Buffon et Daubenton.* 2 vols. Paris, an VI/1798.

[Accarias de Sérionne, Jacques]. *Les intérêts des nations de l'Europe développés relativement au commerce.* 4 vols. Paris, 1767.

An account of the birth, life and negotiations of the Marechal Bellisle. London, 1745.

Adams, Hannah. *An Alphabetical Compendium of the Various Sects which have Appeared in the World from the Beginning of the Christian Era to the Present Day.* Boston, 1784.

Alembert, Jean Le Rond d'. *Miscellaneous Pieces in Literature, History and Philosophy.* London, 1764.

Alès de Corbet, Pierre-Alexandre. *De l'origine du mal, ou examen des principales difficultés de Bayle sur cette matière.* 2 vols. Paris, 1758.

Almanach littéraire, ou étrennes d'Apollon. Paris, 1782.

Anquetil-Duperron, Abraham-Hyacinthe. *Dignité du commerce et de l'état commerçant.* Paris, 1789.

———. *L'Inde en rapport avec l'Europe.* 2 vols. Hamburg, 1798.

Antonelle, Pierre-Antoine. *Lettre au citoyen S . . . rédacteur de l'article "Paris" dans le journal dit "Annales patriotiques, littéraires".* Rochefort, 18 April 1793.

Argenson, René-Louis de Voyer de Paulmy, marquis d'. *Considérations sur le gouvernement ancien et présent de la France.* Amsterdam, 1764.

L'armée française au conseil de la guerre. N.p., n.d.

[Aubert de Vitry, François-Jean-Philibert]. *J. J. Rousseau à l'assemblée nationale.* Paris, 1789.

[Auffray]. "Réflexions sur la guerre." *Courier de l'Europe* 8, no. 30 (13 October 1780).

Bacher, Alexandre. *Cours de droit public.* 4 vols. Paris, 1801.

Bagehot, Walter. *The English Constitution* [1867]. Edited by Paul Smith. Cambridge, CUP, 2001.

Barbauld, Anna Laetitia. "Essay on Akenside's Poem, *The Pleasures of Imagination*" [1794]. In Mark Akenside, *The Pleasures of Imagination.* London, 1796.

Barère, Bertrand. *Montesquieu peint d'après ses ouvrages.* Paris, an V/1797.

Barrett, Jean-Jacques de. *De la loi naturelle.* 2 vols. Paris, 1790.

Barthélémy, Jean-Jacques. "Vie privée de l'abbé de Mably." In Gabriel Bonnot de Mably, *Oeuvres*, vol. 13. 13 vols. London, 1789–90.

Beauty's Triumph, or The Authority of the Fair Sex Invincibly Proved. London, 1751.

Bentham, Jeremy. *Works.* Edited by John Bowring. London, 1843.

Bergasse, Nicolas. *Lettre de M. Bergasse, député de la sénéchaussée de Lyon à ses commettants, au sujet de sa protestation contre les assignats monnaie.* Paris, 1790.

Bergier, Nicolas-Silvestre. *Traité historique et dogmatique de la vraie religion.* 12 vols. Paris, 1780.

Bernardin de Saint-Pierre, Jacques-Henri. *Etudes de la nature* [1784]. Edited by Napoléon Chaix. 2 vols. Paris, 1865.

————. *Voeux d'un solitaire*. Paris, 1793.

Berthelot, Jean-François. *Réponse à quelques propositions hasardées par M. Garat contre le droit romain dans le Mercure de France du 19 février 1785*. Paris, 1785.

Blackburne, Francis. *Memoirs of Thomas Hollis*. 2 vols. London, 1780.

Blackstone, William. *Commentaries on the Laws of England* [1765–9]. 4 vols. Edited by A. W. Brian Simpson. Chicago, University of Chicago Press, 1979.

[Boissel, François]. *Adresse à la nation française. Peuple français, voici ta constitution*. n.p., n.d.

Bonnet, Charles. *Essai de psychologie*. London, 1755.

————. *Oeuvres d'histoire naturelle et de philosophie*. 18 vols., in 8°, or 8 vols., in 4°. Neuchâtel, 1779–83.

Bostock, John. *An Elementary System of Physiology* [1824]. 3rd ed. London, 1836.

[Boureau Deslandes, André-François]. *A Philological Essay, or Reflections on the Death of Free-Thinkers, with the Characters of the Most Eminent Persons of Both Sexes, Ancient and Modern, that Died Pleasantly and Unconcern'd*. London, 1713.

[————]. *Réflexions sur les grands hommes qui sont morts en plaisantant* [1714]. Rochefort, 1755.

Brissot, Jacques-Pierre. *Recherches philosophiques sur le droit de la propriété considéré dans la nature, pour servir de premier chapitre à la "Théorie des loix" de M. Linguet*. N.p., 1780.

————. *Testament politique de l'Angleterre*. London, 1782.

————. *Journal du lycée de Londres*. London, 1784.

————. *A ses commettants sur la situation de la Convention nationale*. Paris, 1793.

————. *Mémoires de Brissot*. Edited by Adolphe Mathurin de Lescure. Paris, 1877.

————. *Mémoires de Brissot*. Edited by Claude Perroud. 2 vols. Paris, 1911.

Brissot, Jacques-Pierre, and Etienne Clavière. *The Commerce of America with Europe, particularly with France and Great-Britain, comparatively stated and explained*. London, 1794.

Brizard, Gabriel. "Eloge historique de l'abbé Mably." In Gabriel Bonnot de Mably, *Oeuvres*, vol. 1. 13 vols. London, 1789–90.

Broglie, Victor de. "Mémoire sur l'état de l'armée" (1769). In Albert Latreille, *L'armée et la nation à la fin de l'ancien régime*, pp. 343–93. Paris, 1914.

[Brossais du Perray, Joseph-Marie]. *Remarques historiques et anecdotiques sur le château de la Bastille*. N. p., 1774.

Brosses, Charles de. *Histoire de la république romaine dans le cours du viiᵉ siècle par Salluste*. 3 vols. Dijon, 1777.

Brown, John. *Essays on the Characteristics*. London, 1751.

————. *An Estimate of the Manners and Principles of the Times*. 2 vols. London, 1757.

————. *An Explanatory Defence of the Estimate of the Manners and Principles of the Times*. London, 1758.

————. *A Dissertation on the Rise, Union, and Power, the Progressions, Separations, and Corruptions, of Poetry and Music*. London, 1763.

————. *Sermons on Various Subjects*. London, 1764.

————. *Histoire de l'origine et des progrès de la poésie dans ses différents genres*. Paris, 1768.

[————]. *De la liberté civile et des factions*. N.p., 1789.

————. *Description of the Lake at Keswick*. In William Roberts, *A Dawn of Imaginative Feeling: The Contribution of John Brown (1715–66) to Eighteenth-Century Thought and Literature*. Carlisle, Northern Academic Press, 1996.

Bryant, Jacob. *A New System, or An Analysis of Ancient Mythology*. 3 vols. London, 1774.

Burlamaqui, Jean-Jacques. *The Principles of Natural and Political Law* [1763]. Edited by Petter Korkman. Indianapolis, Liberty Fund, 2006.

Burton, Thomas. *Parliamentary Diary*. Edited by John Towill Rutt. London, 1828.

Cantillon, Richard. *Essai sur la nature du commerce en général*.

Caraccioli, Louis-Antoine de. *Paris, le modèle des nations étrangères, ou l'Europe française*. Paris, 1777.

[Carl, Ernst Ludwig]. *Traité de la richesse des princes et de leurs états: et des moyens simples et naturels pour y parvenir*. 3 pts. Paris, 1722–3.

Carra, Jean-Louis. *Examen physique du magnétisme animal*. London, 1785.

Carrard, Benjamin. *Essai qui a remporté le prix de la société hollandaise des sciences de Haarlem en 1770 sur cette question: 'Qu'est-ce qui est requis dans l'art d'observer, et jusqu'où cet art contribue-t-il à perfectionner l'entendement?'*. Amsterdam, 1777.

Carte, Thomas. *A General History of England*. 4 vols. London, 1747–55.

[Casaux, Charles, marquis de]. *Considérations sur les principes politiques de mon siècle*. London, 1776.

Castel, Louis-Bertrand. "Lettre sur la politique adressée à Monsieur l'abbé de Saint-Pierre, par le P. Castel Jésuite." *Journal de Trévoux*, April 1725, pp. 698–729.

————. *L'homme moral opposé a l'homme physique de Monsieur R****. Toulouse, 1756. Reprinted in *Supplément aux Oeuvres de J. J. Rousseau, citoyen de Genève*, in Jean-Jacques Rousseau, *Oeuvres*, 15:77–251. 16 vols. Geneva, 1783.

————. "De l'action des hommes sur la nature." Originally published in the *Mémoires de Trévoux* and reprinted in *Esprit, saillies et singularités du père Castel*, pp. 189–222. Amsterdam, 1763.

————. "De la physique par rapport à la politique." In *Esprit, saillies et singularités du père Castel*, pp. 155–83. Amsterdam, 1763.

Castiglione, Giovanni Francesco Mauro Melchiorre Salvemini di. *Discours sur l'origine de l'inégalité parmi les hommes. Pour servir de réponse au discours que M. Rousseau a publié sur le même sujet*. Amsterdam, 1756.

Castilhon, Jean-Louis. *Considérations sur les causes physiques et morales de la diversité du génie des moeurs, et du gouvernement des nations*. 2 vols. Bouillon, 1769.

————. *Le Diogène moderne, ou le désapprobateur*. 2 vols. Bouillon, 1770.

Cerutti, Joseph-Joachim. *Idées simples et précises sur le papier monnaie, les assignats forcés, et les biens ecclésiastiques*. Paris, 1790.

Chabanon, Michel-Paul-Guy de. *Observations sur la musique, et principalement sur la métaphysique de l'art*. Paris, 1779.

————. *De la musique considérée en elle-même et dans ses rapports avec la parole, les langues, la poésie et la théâtre*. Paris, 1785.

[Chaillon de Jonville, Augustin-Jean-François]. *Apologie de la constitution française, ou états républicains et monarchies comparés dans les histoires de Rome et de France*. 2 vols. N.p., 1789.

————. *La vérité dévoilée*. Paris, 1789.

Chamfort, Sébastien-Roch-Nicolas. *Maximes, pensées, caractères et anecdotes*. London, 1796.

[Chas, Jean]. *Exposition de quelques principes politiques et quelques opinions religieuses*. N.p., n.d.

[————]. *Réponse aux réflexions de M. Garat insérées dans le Mercure du 14 mai 1785*. London, 1785.

[————]. *Nouvelle vie de M. François de Salignac de la Mothe Fénelon*. Paris, 1788.

[————]. *A la nation française*. Paris, 1805.

————. *Principes élémentaires des constitutions et des gouvernements*. Paris, 1807.

————. *Sur la souveraineté*, Paris, 1810.

[Chas, Jean, and Henri de Montignot]. *Réflexions sur les immunités ecclésiastiques, considérées dans leurs rapports avec les maximes du droit public et l'intérêt national*. Paris, 1788.

Chaussard, Pierre-Jean-Baptiste (Publicola). *Fêtes et courtisanes de la Grèce*. 4 vols. Paris, 1801.

Chevrier, François-Antoine. *Oeuvres*. 3 vols. London, 1774.

[Christie, Thomas]. *Miscellanies: Literary, Philosophical and Moral*. London, 1788.

Cicero. *Des offices*. In Cicero, *Oeuvres*, vol. 9, translated by Pierre Du Ryer. Paris, 1670.

————. *Des devoirs de l'homme*. Translated by Emmanuel Brosselard. Paris, an IV/1796.

————. *On Duties*. Harmondsworth, Penguin, 1971.

————. *On Duties*. Edited by M. T. Griffin and E. M. Adkins. Cambridge, CUP, 1991.

Claudius Aelianus. *His Various Histories*. Translated by Thomas Stanley. London, 1665.

Clavière, Etienne. *De la foi publique envers les créanciers de l'état*. London, 1788.

————. *Opinions d'un créancier de l'état sur quelques matières de finance importantes dans le moment actuel*. Paris, 1789.

————. "Lettre aux rédacteurs du Courier de Provence." *Courier de Provence* 48 (29 September–1 October 1789): 18–24.

————. "Sur les rapports des provinces et de Paris, relativement à la dette publique." *Courier de Provence* 61 (2–3 November 1789): 34–43.

————. "Réflexions nouvelles sur les assignats." *Courier de Provence* 197 (1790): 413–30.

————. *Observations nécessaires sur la partie du mémoire du premier ministre des finances, relative aux subsides qu'exige le déficit de 1790, et sur la convenance d'une prompte émission d'assignats monnaie*. Paris, 1790.

————. "Seconde suite des observations sur le mémoire de M. Necker." *Courier de Provence* 128 (1790): 303–34.

————. *Dissection du projet de M. l'évêque d'Autun. Sur l'échange universel et direct des créances de l'état contre les biens nationaux*. Paris, 3 July 1790.

————. *Réponse au mémoire de M. Necker concernant les assignats*. Paris, 15 September 1790.

————. *Réflexions sur les formes et les principes auxquels une nation libre doit assujettir l'administration des finances*. Paris, 1791.

————. "De ce qu'il faut faire dans l'état actuel des finances." *Chronique du mois* 2 (December 1791): 4–30.

————. "De la conjuration contre les finances, et des moyens d'en arrêter les effets." *Chronique du mois* 3 (January 1792): 127–8.

Clavière, Etienne, and Jacques-Pierre Brissot. *De la France et des Etats-Unis* [1787]. Edited by Marcel Dorigny. Paris, Editions du C.T.H.S., 1996.

[Clément, Jean-Marie-Bernard, ed.]. *Les cinq années littéraires, ou nouvelles littéraires des années 1748, 1749, 1750, 1751 & 1752.* 4 vols. The Hague, 1754.

Clermont-Tonnerre, Stanislas-Marie-Adelaide de. *Réflexions sur l'opinion de M. l'abbé Sieyès, concernant les municipalités et le veto.* Paris, 1789.

Cloots, Jean-Baptiste, baron du Val de Grace (Anacharsis). *Voeux d'un Gallophile.* Amsterdam, 1786.

————. *Voeux d'un Gallophile.* New ed. Amsterdam, 1786. Reprinted in Anacharsis Cloots, *Oeuvres*, vol. 2, edited by Albert Soboul. 3 vols. Munich, 1980.

————. *L'Orateur du genre humain, ou dépêche du Prussien Cloots au Prussien Herzberg.* Paris, 1791. Reprinted in Anacharsis Cloots, *Oeuvres*, vol. 3, edited by Albert Soboul. 3 vols. Munich, 1980.

Le Club des Dames, ou les deux partis. Avignon, 1787.

Condillac, Etienne Bonnot de. *Les Monades.* Edited by Laurence L. Bongie. *Studies on Voltaire and the Eighteenth Century* 187 (1980).

————. *Traité des animaux* [1755]. Edited by M. Malherbe. Paris, Vrin, 2004.

Condorcet, Marie-Jean-Antoine-Nicolas de Caritat, marquis de. "Discours de réception." In *Recueil des harangues prononcées par Messieurs de l'Académie française dans leur réception*, 8:413–49. 8 vols. Paris, 1787.

————. *Adresse à l'assemblée nationale sur les conditions d'éligibilité. 5 juin 1790.* Reprinted in Condorcet, *Oeuvres*, 10:77–91, edited by A. Condorcet O'Connor and F. Arago, 12 vols. [1847]. Hamburg, 1968.

————. *Sketch for a Historical Picture of the Progress of the Human Mind* [1795]. Edited by Stuart Hampshire. London, 1955.

————. *Tableau historique des progrès de l'esprit humain. Projets, Esquisse, Fragments et Notes (1772–1794).* Edited by Jean-Pierre Schandeler and Pierre Crépel. Paris, Institut National des Etudes Démographiques, 2004.

The Contrast, with corrections and restorations. And an introductory dissertation on the origins of the feuds and animosities in the state. London, 1765.

Court de Gebelin, Antoine. *Le monde primitif, analysé et comparé avec le monde moderne.* 9 vols. Paris, 1773–83.

Coyer, Gabriel-François. *Développement et défense du système de la noblesse commerçante.* 2 vols. Amsterdam, 1757.

Cubières-Palmézeaux, Michel de. *Les états-généraux du Parnasse, de l'Europe, de l'église, et de Cythère, ou les quatre poèmes politiques.* Paris, 1791.

Cuppé, Pierre. *Le ciel ouvert à tous les hommes* [1743]. Translated by Paolo Cristofolini as *Il cielo aperto di Pierre Cuppé.* Florence, Olschki, 1981.

Dagge, Henry. *Considerations on Criminal Law.* 3rd ed. 3 vols. London, 1774.

Dalmas, Victor de. *Mémoire sur le zodiaque en faveur de la religion chrétienne.* Paris, 1823.

Daunou, Pierre-Claude-François. *Le contrat social des français.* Paris, 1789.

————. *Vues rapides sur l'organisation de la république française.* Paris, 1793.

Davies, Edward. *Celtic Researches, on the Origin, Traditions and Language of the Ancient Britons, with some Introductory Sketches on Primitive Society*. London, 1804.

De l'équilibre des trois pouvoirs politiques, ou lettres au représentant du peuple Lanjuinais. Paris, an III/1795.

Décret important de l'assemblée nationale. N.p., n.d.

Delacroix, Jacques-Vincent. *A Review of the Principal States of Europe and of the United States of America*. 2 vols. London, 1792.

Delandine, Antoine-François. "Observations sur les romans et en particulier sur ceux de Mme de Tencin." In Mme de Tencin, *Oeuvres*, vol. 1. 7 vols. Paris, 1786.

Delolme, Jean-Louis. *An Essay on the Constitution of England*. London, 1776.

Deluc, Jean-André. *Lettres sur l'histoire physique de la terre adressées à M. le professeur Blumenbach*. Paris, 1798.

Des principes et des causes de la révolution française. London, 1790

[Desbans, Louis]. *Les principes naturels du droit et de la politique*. Edited by J. F. Dreux du Radier. Paris, 1765.

Descartes, René. *Les passions de l'âme* [1649]. Translated by Stephen H. Voss as *The Passions of the Soul*. Indianapolis, Hackett, 1989.

———. *Traité des passions* [1649]. Edited by François Mizrachi. Paris, 1965.

Deschamps, Léger-Marie. *Lettres sur l'esprit du siècle*. London, 1769.

———. *Le Vrai système de la nature*. In Léger-Marie Deschamps, *Oeuvres philosophiques*, edited by Bernard Delhaume. 2 vols. Paris, Vrin, 1993.

———. *Correspondance générale établie à partir des archives d'Argenson*. Edited by Bernard Delhaume. Paris, Champion, 2006.

Desmoulins, Camille. "Eloge de M. Loustallot" [September 1790]. Reprinted in Alphonse Aulard, *La société des Jacobins. Recueil de documents pour l'histoire du club des Jacobins de Paris*, vol. 1. 6 vols. Paris, 1889–97.

———. *Le Vieux Cordelier* [no. 3, 15 December 1793]. Edited by Henri Calvet. Paris, 1936.

Dialogue de la mode et de la nature. 2nd ed. N.p., 1662.

Diderot, Denis. *Essai sur le mérite et la vertu*. Paris, 1748.

———. *Réfutation suivie de l'ouvrage d' Helvétius intitulé "L'Homme"* [1775] and *Essai sur les règnes de Claude et de Néron* [1780]. In Denis Diderot, *Oeuvres*, vol. 1, *Philosophie*, edited by Laurent Versini. 5 vols. Brussels, Robert Laffont, 1994–7.

———. *Le Neveu de Rameau*. Edited by Jean Fabre. Geneva, Droz, 1950.

———. *Le Neveu de Rameau*. Edited by Henri Coulet. In Denis Diderot, *Oeuvres complètes*, vol. 12. 23 vols. Paris, Hermann, 1989.

———. *Political Writings*. Edited by Robert Wokler and John Hope Mason. Cambridge, CUP, 1992.

Diderot, Denis, and Jean Le Rond d'Alembert, eds. *Encyclopédie*. 17 vols. Paris, 1751–68.

[Dingé, Antoine]. *L'écho de l'Elysée, ou dialogues de quelques morts célèbres sur les etats-généraux de la nation et des provinces*. N.p., October 1788.

Diogenes Laertius. *Les vies des plus illustres philosophes de l'antiquité*. 3 vols. Amsterdam, 1758.

Le disciple de Montesquieu à MM les députés aux états-généraux. N.p., 1789.

Domat, Jean. *A Treatise of Laws* [Paris, 1689]. Translated by William Strahan. London, 1722.

Dubos, Jean-Baptiste. *Réflexions critiques sur la poésie et la peinture* [1719]. Utrecht, 1732.

Duguet, Jacques-Joseph, and Hilarion Monnier. *Réfutation du système de M. Nicole touchant la grâce universelle*. Paris, 1716.

Duport, Adrien. *Des assignats*. Paris, 1790.

Dupuis, Charles-François. *Mémoire sur l'origine des constellations et sur l'explication de la fable par le moyen de l'astronomie*. Paris, 1781.

Durand-Maillane, Pierre-Toussaint. *Examen critique du projet de constitution présenté à la Convention nationale*. Paris, 1793.

Dusaulx, Jean. *De la passion du jeu depuis les temps anciens jusqu'à nos jours*. Paris, 1779.

[———]. *Observations sur l'histoire de la Bastille publiée par Monsieur Linguet*. London, 1784.

———. *Motion faite à la convention nationale, après la pétition des exécuteurs testamentaires de Mably, pour demander en faveur de ce grand homme, les honneurs du Panthéon française*. Paris, 1795.

———. *Satires de Juvénal* [1770]. 2 vols. Paris, 1803.

Dutens, Louis. *The Tocsin, or an appeal to good sense* [1769]. London, 1800.

Eaton, Daniel. *Politics for the People; or a salmagundi for swine*. 2 vols. London, 1794–5.

The Englishman's Miscellany. London, 1742.

Espiard de la Borde, François-Ignace. *Essai sur le génie et le caractère des nations* [1743].

An Essay on the Constitution of England. London, 1765.

Exposé historique des écrits de Sieyès. N.p., an VIII/1799.

Fauchet, Claude. *De la religion nationale*. Paris, 1789.

[———]. *Le despotisme décrété par l'assemblée nationale*. London, 1790.

Fénelon, François de Salignac de la Mothe. *Telemachus* [1715]. Edited by Patrick Riley. Cambridge, CUP, 1994.

———. *The Lives and Most Remarkable Maxims of the Ancient Philosophers* [1726]. London, 1726.

———. *A Dissertation on Pure Love*. Dublin, 1739.

———. *Oeuvres*. Edited by Aimé Martin. 3 vols. Paris, 1835.

Ferrières, Jacques-Annibal. *Plan d'un nouveau banque nationale et territoriale*. Paris, 1789.

Fichte, Johann Gottlieb. *Der Geschlossene Handelsstaat* [1800]. Translated as *L'état commercial fermé*, edited by Daniel Schulthess. Lausanne, L'âge d'homme, 1980.

———. *Conférences sur la destination du savant*. Translated by J. L. Vieillard-Baron. Paris, Vrin, 1980.

———. *Early Philosophical Writings*. Translated and edited by Daniel Breazeale. Ithaca, Cornell UP, 1988.

Filangieri, Gaetano. *The Science of Legislation* [1784]. London, 1791.

Flanders Delineated. London, 1745.

Fleury, Claude. *Moeurs des Israélites* [1681]. Reprinted in his *Oeuvres*, edited by Louis Aimé-Martin. Paris, 1837.

———. *Moeurs*. Lyon, 1808.

———. *Réflexions sur les oeuvres de Machiavel*. Reprinted in his *Oeuvres*, edited by Louis Aimé-Martin. Paris, 1837.

Le fonds des dîmes ecclésiastiques mis en circulation, ou création d'un crédit territorial pour la liquidation de la dette de l'état. N.p., 18 September 1789.

Fontanes, Louis de. "Discours prononcé au nom des professeurs des écoles centrales." *Magasin encyclopédique* 7 (1796): 508–17.

Forster, Nathaniel. *A Sermon Preached at the Visitation of the Rev. Dr. Moss, Archdeacon of Colchester at St. Peter's Colchester, May 20, 1765 and before the University of Oxford, May 24, 1767.* Oxford, 1767.

Fragment d'un roman philosophique du célèbre Haller sur les principes d'un bon gouvernement. N.p., 1790.

Frederick II, King of Prussia. *Letters between Frederick II and M. de Voltaire.* 3 vols. London, 1789.

[Frey, Junius]. *Philosophie sociale. Dédiée au peuple françois.* Paris, 1793.

Fuseli, Henry [Fuessli, Johann Heinrich]. *Remarks on the Writings and Conduct of J. J. Rousseau.* London, 1767.

[Gay, John]. *The Guardian* [1714–5], 3rd ed. 2 vols. London, 1723.

Garat, Dominique-Joseph. *Eloge de Michel de l'Hôpital, chancelier de France.* Paris, 1778.

———. [On Diderot.] *Mercure de France,* 15 February 1779, pp. 172–90

———. Review of Lacretelle, *Mélanges philosophiques de jurisprudence. Mercure de France,* 25 March 1779, pp. 277–89.

———. Review of [André Liquier], *"Discours qui a remporté le prix de l'académie de Marseille,* sur cette question, *Quelle a été dans tous les temps l'influence du commerce sur l'esprit et les moeurs des peuples?" Mercure de France,* 15 April 1779, pp. 149–63.

———. Account of Chamfort's reception speech of 19 July 1781 to the Académie française. *Mercure de France,* 1 September 1781, pp. 14–34.

———. Account of Condorcet's reception speech of 21 February 1782 to the Académie française. *Mercure de France,* 6 April 1782, pp. 9–36.

———. Review of abbé Robin, *Nouveau voyage dans l'Amérique septentrionale en l'année 1781. Mercure de France,* 1 March 1783, pp. 55–73.

———. Review of M.P.D.L.C., *Lettres sur l'état primitif de l'homme jusqu'à la naissance de l'esclavage. Mercure de France,* 19 July 1783, pp. 103–21, 151–77.

———. Review of Pierre Chabrit, *De la monarchie française. Mercure de France,* 6 March 1784, pp. 9–27; 10 April 1784, pp. 58–80.

———. Review of [Anon.], *Loix municipales et économiques du Languedoc. Mercure de France,* 12 December 1784, pp. 54–68; 19 February 1785, pp. 103–32.

———. Account of Morellet's reception speech to the Académie française. *Mercure de France,* 16 June 1785, pp. 114–36.

———. "Réponse de M. Garat à une lettre du docteur du province à un docteur de Paris sur un article du Mercure." *Mercure de France,* August 1785, pp. 155–85.

———. Review of Rivarol, *De l'universalité de la langue française. Mercure de France,* 6 August 1785, pp. 10–34.

———. Review of d'Albisson, *Discours sur l'origine des municipalités de Languedoc. Mercure de France,* 9 June 1787, pp. 55–69.

Garnier, Germain. *De la propriété dans ses rapports avec le droit politique.* Paris, 1792.

Gifford, Richard. *Remarks on Mr. Kennicott's Dissertation upon the Tree of Life in Paradise.* London, 1748.

Gifford, William. "An Essay on the Roman Satirists." In William Gifford, ed., *The Satires of Decimus Junius Juvenalis*. London, 1802.

Gilbert, Nicolas-Joseph-Laurent. *Oeuvres complètes*. Paris, 1823.

Goguet, Antoine-Yves. *De l'origine des loix, des arts, des sciences*. 3 vols. Paris, 1758.

Gordon, John. *A New Estimate of Manners and Principles: Being a Comparison between Ancient and Modern Times*. Cambridge, 1760.

Gordon, Thomas. *The Works of Sallust Translated into English, with Political Discourses on that Author*. London, 1744.

Gorsas, Antoine-Joseph. *Le Courrier de Paris dans les provinces et des provinces à Paris*.

———. *Le Courrier des LXXXIII départements*.

———. *L'âne promeneur, ou Critès promené par son âne*. Paris, 1786.

———. *La Plume du coq de Micille, ou aventures de Critès au salon, pour servir de suites aux Promenades de 1785* [1787]. In René Démoris and Florence Ferran, eds., *La peinture en procès. L'invention de la critique de l'art au siècle des lumières*, pp. 285–369. Paris, Presses de la Sorbonne Nouvelle, 2004.

[———]. *Mais! ... Qu'est-ce qu'un sans-culotte?* Paris, Imprimerie Gorsas, n.d. [1793].

Gouget-Deslandres, Maurice. *Sérieux et dernier examen sur le rachat de la chose publique*. Paris, 1790. Reprinted in Alphonse Aulard, *La société des Jacobins. Recueil de documents pour l'histoire du club des Jacobins de Paris*, 1:204–25. 6 vols. Paris, 1889–97.

[Gourcy, François-Antoine-Etienne de]. *Des droits et des devoirs du citoyen dans les circonstances présentes, avec un jugement impartial sur l'ouvrage de M. l'abbé Mably*. N.p., 1789.

Grégoire, Henri. *Rapport et projet de décret présenté par le comité d'instruction publique à la séance du 8 août*. Paris, 1793.

Grimm, Friedrich-Melchior, and Jacques-Henri Meister. *Correspondance secrète, politique et littéraire*. 18 vols. London, 1787–90.

Grivel, Charles. "Lettre sur les économistes." In *Encyclopédie Méthodique. Economie Politique*, 2:186–96. 4 vols. Paris, 1784–91.

Grosley, Jean-Pierre. *Londres*. 3 vols. Neuchâtel, 1774.

Grouvelle, Philippe-Antoine. *De l'autorité de Montesquieu dans la révolution présente*. Reprinted in *Bibliothèque de l'homme public*, vol. 7. 12 vols. Paris, 1790.

Grove, Henry. *A System of Moral Philosophy*. 2 vols. London, 1749.

Guffroy, Armand-Benoit-Joseph. *Le Tocsin sur la permanence de la garde nationale, sur l'organisation des municipalités et des assemblées provinciales*. Paris, 1789.

Guiraudet, Toussaint. *Qu'est-ce que la nation et qu'est-ce que la France?* N.p., 1789.

Guyot Desfontaines, Pierre-François. *Dictionnaire néologique à l'usage des beaux esprits du siècle, avec l'éloge historique de Pantalon-Phoebus*. N.p., 1726.

Harrington, James. *The Commonwealth of Oceana* [1656]. Edited by J.G.A. Pocock. Cambridge, CUP, 1977.

Hegel, Georg Friedrich Wilhelm. *Phenomenology of Spirit* [1807]. Translated by A. V. Miller. Oxford, OUP, 1977.

Herder, Johann Gottfried. *Selected Early Works, 1764–1767*. Edited by Ernest A. Menze and Karl Menges. Pittsburgh, Penn State UP, 1992.

———. "On the cognition and sensation of the human soul" [1778]. In Johann Gottfried Herder, *Philosophical Writings*, edited by Michael N. Forster. Cambridge, CUP, 2002.

Herrenschwand, Jean-Fréderic. *De l'économie politique moderne. Discours fondamental sur la population.* London, 1786.

Hirzel, Johann Caspar. *Le Socrate rustique, ou description de la conduite économique et morale d'un paysan philosophe.* 2nd ed. Zurich, 1764.

His, Charles. *Théorie du monde politique, ou de la science du gouvernement considérée comme science exacte.* Paris, 1806.

Holbach, Pierre-Paul Thiry, baron d'. *Système social* [1773]. 2 vols. Paris, 1795.

Hooke, Nathaniel. *The Roman History, from the Building of Rome to the Ruin of the Commonwealth.* 4 vols. London, 1738–71.

Huet, Pierre-Daniel. "De l'origine des romans." In Jean-Regnaud de Segrais [but actually Mme de Lafayette], *Zayde, histoire espagnole,* 1:5–67. 2 vols. Paris, 1671.

Hume, David. *The Letters of David Hume.* Edited by J.Y.T. Greig [1932]. 2 vols. Oxford, OUP, 1969.

Idées à communiquer aux états-généraux. N.p., 1789.

Imbert de la Platière, Sulpice. *Vie Philosophique, politique et littéraire de Rivarol.* Paris, 1802.

Iselin, Isaak. *Pariser Tagebuch 1752.* Edited by Ferdinand Schwarz. *Basler Jahrbuch.* Basel, 1923.

Jacobi, Friedrich Heinrich. *The Main Philosophical Writings and the Novel "Allwill".* Edited by George di Giovanni. Montreal, McGill-Queen's UP, 1994.

Jeannot et Diogène à Paris. N.p., n.d.

Jebb, John. *The Works.* 3 vols. London, 1787.

Jefferson, Thomas. *The Papers of Thomas Jefferson.* Edited by Julian Boyd et al. 33 vols. to date. Princeton, Princeton UP, 1950–.

Les jetons. Apologue politico-économique. Paris, 1789.

Jones, Sir William. "Dissertation on the Antiquity of the Indian Zodiac" and "Dissertation on the Chronology of the Hindus." In Sir William Jones, *Dissertations and Miscellaneous Pieces Relating to the History and Antiquities, the Arts, Sciences, and Literature of Asia.* 2 vols. London, 1792.

Joubert, Joseph. *Essais 1779–1821.* Edited by Rémy Tessonneau. Paris, Nizet, 1983.

———. *Carnets.* Edited by David Kinloch and Philippe Mangeot. London, University of London Institute of Romance Studies, 1996.

Joux, Pierre de. *Lettres sur l'Italie.* 2 vols. Paris, 1825.

Kaestner, Abraham Gotthelf. "Réflexions sur l'origine du plaisir, où l'on tache de prouver l'idée de Descartes qu'il naît toujours du sentiment de la perfection de nous-mêmes." In *Le temple du bonheur, ou recueil des plus excellents traités sur le bonheur, extraits des meilleurs auteurs anciens et modernes,* 3:191–204. 3 vols. Bouillon, 1769.

Kant, Immanuel. *Conjectures on the Beginning of Human History.* In Immanuel Kant, *Political Writings,* edited by Hans Reiss. Cambridge, CUP, 1991.

———. *Toward Perpetual Peace* [1795]. In Immanuel Kant, *Practical Philosophy,* translated and edited by Mary J. Gregor. Cambridge, CUP, 1996.

———. *The Metaphysics of Morals* [1797]. In Immanuel Kant, *Practical Philosophy,* translated and edited by Mary Gregor. Cambridge, CUP, 1996.

———. *Lectures on Ethics.* Edited by Peter Heath and J. B. Schneewind. Cambridge, CUP, 1997.

Kennicott, Benjamin. *Two Dissertations: The First on the Tree of Life in Paradise . . . The Second on the Oblations of Cain and Abel.* Oxford, 1747.

Kippis, Andrew. *Biographia Britannica: or The Lives of The Most Eminent Persons who have Flourished in Great Britain, From the Earliest Ages.* 5 vols. London, 1778–93.

[Knox, Vicesimus]. *The Spirit of Despotism.* London, 1795.

[La Barre de Beaumarchais, Antoine de]. *Lettres sérieuses et badines sur les ouvrages des savants et sur d'autres matières.* 8 vols. The Hague, 1729–33.

Laborde, Jean-Benjamin. *Essai sur la musique ancienne et moderne.* 4 vols. Paris, 1780.

Lafitau, Joseph-François. *Customs of the American Indians Compared with the Customs of Primitive Times* [1724]. Edited and translated by William N. Fenton and Elizabeth L. Moore. 2 vols. Toronto, The Champlain Society, 1974.

Laharpe, Jean-François. *Lycée.* 16 vols. Paris, 1799–1805.

Langlès, Louis-Mathieu. *Fables et contes indiens nouvellement traduits avec un discours préliminaire sur la religion, la littérature, les moeurs, etc. des Hindous.* Paris, 1790.

Lanjuinais, Joseph de. *Le monarque accompli, ou prodiges de bonté, de savoir et de sagesse qui font l'éloge de sa majesté impériale Joseph II.* 3 vols. Lausanne, 1774.

Lanthénas, François-Xavier. "De l'influence de la liberté sur la santé, la morale et le Bonheur." *Chronique du mois,* June 1792. Paris, 1792.

———. *Bases fondamentales de l'instruction publique et de toute constitution libre, ou moyens de lier l'opinion publique, la morale, l'éducation, l'enseignement, l'instruction, les fêtes, la propagation des lumières, et le progrès de toutes les connaissances, au Gouvernement national républicain* [Paris, 1793]. 2nd ed. Paris, Vendémiaire an III/1795.

———. *Motifs de faire du 10 août un jubilé fraternel.* Paris, 1793.

Larry, Isaac de. *Histoire des sept sages.* 2 vols. Rotterdam, 1714.

Lavoisier, Antoine. *Réflexions sur les assignats et sur la liquidation de la dette exigible ou arriérée, lue à la société de 1789, le 29 août 1790.* Paris, 1790.

Law, John. *Oeuvres.* Edited by Gabriel de Sénovert. Paris, 1790.

Le Maître de Claville, Charles-François-Nicolas. *Traité du vrai mérite de l'homme* [1734]. Amsterdam, 1759.

Le Mierre, Antoine-Marin. "L'empire de la mode" [1754]. Reprinted in his *Oeuvres,* vol. 3. 3 vols. Paris, 1810.

[Le Gros, Jean-Charles-François]. *Analyse des ouvrages de J. J. Rousseau de Genève, et de M. Court de Gebelin, auteur du Monde primitif, par un solitaire.* Paris, 1785.

[———]. *Examen des systèmes de J. J. Rousseau de Genève, et de M. Court de Gebelin, auteur du Monde primitif, par un solitaire.* Paris, 1786.

[Le Guay de Prémontval, André-Pierre]. *L'esprit de Fontenelle ou recueil de pensées tirés de ses ouvrages.* The Hague, 1753.

Lebrun, Charles-François, *La voix du citoyen* [n.p., 1789]. Paris, 1814.

Lebrun, Pons-Denis Ecouchard. *Oeuvres.* 4 vols. Paris, 1811.

Leibniz, Gottfried Wilhelm. *Essais de Théodicée* [1709]. 2 vols. Edited by Paul Janet. Paris, 1866.

———. *New Essays on Human Understanding.* Cambridge, CUP, 1981.

Lemercier de la Rivière, Pierre-Paul. *L'ordre naturel et essentiel des sociétés politiques* [1767]. Edited by Edgard Depitre. Paris, 1910.

———. *L'intérêt général de l'état ou la liberté du commerce des grains.* Amsterdam and Paris, 1770.

Lenglet, Etienne-Géry. *De la propriété et de ses rapports avec les droits et avec la dette du citoyen.* Paris, an VI/1797.

Lettre à M. D. par M. L., ou examen d'un ouvrage intitule "Réflexions sur les immunités" ecclésiastiques. Paris, 1788.

Lettres sur les préjugés du siècle. The Hague, 1760.

Levesque de Pouilly, Louis-Jean. *Théorie des sentiments agréables.* Dublin, 1749.

Ligne, Charles-Joseph, prince de. *Mémoires et mélanges historiques et littéraires.* 5 vols. Paris, 1827–9.

Linguet, Simon-Nicolas-Henri. *Annales politiques, civiles, et littéraires du dix-huitième siècle.* London, 1777.

———. *Mémoires sur la Bastille, et sur la détention de M. Linguet, écrits par lui-même.* London, 1783.

———. *Memoirs of the Bastille.* London, 1783.

Liste des Sans-Culotte [sic]. Paris, 1791.

Locke, John. *A Letter Concerning Toleration* [1689]. London, 1765.

Longchamps, Pierre de. *Tableau historique des gens de lettres.* 6 vols. Paris, 1767–70.

Le luxe considéré relativement à la population et à l'économie. Lyon, 1762.

Mably, Gabriel Bonnot de. *Observations sur les Grecs* [Geneva, 1749].

——— *Observations sur les Romains* [1751]. Reprinted in his *Oeuvres*, vol. 4. 12 vols. Paris, 1794–5.

———. *Observations on the Romans* [1751]. London, 1751.

———. *Observations sur l'histoire de la Grèce.* [Geneva, 1766].

———. *Du gouvernement et des loix de la Pologne* [1770]. In Mably, *Oeuvres*, vol. 8.

———. *De l'étude de l'histoire* [1775]. In Mably, *Oeuvres*, vol. 12.

———. *De l'étude de l'histoire* [1775]. Edited by Barbara de Negroni. Paris, Fayard, 1988.

———. *De la législation ou principes des lois* [1776]. In Mably, *Collection complète des Oeuvres*, edited by Peter Friedemann, vol. 9. 15 vols. Aalen, Scientia Verlag, 1977.

———. *Le Destin de la France* [1781]. In Mably, *Oeuvres*, vol. 13.

———. *Observations sur le gouvernement et les loix des Etats-Unis.* Amsterdam, 1784.

———. *Remarks concerning the Government and the Laws of the United States of America.* London, 1784.

———. *Observations on the Manners, Government, and Policy of the Greeks.* Oxford, 1784.

———. *Principes de morale* [1784]. In Mably, *Oeuvres*, vol. 10. 14 vols. Paris, 1797.

———. *Des droits et des devoirs du citoyen* [1789]. Edited by Jean-Louis Lecercle. Paris, Marcel Didier, 1972.

———. *Principes des négociations*, in Mably, *Oeuvres*, vol. 5.

———. *Oeuvres complètes.* 13 vols. London, 1789–90.

———. *Le droit public de l'Europe fondé sur les traités.* In Mably, *Oeuvres*, vol. 6..

———. *De la législation.* Reprinted in the *Bibliothèque de l'homme public*, vol. 7. 12 vols. Paris, 1790.

———. "Des talents." In Mably, *Collection complète des Oeuvres* [Paris, 1794–95], edited by Peter Friedemann, vol. 14. 15 vols. Aalen, Scientia Verlag, 1977.

———. "Du développement, des progrès, et des bornes de la raison." In Mably, *Collection complète des Oeuvres* [1797], edited by Peter Friedemann, vol. 15. 15 vols. Ahlen, Scientia Verlag, 1977.

Machiavelli, Niccolò. *Discourses.* Introduced by Max Lerner. New York, 1950.

Madison, James. "Essay on Money" [1791]. In *Selected Writings of James Madison*, edited with an introduction by Ralph Ketcham. Indianapolis, Hackett, 2006.

Maimbourg, Louis. *The History of Arianism*. 2 vols. London, 1728–9.

Mallet du Pan, Jacques. "Deux lettres inédites de Mallet du Pan." *Mémoires et documents de la société d'histoire et d'archéologie de Genève*, 22:9–11. Geneva, 1886.

[Mandrillon, Joseph]. *Révolutions des provinces unies sous l'étendard des divers stadhouders*. 3 vols. Nijmegen, 1788.

[Manuel, Pierre-Louis]. *Essais historiques, critiques, littéraires et philosophiques*. Geneva, 1783.

[Marat, Jean-Paul]. *A Philosophical Essay on Man. Being an Attempt to investigate the Principles and Laws of the Reciprocal Influence of the Soul on the Body*. 2nd ed. 2 vols. London, 1775.

Marivaux, Pierre Carlet de Chamblain de. *La vie de Marianne* [1741]. Edited by Frédéric Deloffre. Paris, Garnier, 1963.

Maurice, Thomas. *Indian Antiquities*. 5 vols. London, 1793–4.

Mayer, M. de. "Origine des étrennes." In [Antoine François Delandine, ed.], *Le conservateur, ou bibliothèque choisie de littérature, de morale et d'histoire*, 1:1 et seq. Paris, 1787.

Mazzei, Filippo. *Historical and Political Researches on the United States* [1788]. Charlottesville, University of Virginia Press, 1976.

Meister, Jacques-Henri. *De la morale naturelle*. Paris, 1787.

Mémoire pour les marchands merciers, et les fabricants d'étoffes de soie, d'or, et d'argent de la ville de Paris. Paris, 1772. B. N. Collection Joly de Fleury, Mss. 1426, fol. 168.

Mémoires de la Bastille, sous les règnes de Louis XIV, Louis XV et Louis XVI. London, 1784.

Mercier, Louis-Sébastien. *L'An deux mille quatre cent quarante quatre, rêve s'il en fut jamais* [1770]. Edited by Raymond Trousson. Bordeaux, Editions Ducros, 1961.

———. *De la littérature et des littérateurs*. Lausanne, 1778.

———. *Tableau de Paris* [1781]. 12 vols. Amsterdam, 1782–8.

———. *Tableau de Paris* [1781]. Edited by Jean-Claude Bonnet, Shelly Charles, and Michel Schlupp. 2 vols. Paris, Mercure de France, 1994.

———. *Mon Bonnet de Nuit* [1784]. Translated as *The Nightcap*. 2 vols. London, 1785.

———. *Notions claires sur les gouvernements*. 2 vols. Amsterdam, 1787.

———. *De Jean-Jacques Rousseau, considéré comme l'un des premiers auteurs de la révolution*. Paris, 1791.

———. "De la ligue." *Chronique du mois*, July 1792, pp. 58–80.

———. "Portrait de Choiseul." *Chronique du mois*, September 1792, pp. 49–60.

———. *Fragments of Politics and History*. 2 vols. London, 1795.

———. *Astraea's Return, or the Halcyon Days of France in the Year 2440*. London, 1797.

———. *Le Nouveau Paris* [1799]. Paris, 1862.

———. *New Picture of Paris*. 2 vols. London, 1800.

Merian, Johann Bernhard. "Parallèle de deux principes de psychologie." In *Histoire de l'Académie Royale des Sciences et Belles Lettres, année 1757*, pp. 375–91. Berlin, 1759.

Merlin de Douai, Philippe-Antoine. *Rapport fait à l'assemblée nationale au nom du comité de féodalité, le 8 février 1790*. Paris, 1790.

[Métra, François]. *Correspondance secrète, politique et littéraire*. 18 vols. London, 1787–90.

[Michaux, P. G.]. *Les coutumes, considérées comme loi de la nation*. Paris, 1783.

Michel, Jean-André. *Discours sur l'immortalité de l'âme*. Paris, 1790.

Mignet, François-Auguste-Marie-Alexis. *History of the French Revolution from 1789 to 1814* [1824]. London, 1846.

Mignot, Etienne. *Traité des droits de l'état et du prince sur les biens possédés par le clergé*. 6 vols. Amsterdam, 1755–7.

[Millot, Claude-François-Xavier]. *Histoire philosophique de l'homme*. London, 1766.

Mirabeau, Honoré Gabriel Riqueti, comte de. *De la monarchie prussienne sous Frédéric le Grand*. 4 vols. London, 1786.

Mirabeau, Victor Riqueti, marquis de. *L'Ami des hommes*. Avignon, 1756.

———. *Philosophie rurale, ou économie générale et politique de l'agriculture* [1763]. Amsterdam, 1764.

———. *Précis de l'ordre légal*. Paris, 1768.

———. *Lettres sur la législation, ou l'ordre légal dépravé, rétabli et perpétué* [London, 1769]. 2nd ed. Berne, 1775.

———. *Hommes à célébrer, pour avoir, en ces dernières âges, mérité de leur siècle et de l'humanité, relativement à l'instruction politique et économique*. 2 vols. N.p., 1789.

[Monnais, Guillaume-Edouard-Désiré, ed.] *Ephémérides universelles*. 13 vols. Paris, 1828–33.

Montesquieu, Charles-Louis de Secondat, baron de. *Lettres persanes* [1721]. Edited by Paul Vernière. Paris, 1960.

———. *The Spirit of Laws* [1748]. Translated by Thomas Nugent. New York, Hafner Publishing Company, 1949.

Moore, Charles. *A Full Inquiry into the Subject of Suicide*. London, 1790.

Moore, John. *A Journal during a Residence in France from the Beginning of August to the Middle of December 1792*. 2 vols. London, 1793.

[Morande, Charles Theveneau de]. *Le philosophe cynique, pour servir de suite aux anecdotes scandaleuses de la cour de France*. London, 1771.

Morellet, André. *De l'expression en musique et de l'imitation dans les arts* [1771]. In André Morellet, *Mélanges de littérature et de philosophie du 18e siècle*, 2:366–413. 2 vols. Paris, 1818.

———, ed. *Eloges de Mme Geoffrin, par MM Morellet, Thomas et d'Alembert*. Paris, 1812.

[Morelly, Etienne-Gabriel]. *Naufrage des isles flottantes, ou Basiliade du célèbre Pilpai. Poème héroïque*. Messina, 1742.

Morhof, Daniel Georg. *Polyhistor*. Lubeck, 1688.

Mouffle d'Angerville, Barthélémy-François-Joseph. *Vie privée de Louis XV*. 4 vols. London, 1781.

Mounier, Jean-Joseph. *Considérations sur les gouvernements, et principalement sur celui qui convient à la France*. Versailles, 1789.

———. *Nouvelles observations sur les états-généraux de France*. N.p., 1789.

———. *Réflexions politiques sur les circonstances présentes*. Geneva, 1790.

Muralt, Béat-Louis de. *Lettres sur les anglais et les français* [1725]. Lausanne, Bibliothèque romande, 1972.

———. *Lettres sur les anglais et les français* [1728]. Edited by Charles Gould. Paris, 1933.

Naigeon, Jean-André. *Théologie portative, ou dictionnaire abrégé de la religion chrétienne.* London, 1768.

———. *Adresse à l'assemblée nationale sur la liberté des opinions, sur celle de la presse, etc.* Paris, 1790.

———. *Mémoires historiques et philosophiques sur la vie et les ouvrages de D. Diderot.* Paris, 1821.

La Nation Sans Culotte. Paris, n.d.

Necker, Jacques. *De la morale naturelle, et du bonheur des sots.* Paris, 1788.

The New Ministry. London, 1742.

Nicole, Pierre. *Traité de la grâce générale.* 2 vols. Paris, 1715.

[Nihell, Laurence]. *Rational Self-Love; or a* Philosophical and Moral Essay *on the Natural Principles of Happiness and Virtue: with Reflections on the various Systems of Philosophers, Ancient and Modern, on this Subject* [1770]. London, 1773.

Oberlin, John Frederick. *Memoirs of John Frederick Oberlin, Pastor of Waldbach in the Ban de la Roche.* 2nd ed. London, 1833.

Observations sur le règlement de 22 May 1782 [sic] *concernant les preuves de noblesse exigées pour entrer au service.* London, 1789.

[Oelsner, Conrad Engelbert]. *Notice sur la vie de Sieyès.* N.p., 1795.

Ogilvie, William. *Essay on the Right of Property in Land with Respect to its Foundation in the Law of Nature; Its Present Establishment by the Municipal Laws of Europe and the Regulations by which It Might be Rendered more Beneficial to the Lower Ranks of Mankind* [1781]. London, 1782.

Palissot de Montenoy, Charles. *Les Courtisanes.* Reprinted in Charles Palissot de Montenoy, *Oeuvres complètes*, vol. 2. 6 vols. Paris, 1809.

Palmer, John, ed. *Tracts on Law, Government and Other Political Subjects.* London, 1836.

Le parchemin en culotte. Amsterdam, 1789.

Parsons, James. *Remains of Japhet: Being Historical Enquiries into the Affinity and Origin of the European Languages.* London, 1767.

[Perreau, Jean-André]. *Le bon politique, ou le sage à la cour.* London, 1789.

Perroud, Claude, ed. *Lettres de Madame Roland.* 2 vols. Paris, 1900–2.

Pétion de Villeneuve, Jérôme. *Les loix civiles et l'administration de la justice ramenées à un ordre simple et uniforme* [1782]. Reprinted in his *Fragments d'un ouvrage sur les loix civiles.* Paris, 1789.

———. *Essai sur le mariage considéré sous des rapports naturels, moraux et politiques.* Geneva, 1785.

———. *Avis aux français sur le salut de la patrie.* Paris, 1789.

———. *Oeuvres.* 3 vols. Paris, 1792.

[Picardet *aîné*, Henri-Claude]. "Considérations sur les écoles où l'on enseigne l'art du dessin et sur l'utilité d'un pareil établissement en faveur des métiers." *Mémoires de l'Académie de Dijon*, n.s., 2:130–56. Paris and Dijon, 1774.

Pichon, Thomas-Jean. *Le physique de l'histoire, ou considérations générales sur les principes élémentaires du tempérament et du caractère naturel des peuples.* Amsterdam, 1765.

Piermont, Fréderic-Henri Strube de. *Recherche nouvelle de l'origine et des fondements du droit de la nature*. St. Petersburg, 1740.

Pinto, Isaac de. *An Essay on Circulation and Credit in Four Parts, and A Letter on the Jealousy of Commerce*. London, 1774.

Piron, Alexis, *Oeuvres complètes*. 7 vols. Paris, 1776.

Plato. *Republic*. In Plato, *The Collected Dialogues*, edited by Edith Hamilton and Huntingdon Cairns. Princeton, Princeton UP, 1963.

Pliny. *Histoire naturelle*. 12 vols. Paris, 1771–82.

Pluche, Noël-Antoine. *Le spectacle de la nature, ou entretiens sur les particularités de l'histoire naturelle*. 8 vols. Paris, 1732–50.

———. *Spectacle de la nature: or Nature Displayed. Being Discourses on such Particulars of Natural History as were thought most proper to excite the curiosity and form the minds of youth. Containing what belongs to man considered in society*. 7 vols. London, 1748.

Plutarch, *Morals*. 5 vols. London, 1704.

Poinsinet de Sivry, Louis. *Traité des causes physiques et morales du rire*. Paris, 1768.

———. *Origine des premières sociétés, des peuples, des sciences, des arts et des idiomes anciens et modernes*. Amsterdam and Paris, 1769.

———. Introduction to Pliny, *Histoire naturelle*. 12 vols. Paris, 1771–82.

Poiret, Pierre. *L'oeconomie divine, ou système universel et démontré des oeuvres et des desseins de Dieu envers les hommes. Ou l'on explique et prouve d'origine, avec une évidence et une certitude métaphysique, les principes et les vérités de la nature et de la grâce, de la philosophie et de la théologie, de la raison et de la foi, de la morale naturelle et de la religion chrétienne, et ou l'on résout entièrement les grandes et épineuses difficultés sur la prédestination, sur la liberté, sur l'universalité de la rédemption et sur la providence, etc.* 7 vols. Amsterdam, 1687.

———. *The Divine Oeconomy: or An Universal System of the Works and Purposes of God towards Men, Demonstrated*. 6 vols. London, 1713.

Poullain de Saint-Foix. *Essais historiques sur Paris*. 5th ed. 5 vols. Paris, 1776.

Le premier aux grands, ou suite du Fanal. N.p., 1789.

Première collection de pétitions, d'écrits et de mémoires présentés à la nation française et à ses représentants aux états-généraux. Paris, 1789.

Priestley, Joseph. *An Essay on a Course of Liberal Education for Civil and Active Life*. London, 1765.

———. *Political Writings*. Edited by Peter Miller. Cambridge, CUP, 1993.

Prudhomme, Louis-Marie. *Louis Prudhomme aux patriotes, le 13 juin 1793*. Paris, 1793.

Pufendorf, Samuel. *The Divine Feudal Law: or Covenants with Mankind, Represented* [1695]. Edited by Simone Zurbuchen. Indianapolis, Liberty Fund, 2002.

Rabaut Saint-Etienne, Jean-Paul. *Lettres à M. Bailly sur l'histoire primitive de la Grèce*. Paris, 1787.

———. "Réflexions politiques sur les circonstances présentes." In Jean-Paul Rabaut Saint-Etienne, *Précis de l'histoire de la révolution française*, edited by François-Antoine Boissy d'Anglas. Paris, 1827.

Radonvilliers, Claude-François Lezarde de. *Oeuvres diverses*. 3 vols. Paris, 1807.

Ramsay, Andrew Michael. "Discours de la poésie épique et de l'excellence du poème Télémaque." In Fénelon, *Télémaque* [1715]. Amsterdam, 1725.

————. "A Discourse on Epic Poetry" [1719]. In François de Salignac de la Mothe-Fénelon, *Telemachus* [1715]. Dublin, 1764.

————. *The Travels of Cyrus* [1726]. Edinburgh, 1800.

Rapin, Nicolas, Jean Passerat, and Florent Chrestien. *Satyre ménippée, de la vertu du Catholicon d'Espagne et de la tenue des Etats de Paris.* Tours, 1594.

Rapport du 22 janvier 1790 fait par MM les commissaires pour l'examen du plan de M. Ferrières au comité générale du district de Henri IV. Paris, 1790.

Raymond, George-Marie. *Essai sur l'émulation dans l'ordre social, et sur son application à l'éducation.* Geneva, 1802.

Réal de Curban, Gaspard de. *La science du gouvernement: ouvrage de morale, de droit, et de politique.* 8 vols. Aix-la-Chapelle and Paris, 1761–5.

Réflexions sur la constitution de l'Angleterre. Translated by Jean Chas. London, 1789.

"Regrets de Madame de Tencin en mourant." In *La Bigarrure, ou Meslance* [sic] *curieux, instructif et amusant,* p. 103. The Hague, 1753.

Reimarus, Hermann Samuel. *The Principal Truths of Natural Religion Defended and Illustrated in Nine Dissertations, wherein the Objections of Lucretius, Buffon, Maupertuis, Rousseau, La Mettrie and Other Ancient and Modern Followers of Epicurus are Considered and their Doctrines Refuted.* London, 1766.

Richer d'Aube, François-René. *Essai sur les principes du droit et de la morale.* Paris, 1743.

Ripert de Monclar, Jean-Pierre-François. *Les commentaires sur l' "Esprit des lois" de Montesquieu.* Paris, Institut Michel Villey, 2006.

Robespierre, Maximilien. *Adresse de la Société des Amis de la Constitution aux Sociétés qui lui sont affiliées.* Paris, 1791.

————. *Oeuvres.* Edited by Victor Barbier, Marc Bouloiseau, Jean Dautry, Gustave Laurent, Georges Lefebvre, Georges Michon, Albert Soboul, and Charles Vellay. 10 vols. Paris, 1910–67.

Robinet, Jean-Baptiste-René. *De la nature.* Amsterdam, 1757.

————. *Considérations philosophiques de la gradation naturelle des formes de l'être, ou les essais de la nature qui apprend à faire l'homme.* Paris, 1768.

————. "De la parure et de la mode." In Société typographique de Bouillon, *Recueils philosophiques et littéraires,* 1:320–40. 5 vols. Bouillon, 1769–70.

————. *Dictionnaire universel des sciences morale, économique, politique et diplomatique, ou Bibliothèque de l'homme d'état et du citoyen.* 30 vols. London, 1772–83.

Rochefoucauld-Liancourt, Gaëtan de la. *Mémoires de Condorcet sur la révolution française.* 2 vols. Paris, 1824.

Rocques de Montgaillard, abbé Jean-Gabriel-Maurice. *Histoire de France.* 9 vols. Paris, 1827.

Roederer, Pierre-Louis. *Journal d'économie publique.* Paris, 1795–97.

————. *De l'usage à faire de l'autorité publique dans les circonstances présentes.* Paris, 1797.

————. *Mémoires pour servir à l'histoire de la société polie en France.* Paris, 1835.

————. *Oeuvres,* ed. A.-M. Roederer. 7 vols. Paris, 1853–9.

[Romieux, Claude]. *Les éléments du contrat social, ou le développement du droit naturel de l'homme sur la propriété.* Paris, 1792.

Roucher, Jean-Antoine. *Les Mois.* Paris, 1779.

Rousseau, Jean-Jacques. *Oeuvres . . . nouvelle édition.* Neufchâtel [Paris], n.d.

————. "Preface to *Narcissus*" [1752]. In Jean-Jacques Rousseau, *The Discourses and Other Early Political Writings*, edited by Victor Gourevitch. Cambridge, CUP, 1997.

————. *A Discourse on the Origin of Inequality* [1755]. Translated by G.D.H. Cole. Revised and augmented by J. H. Brumfitt and John C. Hall. London, J. M. Dent, 1973.

————. *Discourse on the Origin and the Foundations of Inequality among Men* [1755]. In Jean-Jacques Rousseau, *The Discourses and Other Early Political Writings*, edited by Victor Gourevitch. Cambridge, CUP, 1997.

————. *Letter from J. J. Rousseau to M. de Voltaire* [1756]. In Jean-Jacques Rousseau, *The Discourses and Other Early Political Writings*, edited by Victor Gourevitch. Cambridge, CUP, 1997.

————. *A Letter from M. Rousseau of Geneva to M. d'Alembert of Paris, Concerning the Effects of Theatrical Entertainments on the Manners of Mankind.* London, 1759.

————. *A Discourse upon the Origin and Foundation of the Inequality among Mankind.* London, 1761.

————. *A Project for Perpetual Peace.* London, 1761.

————. *Emile, ou de l'éducation* [1762]. Edited by Michel Launay. Paris, Garnier Flammarion, 1966.

————. *Emile, ou de l'éducation* [1762]. In Jean-Jacques Rousseau, *Oeuvres complètes*, edited by Bernard Gagnebin and Marcel Raymond, vol. 4. 5 vols. Paris, Pléiade, 1959–96.

————. *Emile.* 4 vols. London, 1762.

————. *Emilius and Sophia.* 4 vols. London, 1763.

————. *Emilius, or An Essay on Education.* Translated by Thomas Nugent. 2 vols. London, 1763.

————. *An Expostulatory Letter from J. J. Rousseau, Citizen of Geneva, to Christopher de Beaumont, Archbishop of Paris.* London, 1763.

————. *Eloisa, or a series of original letters collected and published by J. J. Rousseau.* 4 vols. London, 1769.

————. *Considérations sur le gouvernement de Pologne* [1772]. Edited by Barbara de Negroni. Paris, Garnier Flammarion, 1990.

————. *Letters Written from the Mountains.* In Jean-Jacques Rousseau, *Miscellaneous Works*, vol. 3. 4 vols. Edinburgh, 1774.

————. *Reveries of a Solitary Walker* [1778]. Edited and translated by Peter France. Harmondsworth, Penguin Books, 1979.

————. *Pièces diverses.* 4 vols. London, P. Cazin, 1782.

————. *Collection complète des Oeuvres.* Geneva, 1782.

————. *Les Confessions* [1783]. 3 vols. London, 1786.

————. *Oeuvres complètes.* Edited by Louis-Sébastien Mercier, Gabriel Brizard, and Louis Le Tourneur. 38 vols. Paris, 1788–93.

————. *An Inquiry into the Nature of the Social Contract, or Principles of Political Right.* London, 1791.

————. *Lettre à M. d'Alembert sur les spectacles.* Edited by M. Fuchs. Geneva, Droz, 1948.

————. *Oeuvres complètes.* Edited by Bernard Gagnebin and Marcel Raymond. 5 vols. Paris, Pléiade, 1959–95.

————. "Notes sur *De l'Esprit*." In Jean-Jacques Rousseau, *Oeuvres complètes*, edited by Bernard Gagnebin and Marcel Raymond, vol. 4. 5 vols. Paris, Pléiade, 1959–95.

————. *Correspondance complète*. Edited by R. A. Leigh. 52 vols. Oxford, Voltaire Foundation, 1967–98.

————. *Discours sur les sciences et les arts. Discours sur l'origine et les fondements de l'inégalité parmi les hommes*. Edited by Jacques Roger. Paris, Garnier Flammarion, 1971.

————. *Emile*. Edited and translated by Alan Bloom. New York, 1979.

————. *Sur l'économie politique, Considérations sur le gouvernement de Pologne, Projet pour la Corse*. Edited by Barbara de Negroni. Paris, Garnier Flammarion, 1990.

————. *Considerations on the Government of Poland*. In Jean-Jacques Rousseau, *The Social Contract and Other Political Writings*, edited by Victor Gourevitch. Cambridge, CUP, 1997.

————. *The Social Contract*. In Jean-Jacques Rousseau, *The Social Contract and Other Later Political Writings*, edited by Victor Gourevitch. Cambridge, CUP, 1997.

————. *The Discourses and Other Early Political Writings*. Edited by Victor Gourevitch. Cambridge, CUP, 1997.

————. *Essay on the Origin of Languages and Writings Related to Music*. In Jean-Jacques Rousseau, *The Collected Writings*, edited by John T. Scott, vol. 7. Hanover and London, UP of New England, 1998.

Rutherforth, Thomas. *Institutes of Natural Law. Being the substance of a course of lectures on "Grotius de Jure Belli et Pacis" read in St John's College Cambridge*. 2 vols. Cambridge, 1754.

Rutledge, Jean-Jacques. *Le Bureau d'esprit* [1776]. Edited by Pierre Peyronnet. Paris, Champion, 1999.

[————]. *Essais politiques sur l'état actuel de quelques puissances*. London, 1777.

————. *Eloge de Montesquieu*. London, 1786.

Sabatier de Castres, Antoine. *Les trois siècles de notre littérature*. 3 vols. Amsterdam, 1772.

[Sablé, Mme de]. "Discours sur les Réflexions, sentences et maximes morales." In François, duc de la Rochefoucauld, *Réflexions, sentences et maximes morales*, edited by Amelot de la Houssaye. Paris, 1714.

Saint Lambert, Jean-François, marquis de. *Oeuvres philosophiques*. 5 vols. Paris, an IX.

Saint-Haippy [a pseudonym for Antoine-Prosper Lottin]. *Discours sur ce sujet: le luxe corrompt les moeurs et détruit les empires*. 2nd ed. Amsterdam and Paris, 1785.

Saint-Hyacinthe, Claude Thémiseul de. *Le chef d'oeuvre d'un inconnu*. Edited by Henri Duranton. Paris, Editions du CNRS, 1991.

Saint-Just, Louis-Antoine. *Esprit de la revolution et de la constitution de la France* [1791]. Edited by Michel Vovelle. Paris, Editions 10/18, 2003.

————. *Oeuvres complètes*. Edited by Michèle Duval. Paris, Editions Gérard Lebovici, 1984.

————. *Oeuvres complètes*. Edited by Anne Kupiec and Miguel Abensour. Paris, Gallimard, 2004.

Saint-Pierre, Charles Irénée Castel, abbé de. *Projet pour rendre la paix perpétuelle en Europe* [1713]. Edited by Simone Goyard-Fabre. Paris, Garnier, 1981.

————. *A Project for Settling an Everlasting Peace in Europe. First Proposed by Henry IV of France, and Approved of by Queen Elizabeth . . . and now Discussed at Large and Made Practical by the Abbot St. Pierre* [1713]. London, 1714.

———. *Les rêves d'un homme de bien, qui peuvent être réalisés.* Paris, 1775.

Salaville, Jean-Baptiste. *Le moraliste mesmérien, ou Lettres philosophiques sur l'influence du magnétisme.* London, 1784.

———. *De l'organisation d'un état monarchique, ou considérations sur les vices de la monarchie française et nécessité de lui donner une constitution.* Paris, 1789.

———. *L'homme et la société, ou nouvelle théorie de la nature humaine et de l'état social.* Paris, an VII/1799.

———. *De la perfectibilité.* Paris, 1801.

Salchli, Emmanuel. *Les causes finales et la direction du mal.* Berne, 1784.

———. *Le mal, poème philosophique en quatre chants, suivi de remarques et dissertations relatives au sujet.* Berne, 1789.

Salchli, Emmanuel. *Le mal, poème philosophique en neuf chants.* Lausanne, 1813.

Saumaize, Antoine Baudeau, sieur de. *Le grand dictionnaire des prétieuses, historique, poétique, géographique, cosmographique et armoirique.* Paris, 1661.

Schiller, Friedrich. *Medicine, Psychology and Literature.* Edited by Kenneth Dewhurst and Nigel Reeves. Oxford, Sandford Publications, 1978.

[Schmid d'Auenstein, Georg-Ludwig]. *Essais sur divers sujets intéressants de politique et de morale.* 2 vols. N.p., 1761.

———. *Principes de la législation universelle.* 2 vols. Amsterdam, 1776.

Schwab, Raymond. *Vie d'Anquetil-Duperron.* Paris, 1934.

Schwarz, C. G. *Le zodiaque expliqué, ou recherches sur l'origine et la signification des constellations de la sphère grecque.* 2nd ed. Paris, 1809.

Sénovert, Gabriel-Etienne de. *Théorie et pratique des assignats.* Paris, 1790.

[———, ed.] *Oeuvres de J. Law.* Paris, 1790.

[Servan, Antoine-Joseph-Michel]. *La seconde aux grands.* N.p., n.d.

Shaftesbury, Anthony Ashley Cooper, Third Earl. *Characteristics of Men, Manners, Opinions, Times* [2nd ed., 1714]. Edited by Lawrence E. Klein. Cambridge, CUP, 1999.

Sieyès, Emmanuel Joseph. *Observations sommaires sur les biens ecclésiastiques.* Paris, 1789.

———. *Political Writings.* Edited by Michael Sonenscher. Indianapolis, Hackett, 2003.

———. *Views of the Executive Means available to the Representatives of France in 1789.* Translated by Michael Sonenscher. In Sieyès, *Political Writings,* dited by Michael Sonenscher. Indianapolis, Hackett, 2003.

———. *What Is the Third Estate?* Translated by Michael Sonenscher. In Sieyès, *Political Writings,* edited by Michael Sonenscher. Indianapolis, Hackett, 2003.

Silence, Samuel. *The Foundling Hospital for Wit.* London, 1743.

Smellie, William. *The Philosophy of Natural History.* 2 vols. Edinburgh, 1790.

Spon, Jacob. *De l'origine des étrennes* [1674]. Paris, 1781.

Steuart, Sir James. *An Enquiry into the Principles of Political Oeconomy* [1767]. Edited by Andrew Skinner. 2 vols. Edinburgh, 1967.

Stewart, Dugald. "Locke on the Sources of Human Knowledge." In Dugald Stewart, *Philosophical Essays,* edited by Sir William Hamilton. 4th ed. Edinburgh, 1855.

Stuart, Gilbert. *Tableau des progrès de la société en Europe.* 2 vols. Paris, 1789.

Suard, Jean-Baptiste-Antoine. *Mélanges de littérature.* 2nd ed. 5 vols. Paris, 1806.

Suard, Jean-Baptiste-Antoine, and Simon-Jérôme Bourlet de Vauxcelles, eds. *Opuscules philosophiques et littéraires.* Paris, 1796.

Sulzer, Johann Georg. *Nouvelle théorie des plaisirs, avec des réflexions sur les origines du plaisir par Mr Kaestner.* N.p., 1767.

The Summer Miscellany. London, 1742.

"Sur les avantages que l'étude de la physique procure à l'oeconomie." *La nouvelliste oeconomique et littéraire, ou choix de ce qui se trouve de plus curieux, et de plus intéressant dans les journaux, ouvrages périodiques, et autres livres qui paraissent en France et ailleurs,* 1:5–19. The Hague, 1754.

[Théveneau de Morande, Charles]. *Le philosophe cynique, pour servir de suite aux anecdotes scandaleuses de la cour de France.* London, 1771.

Théroigne et Populus, ou le triomphe de la démocratie. Drame nationale en vers civiques. London, 1790.

Tissot, Samuel-Auguste-André-David, and Johann Georg Zimmermann. *Correspondance 1754–1797.* Edited by Antoinette Emch-Dériaz. Geneva, Slatkine, 2007.

Titon du Tillet, Evrard. *Le parnasse français.* Paris, 1732.

Tocnaye, Jacques-Louis de la. *Les causes de la révolution de France et les efforts de la noblesse pour en arrêter les progrès.* Edinburgh, 1797.

Tressan, Louis-Elizabeth de la Vergne, comte de. *Oeuvres choisis,* 12 vols. Paris, 1787–91.

———. "Différentes preuves de la métempsycose, adressées à feu Mme de Tencin." In Tressan, *Oeuvres choisis,* 11:91–5.

———. "Lettre écrite de *** à M. le comte de Caylus sur l'incertitude des sciences élevées et des systèmes." In Tressan, *Oeuvres choisis,* 11:131–5.

Velthusyen, Lambert van. *Epistolica Dissertatio de Principiis Justi, et, Decori* [1651]. Translated as *Des principes du juste et du convenable,* edited by Catherine Secrétan. Caen, Presses Universitaires de Caen, 1995.

Vernet, Jacob. *Réflexions sur les moeurs, sur la religion, et sur le culte.* Geneva, 1769.

Vernier, Thomas. *Éléments de finances.* Paris, 1789.

Vico, Giambattista. *New Science* [1744]. Edited by Anthony Grafton. Translated by David Marsh. London, Penguin Books, 1999.

Villemain, Abel-François. *Cours de littérature française. Examen des ouvrages de Thompson, Young, Hume, Robertson, Gibbon, Ossian, Beccaria, Filangieri, Alfieri, etc.* Paris, 1828.

Villers, Charles de. *Le Magnétiseur amoureux* [1787]. Edited by François Azouvi [1978]. 2nd ed. Paris, Vrin, 2006.

Villette, Charles de. *Lettres choisies sur les principaux évènements de la révolution.* Paris, 1792.

Villoteau, Guillaume-André. *Recherches sur l'analogie de la musique avec les arts qui ont pour objet l'imitation du langage, pour servir d'introduction à l'étude des principes naturels de cet art.* Paris, 1807.

Voeux d'un citoyen pour le militaire français. N.p., n.d.

Volney, Constantin-François. *Voyage en Egypte et en Syrie* [1785]. 6th ed. 3 vols. Paris, 1823.

———. *Moyen très simple pour vendre en moins de deux ans, et sans dépréciation, tous les biens appartenant ci-devant au clergé et au domaine* [1790]. In Constantin-François Volney, *Oeuvres,* vol. 2. 3 vols. Paris, Fayard, 1989–98.

———. *Les ruines* [1791]. In Volney, *Oeuvres*, vol. 1. 3 vols. Paris, Fayard, 1989–98.

———. *The Ruins, or A Survey of the Revolutions of Empires* [1791]. London, 1795.

———. *La loi naturelle, ou catéchisme du citoyen français* [1793]. In Volney, *Oeuvres*, vol. 1. 3 vols. Paris, Fayard, 1989–98.

Voltaire, François-Marie Arouet de. *Zaïre*. Paris, 1732.

———. *La pucelle d'Orléans* [1756]. Paris, 1766.

———. *Le pauvre diable*. In *Le joli recueil ou l'histoire de la querelle littéraire, où les auteurs s'amusent en amusant le public*, pp. 49–72. Geneva, 1760.

———. "De la loi naturelle, et de la curiosité" [1768]. In Voltaire, *Dialogues philosophiques*, edited by Raymond Naves, pp. 280–4. Paris, Garnier, 1966.

———. *Correspondance*. Edited by Theodore Besterman. 13 vols. Paris, Pléiade, 1963–93.

Walckenaer, Charles-Athanase. *Essai sur l'histoire de l'espèce humain*. Paris, 1798.

Walker, George. "A Defence of Learning and the Arts, against some charges of Rousseau." *Memoirs of the Literary and Philosophical Society of Manchester*, vol. 5. 5 vols. Warrington, 1785–1802.

[Warburton, William]. Preface to vol. 4 of Samuel Richardson, *Clarissa*. 7 vols. London, 1748.

[Wedekind, Georg Christian Gottlieb]. *Idées d'un allemand sur les rapports extérieurs de la république française, adressées au peuple français et à ses représentants*. N.p., 1795.

Wieland, Christoph Martin. *Sokrates mainomenos oder die Dialoge des Diogenes von Sinope* [1770].

———. *Socrate en délire, ou dialogues de Diogène de Synope*. Paris, 1772.

Williams, David. *Lectures on the Universal Principles and Duties of Religion and Morality*. London, 1779.

———. *Lectures on Political Principles; The Subjects of Eighteen Books in Montesquieu's "Spirit of Laws"*. In David Williams, *Lectures on Education*, vol. 4. 4 vols. London, 1789.

———. *Letters on Political Liberty and the principles of the English and Irish Projects of Reform*. 3rd ed. London, 1789.

———. *Lessons to a Young Prince on the Present Disposition in Europe to a General Revolution*. London, 1790.

Winchester, Elhanan. *The Universal Restoration examined in Four Dialogues between a Minister and his Friend*. Boston, 1831.

Winstanley, John. *Poems*. Dublin, 1742.

Yorke, Henry Redhead. *Letters from France in 1802*. 2 vols. London, 1804.

Young, Arthur. *Rural Oeconomy*. London, 1770.

———. *Political Essays Concerning the Present State of the British Empire*. London, 1772.

Young, Edward. *A Vindication of Providence, or a True Estimate of Human Life. In Which the Passions are Considered in a New Light* [1728]. In Edward Young, *Works*, vol. 6. 6 vols. Edinburgh, 1774.

———. *Night Thoughts* [1742]. Edited by Stephen Cornford. Cambridge, CUP, 1989.

———. *Klagen, oder Nachtgedanken*. Translated by Johann Arnold Ebert. Leipzig, 1794.

SECONDARY SOURCES

Aarsleff, Hans. *From Locke to Saussure: Essays on the Study of Language and Intellectual History.* Minneapolis, University of Minnesota Press, 1982.

Ablondi, Fred. *Gerauld de Cordemoy: Atomist, Occasionalist, Cartesian.* Milwaukee, Marquette UP, 2005.

Adam, Ulrich. "Nobility and Modern Monarchy—J. G. G. Justi and the French Debate on Commercial Nobility at the Beginning of the Seven Years War." *History of European Ideas* 29 (2003): 141–57.

———. *The Political Economy of J. H. G. Justi.* Berne, Peter Lang, 2006.

Advielle, Victor. *Histoire de Gracchus Babeuf et du babouvisme.* 2 vols. Paris, 1884.

Ahnert, Thomas. "The Soul, Natural Religion and Moral Philosophy in the Scottish Enlightenment." In James G. Buickerood, ed., *Eighteenth-Century Thought,* 2:233–53. New York, AMS Press, 2004.

Alder, Ken. "French Engineers Become Professionals: or, How Meritocracy Made Knowledge Objective." In William Clark, Jan Golinksi, and Simon Schaffer, eds., *The Sciences in Enlightened Europe,* pp. 94–125. Chicago, University of Chicago Press, 1999.

Almond, Philip C. *The British Discovery of Buddhism.* Cambridge, CUP, 1988.

———. *Heaven and Hell in Enlightenment England.* Cambridge, CUP, 1994.

———. "Druids, Patriarchs, and the Primordial Religion." *Journal of Contemporary Religion* 15 (2000): 379–94.

Andress, David. "Order, Respectability and the Sans-Culottes." *The French Historian: Bulletin of the Society for the Study of French History* 10, no. 1 (Autumn 1995).

———. "Press and Public in the French Revolution: A Parisian Case-Study from 1791." *European History Quarterly* 28 (1998): 51–80.

———. *Massacre at the Champ de Mars.* London, The Royal Historical Society, Boydell Press, 2000.

Andrews, Richard M. "Social Structures, Political Elites, and Ideology in Revolutionary Paris, 1792–1794: A Critical Evaluation of Albert Soboul's *Les sans-culottes parisiens en l'an II.*" *Journal of Social History* 19 (1985): 71–112.

Antonetti, Guy. "Etienne-Gabriel Morelly, l'homme et sa famille." *Revue d'histoire littéraire de la France* 83 (1983): 390–402.

———. "Etienne-Gabriel Morelly: l'écrivain et ses protecteurs." *Revue d'histoire littéraire de la France* 84 (1984): 19–52.

Appleby, John H. "Daniel Dumaresq D.D., F.R.S. (1712–1805) as a Promoter of Anglo-Russian Science and Culture." *Notes and Records of the Royal Society of London* 44 (1990): 25–50.

Archives parlementaires. Edited by M. J. Mavidal, M. E. Laurent, and M. E. Clavel. 82 vols. Paris, 1878–1913.

Aristotle. *Ethics.* Cambridge, CUP, 2003.

Arvidsson, Stefan. *Aryan Idols: Indo-European Mythology as Ideology and Science.* Chicago, University of Chicago Press, 2006.

Assmann, Jan. *Moses the Egyptian: The Memory of Egypt in Western Monotheism.* Cambridge, Mass., Harvard UP, 1997.

Aston, Nigel. *The End of an Elite: The French Bishops and the Coming of the Revolution 1786–1790.* Oxford, OUP, 1992.

Aulard, F. A. *La Société des Jacobins. Recueil de documents pour l'histoire du club des Jacobins de Paris.* 6 vols. Paris, 1889–97.

Ayres-Bennett, Wendy. "Women and Grammar in Seventeenth-Century France." *Seventeenth-Century French Studies* 12 (1990): 5–25.

———. *Sociolinguistic Variation in Seventeenth-Century France.* Cambridge, CUP, 2004.

Baecque, Antoine de. *The Body Politics: Corporeal Metaphor in Revolutionary France, 1770–1800* [1993]. Stanford, Stanford UP, 1997.

———. *Les éclats du rire. La culture des rieurs au xviiie siècle.* Paris, Calmann-Lévy, 2000.

Baehr, Peter, and Melvin Richter, eds. *Dictatorship in History and Theory: Bonapartism, Caesarism, and Totalitarianism.* Cambridge, CUP, 2004.

Baere, Benoit de. *Trois introductions à l'abbé Pluche: sa vie, son monde, ses livres.* Geneva, Droz, 2002.

Bagehot, Walter. *The English Constitution.* 1867.

Baker, Eric. "Lucretius in the European Enlightenment." In Stuart Gillespie and Philip Hardie, eds., *The Cambridge Companion to Lucretius*, pp. 274–88. Cambridge, CUP, 2007.

Baker, Keith Michael. *Inventing the French Revolution: Essays on French Political Thought in the Eighteenth-Century.* Cambridge, CUP, 1990.

———. "A Script for a French Revolution: The Political Consciousness of the Abbé Mably." In Keith Michael Baker, *Inventing the French Revolution*, pp. 86–106. Cambridge, CUP, 1990.

Baldensperger, Fernand. *Etudes d'histoire littéraire.* 4 vols. Paris, 1907–39.

———. "Les théories de Lavater dans la littérature française." In his *Etudes d'histoire littéraire.* 4 vols. Paris, 1907–39.

Baldi, Marialuisa. "Nature and Man Restored: Mysticism and Millenarianism in Andrew Michael Ramsay." *Anglophonia* 3 (1998): 89–102.

———. "Tra Giacobiti e Massoni. La Libertà secondo Ramsay." In Luisa Simonutti, ed., *Dal necessario al possibile. Determinismo e libertà nel pensiero anglo-olandese del xvii secolo*, pp. 265–80. Milan, FrancoAngeli, 2001.

———. *Verisimile, non Vero. Filosofia e politica in Andrew Michael Ramsay.* Milan, Franco Angeli, 2002.

Bapst, Germain. "Inventaire des bibliothèques de quatre condamnés." *La Révolution française* 21 (1891): 532–6.

Barber, W. H. *Leibniz in France from Arnauld to Voltaire: A Study in French Reactions to Leibnitzianism, 1670–1760.* Oxford, Clarendon Press, 1955.

Barker, Emma. "Mme Geoffrin, Painting and *Galanterie*: Carl Van Loo's *Conversation Espagnole* and *Lecture Espagnole*." *Eighteenth-Century Studies* 40 (2007): 587–614.

Barnes, Annie. *Jean Le Clerc (1657–1736).* Geneva, Droz, 1938.

Barnouw, Jeffrey. "Feeling in Enlightenment Aesthetics." *Studies in Eighteenth-Century Culture* 18 (1988): 323–42.

———. "The Beginnings of 'Aesthetics' and the Leibnizian Conception of Sensation." In Paul Mattick Jr., ed., *Eighteenth-Century Aesthetics and the Reconstructions of Art*, pp. 52–95. Cambridge, CUP, 1993.

Barny, Roger. *L'éclatement révolutionnaire du rousseauisme.* Paris, 1988.

Baum, Manfred. "Herder's Essay on Being." In Kurt Mueller-Vollmer, ed., *Herder Today*, pp. 126–37. Berlin and New York, Walter de Gruyter, 1990.

Beales, Derek. "Joseph II's *Rêveries*." In Derek Beales, *Enlightenment and Reform in Eighteenth-Century Europe*, pp. 157–81. London, I. B. Tauris, 2005.

Becq, Annie. *Genèse de l'esthétique française moderne 1680–1814* [1984]. Paris, Albin Michel, 1994.

Beiser, Frederick. *The Fate of Reason: German Philosophy from Kant to Fichte*. Cambridge, Mass., Harvard UP, 1987.

———. *Enlightenment, Revolution, and Romanticism: The Genesis of Modern German Political Thought 1790–1800*. Cambridge, Mass., Harvard UP, 1992.

Bell, David A. *Lawyers and Citizens: The Making of a Political Elite in Old Regime France*. Oxford, OUP, 1994.

———. *The Cult of the Nation in France: Inventing Nationalism, 1680–1800*. Cambridge, Mass., Harvard UP, 2001.

———. Review of Benedetta Craveri, *The Art of Conversation*. *London Review of Books* 28, no. 9 (2006): 17–9.

Berg, Maxine. *Luxury and Pleasure in Eighteenth-Century Britain*. Oxford, OUP, 2005.

Bernal, Martin. *Black Athena*. 3 vols. London, Free Association Books, 1987–2006.

Bernardi, Bruno. *La fabrique des concepts. Recherches sur l'invention conceptuelle chez Rousseau*. Paris, Champion, 2006.

Beaurepaire, Pierre-Yves. *L'Europe des francs-maçons, xviiie–xxie siècles*. Paris, Belin, 2002.

Bevis, Richard. *The Road to Egdon Heath: The Aesthetics of the Great in Nature*. Montreal and Kingston, McGill-Queen's UP, 1999.

Bianchini, Paolo. "Le annotazioni manoscritti di Augustin Barruel ai *Mémoires pour servir à l'histoire du Jacobinisme*." *Annali della Fondazione Luigi Einaudi* 33 (1999): 367–444.

Bien, David D. "La réaction aristocratique avant 1789: l'exemple de l'armée." *Annales E. S. C.* 29 (1974): 23–48, 505–34.

———. "The Army in the French Enlightenment: Reform, Reaction, and Revolution." *Past & Present* 85 (1979): 68–98.

Bindman, David. *Ape to Apollo: Aesthetics and the Idea of Race in the Eighteenth Century*. London, Reaktion Books, 2002.

Binoche, Bertrand. *Les trois sources des philosophies de l'histoire (1764–1798)*. Paris, Presses universitaires de France, 1994.

———, ed. *Les équivoques de la civilisation*. Seyssel, Champ Vallon, 2005.

Birn, Raymond. "Les 'oeuvres complètes' de Rousseau sous l'ancien régime." *Annales de la Société Jean-Jacques Rousseau* 41 (1997): 229–62.

———. *Forging Rousseau. Print, Commerce and Cultural Manipulation in the Late Enlightenment. SVEC* 2001: 08.

Blaney, David L., and Naeem Inayatullah. "The Savage Smith and the Temporal Walls of Capitalism." In Beate Jahn, ed., *Classical Theory in International Relations*, pp. 123–55. Cambridge, CUP, 2006.

Blanning, T.C.M. *The Origins of the French Revolutionary Wars*. London, Arnold, 1986.

————. *The French Revolution: Aristocrats versus Bourgeois?* London, Macmillan, 1987.

Blaser, Robert-Henri. *Un suisse J. H. Obereit, 1725–1798, médecin et philosophe, tire de l'oubli la chanson des Nibelungen.* Berne, Editions Berlincourt, 1965.

Blaufarb, Rafe. *The French Army 1750–1820: Careers, Talent, Merit.* Manchester, Manchester UP, 2002.

————. "The Social Contours of Meritocracy in the Napoleonic Officer Corps." In Howard G. Brown and Judith A. Miller, eds., *Taking Liberties: Problems of a New Order from the French Revolution to Napoleon,* pp. 126–46. Manchester, Manchester UP, 2002.

Blundell, Mary Whitlock. *Helping Friends and Harming Enemies: A Study in Sophocles and Greek Ethics.* Cambridge, CUP, 1989.

Boas, George, and Arthur O. Lovejoy. *Primitivism and Related Ideas in Antiquity* [1935]. Baltimore, Johns Hopkins UP, 1997.

Boas, George. *Primitivism and Related Ideas in the Middle Ages* [1948]. Baltimore, Johns Hopkins UP, 1997.

Bobé, Louis Theodor Alfred, ed. *Efterladte Papirer fra den Reventlowske Familiekreds I Tidsrummet 1770–1827.* 10 vols. Copenhagen, 1895–1931.

————, ed. *Mémoires de Charles-Claude Flahaut comte de la Billarderie d'Angiviller, avec des notes sur les "Mémoires" de Marmontel, publiés d'après le manuscrit.* Copenhagen, 1933.

Bodinier, Bernard, and Eric Teyssier. *"L'événement le plus important de la révolution": La vente des biens nationaux (1789–1867) en France et dans les territoires annexes.* Paris, Société des études robespierristes, 2000.

Bois, Pierre-André. *Adolph Freiherr Knigge (1752–1796). De la "nouvelle religion" aux Droits de l'Homme.* Wiesbaden, Wolfenbütteler Forschungen, Band 50, 1990.

Bongie, Laurence L. *The Love of a Prince: Bonnie Prince Charlie in France.* Vancouver, University of British Columbia Press, 1986.

————. *David Hume: Prophet of the Counter-Revolution* [1965]. Indianapolis, Liberty Fund, 2000.

Bonnet, Jean-Claude. "Louis-Sébastien Mercier et les *Oeuvres complètes* de Jean-Jacques Rousseau." *Studies on Voltaire and the Eighteenth Century* 370 (1999): 111–24.

Bosher, John. *French Finances 1770–1795: From Business to Bureaucracy.* Cambridge, CUP, 1970.

Bourguinat, Elisabeth. *Le siècle du persiflage 1734–1789.* Paris, Presses universitaires de France, 1998.

Bowman, Frank Paul. *Le Christ romantique.* Geneva, Droz, 1973.

Boyd, Julian P., ed. *The Papers of Thomas Jefferson.* 33 vols. to date. Princeton, Princeton UP, 1950–.

Bracht Branham, R., and Marie-Odile Goulet-Cazé, eds. *The Cynics: The Cynic Movement in Antiquity and Its Legacy.* Berkeley and Los Angeles, University of California Press, 1996.

Bressler, Ann Lee. *The Universalist Movement in America, 1770–1880.* Oxford, OUP, 2001.

Brown, Deborah J. *Descartes and the Passionate Mind.* Cambridge, CUP, 2006.

Brown, Gregory S. "Beaumarchais, Social Experience and Literary Figures in Eighteenth-Century Public Life." *SVEC* 2005: 04, pp. 143–70.

Burrows, Simon. *Blackmail, Scandal, and Revolution: London's French libellistes, 1758–92*. Manchester, Manchester UP, 2006.

Burtin, Nicolas. *Un semeur d'idées au temps de la restauration: le baron d'Eckstein*. Paris, 1931.

Butler, E. M. *The Tyranny of Greece over Germany* [1935]. Boston, Beacon Press, 1958.

Cannon, Garland Hampton. *The Life and Mind of Oriental Jones*. Cambridge, CUP, 1990.

Carcassonne, Elie. *Montesquieu et le problème de la constitution française au xviiie siècle*. Paris, 1927.

Carnochan, W. B. "Satire, Sublimity and Sentiment: Theory and Practice in Post-Augustan Satire." *PMLA* 85 (1970): 260–70.

———. "Juvenal as Sublime Satirist." *PMLA* 87 (1972): 1125–26.

Carson, John. *The Measure of Merit: Talents, Intelligence, and Inequality in the French and American Republics, 1750–1940*. Princeton, Princeton UP, 2007.

Charrak, André. "La question du fondement des lois de la nature au dix-huitième siècle." *SVEC* 2006: 12, pp. 87–99.

Chaussinand-Nogaret, Guy. *Mirabeau entre le roi et la révolution*. Paris, Hachette, 1986.

Chayes, Irene H. "Coleridge, Metempsychosis, and 'Almost All the Followers of Fénelon.'" *English Literary History* 25 (1958): 290–315.

Chérel, Albert. *Fénelon au xviiie siècle en France*. Paris, 1917.

Cherpack, Clifton. "Warburton and the Encyclopédie." *Comparative Literature* 7 (1955): 226–39.

Chevallier, Marjolaine. "La réponse de Poiret à Fénelon." *Revue d'histoire de la spiritualité* 53 (1977): 129–64.

———. *Pierre Poiret (1646–1719), du protestantisme à la mystique*. Geneva, Labor et Fides, 1994.

———. "Deux réactions protestantes à la condamnation de Fénelon." In François-Xavier Cuche and Jacques Le Brun, eds., *Fénelon, Mystique et Politique*, pp. 147–161. Paris, Champion, 2004.

Chinard, Gilbert. *L'Amérique et le rêve exotique dans la littérature française du xviie et xviiie siècles*. Geneva, Droz, 1934.

Chomsky, Noam. *Cartesian Linguistics*. New York, Harper & Row, 1966.

Chouillet-Roche, Anne-Marie. "Le Clavecin oculaire du père Castel." *Dix-Huitième Siècle* 8 (1976): 141–66.

Clark, Henry C. "Commerce, Sociability, and the Public Sphere: Morellet vs Pluquet on Luxury." *Eighteenth Century Life* 22 (1998): 83–103.

———. *Compass of Society: Commerce and Absolutism in Old-Regime France*. New York, Lexington Books, 2007.

Clark, J.C.D. *The Language of Liberty 1660–1832: Political Discourse and Social Dynamics in the Anglo-American World*. Cambridge, CUP. 1994.

Clarke, J. J. *Oriental Enlightenment: The Encounter between Asian and Western Thought*. London, Routledge, 1997.

Clarke, Joseph. *Commemorating the Dead in Revolutionary France*. Cambridge, CUP, 2007.

Cobb, Richard. *Les armées révolutionnaires: instrument de la terreur dans les départements*. 2 vols. The Hague, Mouton, 1961–3.

Coleman, Patrick. "The Enlightened Orthodoxy of the Abbé Pluquet." In John Christian Laursen, ed., *Histories of Heresy in Early Modern Europe: For, against, and beyond Persecution and Toleration*, pp. 223–38. New York, Palgrave, 2002.

———. "Rousseau's Quarrel with Gratitude." In Victoria Kahn, Neil Saccamano, and Daniela Coli, eds., *Politics and the Passions, 1500–1850*, pp. 151–74. Princeton, Princeton UP, 2006.

Coley, Awen A. M. "The Science of Man: Experimental Routes to Happiness in Duclos and Rousseau." *SVEC* 2000:08, pp. 235–327.

Conrad, Stephen. *Citizenship and Common Sense: The Problem of Authority in the Social Background and Social Philosophy of the Wise Club of Aberdeen*. New York, Garland, 1987.

Cook, Malcolm. *Bernardin de Saint Pierre: A Life of Culture*. London, Legenda, 2006.

Cottret, Monique and Bernard. *Jean-Jacques Rousseau en son temps*. Paris, Perrin, 2005.

Coynart, Charles de. *Les Guérin de Tencin (1520–1758)*. Paris, 1910.

Crane, R. S. "Richardson, Warburton and French Fiction." *Modern Language Review* 17 (1922): 17–23.

Cranston, Maurice. *The Noble Savage: Jean-Jacques Rousseau 1754–1762*. London, Allen Lane, 1991.

Craveri, Benedetta. *The Art of Conversation*. New York, New York Review, 2005.

Crimmins, James. *Secular Utilitarianism*. Oxford, OUP, 1990.

Crook, Malcolm. "Citizen Bishops: Episcopal Elections in the French Revolution." *Historical Journal* 43 (2000): 955–76.

Crouzet, François. *La grande inflation. La monnaie en France de Louis XVI à Napoléon*. Paris, Fayard, 1993.

Cuénin, Micheline. *Roman et société sous Louis XIV. Madame de Villedieu*. 2 vols. Lille, Atelier de reproduction des thèses, 1979.

Czarnocka, Anna. "Vernis Martin: The Lacquer Work of the Martin Family in the Eighteenth Century." *Studies in the Decorative Arts* 2 (1994): 56–74.

Dacome, Lucia. "Resurrecting by Numbers in Eighteenth-Century England." *Past & Present* 193 (2006): 73–110.

Daniel Wilson, W. "Wieland's *Diogenes* and the Emancipation of the Critical Intellectual." In Hansjörg Schelle, ed., *Christoph Martin Wieland*, pp. 149–79. Tübingen, Max Niemeyer Verlag, 1984.

Darnton, Robert. *Mesmerism and the End of the Enlightenment in France*. Cambridge, Mass., Harvard UP, 1968.

———. "The High Enlightenment and the Low-Life of Literature in Pre-Revolutionary France." *Past & Present* 51 (1971): 81–115.

———. *The Literary Underground of the Old Regime*. Cambridge, Mass., Harvard UP, 1982.

Darwall, Stephen. *The British Moralists and the Internal 'Ought'*. Cambridge, CUP, 1995.

Davies, Peter. *The Debate on the French Revolution*. Manchester, Manchester UP, 2006.

Davis, Joe Lee. "Mystical versus Enthusiastic Sensibility." *Journal of the History of Ideas* 4 (1943): 301–19.

Davis, Tony. "Borrowed Language: Milton, Jefferson, Mirabeau." In David Armitage, Armand Himy, and Quentin Skinner, eds., *Milton and Republicanism*, pp. 254–71. Cambridge, CUP, 1995.

Deane, Seamus. *The French Revolution and Enlightenment in England, 1789–1832*. Cambridge, Mass., Harvard UP, 1988.

Delehanty, Ann. "Mapping the Aesthetic Mind: John Dennis and Nicolas Boileau." *Journal of the History of Ideas* 68 (2007): 233–53.

Deligiorgi, Katerina. *Kant and the Culture of Enlightenment*. New York, State University of New York Press, 2005.

Dent, N.J.H. *Rousseau*. Oxford, Blackwell, 1988.

———. *A Rousseau Dictionary*. Oxford, Blackwell, 1992.

Dent, N.J.H., and T. O'Hagan. "Rousseau on *Amour-Propre*." *Proceedings of the Aristotelian Society, Supplement* 72 (1998): 57–74.

Deprun, Jean. *La philosophie de l'inquiétude en France au xviiie siècle*. Paris, Vrin, 1979.

Derrida, Jacques. *Of Grammatology* [1967]. Baltimore, Johns Hopkins UP, 1974.

D'Hondt, Jacques. "Le cynisme de Rameau." *Recherches sur Diderot et sur l'Encyclopédie* 36 (2004): 125–37.

Dieckmann, Herbert. "The Relationship between Diderot's *Satire I* and *Satire II*." *Romanic Review* 43 (1952): 12–26.

Dimoff, Paul. *La vie et l'oeuvre d'André Chénier jusqu'à la révolution française*. 2 vols. Geneva, 1936.

———. "Cicéron, Hobbes et Montesquieu." *Annales Universitatis Saraviensis (Philosophie-Lettres)* 1 (1952): 19–47.

Doolittle, James. "Jaucourt's Use of Source Material in the *Encyclopédie*." *Modern Language Notes* 65 (1950): 387–92.

Dorigny, Marcel. "Du 'despotisme vertueux' à la république." In Jean-Claude Bonnet, ed., *Louis-Sébastien Mercier (1740–1814) Un hérétique en littérature*, pp. 247–77. Paris, Mercure de France, 1995.

Dorigny, Marcel, and Bernard Gainot. *La société des amis des noirs 1788–1799: contribution à l'histoire de l'abolition de l'esclavage*. Paris, Editions UNESCO, 1998.

Dossios-Pralat, Odette. *Michel Regnaud de Saint-Jean-d'Angély, serviteur fidèle de Napoléon*. Paris, Editions Historiques Teissèdre, 2007.

Doyle, William. *The Oxford History of the French Revolution* [1989]. 2nd ed. Oxford, OUP, 2002.

———. "The French Revolution and the Abolition of Nobility." In Hamish Scott and Brendan Simms, eds., *Cultures of Power in Europe during the Long Eighteenth Century*, pp. 289–303. Cambridge, CUP, 2007.

Du Bus, Charles. *Stanislas de Clermont-Tonnerre et l'échec de la révolution monarchique*. Paris, 1931.

Ducange, Jean, ed. *Robespierre: Virtue and Terror*. Introduced by Slavoj Ži žek. London, Verso, 2007.

Duchez, Elizabeth. "*Principe de mélodie* et *Origine des langues*: Un brouillon inédit de Jean-Jacques Rousseau sur l'origine de la mélodie." *Revue de musicologie* 60 (1974): 33–86.

Dudley, Donald R. *A History of Cynicism* [1937]. 2nd ed. with a foreword and bibliography by Miriam Griffin. Bristol, Bristol Classical Press, 1998.

Dudley, Edward, and Maximillian E, Novak, eds. *The Wild Man Within: An Image in Western Thought from the Renaissance to Romanticism*. Pittsburgh, University of Pittsburgh Press, 1972.

Dulac, Georges. "Quelques exemples de transferts européens du concept de 'civilisation.'" In Bertrand Binoche, ed., *Les équivoques de la civilisation*, pp. 105–35. Seyssel, Champ Vallon, 2005.

Dunn, John "From Applied Theology to Social Analysis: The Break between John Locke and the Scottish Enlightenment." In Istvan Hont and Michael Ignatieff, eds., *Wealth and Virtue: The Shaping of Political Economy in the Scottish Enlightenment*, pp. 119–35. Cambridge, CUP, 1983.

———. *Setting the People Free: The Story of Democracy*. London, Atlantic Books, 2005.

Dybikowski, James. "David Williams (1738–1816) and Jacques-Pierre Brissot: Their Correspondence." *National Library of Wales Journal* 25 (1987–8): 71–97, 167–90.

———. *On Burning Ground: An Examination of the Ideas, Projects and Life of David Williams. Studies on Voltaire and the Eighteenth Century* 307 (1993).

Eddy, Donald D. "John Brown: 'The Columbus of Keswick.'" *Modern Philology* 73 (1976): S74–S84.

Eggli, Edmond. *Schiller et le romantisme français*. 2 vols. Paris, 1927.

Egret, Jean. *La révolution des notables. Mounier et les Monarchiens*. Paris, Armand Colin, 1950.

Evans, A. W. *Warburton and the Warburtonians: A Study in Some Eighteenth-Century Controversies*. Oxford, OUP, 1932.

Faccarello, Gilbert. *Aux origines de l'économie politique libérale: Pierre de Boisguilbert*. Paris, Anthropos, 1986.

Fairchilds, Cissie. "Fashion and Freedom in the French Revolution." *Continuity and Change* 15 (2000): 419–33.

Fauré, Christine. "Sieyès, lecteur problématique des lumières." *Dix-Huitième Siècle* 37 (2005): 225–41.

———, ed. *Des manuscrits de Sieyès*. 2 vols. Paris, Champion, 1999–2007.

Feher, Ferenc. *The Frozen Revolution: An Essay on Jacobinism*. Cambridge, CUP, 1987.

Feldman, Burton, and Robert D. Richardson, eds. *The Rise of Modern Mythology 1680–1860*. Bloomington, Indiana UP, 1972.

Feldman, Martha, and Bonnie Gordon, eds. *The Courtesan's Arts: Cross Cultural Perspectives*. Oxford, OUP, 2006.

Ferrazzini, Arthur. *Béat de Muralt et Jean-Jacques Rousseau. Etude sur l'histoire des idées au xviiie siècle*. La Neuveville, Switzerland, 1951.

Filippaki, Eleni. "La Mettrie on Descartes, Seneca, and the Happy Life." *SVEC* 2004: 10, pp. 249–72.

Fisher, Philip. *Wonder, the Rainbow, and the Aesthetics of Rare Experiences*. Cambridge, Mass., Harvard UP, 1998.

Flasdieck, Hermann. *John Brown und seine Dissertation on Poetry and Music*. Halle, 1924.

Foner, Philip S., ed. *The Complete Writings of Thomas Paine*. 2 vols. New York, 1945.

Forbes, Duncan. *Hume's Philosophical Politics*. Cambridge, CUP, 1975.

Forster, Harold. *Edward Young, the Poet of the Night Thoughts, 1683–1765.* Harleston, Erskine Press, 1986.

Fort, Sylvain. *Les lumières françaises en Allemagne: le cas Schiller.* Paris, Presses universitaires de France, 2002.

Fott, David. "'Preface' to Translation of Montesquieu's 'Discourse on Cicero.'" *Political Theory* 30 (2002): 728–32.

Freedman, Jeffrey. *A Poisoned Chalice.* Princeton, Princeton UP, 2002.

Freudenberg, Kirk, ed. *The Cambridge Companion to Roman Satire.* Cambridge, CUP, 2005.

Frierson, Patrick R. "Learning to Love: From Egoism to Generosity in Descartes." *Journal of the History of Philosophy* 40 (2002): 313–48.

Furet, François. *Interpreting the French Revolution* [Paris, 1978]. Cambridge, CUP, 1981.

Furet, François, and Mona Ozouf, eds. *Terminer la révolution. Mounier et Barnave dans la révolution française.* Grenoble, Presses Universitaires de Grenoble, 1990.

———, eds. *La Gironde et les Girondins.* Paris, Payot, 1991.

Ganochaud, Colette. *L'Opinion publique chez Jean-Jacques Rousseau.* Lille, Atelier de la Reproduction des Thèses, Université de Lille III, 1980.

Garaud, Marcel. *Histoire générale du droit privé de 1789 à 1804.* 2 vols. Paris, Sirey, 1953–8.

Garnsey, Peter. *Thinking about Property: From Antiquity to the Age of Revolution.* Cambridge, CUP, 2007.

Garrioch, David, *The Making of Revolutionary Paris.* Berkeley and Los Angeles, University of California Press, 2002.

Gaskill, Howard, ed. *Ossian Revisited.* Edinburgh, Edinburgh UP, 1991.

Gaulmier, Jean. *L'idéologue Volney 1757–1820. Contribution à l'histoire de l'orientalisme en France* [1951]. Geneva, Slatkine, 1980.

Gawlick, Gunter. "Cicero and the Enlightenment." *Studies on Voltaire and the Eighteenth Century* 25 (1963): 657–82.

Gay, Peter. *The Enlightenment, an Interpretation* [1966]. 2 vols. London, Wildwood House, 1970.

Gay, Sophie. *Salons célèbres.* Brussels, 1837.

Geffroy, Annie. "Sans-culotte(s)." In Annie Geffroy, Jacques Guilhaumou, and Sylvia Moreno, eds., *Dictionnaire des usages socio-politiques*, pp. 159–86. Paris, Klincksieck, 1985.

Gelbart, Matthew. *The Invention of "Folk Music" and "Art Music": Emerging Categories from Ossian to Wagner.* Cambridge, CUP, 2007.

Gelbart, Nina Rattner. *Feminine and Opposition Journalism in Old Regime France.* Berkeley and Los Angeles, University of California Press, 1987.

Genty, Maurice. *L'apprentissage de la citoyenneté. Paris 1789–1795.* Paris, Messidor, 1987.

Geuss, Raymond. *Public Goods, Private Goods.* Princeton, Princeton UP, 2001.

———. *Outside Ethics.* Princeton, Princeton UP, 2005.

Gevrey, Françoise, Julie Boch, and Jean-Louis Haquette, eds. *Ecrire la nature au xviiie siècle.* Paris, Presses de l'Université Paris-Sorbonne, 2006.

Gill, Christopher. "Personhood and Personality: The Four *Personae* Theory in Cicero, *De Officiis* I." *Oxford Studies in Ancient Philosophy* 6 (1988): 168–99.

Gill, Michael B. *The British Moralists on Human Nature and the Birth of Secular Ethics*. Cambridge, CUP, 2006.

——, Gilmore, Thomas B., and W. B. Carnochan. "The Politics of Eighteenth-Century Satire." *PMLA* 86 (1971): 277–80.

Glass, Bentley, Owsei Temkin, and William L. Straus, eds. *Forerunners of Darwin 1745–1859* [1959]. New ed. Baltimore, Johns Hopkins UP, 1968.

Gode von Aesch, Alexander Gottfried Friedrich. *Natural Science in German Romanticism*. New York, Columbia UP, 1941.

Goggi, Gianluigi. "Diderot et l'abbé Baudeau: les colonies de Saratov et la civilisation de la Russie." *Recherches sur Diderot et sur l'Encyclopédie* 14 (1993): 23–83.

Goodman, Dena. *The Republic of Letters: A Cultural History of the French Enlightenment*. Ithaca, Cornell UP, 1994.

Goodwin, Albert. *The Friends of Liberty: The English Democratic Movement in the Age of the French Revolution*. London, 1979.

Gordon, Daniel. *Citizens without Sovereignty: Equality and Sociability in French Thought 1670–1789*. Princeton, Princeton UP, 1994.

Gourevitch, Victor. "Rousseau on Providence." In Todd Breyfogle, ed., *Literary Imagination, Ancient and Modern*. Chicago, University of Chicago Press, 1999.

——. "Rousseau on Providence." *Review of Metaphysics* 53 (2000): 565–611.

Granderoute, Robert. *Le Roman pédagogique de Fénelon à Rousseau*. 2 vols. Geneva, Slatkine, 1985.

Griffiths, Robert. *Le centre perdu. Malouet et les 'monarchiens' dans la révolution française*. Grenoble, Presses universitaires de Grenoble, 1988.

Groom, Nick. "Celts, Goths, and the Nature of the Literary Source." In Alvaro Ribiero and James G. Basker, eds., *Tradition in Transition: Women Writers, Marginal Texts, and the Eighteenth-Century Canon*, pp. 275–96. Oxford, OUP, 1996.

Grosclaude, Pierre. *Malesherbes, témoin et interprète de son temps*. Paris, Librairie Fischbacher, 1961.

Gross, Jean-Pierre. *Fair Shares for All: Jacobin Egalitarianism in Practice*. Cambridge, CUP, 1997.

Grove, Richard H. *Green Imperialism: Colonial Expansion, Tropical Island Edens and the Origins of Environmentalism, 1600–1860*. Cambridge, CUP, 1995.

Gueniffey, Patrice. *La politique de la terreur. Essai sur la violence révolutionnaire 1789–1794*. Paris, Fayard, 2000.

Guillaume, Jacques, ed. *Procès-verbaux du comité d'instruction publique de la Convention Nationale*. 6 vols. Paris, 1891–1907.

Gunn, J.A.W. "Queen of the World: Opinion in the Public Life of France from the Renaissance to the Revolution." *Studies on Voltaire and the Eighteenth Century* 285. Oxford, Voltaire Foundation, 1995.

Gür, André. "Quête de la richesse et critique des riches chez Etienne Clavière." In Jacques Berchtold and Michel Porret, eds., *Etre riche au siècle de Voltaire*, pp. 97–115. Geneva, Droz, 1996.

Gutwirth, Madelyn. "The 'article Genève' Quarrel and the Reticence of French Enlightenment Discourse on Women in the Public Realm." *SVEC* 2001: 12, pp. 135–66.

Haakonssen, Knud, ed. *Enlightenment and Religion: Rational Dissent in Eighteenth-Century Britain*. Cambridge, CUP, 1996.

Haber, Francis C. *The Age of the World: Moses to Darwin*. Baltimore, Johns Hopkins UP, 1959.

Habermas, Jürgen. *The Structural Transformation of the Public Sphere* [1959]. Cambridge, Mass., MIT Press, 1991.

Halbfass, Wilhelm. *India and Europe: An Essay in Understanding* [1981]. New York, State University of New York Press, 1988.

Hammersley, Rachel. *French Revolutionaries and English Republicans: The Cordeliers Club, 1790–1794*. Woodbridge, Suffolk, The Royal Historical Society & The Boydell Press, 2005.

Hampson, Norman. *Will and Circumstance*. London, Duckworth, 1983.

Hans, N. "Marginalia: Dumaresq, Brown and Some Early Educational Projects of Catherine II." *Slavonic and East-European Review* 40 (1961): 229–35.

Hardman, John. *French Politics 1774–1789*. London, Longman, 1995.

Harris, Henry. *The Birth of the Cell*. New Haven, Yale UP, 1999.

Hartmann, L. *Les officiers de l'armée royale et la révolution*. Paris, 1910.

Head, Brian W. "The Origins of 'la science sociale' in France." *Australian Journal of French Studies* 19 (1982): 115–32.

Heinz, Marion. *Sensualistischer Idealismus. Untersuchungen zur Erkenntnistheorie und Metaphysik des jungen Herder (1763–1778)*. Hamburg, Felix Meiner, 1994.

Hellegouarc'h, Jacqueline. *L'Esprit de société. Cercles et 'salons' parisiens au xviiie siècle*. Paris, Garnier, 2000.

Heller, Henry. *The Bourgeois Revolution in France 1789–1815*. New York, Berghahn Books, 2006.

Hellman, Mimi. "Furniture, Sociability, and the Work of Leisure in Eighteenth-Century France." *Eighteenth-Century Studies* 32 (1999): 415–45.

Henderson, G. D., ed. *Mystics of the North-East*. Aberdeen, 1934.

Henrich, Dieter. *Aesthetic Judgement and the Moral Image of the World*. Stanford, Stanford UP, 1992.

Herding, Klaus. "Diogenes als Bürgerheld." *Boreas* 5 (1982): 232–54.

———. "Diogenes, Symbolic Hero of the French Revolution." In Michel Vovelle, ed., *L'image de la révolution française*, 3:2259–71. 5 vols. Oxford, Pergamon Press, 1989.

Higonnet, Patrice. *Goodness beyond Virtue: Jacobins during the French Revolution*. Cambridge, Mass., Harvard UP, 1998.

Hirschman, Albert. *The Passions and the Interests: Political Arguments for Capitalism before Its Triumph*. Princeton, Princeton UP, 1977.

Hofer, Hermann. "Mercier admirateur de l'Allemagne et ses reflets dans le préclassicisme et le classicisme allemands." In Hermann Hofer, ed., *Louis-Sébastien Mercier précurseur et sa fortune*, pp. 73–116. Munich, Fink, 1977.

Hont, Istvan. *Jealousy of Trade: International Competition and the Nation-State in Historical Perspective*. Cambridge, Mass., Belknap Press, 2005.

———. "The 'Rich Country-Poor Country' Debate in the Scottish Enlightenment." In Istvan Hont, *Jealousy of Trade: International Competition and the Nation-State in Historical Perspective*, pp. 267–322. Cambridge, Mass., Belknap Press, 2005.

———. "The Early Enlightenment Debate on Commerce and Luxury." In Mark Goldie and Robert Wokler, eds., *The Cambridge History of Eighteenth-Century Political Thought*, pp. 379–418. Cambridge, CUP, 2006.

———. "The 'Rich Country-Poor Country' Debate Revisited: The Irish Origins and French Reception of Hume's 'Paradox.'" In Margaret Schabas and Carl Wennerlind, eds., *David Hume's Political Economy*. London, Routledge, 2008.

Hont, Istvan, and Michael Ignatieff. "Needs and Justice in the *Wealth of Nations*." Reprinted in Istvan Hont, *Jealousy of Trade: International Competition and the Nation-State in Historical Perspective*, pp. 389–443. Cambridge, Mass., Belknap Press, 2005.

Hope Mason, John. *The Value of Creativity: The Origins and Emergence of a Modern Belief*. Aldershot, Ashgate Press, 2003.

Hours, Bernard. *La vertu et le secret. Le dauphin, fils de Louis XV*. Paris, Champion, 2006.

Howarth, W. D. "Beaumarchais homme de théâtre et la révolution française." In Philip Robinson, ed., *Beaumarchais, homme de lettres, homme de société*, pp. 69–89. Berne, Peter Lang, 2000–2.

Hulliung, Mark. *The Autocritique of Enlightenment: Rousseau and the Philosophes*. Cambridge, Mass., Harvard UP, 1994.

Hundert, E. J. "A Satire of Self-Disclosure: From Hegel through Rameau to the Augustans." *Journal of the History of Ideas* 47 (1986): 235–48.

Hunt, Lynn. *Inventing Human Rights: A History*. New York, Norton, 2007.

Intermédiaire des chercheurs et curieux. Paris, 1864–.

Irlam, Shaun. *Elations: The Poetics of Enthusiasm in Eighteenth-Century Britain*. Stanford, Stanford UP, 1999.

Israel, Jonathan. *Enlightenment Contested: Philosophy, Modernity, and the Emancipation of Man 1670–1752*. Oxford, OUP, 2006.

Jack, Malcolm. *Corruption and Progress: The Eighteenth-Century Debate*. New York, AMS Press, 1989.

Jacquart, Jean. *L'abbé Trublet, critique et moraliste 1697–1770*. Paris, Auguste Picard, 1926.

Jacques-Lefèvre, Nicole. *Louis-Claude de Saint-Martin, le philosophe inconnu (1743–1803)*. Paris, Editions Dervy, 2003.

James, Susan. "The Passions and the Good Life." In Donald Rutherford, ed., *The Cambridge Companion to Early Modern Philosophy*, pp. 198–220. Cambridge, CUP, 2006.

Jaume, Lucien. *Le discours jacobin et la démocratie*. Paris, Fayard, 1989.

Jennings, Jeremy. "The Debate about Luxury in Eighteenth- and Nineteenth-Century French Political Thought." *Journal of the History of Ideas* 68 (2007): 79–105.

Jimack, Peter. *Diderot. Supplément au Voyage de Bougainville*. London, Grant and Cutler, 1988.

Johnston, Joseph, ed. *Bishop Berkeley's Querist in Historical Perspective*. Dundalk, Dundalgan Press, 1970.

Johnstone, Paul H. "The Rural Socrates." *Journal of the History of Ideas* 5 (1944): 151–75.

Jones, Colin. "The Great Chain of Buying: Medical Advertisement, the Bourgeois Public Sphere, and the Origins of the French Revolution." *American Historical Review* 101 (1996): 13–40.

———. *The Great Nation: France from Louis XV to Napoleon*. London, 2002.

————. "The French Smile Revolution." *Cabinet* 17 (2005): 97–100.

Jones, J. R, ed. *Liberty Secured? Britain before and after 1688*. Stanford, Stanford UP, 1992.

Jones, Jennifer M. *Sexing La Mode: Gender, Fashion and Commercial Culture in Old Regime France*. Oxford, Berg, 2004.

Jones, Peter. "The 'Agrarian Law': Schemes for Land Redistribution during the French Revolution." *Past & Present* 133 (1991): 96–133.

Kahn, Gerard, ed. *Beaumarchais, "Le mariage de Figaro"*. SVEC 2002: 12.

Kale, Steven. *French Salons: High Society and Political Sociability from the Old Regime to the Revolution of 1848*. Baltimore, Johns Hopkins UP, 2004.

Kanuf, Peggy. "The Gift of Clothes: Of Mme de Lafayette and the Origin of Novels." *Novel: A Forum on Fiction* 17 (1984): 233–45.

Kapossy, Béla. *Iselin contra Rousseau: Sociable Patriotism and the History of Mankind*. Basel, Schwabe, 2006.

Kates, Gary. *The* Cercle Social, *the Girondins, and the French Revolution*. Princeton, Princeton UP, 1985.

Keener, Frederick M. *English Dialogues of the Dead: A Critical History, an Anthology, a Check List*. New York, Columbia UP, 1973.

Kelly, Patrick. "Berkeley's Economic Writings." In Kenneth P. Winkler, ed., *The Cambridge Companion to Berkeley*, pp. 339–68. Cambridge, CUP, 2005.

Keohane, Nannerl O. "'The Masterpiece of Policy in Our Century': Rousseau and the Morality of the Enlightenment." *Political Theory* 6 (1974): 457–84.

————. *Philosophy and the State in France: From the Renaissance to the Enlightenment*. Princeton, Princeton UP, 1980.

Kidd, Colin. "Civil Theology and Church Establishment in Revolutionary America." *Historical Journal* 42 (1999): 1007–26.

————. *British Identities before Nationalism: Ethnicity and Nationhood in the Atlantic World 1600–1800*. Cambridge, CUP, 1999.

————. *The Forging of Races: Race and Scripture in the Protestant Atlantic World, 1600–2000*. Cambridge, CUP, 2006.

Kitromilides, Paschalis M., ed. *From Republican Polity to National Community: Reconsiderations of Enlightenment Political Thought*. SVEC 2003: 09.

Kivy, Peter. *The Fine Art of Repetition*. Cambridge, CUP, 1993.

Klein, Lawrence E. "Politeness and the Interpretation of the British Eighteenth Century." *Historical Journal* 45 (2002): 869–98.

Koch, Adrienne. *Jefferson and Madison: The Great Collaboration*. New York, 1964.

Koepke, Wulf, ed. *Johann Gottfried Herder: Academic Disciplines and the Pursuit of Knowledge*. Columbia, S.C., Camden House, 1996.

Koselleck, Reinhart. *Futures Past: On the Semantics of Historical Time*. Cambridge, Mass., MIT Press, 1985.

————. *Critique and Crisis: Enlightenment and the Pathogenesis of the Modern Society*. Cambridge, Mass., MIT Press; Leamington Spa, Berg Press, 1988.

————. *The Practice of Conceptual History*. Stanford, Stanford UP, 2002.

Kristeller, Paul Oskar. "The Modern System of the Arts: A Study in the History of Aesthetics." *Journal of the History of Ideas* 12 (1951): 496–527; 13 (1952): 17–46.

Kuhn, Albert J. "English Deism and the Development of Romantic Mythological Syncretism." *PMLA* 71 (1956): 1094–116.

Kupersmith, William. "Juvenal as Sublime Satirist." *PMLA* 87 (1972): 508–11.

———. "Juvenal as Sublime Satirist." *PMLA* 88 (1973): 144.

Labbé, François. *Anacharsis Cloots le Prussien francophile. Un philosophe au service de la révolution française et universelle*. Paris, L'Harmattan, 1999.

Lacroix, Sigismond. *Actes de la commune de Paris pendant la révolution*. Première série. 7 vols. Paris, 1894–8.

Laffay, Ernest. *Le poète Gilbert (Nicolas-Joseph-Florent [sic]), étude biographique et littéraire*. Paris, 1898.

Landes, David S. "The Statistical Study of French Crises." *Journal of Economic History* 10 (1951): 195–211.

Langlois, Claude. "Religion, culte ou opinion religieuse: la politique des révolutionnaires." *Revue française de sociologie* 30 (1989): 471–96.

Larson, James L. "Vital Forces: Regulative Principles or Constitutive Agents? A Strategy in German Physiology, 1786–1801." *Isis* 70 (1979): 235–49.

Latreille, Albert. *L'armée et la nation à la fin de l'ancien régime*. Paris, 1914.

Le Bozec, Christine. *Boissy d'Anglas. Un grand notable libéral*. Privas, Fédération des Oeuvres Laïques de l'Ardèche, 1995.

Le Guillou, Louis. *Le "baron" d'Eckstein et ses contemporains. Correspondances avec un choix de ses articles*. Paris, Champion, 2003.

Leask, Nigel. *British Romantic Writers and the East: Anxieties of Empire*. Cambridge, CUP, 1992.

Legrand, Robert. *Babeuf et ses compagnons de route*. Paris, Clavreuil, 1981.

Lemay, Edna Hindie. *Dictionnaire des constituants*. 2 vols. Oxford, Voltaire Foundation, 1991.

Leopold, Joan, ed. *The Prix Volney: Its History and Significance for the Development of Linguistic Research*. 3 vols. Dordrecht, Kluwer, 1999.

Lepan, Géraldine. *Jean-Jacques Rousseau et le patriotisme*. Paris, Champion, 2007.

Leterrier, S. A. "Mercier à l'Institut." In Jean-Claude Bonnet, ed., *Louis-Sébastien Mercier (1740–1814). Un hérétique en littérature*, pp. 295–326. Paris, Mercure de France, 1995.

Lever, Maurice, ed. *Bibliothèque Sade (I). Papiers de famille. Le règne du père 1721–1760*. Paris, Fayard, 1993.

Levi, Anthony. *French Moralists: The Theory of the Passions 1585 to 1649*. Oxford, OUP, 1964.

Levitt, Marcus C. "An Antidote to Nervous Juice: Catherine the Great's Debate with Chappe d'Auteroche over Russian Culture." *Eighteenth-Century Studies* 32 (1998): 49–63.

Levy, Darlene Gay. *The Ideas and Careers of Simon-Nicolas Henri Linguet: A Study in Eighteenth-Century French Politics*. Urbana, University of Illinois Press, 1980.

Lilla, Mark. *Gian Battista Vico: The Making of an Anti-Modern*. Cambridge, Mass., Harvard UP, 1993.

Lilti, Antoine. "Sociabilité et mondanité: Les hommes de lettres dans les salons parisiens du xviiie siècle." *French Historical Studies* 28 (2005): 415–45.

———. *Le monde des salons. Sociabilité et mondanité à Paris au xviiie siècle*. Paris, Fayard, 2005.

Lincoln, Bruce. *Theorizing Myth: Narrative, Ideology, and Scholarship*. Chicago, University of Chicago Press, 1999.

Lippman, Edward A., ed. *Musical Aesthetics: A Historical Reader*. 3 vols. New York, Pendragon Press, 1986–90.

Livesey, James. *Making Democracy in the French Revolution*. Cambridge, Mass., Harvard UP, 2001.

Lockwood, Thomas. "On the Relationship of Satire and Poetry after Pope." *Studies in English Literature, 1500–1900* 14 (1974): 387–402.

Loft, Leonore. *Passion, Politics, and* Philosophie: *Rediscovering Jacques-Pierre Brissot*. Westport, Conn.., Greenwood Press, 2002.

Lotterie, Florence. *Progrès et perfectibilité: un dilemme des lumières françaises (1755–1814)*. *SVEC* 2006: 04.

Lovejoy, Arthur O. *The Great Chain of Being*. Cambridge, Mass., Harvard UP, 1936.

———. "The Supposed Primitivism of Rousseau's *Discourse on Inequality*." Reprinted in Lovejoy, *Essays in the History of Ideas*, pp. 14–37. Baltimore, Johns Hopkins UP, 1948.

———. *Reflections on Human Nature*. Baltimore, Johns Hopkins UP, 1961.

Lovejoy, Arthur O., and George Boas. *Primitivism and Related Ideas in Antiquity* [1935]. Baltimore, Johns Hopkins UP, 1997.

Lovering, Stella. *L'activité intellectuelle de l'Angleterre d'après l'ancien "Mercure de France" (1672–1778)*. Paris, 1930.

Lüsebrink, Hans-Jürgen, and Rolf Reichardt. *The Bastille: A History of a Symbol of Despotism and Freedom* [1990]. Translated by Norbert Schürer. Durham, N.C., Duke UP, 1997.

Lüthy, Herbert. *Le passé présent. Combats d'idées de Calvin à Rousseau*. Monaco, Editions du Rocher, 1965.

Macdonald, D. C. *Birthright in Land*. London, 1891.

Macintyre, Alasdair. "The Logical Status of Religious Belief." In Stephen Toulmin, Ronald W. Hepburn, and Alasdair Macintyre, *Metaphysical Beliefs: Three Essays*, pp. 167–211. London, SCM Press, 1957.

Magendie, Maurice. *La politesse mondaine et les théories de l'honnêteté en France au xviie siècle, de 1600–1660*. 2 vols. Paris, 1925.

Maître, Miriam. *Les Précieuses. Naissance des femmes de lettres en France au xviie siècle*. Paris, Champion, 1999.

Major, Vernon Hyde. *The Death of the Baroque and the Rhetoric of Good Taste*. Cambridge, CUP, 2006.

Malvache, Jean-Luc, ed. "Correspondance inédit de Mably à Fellenberg 1763–1778." *Francia* 19 (1992): 47–93.

Mantel, Hilary. *A Place of Greater Safety*. London, Viking, 1992.

Manuel, Frank. *The Eighteenth Century Confronts the Gods*. Cambridge, Mass., Harvard UP, 1959.

Manuel Frank E., and Fritzie P. Manuel. *Utopian Thought in the Western World*. Cambridge, Mass., Harvard UP, 1979.

Margerison, Kenneth. *Pamphlets and Public Opinion: The Campaign for a Union of Orders in the Early French Revolution*. West Lafayette, Purdue UP, 1998.

Markov, Walter, and Albert Soboul. *Die Sansculotten von Paris*. Berlin, Akademie Verlag, 1957.

Marshall P. J., ed. *The British Discovery of Hinduism in the Eighteenth Century*. Cambridge, CUP, 1970.

Marshall, John. *Descartes's Moral Theory*. Ithaca, Cornell UP, 1998.

May, Gita. *De Jean-Jacques Rousseau à Madame Roland*. Geneva, Droz, 1964.

Maza, Sarah C. *Private Lives and Public Affairs. The Causes Célèbres of Pre-revolutionary France*. Berkeley and Los Angeles, University of California Press, 1993.

———. *The Myth of the French Bourgeoisie: An Essay on the Social Imaginary*. Cambridge, Mass., Harvard UP, 2003.

McClelland, Charles E. *The German Historians and England: A Study in Nineteenth-Century Views*. Cambridge, CUP, 1971.

McKendrick, Neil, John Brewer, and J. H. Plumb. *The Birth of a Consumer Society: The Commercialisation of Eighteenth-Century England*. London, Europa, 1982.

McKenna, Stephen J. *Adam Smith: The Rhetoric of Propriety*. Albany, State University of New York Press, 2006.

McMahon, Darrin M. *The Pursuit of Happiness: A History from the Greeks to the Present*. London, Allen Lane, 2006.

McManners, John. *Death and the Enlightenment*. Oxford, OUP, 1981.

McNeil, Maureen. *Under the Banner of Science: Erasmus Darwin and His Age*. Manchester, Manchester UP, 1987.

Megill, Allan. "Aesthetic Theory and Historical Consciousness in the Eighteenth Century." *History and Theory* 17 (1978): 29–62.

Meier, Heinrich. *Carl Schmitt and Leo Strauss: The Hidden Dialogue*. Chicago, University of Chicago Press, 1995.

———. *Leo Strauss and the Theologico-Political Problem*. Cambridge, CUP, 2006.

Meinecke, Friedrich. *Historism: The Rise of A New Historical Outlook* [1936]. New York, 1972.

Mercier, Roger. *La réhabilitation de la nature humaine, 1700–1750*. Villemomble, 1960.

Mercier-Faivre, Anne-Marie. *Un supplément à l'Encyclopédie: Le Monde primitif d'Antoine Court de Gebelin*. Paris, Champion, 1999.

Merrick, Jeffrey. "Corruption versus *honnêteté*: Morellet's Assessment of the French Political Scene in May 1774." *SVEC* 2005: 12, pp. 155–75.

Meyer, Annette. "The Experience of Human Diversity and the Search for Unity: Concepts of Mankind in the Late Enlightenment." *Studi Settecenteschi* 21 (2001): 244–64.

Meyer, Jerry D. "Benjamin West's Chapel of Revealed Religion: A Study in Eighteenth-Century Protestant Religious Art." *Art Bulletin* 57 (1975): 247–65.

Michaud, Louis-Gabriel, ed. *Biographie universelle ancienne et moderne*. 45 vols. Paris, 1843–65.

Michon, Georges. *Essai sur l'histoire du parti feuillant. Adrien Duport*. Paris, 1924.

———. *Robespierre et la guerre révolutionnaire, 1791–92*. Paris, 1937.

Miller, Peter. *Defining the Common Good: Empire, Religion and Philosophy in Eighteenth-Century Britain*. Cambridge, CUP, 1994.

Moles, John. "Cynic Cosmopolitanism." In R. Bracht Branham and Marie-Odile Goulet-Cazé, eds., *The Cynics: The Cynic Movement in Antiquity and Its Legacy*, pp. 105–20. Berkeley and Los Angeles, University of California Press, 1996.

Momigliano, Arnoldo. "Vico's *Scienza Nuova*: Roman '*Bestioni*' and Roman '*Eroi*.'" In Arnoldo Momigliano, *Essays in Ancient and Modern Historiography*, pp. 259–76. Oxford, OUP, 1977.

Monnier, Raymonde. "Tableaux croisés chez Mercier et Rutlidge. Le *Peuple* de Paris et le *Plébéien* Anglais." *Annales historiques de la révolution française* 339 (2005): 1–16.

Monselet, Charles. *Les oubliés et les dédaignés. Figures littéraires de la fin du xviiie siècle*. 2 vols. Alençon, 1857.

Moyn, Samuel. "From Experience to Law: Leo Strauss and the Weimar Crisis of the Philosophy of Religion." *History of European Ideas* 33 (2007): 174–94.

Munro, James S. "Richardson, Marivaux, and the French Romance Tradition." *Modern Language Review* 70 (1975): 752–9.

Nelson, Eric. *The Greek Tradition in Republican Thought*. Cambridge, CUP, 2004.

———. "'Talmudical Commonwealthsmen' and the Rise of Republican Exclusivism." *Historical Journal* 50 (2007): 809–35.

Neuhouser, Frederick. "Freedom, Dependence and the General Will." *Philosophical Review* 102 (1993): 363–95.

———. "Rousseau on the Relation between Reason and Self-Love." *International Yearbook of German Idealism* 1 (2003): 221–39.

Nicolas, Serge. "'Sur la réminiscence': un manuscrit inédit de Charles Bonnet." *Corpus. Revue de philosophie* 29 (1995): 165–221.

———. Introduction to Charles Bonnet, *Essai de psychologie*, edited by Serge Nicolas. Paris, L'Harmattan, 2006.

Nicolet, Claude. *Les Gracques*. Paris, Gallimard, 1980.

Niehues-Pröbsting, Heinrich. "Diogenes in the Enlightenment." In R. Bracht Branham and Marie-Odile Goulet-Cazé, eds., *The Cynics: The Cynic Movement in Antiquity and Its Legacy*, pp. 329–65. Berkeley and Los Angeles, University of California Press, 1996.

Nijenhuis, I.J.A. *Ein Joodse* Philosophe. *Isaac de Pinto (1717–1787)*. Amsterdam, 1992.

Nisbet H. B., and Claude Rawson, eds. *The Cambridge History of Literary Criticism*. Cambridge, CUP, 1997.

Northeast, Catherine M. *The Parisian Jesuits and the Enlightenment 1700–1762. Studies on Voltaire and the Eighteenth Century* 288 (1991).

Norton, Robert E. *The Beautiful Soul: Aesthetic Morality in the Eighteenth Century*. Ithaca, Cornell UP, 1995.

O'Connor, Thomas. *An Irish Theologian in Enlightenment France: Luke Joseph Hooke, 1714–96*. Dublin, 1995.

O'Dea, Michael. "Philosophie, histoire et imagination dans le *Discours sur l'origine de l'inégalité* de Jean-Jacques Rousseau." *SVEC* 2001: 04, pp. 340–60.

O'Gorman, Donal. *Diderot the Satirist*. Toronto, University of Toronto Press, 1971.

O'Neal, John C. *The Authority of Experience: Sensationist Theory in the French Enlightenment*. University Park, Pennsylvania State UP, 1996.

Oncken, August. *Der ältere Mirabeau und die ökonomische Gesellschaft in Bern*. Berne, 1886.

Orcibal, Jean. "L'influence spirituelle de Fénelon dans les pays anglo-saxons au xviiie siècle." In Jean Orcibal, *Etudes d'histoire et de littérature religieuses*, pp. 221–32. Paris, Klincksieck, 1997.

———. "Les spirituels français et espagnols chez Jean Wesley et ses contemporains." In Jean Orcibal, *Etudes d'histoire et de littérature religieuses*, pp. 163–220. Paris, Klincksieck, 1997.

———. *Etudes d'histoire et de littérature religieuses*. Paris, Klincksieck, 1997.

Ozouf, Mona. *La fête révolutionnaire*. Paris, Gallimard, 1976

———. *L'homme régénéré. Essais sur la révolution française*. Paris, Gallimard, 1989.

———. *Varennes: la mort du royauté, 21 juin 1791*. Paris, Gallimard, 2005.

Paganini, Gianni. "'Everything Must Be Redone': Condillac as Critic of Despotism and Defender of Toleration." In Hans Blom, John Christian Laursen, and Luisa Simonutti, eds., *Monarchisms in the Age of Enlightenment*, pp. 144–61. Toronto, University of Toronto Press, 2007.

Pagden, Anthony. *The Fall of Natural Man: The American Indian and the Origins of Comparative Ethnology* [1982]. Cambridge, CUP, 1986.

Palmer, Robert R. *Catholics and Unbelievers in Eighteenth-Century France*. Princeton, Princeton UP, 1939.

Peck, Linda Levy. *Consuming Splendor*. Cambridge, CUP, 2005.

Pekacz, Jolanta T. *Conservative Tradition in Pre-Revolutionary France: Parisian Salon Women*. New York, Peter Lang, 1999.

Peltonen, Markku. "Politeness and Whiggism, 1688–1732." *Historical Journal* 48 (2005): 391–414.

Perelli, Luciano. *I Gracchi*. Rome, Salerno Editrice, 1993.

Perroud, Claude. "Un projet de Brissot pour une association agricole." *La Révolution française* 42 (1902): 260–65.

Pfersmann, Andreas. "Une 'gloire tudesque.'" In Jean-Claude Bonnet, ed., *Louis-Sébastien Mercier (1740–1814). Un hérétique en littérature*, pp. 417–36. Paris, Mercure de France, 1995.

Phillips, Patricia. *The Adventurous Muse: Theories of Originality in English Poetics 1650–1760*. Uppsala, 1984.

Philonenko, Alexis. "Rousseau et Fichte." In Ives Radrizzani, ed., *Fichte et la France*. Paris, Beauchesne, 1997.

Pignol, Claire. "Rousseau et l'argent: autarcie et division du travail dans *La Nouvelle Héloïse*." *SVEC* 2004: 10, pp. 262–74.

Pocock, J.G.A. *The Machiavellian Moment: Florentine Political Thought and the Atlantic Republican Tradition* [1975]. 2nd ed. Princeton, Princeton UP, 2003.

———. *Barbarism and Religion: The First Decline and Fall*. Cambridge, CUP, 2003.

———. *Barbarians, Savages and Empires*. Cambridge, CUP, 2005.

Poliakov, Leon. *The Aryan Myth: A History of Racist and Nationalist Ideas in Europe*. London, Chatto-Heinemann, 1974.

Pomeroy, Sarah B. *Goddesses, Whores, Wives and Slaves: Women in Classical Greece*. New York, Schocken, 1975.

Poni, Carlo. "Fashion as Flexible Production: The Strategies of the Lyons Silk Merchants in the Eighteenth Century." In Charles F. Sabel and Jonathan Zeitlin, eds., *World of Possibilities: Flexibility and Mass Production in Western Industrialization*, pp. 37–74. Cambridge, CUP, 1997.

Popkin, Jeremy D., and Richard H. Popkin, eds. *The Abbé Grégoire and His World*. Dordrecht, Kluwer, 2000.

Popkin, Richard H. *Isaac La Peyrère (1596–1676): His Life, Work and Influence.* Leiden, Brill, 1987.

———. "The Fifth Monarchy Redux." In Hans Blom, John Christian Laursen, and Luisa Simonutti, eds., *Monarchisms in the Age of Enlightenment*, pp. 162–72. Toronto, University of Toronto Press, 2007.

Porset, Charles. "L'inquiétante étrangeté de l'*Essai sur l'origine des langues*: Rousseau et ses exégètes." *Studies on Voltaire and the Eighteenth Century* 154 (1976): 1715–54.

———. "*Grammatista philosophens*. Les sciences du langage de Port-Royal aux Idéologues (1660–1818). Bibliographie." In André Joly and Jean Stefanini, eds., *La Grammaire générale, des modistes aux idéologues*, pp. 11–95. Lille, Presses de l'Université de Lille, 1977.

Postigliola, Alberto. "De Malebranche à Rousseau: les apories de la volonté générale et la revanche du 'raisonneur violent.'" *Annales de la société Jean-Jacques Rousseau* 39 (1972–7): 123–38.

———. "Montesquieu e Bonnet: la controversia sul concetto de legge." In Paolo Casini, ed., *La Politica della Ragione*, pp. 43–69. Bologna, Il Mulino, 1978.

Postle, Martin. "'Painted Women': Reynolds and the Cult of the Courtesan." In Robyn Asleson, ed., *Notorious Muse: The Actress in British Art and Culture, 1776–1812*, pp. 22–56. New Haven, Yale UP, 2003.

Potkay, Adam. *The Story of Joy: From the Bible to Late Romanticism.* Cambridge, CUP, 2007.

Price, Munro. *Preserving the Monarchy: The Comte de Vergennes, 1774–1787.* Cambridge, CUP, 1995.

———. *The Fall of the French Monarchy.* London, Macmillan, 2002.

———. "Mirabeau and the Court: Some New Evidence." *French Historical Studies* 29 (2006): 37–75.

———. "The Court Nobility and the Origins of the French Revolution." In Hamish Scott and Brendan Simms, eds., *Cultures of Power in Europe during the Long Eighteenth Century*, pp. 269–88. Cambridge, CUP, 2007.

Priestman, Martin. *Romantic Atheism: Poetry and Freethought, 1780–1830.* Cambridge, CUP, 1999.

Purdy, Daniel Leonhard. *The Tyranny of Elegance: Consumer Cosmopolitanism in the Age of Goethe.* Baltimore, Johns Hopkins UP, 1998.

———, ed. *The Rise of Fashion: A Reader.* Minneapolis, University of Minnesota Press, 2004.

Pusey, W. W. *Louis-Sébastien Mercier in Germany: His Vogue and Influence in the Eighteenth Century.* New York, Columbia UP, 1939.

Raskolnikoff, Mouza. *Histoire romaine et critique historique au siècle des lumières.* Collection de l'Ecole française de Rome, 163. Strasbourg and Rome, 1992.

Rawson, Claude. *Satire and Sentiment 1660–1830.* New Haven, Yale UP, 2000.

Recchia, Viola. "La via segreta alla rivoluzione. Le *Lettres sur l'esprit du siècle* di Dom Deschamps." *Studi Settecenteschi* 21 (2001): 85–110.

Reill, Peter Hans. *Vitalizing Nature in the Enlightenment.* Berkeley and Los Angeles, University of California Press, 2005.

Reinhard, Marcel. *La légende de Henri IV.* Paris, 1935.

———. "Le voyage de Pétion à Londres, 24 Octobre–11 Novembre 1791." *Revue d'histoire diplomatique* (1970): 1–60.

Relihan, Joel C. "Menippus in Antiquity and the Renaissance." In R. Bracht Branham and Marie-Odile Goulet-Cazé, eds., *The Cynics: The Cynic Movement in Antiquity and Its Legacy*, pp. 265–93. Berkeley and Los Angeles, University of California Press, 1996.

Rétat, Claude. "Lumières et ténèbres du citoyen Dupuis." *Chroniques d'histoire maçonnique* 50 (1999): 5–68.

Rey, Roselyne. "La partie, le tout et l'individu: science et philosophie dans l'oeuvre de Charles Bonnet." In Marino Buscaglia, René Sigrist, Jacques Trembley, and Jean Wüest, eds., *Charles Bonnet, savant et philosophe (1720–1793). Mémoires de la société de physique et d'histoire naturelle de Genève* 47 (1994): 61–75.

Reynold, G de. "J. J. Rousseau et la Suisse." *Annales de la société Jean-Jacques Rousseau* 8 (1912): 161–204.

Richardson, Alan. *British Romanticism and the Science of the Mind*. Cambridge, CUP, 2001.

Riley, Patrick. *The General Will before Rousseau*. Princeton, Princeton UP, 1986.

———. *Leibniz' Universal Jurisprudence: Justice as the Charity of the Wise*. Cambridge, Mass., Harvard UP, 1996.

———. "Rousseau, Fénelon and the Quarrel between the Ancients and the Moderns." In Patrick Riley, ed., *The Cambridge Companion to Rousseau*, pp. 78–93. Cambridge, CUP, 2001.

———. "Fénelon's Republican Monarchism in Telemachus." In Hans Blom, John Christian Laursen, and Luisa Simonutti, eds., *Monarchisms in the Age of Enlightenment*, pp. 78–100. Toronto, University of Toronto Press, 2007.

Riskin, Jessica. *Science in the Age of Sensibility*. Chicago, University of Chicago Press, 2002.

Ritchie, R. L. "Le 'père Hoop' de Diderot: Essai d'identification." In Mary Williams and James A. Rothschild, eds., *A Miscellany of Studies in Romance Languages and Literatures*, pp. 409–26. Cambridge, Heffer, 1932.

Robbins, Caroline. "The Strenuous Whig, Thomas Hollis of Lincoln's Inn." [1950.] In Caroline Robbins, *Absolute Liberty*, edited by Barbara Taft. Hamden, Conn., Archon Books, 1982.

Roberts, William. *A Dawn of Imaginative Feeling: The Contribution of John Brown (1715–66) to Eighteenth-Century Thought and Literature*. Carlisle, Northern Academic Press, 1996.

Robertson, John. *The Case for the Enlightenment: Scotland and Naples 1680–1760*. Cambridge, CUP, 2005.

Roddier, Henri. *J. J. Rousseau en Angleterre au xviiie siècle*. Paris, 1950.

Roger, Jacques. *Les sciences de la vie dans la pensée française du xviiie siècle*. Paris, Armand Colin, 1963.

———. "The Living World." In G. S. Rousseau and Roy Porter, eds., *The Ferment of Knowledge: Studies in the Historiography of Eighteenth-Century Science*, pp. 255–83. Cambridge, CUP, 1980.

Rogers, Robert W. "Critiques of the *Essay on Man* in France and Germany, 1736–1755." *English Literary History* 15 (1948): 176–93.

Roggerone, Giuseppe A. "Rousseau-Mably: Un rapporto umano e culturale difficile." *Il Pensiero Politico* 23 (1990): 219–39.

Rogister, John. *Louis XV and the Parlement of Paris*. Cambridge, CUP, 1995.

Rose, R. B. *Gracchus Babeuf, the First Revolutionary Communist.* London, Arnold, 1978.

————. "The 'Red Scare' of the 1790s: The French Revolution and the 'Agrarian Law.'" *Past & Present* 103 (1984): 113–30.

Rosenblum, Robert. "The Origin of Painting: A Problem in the Iconography of Romantic Classicism." *Art Bulletin* 39 (1957): 279–90.

Rossi, Paolo. *I Segni del Tempo.* Milan, Feltrinelli, 1979.

Rothkrug, Lionel. *Opposition to Louis XIV: The Political and Social Origins of the French Enlightenment.* Princeton, Princeton UP, 1965.

Rousseau, G. S., and Roy Porter, eds. *The Ferment of Knowledge: Studies in the Historiography of Eighteenth-Century Science.* Cambridge, CUP, 1980.

Roux, Philippe de. "Le marquis de Casaux. Un planteur des Antilles inspirateur de Mirabeau." Paris, Société d'histoire des colonies françaises, 1951.

Rubin, James Henry. "Painting and Politics II: J. L. David's Patriotism, or The Conspiracy of Gracchus Babeuf and the Legacy of Topino-Lebrun." *Art Bulletin: A Quarterly Published by the College Art Association of America* 58 (1976): 547–68.

Rudé, George. *The Crowd in the French Revolution.* Oxford, OUP, 1959.

Rufi, Enrico. *Le rêve laïque de Louis-Sébastien Mercier entre littérature et politique. Studies on Voltaire and the Eighteenth Century* 326 (1995).

Russo, Elena. *Styles of Enlightenment: Taste, Politics, and Authorship in Eighteenth-Century France.* Baltimore, Johns Hopkins UP, 2007.

Rutherford, Donald. "Metaphysics, the Late Period." In Nicholas Jolley, ed., *The Cambridge Companion to Leibniz*, pp. 124–75. Cambridge, CUP, 1995.

————. "Leibniz on Spontaneity." In Donald Rutherford and J. A. Cover, eds., *Leibniz: Nature and Freedom*, pp. 156–80. Oxford, OUP, 2005.

Ruwet, Joseph, ed. *Lettres de Turgot à la duchesse d'Enville.* Louvain, 1976.

Ryan, Robert M. *The Romantic Reformation: Religious Politics in English Literature 1789–1824.* Cambridge, CUP, 1997.

Sabel, Charles, and Jonathan Zeitlin. "Historical Alternatives to Mass Production." *Past & Present* 108 (1985): 133–76.

————. *World of Possibilities: Flexibility and Mass Production in Western Industrialization.* Cambridge, CUP, 1997.

Salkever, Stephen G. "Rousseau and the Concept of Happiness." *Polity* 11 (1978): 27–45.

Sandoz, Ellis, ed. *The Roots of Liberty: Magna Carta, Ancient Constitution, and the Anglo-American Tradition of Rule of Law.* Columbia, University of Missouri Press, 1993.

Sareil, Jean. *Les Tencin.* Geneva, Droz, 1969.

Savarian, Norbert. *Louis de Fontanes. Belles-lettres et enseignement de la fin de l'ancien régime à l'Empire. SVEC* 2002: 8.

Savioz, Raymond. *La Philosophie de Charles Bonnet de Genève.* Paris, Vrin, 1948.

Schaffer, Simon. "States of Mind: Enlightenment and Natural Philosophy." In G. S. Rousseau, ed., *The Languages of Psyche: Mind and Body in Enlightenment Thought*, pp. 233–90. Berkeley and Los Angeles, University of California Press, 1990.

Schechter, Ronald. *Obstinate Hebrews: Representations of Jews in France, 1715–1815.* Berkeley and Lose Angeles, University of California Press, 2003.

Schier, Donald S. *Louis-Bertrand Castel, Anti-Newtonian Scientist*. Cedar Rapids, Iowa, 1941.

Schlüter, Gisela. "Exporting Heresiology: Translations and Revisions of Pluquet's *Dictionnaire des hérésies*." In Ian Hunter, John Christian Laursen, and Cary J. Nederman, eds., *Heresy in Transition: Transforming Ideas of Heresy in Medieval and Early Modern Europe*, pp. 169–80. Aldershot, Ashgate, 2005.

Scholem, Gershom. *Du Frankisme au Jacobinisme. La vie de Moses Dobruška alias Thomas von Schönfeld alias Junius Frey*. Paris, Ecole des Hautes Etudes en Sciences Sociales, 1981.

Schui, Florian. *Early Debates about Industry: Voltaire and His Contemporaries*. Basingstoke, Palgrave Macmillan, 2005.

Schwab, Raymond. *The Oriental Renaissance* [1950]. New York, Columbia UP, 1972.

Scott, Katie, and Deborah Cherry, eds. *Between Luxury and the Everyday: Decorative Arts in Eighteenth-Century France*. Oxford, Blackwell, 2005.

Scott, John T. "Rousseau and the Melodious Language of Freedom." *Journal of Politics* 59 (1997): 803–29.

———. "The Harmony between Rousseau's Musical Theory and His Philosophy." *Journal of the History of Ideas* 59 (1998): 287–308.

Sepinwall, Alyssa Goldstein. *The Abbé Grégoire and the French Revolution: The Making of Modern Universalism*. Berkeley and Los Angeles, University of California Press, 2005.

Sewell, William H. *A Rhetoric of Bourgeois Revolution: The Abbé Sieyès and "What Is the Third Estate?"* Durham, Duke UP, 1994.

Sheehan, Jonathan. *The Enlightenment Bible: Translation, Scholarship, Culture*. Princeton, Princeton UP, 2005.

Sher, Richard B. *Church and University in the Scottish Enlightenment: The Moderate Literati of Edinburgh*. Princeton UP, 1985.

Shovlin, John. *The Political Economy of Virtue: Luxury, Patriotism and the Origins of the French Revolution*. Ithaca, Cornell UP, 2006.

Silvestre de Sacy, Jacques. *Le comte d'Angiviller, dernier directeur général des bâtiments du roi*. Paris, 1953.

Simons, Katrin. *Jacques Réattu (1760–1833), peintre de la révolution française*. Paris, Arthéna, 1985.

Skinner, Quentin. *Liberty before Liberalism*. Cambridge, CUP, 2000.

Smentek, Kristel. "Sex, Sentiment, and Speculation: The Market for Genre Prints on the Eve of the French Revolution." In Philip Conisbee, ed., *French Genre Painting in the Eighteenth Century*, pp. 221–43. Washington D.C., National Gallery of Art, 2007.

Smiles, Sam. *The Image of Antiquity: Ancient Britain and the Romantic Imagination*. New Haven, Yale UP, 1994.

Smith, Christopher J. P. *A Quest for Home: Reading Robert Southey*. Liverpool, Liverpool UP, 1997.

Smith, Edwin Burrows. "Jean-Sylvain Bailly: Astronomer, Mystic, Revolutionary, 1736–1793." *Transactions of the American Philosophical Society*, n.s., 44 (1954): 427–538.

Smith, Jay M. *The Culture of Merit: Nobility, Royal Service, and the Making of Absolute Monarchy in France, 1600–1789*. Ann Arbor, University of Michigan Press, 1996.

————. "Social Categories, the Language of Patriotism, and the Origins of the French Revolution: The Debate over *noblesse commerçante*." *Journal of Modern History* 27 (2000): 339–74.

————. *Nobility Reimagined: The Patriotic Nation in Eighteenth-Century France*. Ithaca, Cornell UP, 2005.

————, ed. *The French Nobility in the Eighteenth Century: Reassessments and New Approaches*. University Park, Penn State UP, 2006.

Smith, Ruth. *Handel's Oratorios and Eighteenth-Century Thought*. Cambridge, CUP, 1995.

Smith, Steven B. *Reading Leo Strauss: Politics, Philosophy, Judaism*. Chicago, University of Chicago Press, 2006.

Soboul, Albert. *Les sans-culottes parisiens en l'an II*. Paris, Clavreuil, 1958.

————. *The Parisian Sans-Culottes and the French Revolution*. Translated by Gwynne Lewis. Oxford, OUP, 1964.

Söderhjelm, Alma. *Marie-Antoinette et Barnave. Correspondance secrète (Juillet 1791-Janvier 1792)*. Paris, 1934.

Sonenscher, Michael. "The *Sans-Culottes* of the Year II: Rethinking the Language of Labour in Revolutionary France." *Social History* 9 (1984): 301–28.

————. *Work and Wages: Politics, Natural Law and the Eighteenth-Century French Trades*. Cambridge, CUP, 1989.

————. "Artisans, Sans-Culottes and the French Revolution." In Alan Forrest and Peter Jones, eds., *Reshaping France: Town, Country and Region during the French Revolution*, pp. 105–21. Manchester, Manchester UP, 1991.

————. "The Nation's Debt and the Birth of the Modern Republic: The French Fiscal Deficit and the Politics of the Revolution of 1789." *History of Political Thought* 18 (1997): 64–103, 267–325.

————. "Republicanism, State Finances and the Emergence of Commercial Society in Eighteenth-Century France—or from Royal to Ancient Republicanism, and Back." In Martin Van Gelderen and Quentin Skinner, eds., *Republicanism: A Shared European Heritage*, 2:275–91. 2 vols. Cambridge, CUP, 2002.

————. "Property, Community and Citizenship." In Mark Goldie and Robert Wokler, eds., *The Cambridge History of Eighteenth-Century Political Thought*, pp. 465–94. Cambridge, CUP, 2006.

————. *Before the Deluge: Public Debt, Inequality, and the Intellectual Origins of the French Revolution*. Princeton, Princeton UP, 2007.

Sordi, Marta. "La tradizione storiografica su Tiberio Gracco e la propaganda contemporanea." *Sesta Miscellanea Greca e Romana* (Rome, Istituto Italiano di Storia Antica) (1978): 299–330.

Spang, Rebecca L. "The Ghost of Law: Speculating on Money, Memory and Mississippi in the French Constituent Asssembly." *Historical Reflections* 31 (2005): 3–35.

Speck, W. A. *Robert Southey, Entire Man of Letters*. New Haven, Yale UP, 2006.

Starobinski, Jean. *Blessings in Disguise; or the Morality of Evil* [1989]. Translated by Arthur Goldhammer. Cambridge, Polity Press, 1993.

————. "Rousseau and Revolution." *New York Review of Books* 49, no. 7 (25 April 2002).

Stavan, Henry A. *Gabriel Sénac de Meilhan, 1736–1806. Moraliste, romancier, homme de lettres*. Paris, Lettres modernes, 1968.

Stedman Jones, Gareth. Introduction to Karl Marx and Frederick Engels, *The Communist Manifesto*. London, Penguin, 2002.

Stewart, M. A. "The Stoic Legacy in the Early Scottish Enlightenment." In Margaret J. Osler, ed., *Atoms, Pneuma, and Tranquillity: Epicurean and Stoic Themes in European Thought*, pp. 273–96. Cambridge, CUP, 1991.

Stone, Bailey. *The French Parlements and the Crisis of the Old Regime*. Chapel Hill, University of North Carolina Press, 1986.

Strauss, Leo. "On the Interpretation of Rousseau." *Social Research* 14 (1947): 455–87.

———. *Natural Right and History* [1953]. Chicago, University of Chicago Press, 1965.

———. "What Is Political Philosophy." In Leo Strauss, *What Is Political Philosophy? and Other Studies* [1959]. Chicago, University of Chicago Press, 1988.

Stuart, Tristram. *The Bloodless Revolution: Radical Vegetarians and the Discovery of India*. London, Harper Collins, 2006.

Stunkel, Kenneth R. "India and the Idea of a Primitive Revelation in French Neo-Catholic Thought." *Journal of Religious History* 8 (1974–75): 228–39.

Stuurman, Siep. *François Poulain de la Barre and the Invention of Modern Equality*. Cambridge, Mass., Harvard UP, 2004.

Suderman, Jeffrey M. *Orthodoxy and Enlightenment: George Campbell in the Eighteenth Century*. Montreal and Kingston, McGill-Queen's UP, 2001.

Sutherland, Donald M. G. "Taxation, Representation and Dictatorship in France, 1789–1830." In W. M. Ormrod, Margaret Bonney, and Richard Bonney, eds., *Crises, Revolutions, and Self-Sustained Growth: Essays in European Fiscal History, 1130–1830*, pp. 414–26. Stamford, Shaun Tyas, 1999.

Swann, Julian. *Politics and the Parlement of Paris under Louis XV, 1754–1774*. Cambridge, CUP, 1995.

Swenson, James. *On Jean-Jacques Rousseau Considered as One of the First Authors of the Revolution*. Stanford, Stanford UP, 2000.

Sydenham, Michael J. *Léonard Bourdon: The Career of a Revolutionary 1754–1807*. Waterloo, Ontario, Wilfred Laurier UP, 1999.

Tackett, Timothy. *Becoming a Revolutionary: The Deputies of the French National Assembly and the Emergence of a Revolutionary Culture (1789–1790)*. Princeton, Princeton UP, 1996.

———. *When the King Took Flight*. Cambridge, Mass., Harvard UP, 2003.

Tessonneau, Rémy. *Joseph Joubert, éducateur, d'après des documents inédits, 1754–1824*. Paris, 1944.

Thomas, Downing A. *Music and the Origins of Language: Theories from the French Enlightenment*. Cambridge, CUP, 1995.

Thomas, Walter. *Le poète Edward Young 1683–1765. Etude sur sa vie et ses oeuvres*. Paris, 1901.

Thompson, J. M. *Robespierre*. Oxford, 1939.

Thomson, Ann. *Materialism and Society in the Mid-Eighteenth Century: La Mettrie's "Discours Préliminaire"*. Geneva, Droz, 1981.

———. "Thomas Christie, Paine et la révolution française." In Bernard Vincent, ed., *Thomas Paine, ou la république sans frontières*, pp. 17–32. Nancy, Presses Universitaires de Nancy, 1993.

Tillet, Edouard. *La constitution anglaise, un modèle politique et institutionnel dans la France des lumières*. Aix-en-Provence, Presses universitaires d'Aix-Marseille, 2001.

Tilly, Charles. *Coercion, Capital, and European States, A.D. 900–1990*. Oxford, Blackwell, 1990.

Tomlinson, Gary. "Vico's Songs: Detours at the Origins of (Ethno) Musicology." *Musical Quarterly* 83 (1999): 344–77.

Tornezy, A. *Un bureau d'esprit au xviiie siècle. Le salon de Madame Geoffrin*. Paris, 1895.

Touchard-Lafosse, M. *Souvenirs d'un demi-siècle*. 6 vols. Brussels, 1836.

Toulangeon, François-Emmanuel. *Histoire de France depuis la révolution de 1789*. 7 vols. Paris, 1801.

Trautmann, Thomas R. *Aryans and British India*. Berkeley and Los Angeles, University of California Press, 1997.

Trousson, Raymond. Introduction to Mercier, *L'An deux mille quatre cent quarante quatre*, edited by Raymond Trousson.

———. *Jean-Jacques Rousseau jugé par ses contemporains*. Paris, Champion, 2000.

Tuck, Richard. *Natural Rights Theories: Their Origin and Development*. Cambridge, CUP, 1979.

———. *Philosophy and Government, 1572–1651*. Cambridge, CUP, 1993.

———. *The Rights of War and Peace: Political Thought and International Order from Grotius to Kant*. Oxford, OUP, 1999.

Tucker, Susie I. *Protean Shape: A Study in Eighteenth-Century Vocabulary and Usage*. London, Athlone Press, 1967.

Turgeon, F. K. "Fanny de Beauharnais." Ph.D. diss., Harvard, 1931.

———. "Fanny de Beauharnais: Biographical Notes and a Bibliography." *Modern Philology* 30 (1932): 61–80.

Vaissière, Pierre de. *Lettres d' 'aristocrates'. La révolution racontée par des correspondances privées*. Paris, 1907.

Vallance, Edward. " 'A Holy and Sacramentall Paction': Federal Theology and the Solemn League and Covenant in England." *English Historical Review* 116 (2001): 50–75.

Van Asselt, Willem J. *The Federal Theology of Johannes Cocceius (1603–1669*. Leiden, Brill, 2001.

Van Kley, Dale. "Pierre Nicole, Jansenism, and the Morality of Enlightened Self-Interest." In Alan Charles Kors and Paul J. Korshin, eds., *Anticipations of the Enlightenment in England, France, and Germany*, pp. 69–85. Philadelphia, University of Pennsylvania Press, 1987.

Van Tieghem, Paul. *Ossian en France*. 2 vols. Paris, 1917.

———. *Le Préromantisme*. 3 vols. Paris, 1948.

Velkley, Richard L. *Freedom and the End of Reason: On the Moral Foundations of Kant's Critical Philosophy*. Chicago, University of Chicago Press, 1989.

———. *Being after Rousseau: Philosophy and Culture in Question*. Chicago, University of Chicago Press, 2002.

Venturi, Franco. *Europe des lumières. Recherches sur le 18e siècle*. Paris, 1971.

Verba, Cynthia. *Music in the French Enlightenment*. Oxford, OUP, 1993.

Vidal-Naquet, Pierre. *Politics Ancient and Modern*. Cambridge, Polity Press, 1995.

Vovelle, Michel. *Théodore Desorgues, ou la désorganisation. Aix-Paris, 1763–1809*. Paris, Seuil, 1985.

Wade, Ira O. *The "Philosophe" in the French Drama of the Eighteenth Century*. Princeton, Princeton UP, 1926.

Wahrman, Dror. "Gender in Translation: How the English Wrote Their Juvenal, 1644–1815." *Representations* 65 (1999): 1–41.

Waldron, Jeremy. *God, Locke and Equality: Christian Foundations in Locke's Political Thought*. Cambridge, CUP, 2002.

Walker, D. P. *The Decline of Hell*. London, Routledge, 1962.

Ward, Addison. "The Tory View of Roman History." *Studies in English Literature* 4 (1964): 412–56.

Weinbrot, Howard D. *Menippean Satire Reconsidered; From Antiquity to the Eighteenth Century*. Baltimore, Johns Hopkins UP, 2006.

Weir, David A. *The Origins of the Federal Theology in Sixteenth-Century Reformation Thought*. Oxford, Clarendon Press, 1990.

Whatmore, Richard. *Republicanism in the French Revolution: An Intellectual History of Jean-Baptiste Say's Political Economy*. Oxford, OUP, 2000.

———. "Etienne Dumont, the British Constitution, and the French Revolution." *Historical Journal* 50 (2007): 23–47.

Whitman, James Q. "The Seigneurs Descend to the Rank of Creditors: The Abolition of Respect." *Yale Journal of Law and Humanities* 6 (1994): 249–83.

Whitney, Lois. *Primitivism and the Idea of Progress in English Popular Literature of the Eighteenth Century*. Baltimore, Johns Hopkins UP, 1934.

Williams, Bernard. "Pagan Justice and Christian Love" [1993]. In Bernard Williams, *The Sense of the Past: Essays in the History of Philosophy*, ed. Miles Burnyeat, pp. 71–82. Princeton, Princeton UP, 2006.

Williams, David. "French Opinion concerning the English Constitution in the Eighteenth Century." *Economica* 30 (1930): 295–308.

Williams, Elizabeth A. *The Physical and the Moral: Anthropology, Physiology and Philosophical Medicine in France, 1750–1850*. Cambridge, CUP, 1994.

Williams, Gwyn A. *Artisans and Sans-Culottes* [1968]. 2nd ed. London, Libris, 1989.

Wilson, Catherine. "The Reception of Leibniz in the Eighteenth Century." In Nicholas Jolley, ed., *The Cambridge Companion to Leibniz*, pp. 442–74. Cambridge, CUP, 1995.

Wokler, Robert. "Rameau, Rousseau, and the *Essai sur l'origine des langues*." *Studies on Voltaire and the Eighteenth Century* 117 (1974): 179–238.

———. "The Influence of Diderot on the Political Theory of Rousseau." *Studies on Voltaire and the Eighteenth Century* 132 (1975): 55–111.

———. *Rousseau on Society, Politics, Music and Language: An Historical Interpretation of His Early Writings*. New York, Garland Press, 1987.

———. Introduction to Denis Diderot, *Political Writings*, edited by Robert Wokler and John Hope Mason. Cambridge, CUP, 1992.

———. "Anthropology and Conjectural History in the Enlightenment." In Christopher Fox, Roy Porter, and Robert Wokler, eds., *Inventing Human Science: Eighteenth-Century Domains*, pp. 31–52. Berkeley and Los Angeles, University of California Press, 1995.

Wolf, Erma. *Rutledge's "Bureau d'Esprit"*. Giessener Beitrage zur Romanischen Philologie, 16. Giessen, 1925.

Wood, Paul B. *The Aberdeen Enlightenment: The Arts Curriculum in the Eighteenth Century*. Aberdeen, Aberdeen UP, 1993.

Woolhouse, R. S., and Richard Francks, eds. *Leibniz's New System and Associated Contemporary Texts*. Oxford, OUP, 1997.

Wootton, David. Review of Quentin Skinner and Martin Van Gelderen, eds., *Republicanism: A Shared European Heritage*. 2 vols. Cambridge, CUP, 2002. *English Historical Review* 120 (2005): 135–9.

———. "Liberty, Metaphor, and Mechanism: '*Checks and Balances*' and the Origins *of Modern Constitutionalism*." In David Womersley, ed., *Liberty and American Experience in the Eighteenth Century*, pp. 209–74. Indianapolis, Liberty Fund, 2006.

———. "The True Origins of Republicanism, or *de vera respublica*." In Manuela Albertone, ed., *Il repubblicanismo moderno. L'idea di republicca nella riflessione storica di Franco Venturi*. Naples, Bibliopolis, 2007.

Wright, John P. "Metaphysics and Physiology: Mind, Body and the Animal Economy in Eighteenth-Century Scotland." In M. A. Stewart, ed., *Studies in the Philosophy of the Scottish Enlightenment*, pp. 251–301. Oxford, OUP, 1990.

———. "Locke, Willis and the Seventeenth-Century Epicurean Soul." In Margaret J. Osler, ed., *Atoms, Pneuma, and Tranquillity: Epicurean and Stoic Themes in European Thought*, pp. 239–58. Cambridge, CUP, 1991.

———. "Materialism and the Life Soul in Eighteenth-Century Scottish Physiology." In Paul Wood, ed., *The Scottish Enlightenment: Essays in Reinterpretation*, pp. 177–97. Rochester, N.Y., University of Rochester Press, 2000.

Wright John P., and Paul Potter, eds. *Psyche and Soma: Physicians and Metaphysicians on the Mind-Body Problem from Antiquity to the Enlightenment*. Oxford, OUP, 2000.

Wright, Johnson Kent. *A Classical Republican in Eighteenth-Century France: The Political Thought of Mably*. Stanford, Stanford UP, 1997.

Wrigley, Richard. *The Origins of French Art Criticism: From the Ancien Regime to the Restoration*. Oxford, OUP, 1993.

———. *The Politics of Appearances: Representation of Dress in Revolutionary France*. Oxford, Berg, 2002.

———. "Genre Painting with Italy in Mind." In Philip Conisbee, ed., *French Genre Painting in the Eighteenth Century*, pp. 245–55. Washington D.C., National Gallery of Art, 2007.

Wurst, Karin A. *Fabricating Pleasure: Fashion, Entertainment and Cultural Consumption in Germany 1780–1820*. Detroit, Wayne State UP, 2005.

Yardeni, Miriam. "Linguet contre Montesquieu." In Louis Desgraves, ed., *La fortune de Montesquieu*, pp. 93–105. Bordeaux, Bibliothèque municipale, 1995.

Young, Brian W. *Religion and Enlightenment in Eighteenth-Century England*. Oxford, OUP, 1998.

Zammito, John H. *Kant, Herder and the Birth of Anthropology*. Chicago, University of Chicago Press, 2002.

Zurbuchen, Simone. "Theorizing Enlightened Absolutism: The Swiss Republican Origins of Prussian Monarchism." In Hans Blom, John Christian Laursen, and Luisa Simonutti, eds., *Monarchisms in the Age of Enlightenment*, pp. 240–66. Toronto, University of Toronto Press, 2007.

Adam: in federal theology, 224; Poiret on, 232, 238; as representative of humanity, 224; in Rousseau, 173; and tree of life, 258. *See also* Fall; Kant; Origen

Addison, Joseph, 82

agrarian law, 45, 48, 109, 208, 212–13, 216, 218, 262, 283, 363–65; and agrarian justice, 262; and Cicero, 216, 364–65; in Egypt, 244–45; Fauchet on, 48; Fénelon and, 208; and land bank, 271–72; in Mercier, 109; and Paine, 262; Steuart on, 262. *See also* Argenson; Barère; Bernardin de Saint-Pierre; Fleury; Gracchi; Harrington; Mably

agriculture, 182–83, 197, 253–57, 408–9; and astronomy, 37–38, 253–57; and language, 252; Mably on, 392; and Physiocracy, 249–50; Rousseau on, 183. *See also* Bailly; Brown; Dupuis; Rabaut Saint-Etienne

Aiguillon, Armand-Desiré du Plessis-Richelieu d'Agenois, duc d', 306

Alembert, Jean Le Rond, d', 59, 149; on Cynics, 22

Alfred the Great (Saxon king), 44

altruism, 135. *See also* Rousseau

Americans, native, 172

amour de l'ordre: in Fénelon, 210; in Ramsay, 243; in Rousseau, 112–14

amour-de-soi, 88, 112–14, 150, 160, 195, 210–11; in Dubos, 88–89, 153; in Rousseau, 153. *See also* love

amour-propre, 88, 114, 134, 150, 160, 177, 230; and Cartesian moral theory, 73; in Dubos, 88–89, 153; in Marivaux, 73; and patriotism, 170; in Rousseau, 153, 170; and Mme de Tencin, 73. *See also* morality

Amsterdam, 93, 137

ancients: and glory, 276; and moderns, 3, 116, 136, 158, 161–62, 167, 192, 212, 238, 258, 275–77, 278–79, 280–81, 349, 376–77, 384, 386, 391, 393–94, 400–401

André, Antoine-Balthazar-Joseph d', 335, 356

Angiviller, Charles-Claude Flahaut de la Billarderie, comte d', and Mably, 378

animal magnetism, 35. *See also* mesmerism

animals, versus humans, 89. *See also* Rousseau

Année littéraire: and Gilbert, 102; and Voltaire, 102

Anquetil-Duperron, Abraham-Hyacinthe, on Condillac, 397n91

anthropology, 125–26

Antisthenes, 239

Argenson, Maure-Charles-René de Voyer de Paulmy, comte d', 65

Argenson, René-Louis de Voyer de Paulmy, marquis d', 65, 82, 109, 206, 214, 215, 266, 268, 272, 295; and republican monarchy, 206. *See also* Aubert de Vitry; Bernardin de Saint-Pierre; Dingé; Mercier

Aristophanes, 145

Aristotle, 80–81, 168, 177, 242, 243, 278, 308; in Jansenist political theology, 86, 168; and monarchy, 242; and natural philosophy, 173; Smellie on, 168. *See also* sociability

armies, standing, 137

Arminianism, 231–32

army, French: and Marshal Broglie, 15–16; promotion in, 292–96; reform of, 15–16, 132, 179, 286, 287–96, 362; and Ségur ordinance, 289–96

artisans, and *sans-culottes*, 1, 58

Artois, comte d', 336

arts, 8, 9–10, 92–93, 94–95, 148–49, 153–55, 229; in Brown, 180, 183–88, 203–4; Carl on, 92–95; in Castel, 172; in Castilhon, 183; and civilisation, 411; and commerce, 8, 183–88, 203–4; and culture, 148–49, 153–55, 419; Dubos on, 86–90; and emotions, 10, 25; and fashion, 77–101; Mably on, 391–92; Morelly on, 229; and nature, 197; Rousseau on, 183, 391–92; Saint-Pierre on, 9–10; and sciences, 24, 278, 417. *See also* Diogenes; history; Kant

Aspasia, 10

assignat, 40–41, 305, 316, 328–32, 332, 340, 408–9; Clavière and, 316–24; and debt

assignat (cont.)
  liquidation, 320; Duport on, 41, 323; and emigration, 337; as fiat currency, 321–22; and Hume, 322; and inflation, 321; monetisation of, 321–22; and Smith, 323–24; and trade balance, 322–24; and war of 1792, 340. *See also* church; Law (John)
Astraea, 246
astronomy: and agriculture, 253–57; and natural religion, 257
Asur, 175–76
Athens, 245, 248, 276, 411
Atlantis, 254. *See also* Bailly
Attila the Hun, 401
Aubert de Vitry, François-Jean-Philibert, 266–73, 275, 308
Aubert, abbé Jean-Louis, 295–96
Augustus Caesar, 401
Ayr Bank, 324

Babel, tower of, 175–76
Babeuf, François-Noël (Gracchus), 40, 229, 366, 407; on Rousseau, 407
Bacon, Francis, 256, 258
Bailly, Jean-Silvain, 253–54, 255, 256, 259, 260, 306, 307, 328, 330, 331, 369, 409; and astronomy, 253–54; and church property, 328–29; and Physiocracy, 255
balance of power, 270, 272–73; Mably on, 374. *See also* Rutledge
bankruptcy, voluntary, 296–97
Barbeyrac, Jean, 117
Barère, Bertrand, 364, 366
Barnave, Antoine-Joseph, 50, 305, 306, 323, 327, 328, 332, 335, 371, 372; and emigration, 336–37; on empire, 334–35; and Feuillants, 305; and reason of state, 334–35; on Sieyès, 304
Barthélémy, Jean-Jacques, 374
Bastille, 11, 12–13, 14, 15, 19–20, 57, 399, 401
Baudeau, abbé Nicolas, 255
Beauharnais, Marie-Anne-Françoise de, 307–8
Beaumarchais, Pierre-Auguste Caron de, 345–46, 351
Bentham, Jeremy, 264, 317; on Fénelon, 209–10
Bergasse, Nicolas, 315
Berkeley, George, 382; and John Law, 262

Bernardin de Saint Pierre, Jacques-Henri, 214, 266, 268, 270, 288–89, 295; and d'Argenson, 266; and Hobbism, 214, 266; on merit, 288–89; and reform, 214; and Rousseau, 214; Suard on, 214
Berne, 137, 204
Betica, 349. *See also* Fénelon
Biauzat, Jean-François Gaultier de, 306
Bignon, Louis-Clair Le Beau du, 217, 365
Bion, 239
Blair, Hugh, 350
Blake, William, 236
Blanc, Louis, 423
Bodin, Jean, 294
body, 4; and soul, 4, 121, 135–36, 202, 233–34, 235, 243. *See also* Herder; Poiret; Salchli; vitalism
Boehme, Jacob, 232
Boerhaave, Hermann, 243
Boisguilbert, Pierre Le Pesant, sieur de, 96
Boissy d'Anglas, François-Antoine, 307
Bolingbroke, Henry St John, viscount, 165, 286
Bonaparte, Napoleon, 421–22, 423; and Caesar, 217; and reform, 265
Bonnet, Charles, 120, 121, 122, 125, 223, 235, 418, 423; on palengenesis, 122; on personality, 125; on Rousseau, 120
bonnets de laine, 7, 341, 353; and *sans-culottes*, 341–42
Bonneville, Nicolas, 218
Bossuet, Jacques-Bénigne, 110, 384
Bourdon, Léonard, 364
Boureau Deslandes, André-François, on Cynics, 22
bourgeois, Prudhomme on, 341
bourgeoisie, and *sans-culottes*, 356
Bourignon, Antoinette, 232. *See also* Poiret
breeches, 5, 8, 11, 14, 18, 49, 64, 103, 134; joke about, 5, 8, 11, 49; and Lequesne, 13; and Linguet, 12–13, 399; and New Year's Day gift, 15, 17, 65–70; order of, 19; and salons, 56; 58, 60, 141, 343–51; and *sans-culottes*, 59–63, 65–70; and Mme de Tencin, 15, 17, 65–70, 104; and writers, 64–65. *See also* Geoffrin; Gorsas; Rutledge; *sans-culottes*
Brissot, Jacques-Pierre, 7, 8, 37, 40, 42, 46, 145, 262, 263, 269, 273, 283, 305, 316, 317, 318, 321, 329, 331, 337, 338, 352, 361, 368, 371, 385, 404; on *Figaro*,

346–47; on grocery riots of January 1792, 356; on Mably, 386; and *sans-culottes*, 7, 8, 51, 60–61; and Sir George Staunton, 263–64; and David Williams, 42–43. *See also* Clavière; Gorsas; Mercier; Pétion

Brissotins, 7, 51, 339, 363, 402; and Feuillants, 324–38; and *sans-culotte* ministry, 7, 51, 339; and *sans-culottes*, 7–8, 343–51, 353–61

Britain, 41–42, 206, 243, 285, 298–99, 308–14, 317; constitution of, 41–42, 47, 297, 308–14; Delolme on, 47, 299–300; Mounier on, 298–301; public debt in, 41; stability in, 313. *See also* England

Brizard, abbé Gabriel, 105, 294; and Mably, 294; and Rousseau, 294

Broglie, Victor-François, Marshal de, 15

Brown, John, 23, 25, 26, 178–95, 202, 203–4, 205, 207, 256, 293, 308, 387, 388, 413, 423; and Catherine the Great, 180; on civilisation, 191; as Cynic, 178; and Lafitau, 186–87; and Mably, 386–90; and moral sense theory, 188–89; on music, dance, and poetry, 183–88; and natural religion, 53, 185; and reform, 180–81, 203–4; and Rousseau, 178, 181; and Russia, 180, 203–4; and Shaftesbury, 188–89

Brutus, 268, 394; Mably on, 268

Buffon, Georges Leclerc, comte de, 37, 417

Burke, Edmund, 185, 402, 419

Burlamaqui, Jean-Jacques, 225; and Jefferson, 226; and Pufendorf, 225

Caesar, Augustus, 11

Caesar, Julius, 217, 365, 366, 394; and Napoleon, 217, 422

Cain, 172

calendar, French republican, 16; and *sans-culottides*, 16

Calonne, Charles-Alexandre de, 284, 288, 330

Calvinism, 231

Camus, Armand-Gaston, 306

Cantillon, Richard, 387–89, 392, 397; and Mably, 387–88

Carl, Ernst-Ludwig, 92–97; on equality, 97; on fashion, 92–95, 97; on justice, 97; and John Law, 325

Carneades, 127

carnivorism, 169

Carra, Jean-Louis, 35

Cartesianism, 165. *See also* Descartes

Carthage, 276, 393, 411

Casaux, Charles de, 36, 271, 263

Castel, Louis-Bertrand, 9, 25, 26, 170–77, 186, 207, 212, 228, 406, 412; as Cynic, 23, 170; and Descartes, 173; and Montesquieu, 171; on pastoral life, 176; on Rousseau, 170–77; Voltaire on, 170

Castilhon, Jean-Louis, 182, 190, 193, 203, 340, 350, 414; on Voltaire, 182

Catalina, 364

Catherine the Great (empress of Russia), 180, 203, 387

Cato, 231, 279, 306, 394

Celts, 4

centralisation, of court, 77; and reform, 249. *See also* decentralisation; patronage; salons

Cercle social, 105, 144, 342, 364

cereals, price of: maximum, 404, 408–9; and public credit, 262–63; and taxation, 260, 263, 271, 326, 334–35

Chabanon, Michel-Paul-Guy, 413–14

Chabrit, Louis, 266

Chaldeans, 253

Champ-de-Mars, massacre of, 338–39, 340, 342, 354

Chandos, John, 13–14, 17

character, national, 280–81. *See also* clothing

Charlemagne, 282

Charles VII, 14

Charpentier, Mme, salon of, 64

Chas, Jean, 42, 309, 314, 353

Chateauvieux, regiment of, 341–42, 358

Châtelet, Gabrielle Emilie Le Tonnelier de Breteuil, marquise du, 76

Chatterton, Thomas, 266

Chénier, André, 353, 356, 359

Chénier, Joseph-Marie, 52

Chérin, Gabriel, 294

Chevert, François de, 295

China, 253, 256, 263, 280, 300–301

chivalry, 66n22, 70, 101, 137

Choiseul, Etienne-François, duc de, 291

Christ, in federal theology, 224

Christianity, 165; Mably on, 384; and politics, 63

church, property of, 314, 319, 364–65. See also *assignat*; clergy

Cicero, 4, 10, 49, 81–86, 90, 91, 216, 238, 240, 279, 418, 422; and agrarian law, 216, 364–65; on Cynics, 84; on decorum, 81–86; on Gracchi, 365; moral philosophy of, 26; and Nicole, 96; and seemliness, 85

citizenship, 362; active, 50, 325–26; and taxation, 50–51

civil war: Mably on, 393; Mercier on, 21, 105–7; Rousseau on, 105

civilisation, 26, 55, 191, 199, 203, 259, 270–71, 275, 390; Brown on, 26, 191, 203; Ferguson on, 191n158; Gordon on, 191; Rutledge on, 270; theory of, 363

civility, 24. *See also* Cicero; Dubos

class: in French revolutionary historiography, 55–56, 362; and *sans-culottes*, 342, 356–59

Clavière, Etienne, 36, 40, 46, 145, 316, 318, 319, 320–21, 322, 329, 331, 334, 338, 367–68, 371, 372; and bankruptcy, 51, 337; and debt default, 51; and emigration, 337; and Geneva, 317; on inequality, 316, 320–31; on justice, 316; and John Law, 315–23; on property, 316; on Smith, 323–24; on war, 367–68

Clement of Alexandria, 188

Clement, abbé Jean-Marie-Bernard, 378

clergy, civil constitution of, 305, 327, 331

Clermont-Tonnerre, Stanislas de, 48

Cloots, Jean-Baptiste (Anacharsis), baron du Val-de Grace, 262, 307, 405; on Rousseau, 307–8

clothing, as character, 83

Clovis, 401

Coblenz, 359

Cocceius, Johannes, 232

codpiece, 14. See also *grègues*

Colbert, Jean-Baptiste, 324–25

Coleridge, Samuel Taylor, 236; on Fénelon's followers, 236; and Pantisocracy, 236

commerce: and the arts, 8; versus conquest, 8, 246; and credit, 247. *See also* trade

concupiscence, 74, 90

Condé, Louis-Joseph de Bourbon, prince de, 295

Condillac, abbé Etienne Bonnot de, 112–13, 184, 277, 373, 376, 385; and Leibniz, 375–76; and Locke, 375; discussed by Rousseau, 112–13; and trade, 393, 397n91. *See also* Mably

Condorcet, Marie-Jean-Antoine-Nicolas de Caritat, marquis de, 99, 204–5, 219, 275, 305, 326; on Bailly, 255; on patronage, 132; and Rousseau, 219; on salons, 99; on taxation and representation, 326

conformism, and fashion, 79, 90

conquest, versus commerce, 8, 246

conscience, in Rousseau, 112–13

constituting power, 41, 128, 269, 311–12; and constituted power, 269, 311; and English constitution, 41, 310–12; in Mercier, 128; and public debt, 41–42. *See also* Chas; Sieyès

constitution, English, 298–99, 308–14; English, and Norman conquest, 299

Cordeliers club, 215, 329, 338

Corsica, 368, 370

Court, Antoine, 251

Court de Gebelin, Antoine, 251–53, 254, 255, 256, 259, 260, 279, 307, 369; and Physiocracy, 253; and Rousseau, 251–52

court society, versus salon society, 77, 99–100, 132

courtesans, Greek, 10

Cousin, Victor, 99

Covenant: of grace, 224; of works, 224, 233

covenant theology, 224, 232; and Catholicism, 226

Coyer, Gabriel-François, 179, 291; and commercial nobility, 291

Crates, 140, 239, 346

credit: and commerce, 247–48; public, 3. *See also* public debt

Cromwell, Oliver, 365

Crozat, Antoine, 65

Cubières-Palmézeaux, Michel de, 306–8; on Aristotle, 308

culture, 26, 77–101, 146–50, 248; and the arts, 419; Gorsas and, 349–51; and nature, 147–48, 419; versus nature, 146–50, 197; and Physiocracy, 250–51; and property, 3, 77–101; Rousseau and, 146–50; and wealth, 248. *See also* Brown; fashion; Salchli; salons; Voltaire; women

Cumberland, Richard, 376

Cynic philosophy, 134–47; and music, 24

Cynics, 21, 22, 23, 26, 49, 69, 74, 138–47, 164, 165, 170, 177, 181–82, 194, 199, 202, 203, 207, 238, 240, 242, 391, 406, 422; Castel as, 170; in Cicero, 84; and fashion, 90; in Fénelon, 239–40; and

Gorsas, 50; and Mably, 23, 391; and men of letters, 21–22; and Mercier, 50; and Plato, 21, 139; Rousseau as, 23, 27, 139, 147, 157, 170, 199, 223; and *sans-culottes*, 62; and satire, 49. *See also* Diogenes; Plato; Rousseau; satire

dance, 136, 183–84, 192. *See also* Brown
Danton, Georges, 273
Darnton, Robert, 61, 66
Darwin, Erasmus, 37
Davies, Edward, 279
debt. *See* public debt
decentralisation, of salons, 77. *See also* centralisation; salons
decorum, 10, 12, 24, 49, 81–86, 101, 168, 214, 348, 422; in Bernardin de Saint-Pierre, 214; in Cicero, 81–86; and Jansenism, 84–85; in Nicole, 96. *See also* Cicero
Delandine, Antoine-François, 104
Delolme, Jean-Louis, 47, 281, 299–300, 308, 309; and English constitution, 47; and Mounier, 299–300
Deluc, Jean-André, 316; on Rousseau, 29
democracy, 4, 5, 400; and *bourgeois* politics, 341; Dusaulx on, 400; and magistracy, 404; in Mercier, 128; and public debt, 423; representative, 407–8; and revolutionary government, 404–5; and Rousseau, 154, 403; royal, 266, 272; Saint-Just on, 404–5; and sovereignty, 403; and Terror, 404–5
Dequevauviller, François-Jacques-Barthélemy, 5–6
Descartes, René, 10, 26, 166, 233; and altruism, 75; on language, 89; on morality, 75–76
Deschamps, Dom Léger-Marie, 380
desires: in Physiocracy, 250–51; in Rousseau, 200
Desjardins, Marie-Catherine, 78
Desmoulins, Camille, 36, 306, 365–66, 405
Desorgues, Théodore, 52
despotism, 419; Delolme on, 299; in France, 271; legal, 200, 297; and Louis XIV, 284; and luxury, 371; ministerial, 12; and Norman conquest, 299; Rousseau on, 200, 327; and sovereignty, 310–11. *See also* Linguet
diatribe, 190; Cynic, 141, 361

dictatorship, Mably on, 397–98, 399, 402–3
Diderot, Denis, 59, 141, 142, 145, 177, 180, 216, 221, 223, 407, 419; and Morelly, 229; *Rameau's Nephew*, 141–44; and Rousseau, 142, 147, 165, 189–90; as *sans-culotte*, 60, 103; and Shaftesbury, 189–90; *Supplément au voyage de Bougainville*, 146–47
Dingé, Antoine, 295
Diogenes Laertes, 238
Diogenes of Sinope, 21, 22, 25, 26–27, 49–50, 63, 108, 130, 136, 139, 141, 144, 145, 164, 178, 190, 199, 200, 239, 346, 350, 361, 414; and elitism, 190; Kant on, 26–27, 199; Mably on, 391; Mercier on, 136; modern, 178, 181, 190; and Plato, 239; and Plato's purple carpets, 22, 49, 69, 69n30, 70, 101, 130, 134, 143, 239; Quatorze-oignons as, 144; in Rousseau, 147; Rousseau as, 26–27, 199; and *sans-culottes*, 62. *See also* Cynics
Dionysius the Tyrant, 22
division of labour, 177, 192; Carl on, 94–95; and civility, 95; in *Encyclopédie*, 177; and fashion, 94; in Geneva, 154; in history, 192; and pin factory, 177; and productivity, 94–95; in Pluche, 177; in Rousseau, 115–16, 149–50, 154; and social interdependence, 94–95
Domat, Jean, 92, 226–27
Dorvigny, Louis-Archambault, 345
Dubois de Crancé, Edmond-Louis-Alexis, 306
Dubos, abbé Jean-Baptiste, 10, 86–90, 134, 156, 159–60, 166, 248; on aesthetics, 87–90; on *amour-de-soi* and *amour-propre*, 153; and the arts, 86–90; on morality, 86–90; passions in, 87–90, 156. *See also* Stoics
duelling, Rousseau on, 162
Duguay-Trouin, René, 295
Dumas, Mathieu, 335
Dumont, Etienne, 36
Duponceau, Peter Stephen, 253
Dupont de Nemours, Pierre-Samuel, 322–23, 353, 408, 410
Duport, Adrien, 46, 51, 305, 322, 323, 327, 330, 331, 332, 333, 334, 335, 371, 372; on *assignats*, 41; on John Law, 40–41, 323; and Mississippi, 41, 323; on Sieyès, 304
Dupuis, Charles-François, 254, 257, 369

Dusaulx, Jean, 49, 307, 393, 399–402, 410; on democracy, 400–401; on England, 401–2; on liberty, 399–400; on Linguet, 399, 401; and Mably, 49; on Montesquieu, 399–400; on satire, 49

Eaton, Daniel, 399
Ebert, Johan Arnold, 52; and Young's *Night Thoughts*, 52
Eckstein, Ferdinand, baron d', 145–46
Egypt, 194, 213, 243–45
electorate, and fiscal system, 325–26
Elizabeth I (of England), 312
émigrés, 51, 325, 334, 335–37, 338; and taxation, 50–51, 325, 334, 335–37. *See also* Barnave; Duport; Feuillants
emotions, 4, 222; and the arts, 25; in Dubos, 153; and enthusiasm, 168; and music, 187–88, 412–13; and natural religion, 254–55; in Physiocracy, 250–51; in Rousseau, 153, 160; and sociability, 168–70. *See also* Brown; enthusiasm; passions; Vico; Young
empire, 51, 175, 276, 325, 334, 338, 362; of fashion, 77–101, 423; Ottoman, 289; and property, 175; Roman, 4; and slavery, 334; and taxation, 50, 326, 334
Enclos, Ninon d', 71
England: constitution of, 41–42, 220, 298–99, 308–14; Dusaulx on, 401–2; and French Revolution, 220; political stability in, 41–42, 308–14. *See also* constitution; Delolme; Harrington; Hume; Mounier; Williams
Enlightenment, historiography of, 5, 55–56, 64
enthusiasm, 25, 168, 399; in Brown, 185; in Plato, 193; and sociability, 168–70
Enville, Marie-Louise-Elizabeth de la Rochefoucauld, duchesse d', and Mably, 379; and Turgot, 379
ephors, 44, 373
Epicureanism, 74, 165–66, 170, 189, 377; and fashion, 90; in Greece and Rome, 377; in Rousseau, 150. *See also* concupiscence; Hobbes; Jansenism
Epicureans, 238, 242; in Fénelon, 240–41; and Rousseau, 241
Epicurus, 240–41
equality: Mably on, 396; and monarchy, 214; of opportunity, 288–89; and political

stability, 266–73. *See also* agrarian laws; Babeuf; Brissot; Brown; Clavière; Fénelon; Gorsas; Mercier; Ogilvie; Physiocracy; property; Ramsay; Robespierre; Rousseau; Rutledge; Salchli; Steuart; Williams
étrennes, 58; origin of, 66, 104
evil, problem of, 415–16; Salchli on, 414–20. *See also* Fall; Kant; Leibniz; Rousseau
executive power, in Rousseau, 155

fair trade, and public debt, 46
Falkland, Lewis Clary, viscount, 295
Fall, 63, 165–66, 232–33, 233–34; Mably on, 384; Rousseau on, 195–96
fashion, 9, 10, 77–101, 166, 209, 423; and conformism, 79, 90; and division of labour, 94, 94n96; empire of, 77–101; French, 79–80, 83; versus Gothic gloom, 97; Mirabeau (comte de) on, 97–98; and morality, 77–101; and nature, 78; and prices, 93; and property, 77; Rousseau on, 134, 423; and salons, 77; and trade, 77, 92–95
fashion dolls, 93
Fauchet, Claude, 48–49, 330, 342, 379; on Sieyès, 48–49
Fauchet, Joseph, 306
federalism, in Rousseau, 119, 220
federation, Mably on, 392–93
Fénelon, François de Salignac de la Mothe, archbishop of Cambrai, 38–39, 202, 207, 215, 218, 220, 231, 234–35, 238, 243, 268, 307, 324, 345, 351, 423; and agrarian law, 365; and ancient philosophy, 238–42; Coleridge on, 236; and Cynic philosophy, 238–42; in Gorsas, 345, 349; and John Law, 324–25; on Lucretius, 241–42; and Mably, 219, 395, 411; and Marat, 218; and metempsychosis, 236; and Physiocracy, 249, 260; and Poiret, 231; and Ramsay, 242; and reform, 207–9; and Rousseau, 38, 210–11; *Telemachus*, 207–9, 345; and trade, 209. *See also* Ramsay
Ferguson, Adam, 275, 278, 416; on civilisation, 191n158
Ferrand, Elizabeth, and Condillac, 378; and Mably, 378
Ferrières, Jacques-Annibal, 329
festivals, Rousseau on, 164

feudal system, 272, 276; and English constitution, 300. *See also* government: Gothic

Feuillants, 40, 51, 56, 305–6, 309, 330, 338;
and Brissotins, 324–38; and emigration,
335–37; and Gorsas, 351–59; and Jacobins, 343

Fichte, Johann Gottlieb, 45, 129, 222;
compared to Mercier, 129; on Rousseau,
222

Fielding, Henry, 72

finance, and army reform, 287–88. *See also*
public debt; taxation

fire, discovery of, 168

Fléchier, Valentin-Esprit, 110, 295

Fleury, abbé Claude, 211–13, 243, 384; and
Fénelon, 211–13; and Harrington, 212

Fleury, André-Hercule, cardinal, 271

Fontanes, Louis de, 411

Fontenelle, Bernard Le Bovier de, 15, 65,
69, 76, 96; as Seneca, 91

France, 285, 420; Calonne on, 284; fashion
in, 79–80; history of, 286–87; love in,
159; Mallet du Pan on, 286–87; Rousseau
on, 159; and imperial Rome, 102; women
in, 97–98. *See also* French Revolution

freemasonry, and Physiocracy, 259

free trade, and public debt, 46. *See also*
public debt

French Revolution, ancient thought in, 63;
historiography of, 1–2, 3, 5, 55–56, 213,
217, 218–19, 286, 288, 296, 305, 345–46,
362–63, 367, 398, 423; Jacobin phase of,
2; and Mably's "script," 395

Frey, Junius, 382; and Rousseau, 382

funding system, and political independence,
129. *See also* Clavière; Law (John); public
debt; Steuart

Fuseli, Henry, 179

Gallia braccata, 14

Gallia togata, 14, 16

Garat, Dominique-Joseph, 38, 39, 273–82,
286, 333, 385; on glory, 276; on happiness, 273, 275–76; on history, 275–77; on
Mably, 385; on machinery, 278; on Rousseau, 280–81

Garve, Christian, 418

Gassendi, Pierre, 166

Gay, John, 83

general will, 200; in Barbeyrac, 117; and
Condorcet, 219; in Montesquieu, 117;

in Pufendorf, 117; in Rousseau, 114–19,
151, 211. *See also* Rousseau

Geneva, 155, 202, 204, 317, 342, 374, 379,
390; *cercles* in, 162–63; Mably on, 390n75;
versus Neuchatel, 154; in Rousseau, 116,
153–55

Geoffrin, Marie-Thérèse-Rodet, Mme,
18–19, 59, 64, 71, 141, 215, 344–45; and
breeches, 59–60, 344–45; salon of, 59–60

Gerle, Dom, 331

Germans, 4, 290, 300

Gibbon, Edward, 309

Gilbert, Nicolas-Joseph-Laurent, 17, 18,
19–21, 101–4, 106, 107, 140, 227, 266,
346; and Gorsas, 346; and Mercier,
103–4

Giraldi, Lilio Gregorio, 194

Girondins, 7, 56

glory, 276; and Louis XIV, 284

God, in Rousseau's thought, 151

Godwin, William, 36, 381

Goethe, Johann Wolfgang von, 142

Gordon, John, 191

Gordon, Thomas, 365, 405

Gorsas, Antoine-Joseph, 20, 130, 338,
343–61, 362, 407, 422, 423; on academies, 349; and culture, 349; and Cynic
satire, 50, 343–51; and Fénelon, 345,
349; and Feuillants, 351–59; and Gilbert,
346; on grocery riots of January 1792,
356; on morality, 347–49; and Pétion,
357; and Rousseau, 347–49; and *sans-
culottes*, 20–21, 343–51, 353–61; and
satire, 50, 343–51

Gournay group, 179; and commercial
nobility, 290–91; and military reform,
290–91

government: ancient and modern, 276–77;
Aristotle on, 308; balanced, 298, 308;
composite, 308; constitutional, 297;
constitutional, and public debt, 310–12;
English, 297, 308; feudal, 300, 311–12;
Gothic, 211–12, 300; and happiness,
276–77; and music, 186–87; representative, 412; republican, 54; revolutionary,
404–5; Robespierre on, 54, 404; Saxon,
45. *See also* Britain; democracy; dictatorship; England; representative government

Gracchi, Caius and Tiberius, 215–16, 217,
357, 365, 394

Gracchus, Caius, 357

grace, efficacious, 96; general, 96
Greece, 44, 192, 213, 245, 257, 364, 373, 377, 398, 415
Grégoire, Henri, 62, 379, 410
grègues, 14. *See also* breeches; Voltaire
Gresset, Jean-Baptiste-Louis, 406
Grivel, Charles, 260; and Mirabeau (marquis de), 260
Grotius, Hugo, 3, 161, 164, 168, 210, 383
Guadet, Marguerite-Elie, 361
Gudin de la Brenellerie, Pierre-Paul, 307
Guffroy, Armand-Benoît-Jules, 218
Guyon, Jeanne, 232
Guyot, Joseph-Nicolas, 275
gymnastics, 192; and Olympic games, 192

Haller, Albrecht von, 120, 121, 122; on Rousseau, 127
Ham, 172, 175–76
Hamilton, Emma, as *hetaira*, 71
Hampden, John, 295
happiness, 38, 242; Garat on, 275–76; versus glory, 275–76; Saint-Just on, 38, 275
Harlequin, 15
Harrington, James, 42, 44, 45, 215, 243, 273, 310, 311, 361; Aubert de Vitry on, 267; and Fleury, 212; on Gracchi, 365; and Montesquieu, 215; in Rutledge, 270
Hazard, Pierre-Nicolas-Joseph, 350
Hegel, Georg Friedrich Wilhelm, 145, 223; on Cynic philosophy, 144, on *Rameau's Nephew*, 142–43, 145
Helvétius, Claude-Adrien, 37, 216, 369, 407, 418
Henri IV, 165, 260, 268, 282, 285, 286, 350; and patriotic debt default, 286
Henry VII (of England), 311
Hercules, 16
Herder, Johann Gottfried, 36, 121, 179, 235, 417–18, 421; on Brown, 179
Herrenschwand, Jean Fréderic, 262, 314
hetaira (Greek courtesan), 10, 70
Hipparchia, 140
Hirzel, Johann Caspar, 111
history, conjectural, 169, 173, 186, 195–200, 254, 258, 333, 347–49, 363, 379, 380–81, 387–88, 411, 412, 415, 416–17, 419; Castel on, 172–75; Poiret on, 233, 243; Garat on, 275–77; Mably on, 376, 383–84; Mercier on, 137; in Rousseau, 112–14, 135; scriptural, 167–68, 172,

175, 176, 383; spiritual, 233, 243. *See also* Kant; Vico
Hobbes, 82, 85–86, 90, 115–16, 120, 161, 164, 168, 170, 202, 219, 376, 382; and Epicureanism, 165; compared to Jansenism, 90; on laughter, 169; in Poiret, 237; and Rousseau, 38, 127, 173, 412
Hobbism, 200, 214
Holbach, Pierre-Paul Thiry, baron d', 381–82
Holland, 207, 246, 272, 317, 318
Hollis, Thomas, 8, 310
Homer, 187
hommes à piques, 7
honestum, 10, 62. *See also* Cicero
honour, 10, 62, 110, 134, 162, 293, 357; chivalrous, 101
Hooke, Luke-Joseph, 216
Hooke, Nathaniel, 215–16, 217, 365
Horace, 11, 49, 88
Hotman, François, 354
households, in Rousseau, 114–15
human nature, Castel on, 174; Mably on, 384; Rousseau on, 29–30. *See also* Rousseau
Hume, David, 41, 72, 179, 226, 309, 310, 322, 323, 350
Hurons, described by French Jesuits, 25, 186–87
Hutcheson, Francis, 188

ideology, 414
imagination, in Rousseau, 160
India, 253
Indigents, Society of, 341
inequality, 197, 298; Kant on, 197; Rousseau on, 28. *See also* Brown; Fénelon; Mercier; Mounier; Rutledge
insurrection: of 20 June 1792, 106; right to, 128–29
interest: private, 114; public, 114; self-, in Rousseau, 114–16, 118
interests, and passions, 9. *See also* arts
Iselin, Isaak, on Rousseau, 143
Israel, 211–13
Israelites, 211–13; Fleury on, 211–13

Jacobins, 7, 56, 273, 338; and agrarian law, 363–65; and emigration, 335–37; and Feuillants, 343, 351–59; and Mably, 410–12; and *sans-culottes*, 1–2. *See also* Robespierre; Saint-Just

Jacobites, 267
Jaméry-Duval, Valentin, 295
James I (of England), 312
Jansenism, 10, 74–75, 90, 91, 165, 177,
    202, 210, 226; and Aristotle, 86, 168;
    and charity, 227; and decorum, 84–85;
    compared to Hobbes, 90; and Plato,
    86; and property, 227; and taxation,
    227
Japhet, 172, 175
Jaucourt, Louis, chevalier de, 378
Jebb, John, and Holbach, 381–82
Jefferson, Thomas, 263, 402; on property,
    226
Joan of Arc, 13, 268
Jones, Sir William, 255
Joseph II (Holy Roman Emperor), 108,
    209
Joubert, Joseph, 221
Journal de Paris, 274
Joux, Pierre de, 253
jubilee, 212
judgement, private, 418–19
justice: and merit, 245; versus morality,
    161. *See also* army; Mercier' Rousseau
Juvenal, 11, 49, 102, 140, 238, 240

Kames, Henry Home, Lord, 416
Kant, Immanuel, 3, 37, 195–200, 213,
    223, 275, 383, 407; on China, 198; on
    Diogenes, 199; on golden age, 198; on
    inequality, 197; Mercier on, 124–25;
    on Rousseau, 26–27, 195–200, 223; on
    Rousseau as Cynic, 199; on war, 198
King, Sir Edward, 309
Kircher, Athanasius, 184
Kliyogg, 321. *See also* Hirzel; Socrates
Knox, Vicesimus, 179

L'Hôpital, Michel de, 275, 286
La Bruyère, Jean de, and women, 100–101
La Chalotais, Louis-René de Caradeuc de,
    on Rousseau, 377n36
La Mettrie, Julien Offray de, 122
La Rochefoucauld-Liancourt, François, duc
    de, 332
Laceuil, Mercier on, 18
Lacretelle, Pierre-Louis, 274, 353
Lafayette, Marie-Josèphe-Paul-Yves-Roche
    Gilbert du Motier, marquis de, 306, 336,
    352

Lafitau, Joseph-François, 186–87, 413; in
    Brown, 186–87
Lafontaine, Jean de, 21, 105, 341, 358
Lafrensen, Niclas, 6
Laharpe, Jean-François, 255
Lambert, Anne-Thérèse de Margenat de
    Courcelles, marquise de, 73
Lameth brothers (Alexandre, Charles, and
    Théodore de), 305, 306
Lameth, Charles, 327, 330, 331, 332, 335
Lamourette, Adrien-Antoine, 36, 379
language: Court de Gebelin on, 251–52;
    origin of, 251–52; in Rousseau, 30; and
    writing, 257–58, 259
Lanthénas, François-Xavier, 45, 144–45; on
    grocery riots of January 1792, 356; and
    sans-culottes, 144–45; on Williams, 45. *See
    also* Quatorze-oignons
laughter, 169; Hobbes on, 169
Lavater, Johann Caspar, 37, 123, 209, 224,
    423
Lavoisier, Antoine de, 322, 323
law: in Cynic thought, 139; government of,
    200, 214; of nations, 3, 279; of nature, 3,
    370, 420; and Machiavelli, 3, 278–79. *See
    also* Grotius; Hobbes; Mably; Rousseau
Law, John, 4, 39–41, 47, 260–73, 314,
    318, 320, 323, 324, 325, 423; and *assig-
    nat*, 40–41, 315–23; and Berkeley, 262;
    Carl on, 325; and Clavière, 40, 315–23;
    Colbert and, 324; Duport on, 40–41,
    323; Fénelon and, 324; and French debt
    finance after 1789, 39–40, 47; legacy of,
    260–73; and Mercier, 129; Montesquieu
    on, 324; in Rutledge, 271; Saint-Just on,
    40; and Sieyès, 47; and Smith, 323–24;
    and Steuart, 262, 323; Voltaire on, 32
Le Chapelier, Isaac-René-Guy, 335
Le Maître de Claville, Charles-François-
    Nicolas, 100–101
Le Mercier de la Rivière, Pierre-Paul,
    250–51, 269
Le Mierre, Antoine-Marin, 78, 90
Le Tourneur, Louis, 122, 307
League (Catholic), Mercier on, 106
Lebrun, Charles-François, 293
Lebrun, Pons-Denis (Pindar), 284–85, 288
legion of honour, 162
legislative power, in Rousseau, 155
legislator: and Robespierre, 53; in
    Rousseau, 53

Leibniz, Gottfried Wilhelm, 34, 119, 120, 121, 130, 259, 374, 377, 383, 385, 415, 417; and Condillac, 375–76; Mably on, 385

Lequesne, Pierre, 13, 19; and Linguet, 13

liberty, 55; cap of, 8, 194, 340; Dusaulx on, 399–400; tree of, 8. See also *pileus*

Ligne, Charles-Joseph, prince de, 131

Lindet, Robert, 408

Linguet, Simon-Nicolas-Henri, 11, 12, 15, 18–19, 19–20, 286, 399, 401; and breeches, 18–19, 19–20, 399; on order of the breeches, 19; and property, 12

Locke, John, 86, 120, 164, 168, 184, 230, 264, 376; and Condillac, 375; on property, 264; and religion of magistrate, 313

London, 137

Louis IX, 268

Louis the Fat, 268, 295

Louis XII, 268, 295

Louis XIV, 11, 74, 102, 103, 109, 166, 261, 284–85, 401; and Gothic government, 211

Louis XV, 11, 21, 284–85, 293, 377

Louis XVI, 7, 11, 57, 260, 268, 273, 282, 284, 327, 335, 338–39; and flight to Varennes, 51; and Parisian insurrection of 20 June 1792, 57; as patriot king, 285–86, 288, 296–97

love, 4, 100, 135, 150, 158–59; and music, 169; of order, 112–13, 210, 243; and painting, 169; pure, 231–32; in Rousseau, 112–14, 156–59, 210–11; and vitalism, 36. See also *amour de l'ordre*; *amour-de-soi*; *amour-propre*; Fénelon; Poiret; Ramsay; Rousseau

Lucian, 102, 140

Lucretius, in Fénelon, 241–42

luxury, 10, 90, 136, 152, 208, 244, 248, 276, 278, 285, 312, 371, 373, 374, 386, 397; Brown on, 178–79; 181; historiography of, 138; Mercier on, 128, 136–38; and moderns, 136; and despotism, 371; and Physiocracy, 249–50; in republics, 137; and Rome, 90

Lyon, silk industry of, 92

Mably, Gabriel Bonnot, abbé de, 13, 23, 105, 184, 268, 405, 407, 408, 423; on agriculture, 392; and d'Angiviller, 378; and army reform, 291; on balance of power, 374; Brissot on, 386; and Brizard, 294; and Brown, 386–90; on Brutus, 268; and Cantillon, 388–89; and Christianity, 376–77; and civil war, 393–94; and crisis government, 52; on dictatorship, 397–98, 399, 402–3; on Diogenes, 391; and Dusaulx, 49; Eaton on, 399; on federation, 392–93; and Fénelon, 219, 395, 411; Fontanes on, 411–12; and French Revolution, 395; Garat on, 385; on Geneva, 390n75; on Greece, 373; and Jacobins, 410–12; on luxury, 373; and monarchy, 395; on morality, 376, 391; on passions, 372–73; and Phocion, 23; on Poland, 387; and politics of necessity, 268, 394, 397–98, 402–3, 405; and property, 230–31, 387; on reason, 376, 385; and reform, 394–98; on religion, 377, 383–84; and revolution, 52, 395–98, 405; in Roederer, 403; on Rome, 373; and Rousseau, 24, 231, 372, 374, 377, 385, 390, 391–92, 402–3; on states, 373; on trade, 387–90, 392; and Mme de Vassé, 378; on war, 397–98

Machiavelli, Niccolò, 3, 205, 212, 219, 268, 278–79, 398–99; on Gracchi, 365; in Rousseau, 205n4, 278

machinery, and liberty, 278

Mackintosh, Sir James, 265

Madison, James, 226

magistracy, and democracy, 404

magistrate, religion of, 331. See also Locke

majority rule, in Rousseau, 119

Malebranche, Nicolas, 166, 233–34, 382

Malesherbes, Guillaume-François-Chrétien de Lamoignon de, 415

Mallet du Pan, Jacques-Pierre, 274, 286–87; on French history, 286–87

Manuel, Pierre-Louis, 61

Marat, Jean-Paul, 37, 219, 398; and Fénelon, 218

Maréchal, Sylvain, 229

Maria Leczinska (queen of France), 103, 377

Marie Antoinette (queen of France), 23, 51, 327, 336, 353; and court patronage, 99, 132; and Cynic satire, 51, 353; and Feuillants, 51, 327, 336, 353; and the phrase "let them eat cake," 23; and salon society, 99, 132. See also Rousseau

Marivaux, Pierre Carlet de Chamblain de, 72–74, 100, 156, 248; on gifts, 72–73;

and morality, 72–74; and *Vie de Marianne*, 72–74
Martial, 66
Martin brothers, 71
Martin, Josiah, 209
Mascaron, Jules, 110
Maupeou, René-Nicolas de, 227, 293
maximum, Jacobin, 404, 408
Melon, Jean-François, 46, 290
Menou, Jacques-François, 306, 330; and civil constitution of clergy, 331
Mercier, Louis-Sébastien, 17, 18, 19–20, 28, 34–35, 37, 39, 46, 55, 108–132, 135, 144, 193, 201, 223, 307, 317, 343, 364, 368, 385, 407, 423; *L'an 2440*, 108–10, 420; and d'Argenson, 109; and Brizard, 294; on Choiseul, 292; and civil war, 21, 105–7, 393; as Cynic, 23, 108, 111; and Cynic satire, 50; and equality, 109; on *Figaro*, 346; and Gilbert, 103–4; on Kant, 124–25; on Lavater, 123; on John Law, 40, 129, 263; and Leibniz, 119; on luxury, 136–38; and merit, 109; on Montesquieu, 130n191, 215; on morality, 109; on music, poetry, and dance, 137; on Necker, 129, 263; *New Picture of Paris*, 18; and reform, 108–9, 282; and revolution, 108–9; described by Roederer, 107; and Rousseau, 110–32; on Rousseau, 127–29; and Rutledge, 104, 215; in Salchli, 420, 422; on origin of *sans-culottes*, 17–18, 20; and *sans-culottes*, 342–43; on self-sufficiency, 129; *Tableau de Paris*, 17; and vitalism, 119–26; on writers, 60–61; on Edward Young, 122–23
Mercure de France, 274
merit, 288; and army reform in France, 288; and distinction, 133; and inheritance, 288; and justice, 245; in monarchies, 214, 245; Mercier and, 109; Mounier on, 301; and property, 288; and service, 289–90; and system of ranks, 248
Mesmer, Franz Anton, 35–36, 46
mesmerism, 34
metempsychosis, and Fénelon's followers, 236
Michel, Jean-André, 350
Middleton, Conyers, 216
Millar, John, 275
Milton, John, 193
mind, and body, 233–34. *See also* soul; vitalism

mind-body problem, 4, 121. *See also* soul; vitalism
Minos, laws of, 246
Mirabeau, André-Boniface-Louis Riqueti, vicomte de, 354
Mirabeau, Honoré-Gabriel Riqueti, comte de, 36, 47, 97–98, 304, 316, 318, 327, 332, 334, 335; on fashion, 97–98; on Feuillants, 327–28; and Sieyès, 304; on women, 97–98
Mirabeau, Victor Riqueti, marquis de, 200–201, 248, 253, 258, 266, 268, 279, 309; on civilisation, 191n158; and Court de Gebelin, 253; and Rousseau, 200–201, 259
Mississippi, 41, 323. *See also* Law (John)
Mississippi Company, 39–40. *See also* Law (John)
modesty: among ancients, 158; Rousseau on, 157–58; in women, 157–58
moi commun, in Rousseau, 118
Molière, Jean-Baptiste Poquelin, 59, 68, 344–45, 351
Monarchiens, 47, 56, 298–301, 308; and Mounier, 47, 298–301
monarchy, 362; Brown on, 203–4; and civilisation, 203–4; constitutional, 423; Delolme on, 299–300; democratic, 267; and Gothic government, 211–12; and justice, 214; Mably on, 395; and military reform, 290–96; in Montesquieu, 154, 159; Mounier on, 298–301; and reform, 203–4, 207–9, 267, 395; republican, 205–6, 266; and republicanism, 423; and republics, 211, 214, 217, 242, 245, 265; in Rousseau, 154; virtue in, 203–4. *See also* Argenson (marquis d'); Bernardin de Saint-Pierre; Fénelon; Hooke (Nathaniel); Ramsay; Rutledge
Montesquieu, Charles Louis de Secondat, baron de, 25, 28, 65, 70, 78, 82, 115–16, 120, 165, 186, 206, 215, 217, 219, 225, 248, 278, 288, 293, 298–99, 308, 349, 351, 376, 399–400; and Castel, 171; on English constitution, 220; as covert Harringtonian, 45, 130, 215; and John Law, 45, 324; on liberty, 399–400; on liberty and necessity, 335–36; Mercier on, 130n191, 215; Mounier on, 298–99; and reform, 203, 205; as covert republican, 45, 130, 215; and Rousseau, 154, 158–59, 171, 206–7; Williams on, 44

Montesquiou-Fezensac, Anne-Pierre de, 320

Moore, John, 57

moral, versus physical, 146–47

moral theory: Cartesian, 91, 100; Ciceronian, 81–85, 91

morality, 29, 37, 72, 228, 248; and beauty, 91; Cartesian, 75–76, 96; in Cicero, 81–85, 91, 418; and civilisation, 26, 55, 191, 199, 203, 259, 271, 275, 390; Condillac on, 376; in Cynic philosophy, 134–47; in Descartes, 75–76; Diderot on, 146; Dom Deschamps on, 380; Dubos on, 86–90; and fashion, 77–101; Frey on, 382–83; Garat on, 278; in Gorsas, 347–49; Holbach on, 381; and immortality of soul, 350; and industry, 357; and Jansenism, 96; versus justice, 161; in Le Maître de Claville, 100–101; and Mably, 376, 408; Machiavelli and, 278–79; in Marivaux, 72–74; in Mercier, 109–10, 123; and moral sense, 188; and natural religion, 251–52, 254–55, 256–60; Periander and, 70; Pétion on, 352–53; and pity, 29–31, 37, 112, 376; in Poiret, 237–38; republican, 409; and Rousseau, 29–31, 31–32, 37, 112, 134–35, 150, 188, 223, 241, 256, 376, 408; Salchli on, 418–19; and trade, 409; and vitalism, 123; and women, 77–101; and wonder, 75–76. See also Brown; enthusiasm; Hobbes; love

More, Thomas, 219

Moreau, Mme, salon of, 64

Morellet, André, 274; on music, 412–13

Morelly, Etienne-Gabriel, 229–30; and Diderot, 229; and property, 229–30

Mounier, Jean-Joseph, 47, 48, 51, 308, 309, 327; and Delolme, 299–300; and Monarchiens, 48, 298–301; and Montesquieu, 298, 299

Muralt, Béat-Louis de, 79–80

music, 32, 136, 169, 183–84, 191, 192; Brown on, 181–82; Chabanon on, 413–14; in Cynic philosophy, 24; and emotions, 187–88; and enthusiasm, 169; and government, 186–87; and language, 184, 190; and love, 169; and morality, 4; Morellet on, 412–13; and Rousseau, 32, 153, 412–14; Villoteau on, 414

Naples, 137

Napoleon. See Bonaparte

national guard, 305

nations, law of, 3

natural law, 3, 279, 370; Mably on, 384. See also Garat; Grotius; Machiavelli; Rousseau

naturalism, 25, 26, 171–72, 228

nature, 146; and culture, 146–47, 148, 197, 419; in Cynic thought, 139; human, 281, 384; law of, 3, 243. See also Mercier; Rousseau

Nebuchadnezzar, 244

necessity: politics of, 3; and property, 227. See also Barnave; Clavière; Mably; Saint-Just

Necker, Jacques, 320, 329, 331, 263, 409; Mercier on, 136

Needs: Mably on, 389; and machinery, 278; and property, 95; in Rousseau, 153, 200. See also culture; nature; Sparta; trade

Nelson, Horatio, 71

Neuchatel: versus Geneva, 154; described by Rousseau, 148–49, 154

Neuville, Bon-Pierre-Charles, Frey de, 110

New Year's Day gift, 18. See also breeches; étrennes; sans-culottes; Tencin

Newton, Sir Isaac, 76, 243, 257; compared to Mesmer, 35

Nicole, Pierre, 92, 96, 384; and general grace, 96

Nimrod, 175–76

Noah, 175

nobility, 362; abolition of, 305, 327; and army reform, 288; commercial versus military, 179, 290–91; French, 290–92, 300; and venality, 289–93

notables, assembly of, 284, 288

Oberlin, Jean-Frédéric, 379

Ogilvie, William, 263–66, 272, 314, 423

opinion. See public opinion

Origen, 232–33, 237, 243, 379

Ossian, 25, 187, 193, 266, 350

Ottoman Empire, 12

Paine, Tom, 218, 262; and agrarian justice, 262

painting, and love, 169

Palissot, Charles, 148

Pantisocracy, 236

Paris, 137, 409; articles de, 92–93; and assignats, 328–29; fashions of, 93; and French finances, 319; and French politics in 1791, 339; tailoring trade of, 94–95

passions, 9, 10; artificial, 153, 166; in Descartes, 75–76; in Dubos, 87–90; and interests, 9; Mably on, 372–73, 374; and property, 228–29. *See also* arts; Brown; emotions; enthusiasm; fashion; Rousseau; Vico; Young

Pastoret, Charles-Emmanuel-Joseph-Pierre, baron de, 336

Patriotic Society of Switzerland, and Brown, Mably, and Rousseau, 23

patriotism, 284–85, 371; Clavière and, 367–68; versus despotism, 371; and *don patriotique*, 318; and Mounier, 298–99; and patriot king, 285–86, 296–97; and public debt, 317; Volney and, 371; and war of 1792, 367–68. *See also* army

patronage, 132–33; and court, 77, 99, 132–33; and Marie Antoinette, 132–33; and salons, 77, 132–33. *See also* centralisation; decentralisation

perfectibility, 251, 275, 411; in Condorcet, 204–5; in Rousseau, 120, 204. *See also* Court de Gebelin

Periander, 132; banquet of, 70; morality of, 70, 71

Persia, 253, 281

personality, in Bonnet, 125

Peter the Great (emperor of Russia), 203

Pétion, Jerome, 43, 46, 145, 263, 306, 329, 330, 333, 339, 342, 352–53, 356–57; and Brissot, 43; and Gorsas, 357; on grocery riots of January 1792, 356; and Williams, 43, 352

Petronius, 102

philosophy: ancient, 63, 238–42; ancient, in eighteenth-century thought, 63; common sense, 226. *See also* Cicero; Cynics; Diogenes; Epicureanism; morality; Stoics

Phocion, 23, 306. *See also* Cynics; Mably

Phoenicians, 257; and trade, 247–48

phrygian bonnets, 8, 57. See also *pileus*

Phryne, 139

physical, versus moral, 146–47. *See also* Rousseau; vitalism

Physiocracy, 200, 202–3, 248–51, 258, 260, 268, 272, 275, 297, 390; ancients and moderns in, 258; and astronomy, 253–54; and Court de Gebelin, 251–53; and culture, 250–51; and equality, 250–51;

and Fénelon, 249, 260; and freemasonry, 259; and general will, 200; Mably on, 390; and natural religion, 256–60; needs and desires in, 250–51; and reform, 249–50; and Rousseau, 259; and sovereignty, 249

physiology, 126; and moral theory, 100

Pico della Mirandola, 194

pileus, 8, 194, 340

Pilnitz, declaration of, 336, 339

Pindar, 284–85

Pinto, Isaac de, 309, 371

Piron, Alexis, 67

Pitt, William (the elder), 179

Pitt, William (the younger), 179

pity, 37, 376; in Rousseau, 29–30. *See also* morality

Plato, 10, 21, 22, 86, 138–39, 160, 164, 188, 219, 238, 278, 383, 386, 387, 389; on Cynics, 138–39; and Diogenes, 21, 139; and enthusiasm, 193; and Periander, 70–71; and his purple carpets, 22, 49, 69, 70, 101, 130, 134, 143, 239; *Republic*, 71; Rousseau on, 160, 164; *Symposium*, 70

Platonism, 189

Pliny, 151–52

Pluche, François-Noël, 86, 86n73, 91–92, 177

Pluquet, François-André-Adrien, 230

Plutarch, 71, 238

poetry, 136, 183–84, 192. *See also* Brown

Poiret, Pierre, 231–38, 243; and Fénelon, 231; on Hobbes, 237

Poland, 204, 280, 368, 384; Rousseau on, 30–31, 204; Mably on, 387; and Valais, 204

polytheism, 313. *See also* Condillac; Mably

poor, versus rich, 283

Pope, Alexander, 52, 215, 376, 382, 415

possession, and property, 95. *See also* property

Poultier, François, 408

Poussin, Nicolas, 86

power, constituting, 128

Prades, Jean-Martin, abbé de, 216, 376

préciosité, 71, 78. *See also* salons

Price, Richard, 386

Pride: Cynic, 177; in Mably, 231

Priestley, Joseph, on Brown, 179

primitivism, 166; and naturalism, 26

product cycle, and fashion, 93

property, 2–3, 4, 9, 38, 175, 197, 202, 208, 212, 218, 228–29, 244, 306; and *assignat*, 324–32; Babeuf on, 366; balance of, 310, 335; Brissot on, 37; Carl on, 95; and Catholicism, 224; common, 225, 229, 264; in common sense philosophy, 226; in Cynic philosophy, 239; of *émigrés*, 366; and empire, 175; and fashion, 77; of French church, 305, 314, 319, 324–32, 332, 364–65, 366; Harrington on, 310; in Jefferson, 226; and labour, 264; and Linguet, 12; and Locke, 230, 264; Mably on, 230–31, 387; in Morelly, 229–30; and necessity, 227; Ogilvie on, 264–66; origin of, 228–29; and passions, 228–29; and pastoral life, 176, 212; Pétion on, 353; in Poiret, 231–38; and political power, 310; and possession, 95; and Protestantism, 224; in Pufendorf, 224–25; in Ramsay, 246; Rousseau on, 28, 209, 221; Saint-Pierre on, 9; and social divisions, 9; and social interdependence, 95; and state power, 221–82; and taxation, 326–27; and towns, 176; and utility, 224–27

Proudhon, Pierre-Joseph, 423

Provence, comte de, 336

prudence, ancient, 212. *See also* Harrington

Prudhomme, Louis-Marie, 341

Prussia, 289

puberty, 169

public credit, 201; and free trade, 46l; and land ownership, 264–66; Mercier on, 129; and Physiocracy, 203, 260–73. *See also* Law (John)

public debt, 3, 29, 40, 46, 50, 129, 297, 362; and agrarian law, 262; British, 41, 47, 310–12; as cement of society, 42, 45; and English political stability, 41, 44–45, 310–12; and human history, 4; and patriotism, 317, 318; and political conflict, 51; and political stability, 41, 42, 44–45, 308, 310–12; properties of, 3; and taxation, 50, 297; and trade, 318; and War of Spanish Succession, 312; Williams on, 44–45. *See also* Clavière; Harrington; Law (John); Mercier; Necker; Saint-Just; Steuart

public finance, and political representation, 54, 325–26

public opinion, 161–63; historiography of, 161; Rousseau on, 161–63, 170

Pufendorf, Samuel, 77, 82, 117, 120, 161, 164, 168, 210; in Jansenist political theology, 86; on property, 224–25

Pythagoras, 240, 344

Quatorze-oignons, 144, 356, 423; as Diogenes, 144. *See also* *sans-culottes*

Quesnay, François, 248, 258

Rabaut Saint-Etienne, Jean-Paul, 37, 39, 256–60, 307, 369, 370–71, 385

Rabelais, François, 350

Racine, Jean, 344, 351

Rambouillet, Catherine de Vivonne, marquise de, 98; salon of, 98n106

Ramsay, Andrew Michael, chevalier, 210, 215, 236, 238, 379; and natural law, 243; *Travels of Cyrus*, 242–48. *See also* Fénelon

ranks, 244; and merit, 245, 248

Raynal, Guillaume-Thomas, 419

reason: in Mably, 376, 385; in Rousseau, 151, 159–60, 162, 196

Réattu, Jacques, 26, 55–56

Réaumur, René-Antoine Ferchault de, 69

reform, 131, 220; d'Argenson and, 206; of army, 286; Bonaparte and, 265–66; Brown on, 203–4; dilemmas of, 220–21; and Fénelon, 207–9; indirect, 249; Mably on, 394–98; and monarchy, 281, 395; Montesquieu on, 203; Ogilvie on, 265; and Physiocracy, 249–50; and public credit, 267, 271; and republics, 205; and revolution, 207, 219; Robespierre on, 281–82; royal, 208–9, 213, 217, 220, 281–82, 288, 296; and Rousseau, 220; in Salchli, 421; in 1789, 47; and sovereignty, 205; and state power, 220–21, 249. *See also* Louis XVI

Regnault de Saint-Jean-d'Angély, Michel-Louis-Etienne, 358

religion: and astronomy, 257; and emotions, 255, 257; in Mably, 383–84; of magistrate, 312–13; natural, 185, 190, 254–55, 256, 257, 307; and Physiocracy, 256–60

representation: in Hobbes, 116; in Montesquieu, 116; political, after 1789, 325–26; in Rousseau, 116; and taxation, 325–26

representative government, Robespierre on, 53. *See also* Sieyès

republicanism, 4; and constitutional monarchy, 423; in 1848, 423; in French

Revolution, 1; and morality, 29; and Napoleon, 421–22. *See also* Brissot; Clavière; Cubières-Palmézeaux; Desmoulins; Gorsas; Mercier; Robespierre; Rousseau; Saint-Just

republics, 203; Dutch, 8; Garat on, 281; luxury in, 137; Mercier on, 108–9; and monarchies, 203, 205, 211, 217, 242, 245; Montesquieu on, 203; and reform, 205; Roman, 4; Swiss, 8; virtue in, 203. *See also* Fénelon; Harrington

Restif de la Bretonne, Nicolas-Anne-Edmé, 307

revolution, 108–10, 131, 221; Aubert de Vitry on, 268; consumer, 138; Garat on, 279–80; Mably on, 399; Mercier on, 108–10; and reform, 38, 219; Rousseau on, 28, 31, 33, 206–7, 368, 371–72; Salchli on, 420–21; Volney on, 369–70. *See also* French Revolution

revolutionary government, 21, 367–68, 370–71, 404–5. *See also* Clavière; Mably; Robespierre; Saint-Just; Volney

rich, versus poor, 283

Richardson, Samuel, 72

Richelieu, Louis-François Armand de Vignerot du Plessis, duc de, 77

Richer d'Aube, François-René, 70, 225; and Montesquieu, 225; and Pufendorf, 225; Sade on, 225

Rivarol, Antoine de, 64

Robespierre, Maximilien, 7, 8, 16, 21, 39, 50, 52–53, 54, 55, 273, 282, 283, 285, 305, 306, 307, 332, 333, 352, 363, 366, 402, 405–6, 407; and Brown, 406; and Fénelon, 406; and Festival of Supreme Being, 52; on legislator, 53; on d' Orléans de la Motte, bishop of Amiens, 406; and popular economy, 54; on reform, 281–82; and religion, 52–53, 406; on representative government, 53, 404; and republican government, 54; and revolutionary government, 404–5; and Rousseau, 406; and *sans-culottes*, 55, 283; and Sieyès, 53; and virtue, 16; on war, 368; and Young, 52, 406. *See also* Dusaulx; Mably

Rochefoucauld, François duc de la, 74

Roederer, Pierre-Louis, 99, 274, 403; on court society and Versailles, 99–100; on Mably, 403; on Mercier, 107; and morality, 100; on patronage, 132; on Rousseau,

407–8; on salons, 99–100; on women, 99–100

Rohan, Edouard de, cardinal, 354

Roland de la Platière, Jean-Marie, 145

Roland, Marie-Jeanne Phlipon, Mme, 28

Romans, 300

Rome, 4, 14, 44, 90, 172, 194–95, 207, 215–16, 217, 246, 276, 290, 301, 312, 340, 341, 365, 368, 371, 372, 373, 376, 377, 393, 394, 397–98, 400, 411, 415; Cretan dances in, 187; compared to France, 102; satire in, 11. *See also* Gilbert

Romney, George, 71

Roucher, Jean-Antoine, 254, 255, 275, 352, 353, 359; and Garat, 278; Laharpe on, 255n137

Rousseau, Jean-Jacques, 1, 5, 22–23, 24, 26, 29–40, 55, 105, 120, 124–25, 134, 136, 139, 147–51, 198, 202, 204, 217, 219, 228, 229, 235, 248, 256, 270, 275, 278, 307, 316, 327, 333, 336, 342, 363, 374, 376, 378, 379, 395, 401, 405, 407, 408, 412, 416, 422, 423; on agriculture, 183; on *amour-de-soi*, 112; and *amour-propre*, 153, 170; on ancients and moderns, 116; and arts and sciences, 193, 229; Aubert de Vitry on, 266–73; and Bernardin de Saint-Pierre, 214; Bonnet on, 120; on Britain, 206; and Brizard, 294; and Brown, 23–24, 178; as Carneades, 127; in Castel, 170–77; on *cercles*, 162–63; on chivalry, 158; on civil war, 105; on Condillac, 112–13; and Condorcet, 219; and conjectural history, 32–33, 170; on conscience, 112; and Corsica, 31; in Court de Gebelin, 251–52; and his critics, 5, 30, 33, 38; and culture, 147–51; as a Cynic, 22–23, 24, 26–27, 111, 139, 170, 177, 181, 194, 199, 351; and democracy, 154–55, 403; on desires, 200; and Diderot, 142–43, 147, 165, 189–90, 223; and Diogenes, 23, 25, 26–27, 139, 147, 157, 223; and division of labour, 115–16, 149–50, 154; Dom Deschamps on, 380; and Dubos, 156; on duelling, 162; and Duport, 333; on emotions, 159–160, 222; and Epicureanism, 150, 172; and evil, 173, 413; and executive power, 155; and federalism, 119; and Fénelon, 38–39, 210–11, 219; and festivals, 164; Fichte on, 222; freedom in, 194; Frey on,

Rousseau, Jean-Jacques (*cont.*)
382–83; Garat on, 275, 280–81; on general will, 114–19; and Geneva, 153–55; on Geneva as "mansion of reason," 159; on God, 151; on government, 116–17, 155; Haller on, 127; on happiness, 150, 241; and history, 31, 112–14; and Hobbes, 27, 38–39, 127, 173, 175, 200; Holbach on, 381; and human nature, 29–30, 33; on imagination, 160; described by Iselin, 143; on justice, 112; Kant on, 26–27, 195–200, 223; on Kliyogg, 111; La Chalotais on, 377n36; on language, 30–31; and legion of honour, 162; and legislative power, 155; on legislator, 53; Linguet and, 12; on love, 31, 156–59; on love of order, 112–14; and Mably, 24, 231, 372, 374, 377, 385, 390, 391–92, 402–3, 410; on Machiavelli, 278; and majority rule, 119; compared to Mercier, 110–32, 138; and migrations of population, 32; and marquis de Mirabeau, 200–201, 259; on modesty, 157–58; and *moi commun*, 118; and Montesquieu, 28, 154, 158, 172; and morality, 134–35, 223, 256; and moral sense theory, 188; on music and language, 31–32, 412–13; on needs, 153, 200; on Neufchatel, 148–49; "noble savage" in, 134–35; and perfectibility, 24, 36; on personality, 31–32, 125–26; and Physiocracy, 259, 260, 269; on pity, 29–32, 112; on Plato, 160, 164; on pleasure, 150; and Pliny, 151–52; and Poland, 30–31; on political society, 114–19; on politics, 135; on property, 27, 31, 209, 221–22; on public opinion, 110–11, 161–63; on reason, 151, 159–160, 162, 196; and reform, 203, 205, 206; on representation, 116; and revolution, 28, 31, 33, 52, 206–7, 221, 368, 371–72; Roederer on, 407–8; Saint-Martin on, 379; as *sans-culotte*, 60, 103; on selfhood, 124; on self-interest, 134–36; on sexuality, 196; and Shaftesbury, 188–90; and Sieyès, 117, 201, 222; *Social Contract*, 114–19; on sovereignty, 114–19, 155; state and property in, 31, 221–22; on taste, 113; on taxation, 117; on theatre, 152, 155; on towns, 176; Wieland on, 139; on women, 155–59. *See also* Marie Antoinette
royalty, and merit, 245

Rush, Benjamin, 236
Russia, 203, 207, 280, 281
Rutledge, Jean-Jacques, 59, 68, 70, 107, 130 141, 215, 267, 270–73, 314, 329, 343, 345; and *Le Bureau d'esprit*, 59–60; on civilisation, 270; on feudalism, 272; and Harrington, 270; on international relations, 270–73; on John Law, 271; and Mercier, 104; on Montesquieu, 215

Sabatier de Castres, abbé Antoine, 378
Sablé, Madeleine de Souvré, marquise de, 74
Sablière, Marguerite de, and Lafontaine, 21, 105, 358
Sade, Jean-Baptiste-François-Joseph, comte de, 225
Saint Jerome, 145
Saint Petersburg, 137
Saint-André, Jean-Bon, 409
Saint-Antoine, *faubourg*, 18, 19, 57, 341, 342, 353
Saint-Hyacinthe, Claude Thémiseul de, 344
Saint-Just, Louis-Antoine, 21, 38, 273, 361, 363; on happiness, 38, 275; on John Law, 40; on maximum, 404; on revolutionary government, 404–5; and Cynic satire, 50
Saint-Lambert, Jean-François, marquis de, 127, 277, 254; on Rousseau, 127
Saint-Marcel, *faubourg*, 18, 57, 341, 353
Saint-Martin, Louis-Claude de, 379
Saint-Pierre, Charles-Irénée, abbé de, 9–10, 23, 96, 260, 272, 290–91; and army reform, 290–91; on property, 9–10
Salaville, Jean-Baptiste, 35, 37; on perfectibility, 36
Salchli, Emmanuel, 414–22; on evil, 415–17; on Herder, 417; and Mercier, 420; on morality, 418–19; on Rousseau, 417
salons, 1, 5–6, 21, 58–59, 64, 66, 99–100, 132–33, 190, 248; and breeches, 60, 66, 141; Condorcet on, 99; and court society, 77, 99–100, 132–33; etymology of, 5–6, 58–59; and fashion, 77; of Mme Geoffrin, 18–19, 59–60, 64, 71, 141, 215, 344–45; and patronage, 132–33; Roederer on, 99–100; and *sans-culottes*, 6–7; and Plato's *Symposium*, 10; of Mme de Tencin, 15, 17, 18–19, 21, 64, 66–67; and troubadours, 66n22. *See also* Charpentier; *étrennes*; Moreau; Rutledge; Tencin

San Domingo, 342

sans-culottes, 1, 7, 11, 16, 51, 338, 363, 402, 404, 412; alternative names for, 7; and bourgeoisie, 356, 357–58; and breeches, 59–63; Brissot and, 7, 283; and Brissotins, 7, 339–40; and *bonnets de laine*, 341–42; and *canaille*, 359; defined, 1–2, 5, 58–63; and Feuillants, 353–59; and Gorsas, 20, 353–61; and Greeks, 107; Grégoire on, 62, 379; and "Harrington," 273; historiography of, 1, 61–63, 423; imagery of, 2; literal meaning of, 5; and Jacobins, 2; and Jesus, 355; Mercier on origin of, 20, 106; origin of name, 21–22, 103, 129–30; and Parisian insurrection of 20 June 1792, 57; and Parisians, 355; and Quatorze-oignons, 144; Robespierre on, 55, 283, 339; and Romans, 107; and salons, 5; and *sans-culotte* ministry, 7, 51, 339; and satire, 353–54; and social conflict, 342, 356–58; Wedekind on, 407. *See also* breeches; Geoffrin; Rutledge; salons; Tencin

sans-culottides, 16

Santerre, Antoine-Joseph, 342

satire, 11, 25, 49, 267; and Beaumarchais, 345–47; Cynic, 49, 140, 190, 343–44; definition of, 11–12; Dusaulx on, 49; and Gilbert, 102, 346; Gorsas and, 343–51; Menippean, 140, 345; neo-Roman, 102; and *sans-culottes*, 353–54; types of, 49. *See also* Mercier

Saurin, Joseph, 70

Saxons, 4

Schiller, Friedrich, 108

Scythians, 4, 194

Ségur ordinance, 132, 289; and army reform, 289–96

Seneca, Fontenelle as, 91

Sénovert, Etienne de, 314–15

sentiment, defined, 126

Sesostris, 244

sexuality, Rousseau on, 196

Shaftesbury, Anthony Ashley Cooper, third earl of, 83, 127, 135–36; 188; and Brown, 188–89

Shakespeare, William, 193

Shem, 172, 175–76

Sidney, Algernon, 107

Sieyès, abbé Emmanuel-Joseph, 28, 36, 46, 47–48, 49, 51, 128, 130, 132, 217, 223, 296, 301, 305, 306, 307, 309, 315, 327, 330, 334, 370, 396, 403, 407, 412; Aubert de Vitry on, 269; and Barnave, 304; and constituent power, 42; and deficit, 302; and Duport, 304; and elections, 303; and gradual promotion, 303–4; and legion of honour, 304; and Mirabeau (comte de), 304; and natural philosophy, 35; and patriotism, 302; and political reform, 47–48, 131; and public finance, 315–16; and representative system, 302–4; Robespierre on, 53; and Rousseau, 117, 201; on Rousseau, 222–23; and social science, 33, 414; and taxation, 303

slavery, 334; and empire, 334–35; and liberty, 194. *See also pileus*

Smellie, William, 168, 177; on Aristotle, 168

Smith, Adam, 40, 72, 226, 256, 323, 325, 350, 352; Clavière on, 323–24

sociability, 4, 26, 85, 220, 230–31; and Aristotle, 86; and emotions, 168–70; and Hobbes, 85–86; and Physiocracy, 250–51; and Rousseau, 220. *See also* Brown; Castel; Mercier; naturalism

social contract: in Mercier, 128; in Williams, 43. *See also* Rousseau

social science, 33, 414

society, polite, 68–69. *See also* salons

Socinianism, 231–32

Socrates, 238, 239, 383

Socrates, rural (Kliyogg), 111, 114, 116, 321

Solomon, 258; wisdom of, 213

Solon, 245–46, 279

Sorel, Agnès, 14

soul, 4; and body, 4, 121, 135–36, 202, 233–34, 235, 243; immortality of, and morality, 350. *See also* Bonnet; Herder; Mercier; mesmerism; vitalism

sovereignty: and democracy, 403; and despotism, 310–11; in French revolutionary historiography, 55–56, 362; in Montesquieu, 115–16; and reform, 205; representative, 115; in Rousseau, 116–17, 155

Spain, 285

Spallanzani, Lazzaro, 120, 121, 125

Spanish Succession, war of, and public debt, 312

Sparta, 207, 212, 245–46, 276, 281, 368, 371, 372, 373, 376, 393, 402, 411

Spartans, 194, 367–68

Spinoza, 82

Spinozism, 381

Staël, Germaine de, 353

state, 3; Mably on, 373; and property, 221–22. *See also* government; Mercier; Rousseau; Williams

Staunton, Sir George, 263–64

Sterne, Lawrence, 141

Steuart, Sir James, 40, 45, 272, 314, 325, 317, 325; Aubert de Vitry on, 267; and John Law, 262; and modern liberty, 267; and public debt, 267; Williams on, 44. *See also* Barnave; Clavière; Duport

Stoics, 74, 144, 238, 239, 240, 242; in Cicero, 84; and Dubos, 87–88; and fashion, 90. *See also* Fontenelle; Seneca

Strauss, Leo, 45, 63

Suard, Jean-Baptiste-Antoine, 61, 66, 146, 214, 274

Suger, abbot of Saint-Denis, 268

Sully, Maximilien de Béthune, duc de, 286; and patriotic debt default, 286. *See also* Mallet du Pan

Sweden, constitution of, 295

Swift, Jonathan, 83, 141

Switzerland, 207, 318

symposium, Greek, 70; and Plato, 70

Tacitus, 82; on Germans, 300–301; in Mounier, 300–301

Tahiti, Diderot on, 146–47

Talleyrand, Charles-Maurice de, 307, 319, 320, 321

Tartars, 176, 212, 253, 300; and pastoral life, 176

taste, in Rousseau, 113; versus fashion, 113. *See also* Cicero; decorum; Dubos

taxation, 50, 284, 334; and active citizenship, 325–26; and army reform, 288; and cereal prices, 260, 271, 297, 326, 334–35; direct, 326, 334; and electorate, 325–26; and *émigrés*, 50, 334; and empire, 50, 326, 334–35; indirect, 326, 334; and political stability, 326; and public debt, 50, 297; and representation, 50, 325–26

Temple, Sir William, 309

Tencin, Claudine-Alexandrine Guérin de, 15, 17, 18–19, 21, 64, 66–67, 69, 73, 76, 101, 103, 104, 132, 156; and men of letters, 64–70; and New Year's Day

gift of breeches, 15, 17, 104; salon of, 64; described by Trublet, 104; in *Vie de Marianne*, 72–73

Terror, 218, 404–5; and *sans-culottes*, 2, 58

theatre, 159–60; Greek, 163–64; Rousseau on, 152, 155, 163–64

theology: covenant, 224; federal, 224. *See also* Adam; Fénelon; Jansenism; Poiret; Ramsay

Thomasius, Christian, 82

towns, Castel on, 176

trade, 46, 203–4, 209, 246–48, 387–89, 393, 408–9; and army reform, 290–91; and *assignat*, 322–23; Brown on, 203–4, 387–88; Cantillon on, 387–88; Condillac on, 393; fair, 46, 203–4, 393; and fashion, 9, 77, 91, 92–95; Mably on, 387–89, 392; in Physiocracy, 250; and public debt, 318; and republican morality, 409. *See also* free trade; Law (John)

Tressan, Louis-Elizabeth de la Vergne, comte de, 68–70, 71, 76, 77, 101; and polite society, 69–70. *See also* Tencin; troubadours

tribunes, 44, 373

troubadours, 70, 101; and salons, 66n22

Trublet, abbé Nicolas, 104; and Mme de Tencin, 104

Tscharner, Vincenz Bernhard, 204

Turgot, Anne-Robert-Jacques, 260, 268, 271, 322, 379

Tyre, 246, 247, 248, 276

Ulysses, 213

United States of America, 318, 334, 397, 420; Mably on, 386–90

utile, 10, 62. *See also* Cicero; honour

utility, and property, 224–27

Utrecht, treaty of, 270

Valais, described by Rousseau, 148–52; and Poland, 204

Van Helmont, Francis Mercurius, 235

vanitas, 101

vanity, 100–101

Vassé, Antoinette-Louise-Gabrielle des Gentils du Bessay, comtesse de, and Mably, 378

vegetarianism, 169

Velthusyen, Lambert van, 82

venality, and nobility, 289–93

Venice, 137, 246
Vergniaud, Pierre-Victurnien, 361
Versailles, 109, 211
veto, royal, 298
vice, 12. *See also* satire
Vico, Giambattista, 166, 167, 168, 172
Vienna, 137
Villedieu, Mme de. *See* Desjardins
Villers, Charles de, 35
Villoteau, Guillaume-André, 414
virtue, 12; and Cynics, 23; political, 203; and
    wealth, 136, 348. See also *amour de l'ordre*;
    Clavière; Fénelon; love of order; Mably;
    Ramsay; Robespierre; Rousseau; Volney
vitalism, 4, 34, 119–26, 128, 135, 201, 235,
    375, 383, 417–18, 421, 423; and body
    politic, 43; and love, 36; in Mercier, 107;
    and morality, 123; and social stability,
    130; in Williams's political thought, 43,
    45. *See also* Herder; Leibniz; mesmerism;
    Salchli
Volney, Constantin-François, 307, 369–71;
    on law of nature, 370
Voltaire, François Arouet de, 13, 16, 25–26,
    59, 76, 77, 78, 82, 120, 127, 134, 135,
    159, 166, 168, 170, 179, 182, 206, 207,
    248, 254, 268, 277, 290, 340, 350, 358,
    408; on Castel as Cynic, 170; Castilhon
    on, 182; and Gournay group, 290; on
    John Law, 324; *Le Mondain*, 76, 78, 135;
    on natural law and curiosity, 76; *Le pau-
    vre diable*, 101–2; *La pucelle d'Orléans*, 13;
    on Rousseau, 170; as *sans-culotte*, 60, 103;
    on Trublet, 104; on women, 156
voting: and citizenship, 50; and taxation,
    50–51. *See also* citizenship

Walker, George, on Rousseau, 158n68
Walpole, Sir Robert, 271
war: civil, 21, 105–7, 128, 393; Clavière on,
    367–68; Mably on, 397–98; Robespierre

on, 368; of 1792, 51; Volney on, 371. *See
    also* civil war
Warburton, William, 72, 186; and French
    novels, 72
Wealth: and culture, 248; and virtue, 136,
    165, 348. *See also* Carl; fashion; trade
Wedekind, Georg Christian Gottlieb, 407
Wesley, John, 209
Westphalia, treaty of, 270
Wieland, Christoph Martin, 108, 139, 140
Wilkes, John, 308, 310
Williams, David, 42–45, 262, 314, 317, 318,
    352; and Brissot, 42–43; on Harrington,
    44; on Montesquieu, 44; on Necker, 44;
    and Pétion, 352; on public debt, 44–45;
    on revolution, 43; on Rousseau, 43,
    43n77; on Steuart, 44; and vitalism, 43
Winchester, Elhanan, 236
women, 248; and chivalry, 158; and gossip,
    163; La Bruyère and, 100–101; and
    love, 156; Mirabeau (comte de) on,
    97–98; modern, 158; modesty in,
    157–58; and morality, 77–101; and pa-
    tronage, 132; Roederer on, 99–100; in
    Rousseau, 155–59; in Voltaire, 156. *See
    also* salons
wonder, in Descartes, 75–76. *See also*
    emotions
Woodward, John, 243
writers: and breeches, 64–65; and Mme de
    Tencin, 64–70; and *sans-culottes*, 5, 58,
    60. *See also* Diogenes; Tencin

Xenophon, 238

Young, Edward, 25–26, 52, 103, 122, 193,
    307, 380, 415; and Festival of Supreme
    Being, 52; *Night Thoughts*, 52

Zeno, 239, 240
zodiac, 254, 255n116